Globalization

The Macroeconomic Implications of Microeconomic Heterogeneity

World Scientific Studies in International Economics

(ISSN: 1793-3641)

Vol. 44 Non-Tariff Barriers, Regionalism and Poverty: Essays in Applied International Trade Analysis
by L. Alan Winters (University of Sussex, UK)

Vol. 45 Trade Law, Domestic Regulation and Development
by Joel P. Trachtman (Tufts University, USA)

Vol. 46 The Political Economy of International Trade
by Edward D. Mansfield (University of Pennsylvania, USA)

Vol. 47 Trade-Related Agricultural Policy Analysis
by *David Orden (Virginia Polytechnic Institute and State University, USA)*

Vol. 48 The New International Financial System: Analyzing the Cumulative Impact of Regulatory Reform
edited by Douglas Evanoff (Federal Reserve Bank of Chicago, USA), Andrew G. Haldane (Bank of England, UK) & George Kaufman (Loyola University Chicago, USA)

Vol. 49 The Economics of International Migration
by Giovanni Peri (UC Davis)

Vol. 50 The Legal and Economic Analysis of the WTO/FTA System
by Dukgeun Ahn (Seoul National University, Korea)

Vol. 51 The Political Economy of Trade Policy: Theory, Evidence and Applications
by Devashish Mitra (Syracuse University, USA)

Vol. 52 Microeconometrics of International Trade
by Joachim Wagner (Leuphana University Lueneburg, Germany)

Vol. 53 Multinational Enterprises and Host Country Development
by Holger Görg (Kiel Institute for the World Economy, Germany)

Vol. 54 Globalization: The Macroeconomic Implications of Microeconomic Heterogeneity
by Andrei A. Levchenko (University of Michigan, USA)

The complete list of the published volumes in the series can be found at
http://www.worldscientific.com/series/wssie

54 World Scientific Studies in International Economics

Globalization

The Macroeconomic Implications of Microeconomic Heterogeneity

Andrei A. Levchenko
University of Michigan, USA

World Scientific

NEW JERSEY • LONDON • SINGAPORE • BEIJING • SHANGHAI • HONG KONG • TAIPEI • CHENNAI • TOKYO

Published by

World Scientific Publishing Co. Pte. Ltd.
5 Toh Tuck Link, Singapore 596224
USA office: 27 Warren Street, Suite 401-402, Hackensack, NJ 07601
UK office: 57 Shelton Street, Covent Garden, London WC2H 9HE

British Library Cataloguing-in-Publication Data
A catalogue record for this book is available from the British Library.

World Scientific Studies in International Economics — Vol. 54
GLOBALIZATION
The Macroeconomic Implications of Microeconomic Heterogeneity

ISBN 978-981-4663-00-7

Desk Editor: Philly Lim

Typeset by Stallion Press
Email: enquiries@stallionpress.com

Printed in Singapore

Dedication

To Agnieszka

Contents

About the Author

Andrei A. Levchenko is a Professor of Economics at the University of Michigan, a Research Associate at the National Bureau of Economic Research and a Research Fellow at the Centre for Economic Policy Research. Previously, he was an Economist in the Research Department of the International Monetary Fund, and has held visiting positions at the University of Chicago Booth School of Business and the University of Zurich. He earned a Ph.D. in Economics from the Massachusetts Institute of Technology in 2004 and a B.A. in Economics, Mathematics, and Italian from Indiana University in 1999. Prof. Levchenko's research focuses on the interactions between globalization, economic development, and macroeconomics. His research has been funded by the National Science Foundation and has appeared in a variety of journals including *Econometrica*, *Journal of Political Economy*, *Review of Economic Studies*, *Journal of Economic Theory*, *Review of Economics and Statistics*, *American Economic Journal: Macroeconomics*, and *Journal of International Economics*.

Acknowledgements

This book would not be possible without Julian di Giovanni and Jing Zhang, my coauthors of all but one of the chapters that follow. I could not wish for better collaborators than Julian and Jing. The friendship and camaraderie we built over the course of working together on this research will last a lifetime. I am also deeply grateful to Pravin Krishna, Isabelle Méjean, Francesc Ortega, and Romain Rancière, with whom some of the papers below are written. I am thankful for the chance to have them in my professional and personal life. I am lucky to be part of the University of Michigan's Economics Department, which provided an academic environment at the same time intellectually stimulating and warm and collegial. The book is dedicated to my wife Agnieszka, as a small token of gratitude for her unwavering love and support before, during, and after these papers were written.

Also, I would like to thank the following publishers, for granting the permissions to make this book possible. In alphabetical order:

American Economic Association

The Global Welfare Impact of China: Trade Integration and Technological Change. *American Economic Journal: Macroeconomics*, July 2014, *6*(3), 153–183.

Elsevier

Ricardian Productivity Differences and the Gains from Trade. *European Economic Review*, January 2014, *65*, 45–65.

Comparative Advantage, Complexity, and Volatility. *Journal of Economic Behavior and Organization*, October 2013, *94*, 314–329.

Power Laws in Firm Size and Openness to Trade: Measurement and Implications. *Journal of International Economics*, September 2011, *85*(1), 42–52.

Firm Entry, Trade, and Welfare in Zipf's World. *Journal of International Economics*, March 2013, *89*(2), 283–296.

Oxford University Press

Comparative Advantage and the Welfare Impact of European Integration. *Economic Policy*, October 2012, *27*(72), 567–602.

Palgrave Macmillian

The Global Labor Market Impact of Emerging Giants: A Quantitative Assessment. *IMF Economic Review*, August 2013, *61*(3), 479–519.

University of Chicago Press

Country Size, International Trade, and Aggregate Fluctuations in Granular Economies. *Journal of Political Economy*, December 2012, *120*(6), 1083–1132.

Wiley

Firms, Destinations, and Aggregate Fluctuations. *Econometrica*, July 2014, *82*(4), 1303–1340.

A Global View of Cross-Border Migration. *Journal of the European Economic Association*, February 2015, *13*(1), 168–202.

Introduction

We live in an era of globalization: ever increasing international integration of goods, capital, and labor markets. The benefits and costs of global integration in the world today continue to be hotly debated. Among the most pressing questions in the past few years are: what is the impact on the world economy of the rapid integration of "emerging giants" — China, India, and former Communist bloc countries? How does migration affect the welfare of natives in both the receiving and the sending countries? How does increased globalization affect macroeconomic volatility?

These are open questions for two reasons. First, theoretically the impact of these different facets of globalization is often nuanced, and theory reveals many possibilities. And second, even in cases when theory delivers clear and unambiguous qualitative predictions, the magnitudes of the effects still need to be established. For both of these reasons, the impact of globalization on macroeconomic outcomes remains an empirical and quantitative question.

This book collects in one volume the results of a multi-year research program to build heterogeneous firm and sector models for the quantitative evaluation of globalization. The research in the book builds on the transformative innovations in the field of international economics of the past 15 years. This period has witnessed unprecedented dynamism in the field, which is now reaching a synthesis of theory, quantitative work, and data.

International trade has always been a field rich in theory. Going back to David Ricardo in the 19th century, the field advanced through brilliant theoretical insights that described how international trade arises and in turn how it affects people's welfare in the trading countries. International trade theory offers an array of theoretical possibilities and often reveals unexpected results. However, pre-2000 international trade theory was not well-suited for answering the question of what are the actual effects of a particular development in the international economy. This is because traditional theory was largely carried out using stylized models — often with two countries and two sectors, often without trade costs, and in which if there were firms, they were all identical. As such, traditional models did not resemble much the world economy, and "putting numbers on them" was not feasible.

That all changed starting in the early 2000s with the arrival of two seminal contributions, Eaton and Kortum (2002), and Melitz (2003). These breakthroughs became building blocks of rich and tractable theoretical models that can be implemented numerically and used to evaluate quantitatively the impact of a variety of real-world phenomena. The resulting quantitative models are global in scale — encompassing as many as 80 countries as well as multiple sectors — and at the same time feature rich micro-foundations of firm and technological heterogeneity. This quantum leap in realism means it is now possible to dramatically expand the set of questions that can be answered, in particular regarding the consequences of real-world heterogeneity present in the global economy, both at the firm and sector level.

Finally, the third pillar in the field's synthesis is data. Over the same time period, the use of rich micro datasets on firm production and exports has expanded dramatically. While in the mid-1990s firm-level data on international trade were virtually unheard of, now Census, tax authority, and customs datasets that cover (nearly) the universe of firms and trade flows in a particular country are a standard part of the toolkit of the international economist. The firm-level data and the Melitz model fit together like a hand in glove. Using the data, we can now calibrate the heterogeneous firms model to feature a realistic distribution of firm size, something that turns out to matter a great deal both economically and quantitatively, as will become clear below.

This book deploys all three of these ingredients — theory, quantitative analysis, and data — to address the central questions about globalization around the world: the impacts of reductions in trade costs, long-run changes in comparative advantage, and migration of labor, among others. The ultimate goal of the research presented here is not to innovate methodologically (although sometimes that happens along the way). Rather, it is to use these new powerful tools to answer the first-order questions about today's process of globalization. The running theme of the book is that in order to understand the macroeconomic impact of globalization, it is essential to both model and measure the microeconomic heterogeneity in the economy.

The book consists of two parts. Part I explores the consequences of sectoral heterogeneity — "comparative advantage." It is based in large part on the research program joint with Jing Zhang, that developed, estimated, and solved a large-scale quantitative model of the world economy that features productivity differences across countries and sectors — Ricardian comparative advantage. Chapter 1 presents a detailed exposition of the quantitative framework, and provides details of the data, estimation, calibration, and solution of the model. We use this framework to study a series of questions.

Chapter 2, "Ricardian Productivity Differences and the Gains from Trade," goes back to an old insight in the Ricardian trade literature: gains from trade are larger the "stronger" is comparative advantage. That is, greater relative productivity differences between countries produce larger gains from trade. The chapter takes this qualitative insight and makes it quantitative by exploring *how much* observed sectoral productivity differences affect the gains from trade, building on the "sufficient statistic" literature (Arkolakis, Costinot, and Rodriguez-Clare, 2012). It shows that gains from trade calculated ignoring sectoral heterogeneity often dramatically understate the gains from trade.

We next turn our attention to assessing the global welfare impact of two of the most important developments in the international trading system over the last 20 years: the integration of China and the integration of Eastern Europe after the fall of the Iron Curtain. In developed countries, a common concern is that China's growth will be biased towards sectors in which the developed world currently has a comparative advantage. Samuelson (2004) argued that this pattern of Chinese productivity growth can lead to absolute welfare losses in developed countries. Chapter 3, "The Global Welfare Impact of China: Trade Integration and Technological Change," evaluates this conjecture using our 75-country quantitative model of the world economy. The results are striking. The mean welfare gains to the rest of the world when China's comparative disadvantage sectors grow disproportionately faster are actually far larger than the mean gains under balanced productivity growth. Thus, when evaluated quantitatively the welfare impact of China's growth on the rest of the world turns out to be the opposite of what had been conjectured by Samuelson (2004).

Chapter 4, "Comparative Advantage and the Welfare Impact of European Integration" then examines the trade integration of Eastern Europe following the fall of the Iron Curtain. We use this episode as a "laboratory" to study the role of Ricardian comparative advantage in determining the gains from trade. For Eastern Europe, comparative advantage is a key determinant of the variation in the welfare gains: countries whose comparative advantage is most similar to Western Europe tend to gain less, while countries with technology most different from Western Europe gain the most.

In Chapter 5, "The Global Labor Market Impact of Emerging Giants: a Quantitative Assessment" we turn our attention to the distributional impact the trade integration of these countries. As in the cases above, the theoretical insights are well-known. The Specific Factors model (Jones, 1971, Mussa, 1974) describes the winners and losers from international trade: factors of production specific to import-competing sectors suffer from trade opening, whereas specific factors in exporting sectors benefit. While the qualitative result is well-established, how it translates to actual experiences of workers in individual countries and sectors is far from clear. The chapter evaluates the distributional impact of the trade integration of the emerging giants (China, India, Central and Eastern Europe). While the aggregate impact of the trade opening of emerging giants tends to be a fraction of 1% of real income, the distributional effects are an order of magnitude larger, with changes in real wages ranging from −5% to 5% across sectors in most countries. The workers and capital owners in emerging giants' comparative advantage sectors such as Textiles and Wearing Apparel experience greatest losses, while factor owners in Printing and Medical, Precision and Optical Instruments normally gain the most.

Chapter 6, "Comparative Advantage, Complexity, and Volatility," (joint with Pravin Krishna) switches gears and studies instead the impact of comparative advantage on volatility. It has been observed that poorer countries tend to produce disproportionately in more volatile sectors, which in turn contributes to higher macroeconomic volatility in those countries (Koren and Tenreyro, 2007). This chapter proposes a novel source of comparative advantage in more (or less) volatile sectors, with the complexity of the goods playing a central role. Less developed countries with lower institutional ability to enforce contracts, or alternately, with low levels of human capital will specialize in less complex goods which are also characterized by higher levels of output volatility.

Part II explores the consequences of firm heterogeneity. It builds on the seminal work of Melitz (2003) that develops a model of trade and production in which firms are heterogeneous in size. The papers in Part II feature the research program developed jointly with Julian di Giovanni and several other co-authors. The chapters connect the Melitz model more closely with firm-level data, and use it to explore the consequences of observed firm heterogeneity for welfare, macroeconomic volatility, and the impact of migration.

Chapter 7, "Power Laws in Firm Size and Openness to Trade: Measurement and Implications" builds a bridge between the theory and firm-level data. An active literature estimates firm size distributions in the data, effectively fitting a parametric distribution — usually a power law — on the cross-section of firms' total sales. The chapter observes that international trade systematically affects the distribution of firm size: the power law exponent among exporting firms should be strictly lower in absolute value than the power law exponent among non-exporting firms. We use a dataset of French firms to demonstrate that this prediction is strongly supported by the data. While estimates of power law exponents have been used to pin down structural parameters in theoretical and quantitative models, our analysis implies that the existing estimates are systematically lower than the true values. We propose two simple ways of estimating power law parameters that take explicit account of exporting behavior.

This methodological contribution is then used to help calibrate the quantitative heterogeneous firm models in subsequent chapters. Chapter 8, "Firm Entry, Trade, and Welfare in Zipf's World," is motivated by an influential recent literature that combines fixed costs of production and exporting with firm heterogeneity to study firm-level participation in international trade. Naturally, when the unit of the analysis is the firm, much of the emphasis has been placed on the entry decision into export markets — the so-called "extensive margin." This literature is closely related to the research agenda in economic growth that documents the existence of large impediments to entry and cross-border trade, especially in developing countries. The chapter evaluates the importance of fixed costs of production and trade and the extensive margin of imports for welfare. The key ingredient is the observation that firm size follows Zipf's Law, a very fat-tailed distribution that implies a few large firms account for a disproportionate share of overall economic activity. The main result is that once Zipf's Law in firm size is accounted for, the impact of fixed costs and the extensive margin on welfare is vanishingly small. Paradoxically, when the canonical heterogeneous firms framework ideally suited to study the extensive margin of trade is actually calibrated to the observed degree of firm heterogeneity, the extensive margin ceases to matter. This is because under Zipf's Law, the large, infra-marginal firms have a far greater welfare impact than the much smaller firms that comprise the extensive margin in these policy experiments.

The next two chapters turn attention to the role of firms in aggregate fluctuations. Chapter 9, "Country Size, International Trade, and Aggregate Fluctuations in Granular Economies" proposes a new channel through which international trade affects macroeconomic volatility. It studies a multi-country model with heterogeneous firms that are subject to idiosyncratic firm-specific shocks. When the distribution of firm sizes follows Zipf's Law, the idiosyncratic shocks to large firms have an impact on aggregate volatility. Opening to trade increases the importance of large firms to the economy, thus raising macroeconomic volatility. Our simulation exercise shows that the contribution of trade to aggregate fluctuations depends strongly on country size: in the largest economy in the world by total GDP — the US — international trade increases volatility by about 3.5%. By contrast, trade increases aggregate volatility by some 15–20% in small open economies, such as Denmark or Romania.

Chapter 10, "Firms, Destinations, and Aggregate Fluctuations," further explores the idea that idiosyncratic shocks to firms contribute to aggregate fluctuations. It uses a database covering the universe of French manufacturing firms for the period 1990–2007 to provide a forensic account of the role of individual firms in generating aggregate fluctuations. The estimates show that the idiosyncratic firm components do contribute substantially to aggregate volatility, mattering about as much as the country-level and sectoral components.

Finally, building on this modeling and estimation work, Chapter 11, "A Global View of Cross-Border Migration," considers migration in a world with heterogeneous firms. It evaluates the global welfare impact of observed levels of migration and remittances in both origin and destination countries, using a quantitative multi-sector model of the global economy calibrated to aggregate and firm-level data on 60 developed and developing countries. The framework accounts jointly for origin and destination characteristics, as well as the inherently multi-country nature of both migration and other forms of integration, such as international trade and remittance flows. The quantitative results show that the welfare impact of observed levels of migration is substantial, at about 5 to 10% of real income for natives of the main receiving countries and about 10% for the main sending countries.

To summarize, the research collected in this book has implemented some of the largest-scale heterogeneous firms and Ricardian models in the literature, and used these quantitative models to examine the welfare impact of trade integration, technological change, and migration. What emerged is a more complete picture of the global effects of various economic developments and policy changes. A running theme, and a repeated finding, of this book is that microeconomic structure is crucial for understanding the impact of globalization on macroeconomic outcomes. Time and again, attention to detail leads to new insights and unexpected conclusions, such as demonstrating the vanishingly small impact of the extensive margin of trade, or overturning Samuelson's conjecture about the global impact of technological change.

References

Arkolakis, C., A. Costinot and A. Rodríguez-Clare, "New Trade Models Same Old Gains?" *American Economic Review*, February 2012, *102*(1), 94–130.

Eaton, J. and S. Kortum, "Technology, Geography, and Trade," *Econometrica*, September 2002, *70* (5), 1741–1779.

Jones, R., "A Three-Factor Model in Theory, Trade, and History," in Jagdish Bhagwati, ed., *Trade, Balance of Payments, and Growth: Papers in International Economics in Honor of Charles P. Kindleberger*, Amsterdam: North-Holland, 1971, pp. 3–21.

Koren, M. and S. Tenreyro, "Volatility and Development," *Quarterly Journal of Economics*, February 2007, *122*(1), 243–287.

Melitz, M.J., "The Impact of Trade on Intra-Industry Reallocations and Aggregate Industry Productivity," *Econometrica*, November 2003, *71*(6), 1695–1725.

Mussa, M., "Tariffs and the Distribution of Income: The Importance of Factor Specificity, Substitutability, an Intensity in the Short and Long Run," *Journal of Political Economy*, November–December 1974, *82*(6), 1191–1203.

Samuelson, P.A., "Where Ricardo and Mill Rebut and Confirm Arguments of Mainstream Economists Supporting Globalization," *Journal of Economic Perspectives*, Summer 2004, *18*(3), 135–46.

Part I
Sectoral Heterogeneity

Chapter 1

A Multi-Country, Multi-Sector Model of Production and Trade

This chapter lays out the quantitative model of production and trade developed in a series of papers with Jing Zhang. It describes in detail the theoretical structure, the data and assumptions underlying the estimation and calibration of the key parameters, and the algorithm used to solve for the model's equilibrium. Chapters 2–5 then apply the model to a series of quantitative questions. While each subsequent chapter is self-contained in its presentation of the model and implementation details, readers who went through this chapter can skip: (i) Chapter 2, Sections 4.1, 4.2, 4.3, Table A1, Table A2, and Appendix A; (ii) Chapter 3, Section II except II.E and Table A2; (iii) Chapter 4, Tables A1 and A2; and (iv) Chapter 5, Section I (except "Factor Market clearing in the Four Equbria," "Welfare," and "Summary of the Estimates and the Basic Patterns"), and the Appendix.

1.1 The Environment

The world is comprised of N countries, indexed by n and i, and $J+1$ sectors, indexed by j and k. There are two factors of production, labor (L) and capital (K). Each sector produces a continuum of goods. The first J sectors are tradeable subject to barriers to trade, and the $J+1$-th sector is non-tradeable. Both capital and labor are mobile across sectors and immobile across countries.

Period utility of the representative consumer in country n is homothetic, given by

$$U_n = \left(\sum_{j=1}^{J} \omega_j^{\frac{1}{\eta}} \left(Y_n^j\right)^{\frac{\eta-1}{\eta}} \right)^{\frac{\eta}{\eta-1}\xi_n} \left(Y_n^{J+1}\right)^{1-\xi_n}, \tag{1.1}$$

where ξ_n denotes the Cobb-Douglas weight for the tradeable sector composite good, η is the elasticity of substitution between the tradeable sectors, ω_j is the taste parameter for tradeable sector j, Y_n^{J+1} is the nontradeable-sector composite good, and Y_n^j is the composite good in tradeable sector j. Trade is balanced.[1] The budget constraint (or the resource constraint) of the consumer is given by

$$\sum_{j=1}^{J+1} p_n^j Y_n^j = w_n L_n + r_n K_n, \tag{1.2}$$

where p_n^j is the price of the sector j composite, K_n and L_n are the exogenous capital and labor endowments, and w_n and r_n are the wage rate and the rental return of capital, respectively. The consumption price index in country n is thus:

$$P_n = B_n \left(\sum_{j=1}^{J} \omega_j (p_n^j)^{1-\eta} \right)^{\frac{1}{1-\eta}\xi_n} (p_n^{J+1})^{1-\xi_n},$$

where $B_n = \xi_n^{-\xi_n}(1-\xi_n)^{-(1-\xi_n)}$.

Output in each sector j is produced using a CES production function that aggregates a continuum of varieties $q \in [0,1]$ unique to each sector:

$$Q_n^j = \left[\int_0^1 Q_n^j(q)^{\frac{\varepsilon-1}{\varepsilon}} dq \right]^{\frac{\varepsilon}{\varepsilon-1}},$$

where ε denotes the elasticity of substitution across varieties q, Q_n^j is the total output of sector j in country n, and $Q_n^j(q)$ is the amount of variety q that is used in production in sector j and country n. It is well known that the price of sector j's output is given by:

$$p_n^j = \left[\int_0^1 p_n^j(q)^{1-\varepsilon} dq \right]^{\frac{1}{1-\varepsilon}}.$$

The production function of each sectoral variety q is:

$$y_n^j(q) = z_n^j(q) \left(k_n^j(q)^{1-\alpha_j} l_n^j(q)^{\alpha_j} \right)^{\beta_j} \left(\prod_{j'=1}^{J+1} m_n^{j'j}(q)^{\gamma_{j'j}} \right)^{1-\beta_j},$$

[1]The following chapters will present extensions that allow for unbalanced trade. Relaxing the balanced trade assumption is never consequential for the results that follow.

where $z_n^j(q)$ denotes variety-specific productivity, $k_n^j(q)$ and $l_n^j(q)$ denote inputs of capital and labor, and $m_n^{j'j}$ denotes the intermediate input from sector j' used in producing sector-j goods. The value-added based labor intensity is given by α_j, while the share of value added in total output is given by β_j. Both of these vary by sector. The weights on inputs from other sectors, $\gamma_{j'j}$, vary by output industry j as well as input industry j'.

Productivity $z_n^j(q)$ for each $q \in [0,1]$ in each sector j is equally available to all agents in country n, and product and factor markets are perfectly competitive. Following Eaton and Kortum (2002, henceforth EK), the productivity draw $z_n^j(q)$ is random and comes from the Fréchet distribution with the cumulative distribution function

$$F_n^j(z) = e^{-T_n^j z^{-\theta}}.$$

In this distribution, the absolute advantage term T_n^j varies by country and sector, with higher values of T_n^j implying higher average productivity draws in sector j in country n. The parameter θ captures dispersion, with larger values of θ implying smaller dispersion in draws.

It will be convenient to define the cost of an "input bundle" faced by sector j producers in country n:

$$c_n^j = \left(w_n^{\alpha_j} r_n^{1-\alpha_j}\right)^{\beta_j} \left(\prod_{j'=1}^{J+1} \left(p_n^{j'}\right)^{\gamma_{j'j}}\right)^{1-\beta_j}.$$

Then, producing one unit of good q in sector j in country n requires $\frac{1}{z_n^j(q)}$ input bundles, and thus the cost of producing one unit of good q is $c_n^j / z_n^j(q)$.

International trade is subject to iceberg costs: in order for one unit of good q produced in sector j to arrive at country n from country i, $d_{ni}^j > 1$ units of the good must be shipped. We normalize $d_{nn}^j = 1$ for each country n in each tradeable sector j. Note that the trade costs will vary by destination pair and by sector, and in general will not be symmetric: d_{ni}^j need not equal d_{in}^j. Under perfect competition, the price at which country i can supply tradeable good q in sector j to country n is equal to:

$$p_{ni}^j(q) = \left(\frac{c_i^j}{z_i^j(q)}\right) d_{ni}^j.$$

Buyers of each good q in tradeable sector j in country n will select to buy from the cheapest source country. Thus, the price actually paid for this good in country n will be:

$$p_n^j(q) = \min_{i=1,\ldots,N} \{p_{ni}^j(q)\}.$$

Following the standard EK approach, define the "multilateral resistance" term

$$\Phi_n^j = \sum_{i=1}^{N} T_i^j \left(c_i^j d_{ni}^j\right)^{-\theta}.$$

This value summarizes, for country n, the access to production technologies in sector j. Its value will be higher if in sector j, country n's trading partners have high productivity (T_i^j) or low cost (c_i^j). It will also be higher if the trade costs that country n faces in this sector are low. Standard steps lead to the familiar result that the probability of importing good q from country i, π_{ni}^j is equal to the share of total spending on goods coming from country i, X_{ni}^j/X_n^j, and is given by:

$$\frac{X_{ni}^j}{X_n^j} = \pi_{ni}^j = \frac{T_i^j \left(c_i^j d_{ni}^j\right)^{-\theta}}{\Phi_n^j}.$$

In addition, the price of good j in country n is simply

$$p_n^j = \Gamma\left(\Phi_n^j\right)^{-\frac{1}{\theta}}, \tag{1.3}$$

where $\Gamma = \left[\boldsymbol{\Gamma}\left(\frac{\theta+1-\varepsilon}{\theta}\right)\right]^{\frac{1}{1-\varepsilon}}$, with $\boldsymbol{\Gamma}$ the Gamma function.

1.2 Equilibrium

The competitive equilibrium of this model world economy consists of a set of prices, allocation rules, and trade shares such that (i) given the prices, all firms' inputs satisfy the first-order conditions, and their output is given by the production function; (ii) given the prices, the consumers' demand satisfies the first-order conditions; (iii) the prices ensure the market clearing conditions for labor, capital, tradeable goods and nontradeable goods; (iv) trade shares ensure balanced trade for each country.

The set of prices includes the wage rate w_n, the rental rate r_n, the sectoral prices $\{p_n^j\}_{j=1}^{J+1}$, and the aggregate price P_n in each country n. The allocation rules include the capital and labor allocation across sectors $\{K_n^j, L_n^j\}_{j=1}^{J+1}$, final consumption demand $\{Y_n^j\}_{j=1}^{J+1}$, and total demand $\{Q_n^j\}_{j=1}^{J+1}$ (both final and intermediate goods) for each sector. The trade shares include the expenditure share π^j_{ni} in country n on goods coming from country i in sector j.

1.2.1 *Characterization of Equilibrium*

Given the set of prices $\{w_n, r_n, P_n, \{p^j_n\}^{J+1}_{j=1}\}^N_{n=1}$, we first characterize the optimal allocations from final demand. Consumers maximize utility (1.1) subject to the budget constraint (1.2). The first order conditions associated with this optimization problem imply the following final demand:

$$p^j_n Y^j_n = \xi_n(w_n L_n + r_n K_n)\frac{\omega_j (p^j_n)^{1-\eta}}{\sum_{k=1}^J \omega_k (p^k_n)^{1-\eta}}, \quad \text{for all } j = \{1, \ldots, J\} \quad (1.4)$$

and

$$p^{J+1}_n Y^{J+1}_n = (1 - \xi_n)(w_n L_n + r_n K_n).$$

We next characterize the production and factor allocations across the world. Let Q^j_n denote the total sectoral demand in country n and sector j. Q^j_n is used for both final consumption and intermediate inputs in domestic production of all sectors. That is,

$$\begin{aligned} p^j_n Q^j_n = p^j_n Y^j_n &+ \sum_{j'=1}^{J} (1 - \beta'_j)\gamma_{j,j'} \left(\sum_{i=1}^{N} \pi^{j'}_{in} p^{j'}_i Q^{j'}_i \right) \\ &+ (1 - \beta_{J+1})\gamma_{j,J+1} p^{J+1}_n Q^{J+1}_n. \end{aligned}$$

Total expenditure in sector $j = 1, \ldots, J+1$ of country n, $p^j_n Q^j_n$, is the sum of (i) domestic final consumption expenditure $p^j_n Y^j_n$; (ii) expenditure on sector j goods as intermediate inputs in all the traded sectors $\sum_{j'=1}^J (1 - \beta'_j)\gamma_{j,j'} \left(\sum_{i=1}^N \pi^{j'}_{in} p^{j'}_i Q^{j'}_i\right)$, and (iii) expenditure on the j's sector intermediate inputs in the domestic non-traded sector $(1 - \beta_{J+1})\gamma_{j,J+1} p^{J+1}_n Q^{J+1}_n$. These market clearing conditions summarize the two important features of the world economy captured by the model: complex international production linkages, as much of world trade is in intermediate inputs, and a good crosses borders multiple times before being consumed Hummels, Ishii and Yi 2001); and two-way input linkages between the tradeable and the nontradeable sectors.

In each tradeable sector j, some goods q are imported from abroad and some goods q are exported to the rest of the world. Country n's exports in sector j are given by $EX^j_n = \sum_{i=1}^N \mathbb{1}_{i \neq n} \pi^j_{in} p^j_i Q^j_i$, and its imports in sector

j are given by $IM_n^j = \sum_{i=1}^N \mathbb{I}_{i\neq n}\pi_{ni}^j p_n^j Q_n^j$, where $\mathbb{I}_{i\neq n}$ is the indicator function. The total exports of country n are then $EX_n = \sum_{j=1}^J EX_n^j$, and total imports are $IM_n = \sum_{j=1}^J IM_n^j$. Trade balance requires that for any country n, $EX_n - IM_n = 0$.

We now study the factor allocations across sectors. The total production revenue in tradeable sector j in country n is given by $\sum_{i=1}^N \pi_{in}^j p_i^j Q_i^j$. The optimal sectoral factor allocations in country n and tradeable sector j must thus satisfy

$$\sum_{i=1}^{N} \pi_{in}^j p_i^j Q_i^j = \frac{w_n L_n^j}{\alpha_j \beta_j} = \frac{r_n K_n^j}{(1-\alpha_j)\beta_j}.$$

For the nontradeable sector $J+1$, the optimal factor allocations in country n are simply given by

$$p_n^{J+1} Q_n^{J+1} = \frac{w_n L_n^{J+1}}{\alpha_{J+1}\beta_{J+1}} = \frac{r_n K_n^{J+1}}{(1-\alpha_{J+1})\beta_{J+1}}.$$

Finally, the feasibility conditions for factors are given by, for any n,

$$\sum_{j=1}^{J+1} L_n^j = L_n \quad \text{and} \quad \sum_{j=1}^{J+1} K_n^j = K_n.$$

Given all of the model parameters, factor endowments, trade costs, and productivities, the model is solved using the algorithm described in Section 1.5.

1.3 Estimating Model Parameters

This section describes the estimation of the sector-level technology parameters T_n^j for a large set of countries, in three steps. First, we estimate the technology parameters in the tradeable sectors relative to the U.S. using data on sectoral output and bilateral trade. The procedure relies on fitting a structural gravity equation implied by the model. Intuitively, if controlling for the typical gravity determinants of trade, a country spends relatively more on domestically produced goods in a particular sector, it is revealed to have either a high relative productivity or a low relative unit cost in that sector. We then use data on factor and intermediate input prices to net out the role of factor costs, yielding an estimate of relative productivity. This step also produces estimates of bilateral trade costs at the sectoral level over time. Second, we estimate the technology parameters in the tradeable sectors for the U.S.. This procedure requires directly measuring TFP at the sectoral level using data on real output and inputs, and then correcting measured TFP for selection due to trade. The taste parameters for all tradeable sectors ω_j are also calibrated in this step. Third, we calibrate the nontradeable technology for all countries using the first-order condition of the model and the relative prices observed in the data.

The calibration of the remaining parameters is more straightforward. Some parameters — $\alpha_j, \beta_j, \gamma_{j',j}, \xi_n, L_n$, and K_n — come directly from the data. For a small number of parameters — θ, η, and ε – we take values estimated elsewhere in the literature. We discuss the data sources used to calibrate these parameters in detail in Section 1.4.

1.3.1 *Tradeable Sector Relative Technology*

We now focus on the tradeable sectors. Following the standard EK approach, first divide trade shares by their domestic counterpart:

$$\frac{\pi_{ni}^j}{\pi_{nn}^j} = \frac{X_{ni}^j}{X_{nn}^j} = \frac{T_i^j \left(c_i^j d_{ni}^j\right)^{-\theta}}{T_n^j \left(c_n^j\right)^{-\theta}},$$

which in logs becomes:

$$\ln\left(\frac{X_{ni}^j}{X_{nn}^j}\right) = \ln\left(T_i^j (c_i^j)^{-\theta}\right) - \ln\left(T_n^j (c_n^j)^{-\theta}\right) - \theta \ln d_{ni}^j.$$

Let the (log) iceberg costs be given by the following expression:

$$\ln d_{ni}^j = d_k^j + b_{ni}^j + CU_{ni}^j + RTA_{ni}^j + ex_i^j + \nu_{ni}^j,$$

where d_k^j is an indicator variable for a distance interval. Following EK, we set the distance intervals, in miles, to [0, 350], [350, 750], [750, 1500], [1500, 3000], [3000, 6000], [6000, maximum). Additional variables are whether the two countries share a common border (b_{ni}^j), belong to a currency union (CU_{ni}^j), or to a regional trade agreement (RTA_{ni}^j). We include an exporter fixed effect ex_i^j following Waugh (2010), who shows that the exporter fixed effect specification does a better job at matching the patterns in both country incomes and observed price levels. Finally, there is an error term ν_{ni}^j. Note that all the variables have a sector superscript j: we allow all the trade cost proxy variables to affect true iceberg trade costs d_{ni}^j differentially across sectors. There is a range of evidence that trade volumes at sector level vary in their sensitivity to distance or common border (see, among many others, Do and Levchenko, 2007; Berthelon and Freund, 2008).

This leads to the following final estimating equation:

$$\ln\left(\frac{X_{ni}^j}{X_{nn}^j}\right) = \underbrace{\ln\left(T_i^j(c_i^j)^{-\theta}\right) - \theta ex_i^j}_{\text{Exporter Fixed Effect}} \underbrace{- \ln\left(T_n^j\left(c_n^j\right)^{-\theta}\right)}_{\text{Importer Fixed Effect}}$$

$$\underbrace{-\theta d_k^j - \theta b_{ni}^j - \theta CU_{ni}^j - \theta RTA_{ni}^j}_{\text{Bilateral Observables}} \underbrace{-\theta \nu_{ni}^j}_{\text{Error Term}}.$$

This specification is estimated for each sector and decade separately, allowing for complete flexibility in how the coefficients vary both across sectors and over time. Estimating this relationship will thus yield, for each country, an estimate of its technology-cum-unit-cost term in each sector j, $T_n^j(c_n^j)^{-\theta}$, which is obtained by exponentiating the importer fixed effect.[2] The available degrees of freedom imply that these estimates are of each country's $T_n^j(c_n^j)^{-\theta}$ relative to a reference country, which in our estimation is the United States. We denote this estimated value by S_n^j:

$$S_n^j = \frac{T_n^j}{T_{us}^j}\left(\frac{c_n^j}{c_{us}^j}\right)^{-\theta},$$

where the subscript us denotes the United States. It is immediate from this expression that estimation delivers a convolution of technology parameters T_n^j and cost parameters c_n^j. Both will of course affect trade volumes, but we would like to extract technology T_n^j from these estimates. In order to do that, we follow the approach of Shikher (2012). In particular, for each country n, the share of total spending going to home-produced goods is

[2] A standard feature of this procedure is that the trade shares are logged, so that the zero bilateral import flows are dropped from the estimation sample (Eaton and Kortum, 2002; Waugh, 2010). Unfortunately, our large-scale model cannot be tractably enriched to explicitly account for zeros in trade and at the same time retain the structural interpretation linking the fixed effects to underlying productivity. However, we can check the ex-post performance of the estimated model with respect to zeros by solving the full model, and computing within the model the sum of the π_{ni}^j's in the importer-exporter-sector observations that are zeros in the actual data. We can then examine whether these observations account for large shares of absorption inside the model. If the resulting numbers are large, then the quantitative model predicts substantial trade flows where in reality there is zero. However, if these numbers are small, the model predicts very small flows where the actual flows are zero, providing a good approximation to the data even though productivities are estimated dropping zero trade. It turns out that observations for which actual data exhibit zero trade account for a tiny share of overall absorption in our quantitative model. We conclude from this exercise that in spite of ignoring the zero trade observations in estimation, our quantitative model is quite close to the data when it comes to small/zero trade flows.

given by

$$\frac{X^j_{nn}}{X^j_n} = T^j_n \left(\frac{\Gamma c^j_n}{p^j_n}\right)^{-\theta}.$$

Dividing by its U.S. counterpart yields:

$$\frac{X^j_{nn}/X^j_n}{X^j_{us,us}/X^j_{us}} = \frac{T^j_n}{T^j_{us}} \left(\frac{c^j_n}{c^j_{us}}\frac{p^j_{us}}{p^j_n}\right)^{-\theta} = S^j_n \left(\frac{p^j_{us}}{p^j_n}\right)^{-\theta},$$

and thus the ratio of price levels in sector j relative to the U.S. becomes:

$$\frac{p^j_n}{p^j_{us}} = \left(\frac{X^j_{nn}/X^j_n}{X^j_{us,us}/X^j_{us}}\frac{1}{S^j_n}\right)^{\frac{1}{\theta}}. \tag{1.5}$$

The entire right-hand side of this expression is either observable or estimated. Thus, we can impute the price levels relative to the U.S. in each country and each tradeable sector.

The cost of the input bundles relative to the U.S. can be written as:

$$\frac{c^j_n}{c^j_{us}} = \left(\frac{w_n}{w_{us}}\right)^{\alpha_j\beta_j} \left(\frac{r_n}{r_{us}}\right)^{(1-\alpha_j)\beta_j} \left(\prod_{k=1}^{J}\left(\frac{p^k_n}{p^k_{us}}\right)^{\gamma_{k,j}}\right)^{1-\beta_j}$$
$$\times \left(\frac{p^{J+1}_n}{p^{J+1}_{us}}\right)^{\gamma_{J+1,j}(1-\beta_j)}.$$

Using information on relative wages, returns to capital, price in each tradeable sector from equation (1.5), and the nontradeable sector price relative to the U.S., we can thus impute the costs of the input bundles relative to the U.S. in each country and each sector. Armed with those values, it is straightforward to back out the relative technology parameters:

$$\frac{T^j_n}{T^j_{us}} = S^j_n \left(\frac{c^j_n}{c^j_{us}}\right)^{\theta}.$$

1.3.2 *Trade Costs*

The bilateral, directional, sector-level trade costs of shipping from country i to country n in sector j are then computed based on the estimated coefficients as:

$$\ln \hat{d}^j_{ni} = \theta\hat{d}^j_k + \theta\hat{b}^j_{ni} + \theta\widehat{CU}^j_{ni} + \theta\widehat{RTA}^j_{ni} + \theta\widehat{ex}^j_i + \theta\widehat{\nu}^j_{ni},$$

for an assumed value of θ. Note that the estimate of the trade costs includes the residual from the gravity regression $\theta\widehat{\nu}^j_{ni}$. Thus, the trade costs computed as above will fit bilateral sectoral trade flows exactly, given the estimated fixed effects. Note also that the exporter component of the trade costs $\widehat{ex}^j_i$ is part of the exporter fixed effect. Since each country in the sample appears as both an exporter and an importer, the exporter and importer estimated fixed effects are combined to extract an estimate of $\theta\widehat{ex}^j_i$.

1.3.3 *Complete Estimation*

So far we have estimated the levels of technology of the tradeable sectors relative to the United States. To complete our estimation, we still need to find (i) the levels of T for the tradeable sectors in the United States; (ii) the taste parameters ω_j, and (iii) the nontradeable technology levels for all countries.

To obtain (i), we use the NBER-CES Manufacturing Industry Database for the U.S. (Bartelsman and Gray 1996). We start by measuring the observed TFP levels for the tradeable sectors in the U.S.. The form of the production function gives

$$\ln Z^j_{us} = \ln \Lambda^j_{us} + \beta_j\alpha_j \ln L^j_{us} + \beta_j(1-\alpha_j)\ln K^j_{us} + (1-\beta_j)\sum_{k=1}^{J+1}\gamma_{k,j}\ln M^{k,j}_{us}, \tag{1.6}$$

where Λ^j denotes the measured TFP in sector j, Z^j denotes the output, L^j denotes the labor input, K^j denotes the capital input, and $M^{k,j}$ denotes the intermediate input from sector k. The NBER-CES Manufacturing Industry Database offers information on output, and inputs of labor, capital, and intermediates, along with deflators for each. Thus, we can estimate the observed TFP level for each manufacturing tradeable sector using the above equation.

If the United States were a closed economy, the observed TFP level for sector j would be given by $\Lambda^j_{us} = (T^j_{us})^{\frac{1}{\theta}}$. In the open economies, the goods with inefficient domestic productivity draws will not be produced and will be imported instead. Thus, international trade and competition introduce selection in the observed TFP level, as demonstrated by Finicelli, Pagano and Sbracia (2013). We thus use the model to back out the true level of T^j_{us} of each tradeable sector in the United States. Here we follow Finicelli,

Pagano and Sbracia (2013) and use the following relationship:

$$(\Lambda_{us}^j)^\theta = T_{us}^j + \sum_{i \neq us} T_i^j \left(\frac{c_i^j d_{us,i}^j}{c_{us}^j} \right)^{-\theta}.$$

Thus, we have

$$(\Lambda_{us}^j)^\theta = T_{us}^j \left[1 + \sum_{i \neq us} \frac{T_i^j}{T_{us}^j} \left(\frac{c_i^j d_{us,i}^j}{c_{us}^j} \right)^{-\theta} \right] = T_{us}^j \left[1 + \sum_{i \neq us} S_i^j \left(d_{us,i}^j \right)^{-\theta} \right]. \tag{1.7}$$

This equation can be solved for underlying technology parameters T_{us}^j in the U.S., given estimated observed TFP Λ_{us}^j, and all the S_i^j's and $d_{us,i}^j$'s estimated in the previous subsection.

To estimate the taste parameters $\{\omega_j\}_{j=1}^J$, we use information on final consumption shares in the tradeable sectors in the U.S.. We start with a guess of $\{\omega_j\}_{j=1}^J$ and find sectoral prices p_n^k as follows. For an initial guess of sectoral prices, we compute the tradeable sector aggregate price and the nontradeable sector price using the data on the relative prices of nontradeables to tradeables. Using these prices, we calculate sectoral unit costs and Φ_n^j's, and update prices according to equation (1.3), iterating until the prices converge. We then update the taste parameters according to equation (1.4), using the data on final sectoral expenditure shares in the U.S.. We normalize the vector of ω_j's to have a sum of one, and repeat the above procedure until the values for the taste parameters converge.

Finally, we estimate the nontradeable sector TFP using the relative prices. In the model, the nontradeable sector price is given by

$$p_n^{J+1} = \Gamma (T_n^{J+1})^{-\frac{1}{\theta}} c_n^{J+1}.$$

Since we know the aggregate price level in the tradeable sector p_n^T, c_n^{J+1}, and the relative price of nontradeables (which we take from the data), we can back out T_n^{J+1} from the equation above for all countries.

1.4 Data Description and Implementation

In order to carry out the estimation and model implementation, we assemble data on production and trade for a sample of up to 75 countries, 19 manufacturing sectors, and spanning five decades, from the 1960s to the 2000s. Production data come from the 2009 UNIDO Industrial Statistics Database, which reports output, value added, employment, and wage bills at roughly 2-digit ISIC Revision 3 level of disaggregation for the period 1962–2007 in the best of cases. The corresponding trade data comes from the COMTRADE database compiled by the United Nations. The trade data are collected at the 4-digit SITC level, and aggregated up to the 2-digit ISIC level using a concordance developed by the authors. Production and trade data were extensively checked for quality, and a number of countries were discarded due to poor data quality. In addition, in less than 5% of country-year-sector observations, the reported total output was below total exports, and thus had to be imputed based on earlier values and the evolution of exports. Table 1.1 lists the countries used in the analysis along

Table 1.1. Country Coverage

Country	Period	Country	Period
OECD		Non-OECD	
Australia	1960s–2000s	Argentina	1980s–2000s
Austria	1960s–2000s	Bangladesh	1970s–2000s
Belgium-Luxembourg	1960s–2000s	Bolivia	1960s–2000s
Canada	1960s–2000s	Brazil	1980s–2000s
Denmark	1960s–2000s	Bulgaria	1990s–2000s
Finland	1960s–2000s	Chile	1960s–2000s
France	1960s–2000s	China	1970s–2000s
Germany	1960s–2000s	Colombia	1960s–2000s
Greece	1960s–2000s	Costa Rica	1960s–2000s
Iceland	1960s–2000s	Czech Republic	1990s–2000s
Ireland	1960s–2000s	Ecuador	1960s–2000s
Italy	1960s–2000s	Egypt, Arab Rep.	1960s–2000s
Japan	1960s–2000s	El Salvador	1960s–2000s
Netherlands	1960s–2000s	Ethiopia	1980s–2000s
New Zealand	1960s–2000s	Fiji	1960s–2000s
Norway	1960s–2000s	Ghana	1960s–2000s
Portugal	1960s–2000s	Guatemala	1960s–2000s
Spain	1960s–2000s	Honduras	1960s–2000s
Sweden	1960s–2000s	Hungary	1990s–2000s
Switzerland	1980s–2000s	India	1960s–2000s
United Kingdom	1960s–2000s	Indonesia	1960s–2000s
United States	1960s–2000s	Iran, Islamic Rep.	1960s–2000s
		Israel	1960s–2000s
		Jordan	1960s–2000s
		Kazakhstan	1990s–2000s
		Kenya	1960s–2000s
		Korea, Rep.	1960s–2000s
		Kuwait	1960s–2000s
		Malaysia	1960s–2000s
		Mauritius	1960s–2000s

(*Continued*)

Table 1.1. (*Continued*)

Country	Period	Country	Period
		Mexico	1960s–2000s
		Nigeria	1960s–2000s
		Pakistan	1960s–2000s
		Peru	1980s–2000s
		Philippines	1960s–2000s
		Poland	1990s–2000s
		Romania	1990s–2000s
		Russian Federation	1990s–2000s
		Saudi Arabia	1980s–2000s
		Senegal	1970s–2000s
		Slovak Republic	1990s–2000s
		Slovenia	1990s–2000s
		South Africa	1960s–2000s
		Sri Lanka	1960s–2000s
		Taiwan Province of China	1970s–2000s
		Tanzania	1960s–2000s
		Thailand	1960s–2000s
		Trinidad and Tobago	1960s–2000s
		Turkey	1960s–2000s
		Ukraine	1990s–2000s
		Uruguay	1960s–2000s
		Venezuela, RB	1960s–2000s
		Vietnam	1990s–2000s

Note: This table reports the countries in the sample and the decades for which data are available for each country.

with the time periods for which data are available for each country, and Table 1.2 lists the sectors along with the key parameter values for each sector: α_j, β_j, the share of nontradeable inputs in total inputs $\gamma_{J+1,j}$, and the taste parameter ω_j.

The distance and common border variables are obtained from the comprehensive geography database compiled by CEPII. Information on regional trade agreements comes from the RTA database maintained by the WTO. The currency union indicator comes from Rose (2004), and was updated for the post-2000 period using publicly available information (such as the membership in the Euro area, and the dollarization of Ecuador and El Salvador).

In addition to providing data on output for gravity estimation, the UNIDO data are used to estimate production function parameters α_j and β_j. To compute α_j for each sector, we calculate the share of the total wage bill in value added, and take a simple median across countries (taking the

Table 1.2. Sectors

ISIC code	Sector Name	α_j	β_j	$\gamma_{J+1,j}$	ω_j
15	Food and Beverages	0.315	0.281	0.303	0.148
16	Tobacco Products	0.264	0.520	0.527	0.013
17	Textiles	0.467	0.371	0.295	0.024
18	Wearing Apparel, Fur	0.493	0.377	0.320	0.141
19	Leather, Leather Products, Footwear	0.485	0.359	0.330	0.016
20	Wood Products (Excl. Furniture)	0.452	0.372	0.288	0.011
21	Paper and Paper Products	0.366	0.344	0.407	0.014
22	Printing and Publishing	0.484	0.469	0.407	0.005
23	Coke, Refined Petroleum Products, Nuclear Fuel	0.244	0.243	0.246	0.029
24	Chemicals and Chemical Products	0.308	0.373	0.479	0.009
25	Rubber and Plastics Products	0.385	0.387	0.350	0.003
26	Non-Metallic Mineral Products	0.365	0.459	0.499	0.079
27	Basic Metals	0.381	0.299	0.451	0.002
28	Fabricated Metal Products	0.448	0.398	0.364	0.016
29C	Office, Accounting, Computing, and Other Machinery	0.473	0.390	0.388	0.073
31A	Electrical Machinery, Communication Equipment	0.405	0.380	0.416	0.037
33	Medical, Precision, and Optical Instruments	0.456	0.428	0.441	0.051
34A	Transport Equipment	0.464	0.343	0.286	0.236
36	Furniture and Other Manufacturing	0.460	0.407	0.397	0.091
4A	Nontradeables	0.561	0.651	0.788	
	Mean	0.414	0.393	0.399	0.053
	Min	0.244	0.243	0.246	0.002
	Max	0.561	0.651	0.788	0.236

Notes: This table reports the sectors used in the analysis. The classification corresponds to the ISIC Revision 3 2-digit, aggregated further due to data availability. α_j is the value-added based labor intensity; β_j is the share of value added in total output; $\gamma_{J+1,j}$ is the share of nontradeable inputs in total intermediate inputs; ω_j is the taste parameter for tradeable sector j, estimated using the procedure described in Section 1.3.3. Variable definitions and sources are described in detail in the text.

mean yields essentially the same results). To compute β_j, take the median of value added divided by total output.

The intermediate input coefficients $\gamma_{j',j}$ are obtained from the Direct Requirements Table for the United States. We use the 1997 Benchmark Detailed Make and Use Tables (covering approximately 500 distinct sectors), as well as a concordance to the ISIC Revision 3 classification to build a Direct Requirements Table at the 2-digit ISIC level. The Direct Requirements Table gives the value of the intermediate input in row j' required to produce one dollar of final output in column j. Thus, it is the direct counterpart of the input coefficients $\gamma_{j',j}$. Note that the bulk of our analysis assumes these to be the same in all countries.[3] In addition, we use the U.S. I-O matrix to obtain the shares of total final consumption expenditure going to each sector, which we use to pin down taste parameters ω_j in traded sectors $1, \ldots, J$; as well as α_{J+1} and β_{J+1} in the nontradeable sector, which cannot be obtained from UNIDO.[4]

The computation of relative costs of the input bundle requires information on wages and the returns to capital. To compute wages, we divide the total manufacturing sector wage bill by total manufacturing employment in each country, and take that value relative to the U.S.. Consistent with the model, this procedure delivers wages that differ by country but not by sector.[5]

Obtaining information on the return to capital, r_n, is less straightforward, since it is not observable directly. In the baseline analysis, we assume that the wage-rental ratio is determined by the aggregate capital-labor ratio through an aggregate market clearing condition: $r_n/w_n = ((1-\alpha)L_n) / (\alpha K_n)$, where α is the aggregate share of labor in GDP, which we set to 2/3.[6]

The price of nontradeables relative to the U.S., p_n^{J+1}/p_{us}^{J+1}, and the price of nontradeables relative to tradeables in each country, p_n^{J+1}/p_n^T, are computed using the detailed price data collected by the International Comparison of Prices Program (ICP). For a few countries and decades, these relative prices are extrapolated using a simple linear fit to log PPP-adjusted

[3]The following chapters discuss robustness checks that use country-specific I-O matrices. Whether or not we use country-specific I-O matrices is never consequential for the results that follow.

[4]The U.S. I-O matrix provides an alternative way of computing α_j and β_j. These parameters calculated based on the U.S. I-O table are very similar to those obtained from UNIDO, with the correlation coefficients between them above 0.85 in each case. The U.S. I-O table implies greater variability in α_j's and β_j's across sectors than does UNIDO.

[5]In less than 1% of country-decade observations, either the total wage bill or employment are missing from the UNIDO data. In those cases, the wage relative to the U.S. is proxied by the GDP per capita relative to the U.S.

[6]The return to capital will be affected by country characteristics other than capital abundance, such as the quality of the country's regulatory environment, corruption, and expropriation risk, among other factors. Indeed, Caselli and Feyrer (2007) document that the marginal product of capital is remarkably similar across a wide range countries. Alternatively, the return to capital will be the same in all countries under international capital mobility. None of the results below are affected if we assume instead that the return to capital, r_n, does not differ across countries.

per capita GDP from the Penn World Tables 6.3 (Heston, Summers and Aten 2002).

The total labor force in each country, L_n, and the total capital stock, K_n, are obtained from the Penn World Tables 6.3. Following the standard approach in the literature (see, e.g. Hall and Jones 1999, Bernanke and Gürkaynak 2001, Caselli 2005), the total labor force is calculated from the data on the total GDP per capita and per worker.[7] The total capital is calculated using the perpetual inventory method that assumes a depreciation rate of 6%: $K_{n,t} = (1 - 0.06)K_{n,t-1} + I_{n,t}$, where $I_{n,t}$ is total investment in country n in period t. For most countries, investment data start in 1950, and the initial value of K_n is set equal to $I_{n,0}/(\gamma + 0.06)$, where γ is the average growth rate of investment in the first 10 years for which data are available.

In order to estimate the relative TFP's in the tradedable sectors in the U.S., we use the 2009 version of the NBER-CES Manufacturing Industry Database, that reports the total output, total input usage, employment, and capital stock, along with deflators for each of these in each sector. The data are available in the 6-digit NAICS classification for the period 1958 to 2005, and are converted into ISIC 2-digit sectors using a concordance developed by the authors. The procedure yields sectoral measured TFP's for the U.S. in each tradeable sector $j = 1, \ldots, J$ and each decade.

The share of expenditure on traded goods, ξ_n in each country and decade is sourced from Uy, Yi and Zhang (2013), who compile this information for 30 developed and developing countries. For countries unavailable in the Yi and Zhang data, values of ξ_n are imputed based on fitting a simple linear relationship to log PPP-adjusted per capita GDP from the Penn World Tables. In each decade, the fit of this simple linear relationship was typically quite good, with R^2's of 0.30 to 0.80 across decades.

The baseline analysis assumes that the dispersion parameter θ does not vary across sectors and sets $\theta = 8.28$, which is the preferred estimate of EK.[8] We choose the elasticity of substitution between broad sectors within the tradeable bundle, η, to be equal to 2. Since these are very large product

[7]Using the variable name conventions in the Penn World Tables 6.3, $L_n = 1000 * pop * rgdpch/rgdpwok$.

[8]The following chapters present two types of robustness checks on θ. First, they implement a model under $\theta = 4$, which has been advocated by Simonovska and Waugh (2014) and is at or near the bottom of the range that has been used in the literature. Second, they use values of θ_j that vary across sectors, sourced from Caliendo and Parro (2015). Neither of these alternative assumptions on θ changes any of the results that follow.

categories, it is sensible that this elasticity would be relatively low. It is higher, however, than the elasticity of substitution between tradeable and nontradeable goods, which is set to 1 by the Cobb-Douglas assumption. The elasticity of substitution between varieties within each tradeable sector, ε, is set to 4 (as is well known, in the EK model this elasticity plays no role, entering only the constant Γ).

All of the variables that vary over time are averaged for each decade, from the 1960s to the 2000s, and these decennial averages are used in the analysis throughout. Thus, our unit of time is a decade.

1.5 Solution Algorithm

The model equilibrium is found iteratively starting with an initial guess. Given $\{L_n, K_n, \{T_n^j\}_{j=1}^{J+1}, \xi_n\}_{n=1}^N$, $\{\varepsilon, \alpha_j, \theta, \beta_j, \{\gamma_{k,j}\}_{k=1}^{J+1}, \{d_{ni}^j\}_{N\times N}\}_{j=1}^{J+1}$, and η, we compute the competitive equilibrium of the model as follows.

1. Guess $\{w_n, r_n\}_{n=1}^N$.
   - Compute prices from the following equations:

$$c_n^j = \left(w_n^{\alpha_j} r_n^{1-\alpha_j}\right)^{\beta_j} \left(\prod_{k=1}^{J+1} \left(p_n^k\right)^{\gamma_{k,j}}\right)^{1-\beta_j}$$
$$\text{for all } n \in \{1, \dots, N\} \text{ and } j \in \{1, \dots, J+1\},$$

$$\Phi_n^j = \sum_{i=1}^{N} T_i^j \left(c_i^j d_{ni}^j\right)^{-\theta} \quad \text{for all } n \in \{1, \dots, N\} \text{ and } j \in \{1, \dots, J\},$$

$$\Phi_n^{J+1} = T_n^{J+1} \left(c_n^{J+1}\right)^{-\theta} \quad \text{for all } n \in \{1, \dots, N\},$$

$$p_n^j = \Gamma \left(\Phi_n^j\right)^{-\frac{1}{\theta}} \quad \text{for all } n \in \{1, \dots, N\} \text{ and } j \in \{1, \dots, J+1\},$$

$$P_n = B_n \left(\sum_{j=1}^{J} \omega_j (p_n^j)^{1-\eta}\right)^{\frac{1}{1-\eta}\xi_n} (p_n^{J+1})^{1-\xi_n} \quad \text{for all } n \in \{1, \dots, N\}.$$

   - Compute the final demand as follows: for any country n,

$$Y_n^j = \xi_n \frac{w_n L_n + r_n K_n}{p_n^j} \frac{\omega_j (p_n^j)^{1-\eta}}{\sum_{k=1}^{J} \omega_k (p_n^k)^{1-\eta}}, \quad \text{for all } j = \{1, .., J\},$$

$$Y_n^{J+1} = (1 - \xi_n) \frac{w_n L_n + r_n K_n}{p_n^{J+1}}.$$

- Compute the trade shares π_{ni}^j as follows:

$$\pi_{ni}^j = \frac{T_i^j \left(c_i^j d_{ni}^j\right)^{-\theta}}{\Phi_n^j}.$$

- Compute the total demand as follows: for any country n and any sector j

$$p_n^j Y_n^j + \sum_{k=1}^{J} \left(\sum_{i=1}^{N} Q_i^k p_i^k \pi_{in}^k \right) (1-\beta_k)\gamma_{j,k} + Q_n^{J+1} p_n^{J+1} (1-\beta_{J+1})\gamma_{j,J+1} = p_n^j Q_n^j.$$

- Compute the factor allocations across sectors as follows: for any country n,

$$\sum_{i=1}^{N} p_i^j Q_i^j \pi_{in}^j = \frac{w_n L_n^j}{\alpha_j \beta_j} = \frac{r_n K_n^j}{(1-\alpha_j)\beta_j}, \quad \text{for all } j = \{1, \dots, J\},$$

$$p_n^{J+1} Q_n^{J+1} = \frac{w_n L_n^{J+1}}{\alpha_{J+1}\beta_{J+1}} = \frac{r_n K_n^{J+1}}{(1-\alpha_{J+1})\beta_{J+1}}.$$

2. Update $\{w_n', r_n'\}_{n=1}^N$ with the feasibility conditions for factors: for any n,

$$\sum_{j=1}^{J+1} L_n^j = L_n, \quad \sum_{j=1}^{J+1} K_n^j = K_n.$$

3. Repeat the above procedures until $\{w_n', r_n'\}_{n=1}^N$ is close enough to $\{w_n, r_n\}_{n=1}^N$.

References

Bartelsman, E. J. and W. Gray, "The NBER Manufacturing Productivity Database," October 1996. NBER Technical Working Paper 205.

Bernanke, B. and R. Gürkaynak, "Is Growth Exogenous? Taking Mankiw, Romer, and Weil Seriously," *NBER Macroeconomics Annual*, 2001, *16*, 11–57.

Berthelon, M. and C. Freund, "On the Conservation of Distance in International Trade," *Journal of International Economics*, July 2008, *75*(2), 310–320.

Caliendo, L. and F. Parro, "Estimates of the Trade and Welfare Effects of NAFTA," *Review of Economic Studies*, January 2015, *82*(1), 1–44.

Caselli, F., "Accounting for Cross-Country Income Differences," in Steven Durlauf Philippe Aghion, ed., *Handbook of Economic Growth*, Vol. 1, Elsevier-North Holland, 2005, pp. 679–741.

Caselli, F. and J. Feyrer, "The Marginal Product of Capital," *Quarterly Journal of Economics*, May 2007, *122*(2), 535–568.

Do, Q.-T. and A. A. Levchenko, "Comparative Advantage, Demand for External Finance, and Financial Development," *Journal of Financial Economics*, December 2007, *86*(3), 796–834.

Eaton, J. and S. Kortum, "Technology, Geography, and Trade," *Econometrica*, September 2002, *70*(5), 1741–1779.

Finicelli, A., P. Pagano, and M. Sbracia, "Ricardian Selection," *Journal of International Economics*, 2013, *89*(1), 96–109.

Hall, R. and C. I. Jones, "Why Do Some Countries Produce So Much More Output per Worker then Others," *Quarterly Journal of Economics*, 1999, *114*, 83–116.

Heston, A., R. Summers and B. Aten, "Penn World Table Version 6.1," October 2002. Center for International Comparisons at the University of Pennsylvania (CICUP).

Hummels, D., J. Ishii, and K.-M. Yi, "The Nature and Growth of Vertical Specialization in World Trade," *Journal of International Economics*, June 2001, *54*, 75–96.

Rose, A. K., "Do We Really Know That the WTO Increases Trade?," *American Economic Review*, March 2004, *94*(1), 98–114.

Shikher, S., "Putting industries into the Eaton-Kortum model," *Journal of International Trade and Economic Development*, 2012, *21*(6), 807–837.

Simonovska, I. and M. E. Waugh, "The Elasticity of Trade: Estimates and Evidence," *Journal of International Economics*, January 2014, *92*(1), 34–50.

Uy, T., K.-M. Yi, and J. Zhang, "Structural Change in an Open Economy," *Journal of Monetary Economics*, September 2013, *60*(6), 667–682.

Waugh, M. E., "International Trade and Income Differences," *American Economic Review*, December 2010, *100*(5), 2093–2124.

European Economic Review 65 (2014) 45–65

Contents lists available at ScienceDirect

European Economic Review

journal homepage: www.elsevier.com/locate/eer

Ricardian productivity differences and the gains from trade ☆

Andrei A. Levchenko [a,b,c,*], Jing Zhang [d]

[a] University of Michigan, United States
[b] NBER, United States
[c] CEPR, United Kingdom
[d] Federal Reserve Bank of Chicago, United States

ARTICLE INFO

Article history:
Received 4 June 2013
Accepted 18 October 2013
Available online 6 November 2013

JEL classification:
F4

Keywords:
Gains from trade
Comparative advantage
Sufficient statistics

ABSTRACT

This paper evaluates the role of sectoral heterogeneity in determining the gains from trade. We first show analytically that in the presence of sectoral Ricardian comparative advantage, a one-sector sufficient statistic formula that uses total trade volumes as a share of total absorption systematically understates the true gains from trade. Greater relative sectoral productivity differences lead to larger disparities between the gains implied by the one-sector formula and the true gains. Using data on overall and sectoral trade shares in a sample of 79 countries and 19 sectors we show that the multi-sector formula implies on average 30% higher gains from trade than the one-sector formula, and as much as 100% higher gains for some countries. We then set up and estimate a quantitative Ricardian-Heckscher-Ohlin model in which no version of the formula applies exactly, and compare a range of sufficient statistic formulas to the true gains in this model. Confirming the earlier results, formulas that do not take into account the sectoral heterogeneity understate the true gains from trade in the model by as much as two-thirds. The one-sector formulas understate the gains by more in countries with greater dispersion in sectoral productivities.

1. Introduction

It has recently been discovered that under certain restrictions, models with different micro-structures – Armington, Eaton-Kortum, and Melitz – deliver an identical expression for gains from trade (Arkolakis et al., 2012). In its simplest form, the gross proportional gains from trade can be expressed as $\pi_{ii}^{-1/\theta}$, where π_{ii} is the share of spending on domestically produced goods in total spending of the economy, and θ is the elasticity of trade flows with respect to iceberg trade costs.

This result is potentially powerful for two closely related and mutually reinforcing reasons. The first is that one need not even take a precise stand on the micro-structure of the economy or motives for international exchange when evaluating the gains from trade. The second is that the gains are in fact expressed in terms of only a couple of (in principle) observable values. Thus, if the right data are available, and/or one is willing to take a stand on the value of just one or two reduced-form parameters, one could compute a country's gain from trade easily, without the heavy lifting of setting up, estimating/

☆ We are grateful to Alan Deardorff, Andrés Rodríguez-Clare, Linda Tesar, an anonymous referee, and seminar participants at the University of Michigan, University of Nottingham, University of Warwick, and the 2013 NBER ITI Spring Meetings for helpful suggestions. The views expressed here are those of the authors and do not necessarily represent those of the Federal Reserve Bank of Chicago, the Federal Reserve System, or its Board of Governors.

* Corresponding author at: Department of Economics, University of Michigan, 611 Tappan Street, Ann Arbor, MI 48104, USA. Tel. +1 734 764 3296.
E-mail addresses: alev@umich.edu (A.A. Levchenko), jzhang@chifrb.org (J. Zhang).
URLS: http://alevchenko.com (A.A. Levchenko), https://sites.google.com/site/jzhangzn/ (J. Zhang).

0014-2921/$ - see front matter © 2013 Elsevier B.V. All rights reserved.
http://dx.doi.org/10.1016/j.euroecorev.2013.10.006

calibrating, and solving a large-scale quantitative trade model. This promises to dramatically lower barriers to applied policy analysis, and transform the way policy research on the benefits of trade is conducted.

Since the formula features the share of spending on domestically produced goods in total spending, an (over-)simplified message from this literature can easily be taken to be "all you need to know is the overall trade volume." By contrast, it has been understood since Ricardo (1817) that when sectors are imperfect substitutes in consumption, comparative advantage in international trade matters for the magnitude of the gains. Broadly speaking, the stronger the comparative advantage – the more different countries are in their relative technology – the larger are the gains from trade. In turn, cross-sectoral Ricardian comparative advantage will manifest itself in differences in trade shares across sectors, as countries will have less imports as a share of total spending in their comparative advantage sectors, and more imports in their comparative disadvantage sectors. Does the simple formula featuring the overall trade openness adequately capture this source of gains from trade? Arkolakis et al. (2012) show how under certain conditions, the formula can be extended to a setting with multiple sectors, but do not discuss how the gains from trade in a multi-sector formula differ from the gains implied by the one-sector formula.

This paper shows that by ignoring the sectoral heterogeneity in productivity – and hence in trade volumes – the one-sector formula systematically understates the gains from trade. We develop this result in three ways. First, we use a simplified 2-sector, 2-country model to show analytically that the gains from trade according to the one-sector formula coincide with the true gains only when the trade volumes relative to absorption are the same in every sector. *Any* deviation from equal trade volumes across sectors – holding aggregate trade volumes relative to absorption constant – leads to larger gains than what is implied by the one-sector formula. Greater differences in relative sectoral productivities, implying greater dispersion in sectoral trade shares, increase both the gains from trade and the disparity between the true gains and those implied by the one-sector formula.

Second, the differences between one- and multi-sector formula gains are large in magnitude when computed on observed trade flows. We use actual data on output and cross-border trade at sector level in a large sample of countries to compare the gains implied by the one-sector formula to those implied by the formula that uses information on sectoral trade shares. Almost without exception, the gains according to the one-sector formula are lower than those according to the multi-sector formula, confirming the analytical results. The multi-sector formula produces 30% higher gains from trade on average, and as much as 100% higher in countries with a large dispersion in sectoral trade shares. The disparity is also highly non-uniform across countries. There are many examples in which total trade volumes – and thus the gains according to the one-sector formula – are quite similar for a pair of countries, but the multi-sector formula gains differ substantially because of very different degrees of dispersion in sectoral trade shares.

The third part of the paper relates the dispersion in the sectoral trade shares and the resulting bias in the one-sector formulas explicitly to Ricardian comparative advantage. We use the sectoral productivity estimates and the large-scale 79-country 20-sector Ricardian–Heckscher–Ohlin model built by Levchenko and Zhang (2011, 2012). In addition to Ricardian productivity differences, the framework incorporates multiple factors of production, a non-tradeable sector, and intermediate input linkages between and within the sectors. The parameters are calibrated using observed production technologies and input–output matrices, and estimated using bilateral sector-level trade. The model matches relative factor prices and both overall and bilateral trade quite well. In this framework, no version of the formula applies. Because we fully solved it, we can compute the true gains from trade inside this model. We then compare these gains to a series of sufficient statistic formulas, to evaluate which types of formulas work best, and thus which features of the real world are a must to include in any formula-based analysis. It is important to emphasize that we do not claim that gains from trade computed in this model coincide with the true gains from trade in reality. No matter how rich the model, the real world will inevitably be more complex. In our view, the exercise is nonetheless informative because the model does capture, in a quantitative way, several distinct sources of the gains from trade, which can then be compared to the sufficient statistic formulas' attempts to also capture (some of) those gains.

Our main finding is that the simpler formulas that do not use information on sectoral trade volumes understate the true gains from trade dramatically, often by more than two-thirds. The error in the formulas across countries is strongly negatively correlated to the strength of Ricardian comparative advantage: the one-sector formula-implied gains understate the true gains from trade by more in countries with greater dispersion in sectoral productivity. The model-based exercise thus reinforces the main result of the paper that accounting for sectoral heterogeneity in productivity is essential for a reliable assessment of the gains from trade.

We conclude from the analytical results, the data-based evaluation, and the model-based evaluation that policy analysis must take sectoral variation in trade volumes into account when computing the gains from trade using the sufficient statistic approach.

This paper contributes to the recent literature on the welfare gains from trade that arose in parallel with, and in response to, Arkolakis et al. (2012). A number of papers explore the impact of market structure (the extensive margin, variable markups) on the gains from trade (see, among others, Arkolakis et al., 2008, 2012; Atkeson and Burstein, 2010; Feenstra, 2010; Corcos et al., 2012; deBlas and Russ, 2012; di Giovanni and Levchenko, 2013).

This paper addresses sectoral heterogeneity instead. In that respect, our analysis is most closely related to Imbs and Méjean (2011) and Ossa (2012), who explore the biases in the one-sector gains from trade formula induced by sectoral heterogeneity, and Costinot and Rodríguez-Clare (forthcoming), who provide a series of gains from trade results under different assumptions, including one-sector and multi-sector formulas. Relative to these papers, our substantive point is complementary and distinct. We explore variation in sectoral productivity and trade volumes, whereas Imbs and Méjean (2011), Ossa (2012), and Costinot and Rodríguez-Clare (forthcoming) focus on the variation in the trade elasticities across sectors. To make this distinction as transparent as possible, our analysis is carried out under the same trade elasticity in all sectors. While Imbs and Méjean (2011) and Costinot and Rodríguez-Clare (forthcoming) also allude to the dispersion in trade shares across sectors, we relate it explicitly to Ricardian comparative advantage and present a complete elaboration of this effect both analytically and quantitatively. In addition, we provide a model-based evaluation of the performance of the different sufficient statistic formulas. Our argument that sectoral productivity heterogeneity increases the gains from trade is related to the arguments in Melitz and Redding (2013) regarding the impact of firm heterogeneity.

The last part of the paper is based on the quantitative Ricardian–Heckscher–Ohlin model developed and estimated by Levchenko and Zhang (2011, 2012) and di Giovanni et al. (forthcoming). This paper shares with our earlier work the emphasis on the quantitative welfare impact of sectoral technology differences. While our earlier papers focus on technological change or trade integration of individual regions (China, Eastern Europe), this paper investigates the performance of the various sufficient statistic formulas for the gains from trade. The model-based exercise in the last part of the paper is methodologically related to studies that evaluate empirical estimation approaches by applying them to model-simulated data in which the true data-generating process is by construction known. See, for instance, Chari et al. (2008) for an application of this strategy in the business cycle context, and Hauk and Wacziarg (2009) for an application in the economic growth context. Our approach of looking for observables that accurately capture the gains from trade bears an affinity to Burstein and Cravino (2012), who explore the conditions under which real GDP data will reflect the welfare gains from reductions in trade costs.

The rest of the paper is organized as follows. Section 2 derives the analytical results on the impact of sectoral dispersion in trade flows on the gains from trade. Section 3 compares one-sector and multi-sector sufficient statistic formulas for the gains from trade using data on the trade volumes and production. Section 4 sets up the quantitative framework and discusses the results of comparing a range of sufficient statistic formulas to the true gains from trade. Section 5 concludes.

2. Analytical results

This section presents a simple model to illustrate the role of sectoral heterogeneity in determining the gains from trade. The exercise makes two main points. First, the one-sector formula for the gains from trade systematically understates the true gains from trade when there is dispersion in trade volumes across sectors. Holding the overall trade volume – and thus the gains implied by the one-sector formula – constant, the true gains from trade increase in the cross-sectoral dispersion in trade shares. And second, the degree of dispersion in trade shares across sectors is intimately related to the strength of Ricardian comparative advantage.

Consider a two-country (1 and 2) two-sector (a and b) (Eaton and Kortum, 2002, henceforth EK) model. Labor is the only input in production, and both countries are endowed with one unit: $L_1 = L_2 = 1$. International trade is costless. Each sector is a CES composite of a continuum of varieties [0, 1] that do not overlap across sectors, and country i can produce each infinitesimal variety with productivity drawn randomly from the Fréchet distribution with dispersion parameter θ common to all countries and sectors, and central tendency parameter T_i^j in country i, sector j. The parameter T_i^j determines the average productivity draw in country i sector j. Thus, as a shorthand we will refer to T_i^j as country i's "productivity" in sector j. As the structure of the EK model is standard, we do not reproduce the functional forms and derivations here (the more full-fledged multi-sector EK model is described in Section 4), and focus instead on the outcomes.

Preferences are Cobb–Douglas over the broad sectors of the economy, an assumption adopted throughout the paper. Costinot and Rodríguez-Clare (forthcoming) show that the overall gains from trade depend heavily on the "upper level" elasticity of substitution, and point out that we currently have no reliable estimates of what that elasticity would be across broad sectors of the economy. The level of sectoral disaggregation we employ throughout the paper is quite coarse – 19 tradeable sectors – making the Cobb–Douglas assumption relatively more plausible than it would be with finely disaggregated sectors.[1] The result that sectoral dispersion in trade shares will increase the gains from trade conditional on the overall trade volume is more general, however, and would obtain whenever the elasticity of substitution between sectors is lower than the elasticity of substitution within sectors – a reasonable assumption.

To obtain analytical results under endogenous factor price determination, we assume (i) equal expenditure shares in the two sectors and (ii) a mirror image of productivities across sectors and countries: $T_1^a = T_2^b$ and $T_1^b = T_2^a$. Of course, relative productivities are not generically the same in the two countries, $T_1^a/T_1^b \neq T_2^a/T_2^b$, and thus the strength of comparative advantage can vary. The mirror image assumption on sectoral productivity and symmetry in the utility function ensure that the wages are equal in the two countries, $w_1 = w_2$, which we set as the numeraire. Together with the normalization of labor

---

[1] As a related point, our results cannot be "extrapolated" to argue that adopting an ever finer level of sectoral disaggregation will lead to ever higher implied gains from trade, for two reasons. First, the multi-sector gains from trade formulas explored in the paper only apply if the utility over these sectors is Cobb–Douglas. As we disaggregate sectors further and further, the Cobb–Douglas assumption will become implausible. While the assumption of unitary elasticity of substitution is palatable at the 19-sector level of disaggregation (Food Products, Textiles, Apparel, etc.), it will be implausible for a 190-sector level of disaggregation, since by construction more finely disaggregated products will be more similar to each other, and thus more substitutable. Second, the model relies on the EK structure within each sector – that is, there is a continuum of varieties within each sector, and at the sector level countries have interior trade shares. Under much more disaggregated sectors, the EK assumption within each sector will be strained.

endowments to 1 this implies that the total income/expenditure in each country is equal to 1, and trade flows expressed as shares of total expenditure also equal absolute trade flows.

Denote by π^j_{ni} the share of total expenditure in country n on goods coming from country i in sector j. The import shares in country 1 from country 2 are given by

$$\pi^a_{12} = \frac{T^a_2 w_2^{-\theta}}{T^a_1 w_1^{-\theta} + T^a_2 w_2^{-\theta}} = \frac{T^a_2}{T^a_1 + T^a_2}, \tag{1}$$

$$\pi^b_{12} = \frac{T^b_2 w_2^{-\theta}}{T^b_1 w_1^{-\theta} + T^b_2 w_2^{-\theta}} = \frac{T^b_2}{T^b_1 + T^b_2} = \frac{T^a_1}{T^a_1 + T^a_2}, \tag{2}$$

where the last equality uses the mirror image assumption we put on the relative productivities ($T^a_1 = T^b_2$ and $T^b_1 = T^a_2$).

Importantly, regardless of the sectoral import shares, the assumptions on preferences and technology imply that the overall imports (and thus domestically produced goods) as a share of total absorption are always one-half: $\pi_{11} = \pi_{22} = \frac{1}{2}$, regardless of the strength of comparative advantage.[2] An "econometrician" that assumes this economy is well-characterized by a one-sector EK model with labor as the only input in production will compute the (gross) gains from trade as[3]

$$\pi_{ii}^{-1/\theta}. \tag{3}$$

This implies that gains from trade computed using only aggregate trade volumes are always constant in this model.

However, as comparative advantage and thus sectoral trade shares change, the true gains from trade will change as well. Welfare in country i is given by the indirect utility function, and corresponds to real income:

$$\frac{w_i}{(p^a p^b)^{1/2}}, \tag{4}$$

where p^j is the price of sector $j = a, b$ composite, which does not vary by country since trade is costless. Standard steps lead to the expression for welfare as a function of technology and trade shares by sector:[4]

$$\frac{w_i}{(p^a p^b)^{1/2}} = \Gamma^{-1}(T^a_i T^b_i)^{1/(2\theta)}(\pi^a_{ii}\pi^b_{ii})^{-1/(2\theta)}, \tag{5}$$

where Γ is a constant. Thus, the true gains from trade in this model are expressed as

$$(\pi^a_{ii}\pi^b_{ii})^{-1/(2\theta)} = (\pi^a_{ii}(1-\pi^a_{ii}))^{-1/(2\theta)}, \tag{6}$$

where the second equality is due to the fact that $\pi^b_{11} = \pi^a_{22} = 1 - \pi^a_{21} = 1 - \pi^a_{12}$. The following result is immediate, coming from differentiation of (6) with respect to π^a_{ii}:

Proposition 1. *When the share of absorption spent on domestically produced goods is the same across sectors, $\pi^a_{ii} = \pi^b_{ii}$, (i) the true gains from trade attain their minimum, and (ii) the gains from trade implied by the one-sector formula (3) and computed based on aggregate imports and absorption coincide with the true gains from trade. Therefore, the one-sector formula understates the true gains from trade as long as $\pi^a_{ii} \neq \pi^b_{ii}$.*

The result stated in the proposition is illustrated in Fig. 1(a). It plots the true gains from trade and the gains from trade implied by the one-sector formula against the share of spending on domestic goods in sector a, π^a_{ii}. Because of the symmetry assumptions we imposed the total trade volume as a share of absorption is fixed throughout, and so the gains implied by the one-sector model are constant as π^a_{ii} varies. The true gains from trade, computed using information on sectoral trade volumes, are always at least as great as the gains implied by the one-sector formula, and the deviation gets larger the larger is the asymmetry between the sectoral trade shares π^j_{ii}. The one-sector formula yields the true gains from trade only when the trade shares are identical in the two sectors: $\pi^a_{ii} = \pi^b_{ii} = \frac{1}{2}$.

Finally we draw the connection between the magnitude of the gains from trade and the strength of comparative advantage.

Corollary 1. *The deviation between the true gains and the gains implied by the one-sector formula increases as the comparative advantage becomes stronger – that is, as the differences in relative T^j_i's grow.*

[2] To see this, note that the total imports as a share of spending in country 1 are given by

$$\pi_{12} = \frac{w_1 L_1 \frac{1}{2}\pi^a_{12} + w_1 L_1 \frac{1}{2}\pi^b_{12}}{w_1 L_1} = \frac{1}{2},$$

where the last equality comes from the fact, immediate from (1) to (2), that $\pi^b_{12} = 1 - \pi^a_{12}$. Since the share of total spending on domestically produced goods and on imports sum to 1, $\pi_{11} = 1 - \pi_{12} = \frac{1}{2}$.

[3] See Eaton and Kortum (2002) and Arkolakis et al. (2012).

[4] The price index in sector j is given by $p^j = \Gamma(T^j_1 + T^j_2)^{1/\theta}$ (Eaton and Kortum, 2002). Combining this expression with the trade shares (1) and (2) to write p^j as a function of π^j_{ii} and plugging into (4) yields (5).

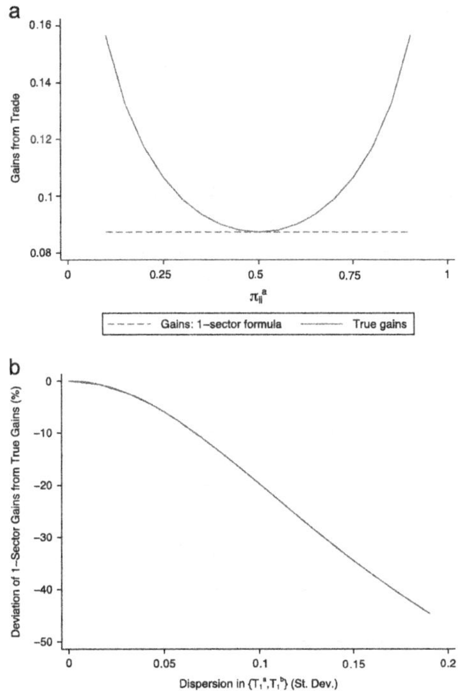

Fig. 1. Illustration of analytical results. (a) Sectoral trade shares and the gains from trade. (b) Comparative advantage and the gains from trade. *Notes:* The top panel depicts the true gains from trade in the 2-sector analytical model as well as the gains from trade implied by the one-sector formula that only uses aggregate trade as a share of absorption. The bottom panel displays the percentage difference between the gains implied by the one-sector formula and true gains as a function of the dispersion in T_1^a and T_1^b, with dispersion measured by the standard deviation among them.

The corollary is immediate from Eqs. (1) and (2). The point at which the welfare gain implied by the one-sector formula coincides with the true gains corresponds to identical technology in the two countries: $T_1^a = T_1^b = T_2^a = T_2^b$. The more different the sectoral absorption shares in the gains from trade formula (6) the more different are T_1^a and T_1^b. Fig. 1b depicts this relationship. It plots the percentage difference between the gains from trade implied by the one-sector formula and the true gains against the dispersion in sectoral T_i^j's, measured by the standard deviation between T_1^a and T_1^b. As expected, greater dispersion in T_i^j's results in the one-sector formula missing the true gains by more.

3. Dispersion in sectoral trade shares and gains from trade

It is possible that while analytically we can show that the one-sector formula systematically understates the gains from trade in a multi-sector environment, real-world sectoral trade shares are such that this understatement is not large in magnitude. In this section we use actual data on manufacturing production and trade for a sample of 79 countries to assess how large are the disparities between the gains from trade implied by the one-sector and the multi-sector formulas under the observed sectoral trade shares.

For 52 countries in the sample, information on output comes from the 2009 UNIDO Industrial Statistics Database. For the 27 European Union countries plus FYR Macedonia, the EUROSTAT database contains data of superior quality, and thus for those countries we used EUROSTAT production data. The two output data sources are merged at the roughly 2-digit ISIC Revision 3 level of disaggregation, yielding 19 manufacturing sectors. Bilateral trade data come from the United Nations' COMTRADE database, concorded to the same sectoral classification. Sectoral absorption shares are averaged for the period

2000–2007, which is the time period on which we carry out the analysis. Appendix Table A1 lists the countries used in the analysis, while Appendix Table A2 lists the sectors.

We compare the gains from trade implied by two formulas: a one-sector formula in which the manufacturing sector is treated as one, and a multi-sector formula. To scale the aggregate gains from trade appropriately, we augment these formulas with a non-tradeable sector. The one-sector formula is

$$\pi_{ii}^{-\xi/\theta} - 1. \tag{7}$$

The multi-sector formula (see Arkolakis et al., 2012, Section IV.A) is

$$\prod_{j=1}^{J} (\pi_{ii}^{j})^{-\xi\omega_j/\theta} - 1, \tag{8}$$

where j indexes sectors.

To be precise, (7) is the gains from trade in a model with labor as the only input in production, one tradeable and one non-tradeable sector, with utility Cobb–Douglas in the two sectors and ξ as the expenditure share of tradeables. The tradeable sector can be an EK-type sector as in Sections 2 and 4, or an Armington-type sector that aggregates goods from different origin countries. The non-tradeable sector can be either an EK-type sector or a sector producing a homogeneous good. The model that yields (8) as the gains from trade is the same except tradeables are composed of j sectors, over which utility is Cobb–Douglas with expenditure shares ω_j. Once again, each tradeable sector can be either EK or Armington.

Table 1
Welfare gains from trade implied by the one- and multi-sector formulas.

	Mean	Std. Dev.	Min	Max
$\pi_{ii}^{-\xi/\theta} - 1$	0.022	0.010	0.005	0.051
$\prod_{j=1}^{J}(\pi_{ii}^{j})^{-\xi\omega_j/\theta} - 1$, Equal-weighted	0.035	0.017	0.006	0.067
$\prod_{j=1}^{J}(\pi_{ii}^{j})^{-\xi\omega_j/\theta} - 1$, Expenditure-weighted	0.030	0.016	0.005	0.080
Pct difference, equal-weighted to one-sector	0.567	0.421	−0.069	1.706
Pct difference, exp.-weighted to one-sector	0.321	0.222	0.032	0.990

Notes: This table presents the summary statistics for the gains from trade implied by the one-sector formula, the equal-weighted multi-sector formula, and the expenditure-weighted multi-sector formula in the sample of 79 countries. The bottom two rows present the summary statistics for the proportional deviations of the multi-sector formulas relative to the one-sector one.

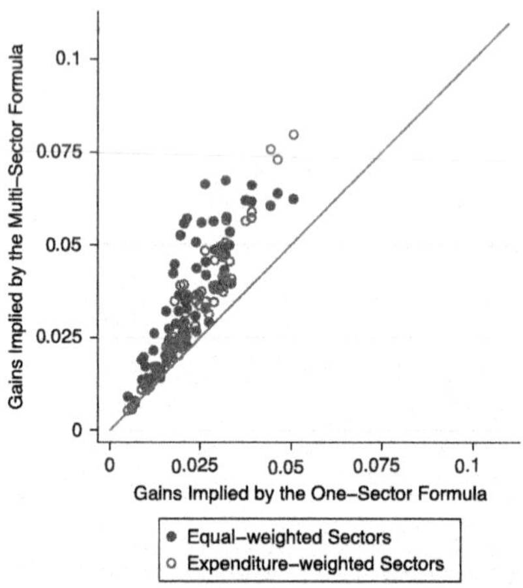

Fig. 2. Estimated gains from trade according to one-sector and multi-sector formulas. *Notes:* This figure plots the gains from trade implied by the one-sector formula on the x-axis against the gains from trade for the same country implied by the equal-weighted (solid dots) and the expenditure-share-weighted (hollow dots) multi-sector formulas, along with the 45-degree line.

For a fully fledged description of one particular model that can lead to these gains from trade formulas, we can refer to Section 4 below. Formula (7) captures the gains from trade in the model set out in Section 4 when (i) there is only 1 traded sector ($J=1$), (ii) there is no capital ($K_n=0\ \forall n$ and $\alpha_j=1\ \forall j$) and (iii) there are no input–output linkages ($\beta_j=1\ \forall j$). Formula (8) captures the gains from trade in the model in Section 4 under conditions (ii)–(iii), but with $J>1$.

In formulas (7) and (8), the absorption shares in manufacturing, both in aggregate (π_{ii}) and at the sector level (π^j_{ii}) come directly from the data on production and trade. To implement these formulas, we must take a stand on a number of parameters. We adopt two alternative assumptions on the Cobb–Douglas shares of sectors in consumption ω_j. First, to make the mechanics behind sectoral heterogeneity's effect as transparent as possible, we set those weights to be equal across sectors. Second, since ω_j's are equivalent to consumption shares, we set them to the actual absorption shares of each manufacturing sector in each country. Since those shares differ across countries, and since a great deal of gross absorption of manufacturing output goes to intermediate input usage, this approach may be less transparent, but it will account for inherent differences in sector sizes. The other two parameters (θ and ξ) do not matter for the qualitative conclusions about the direction of the effect, since they both exponentiate the whole formula. Anticipating the quantitative exercise below, in which this elasticity has a concrete interpretation in the context of the Eaton–Kortum model, we set θ to 8.28, which is the preferred value in Eaton and Kortum (2002). We set the Cobb–Douglas utility weight of the manufacturing sector to 0.35 (Alvarez and Lucas, 2007).

Table 1 presents the summary statistics for the gains from trade implied by the one-sector formula (7) and the multi-sector formula (8), under two assumptions on the utility weights ω_j. The bottom two rows report the summary statistics for the proportional difference between the multi-sector gains from trade and the one-sector gains from trade. The clear result is that the one-sector formula systematically understates the gains from trade relative to the multi-sector formula. The difference is substantial in proportional terms: the gains implied by the multi-sector formulas are 32% and 56% larger, on average, than the one-sector gains. In the more extreme cases, the gains implied by the multi-sector formulas are twice as large as the gains implied by the one-sector formula. The direction of the bias is also (nearly) universal: in every single one of the 79 countries, the expenditure-weighted formula implies larger gains than the one-sector formula, and in 78 out of 79 countries, the equal-weighted formula implies larger gains.

Fig. 2 presents the results graphically by plotting the multi-sector formula gains on the y-axis against the one-sector formula gains on the x-axis. The solid dots denote the gains implied by the equal-weighted sectors, while the hollow dots denote the gains under the expenditure weights. For convenience, a 45° line is added to the plot. It is immediate that nearly all the dots are above the 45° line – the multi-sector gains are larger than the one-sector gains. It is also clear that the larger are the total gains, the greater is the deviation between the one-sector and the multi-sector formulas.

To provide intuition for how sectoral heterogeneity conditions the gains from trade, consider the comparison between Bolivia and the Czech Republic. In the data, these two countries have similar overall openness in the manufacturing sector, and thus similar gains from trade according to the one-sector formula. In fact, Czech Republic's one-sector formula gains, at 2.39%, are slightly larger than the one-sector formula gains for Bolivia, which are 2.06%. However, at a similar – in fact slightly lower – level of overall openness, the dispersion in trade volumes across sectors is much greater in Bolivia. Fig. 3 depicts the shares of domestically produced goods in sectoral spending, π^j_{ii}, for Bolivia and Czech Republic, ranking sectors from the most open (lowest π^j_{ii}) to the least open for each country. It is immediate that the variation in openness across sectors in Bolivia is higher. In its most open sectors, a far greater share of total expenditure goes to imported goods, and in its least open sector, a lower share of expenditure goes to imports, compared to the Czech Republic. This greater heterogeneity implies that Bolivia's gains from trade are actually higher than Czech Republic's, not lower as implied by the one-sector formula. The differences in sectoral heterogeneity also mean that the deviation between the one- and the multi-sector gains

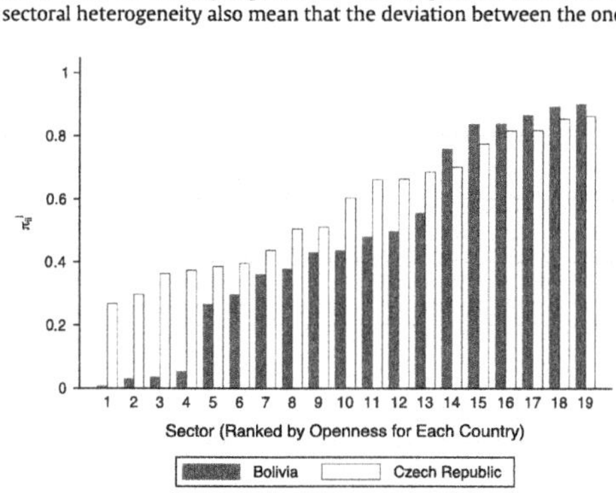

Fig. 3. Dispersion in sectoral trade shares: Bolivia and the Czech republic. *Notes:* This figure displays the π^j_{ii} in the 19 manufacturing sectors for Bolivia and the Czech Republic, ranked for each country by sectoral trade openness (sectors with lower π_{ii} correspond to sectors with lower shares of spending on domestic goods in the total sectoral spending).

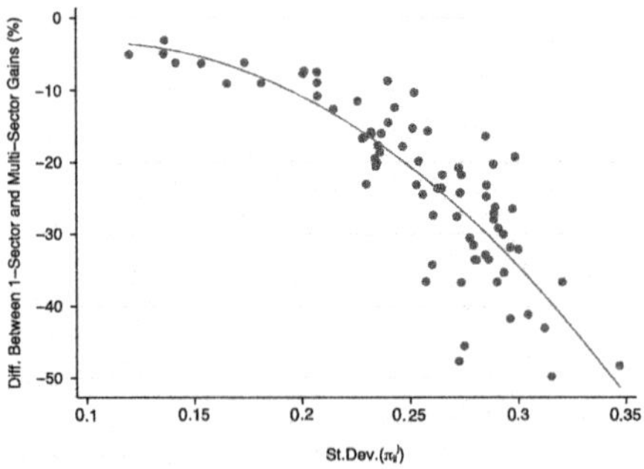

Fig. 4. Dispersion in sectoral trade shares and the gains from trade. *Notes:* This figure plots the percentage difference between the gains from trade implied by the one-sector formula relative to the multi-sector formula against the standard deviation of π_{ii}^j for that country. The curve through the data is the quadratic fit.

is much larger in Bolivia. The expenditure-weighted multi-sector gains in Bolivia are 3.93%, nearly double the gains implied by the one-sector formula, and the equal-weighted gains are 5.57%, or 2.7 times larger. By contrast, for the Czech Republic, the multi-sector gains are 2.67% and 2.68%, or only 11–12% larger than the one-sector gains.

The pattern that greater dispersion in sectoral π_{ii}^j's implies greater deviations between multi- and one-sector gains is a general one. Fig. 4 plots the proportional difference between the one-sector gains and the expenditure-weighted multi-sector gains against the standard deviation of π_{ii}^j's across sectors in each country, which we use as a measure of dispersion in trade shares across sectors. The correlation between the two is -0.82. In countries with larger dispersion in trade shares across sectors, the one-sector formula understates the gains by more, relative to the multi-sector formula.

4. Quantitative assessment

The previous section performed a data-driven exercise: it used actual trade shares by sector to compare the gains implied by the different formulas. However, variation in sectoral trade shares alone does not itself establish Ricardian comparative advantage, since trade shares can differ for a variety of reasons. In addition, the world economy is much more complex than the models that lead to either formula (7) or formula (8), what we cannot do purely with the data is compare the formula-implied gains to the true gains from trade.

While we cannot ever know the true gains from trade in the real world, in this section we implement a large-scale quantitative trade model, and conduct a model-based exercise in which we compare the true gains from trade in that model to a range of possible sufficient statistic formulas calculated based on model quantities that can (in principle) be measured in actual data.

The exercise has two goals. First, we relate the performance of the different sufficient statistic formulas explicitly to Ricardian comparative advantage. And second, we evaluate which, if any, sufficient statistic formulas that can be computed using real-world data are a good approximation to the true gains from trade in a world that is more complex. Aside from the sufficient statistic formula extensions that account for sectoral heterogeneity such as (8), a number of other extensions are known. For instance, sufficient statistic formulas can be enriched to take into account the input linkages, which are well-known to increase the gains from trade. In the world characterized by multiple sectors, input linkages, as well as many additional features at the same time, it is an open quantitative question in which extensions to the sufficient statistic formula are essential to get closer to the true gains. This exercise can thus assess the relative importance of the main mechanism in this paper – cross-sectoral dispersion in trade shares – compared to other sources of error in the simple gains from trade formulas.

Different sufficient statistic formulas also have very different data requirements. Clearly, a one-sector formula that uses only total trade flows and gross output requires less data than a multi-sector formula. Thus, from the perspective of applied trade policy evaluation using the sufficient statistic approach, it is important to know what are the minimum data requirements for a reliable assessment of the gains from trade.

4.1. The environment

The world is composed of N countries, indexed by n and i. There are J tradeable sectors, plus one non-tradeable sector $J+1$. Utility over these sectors in country n is given by

$$U_n = \left(\prod_{j=1}^{J} \left(Y_n^j \right)^{\omega_j} \right)^{\xi_n} (Y_n^{J+1})^{1-\xi_n}, \tag{9}$$

where ξ_n denotes the Cobb–Douglas weight of the tradeable sector composite good, ω_j is the share of tradeable sector j in total tradeable expenditure (and $\sum_{j=1}^{J}\omega_j = 1$), Y_n^{J+1} is the non-tradeable-sector composite good, and Y_n^j is the composite good in tradeable sector j.[5]

Each sector j aggregates a continuum of varieties $q \in [0, 1]$ unique to each sector using a CES production function:

$$Q_n^j = \left[\int_0^1 Q_n^j(q)^{(\varepsilon-1)/\varepsilon} dq\right]^{\varepsilon/(\varepsilon-1)},$$

where ε denotes the elasticity of substitution across varieties q, Q_n^j is the total output of sector j in country n, and $Q_n^j(q)$ is the amount of variety q that is used in production in sector j and country n. Producing one unit of good q in sector j in country n requires $1/z_n^j(q)$ input bundles.

Production uses labor (L), capital (K), and intermediate inputs from other sectors. The cost of an input bundle is

$$c_n^j = (w_n^{\alpha_j} r_n^{1-\alpha_j})^{\beta_j} \left(\prod_{k=1}^{J+1} (p_n^k)^{\gamma_{kj}}\right)^{1-\beta_j},$$

where w_n is the wage, r_n is the return to capital, and p_n^k is the price of intermediate input from sector k. The value-added based labor intensity is given by α_j, and the share of value added in total output by β_j. Both vary by sector. The shares of inputs from other sectors, γ_{kj}, vary by output industry j as well as input industry k.

As standard in the EK model, productivity $z_n^j(q)$ for each $q \in [0, 1]$ in each sector j is random, and drawn from the Fréchet distribution with cdf:

$$F_n^j(z) = e^{-T_n^j z^{-\theta}}.$$

In this distribution, the absolute advantage term T_n^j varies by both country and sector, with higher values of T_n^j implying higher average productivity draws in sector j in country n. The parameter θ captures dispersion, with larger values of θ implying smaller dispersion in draws.

The production cost of one unit of goods q in sector j and country n is thus equal to $c_n^j/z_n^j(q)$. Each country can produce each goods in each sector, and international trade is subject to iceberg costs: $d_{ni}^j > 1$ unit of goods q produced in sector j in country i must be shipped to country n in order for one unit to be available for consumption there. The trade costs need not be symmetric – d_{ni}^j need not equal d_{in}^j – and will vary by sector. We normalize $d_{nn}^j = 1$ for any n and j.

All the product and factor markets are perfectly competitive, and thus the price at which country i supplies tradeable good q in sector j to country n is

$$p_{ni}^j(q) = \left(\frac{c_i^j}{z_i^j(q)}\right) d_{ni}^j.$$

Buyers of each good q in tradeable sector j in country n will only buy from the cheapest source country, and thus the price actually paid for this good in country n will be

$$p_n^j(q) = \min_{i=1,\ldots,N}\left\{p_{ni}^j(q)\right\}.$$

The model thus contains two features that make a closed-form expression for gains from trade impossible (or at least currently unknown): multiple factors of production and cross-sectoral input–output linkages, both within the tradeable sector, and between tradeables and non-tradeables.

4.2. Characterization of equilibrium

The *competitive equilibrium* of this model world economy consists of a set of prices, allocation rules, and trade shares such that (i) given the prices, all firms' inputs satisfy the first-order conditions, and their output is given by the production function; (ii) given the prices, the consumers' demand satisfies the first-order conditions; (iii) the prices ensure the market clearing conditions for labor, capital, tradeable goods and non-tradeable goods; (iv) trade shares ensure balanced trade for each country.

The set of prices includes the wage rate w_n, the rental rate r_n, the sectoral prices $\{p_n^j\}_{j=1}^{J+1}$, and the aggregate price P_n in each country n. The allocation rules include the capital and labor allocation across sectors $\{K_n^j, L_n^j\}_{j=1}^{J+1}$, final consumption demand $\{Y_n^j\}_{j=1}^{J+1}$, and total demand $\{Q_n^j\}_{j=1}^{J+1}$ (both final and intermediate goods) for each sector. The trade shares include the expenditure share π_{ni}^j in country n on goods coming from country i in sector j.

[5] Note that unlike in Sections 2 and 3, the expenditure share of tradeables ξ_n will differ across countries and calibrated using data as described below.

4.2.1. Demand and prices

It can be easily shown that the price of sector j's output will be given by

$$p_n^j = \left[\int_0^1 p_n^j(q)^{1-\varepsilon} dq\right]^{1/(1-\varepsilon)}.$$

Following the standard EK approach, it is helpful to define

$$\Phi_n^j = \sum_{i=1}^N T_i^j (c_i^j d_{ni}^j)^{-\theta}.$$

This value summarizes, for country n, the access to production technologies in sector j. Its value will be higher if in sector j, country n's trading partners have high productivity (T_i^j) or low cost (c_i^j). It will also be higher if the trade costs that country n faces in this sector are low. Standard steps lead to the familiar result that the price of good j in country n is simply

$$p_n^j = \Gamma(\Phi_n^j)^{-1/\theta}, \tag{10}$$

where $\Gamma = [\mathbf{\Gamma}((\theta+1-\varepsilon)/\theta)]^{1/(1-\varepsilon)}$, with $\mathbf{\Gamma}$ the Gamma function. The consumption price index in country n is then

$$P_n = B_n \left(\prod_{j=1}^J (p_n^j)^{\omega_j}\right)^{\xi_n} (p_n^{J+1})^{1-\xi_n}, \tag{11}$$

where $B_n = \xi_n^{-\xi_n}(1-\xi_n)^{-(1-\xi_n)}$.

Both capital and labor are mobile across sectors and immobile across countries, and trade is balanced. The budget constraint (or the resource constraint) of the consumer is thus given by

$$\sum_{j=1}^{J+1} p_n^j Y_n^j = w_n L_n + r_n K_n, \tag{12}$$

where K_n and L_n are the endowments of capital and labor in country n.

Given the set of prices $\{w_n, r_n, P_n, \{p_n^j\}_{j=1}^{J+1}\}_{n=1}^N$, we first characterize the optimal allocations from final demand. Consumers maximize utility (9) subject to the budget constraint (12). The first order conditions associated with this optimization problem imply the following final demand:

$$p_n^j Y_n^j = \xi_n \omega_j (w_n L_n + r_n K_n), \quad \text{for all } j = \{1, .., J\}$$

and

$$p_n^{J+1} Y_n^{J+1} = (1-\xi_n)(w_n L_n + r_n K_n).$$

4.2.2. Production allocation and market clearing

Let Q_n^j denote the total sectoral demand in country n and sector j. Q_n^j is used for both final consumption and as intermediate inputs in domestic production of all sectors. Denote by $X_n^j = p_n^j Q_n^j$ the total *spending* on the sector j goods in country n, and by X_{ni}^j country n's total spending on sector j goods coming from country i, i.e. n's imports of j from country i. The EK structure in each sector j delivers the standard result that the probability of importing good q from country i, π_{ni}^j is equal to the share of total spending on goods coming from country i, X_{ni}^j / X_n^j, and is given by

$$\frac{X_{ni}^j}{X_n^j} = \pi_{ni}^j = \frac{T_i^j (c_i^j d_{ni}^j)^{-\theta}}{\Phi_n^j}. \tag{13}$$

The market clearing condition for expenditures on sector j in country n is

$$p_n^j Q_n^j = p_n^j Y_n^j + \sum_{k=1}^J (1-\beta_k)\gamma_{j,k}\left(\sum_{i=1}^N \pi_{in}^k p_i^k Q_i^k\right) + (1-\beta_{J+1})\gamma_{j,J+1} p_n^{J+1} Q_n^{J+1}.$$

Total expenditure in sector $j = 1, \ldots, J+1$ in country n, $p_n^j Q_n^j$, is the sum of (i) domestic final consumption expenditure $p_n^j Y_n^j$; (ii) expenditure on sector j goods as intermediate inputs in all the traded sectors $\sum_{k=1}^J (1-\beta_k)\gamma_{j,k}(\sum_{i=1}^N \pi_{in}^k p_i^k Q_i^k)$, and (iii) expenditure on the j's sector intermediate inputs in the domestic non-traded sector $(1-\beta_{J+1})\gamma_{jJ+1} p_n^{J+1} Q_n^{J+1}$. These market clearing conditions summarize two important features of the world economy captured by our model: complex international production linkages, as much of world trade is in intermediate inputs, and a good crosses borders multiple times before being consumed (Hummels et al., 2001); and two-way input linkages between the tradeable and the non-tradeable sectors.

In each tradeable sector j, some goods q are imported from abroad and some goods q are exported to the rest of the world. Country n's exports in sector j are given by $EX_n^j = \sum_{i=1}^N 1_{i \neq n} \pi_{in}^j p_i^j Q_i^j$, and its imports in sector j are given by

$IM_n^j = \sum_{i=1}^N 1_{i \neq n} \pi_{ni}^j p_n^j Q_n^j$, where $1_{i \neq n}$ is the indicator function. The total exports of country n are then $EX_n = \sum_{j=1}^J EX_n^j$, and total imports are $IM_n = \sum_{j=1}^J IM_n^j$. Trade balance requires that for any country n, $EX_n - IM_n = 0$.

Given the total production revenue in tradeable sector j in country n, $\sum_{i=1}^N \pi_{in}^j p_i^j Q_i^j$, the optimal sectoral factor allocations must satisfy

$$\sum_{i=1}^{N} \pi_{in}^j p_i^j Q_i^j = \frac{w_n L_n^j}{\alpha_j \beta_j} = \frac{r_n K_n^j}{(1-\alpha_j)\beta_j}.$$

For the non-tradeable sector $J+1$, the optimal factor allocations in country n are simply given by

$$p_n^{J+1} Q_n^{J+1} = \frac{w_n L_n^{J+1}}{\alpha_{J+1}\beta_{J+1}} = \frac{r_n K_n^{J+1}}{(1-\alpha_{J+1})\beta_{J+1}}.$$

Finally, the feasibility conditions for factors are given by, for any n,

$$\sum_{j=1}^{J+1} L_n^j = L_n \quad \text{and} \quad \sum_{j=1}^{J+1} K_n^j = K_n.$$

4.3. *Estimation, calibration, and solution*

The core implementation step of this model is the estimation of the sector-level technology parameters T_n^j for a large set of countries. The technology parameters in the tradeable sectors relative to a reference country (the U.S.) are estimated using data on sectoral output and bilateral trade. The procedure relies on fitting a structural gravity equation implied by the model. Intuitively, if controlling for the typical gravity determinants of trade, a country spends relatively more on domestically produced goods in a particular sector, it is revealed to have either a high relative productivity or a low relative unit cost in that sector. The procedure then uses data on factor and intermediate input prices to net out the role of factor costs, yielding an estimate of relative productivity. This step also produces estimates of bilateral, sector-level trade costs d_{ni}^j. The next step is to estimate the technology parameters in the tradeable sectors for the U.S. This procedure requires directly measuring TFP at the sectoral level using data on real output and inputs, and then correcting measured TFP for selection due to trade. Third, the non-tradeable technology for all countries is calibrated using the first-order condition of the model and the relative prices of non-tradeables observed in the data. The detailed procedures for all three steps are described in Levchenko and Zhang (2011) and reproduced in Appendix A.

Estimation of sectoral productivity parameters T_n^j and trade costs d_{ni}^j requires data on total output by sector, as well as sectoral data on bilateral trade, that are described at the beginning of Section 3. Productivity and trade cost estimation requires an assumption on the dispersion parameter θ. We pick the value of $\theta = 8.28$, which is the preferred estimate of EK, and in addition assume that it does not vary across sectors.[6]

In order to implement the model numerically, we must in addition calibrate the following sets of parameters: (i) preference parameters ω_j and ξ_n; (ii) production function parameters ε, α_j, β_j, γ_{kj} for all sectors j and k; (iii) country factor endowments L_n and K_n.

The share of expenditure on traded goods, ξ_n in each country is sourced from Yi and Zhang (2010), who compile this information for 30 developed and developing countries. For countries unavailable in the Yi and Zhang data, values of ξ_n are imputed based on fitting a simple linear relationship to log PPP-adjusted per capita GDP from the Penn World Tables. The fit of this simple bivariate linear relationship is quite good, with the R^2 of 0.55. The taste parameters for tradeable sectors ω_j were set equal to final consumption expenditure shares in the U.S. sourced from the U.S. Input–Output matrix.

The production function parameters α_j and β_j are estimated using the output, value added, and wage bill data from EUROSTAT and UNIDO. To compute α_j for each sector, we calculate the share of the total wage bill in value added, and take a simple median across countries (taking the mean yields essentially the same results). To compute β_j, we calculate the ratio of value added to total output for each country and sector, and take the median across countries.

The intermediate input coefficients γ_{kj} are obtained from the Direct Requirements Table for the United States. We use the 1997 Benchmark Detailed Make and Use Tables (covering approximately 500 distinct sectors), as well as a concordance to the ISIC Revision 3 classification to build a Direct Requirements Table at the 2-digit ISIC level. The Direct Requirements Table gives the value of the intermediate input in row k required to produce one dollar of final output in column j. Thus, it is the

[6] There are no reliable estimates of how θ varies across sectors, and thus we do not model this variation. Shikher (2005, 2011, 2012), Eaton et al. (2011), and Burstein and Vogel (2012), among others, follow the same approach of assuming the same θ across sectors. Caliendo and Parro (2010) use tariff data and triple differencing to estimate sector-level θ. However, their approach may impose too much structure and/or be dominated by measurement error: at times the values of θ they estimate are negative. In addition, in each sector the restriction that $\theta > \varepsilon - 1$ must be satisfied, and it is not clear whether Caliendo and Parro (2010)'s estimated sectoral θ's meet this restriction in every case. Our approach is thus conservative by being agnostic on this variation across sectors. It is also important to assess how the results below are affected by the value of this parameter. One may be especially concerned about how the results change under lower values of θ. Lower θ implies greater within-sector heterogeneity in the random productivity draws. Thus, trade flows become less sensitive to the costs of the input bundles (c_i), and the gains from intra-sectoral trade become larger relative to the gains from inter-sectoral trade. In Levchenko and Zhang (2011), we estimated the sectoral productivities for a sample of 75 countries assuming instead a value of $\theta = 4$, which has been advocated by Simonovska and Waugh (2011) and is at or near the bottom of the range that has been used in the literature. Overall, the results are remarkably similar. The correlation between estimated T_i^j's under $\theta = 4$ and under $\theta = 8.28$ is above 0.95, and there is actually somewhat greater variability in T_i^j's under $\theta = 4$.

direct counterpart of the input coefficients γ_{kj}. Note that we assume these to be the same in all countries.[7] In addition, we use the U.S. I–O matrix to obtain α_{J+1} and β_{J+1} in the non-tradeable sector.[8] The elasticity of substitution between varieties within each tradeable sector, ε, is set to 4 (of course, as is well known, this value plays no role in this model, beyond affecting the value of the constant Γ). Appendix Table A2 lists the key parameter values for each sector: α_j, β_j, the share of non-tradeable inputs in total inputs $\gamma_{J+1,j}$, and the taste parameter ω_j.

The total labor force in each country, L_n, and the total capital stock, K_n, are computed based on the Penn World Tables 6.3. Following the standard approach in the literature (see, e.g., Hall and Jones, 1999; Bernanke and Gürkaynak, 2001; Caselli, 2005), the total labor force is calculated from data on the total GDP per capita and per worker.[9] The total capital stock is calculated using the perpetual inventory method that assumes a depreciation rate of 6%: $K_{n,t} = (1-0.06)K_{n,t-1} + I_{n,t}$, where $I_{n,t}$ is total investment in country n in period t. For most countries, investment data start in 1950, and the initial value of K_n is set equal to $I_{n,0}/(\gamma+0.06)$, where γ is the average growth rate of investment in the first 10 years for which data are available.

Given the estimated sectoral productivities, factor endowments, trade costs, and model parameters, we solve the system of equations defining the equilibrium under the baseline values. The algorithm for solving the model is described in Levchenko and Zhang (2011). Then, to compute the true gains from trade in the model we re-solve it under the assumption that each country is in autarky, and compare the autarky welfare to the welfare in the baseline. Finally, we compute in the baseline model a range of values that are (potentially) observable in the real-world data, and that are then used to compute gains from trade according to a range of formulas.

4.4. *Model fit*

Table 2 compares the wages, returns to capital, and the trade shares in the baseline model solution and in the data. The top panel shows that mean and median wages implied by the model are very close to the data. The correlation coefficient between model-implied wages and those in the data is above 0.99. The second panel performs the same comparison for the return to capital. Since it is difficult to observe the return to capital in the data, we follow the approach adopted in the estimation of T_n^j's and impute r_n from an aggregate factor market clearing condition: $r_n/w_n = (1-\alpha)L_n/(\alpha K_n)$, where α is the aggregate share of labor in GDP, assumed to be 2/3. Once again, the average levels of r_n are very similar in the model and the data, and the correlation between the two is about 0.95.

Next, we compare the trade shares implied by the model to those in the data. The third panel of Table 2 reports the spending on domestically produced goods as a share of overall spending, π_{nn}^j. These values reflect the overall trade openness, with lower values implying higher international trade as a share of absorption. Though we under-predict overall trade slightly (model π_{nn}^j's tend to be higher), the averages are quite similar, and the correlation between the model and data values is 0.92. Finally, the bottom panel compares the international trade flows in the model and the data. The averages are very close, and the correlation between model and data is about 0.91.

We conclude from this exercise that our model matches quite closely the relative incomes of countries as well as bilateral and overall trade flows observed in the data.

4.5. *Comparison of candidate gains from trade formulas*

All throughout, welfare is defined as the indirect utility function. Straightforward steps can be used to show that indirect utility in each country i is equal to total income divided by the price level. Since the model is competitive, total income equals the total returns to factors of production. Expressed in per capita terms welfare is thus

$$\frac{w_i + r_i k_i}{P_i},$$

where $k_i = K_i/L_i$ is capital per worker, and P_i comes from Eq. (11).

The true gains from trade in this model are computed by solving the baseline model, calculating welfare, and comparing this welfare to a counterfactual scenario in which all countries are assumed to be in autarky. The question is, from a pragmatic perspective, whether there is a formula based on quantities potentially observable in the data that can approximate the true gains from trade well. We go through a sequence of candidate formulas, with different data requirements, to see which data are essential to reliably compute the gains from trade using a formula.

To facilitate comparisons, Table 3 summarizes the formulas, the underlying models that deliver those formulas as the exact gains from trade, and the data requirements for implementing each formula. We proceed in the increasing order of

---

[7] di Giovanni and Levchenko (2010) provide suggestive evidence that at such a coarse level of aggregation, Input–Output matrices are indeed similar across countries. To check robustness of the results, Levchenko and Zhang (2011) collected country-specific I–O matrices from the GTAP database. Productivities computed based on country-specific I–O matrices were very similar to the baseline values, with the median correlation of 0.98, and all but 3 out of 75 countries with a correlation of 0.93 or above, and the minimum correlation of 0.65.

[8] The U.S. I–O matrix provides an alternative way of computing α_j and β_j. These parameters calculated based on the U.S. I–O table are very similar to those obtained from UNIDO, with the correlation coefficients between them above 0.85 in each case. The U.S. I–O table implies greater variability in α_j's and β_j's across sectors than does UNIDO.

[9] Using the variable name conventions in the Penn World Tables, $L_n = 1000 * pop * rgdpch/rgdpwok$.

Table 2
The fit of the baseline model with the data.

	Model		Data
Wages			
Mean	0.387		0.351
Median	0.131		0.150
Corr(model, data)		*0.994*	
Return to capital			
Mean	0.881		0.939
Median	0.664		0.698
Corr(model, data)		*0.946*	
π_{nn}^j			
Mean	0.621		0.569
Median	0.682		0.609
Corr(model, data)		*0.918*	
π_{ni}^j, $i \neq n$			
Mean	0.0052		0.0056
Median	0.0001		0.0001
Corr(model, data)		*0.908*	

Notes: This table reports the means and medians of wages relative to the U. S. (top panel); return to capital relative to the U.S. (second panel), share of domestically produced goods in overall spending (third panel), and share of goods from country i in overall spending (bottom panel) in the model and in the data. Wages and return to capital in the data are calculated as described in Appendix A.

Table 3
Formulas, underlying models, and data requirements.

Formula	Model	Data requirements
$\pi_{ii}^{-1/\theta}-1$	One-sector, no linkages	(1): Aggregate imports, exports, gross output
$\pi_{ii}^{-1/\beta\theta}-1$	One-sector, with linkages	(2): (1) + aggregate value added
$\pi_{ii}^{-\xi_i/\theta}-1$	Tradeable and non-tradeable sectors, no linkages	(3): (2) + breakdown of gross output and value added into tradeables and non-tradeables
$\pi_{ii}^{-\xi_i/\beta\theta}-1$:	Tradeable and non-tradeable sectors, within-sector linkages	
β=total interm. use		(3)
β=within-sector interm. use		(4): (3) + T/NT IO matrix
$\prod_{j=1}^{J}(\pi_{ii}^j)^{-\xi_i\omega_j/\theta}-1$	Multi-sector, no linkages	(5): sector-level output, imports, and exports, share of non-tradeables in aggregate value added
$\prod_{j=1}^{J}(\pi_{ii}^j)^{-\xi_i\omega_j/\beta_j\theta}-1$:	Multi-sector, within-sector linkages	
β_j=total linkages		(6): (5) + sectoral value added
β_j=tradeable only sectoral linkages		(7): (6) + full IO matrix

Notes: This table presents the formulas for the gains from trade, underlying models that yield those formulas, and the data requirements necessary to compute them.

data requirements. The simplest is a one-sector formula that does not distinguish explicitly between the traded and the non-traded sector, and relies only on observing the aggregate trade volume relative to the total gross output. To compute it, one would only need to collect data on aggregate imports and exports, as well as the gross output in the economy. The latter may not be as readily available as total GDP, but could be approximated, for instance, by "grossing up" total GDP by a factor that corresponds to one minus the share of intermediates in total output. One would then take these data and apply the formula $\pi_{ii}^{-1/\theta}-1$ where π_{ii}=(OUTPUT−EXPORTS)/(OUTPUT−EXPORTS+IMPORTS).

This formula can be augmented to account for intermediate input linkages. Since it does not distinguish between the tradeable and the non-tradeable sectors, the strength of the intermediate input linkages simply becomes the share of value added to total gross output, and thus to augment this formula to include input linkages, no extra data are required beyond aggregate value added, which is just total GDP. The augmented formula becomes $\pi_{ii}^{-1/\beta\theta}-1$, where β=VALUE ADDED/OUTPUT in the aggregate economy.

To take explicit account of the fact that much of the domestic GDP is in the non-tradeable sector, one could use some information on the output of tradeables, and the share of tradeables in value added, to refine this formula. The data requirements for implementing this formula call only for aggregate imports and exports, the gross output of the tradeable sector, and the share of tradeables in total value added. The formula for the gains from trade is then given by (7) (where now ξ_i can vary by country).

This formula can also be augmented with intermediate input linkages, under the assumption that these input linkages are strictly within-sector. That is, the tradeable sector only uses tradeable intermediates, and the non-tradeable only non-tradeable intermediates. The formula then becomes

$$\pi_{ii}^{-\xi_i/\beta\theta} - 1. \tag{14}$$

In terms of measuring intermediate input linkages, there are now a couple of ways to proceed. The first, less data-demanding way is to measure the linkages by the share of value added to output in the tradeable and the non-tradeable sectors, exactly as above. That approach would give the input linkages the maximum strength, but may potentially overstate the true gains from trade. This is because a significant share of input usage in the tradeable sector goes to non-tradeables (see Appendix Table A2), and those are not subject to comparative-advantage driven gains from trade. Thus, measuring the strength of input linkages simply by the share of value added in total output overstates international trade's benefits acting through this channel.

The second approach to calibrating the linkages is to isolate the share of intermediate input usage in the tradeable sector that goes to tradeables. This will quantify the intermediate-input driven gains more precisely, but raises the data requirements. In particular, now we need to know not just the total value added and total output, but the breakdown of the input usage into tradeables and non-tradeables. In other words, we now need the (2-sector) input–output table, and the β in (14) is now one minus the share of spending on tradeable intermediate inputs in the tradeable sector gross output.

Finally, one can implement explicitly multi-sector formulas. The data requirements are much higher in this case, as we now need imports, exports, and gross output at the sector level for tradeables. Without input–output linkages, the formula for the gains from trade in an explicitly multi-sector context is given by (8) (where again ξ_i is now country-specific).

This formula can be extended to incorporate within-sector intermediate linkages, in the two ways that parallel the two-sector tradeable-non-tradeable formula. The first way, that does not require any additional data, is to proxy for the strength of intermediate input linkages by the share of value added to total output in each sector. In that case, the gains from trade formula becomes

$$\prod_{j=1}^{J} (\pi_{ii}^{j})^{-\xi_i\omega_j/\beta_j\theta} - 1, \tag{15}$$

where β_j is simply the value added over output in sector j.

Once again, this approach will overstate the contribution of international trade through the input channel because some intermediates used in the tradeable sector are non-tradeable, and thus not subject to the productivity gains from trade. To confine the impact of intermediate inputs to the tradeable inputs only, one must use the full multi-sector input–output table, and for each sector j set β_j to one minus the share of tradeable inputs in total output in each sector. Note that this last option is the most data-intensive, requiring the complete input–output table in addition to data on sectoral output and cross-border trade. While formula (15) does capture some important intermediate input linkages, it still mismeasures the nature of the real-world input linkages because it assumes that all of the linkages are within-sector. That is, the Textile sector uses only Textiles as intermediate inputs, the Apparel sector uses only Apparel, and so on. Thus, to the extent that cross-sectoral input linkages are important – for instance, Apparel uses a great deal of Textiles as intermediates – this formula will miss those. It is ultimately a quantitative question, given the observed Input–Output matrices, how much those linkages matter.

Before moving on to the results, we pause to clarify the nature of the exercise. Each of the formulas offered above can be calculated based on observable data, and thus would not require the researcher to implement, estimate/calibrate, and perform counterfactuals in a complete quantitative model. Thus, the potential promise of these formulas is to enable researchers to estimate gains from trade quickly and easily.

For each of the formulas offered above, there is a model under which that formula represents the exact gains from trade. However, all of these behind-the-scenes models are simplifications, both with respect to reality, and with respect to the full quantitative model. The question we answer below is whether, for the purposes of computing the gains from trade, any of these simplified models represent reasonable approximations to (i) the full quantitative model and (ii) the real world. Our exercise provides the complete answer to (i). With respect to (ii), our results are of course more suggestive, but here the discipline of the estimation and calibration of the quantitative model to real world data, and the match to observed trade flows is helpful.

Table 4 reports the summary statistics for the gains from trade in our 79-country model. The top row reports the true gains from trade implied by the model. On average, the gains are 7.22%, ranging from 1% to 22% in this sample of countries. The rest of the table presents the results of using the formulas to compute the gains from trade. By and large, the message from this table is that the formulas tend to under-predict the gains from trade, often by a significant margin. At the extreme, the one-sector, no-intermediate formula delivers the gains from trade of 1.88% at the mean, or less than a third of the true model gains. The range of gains across countries predicted by these formulas is also much narrower than the range of true gains. Thus, the formulas tend to understate both the mean and the variation in the gains from trade.

The one exception to this regularity is the multi-sector formula that assumes all of the intermediate good usage to come from the sector itself (second-to-last row). That formula overstates both the average gains and the dispersion. As we mentioned above, this overstatement is due to the fact that in the real world and in the quantitative model, a large share

Table 4
Welfare gains from trade.

Formula	Mean	Std. Dev.	Min	Max	No. countries
True gains	7.22	4.92	1.05	22.12	79
$\pi_{ii}^{-1/\theta}-1$	1.88	0.83	0.35	4.11	79
$\pi_{ii}^{-1/\beta\theta}-1$	3.62	1.67	0.70	8.13	79
$\pi_{ii}^{-\xi_i/\theta}-1$	1.97	1.08	0.37	5.11	79
$\pi_{ii}^{-\xi_i/\beta\theta}-1$, β=total linkages	5.81	3.16	1.05	14.83	79
$\pi_{ii}^{-\xi_i/\beta\theta}-1$, β=within-sector linkages	3.46	1.90	0.63	9.09	79
$\prod_{j=1}^{J}(\pi_{ii}^{j})^{-\xi_i\omega_j/\theta}-1$	3.65	2.46	0.52	10.81	79
$\prod_{j=1}^{J}(\pi_{ii}^{j})^{-\xi_i\omega_j/\beta_j\theta}-1$, β_j=total linkages	10.87	7.85	1.45	35.30	79
$\prod_{j=1}^{J}(\pi_{ii}^{j})^{-\xi_i\omega_j/\beta_j\theta}-1$, β_j=tradeable only sectoral linkages	6.49	4.54	0.89	20.21	79

Notes: This table presents the summary statistics for the gains from trade. In the first row are the true gains computed using the full quantitative model. The rest of the rows summarize the gains from trade in this sample of countries implied by various formulas.

Table 5
Comparison of formula-implied gains to true model-implied gains.

Formula	(1)	(2)	(3)	(4)	(5)	(6)	(7)
	Prop. deviation from true gains				Mean	Mean	Corr
	Mean	Std. Dev.	Min	Max	sq. error	abs. error	(Error, $cv((T_i^j)^{1/\theta})$)
$\pi_{ii}^{-1/\theta}-1$	−0.69	0.09	−0.90	−0.50	46.15	5.34	−0.531***
$\pi_{ii}^{-1/\beta\theta}-1$	−0.41	0.17	−0.78	−0.10	25.50	3.60	−0.438***
$\pi_{ii}^{-\xi_i/\theta}-1$	−0.70	0.08	−0.89	−0.56	43.60	5.25	−0.300***
$\pi_{ii}^{-\xi_i/\beta\theta}-1$, β=total linkages	−0.11	0.22	−0.64	0.28	9.02	1.77	−0.287**
$\pi_{ii}^{-\xi_i/\beta\theta}-1$, β = within−sector linkages	−0.47	0.13	−0.78	−0.23	25.49	3.76	−0.273**
$\prod_{j=1}^{J}(\pi_{ii}^{j})^{-\xi_i\omega_j/\theta}-1$	−0.49	0.07	−0.65	−0.27	19.50	3.58	0.030
$\prod_{j=1}^{J}(\pi_{ii}^{j})^{-\xi_i\omega_j/\beta_j\theta}-1$, β_j=total linkages	0.48	0.18	0.04	1.02	23.45	3.65	0.275**
$\prod_{j=1}^{J}(\pi_{ii}^{j})^{-\xi_i\omega_j/\beta_j\theta}-1$, β_j=tradeable only sectoral linkages	−0.11	0.11	−0.38	0.23	1.73	0.94	0.162

Notes: This table presents the comparison of the gains from trade implied by each formula and the true gains from trade. The first 4 columns report the summary statistics for the proportional deviations in the gains from trade according to the formula compared to the true gains. Columns (5) and (6) present respectively the mean squared error and the mean absolute error for the formula-based gains from trade relative to the true ones. Column (7) reports the correlation of the error of the formula with respect to the true gains from trade with the coefficient of variation of a country's average sectoral productivities $(T_i^j)^{1/\theta}$'s relative to the world frontier, along with the level of significance.

*** Significant at 1%.

** Significant at 5%.

(about 40%) of intermediates are actually non-tradeables. These non-tradeables do not benefit from imported, more productive varieties when the country opens to trade, and thus the formula featuring the total intermediate input usage in effect overstates the productivity-enhancing impact of imported intermediates.

Table 5 summarizes the performance of the different formulas relative to the true gains. The first 4 columns present the summary statistics for the proportional deviation of the formula-implied gains from the true ones. We see that most of the formulas understate the true gains by 40–70%, with the exception of the second-to-last formula, which overstates them by nearly 50%. For most formulas, deviations can be quite large for individual countries. At the extreme, some formulas miss 80–90% of the true gains from trade, while the multi-sector, total linkage formula overstates the gains for one of the countries by 100%. We can also see that the bias is quite systematic, with most of the formulas understating the gains for every single country, while one of the formulas overstates the gains for every country.

The clear winner is in the last row. The formula that features multiple sectors, intermediate inputs, and that only uses tradeable intermediate inputs to reflect the intermediate input linkages gets closest to the true gains. This is not surprising, given that it is the most sophisticated and data-intensive approach. However, what is striking is how much better the results are compared to the simpler alternatives. On average, the last formula understates the gains by a relatively modest 11%. The range of its deviations from the true model gains is narrow, from −0.38 to 0.23, and nearly symmetric around zero. Columns (5) and (6) of Table 5 report respectively the mean squared error and the mean absolute error for each formula relative to the true gains. The last row emerges as the clear winner, with both the mean squared error and the mean absolute errors nearly an order of magnitude lower than every other formula, and with the mean absolute error being nearly 2 times smaller than the next best formula.

We conclude from this exercise that, not surprisingly, in order to obtain reliable results for the gains from trade, it is essential to both (i) use sector-level data, and (ii) reflect input-output linkages carefully using input–output tables. Point (i) thus confirms analytical results in Section 2 and the data-driven exercise in Section 3.

Finally, it turns out that the second-best formula is not also the second-most complicated or data-intensive. Instead, the second-best formula is a two sector (tradeable/non-tradeable) formula with input linkages, that features the ratio of tradeable value added to tradeable output as the measure of linkages. The average deviation for that formula from the true gains is also -11%, just as for the best one. It is also the only formula aside from the winner that produces both positive and negative deviations from true gains. Finally, its mean squared and absolute errors are substantially lower than the rest of the field, though still much higher than the winner's.

This potentially suggests that one could get fairly close to the true gains with much lower data requirements. To compute that formula, one needs total imports and exports, and total tradeable and non-tradeable output and value added. No sectoral output and trade flows, and no Input–Output matrices are required to implement that formula. However, it should be clear from the discussion above that this a case of "two wrongs make a right." As shown throughout the paper, ignoring the dispersion among tradeable sectors leads to a systematic understatement of the true gains. On the other hand, attributing all of the intermediate usage in the tradeable sector to tradeables overstates the gains from trade coming from input linkages. Those two opposing forces apparently largely cancel out. Since this cancelling out is clearly not a general feature of all models and calibrations, we would be cautious to conclude that one could use this simpler and easier to calculate formula as a good surrogate when sectoral data and IO matrices are not available.

4.6. *The role of Ricardian comparative advantage*

The simple analytical framework in Section 2 illustrates that the one-sector formula will understate the gains by more the stronger is Ricardian comparative advantage – that is, the greater is the dispersion in T_i^j's. Column (7) of Table 5 reports the correlation between the error of the formula relative to the true gains and a simple heuristic measure of how strong is a country's comparative advantage, namely the coefficient of variation in sectoral productivities relative to the world frontier. Countries with a high coefficient of variation are considered to have "strong comparative advantage," in the sense that their technology has high relative dispersion across sectors. The intuition we built using analytical results suggests that in countries with a high coefficient of variation in technology the one-sector formulas will understate the gains by more: a negative correlation. This is confirmed in the quantitative exercise: the correlations between the strength of comparative advantage and the errors in the one-sector formulas are all negative and highly significant. These negative correlations disappear when we go to the multi-sector formulas (bottom 3 rows). Since the multi-sector formulas take proper account of sectoral heterogeneity, in those formulas there is no longer a systematically greater understatement of the gains for countries with stronger comparative advantage.

The negative relationship is depicted graphically in Fig. 5. In countries with greater dispersion in sectoral productivity, the one-sector formula understates the true gains by more. This is the quantitative, productivity estimates-based counterpart of Fig. 1b in the analytical section.

5. Conclusion

The discovery that several models with very different micro-structures deliver closed-form expressions for the gains from trade that are both (i) identical to each other and (ii) computable based on a small number of observables is a

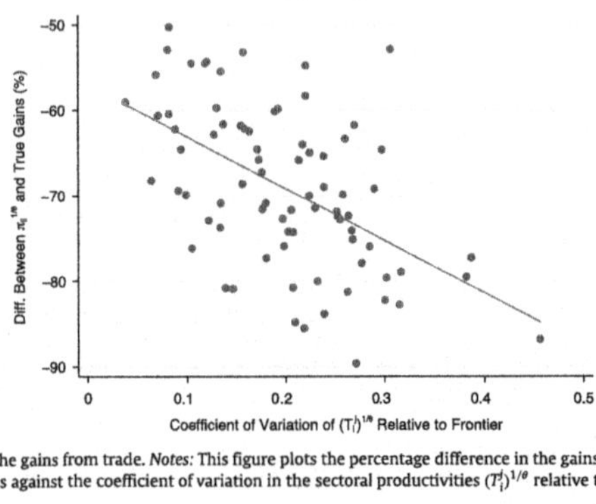

Fig. 5. Comparative advantage and the gains from trade. *Notes:* This figure plots the percentage difference in the gains from trade implied by the one-sector formula $\pi_{ii}^{1/\theta}$ relative to the true gains against the coefficient of variation in the sectoral productivities $(T_i^j)^{1/\theta}$ relative to the world frontier. The line through the data is the OLS fit.

potentially transformative one in the realm of policy research. If made operational, this approach can at the same time dramatically lower barriers to quantitative evaluation of trade policy, and render the results much more general.

This paper takes a step toward assessing the applicability of this approach to real-world policy analysis. It starts from the observation that when there are multiple sectors, a one-sector formula that only incorporates information on the total trade volume relative to absorption systematically understates the true gains from trade. The basic economic intuition for this result can be gleaned from the Ricardian motive for trade: larger sectoral productivity differences will raise the gains from trade even holding constant the overall trade volume. We then use actual data on sectoral and aggregate absorption shares in the manufacturing sector in a sample of 79 countries to show that this effect is large quantitatively: the multi-sector formula implies gains from trade that are 30% higher on average than the gains according to the one-sector formula, and as much as 100% higher in countries with large dispersion in sectoral trade shares.

Finally, we set up a quantitative model with many features relevant in the real world, such as multiple factors of production, a non-tradeable sector, and the full set of input–output linkages between sectors. The model is implemented using actual data on production functions, Input–Output matrices, and trade flows. It matches relative incomes and bilateral and overall trade flows quite closely. We evaluate whether there are sufficient statistic formulas that, when computed inside this model, can approximate well the true gains from trade in the model. It turns out that augmented formulas that take into account input–output linkages but not sectoral trade shares, or sectoral trade shares but not input–output linkages understate the true model gains substantially. However, an appropriate combination of information on sectoral trade flows and input linkages performs quite well relative to others, understating the true model gains by only 11% on average.

We conclude that sectoral heterogeneity in productivity and trade volumes has a first-order impact on the gains from trade, and that it should be taken into account in exercises that use the sufficient statistic approach to compute the gains from trade.

Table A1
Country coverage.

Argentina	Korea, Rep.
Australia	Kuwait
Austria	Latvia
Bangladesh	Lithuania
Belgium-Luxembourg	Macedonia, FYR
Bolivia	Malaysia
Brazil	Mauritius
Bulgaria	Mexico
Canada	Netherlands
Chile	New Zealand
China	Nigeria
Colombia	Norway
Costa Rica	Pakistan
Czech Republic	Peru
Denmark	Philippines
Ecuador	Poland
Egypt, Arab Rep.	Portugal
El Salvador	Romania
Estonia	Russian Federation
Ethiopia	Saudi Arabia
Fiji	Senegal
Finland	Slovak Republic
France	Slovenia
Germany	South Africa
Ghana	Spain
Greece	Sri Lanka
Guatemala	Sweden
Honduras	Switzerland
Hungary	Taiwan Province of China
Iceland	Tanzania
India	Thailand
Indonesia	Trinidad and Tobago
Iran, Islamic Rep.	Turkey
Ireland	Ukraine
Israel	United Kingdom
Italy	United States
Japan	Uruguay
Jordan	Venezuela, RB
Kazakhstan	Vietnam
Kenya	

Notes: This table reports the countries in the sample.

Table A2
Sectors.

ISIC code	Sector name	α_j	β_j	$\gamma_{J+1,j}$	ω_j
15	Food and Beverages	0.290	0.290	0.303	0.166
16	Tobacco Products	0.272	0.490	0.527	0.019
17	Textiles	0.444	0.368	0.295	0.015
18	Wearing Apparel, Fur	0.468	0.369	0.320	0.059
19	Leather, Leather Products, Footwear	0.469	0.350	0.330	0.014
20	Wood Products (Excl. Furniture)	0.455	0.368	0.288	0.008
21	Paper and Paper Products	0.351	0.341	0.407	0.012
22	Printing and Publishing	0.484	0.453	0.407	0.005
23	Coke, Refined Petroleum Products, Nuclear Fuel	0.248	0.246	0.246	0.043
24	Chemical and Chemical Products	0.297	0.368	0.479	0.006
25	Rubber and Plastics Products	0.366	0.375	0.350	0.012
26	Non-Metallic Mineral Products	0.350	0.448	0.499	0.072
27	Basic Metals	0.345	0.298	0.451	0.002
28	Fabricated Metal Products	0.424	0.387	0.364	0.014
29C	Office, Accounting, Computing, and Other Machinery	0.481	0.381	0.388	0.134
31A	Electrical Machinery, Communication Equipment	0.369	0.368	0.416	0.074
33	Medical, Precision, and Optical Instruments	0.451	0.428	0.441	0.060
34A	Transport Equipment	0.437	0.329	0.286	0.219
36	Furniture and Other Manufacturing	0.447	0.396	0.397	0.067
4A	Nontradeables	0.561	0.651	0.788	
	Mean	0.414	0.393	0.399	0.053
	Min	0.244	0.243	0.246	0.002
	Max	0.561	0.651	0.788	0.219

Notes: This table reports the sectors used in the analysis. The classification corresponds to the ISIC Revision 3 2-digit, aggregated further due to data availability. α_j is the value-added based labor intensity; β_j is the share of value added in total output; $\gamma_{J+1,j}$ is the share of non-tradeable inputs in total intermediate inputs; ω_j is the tradeable sector j's share of total tradeable expenditure. Variable definitions and sources are described in detail in the text.

Appendix A. Procedure for estimating T_n^j, d_{ni}^j, and ω_j

This appendix reproduces from Levchenko and Zhang (2011) the details of the procedure for estimating technology, trade costs, and taste parameters required to implement the model. Interested readers should consult that paper for further details on estimation steps and data sources.

A.1. Tradeable sector relative technology

We now focus on the tradeable sectors. Following the standard EK approach, first divide trade shares by their domestic counterpart:

$$\frac{\pi_{ni}^j}{\pi_{nn}^j}=\frac{X_{ni}^j}{X_{nn}^j}=\frac{T_i^j(c_i^j d_{ni}^j)^{-\theta}}{T_n^j(c_n^j)^{-\theta}},$$

which in logs becomes

$$\ln\left(\frac{X_{ni}^j}{X_{nn}^j}\right)=\ln\left(T_i^j(c_i^j)^{-\theta}\right)-\ln\left(T_n^j(c_n^j)^{-\theta}\right)-\theta\ln d_{ni}^j.$$

Let the (log) iceberg costs be given by the following expression:

$$\ln d_{ni}^j=d_k^j+b_{ni}^j+CU_{ni}^j+RTA_{ni}^j+ex_i^j+\nu_{ni}^j,$$

where d_k^j is an indicator variable for a distance interval. Following EK, we set the distance intervals, in miles, to [0, 350], [350, 750], [750, 1500], [1500, 3000], [3000, 6000], [6000, maximum). Additional variables are whether the two countries share a common border (b_{ni}^j), belong to a currency union (CU_{ni}^j), or to a regional trade agreement (RTA_{ni}^j). Following the arguments in Waugh (2010), we include an exporter fixed effect ex_i^j. Finally, there is an error term ν_{ni}^j. Note that all the variables have a sector superscript j: we allow all the trade cost proxy variables to affect true iceberg trade costs d_{ni}^j differentially across sectors. There is a range of evidence that trade volumes at sector level vary in their sensitivity to distance or common border (see, among many others, Do and Levchenko, 2007; Berthelon and Freund, 2008).

This leads to the following final estimating equation:

$$\ln\left(\frac{X_{ni}^j}{X_{nn}^j}\right)=\underbrace{\ln(T_i^j(c_i^j)^{-\theta})-\theta ex_i^j}_{\text{Exporter fixed effect}}\underbrace{-\ln(T_n^j(c_n^j)^{-\theta})}_{\text{importer fixed effect}}\underbrace{-\theta d_k^j-\theta b_{ni}^j-\theta CU_{ni}^j-\theta RTA_{ni}^j}_{\text{Bilateral observables}}\underbrace{-\theta\nu_{ni}^j}_{\text{Error term}}.$$

This equation is estimated for each tradeable sector $j=1,\ldots J$. Estimating this relationship will thus yield, for each country, an estimate of its technology-cum-unit-cost term in each sector j, $T_n^j(c_n^j)^{-\theta}$, which is obtained by exponentiating the importer fixed effect. The available degrees of freedom imply that these estimates are of each country's $T_n^j(c_n^j)^{-\theta}$ relative to a reference country, which in our estimation is the United States. We denote this estimated value by S_n^j:

$$S_n^j = \frac{T_n^j}{T_{us}^j}\left(\frac{c_n^j}{c_{us}^j}\right)^{-\theta},$$

where the subscript us denotes the United States. It is immediate from this expression that estimation delivers a convolution of technology parameters T_n^j and cost parameters c_n^j. Both will of course affect trade volumes, but we would like to extract technology T_n^j from these estimates. In order to do that, we follow the approach of Shikher (2012). In particular, for each country n, the share of total spending going to home-produced goods is given by

$$\frac{X_{nn}^j}{X_n^j} = T_n^j\left(\frac{\Gamma c_n^j}{p_n^j}\right)^{-\theta}.$$

Dividing by its U.S. counterpart yields

$$\frac{X_{nn}^j/X_n^j}{X_{us,us}^j/X_{us}^j} = \frac{T_n^j}{T_{us}^j}\left(\frac{c_n^j\,p_{us}^j}{c_{us}^j\,p_n^j}\right)^{-\theta} = S_n^j\left(\frac{p_{us}^j}{p_n^j}\right)^{-\theta},$$

and thus the ratio of price levels in sector j relative to the U.S. becomes

$$\frac{p_n^j}{p_{us}^j} = \left(\frac{X_{nn}^j/X_n^j}{X_{us,us}^j/X_{us}^j\,\frac{1}{S_n^j}}\right)^{1/\theta}. \tag{A.1}$$

The entire right-hand side of this expression is either observable or estimated. Thus, we can impute the price levels relative to the U.S. in each country and each tradeable sector.

The cost of the input bundles relative to the U.S. can be written as

$$\frac{c_n^j}{c_{us}^j} = \left(\frac{w_n}{w_{us}}\right)^{\alpha_j\beta_j}\left(\frac{r_n}{r_{us}}\right)^{(1-\alpha_j)\beta_j}\left(\prod_{k=1}^{J}\left(\frac{p_n^k}{p_{us}^k}\right)^{\gamma_{kj}}\right)^{1-\beta_j}\left(\frac{p_n^{J+1}}{p_{us}^{J+1}}\right)^{\gamma_{J+1,j}(1-\beta_j)}.$$

Using information on relative wages, returns to capital, price in each tradeable sector from (A.1), and the non-tradeable sector price relative to the U.S., we can thus impute the costs of the input bundles relative to the U.S. in each country and each sector. Armed with those values, it is straightforward to back out the relative technology parameters:

$$\frac{T_n^j}{T_{us}^j} = S_n^j\left(\frac{c_n^j}{c_{us}^j}\right)^{\theta}.$$

A.2. Trade costs

The bilateral, directional, sector-level trade costs of shipping from country i to country n in sector j are then computed based on the estimated coefficients as

$$\ln \hat{d}_{ni}^j = \theta\hat{d}_k^j + \theta\hat{b}_{ni}^j + \theta\widehat{CU}_{ni}^j + \theta\widehat{RTA}_{ni}^j + \theta\widehat{ex}_i^j + \theta\hat{\nu}_{ni}^j,$$

for an assumed value of θ. Note that the estimate of the trade costs includes the residual from the gravity regression $\theta\hat{\nu}_{ni}^j$. Thus, the trade costs computed as above will fit bilateral sectoral trade flows exactly, given the estimated fixed effects. Note also that the exporter component of the trade costs $\widehat{ex}_i^j$ is part of the exporter fixed effect. Since each country in the sample appears as both an exporter and an importer, the exporter and importer estimated fixed effects are combined to extract an estimate of $\theta\widehat{ex}_i^j$.

A.3. Complete estimation

So far we have estimated the levels of technology of the tradeable sectors relative to the United States. To complete our estimation, we still need to find (i) the levels of T for the tradeable sectors in the United States; (ii) the taste parameters ω_j, and (iii) the non-tradeable technology levels for all countries.

To obtain (i), we use the NBER-CES Manufacturing Industry Database for the U.S. (Bartelsman and Gray, 1996). We start by measuring the observed TFP levels for the tradeable sectors in the U.S.. The form of the production function gives

$$\ln Z_{us}^j = \ln A_{us}^j + \beta_j\alpha_j \ln L_{us}^j + \beta_j(1-\alpha_j)\ln K_{us}^j + (1-\beta_j)\sum_{k=1}^{J+1}\gamma_{kj}\ln M_{us}^{kj}, \tag{A.2}$$

where A^j denotes the measured TFP in sector j, Z^j denotes the output, L^j denotes the labor input, K^j denotes the capital input, and $M^{k,j}$ denotes the intermediate input from sector k. The NBER-CES Manufacturing Industry Database offers information on output, and inputs of labor, capital, and intermediates, along with deflators for each. Thus, we can estimate the observed TFP level for each manufacturing tradeable sector using the above equation.

If the United States were a closed economy, the observed TFP level for sector j would be given by $A^j_{us} = (T^j_{us})^{1/\theta}$. In the open economies, the goods with inefficient domestic productivity draws will not be produced and will be imported instead. Thus, international trade and competition introduce selection in the observed TFP level, as demonstrated by Finicelli et al. (2013). We thus use the model to back out the true level of T^j_{us} of each tradeable sector in the United States. Here we follow Finicelli et al. (2013) and use the following relationship:

$$(A^j_{us})^\theta = T^j_{us} + \sum_{i \neq us} T^j_i \left(\frac{c^j_i d^j_{us,i}}{c^j_{us}} \right)^{-\theta}.$$

Thus, we have

$$(A^j_{us})^\theta = T^j_{us} \left[1 + \sum_{i \neq us} \frac{T^j_i}{T^j_{us}} \left(\frac{c^j_i d^j_{us,i}}{c^j_{us}} \right)^{-\theta} \right] = T^j_{us} \left[1 + \sum_{i \neq us} S^j_i (d^j_{us,i})^{-\theta} \right]. \tag{A.3}$$

This equation can be solved for underlying technology parameters T^j_{us} in the U.S., given estimated observed TFP A^j_{us}, and all the S^j_i's and $d^j_{us,i}$'s estimated in the previous subsection.

Finally, we estimate the non-tradeable sector TFP using the relative prices. In the model, the non-tradeable sector price is given by

$$p^{J+1}_n = \Gamma (T^{J+1}_n)^{-1/\theta} c^{J+1}_n.$$

Since we know the aggregate price level in the tradeable sector p^T_n, c^{J+1}_n, and the relative price of non-tradeables (which we take from the data), we can back out T^{J+1}_n from the equation above for all countries.

Appendix B. Supplementary data

Supplementary data associated with this paper can be found in the online version at http://dx.doi.org/10.1016/j.euroecorev.2013.10.006.

References

Alvarez, Fernando, Lucas Jr., Robert E., 2007. General equilibrium analysis of the Eaton–Kortum model of international trade. J. Monet. Econ. 54 (September (6)), 1726–1768.

Arkolakis, Costas, Costinot, Arnaud, Rodríguez-Clare, Andrés, 2012. New trade models same old gains? Am. Econ. Rev. 102 (February (1)), 94–130.

Arkolakis, Costas, Costinot, Arnaud, Donaldson, Dave, Rodríguez-Clare, Andrés, March 2012. The Elusive Pro-Competitive Effects of Trade. Mimeo, Yale University, MIT, and UC Berkeley.

Arkolakis, Costas, Demidova, Svetlana, Klenow, Peter J., Rodríguez-Clare, Andrés, May 2008. Endogenous Variety and the Gains from Trade. Am. Econ. Rev. Pap. Proc. 98(2), 444–450.

Atkeson, Andrew, Burstein, Ariel, 2010. Innovation, firm dynamics, and international trade. J. Polit. Econ. 118 (3), 433–484.

Bartelsman, Eric J., Gray, Wayne, 1996. The NBER Manufacturing Productivity Database, October 1996. NBER Technical Working Paper 205.

Bernanke, Ben, Gürkaynak, Refet, 2001. Is growth exogenous? Taking Mankiw, Romer, and Weil seriously. NBER Macroecon. Annu. 16, 11–57.

Berthelon, Matias, Freund, Caroline, 2008. On the conservation of distance in international trade. J. Int. Econ. 75 (2), 310–320.

Burstein, Ariel, Cravino, Javier, January 2012. Measured Aggregate Gains from International Trade. Mimeo, UCLA.

Burstein, Ariel, Vogel, Jonathan, April 2012. International Trade, Technology, and the Skill Premium. Mimeo, UCLA and Columbia University.

Caliendo, Lorenzo, Parro, Fernando, January 2010. Estimates of the Trade and Welfare Effects of NAFTA. Mimeo, University of Chicago.

Caselli, Francesco, 2005. Accounting for cross-country income differences. In: Durlauf, Steven, Aghion, Philippe (Eds.), Handbook of Economic Growth, vol. 1, , Elsevier-North Holland, pp. 679–741. (Chapter 9).

Chari, V.V., Kehoe, Patrick J., McGrattan, Ellen R., 2008. Are structural VARs with long-run restrictions useful in developing business cycle theory? J. Monet. Econ. 55 (8), 1337–1352.

Corcos, Gregory, Gatto, Massimo Del, Mion, Giordano, Ottaviano, Gianmarco I.P., 2012. Productivity and firm selection: quantifying the 'new' gains from trade. Econ. J. 122 (June (561)), 754–798.

Costinot, Arnaud, Rodríguez-Clare, Andrés. Trade theory with numbers: quantifying the consequences of globalization. Handbook of International Economics, forthcoming.

de Blas, Beatriz, Russ, Katheryn, 2012. Understanding Markups in the Open Economy. Mimeo, Universidad Autónoma de Madrid and UC Davis.

di Giovanni, Julian, Levchenko, Andrei A., 2010. Putting the parts together: trade, vertical linkages, and business cycle comovement. Am. Econ. J. Macroecon. 2 (2), 95–124.

di Giovanni, Julian, Levchenko, Andrei A., 2013. Firm entry, trade, and welfare in Zipf's world. J. Int. Econ. 89 (2), 283–296.

di Giovanni, Julian, Levchenko, Andrei A., Zhang, Jing. The global welfare impact of China: trade integration and technological change, Am. Econ. J. Macroecon, forthcoming.

Do, Quy-Toan, Levchenko, Andrei A., 2007. Comparative advantage, demand for external finance, and financial development. J. Financ. Econ. 86 (3).

Eaton, Jonathan, Kortum, Samuel, 2002. Technology, geography, and trade. Econometrica 70 (September (5)), 1741–1779.

Eaton, Jonathan, Kortum, Samuel, Neiman, Brent, Romalis, John, January 2011. Trade and the Global Recession. NBER Working Paper No. 16666.

Feenstra, Robert C., 2010. Measuring the gains from trade under monopolistic competition. Can. J. Econ. 43 (February (1)), 1–28.

Finicelli, Andrea, Pagano, Patrizio, Sbracia, Massimo, 2013. Ricardian selection. J. Int. Econ. 89 (January (1)), 96–109.

Hall, Robert, Jones, Charles, 1999. Why do some countries produce so much more output per worker then others. Q. J. Econ. 114, 83–116.

Hauk, William, Wacziarg, Romain, 2009. A Monte Carlo study of growth regressions. J. Econ. Growth 14 (June (2)), 103–147.
Hummels, David, Ishii, Jun, Yi, Kei-Mu, 2001. The nature and growth of vertical specialization in world trade. J. Int. Econ. 54, 75–96.
Imbs, Jean, Méjean, Isabelle, August 2011. Trade Elasticities. Mimeo, Paris School of Economics and Ecole Polytechnique.
Levchenko, Andrei A., Zhang, Jing, February 2011. The Evolution of Comparative Advantage: Measurement and Welfare Implications. NBER Working Paper No. 16806.
Levchenko, Andrei A., Zhang, Jing, 2012. Comparative advantage and the welfare impact of European integration. Econ. Policy 27 (October (72)), 567–602.
Melitz, Marc J., Redding, Stephen J., March 2013. Firm Heterogeneity and Aggregate Welfare. Mimeo, Harvard University and Princeton University.
Ossa, Ralph, May 2012. Why Trade Matters After All. NBER Working Paper No. 18113.
Ricardo, David, 1817. On the Principles of Political Economy and Taxation, Works and Correspondence of David Ricardo, vol. 1, Cambridge University Press.
Shikher, Serge, 2012. Putting industries into the Eaton–Kortum model. J. Int. Trade Econ. Dev. 21 (December (6)), 807–837.
Shikher, Serge, August 2005. Accounting for International Trade. Mimeo, Suffolk University.
Shikher, Serge, 2011. Capital technology and specialization in the neoclassical model. J. Int. Econ. 83 (March (2)), 229–242.
Simonovska, Ina, Waugh, Michael E., February 2011. The Elasticity of Trade: Estimates and Evidence. UC Davis Working Paper No. 11-2.
Waugh, Michael, 2010. International trade and income differences. Am. Econ. Rev. 100 (December (5)), 2093–2124.
Yi, Kei-Mu, Jing Zhang, April 2010. Structural Change in an Open Economy. Mimeo, Federal Reserve Bank of Philadelphia and University of Michigan.

American Economic Journal: Macroeconomics 2014, 6(3): 153–183
http://dx.doi.org/10.1257/mac.6.3.153

The Global Welfare Impact of China: Trade Integration and Technological Change[†]

By Julian di Giovanni, Andrei A. Levchenko, and Jing Zhang*

This paper evaluates the global welfare impact of China's trade integration and technological change in a multi-country quantitative Ricardian-Heckscher-Ohlin model. We simulate two alternative growth scenarios: a "balanced" one in which China's productivity grows at the same rate in each sector, and an "unbalanced" one in which China's comparative disadvantage sectors catch up disproportionately faster to the world productivity frontier. Contrary to a well-known conjecture (Samuelson 2004), the large majority of countries experience significantly larger welfare gains when China's productivity growth is biased toward its comparative disadvantage sectors. This finding is driven by the inherently multilateral nature of world trade. (*JEL* F14, F43, 019, 033, 047, P24, P33)

The real value of Chinese exports has increased by a factor of 12 between 1990 and 2007, far outpacing the three-fold expansion of overall global trade during this period. Naturally, such rapid integration and growth leads to some anxiety. In developed countries, a common concern is that China's productivity growth will be biased toward sectors in which the developed world currently has a comparative advantage. In a two-country setting, a well-known theoretical result is that a country can experience welfare losses when its trading partner becomes more similar in relative technology (Hicks 1953; Dornbusch, Fischer, and Samuelson 1977; Samuelson 2004; Ju and Yang 2009).

This paper explores, both qualitatively and quantitatively, the global welfare consequences of different productivity growth scenarios in China. Analytically, we show that in a multi-country world, third-country effects are a key determinant of how a country's sectoral productivity changes affect welfare of all trading partners. For instance, greater similarity in China's relative sectoral technology to that of the United States per se does not necessarily lower United States' welfare. Rather, what drives welfare changes in the United States is how (dis)similar China becomes to

* di Giovanni: Department of Economics and Business, Universitat Pompeu Fabra Roma Trias Fargas 25-27, 08005 Barcelona, Spain, and Barcelona GSE, CREI, and CEPR (e-mail: julian.digiovanni@upf.edu); Levchenko: University of Michigan, 611 Tappan Street, Ann Arbor, MI 48109, NBER and CEPR (e-mail: alev@umich.edu); Zhang: Federal Reserve Bank of Chicago, 230 South LaSalle Street, Chicago, IL 60604 (e-mail: jing.zhang@chi.frb.org). We are grateful to Olivier Blanchard, Alan Deardorff, Gino Gancia, Juan Carlos Hallak, Chris House, Thierry Mayer, Fernando Parro, Matthew Shapiro, Bob Staiger, Heiwai Tang, Linda Tesar, and to seminar participants at numerous institutions for helpful suggestions, and to Aaron Flaaen for superb research assistance. The views expressed here are those of the authors and do not necessarily represent those of the Federal Reserve Bank of Chicago, the Federal Reserve System, or its Board of Governors.

[†]Go to http://dx.doi.org/10.1257/mac.6.3.153 to visit the article page for additional materials and author disclosure statement(s) or to comment in the online discussion forum.

an appropriately input-and-trade-cost-weighted average productivity of the United States and all other countries serving the United States market.

The analytical results underscore the need for a quantitative assessment. Since the welfare outcomes hinge on third-country effects and the specifics of productivity distributions of all trading partners, two key inputs are necessary to reach reliable conclusions. The first is a quantitative framework that is global both in country coverage and in the nature of equilibrium adjustments. The second is a comprehensive set of sectoral productivity estimates for a large set of countries. Our analysis employs the productivity estimates recently developed by Levchenko and Zhang (2011) for a sample of 19 manufacturing sectors and 75 economies that includes China along with a variety of countries representing all continents and a wide range of income levels and other characteristics. We embed these productivity estimates within a quantitative multi-country, multi-sector model with a number of realistic features, such as multiple factors of production, an explicit nontraded sector, the full specification of input-output linkages between the sectors, and both inter- and intra-industry trade, among others.

We simulate two counterfactual growth scenarios starting from the present day. In the first, China's productivity growth rate in each sector is identical, and equal to the average productivity growth we estimate for China between the 1990s and the 2000s, which is 14 percent (i.e., an average of 1.32 percent per annum). In this "balanced" growth scenario, China's comparative advantage vis-à-vis the world remains unchanged. In the second scenario, China's comparative disadvantage sectors grow disproportionally faster. Specifically, in the "unbalanced" counterfactual, China's relative productivity differences with respect to the world frontier are eliminated, and China's productivity in every sector becomes a constant ratio of the world frontier. By design, the average productivity in China is the same in the two counterfactuals. What differs is the relative productivities across sectors.

Our main result is that the mean welfare gains (the percentage change in real consumption) from the unbalanced growth in China, 0.42 percent in our sample of 74 countries, are an order of magnitude larger than the mean gains in the balanced scenario, which are nearly nil at 0.01 percent. This pattern holds for every region and broad country group. Importantly, the large majority of countries that become more similar to China in the unbalanced growth scenario—most prominently the United States and the rest of the OECD—still gain much more from unbalanced growth in China compared to balanced growth.

The analytical results help us understand why this is the case. What matters is not China's similarity to any individual country, but its similarity to the world weighted average productivity (although the theoretically correct weights will differ from country to country because of trade costs). Closer inspection reveals that China's current productivity is relatively high in sectors, such as wearing apparel, that are "common," in the sense that many countries also have high productivity in those sectors. By contrast, China's comparative disadvantage sectors, such as office, accounting, and computing machinery, are "scarce," in the sense that not many other countries are close to the global productivity frontier in those sectors. Put another way, China's pattern of sectoral productivity is actually fairly similar to the world average. Thus, while balanced growth in China keeps it similar to the typical country, unbalanced growth actually makes it more different.

As a related exercise of independent interest, we also compare welfare in the baseline model estimated on the world today to a counterfactual in which China is in autarky. This reveals the global distribution of the gains from trade with China as it stands today. The mean welfare gain from adding China to world trade is 0.13 percent. Dispersion across countries within each region turns out to be large; in nearly every major region or country group, gains range from positive to negative. Aside from China itself, for which the model implies gains of 3.72 percent relative to autarky, the economies with the largest positive welfare changes are Malaysia (0.80 percent), Kazakhstan (0.78 percent), and Taiwan, POC (0.63 percent). Nine out of 75 countries experience welfare losses, the largest for Honduras (−0.27 percent) and El Salvador (−0.21 percent).

Our paper is related to recent quantitative welfare assessments of trade integration and technological change in multi-sector Ricardian models (Caliendo and Parro 2010; Shikher 2011; Costinot, Donaldson, and Komunjer 2012), as well as Computable General Equilibrium (CGE) assessments of China's trade integration (e.g., Francois and Wignaraja 2008; Ghosh and Rao 2010; Tokarick 2011). Most closely related is the work of Hsieh and Ossa (2011), who consider the welfare impact of the observed pattern of sector-level growth in China from 1992 to 2007 on 14 major countries and four broad world regions, and Levchenko and Zhang (2011), who examine the long-run evolution of sectoral technology between the 1960s and the 2000s in a broad range of countries.

The main contribution of this paper relative to existing literature is to reveal the importance of third-country effects, which were not well understood either theoretically or quantitatively. From a theoretical standpoint, we show that any comparative statics exercise on the impact of parameter changes in one country on another country could be fundamentally misleading if carried out in a two-country setting. Our quantitative analysis then shows that these effects are strong enough to overturn an influential conjecture about the global impact of changes in China's comparative advantage. To demonstrate our result as transparently as possible, our counterfactual growth scenarios are prospective and designed as a test of a particular hypothesis, rather than retrospective as in Hsieh and Ossa (2011). Aside from the novel theoretical results on the third-country effects, this paper differs from Levchenko and Zhang (2011) in its set of substantive questions. Levchenko and Zhang (2011) documents the long-run evolution of comparative advantage and emphasizes how comparative advantage changes in individual countries affected their own welfare. This paper's focus is instead on the impact of changes in one country's comparative advantage on the rest of the world, with a particular emphasis on China. Our global general equilibrium approach complements recent micro-level studies of the impact of China on developed (e.g., Autor, Dorn, and Hanson 2013; Bloom, Draca, and Van Reenen 2011; Bitzer, Görg, and Schröder 2012) as well as developing (e.g., Hanson and Robertson 2010) countries.

The rest of the paper is organized as follows. Section I derives a set of analytical results using a simplified multi-sector N-country Eaton and Kortum (2002)—henceforth, EK—model of Ricardian trade. Section II lays out the quantitative framework and describes the details of the calibration. Section III examines the welfare implications of both the trade integration of China, and the hypothetical scenarios for Chinese growth. Section IV concludes. The online Appendix collects a number of additional results and exercises, including (i) further analytical results; (ii) details of model estimation; and (iii) an extensive set of robustness checks on the quantitative results.

I. Analytical Results

How will the evolution of relative sectoral technology in a country affect its own welfare and the welfare of its trading partners? The answer, based on a two-country costless trade model, such as the one employed by Samuelson (2004), is that both countries' welfare is minimized when they have the same relative sectoral productivity. This influential insight must be modified when we step out of this simple environment and consider more than two countries and costly trade. This section derives analytical results and builds intuition in a simplified version of the quantitative model of the next section. We analyze a multi-sector EK model, in which relative factor prices in all countries are fixed, and sectoral productivity affects welfare only through the consumption price level. This simplification makes analytical results possible, and allows us to demonstrate most transparently the role of third countries in how sectoral technological similarity between two trading partners affects welfare. Online Appendix A uses numerical examples to show that the results still hold when relative wages adjust in general equilibrium.

The objective of these simple analytical examples is not to use a two-sector, three-country setting to capture the precise story of China, the United States, and the rest of the world—that is the job of the quantitative exercise. Rather, the analytical examples serve to illustrate two main points. First, the exact same productivity change in country 1 can result in welfare changes of opposite signs in country 2, depending on whether there are two or three countries. Second, when there are more than two countries, it is easy to construct examples in which as relative productivity in country 1 becomes *more* similar to country 2, country 2's welfare actually rises. These two points help understand the mechanisms behind the quantitative results.

A. *The Environment*

There are N countries, indexed by n and i. For concreteness, we can think of country 1 as China, and evaluate the impact of technological changes in country 1 on itself and country 2, which we can think of as the United States. There are multiple sectors, indexed by j. Production in each sector follows the EK structure. Output Q_n^j of sector j in country n is a CES aggregate of a continuum of varieties $q = [0,1]$ unique to each sector:

$$Q_n^j = \left[\int_0^1 Q_n^j(q)^{\frac{\varepsilon-1}{\varepsilon}} dq\right]^{\frac{\varepsilon}{\varepsilon-1}}, \tag{1}$$

where ε denotes the elasticity of substitution across varieties q, and $Q_n^j(q)$ is the amount of variety q that is used in production in sector j and country n.

Producing one unit of good q in sector j in country i requires $\frac{1}{z_i^j(q)}$ units of labor. Productivity $z_i^j(q)$ for each $q \in [0,1]$ in each country i and sector j is random, drawn from the Fréchet distribution with cumulative distribution function

$$F_i^j(z) = e^{-T_i^j z^{-\theta}}. \tag{2}$$

In this distribution, the absolute advantage term T_i^j varies by both country and sector, with higher values of T_i^j implying higher average productivity draws in sector j in country i. The parameter θ captures dispersion, with larger values of θ implying smaller dispersion in draws.

Labor is the only factor of production, with country endowments given by L_n and wages denoted by w_n. The production cost of one unit of good q in sector j and country i is thus equal to $w_i/z_i^j(q)$. Each country can produce each good in each sector, and international trade is subject to iceberg costs: $d_{ni}^j > 1$ units of good q produced in sector j in country i must be shipped to country n in order for one unit to be available for consumption there. The trade costs need not be symmetric—d_{ni}^j need not equal d_{in}^j—and will vary by sector. We normalize $d_{nn}^j = 1 \;\forall\; n$ and j.

All the product and factor markets are perfectly competitive, and thus the price at which country i can supply tradeable good q in sector j to country n is

$$p_{ni}^j(q) = \left(\frac{w_i}{z_i^j(q)}\right) d_{ni}^j.$$

Buyers of each good q in tradeable sector j in country n will only buy from the cheapest source country, and thus the price actually paid for this good in country n will be

$$p_n^j(q) = \min_{i=1,\ldots,N} \{p_{ni}^j(q)\}. \tag{3}$$

It is well-known that the price of sector j's output is given by

$$p_n^j = \left[\int_0^1 p_n^j(q)^{1-\varepsilon}\, dq\right]^{\frac{1}{1-\varepsilon}}.$$

Following the standard EK approach, it is heplful to define

$$\Phi_n^j = \sum_{i=1}^{N} T_i^j (w_i d_{ni}^j)^{-\theta}. \tag{4}$$

This value summarizes, for country n, the access to production technologies in sector j. Its value will be higher if in sector j, country n's trading partners have high productivity (T_i^j) or low cost (w_i). It will also be higher if the trade costs that country n

faces in this sector are low. Standard steps (EK) lead to the familiar result that the price of good j in country n is simply

$$p_n^j = \Gamma(\Phi_n^j)^{-\frac{1}{\theta}}, \tag{5}$$

where $\Gamma = \left[\text{Gamma}\left(\frac{\theta + 1 - \varepsilon}{\theta}\right)\right]^{\frac{1}{1-\varepsilon}}$.

Consumer utility is identical across countries and Cobb-Douglas with sector j receiving expenditure share η_j. The consumption price level in country n is then proportional to

$$P_n \propto \prod_j (p_n^j)^{\eta_j}, \tag{6}$$

and welfare (indirect utility) is given by the real income w_n/P_n.

B. *Main Analytical Result*

Consider the case in which relative wages are fixed. In particular, suppose there are three sectors, $j = A, B, H$. Sectors A and B have the EK structure described above. As in Helpman, Melitz, and Yeaple (2004) and Chaney (2008), good H is homogeneous and can be costlessly traded between any two countries in the world. Let the price of H be the numeraire. In country n, one worker can produce w_n units of H, implying that the wage in n is given by w_n. To obtain the cleanest results, let A and B enter symmetrically in the utility function

$$U_n = \left(A_n^{\frac{1}{2}} B_n^{\frac{1}{2}}\right)^{\alpha} H_n^{1-\alpha}. \tag{7}$$

Throughout, we assume that α is sufficiently small so that some amount of H is always produced in all the countries in the world. This assumption pins down wages in all the countries, making analytical results possible.

We are now ready to perform the main comparative static: the welfare impact of changes in the relative technology in country 1, T_1^A/T_1^B, subject to the constraint that its geometric average stays the same, $(T_1^A T_1^B)^{\frac{1}{2}} = c$ for some constant c. The exercise informs us of the welfare impact of the different growth scenarios in China, when we hold its average growth rate fixed.

LEMMA 1: *Country 1's relative technology* $(T_1^A/T_1^B)_n$*, which minimizes welfare in country n subject to the constraint* $(T_1^A T_1^B)_n^{\frac{1}{2}} = c$*, is given by*

$$\left(\frac{T_1^A}{T_1^B}\right)_n = \frac{\sum_{i=2}^{N} T_i^A \left(\frac{w_i d_{ni}^A}{w_1 d_{n1}^A}\right)^{-\theta}}{\sum_{i=2}^{N} T_i^B \left(\frac{w_i d_{ni}^B}{w_1 d_{n1}^B}\right)^{-\theta}}. \tag{8}$$

PROOF.
See online Appendix A.

Lemma 1 says that the country 1 relative technology that minimizes welfare in country n is not the one that makes country 1 most similar to country n. That is, generically country n's welfare is not minimized when $T_1^A/T_1^B = T_n^A/T_n^B$. What matters instead is the relative-unit-cost-weighted average technologies *of all the other countries serving n (including itself)*. Third countries matter through their technology, but also through their relative unit costs and trade costs of serving market n. Because of third country effects, it is easy to construct examples in which country 1 becomes more technologically similar to country n, and yet country n's welfare increases. Two simple examples under frictionless trade can illustrate the point most clearly.

EXAMPLE 1: *Suppose there are two countries and trade is costless. Then the country 1 relative technology T_1^A/T_1^B that minimizes welfare in countries 1 and 2 is*

$$\left(\frac{T_1^A}{T_1^B}\right)_1 = \left(\frac{T_1^A}{T_1^B}\right)_2 = \frac{T_2^A}{T_2^B}.$$

EXAMPLE 2: *Suppose there are three countries and trade is costless. Then the country 1 relative technology T_1^A/T_1^B that minimizes welfare in the three countries is*

$$\left(\frac{T_1^A}{T_1^B}\right)_1 = \left(\frac{T_1^A}{T_1^B}\right)_2 = \left(\frac{T_1^A}{T_1^B}\right)_3 = \frac{T_2^A w_2^{-\theta} + T_3^A w_3^{-\theta}}{T_2^B w_2^{-\theta} + T_3^B w_3^{-\theta}}. \tag{9}$$

In the simple 2-country example the familiar Samuelson (2004) result obtains: both countries are worst off when $T_1^A/T_1^B = T_2^A/T_2^B$. The third country effect is immediate in expression (9). From the perspective of an individual country, it is generically not the case that in any country, welfare is minimized when it is most similar to country 1. In the absence of unit production cost differences ($w_2 = w_3$), welfare is lowest when country 1 is most similar to the simple average productivity of countries other than country 1. When unit costs differ, what matters for welfare is the production-cost-weighted average, and the lower-wage countries will receive a higher weight in this productivity average. Furthermore, as revealed by equation (8), in the presence of trade costs, the welfare-minimizing relative productivity is no longer the same for each country, as is the case under frictionless trade.

By comparing the three-country expression in (9) to the N-country case in (8), it is also clear that as the number of countries increases, the bilateral technological similarity starts to matter less and less, as the weight of the country itself in the summation decreases. As the number of countries goes up, for country n's welfare, it becomes more and more important how country 1 compares to the countries other than country n rather than to country n itself.

II. Quantitative Framework

To evaluate quantitatively the global welfare impact of balanced and unbalanced sectoral productivity growth in China, we build on the conceptual framework and results above in two respects. First, we enrich the model in a number of dimensions to make it suitable for quantitative analysis. Relative to the simple model in Section I, the complete quantitative framework features (i) full general equilibrium with endogenous relative factor prices; (ii) multiple factors of production—capital and labor; (iii) an explicit nontradeable sector; (iv) input-output linkages between all sectors; (v) CES aggregation of tradeable consumption goods, with taste differences across goods.

Second, we require sectoral productivity estimates (T_n^j) for a large number of countries and sectors in the world. Sectoral productivities are obtained from Levchenko and Zhang (2011), which extends the approach of EK (2002) and uses bilateral trade data at sector level combined with a model-implied gravity relationship to estimate sector-level productivities.The quantitative framework is implemented on a sample of 75 countries, which in addition to China includes countries from all continents and major world regions.

A. *Preferences and Technology*

There are n, $i = 1, \ldots, N$ countries, J tradeable sectors, and one nontradeable sector $J+1$. Utility over the sectors in country n is given by

$$U_n = \left(\sum_{j=1}^{J} \omega_j^{\frac{1}{\eta}} (Y_n^j)^{\frac{\eta-1}{\eta}} \right)^{\frac{\eta}{\eta-1}\xi_n} (Y_n^{J+1})^{1-\xi_n}, \tag{10}$$

where ξ_n denotes the Cobb-Douglas weight for the tradeable sector composite good, η is the elasticity of substitution between the tradeable sectors, Y_n^{J+1} is final consumption of the nontradeable-sector composite good, and Y_n^j is the final consumption of the composite good in tradeable sector j. Importantly, while Section I relied on Cobb-Douglas preferences and symmetry of the tradeable sectors in the utility function, the quantitative model adopts CES preferences and allows ω_j—the taste parameter for tradeable sector j—to differ across sectors.

As in Section I, output in sector j aggregates a continuum of varieties $q \in [0,1]$ according to equation (1), and the unit input requirement $\frac{1}{z_i^j(q)}$ for variety q is drawn from the country- and sector-specific productivity distribution given by equation (2). Production uses labor, capital, and intermediate inputs from other sectors. The cost of an input bundle in country i is

$$c_i^j = \left(w_i^{\alpha_j} r_i^{1-\alpha_j}\right)^{\beta_j} \left(\prod_{k=1}^{J+1} (p_i^k)^{\gamma_{k,j}} \right)^{1-\beta_j},$$

where w_i is the wage, r_i is the return to capital, and p_i^k is the price of intermediate input from sector k. The value-added based labor intensity is given by α_j, and the share of value added in total output by β_j. Both vary by sector. The shares of inputs from other sectors $\gamma_{k,j}$ vary by output industry j as well as input industry k. The production cost of one unit of good q in sector j and country n is thus equal to $c_i^j/z_i^j(q)$, and the price at which country i can serve market n is $p_{ni}^j(q) = \left(\frac{c_i^j}{z_i^j(q)}\right)d_{ni}^j$. The price $p_n^j(q)$ that country n actually pays for good q is given by equation (3).

B. *Characterization of Equilibrium*

The **competitive equilibrium** of this model world economy consists of a set of prices, allocation rules, and trade shares such that (i) given the prices, all firms' inputs satisfy the first-order conditions, and their output is given by the production function; (ii) given the prices, the consumers' demand satisfies the first-order conditions; (iii) the prices ensure the market clearing conditions for labor, capital, tradeable goods, and nontradeable goods; and (iv) trade shares ensure balanced trade for each country.[1]

The set of prices includes the wage rate w_n, the rental rate r_n, the sectoral prices $\{p_n^j\}_{j=1}^{J+1}$, and the aggregate price P_n in each country n. The allocation rules include the capital and labor allocation across sectors $\{K_n^j, L_n^j\}_{j=1}^{J+1}$, final consumption demand $\{Y_n^j\}_{j=1}^{J+1}$, and total demand $\{Q_n^j\}_{j=1}^{J+1}$ (both final and intermediate goods) for each sector. The trade shares include the expenditure share π_{ni}^j in country n on goods coming from country i in sector j.

Demand and Prices.—The price of sector j output in country n is given by equations (4) and (5), with the only difference that the expression for Φ_n^j in equation (4) features c_i^j instead of w_i. The consumption price index in country n is then

$$P_n = B_n\left(\sum_{j=1}^{J} \omega_j (p_n^j)^{1-\eta}\right)^{\frac{1}{1-\eta}\xi_n} (p_n^{J+1})^{1-\xi_n}, \tag{11}$$

where $B_n = \xi_n^{-\xi_n}(1-\xi_n)^{-(1-\xi_n)}$.

Both capital and labor are mobile across sectors and immobile across countries, and trade is balanced. The budget constraint (or the resource constraint) of the consumer is thus given by

$$\sum_{j=1}^{J+1} p_n^j Y_n^j = w_n L_n + r_n K_n, \tag{12}$$

[1] The assumption of balanced trade is not crucial for the results. Online Appendix Section C.1 implements a model with unbalanced trade following the approach of Dekle, Eaton, and Kortum (2007, 2008), and shows that the conclusions are quite similar.

where K_n and L_n are the endowments of capital and labor in country n.

Given the set of prices $\{w_n, r_n, P_n, \{p_n^j\}_{j=1}^{J+1}\}_{n=1}^{N}$, we first characterize the optimal allocations from final demand. Consumers maximize utility (10) subject to the budget constraint (12). The first-order conditions associated with this optimization problem imply the following final demand:

$$(13) \qquad p_n^j Y_n^j = \xi_n(w_n L_n + r_n K_n) \frac{\omega_j (p_n^j)^{1-\eta}}{\sum_{k=1}^{J} \omega_k (p_n^k)^{1-\eta}}, \quad \text{for all} \quad j = \{1, \ldots, J\}$$

and

$$p_n^{J+1} Y_n^{J+1} = (1 - \xi_n)(w_n L_n + r_n K_n).$$

Production Allocation and Market Clearing.—The EK structure in each sector j delivers the standard result that the probability of importing good q from country i, π_{ni}^j, is equal to the share of total spending on goods coming from country i, X_{ni}^j / X_n^j, and is given by

$$\frac{X_{ni}^j}{X_n^j} = \pi_{ni}^j = \frac{T_i^j (c_i^j d_{ni}^j)^{-\theta}}{\Phi_n^j}.$$

Let Q_n^j denote the total sectoral demand in country n and sector j. Q_n^j is used for both final consumption and intermediate inputs in domestic production of all sectors. That is,

$$p_n^j Q_n^j = p_n^j Y_n^j + \sum_{k=1}^{J} (1 - \beta_k) \gamma_{j,k} \left(\sum_{i=1}^{N} \pi_{in}^k p_i^k Q_i^k \right) + (1 - \beta_{J+1}) \gamma_{j,J+1} p_n^{J+1} Q_n^{J+1}.$$

Total expenditure in sector $j = 1, \ldots, J+1$ of country n, $p_n^j Q_n^j$, is the sum of (i) domestic final consumption expenditure $p_n^j Y_n^j$; (ii) expenditure on sector j goods as intermediate inputs in all the traded sectors $\sum_{k=1}^{J} (1 - \beta_k) \gamma_{j,k} \left(\sum_{i=1}^{N} \pi_{in}^k p_i^k Q_i^k \right)$, and (iii) expenditure on the j's sector intermediate inputs in the domestic nontraded sector $(1 - \beta_{J+1}) \gamma_{j,J+1} p_n^{J+1} Q_n^{J+1}$. These market clearing conditions summarize the two important features of the world economy captured by our model: complex international production linkages, as much of world trade is in intermediate inputs, and a good crosses borders multiple times before being consumed (Hummels, Ishii, and Yi 2001); and two-way input linkages between the tradeable and the nontradeable sectors.

In each tradeable sector j, some goods q are imported from abroad and some goods q are exported to the rest of the world. Country n's exports in sector j are given by $EX_n^j = \sum_{i=1}^{N} \mathbb{I}_{i \neq n} \pi_{in}^j p_i^j Q_i^j$, and its imports in sector j are given by $IM_n^j = \sum_{i=1}^{N} \mathbb{I}_{i \neq n} \pi_{ni}^j p_n^j Q_n^j$, where $\mathbb{I}_{i \neq n}$ is the indicator function. The total exports of country n are then $EX_n = \sum_{j=1}^{J} EX_n^j$, and total imports are $IM_n = \sum_{j=1}^{J} IM_n^j$. Trade balance requires that for any country n, $EX_n - IM_n = 0$.

Given the total production revenue in tradeable sector j in country n, $\sum_{i=1}^{N} \pi_{in}^j p_i^j Q_i^j$, the optimal sectoral factor allocations must satisfy

$$\sum_{i=1}^{N} \pi_{in}^j p_i^j Q_i^j = \frac{w_n L_n^j}{\alpha_j \beta_j} = \frac{r_n K_n^j}{(1 - \alpha_j)\beta_j}.$$

For the nontradeable sector $J + 1$, the optimal factor allocations in country n are simply given by

$$p_n^{J+1} Q_n^{J+1} = \frac{w_n L_n^{J+1}}{\alpha_{J+1}\beta_{J+1}} = \frac{r_n K_n^{J+1}}{(1 - \alpha_{J+1})\beta_{J+1}}.$$

Finally, for any n the feasibility conditions for factors are given by

$$\sum_{j=1}^{J+1} L_n^j = L_n \quad \text{and} \quad \sum_{j=1}^{J+1} K_n^j = K_n.$$

C. *Welfare*

Welfare in this framework corresponds to the indirect utility function. Straightforward steps using the CES functional form can be used to show that the indirect utility in each country n is equal to total income divided by the price level. Since both goods and factor markets are competitive, total income equals the total returns to factors of production. Thus total welfare in a country is given by $(w_n L_n + r_n K_n)/P_n$, where the consumption price level P_n comes from equation (11). Expressed in per capita terms it becomes

$$\frac{w_n + r_n k_n}{P_n}, \tag{14}$$

where $k_n = K_n/L_n$ is capital per worker. This expression is the metric of welfare in all counterfactual exercises below.

D. *Calibration*

In order to implement the model numerically, we must calibrate the following sets of parameters: (i) moments of the productivity distributions T_n^j and θ; (ii) trade costs d_{ni}^j; (iii) production function parameters α_j, β_j, $\gamma_{k,j}$, and ε; (iv) country factor endowments L_n and K_n; and (v) preference parameters ξ_n, ω_j, and η. We discuss the calibration of each in turn.

The structure of the model is used to estimate many of its parameters, most importantly the sector-level technology parameters T_n^j for a large set of countries. The first step, most relevant to this study, is to estimate the technology parameters in the tradeable sectors relative to a reference country (the United States) using data on sectoral output and bilateral trade. The procedure relies on fitting a structural gravity equation implied by the model, and using the resulting estimates along with data on input costs to back out underlying technology. Intuitively, if controlling for the typical gravity determinants of trade, a country spends relatively more on domestically produced goods in a particular sector, it is revealed to have either a high relative productivity or a low relative unit cost in that sector. The procedure then uses data on factor and intermediate input prices to net out the role of factor costs, yielding an estimate of relative productivity. This step also produces estimates of bilateral sector-level trade costs d_{ni}^j. The parametric model for iceberg trade costs includes common geographic variables, such as distance and common border, as well as policy variables, such as regional trade agreements and currency unions.

The second step is to estimate the technology parameters in the tradeable sectors for the United States. This procedure requires directly measuring TFP at the sectoral level using data on real output and inputs, and then correcting measured TFP for selection due to trade. The taste parameters for all tradeable sectors ω_j are also calibrated in this step. The third step is to calibrate the nontradeable technology for all countries using the first-order condition of the model and the relative prices of nontradeables observed in the data. The detailed procedures for all three steps are described in Levchenko and Zhang (2011) and reproduced in online Appendix B.

In the baseline analysis, we assume that the dispersion parameter θ does not vary across sectors and set $\theta = 8.28$, which is the preferred estimate of EK. Online Appendix Section C.4 checks the robustness of the results to this assumption in two ways. First, one may be concerned about how the results change under lower values of θ. A lower θ implies greater within-sector heterogeneity in the random productivity draws. Thus, trade flows become less sensitive to the costs of the input bundles (c_i^j), and the gains from intra-sectoral trade become larger relative to the gains from inter-sectoral trade. We repeat the analysis under the assumption that $\theta = 4$, a value that has been advocated by Simonovska and Waugh (2014). This value is at or near the bottom of the range that has been used in the literature. The main conclusions are robust to this alternative value of θ. Second, a number of studies have suggested that θ varies across sectors (see, e.g., Imbs and Méjean 2009; Caliendo and Parro 2010; Chen and Novy 2011). We repeat the analysis allowing θ to be sector-specific, with sectoral values of θ sourced from Caliendo and Parro (2010). Our results are robust to this alternative specification of θ.

The production function parameters α_j and β_j are estimated using the UNIDO Industrial Statistics Database, which reports output, value added, employment, and wage bills at the roughly 2-digit ISIC Revision 3 level of disaggregation. To compute α_j for each sector, we calculate the share of the total wage bill in value added, and take a simple median across countries (taking the mean yields essentially the same results). To compute β_j, we take the median of value added divided by total output.

The intermediate input coefficients $\gamma_{k,j}$ are obtained from the Direct Requirements Table for the United States. We use the 1997 Benchmark Detailed Make and Use

Tables (covering approximately 500 distinct sectors), as well as a concordance to the ISIC Revision 3 classification to build a Direct Requirements Table at the 2-digit ISIC level. The Direct Requirements Table gives the value of the intermediate input in row k required to produce one dollar of final output in column j. Thus, it is the direct counterpart to the input coefficients $\gamma_{k,j}$. Note that in the baseline analysis we assume these to be the same in all countries. Online Appendix Section C.5 establishes the robustness of the results to using country-specific I-O matrices instead. In addition, we use the US I-O matrix to obtain α_{J+1} and β_{J+1} in the nontradeable sector, which cannot be obtained from UNIDO.[2] The elasticity of substitution between varieties within each tradeable sector, ε, is set to 4 (as is well known, in the EK model this elasticity plays no role, entering only the constant Γ).

The total labor force in each country, L_n, and the total capital stock, K_n, are obtained from the Penn World Tables 6.3. Following the standard approach in the literature (see, e.g., Hall and Jones 1999; Bernanke and Gürkaynak 2001; Caselli 2005), the total labor force is calculated from the data on the total GDP per capita and per worker.[3] The total capital is calculated using the perpetual inventory method that assumes a depreciation rate of 6 percent: $K_{n,t} = (1 - 0.06)K_{n,t-1} + I_{n,t}$, where $I_{n,t}$ is total investment in country n in period t. For most countries, investment data start in 1950, and the initial value of K_n is set equal to $I_{n,0}/(\gamma + 0.06)$, where γ is the average growth rate of investment in the first 10 years for which data are available.

The share of expenditure on traded goods, ξ_n in each country is sourced from Yi and Zhang (2013), who compile this information for 36 developed and developing countries. For countries unavailable in the Yi and Zhang data, values of ξ_n are imputed based on their level of development. We fit a simple linear relationship between ξ_n and log PPP-adjusted per capita GDP from the Penn World Tables on the countries in the Yi and Zhang (2013) dataset. The fit of this simple bivariate linear relationship is quite good, with an R^2 of 0.55. For the remaining countries, we then set ξ_n to the value predicted by this bivariate regression at their level of income. The taste parameters for tradeable sectors ω_j were estimated by combining the model structure above with data on final consumption expenditure shares in the United States sourced from the US Input-Output matrix, as described in online Appendix B. The elasticity of substitution between broad sectors within the tradeable bundle, η, is set to 2. Since these are very large product categories, it is sensible that this elasticity would be relatively low. It is higher, however, than the elasticity of substitution between tradeable and nontradeable goods, which is set to 1 by the Cobb-Douglas assumption.

E. *Summary of the Estimates and Basic Patterns*

All of the variables that vary over time are averaged for the period 2000–2007 (the latest available year), which is the time period on which we carry out the analysis.

[2] The US I-O matrix provides an alternative way of computing α_j and β_j. These parameters calculated based on the US I-O table are very similar to those obtained from UNIDO, with the correlation coefficients between them above 0.85 in each case. The US I-O table implies greater variability in α_js and β_js across sectors than does UNIDO.

[3] Using the variable name conventions in the Penn World Tables, $L_n = 1000 \times pop \times rgdpch/rgdpwok$.

Table 1—Top and Bottom Trade Costs and Technological Similarity

Panel A. Trade costs (average d^j_{ni})

Top ten lowest		Top ten highest	
Japan	1.638	Trinidad and Tobago	3.952
Korea, Rep.	1.653	Ghana	3.944
United States	1.699	Ethiopia	3.783
Malaysia	1.760	Senegal	3.777
Taiwan Province of China	1.784	Bolivia	3.639
Germany	1.846	Honduras	3.631
Australia	1.880	Jordan	3.614
Canada	1.890	Mauritius	3.506
United Kingdom	1.931	Nigeria	3.503
Indonesia	1.933	El Salvador	3.486

Panel B. Technological similarity

Top ten highest		Top ten lowest	
India	0.928	Sri Lanka	0.578
Turkey	0.907	Bolivia	0.592
Indonesia	0.904	Iceland	0.595
Hungary	0.897	Honduras	0.611
Brazil	0.896	El Salvador	0.654
Philippines	0.889	Fiji	0.662
Mexico	0.879	Ethiopia	0.662
Egypt, Arab Rep.	0.873	Bangladesh	0.663
Vietnam	0.868	Iran, Islamic Rep.	0.665
Korea, Rep.	0.862	Saudi Arabia	0.710

Notes: This table reports the top and bottom ten countries in terms of the average iceberg costs (d^j_{ni}) with China in the top panel, and in terms of technological similarity, defined as the correlation between the $(T^j_n)^{1/\theta}$s of each country with China in the bottom panel.

Appendix Table A1 lists the 74 countries (besides China) used in the analysis, separating them into the major country groups and regions. Appendix Table A2 lists the 20 sectors along with the key parameter values for each sector: α_j, β_j, the share of nontradeable inputs in total inputs $\gamma_{J+1,j}$, and the taste parameter ω_j. In the baseline analysis tradeables are comprised of manufacturing sectors. Online Appendix Section C.3 presents the results of augmenting the model to include nonmanufacturing tradeables (agriculture and mining) and shows that all of the results are robust.

Countries differ markedly with respect to their trade relationship with China. The top panel of Table 1 lists the top ten and bottom ten countries in terms of the average trade costs (d^j_{ni}) with China, while the bottom panel reports the top ten and bottom ten countries in terms of the correlation between the tradeable sector productivities with China. Since average sectoral productivity scales with $(T^j_n)^{1/\theta}$ rather than T^j_n, and since we want to focus on differences in comparative rather than absolute advantage, we compute the correlations on the vectors of $(T^j_n)^{1/\theta}$ demeaned by each country's geometric average of those sectoral productivities.

Average trade costs vary from 1.6–1.7 for Japan, Korea, and the United States, to 3.95 for Trinidad and Tobago and Ethiopia. Not surprisingly, the trade costs implied by our model correlate positively with distance, with the countries in Asia as the ones with lowest trade costs, though not without exception: the United States, the United Kingdom, and Germany are in the bottom ten. Technological similarity varies a great deal as well, from correlations in excess of 0.9 with India, Turkey, and Indonesia, to correlations below 0.6 with Sri Lanka, Bolivia, and Iceland. It is clear

TABLE 2—THE FIT OF THE BASELINE MODEL WITH THE DATA

	Model	Data
Panel A. Wages		
Mean	0.369	0.333
Median	0.133	0.145
corr(model, data)	*0.993*	
Panel B. Return to capital		
Mean	0.850	0.919
Median	0.718	0.698
corr(model, data)	*0.955*	
Panel C. π^j_{nn}		
Mean	0.626	0.568
Median	0.690	0.611
corr(model, data)	*0.911*	
Panel D. π^j_{ni}, $i \neq n$		
Mean	0.0054	0.0058
Median	0.0002	0.0002
corr(model, data)	*0.902*	

Notes: This table reports the means and medians of wages relative to the United States (panel A); return to capital relative to the United States (panel B), share of domestically produced goods in overall spending (panel C), and share of goods from country *i* in overall spending (panel D) in the model and in the data.

that the regional component is not as prevalent here, with both most similar and most different countries drawn from different parts of the world.

III. Welfare Analysis

This section analyzes the global welfare impact of China's trade integration and various productivity growth scenarios. We proceed by first solving the model under the baseline values of all the estimated parameters, and present a number of checks on the model fit with respect to observed data. Then, we compute counterfactual welfare under two main sets of experiments. The first assumes that China is in autarky, and is intended to give a measure of the worldwide gains from trade with China. The second instead starts from today's equilibrium, and evaluates the implications of alternative patterns of China's productivity growth going forward. The model solution algorithm is described in Levchenko and Zhang (2011).

A. *Model Fit*

Table 2 compares the wages, returns to capital, and the trade shares in the baseline model solution and in the data. Panel A shows that mean and median wages implied by the model are very close to the data. The correlation coefficient between model-implied wages and those in the data is above 0.99. Panel B performs the same comparison for the return to capital. Since it is difficult to observe the return to capital in the data, we follow the approach adopted in the estimation of T^j_n's and impute r_n from an aggregate factor market clearing condition: $r_n/w_n = (1-\alpha)L_n/(\alpha K_n)$, where α is the aggregate share of labor in GDP, assumed

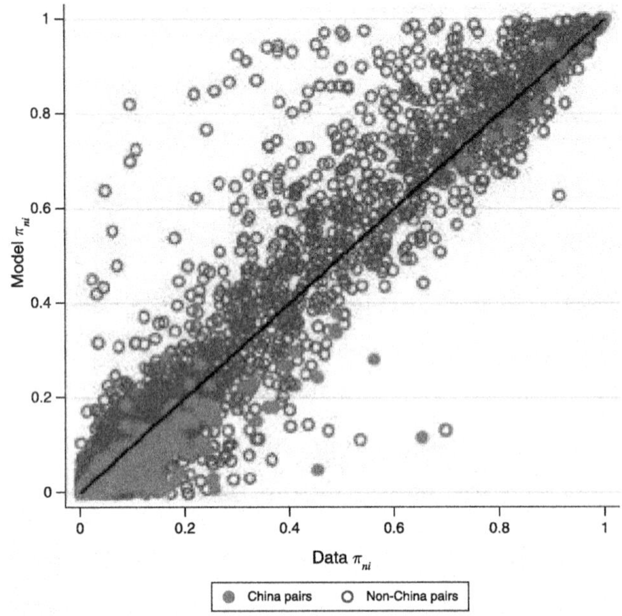

FIGURE 1. BENCHMARK MODEL VERSUS DATA: π_{ni}^{j} FOR CHINA AND THE REST OF THE SAMPLE

Notes: This figure displays the model-implied values of π_{ni}^{j} on the *y*-axis against the values of π_{ni}^{j} in the data on the *x*-axis. Solid dots depict π_{ni}^{j} in which either *n* or *i* equals China. Hollow dots represent the non-China π_{ni}^{j}s. The line through the points is the 45-degree line.

to be 2/3. Once again, the average levels of r_n are very similar in the model and the data, and the correlation between the two is in excess of 0.95.

Next, we compare the trade shares implied by the model to those in the data. Panel C of Table 2 reports the spending on domestically produced goods as a share of overall spending, π_{nn}^{j}. These values reflect the overall trade openness, with lower values implying higher international trade as a share of absorption. Though we underpredict overall trade slightly (model π_{nn}^{j}'s tend to be higher), the averages are quite similar, and the correlation between the model and data values is 0.91. Finally, the panel D compares the international trade flows in the model and the data. The averages are very close, and the correlation between model and data is 0.9.

Figure 1 presents the comparison of trade flows graphically, by depicting the model-implied trade values against the data, along with a 45-degree line. Solid dots indicate π_{ni}^{j}s that involve China, that is, trade flows in which China is either an exporter or an importer. All in all the fit of the model to trade flows is quite good. China is unexceptional, with Chinese flows clustered together with the rest of the observations.

We conclude from this exercise that our model matches quite closely the relative incomes of countries as well as bilateral and overall trade flows observed in the data. We now use the model to carry out the two counterfactual scenarios. One captures

TABLE 3—WELFARE CHANGES

	Mean	Median	Min	Max	Countries
Panel A. Welfare gains from trade with China					
China	3.72				
OECD	0.13	0.12	−0.03	0.30	22
East and South Asia	0.23	0.20	−0.20	0.80	12
East. Europe and Cent. Asia	0.14	0.09	−0.08	0.78	11
Latin America and Caribbean	0.09	0.09	−0.27	0.39	15
Middle East and North Africa	0.12	0.13	0.04	0.22	6
Sub-Saharan Africa	0.08	0.06	−0.04	0.21	8
Panel B. Welfare gains from balanced growth in China					
China	11.43				
OECD	0.01	0.02	−0.01	0.04	22
East and South Asia	0.03	0.04	−0.05	0.09	12
East. Europe and Cent. Asia	0.01	0.01	−0.02	0.06	11
Latin America and Caribbean	−0.01	0.00	−0.06	0.04	15
Middle East and North Africa	−0.01	−0.01	−0.07	0.02	6
Sub-Saharan Africa	0.00	0.01	−0.02	0.02	8
Panel C. Welfare gains from unbalanced growth in China					
China	10.57				
OECD	0.17	0.12	−0.07	0.77	22
East and South Asia	0.84	0.74	0.22	1.70	12
East. Europe and Cent. Asia	0.42	0.34	0.07	1.52	11
Latin America and Caribbean	0.50	0.49	0.09	1.68	15
Middle East and North Africa	0.48	0.52	0.19	0.77	6
Sub-Saharan Africa	0.23	0.21	−0.03	0.57	8

Notes: Units are in percentage points. This table reports the changes in welfare from three counterfactual scenarios. Panel A presents the welfare gains in the benchmark for the 2000s, relative to the scenario in which China is in autarky. Panel B presents the changes in welfare under the counterfactual scenario that growth is balanced in China across sectors, relative to the benchmark. Panel C presents the changes in welfare under the counterfactual scenario of unbalanced growth in China, relative to the benchmark. The technological changes assumed under the counterfactual scenarios are described in detail in the text.

the gains from trade with China as it stands now. The other considers two possible growth patterns for China.

B. *Gains from Trade with China*

Panel A of Table 3 reports the gains from trade with China around the world. To compute these, we compare welfare of each country in the baseline (current levels of trade costs and productivities as we estimate them in the world today) against a counterfactual scenario in which China is in autarky. The table reports the change in welfare for China itself, as well as the summary statistics for each region and country group. China's gains from trade relative to complete autarky are 3.72 percent. Elsewhere in the world, the gains range from −0.27 percent to 0.80 percent, with the mean of 0.13 percent.[4] The gains for the rest of the world from China's trade

[4] This is the unweighted mean across the 74 countries. The population-weighted mean is very close at 0.12 percent. One may also be interested in comparing the gains from trade with China to other commonly calculated magnitudes in these types of models, such as the total gains from trade. Elsewhere (Levchenko and Zhang 2011) we report that the median gain from trade in this type of model among these 75 countries is 4.5 percent, with the range from 0.5 percent to 12.2 percent.

integration are smaller than for China itself because these gains are relative to the counterfactual that preserves all the global trade relationships other than with China.

The countries gaining the most tend to be close to China geographically: Malaysia (0.80 percent), Kazakhstan (0.78 percent), and Taiwan, POC (0.63 percent). Of the top ten, seven are in Asia, and the remaining three are Peru (0.39 percent), Chile (0.37 percent), and Australia (0.30 percent). The OECD countries to gain the most are Australia, New Zealand, and Japan at 0.26 percent–0.30 percent. The mean gain in the OECD is 0.13 percent, and the welfare change for the United States is 0.11 percent. Table 3 also reveals that in nearly every major country group, the welfare changes range from negative to positive. The countries to lose the most from entry of China into world trade are Honduras (−0.27 percent) and El Salvador (−21 percent). All in all, 9 out of 75 countries experience negative welfare changes. By and large, countries that lose tend to be producers of textiles and apparel: Sri Lanka, Bulgaria, Vietnam, Mauritius, and Portugal are all among the losing countries.[5]

Our multi-country, multi-sector model does not admit an analytical expression for the magnitude of the gains from trade with China, as those gains depend on all the parameters characterizing the country and all of its trading partners. Nonetheless, we investigate whether the variation in the gains from trade with China across countries can be explained—in the least-squares sense—by three simple measures of countries' multilateral trade linkages with China. The first is the correlation between a country's export shares and China's export shares. This measure is meant to capture the extent to which China competes with the country in world product markets. A high correlation means that the country has a very similar export basket to China, and thus will compete with it head-to-head. All else equal, we would expect countries with a higher correlation to experience smaller gains from integration of China.

The second measure is the correlation between a country's export shares and China's import shares. This indicator is meant to reflect China's demand for the goods that the country exports. If the correlation is high, this means China imports a lot of the goods that the country exports, and thus all else equal the country's gains from introducing China into the world economy should be higher. Finally, the last indicator is the correlation between China's export shares and the country's import shares. It is meant to measure the extent to which a country values the goods produced by China. A high correlation means that the country imports a lot of the goods that China exports, which should lead to greater gains, ceteris paribus.

In our sample of countries, we regress gains from integration of China on these three heuristic indicators, controlling for the (log) average d_{ni}^{j} between the country

[5]The magnitudes of our welfare results are quite typical for the large literature on the quantitative gains from trade. This literature normally finds total gains from trade relative to complete autarky of a few percent. More incremental comparative statics (introduction of a new trade partner, signing a free trade agreement) normally produce welfare changes on the order of a fraction of 1 percent. To give but a few examples, Baldwin, Francois, and Portes (1997) and Brown et al. (1997) find that Western Europe's gains from integration of Central and Eastern European countries about 0.1–0.2 percent. More recently, using a quantitative framework similar to ours, Caliendo and Parro (2010) report US gains from NAFTA of 0.17 percent.

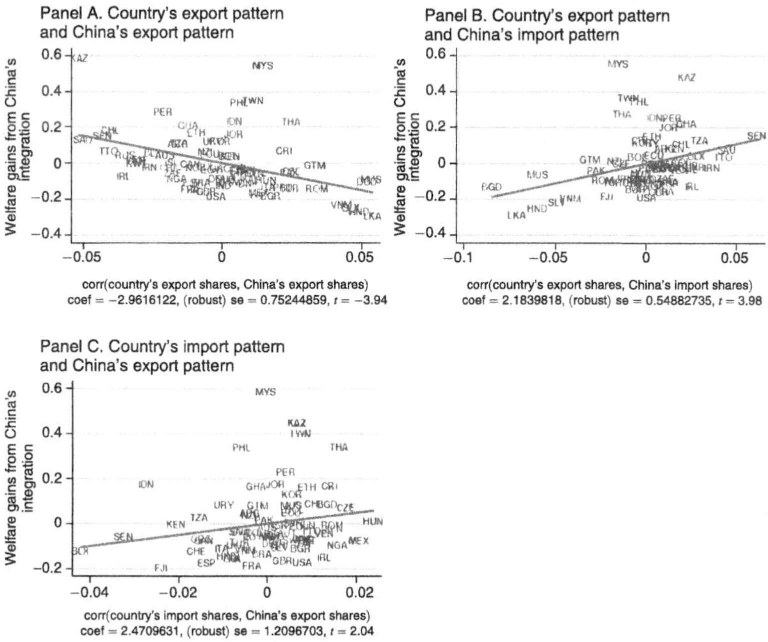

FIGURE 2. GAINS FROM TRADE WITH CHINA

Notes: This figure reports the partial correlation plots between the gains from trade with China on the y-axis against the indicator on the x-axis. The units on the y-axis are percentage points. In each plot, the other two indicators, log average d^j_{ni}, and log population are the control variables. The R^2 of the regression that includes all variables is 0.38.

and China, and (log) country population.[6] The overall R^2 in this regression is 0.38. All three are significant and have the expected sign. It is important to emphasize that we do not seek any kind of causal interpretation in this exercise. Instead, the goal is only to find some simple and intuitive indicators that can account for some of the cross-country variation in gains. With that caveat, Figure 2 depicts the partial correlations between the three indicators of interest and the welfare gains from China's integration. The top left panel shows that countries with similar export baskets to China tend to gain less. The relationship is highly significant, with a t-statistic of nearly four. The top right panel illustrates that countries that export goods imported by China tend to benefit more. The relationship is once again highly significant, with a t-statistic of four. Finally, the bottom panel shows that countries whose import basket is similar to China's export basket tend to gain more. The relationship is less strong than the other two, but still significant at the 5 percent level. We conclude from this exercise that the gains from trade with China are well explained by some

[6] All the results are unchanged if we use total country GDP instead of population as a measure of size, or if we use levels of d^j_{ni} and population or GDP instead of logs.

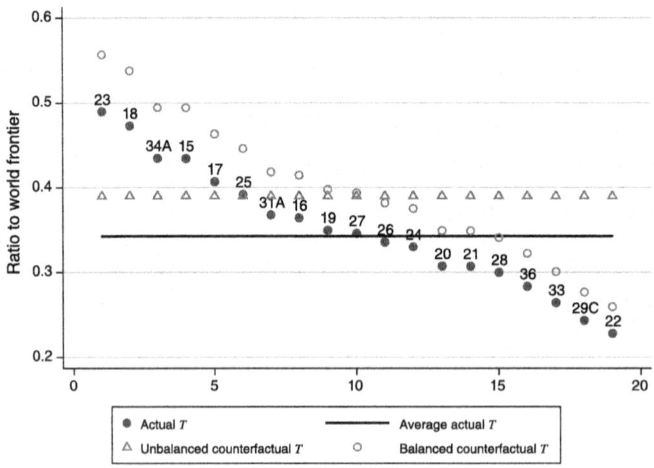

FIGURE 3. CHINA: ACTUAL AND COUNTERFACTUAL PRODUCTIVITIES

Notes: This figure displays the actual and counterfactual productivities in China, by sector. The key for sector labels is reported in Table A2. The formula for the balanced counterfactual Ts is: $(T_n^j)_{balanced} = (T_n^j)_{2000s} \times g_T$, where $g_T = \left(\prod_{k=1}^{j} (T_n^k/T_F^k)_{2000s}\right)^{\frac{1}{J}} / \left(\prod_{k=1}^{j} (T_n^k/T_F^k)_{1990s}\right)^{\frac{1}{J}}$ is the growth rate of the average productivity relative to world frontier between the 1990s and the 2000s, with T_F^j the world frontier productivity in sector j, calculated as the geometric average of the top two values of T_n^j in the world. The formula for the unbalanced counterfactual T's is $(T_n^j)_{unbalanced} = (T_F^j)_{2000s} \times \left(\prod_{k=1}^{j} (T_n^k/T_F^k)_{2000s}\right)^{\frac{1}{J}} \times g_T$.

simple heuristic measures of head-to-head competition with China in world markets, Chinese demand for a country's goods, and Chinese supply of the goods that a country imports.

C. *Balanced and Unbalanced Growth*

The preceding counterfactual was with respect to trade costs. It assumed that trade costs faced by China were prohibitive, and thus it was in autarky. The conjecture put forward by Samuelson (2004) is about uneven technical change in China going forward. Given the prevailing level of trade costs, global welfare will be affected differently depending on the pattern of sectoral productivity growth in China.

To evaluate Samuelson's conjecture, we simulate two productivity growth scenarios starting from today's values of China's T_n^js. Figure 3 depicts these two counterfactuals graphically. The solid dots, labeled by the sector number, represent the actual ratio of productivity to the global frontier in each sector in China in the 2000s. We can see that the comparative advantage sectors are coke, refined petroleum products, nuclear fuel; wearing apparel; and transport equipment. The productivity of these sectors is about 0.45–0.5 of the world frontier productivity. The sectors at the greatest comparative disadvantage are printing and publishing; office, accounting, computing, and other machinery; and medical, precision, and optical instruments.

The productivity of these sectors is around 0.25 of the world frontier. The solid line denotes the geometric average of China's productivity as a ratio to the world frontier productivity in the 2000s, which is about 0.34.[7]

The two counterfactual productivity scenarios are plotted in the figure. In the balanced growth scenario, we assume that in each sector China's distance to the global frontier has grown by the same proportional rate of 14 percent (or 1.32 percent per annum), which is the observed growth of average T_n^js in China relative to the world frontier over a decade between the 1990s and the 2000s. The balanced counterfactual productivities are depicted by the hollow dots. In the unbalanced growth counterfactual, we assume that China's average productivity grows by the same rate, but its comparative advantage relative to world frontier is erased; in each sector, its productivity is a constant fraction of world frontier. That scenario is depicted by the hollow triangles.[8] An attractive feature of this setup is that in the two counterfactuals, the geometric average productivity across sectors in China is the same. The only thing that is different is the comparative advantage.[9]

Panels B and C of Table 3 present the results for the balanced and the unbalanced counterfactuals, respectively. Appendix Table A1 reports the welfare changes for each individual country. The rest of the world gains much more from unbalanced growth in China. The difference is of an order of magnitude or more. While mean and median gains from balanced growth for the OECD are 0.01–0.02 percent, they are 0.12–0.17 percent in the unbalanced growth case. For other regions the difference is even larger: 0.23–0.84 percent at the mean in the unbalanced case, compared to essentially zero in the balanced case.[10] Figure 4, panel A presents the contrast between the the welfare changes in the two counterfactual scenarios graphically, by plotting the welfare changes in each country in the balanced case on the y-axis against the welfare changes in the unbalanced case on the x-axis, along with a 45-degree line. While there is a great deal of variation in the welfare changes under the unbalanced case, the balanced counterfactual welfare changes are all very close to zero. In the large majority of cases, the observation is well below the 45-degree line; the country gains more in the unbalanced counterfactual.

These results are diametrically opposite to what has been conjectured by Samuelson (2004), who feared that China's growth in its comparative disadvantage sectors will hurt the rest of the world. We devote the rest of this section to exploring the mechanisms behind this finding. The analytical section derives the multilateral

[7] Since mean productivity in each sector is equal to $T^{1/\theta}$, the figure reports the distance to the global frontier expressed in terms of $T^{1/\theta}$, rather than T.

[8] Between the 1990s and the 2000s, actual productivity growth has been balanced according to our estimates. While there is some dispersion in sectoral growth rates, comparative disadvantage sectors as of the 1990s had not caught up disproportionately faster to the world frontier.

[9] These counterfactuals match unweighted average productivities. Online Appendix Section C.6 considers an alternative counterfactual scenario in which weighted-average productivities are matched instead, with the weights being shares of value added or employment. The results are virtually indistinguishable from the main results. We keep productivity in the nontradeable sector at the benchmark value in all the counterfactual experiments, since our focus is on the welfare impact of changes in comparative advantage.

[10] Once again, while we report the simple means across countries throughout, population-weighted averages turn out to be very similar. In the sample of 74 countries, under the balanced counterfactual both unweighted and population-weighted mean welfare changes are 0.01 percent. In the unbalanced counterfactual, the unweighted mean welfare change is 0.42 percent, compared to the population-weighted average of 0.39 percent.

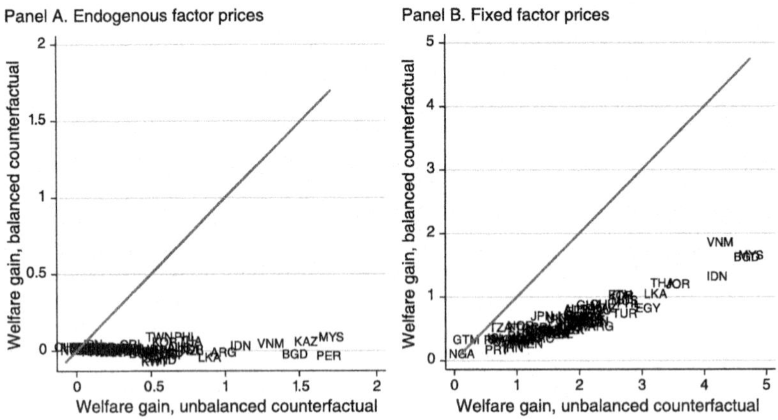

FIGURE 4. WELFARE GAINS IN THE BALANCED AND UNBALANCED COUNTERFACTUALS

Notes: This figure displays the scatterplots of the welfare gains in the balanced counterfactual on the *y*-axis against the welfare gain in the unbalanced counterfactual on the *x*-axis. The units on all of the axes are percentage points. The left panel reports the results from the complete model in which the factor prices w and r adjust to clear goods and factor markets. The right panel reports the welfare changes under the assumption that w and r remain constant at their baseline values. The 45-degree line is added to both plots.

similarity effect in a simple model with exogenously fixed wages. To isolate the channel emphasized by the analytical results, as an intermediate step we compute an alternative change in welfare under the assumption that w and r do not change from their baseline values.[11] Doing so allows us to focus on the changes in the price levels driven purely by changes in technology parameters rather than relative factor prices. Figure 4, panel B presents a scatterplot of the welfare changes in the balanced counterfactual against the welfare changes in the unbalanced one under fixed factor prices. The essential result that the world gains much more from unbalanced growth in China still obtains when factor prices do not change. The mechanism highlighted in the analytical section clearly contributes to generating the quantitative results.

As demonstrated in Section I, what matters for an individual country is how China's technology compares not to itself, but to appropriately averaged world productivity. Figure 5 plots China's distance to the global frontier in each sector against the simple average of the distance to the global frontier in all the countries in the sample except China, along with the least-squares fit. The world average distance to the frontier captures in a simple way how productive countries are, on average, in each sector. Higher values imply that the world as a whole is fairly productive in those sectors. Lower values imply that the world is fairly unproductive in those sectors.

[11] Note that this of course does not involve a solution to the model, and these values do not correspond to any actual equilibrium. They are simply the hypothetical values of the change in the welfare expression (14) that obtain when w_n and r_n remain at their baseline values but T_n^js for China change to their counterfactual values.

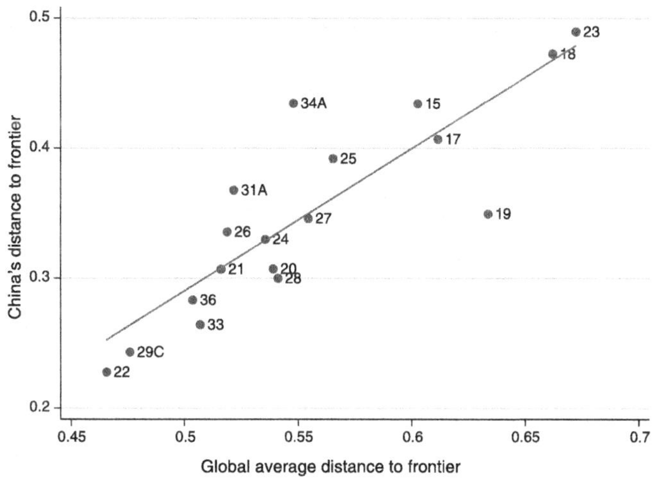

FIGURE 5. CHINA'S AND WORLD AVERAGE COMPARATIVE ADVANTAGE

Notes: This figure displays the distance to the global frontier in each sector in China (y-axis) against the simple average of the distance to frontier in that sector in the world excluding China. The key for sector labels is reported in Table A2.

China's comparative advantage sectors are also the ones in which other countries tend to be more productive. The simple correlation between these two variables is 0.86.[12] Thus, China's comparative advantage is in "common" sectors, those in which many other countries are already productive, most obviously wearing apparel. By contrast, China's comparative disadvantage is in "scarce" sectors in which not many countries are productive, for example, medical, precision, and optical instruments. Thus, it is more valuable for the world if China improves productivity in the globally scarce sectors.

Having isolated the impact of multilateral similarity by fixing w and r, we next explore the role of endogenous factor prices. Figure 6 plots the welfare change under endogenous w and r on the y-axis against the welfare change under fixed w and r on the x-axis. Panel A reports the scatterplot for the balanced counterfactual, while panel B for the unbalanced counterfactual. Several things stand out about the role of endogenous factor prices. First, in all countries (of course, except China) and both counterfactuals, the gains are larger under fixed factor prices. This is not surprising. When factor prices are fixed, the technological improvement in China is not accompanied by rising factor costs, giving all the countries except China a benefit of better technology without the cost of higher Chinese wages and returns to capital.

[12]The plot and the reported correlation drop tobacco, which is a small sector and an outlier. With tobacco, the correlation is 0.78.

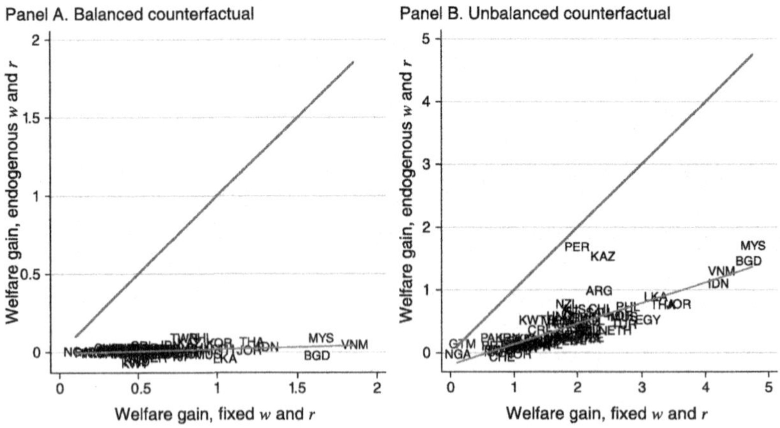

Figure 6. Welfare Gains under Fixed and Endogenous Factor Prices

Notes: This figure displays the scatterplots of the welfare gains under fixed factor prices on the x-axis against the welfare gains under endogenous factor prices on the y-axis in the balanced counterfactual (panel A) and the unbalanced counterfactual (panel B). The units on all of the axes are percentage points. The 45-degree line is added to both plots.

Second, in the balanced counterfactual, from the perspective of almost every country, the benefit from better Chinese technology is essentially perfectly canceled out by the higher factor prices in China. While there is some dispersion in how much countries gain under fixed factor prices (from zero to 2 percent), that dispersion disappears when factor prices are allowed to adjust. Countries that gain more from better Chinese technology when w and r are fixed also lose more from higher w and r in China, such that the net gains to them are nil.

Third, the counteracting movements in w and r are weaker in the unbalanced counterfactual. In contrast to the balanced growth case, it is not generally the case that the benefits to countries from Chinese technological change are perfectly undone by movements in factor prices. That offsetting effect exists, but it is much less strong. There is a clear positive relationship between welfare gains under fixed factor prices and gains with flexible ones; countries that gain the most from changes in Chinese technology when factor prices are fixed continue to gain more when factor prices adjust. Thus, there is an additional effect of unbalanced growth that works through endogenous factor prices. Compared to balanced growth, Chinese relative factor prices do not rise as much, and thus wipe out less of the gains to other countries from average productivity increases in China.

Next we explore technological similarity as a determinant of the gains from unbalanced growth in China. Figure 7, panel A plots the welfare change in the unbalanced counterfactual against the simple change in the correlation of Ts between the country and China. In other words, unbalanced growth in China makes China less technologically similar to the countries below zero on the x-axis, and more similar to the countries above zero on the x-axis. The figure also depicts the OLS fit

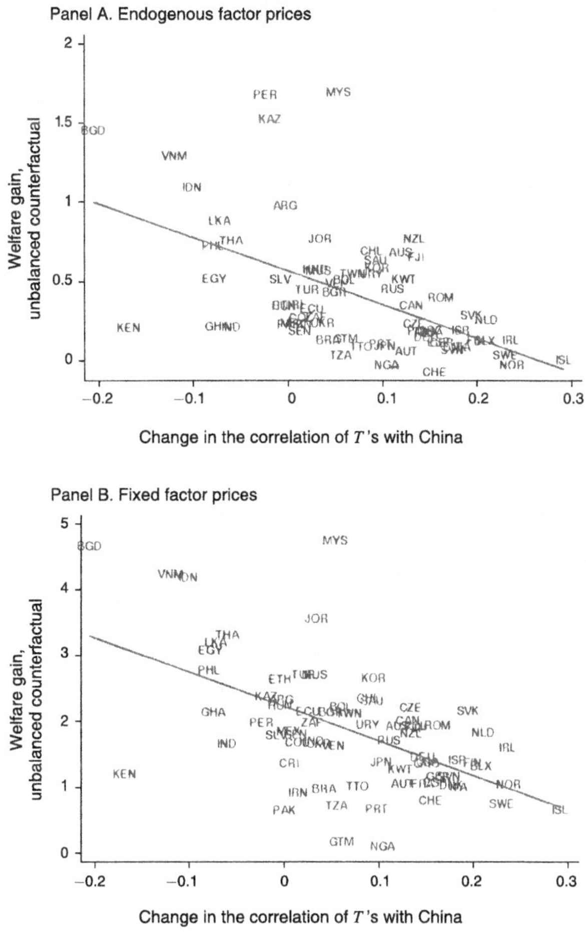

FIGURE 7. UNBALANCED COUNTERFACTUAL WELFARE GAINS AND TECHNOLOGICAL SIMILARITY

Notes: This figure displays the scatterplots of the welfare gains in the unbalanced counterfactual on the *y*-axis against the change in the technological between the country and China. The units on the *y*-axis are percentage points. Technological similarity is measured as the correlation coefficient of the *T*'s between the country and China. On the *y*-axis is the simple change in that correlation coefficient. The top panel reports the results from the complete model in which the factor prices *w* and *r* adjust to clear goods and factor markets. The bottom panel reports the welfare changes under the assumption that *w* and *r* remain constant at their baseline values. The OLS best fit line is added to both plots.

through the data. The relationship is negative and very significant: in this bivariate regression, the R^2 is 0.3 and the robust t-statistic on the change in technological similarity variable is five. Countries that become more similar to China as a result of China's unbalanced growth thus tend to gain less from that growth. (Note that as shown in Figure 4, panel A, nearly all countries, including ones that become more similar to China, none the less gain more from unbalanced growth compared to the balanced one.)

There could be two explanations for this robust negative correlation. The first is that when China becomes more similar, demand for the country's output goes down, pushing down factor prices. As a result, the country would gain less. The second explanation is about how trade costs affect multilateral similarity. Equation (8) shows that in the presence of trade costs, T_n^A and T_n^B will get a larger weight in the right-hand side expression for country n. That is, when d_{ni}^js are substantial, country n's similarity with China matters more than China's similarity to some other country i. The multilateral similarity effect is still of first-order importance in explaining the difference between the balanced and unbalanced growth outcomes. But when examining the variation in welfare gains across countries under the unbalanced counterfactual, the changes in bilateral technological similarity with China become relevant. To isolate the second effect, Figure 7, panel B relates changes in technological similarity to welfare changes in the unbalanced counterfactual, but this time under fixed factor prices. The strength of the negative relationship is the same: both the R^2 and the t-statistic on the coefficient are virtually identical to the plot with endogenous wages. We conclude that the negative relationship in Figure 7, panel A is not due purely to movements in factor prices.

Finally, China itself gains slightly more from a balanced growth scenario than from unbalanced growth, 11.43 percent compared to 10.57 percent, a difference of almost a percentage point. This result is driven by uneven consumption weights across sectors. It turns out that Chinese sectoral productivity today is strongly positively correlated with the sectoral taste parameter ω_j, with a correlation of nearly 0.5. In a world characterized by high trade costs, a country would be better off with higher productivity in sectors with high taste parameters, all else equal. In the unbalanced counterfactual, China's productivity in high-consumption-weight sectors becomes relatively lower.

Online Appendix C describes an extensive set of robustness checks on the main results, including (i) incorporating trade imbalances; (ii) adding nonmanufacturing production and trade; (iii) using directly measured productivities in countries where they are available; (iv) carrying out all of the analysis under alternative assumptions on the dispersion parameter θ; (v) using country-specific I-O matrices; and (vi) considering alternative specifications of the unbalanced counterfactual. The essential contrast between the balanced and the unbalanced cases is robust to all of these alternative approaches. In all cases, the world benefits much more from unbalanced growth in China.

IV. Conclusion

The sheer size of the Chinese economy and the breathtaking speed of its integration into global trade have led to concerns about the possible negative welfare effects of China's integration and productivity growth. These concerns correspond to the theoretically possible, though not necessary, outcomes in fully articulated models of international trade, and thus have been taken seriously by economists.

However, it is ultimately a quantitative question whether the negative welfare effects of China on its trading partners actually obtain in a calibrated model of the world economy with a realistic production structure, trade costs, and the inherently multilateral nature of international trade.

This paper investigates the global welfare impact of China's trade integration and productivity growth in a multi-country, multi-sector Ricardian-Heckscher-Ohlin model of production and trade. With respect to China's trade integration, our main finding is that the gains range from negative to positive, with Asian countries on average gaining more, while many countries in which textile and apparel sectors are important actually experiencing small welfare losses. With respect to technological change, our results are more surprising: contrary to a well-known conjecture, the world will actually gain much more in welfare if China's growth is unbalanced. This is because China's current pattern of comparative advantage is common in the world, and thus unbalanced growth in China actually makes it more different than the average country. Both analytical and quantitative results point to the crucial importance of taking explicit account of the multilateral nature of both Ricardian comparative advantage and trade flows in evaluating the global welfare impact of China.

Appendix

Table A1—Country Coverage and Welfare Changes in the Main Counterfactuals

Country	ΔWelfare Balanced	ΔWelfare Unbalanced	Country	ΔWelfare Balanced	ΔWelfare Unbalanced
OECD			*East and South Asia*		
Australia	0.020	0.684	Bangladesh	−0.026	1.452
Austria	0.014	0.059	Fiji	−0.028	0.654
Belgium-Luxembourg	0.019	0.125	India	0.000	0.215
Canada	0.018	0.350	Indonesia	0.030	1.096
Denmark	0.016	0.085	Korea, Rep.	0.054	0.586
Finland	0.024	0.131	Malaysia	0.086	1.698
France	0.008	0.177	Pakistan	−0.011	0.229
Germany	0.023	0.153	Philippines	0.089	0.726
Greece	−0.001	0.193	Sri Lanka	−0.045	0.886
Iceland	0.008	0.008	Taiwan Province of China	0.088	0.547
Ireland	0.022	0.130	Thailand	0.061	0.758
Italy	0.006	0.089	Vietnam	0.044	1.291
Japan	0.042	0.095			
Netherlands	0.019	0.258	*Eastern Europe and Central Asia*		
New Zealand	−0.001	0.769	Bulgaria	−0.019	0.431
Norway	0.024	−0.027	Czech Republic	0.018	0.234
Portugal	−0.006	0.107	Hungary	0.009	0.345
Spain	0.004	0.118	Kazakhstan	0.056	1.524
Sweden	0.017	0.037	Poland	0.011	0.190
Switzerland	0.024	−0.070	Romania	−0.008	0.397
United Kingdom	0.012	0.113	Russian Federation	0.010	0.454
United States	0.014	0.178	Slovak Republic	0.005	0.288
			Slovenia	0.003	0.070
			Turkey	−0.011	0.446
			Ukraine	0.014	0.240
Latin America and Caribbean			*Middle East and North Africa*		
Argentina	−0.013	0.980	Egypt, Arab Rep.	−0.005	0.517
Bolivia	−0.012	0.508	Iran, Islamic Rep.	−0.009	0.229
Brazil	0.001	0.130	Israel	0.023	0.194
Chile	0.026	0.690	Jordan	0.008	0.768
Colombia	−0.002	0.271	Kuwait	−0.074	0.515
Costa Rica	0.039	0.354	Saudi Arabia	−0.013	0.633
Ecuador	0.005	0.328	Ethiopia	0.014	0.351
El Salvador	−0.048	0.512	Ghana	0.009	0.218
Guatemala	−0.001	0.137	Kenya	−0.006	0.210
Honduras	−0.061	0.575	Mauritius	−0.017	0.567
Mexico	0.012	0.239	Nigeria	0.003	−0.028
Peru	−0.036	1.678	Senegal	0.003	0.190
Trinidad and Tobago	0.008	0.090	South Africa	0.018	0.274
Uruguay	0.002	0.548	Tanzania	0.013	0.036
Venezuela, RB	−0.012	0.488			

Notes: This table reports the countries in the sample, in addition to China, and the welfare change in each country under the balanced and the unbalanced counterfactuals relative to the benchmark. Units are in percentage points.

TABLE A2—SECTORS

SIC code	Sector name	α_j	β_j	$\gamma_{J+1,j}$	ω_j
15	Food and beverages	0.315	0.281	0.303	0.209
16	Tobacco products	0.264	0.520	0.527	0.010
17	Textiles	0.467	0.371	0.295	0.025
18	Wearing apparel, fur	0.493	0.377	0.320	0.089
19	Leather, leather products, footwear	0.485	0.359	0.330	0.014
20	Wood products (excl. furniture)	0.452	0.372	0.288	0.009
21	Paper and paper products	0.366	0.344	0.407	0.012
22	Printing and publishing	0.484	0.469	0.407	0.004
23	Coke, refined petroleum products, nuclear fuel	0.244	0.243	0.246	0.092
24	Chemical and chemical products	0.308	0.373	0.479	0.008
25	Rubber and plastics products	0.385	0.387	0.350	0.014
26	Nonmetallic mineral products	0.365	0.459	0.499	0.071
27	Basic metals	0.381	0.299	0.451	0.002
28	Fabricated metal products	0.448	0.398	0.364	0.012
29C	Office, accounting, computing, and other machinery	0.473	0.390	0.388	0.094
31A	Electrical machinery, communication equipment	0.405	0.380	0.416	0.057
33	Medical, precision, and optical instruments	0.456	0.428	0.441	0.036
34A	Transport equipment	0.464	0.343	0.286	0.175
36	Furniture and other manufacturing	0.460	0.407	0.397	0.065
4A	Nontradeables	0.561	0.651	0.788	
	Mean	0.414	0.393	0.399	0.053
	Min	0.244	0.243	0.246	0.002
	Max	0.561	0.651	0.788	0.209

Notes: This table reports the sectors used in the analysis. The classification corresponds to the ISIC Revision 3 2-digit, aggregated further due to data availability. α_j is the value-added based labor intensity; β_j is the share of value added in total output; $\gamma_{J+1,j}$ is the share of nontradeable inputs in total intermediate inputs; ω_j is the taste parameter for tradeable sector j, estimated using the procedure described in online Appendix B.3. Variable definitions and sources are described in detail in the text.

REFERENCES

Autor, David H., David Dorn, and Gordon H. Hanson. 2011. "The China Syndrome: Local Labor Market Effects of Import Competition in the United States." http://ideas.repec.org/a/bla/ecpoli/v12y1997i24p125-176.html.

Baldwin, Richard E., Joseph F. Francois, and Richard Portes. 1997. "The Costs and Benefits of Eastern Enlargement: The Impact on the EU and Central Europe." *Economic Policy* 12 (24): 125–76.

Bernanke, Ben, and Refet Gürkaynak. 2001. "Is Growth Exogenous? Taking Mankiw, Romer, and Weil Seriously." *NBER Macroeconomics Annual* 16 (1): 11–57.

Bitzer, Jürgen, Holger Görg, and Philipp J. H. Schröder. 2012. "Can Trade Really Hurt? An Empirical Follow-up on Samuelson's Controversial Paper." *Economic Inquiry* 50 (3): 724–38.

Bloom, Nicholas, Mirko Draca, and John Van Reenen. 2011. "Trade Induced Technical Change? The Impact of Chinese Imports on Innovation, IT and Productivity." National Bureau of Economic Research (NBER) Working Paper16717.

Brown, Drusilla, Alan Deardorff, Simeon Djankov, and Robert Stern. 1997. "An economic assessment of the integration of Czechoslovakia, Hungary, and Poland into the European Union." In *Europe's Economy Looks East: Implications for Germany and the European Union,* edited by Stanley W. Black, 23–60. New York: Cambridge University Press.

Caliendo, Lorenzo, and Fernando Parro. 2010. "Estimates of the Trade and Welfare Effects of NAFTA." Unpublished.

Caselli, Francesco. 2005. "Accounting for Cross-Country Income Differences." In *Handbook of Economic Growth,* Vol. 1, edited by Steven Durlauf and Philippe Aghion, 679–741. Amsterdam: North-Holland.

Chaney, Thomas. 2008. "Distorted Gravity: The Intensive and Extensive Margins of International Trade." *American Economic Review* 98 (4): 1707–21.

Chen, Natalie, and Dennis Novy. 2011. "Gravity, trade integration, and heterogeneity across industries." *Journal of International Economics* 85 (2): 206–21.

Costinot, Arnaud, Dave Donaldson, and Ivana Komunjer. 2012. "What Goods Do Countries Trade? A Quantitative Exploration of Ricardo's Ideas." *Review of Economic Studies* 79 (2): 581–608.

Dekle, Robert, Jonathan Eaton, and Samuel Kortum. 2007. "Unbalanced Trade." *American Economic Review* 97 (2): 351–55.

Dekle, Robert, Jonathan Eaton, and Samuel Kortum. 2008. "Global Rebalancing with Gravity: Measuring the Burden of Adjustment." *IMF Staff Papers* 55 (3): 511–40.

di Giovanni, Julian, Andrei A. Levchenko, and Jing Zhang. 2014. "The Global Welfare Impact of China: Trade Integration and Technological Change: Dataset." *American Economic Journal: Macroeconomics.* http://dx.doi.org/10.1257/mac.6.3.153.

Dornbusch, Rüdiger, Stanley Fischer, and Paul A. Samuelson. 1977. "Comparative Advantage, Trade, and Payments in a Ricardian Model with a Continuum of Goods." *American Economic Review* 67 (5): 823–39.

Eaton, Jonathan, and Samuel Kortum. 2002. "Technology, Geography, and Trade." *Econometrica* 70 (5): 1741–79.

Francois, Joseph F., and Ganeshan Wignaraja. 2008. "Economic Implications of Asian Integration." *Global Economy Journal* 8 (3): Article 1.

Ghosh, Madanmohan, and Someshwar Rao. 2010. "Chinese accession to the WTO: Economic implications for China, other Asian and North American economies." *Journal of Policy Modeling* 32 (3): 389–98.

Hall, Robert E., and Charles I. Jones. 1999. "Why do Some Countries Produce So Much More Output Per Worker than Others?" *Quarterly Journal of Economics* 114 (1): 83–116.

Hanson, Gordon H., and Raymond Robertson. 2010. "China and the Manufacturing Exports of Other Developing Countries." In *China's Growing Role in World Trade,* edited by Robert C. Feenstra and Shang-Jin Wei, 137–59. Chicago: University of Chicago Press.

Helpman, Elhanan, Marc J. Melitz, and Stephen R. Yeaple. 2004. "Export Versus FDI with Heterogeneous Firms." *American Economic Review* 94 (1): 300–316.

Hicks, John R. 1953. "An Inaugural Lecture." *Oxford Economic Papers* 5 (2): 117–35.

Hsieh, Chang-Tai, and Ralph Ossa. 2011. "A Global View of Productivity Growth in China." National Bureau of Economic Research (NBER) Working Paper 16778.

Hummels, David, Jun Ishii, and Kei-Mu Yi. 2001. "The nature and growth of vertical specialization in world trade." *Journal of International Economics* 54 (1): 75–96.

Imbs, Jean M., and Isabelle Jeanne Méjean. 2009. "Elasticity Optimism." Centre of Economic Policy Research (CEPR) Discussion Paper 7177.

Ju, Jiandong, and Xuebing Yang. 2009. "Hicks theorem: Effects of technological improvement in the Ricardian model." *International Review of Economics and Finance* 18 (2): 239–47.

Levchenko, Andrei A., and Jing Zhang. 2011. "The Evolution of Comparative Advantage: Measurement and Welfare Implications." National Bureau of Economic Research (NBER) Working Paper 16806.

Levchenko, Andrei A., and Jing Zhang. 2012. "Comparative advantage and the welfare impact of European integration." *Economic Policy* 27 (72): 567–602.

Samuelson, Paul A. 2004. "Where Ricardo and Mill Rebut and Confirm Arguments of Mainstream Economists Supporting Globalization." *Journal of Economic Perspectives* 18 (3): 135–46.

Shikher, Serge. 2011. "Capital, technology, and specialization in the neoclassical model." *Journal of International Economics* 83 (2): 229–42.

Simonovska, Ina, and Michael E. Waugh. 2014. "The Elasticity of Trade: Estimates and Evidence." *Journal of International Economics* 92 (1): 34–50.

Tokarick, Stephen. 2011. "The Implications of China's Pattern of Growth For the Rest of the World." Unpublished.

Yi, Kei-Mu, and Jing Zhang. 2013. "Structural Change in an Open Economy." *Journal of Monetary Economics* 60 (6): 667–82.

Comparative advantage and the welfare impact of European integration

Andrei A. Levchenko and Jing Zhang
University of Michigan and NBER, University of Michigan

1. INTRODUCTION

The fall of the Iron Curtain 20 years ago led to one of the largest episodes of abrupt trade integration in postwar history. It brought some 375 million people of the former communist bloc out of the politically imposed isolation and into the world trading system. Indeed, trade integration has been rapid. Figure 1(a) plots total inflation-adjusted exports of the East European countries between 1962 and 2007, expressed as an index number relative to 1990. The nearly eight-fold expansion in East European exports between 1990 and 2007 far outpaces the growth of overall world trade. For geographical, historical and political reasons, Western Europe is the region most affected by the integration of ex-communist countries. Figure 1(b) plots the share of Eastern

We are grateful to three anonymous referees, Chiara Fumagalli, Ayhan Kose, Marcelo Olarreaga, Daniel Sturm, and seminar participants at the IMF, University of Michigan, 2011 SED (Gent), 2011 ELSNIT (St. Gallen), 2012 AEA Meetings (Chicago), and the 55th Panel Meeting of *Economic Policy* (Copenhagen) for helpful suggestions, and to Lin Ma and Aaron Flaaen for excellent research assistance. E-mail (URL): alev@umich.edu (http://alevchenko.com), jzhang@umich.edu (http://www-personal.umich.edu/~jzhang).
The Managing Editor in charge of this paper was Tullio Jappelli.

Economic Policy October 2012 pp. 567–602 Printed in Great Britain

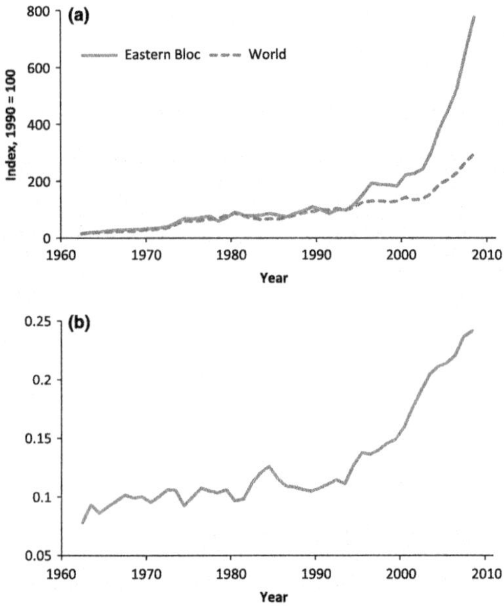

Figure 1. International trade in Eastern Europe, 1962–2007: (a) East European and World Trade, Index Number, 1990 = 100; (b) Share of imports from Eastern Europe in total West European imports

Notes: Figure 1(a) plots the total real (inflation-adjusted) exports from Eastern Europe (solid line), and the total real (inflation-adjusted) world exports (dashed line), for the period 1962–2007. Both series are normalized such that the 1990 value equals 100. Figure 1(b) plots the share of imports coming from Eastern Europe in the total imports of Western Europe from the rest of the world, 1962–2007.

Source: UN COMTRADE.

Europe in total West European imports from the rest of the world. After remaining stable at about 10% from the early 1960s to the early 1990s, it reached 24% by 2007.

Such episodes of rapid trade integration of large regions are relatively rare, and provide an important 'laboratory' for a quantitative study of the welfare gains from trade. This paper provides a comprehensive quantitative assessment of the welfare gains from the post-Cold War European trade integration. The analysis extends the quantitative framework recently developed by Levchenko and Zhang (2011). We build a multisector Ricardian-Heckscher–Ohlin model that incorporates a number of realistic features, such as multiple factors of production, an explicit non-traded sector, the full specification of input–output linkages between the sectors, and both inter- and intra-industry trade. We use the model to estimate sector-level productivities – comparative advantage – for 19 manufacturing sectors and a sample of 79 countries that includes 17 West European and 14 East European countries, as well as virtually all important economies in the rest of the world.

The key advantage of our multi-sector framework is that unlike quantitative assessments based on one-sector models (e.g. Eaton and Kortum, 2002; Alvarez and Lucas, 2007; Arkolakis *et al.*, 2012), we can examine the role of an often neglected determinant of welfare gains from trade: the Ricardian comparative advantage. Standard theories tell us that while trade integration should be beneficial to the countries involved, *how much* countries gain depends on the nature of comparative advantage. Generally, countries that are very different from each other will tend to gain more from trade opening than similar countries. Though qualitatively this idea is well understood, quantitatively we still do not have a clear understanding of the role that Ricardian comparative advantage plays in general, and for welfare gains from European integration in particular.

We first use our sectoral productivity estimates to document that there is indeed a great deal of variation in relative technology among the different countries in our sample. Correlations of sectoral productivities range from 0.16 between Russia and the Netherlands, to virtually 1 between Finland and Poland. Among the West European countries, average (GDP-weighted) correlations in sectoral technology with the Eastern bloc countries as a group range from 0.285 and 0.417 for the Netherlands and Ireland to 0.928 and 0.926 for Switzerland and Finland. Similarly, for Eastern Europe, GDP-weighted average correlations with Western Europe range from 0.533 and 0.537 for Estonia and Kazakhstan to 0.921 and 0.916 for Poland and Slovenia.

We then quantify the welfare gains from the trade integration of Eastern Europe, by comparing welfare in each West and East European country to a counterfactual scenario in which Eastern Europe is closed to trade. For each East European country, this comparison reveals the total gains from trade relative to autarky. The mean gain for Eastern Europe is 9.23%, ranging from 2.85% for Russia to 20% for Estonia. Ricardian comparative advantage plays an important role in explaining the variation in welfare gains in Eastern Europe. Controlling for country size and average trade costs, East European countries that are similar in relative technology to Western Europe – the wealthier Central European countries – tend to gain less. The most technologically different countries – Estonia and Kazakhstan – gain the most. The impact of similarity in comparative advantage is significant in magnitude: a one-standard deviation change in similarity to Western Europe increases the welfare gains for an East European country by 2.4%, all else equal.

For Western Europe, the mean gain from East European trade integration is 0.16%, ranging from zero for Portugal to 0.4% for Austria. Technological similarity to Eastern Europe does not help account – in the least-squares sense – for the variation in the gains to Western Europe. Trade costs with the East European countries are the predominant determinant of the variation in gains.

Not surprisingly, West European gains are much smaller, since for each West European country, this comparison represents the gains from the ability to trade with Eastern Europe, given that it trades with the rest of the world as well. Even at the peak, imports from Eastern Europe take up only a quarter of total West European imports from outside the region. Probing further, the main reason for the negligible role of comparative advantage is that the rest of the world has very similar sectoral productivity to the East European countries as a group. The simple correlation of average sectoral productivities in Eastern Europe with average sectoral productivities in the other countries serving the West European market – the Americas, Asia and the Pacific, the Middle East and sub-Saharan Africa – is in excess of 0.9. Thus, from the perspective of Western Europe, taken as a group Eastern Europe looks much like the rest of the world economy with which it trades. This is not to say that individual East European countries are not very different from the rest of the world – they are. But on the whole, Eastern Europe is a collection of diverse economies that looks quite similar to the world as a whole in terms of comparative advantage.

As a result, when Western Europe opens to trade with the East European countries, its imports from all other regions decrease somewhat and total West European imports expand by a modest 5%. Opening to trade with Eastern Europe also has a negligible effect on the sectoral structure in the West: value added shares of individual sectors never change by more than a fraction of a percentage point. This implies that Western Europe's gains come largely from within-industry specialization. Thus, part of the reason for small welfare gains in Western Europe is that without East European trade Western Europe easily substitutes towards other source countries, and its industrial structure remains largely unchanged.

We place our analysis in a broader context by evaluating the impact of other policy experiments in the European economy, benchmarking the main results and informing the policy priorities. Our first exercise compares deeper trade integration within Western Europe and the EU to broader but shallower trade integration with countries farther afield. For the West European countries the welfare gains from greater intra-West European integration are on average 16 times larger than the gains from integration with Eastern Europe.[1] In addition, more than two-thirds of the West European gains from East European trade are due to the EU accession countries. Both of these results suggest that deeper integration brings much greater welfare gains than shallower integration with more distant economies.

Next, we compare the welfare benefits of different types of integration. Western Europe gains far less from the observed productivity growth in Eastern Europe than from trade integration *per se*. This suggests that the West derives negligible welfare benefits from technology transfer to Eastern Europe, and that the majority of those benefits accrue to the East European countries. Finally, we examine the impact of barriers to factor reallocation. Our results reveal an important role for the cross-sectoral reallocation of labour and capital in Eastern Europe. When factors of produc-

[1] Indeed, the welfare gains from the observed fall in trade costs within Western Europe from the 1960s to the 2000s are equivalent to more than half of the total West European gains from trade relative to complete autarky in the 2000s. Put simply, for a West European country the majority of the total benefits from international trade come from trading with other West European countries.

tion cannot reallocate across sectors, East European gains from trade integration are reduced by 14%. Equally important as the impact on aggregate gains, trade opening without sectoral reallocation can have dramatic distributional effects. The policy implications are twofold. In order to reap the full gains from trade, opening must be accompanied by policies that promote smooth functioning of both labour and capital markets. And, since wages and returns to capital can fall dramatically in some import-competing sectors, it is essential to supplement trade opening with appropriate social safety net programmes, especially in cases where trade liberalization is expected to lead to large cross-sectoral reallocations of resources.

This paper relates to the broad line of research that studies regional economic integration using quantitative models (see Baldwin and Venables, 1995, for a survey). With respect to its focus on Europe, our analysis is most closely related to computable general equilibrium (CGE) assessments of the welfare impact of East European trade integration (e.g. Baldwin *et al.,* 1997; Brown *et al.*, 1997; Hertel *et al.*, 1997; Baourakis *et al.*, 2008), and to the quantitative industry equilibrium studies of West European integration under imperfect competition (e.g. Smith and Venables, 1988; Ottaviano *et al.*, 2009; Corcos *et al.*, 2012).

The average magnitudes of the welfare effects in our paper are broadly in line with existing literature. For instance, Baldwin *et al.* (1997) find that the welfare gains from East European integration are about 0.1–0.2% for Western Europe, and 1.5–18.8% for Eastern Europe. Similarly, Brown *et al.* (1997) find that the gains from integration of Central Europe are well under 0.5% for Western Europe, and 4–7% for Central European countries themselves. Our main contribution to this literature is to focus on a neglected determinant of the gains from trade: Ricardian comparative advantage. We thus build on the CGE approach by incorporating the multi-sector Eaton and Kortum (2002) structure explicitly into a global general equilibrium framework. Our results are more complementary to the industry equilibrium investigations of Smith and Venables (1998), Ottaviano *et al.* (2009), and Corcos *et al.* (2012). While we ignore the pro-competitive effects of liberalization on firm scale, mark-ups and firm selection, we explicitly model cross-industry Ricardian specialization. Methodologically, our work builds on recent quantitative welfare assessments of trade integration and technological change in multi-sector Ricardian models (Shikher, 2011; Caliendo and Parro, 2010; Costinot *et al.*, 2012; Hsieh and Ossa, 2011; Levchenko and Zhang, 2011; di Giovanni *et al.*, 2012). This paper is the first to apply this type of analysis to the trade integration of Eastern Europe.

Before moving on to the description of the model and the results, we outline some limitations of our analysis. Though our estimates of capital stocks and productivity are taken from the data, our counterfactuals ignore any endogenous responses of factor endowments and technology to trade opening. For instance, our analysis abstracts from endogenous cross-border movements of capital in response to trade opening, and any resulting impacts on factor prices. Similarly, we do not model the possibility that trade opening was itself responsible for technology transfer from West to East, and thus in the absence of trade productivity would be lower in Eastern Europe.[2] Similarly, it may be that trade openness will also result in changes in institutions, such as contract enforcement, property rights, or financial development. Our counterfactual exercises abstract from this potential indirect benefit of trade integration. In addition, because the model has no aggregate uncertainty, it also cannot be used to study the welfare benefits of improved international risk sharing.

The rest of the paper is organized as follows. Section 2 describes the basic features of the model and the quantitative implementation. Section 3 examines the welfare implications of East European integration, paying special attention to the role of comparative advantage. Section 4 performs a number of other policy experiments and discusses the policy implications of the results. Section 5 concludes. The Appendices collect the formal statement of the model equations, the description of the productivity estimation procedure, and the details of data collection.

2. ANALYTICAL AND QUANTITATIVE FRAMEWORK

The model is comprised of 79 countries, including 17 West European countries, 14 East European countries, and 48 non-European countries. The sample of countries is listed in Appendix Table A1.[3] There are 20 large sectors: 19 tradable manufacturing sectors, and one non-tradable sector. The sectors along with a number of salient sectoral characteristics in production and consumption are listed in Appendix Table A2.

Utility in each country aggregates consumption of these sectors. In our model, taste parameters associated with each sector are different, allowing for the possibility that some sectors (such as Food Products) carry a large weight in consumption, while others, such as Basic Metals, are not used much in final consumption. In addition, the share of tradables in the total consumption expenditure differs across countries according to income, to capture the well-known empirical regularity that the share of tradables in consumption tends to be higher in poorer countries. The parameters of the utility function are estimated based on country and sector-level consumption data, as detailed in the Web Appendix.

Each large sector aggregates a large number (formally a continuum) of varieties unique to each sector.[4] Each country can in principle produce each individual variety in each sector, but productivities will differ across countries, and be drawn from a country-specific random productivity distribution. In each individual sector, some

[2] The *cross-border* impact of technology transfer is quantitatively negligible, as we show in Section 4.2. Technology transfer accompanying trade opening may have a large impact on the country receiving the technology, but not on its trading partners.

[3] Due to lack of required data, a number of East European countries are missing. The missing countries include all but two of the countries comprising former Yugoslavia (Bosnia and Herzegovina, Croatia, Montenegro and Serbia), the trans-Caucasus countries (Armenia, Azerbaijan, Georgia), Albania, Belarus and Moldova. These countries together account for 14% of total Eastern bloc population and 10% of its GDP, but less than 6% of its exports.

[4] For instance, we can think of the Wearing Apparel sector as comprising of a large number of different garments.

countries will be on average more productive than others, and these relative differences in sectoral average productivity across countries – for which we adopt the shorthand 'Ricardian comparative advantage' – are central to our analysis. Countries that are on average relatively more productive in a particular sector will tend to be net exporters in that sector, as basic trade theory would predict. At the same time, because of the random nature of productivity draws in each country, even the relatively unproductive countries will produce and export some varieties in each sector. Because of this, the model will exhibit two-way, intra-industry trade between countries, which is a prominent feature of the data. The attractive feature of our model is that we can speak of classical, Ricardian predictions of trade theory while at the same time matching the observed, intra-industry trade between countries.

Following Chor (2010), we adopt a broad interpretation of sectoral productivity. Countries differ in a variety of ways, for instance in the quality of contract enforcement and property rights, financial development, and labour market institutions, among others. Recent empirical and theoretical literature has shown that all of these are sources of comparative advantage in international trade. Our paper adopts a reduced-form approach, under which institutions, financial development, and other country characteristics manifest themselves in productivity. For instance, countries with worse contracting institutions will have lower productivities in the more institutionally intensive sectors. Chor (2010) provides empirical evidence that sector-level trade patterns can indeed be modelled this way. We follow this approach by necessity, since it would be impractical to explicitly incorporate all of these various sources of comparative advantage into a quantitative framework of this scale.

All factor and goods markets are competitive. International trade in goods is subject to *ad valorem* ('iceberg') trade costs, while factors of production are immobile internationally. Production in each sector uses capital, labour and intermediate inputs from (potentially) all the sectors of the economy. Several features of the production structure are worth noting. First, labour (and conversely capital) intensity will differ across sectors, introducing a factor-proportions (Heckscher–Ohlin) motive for trade. On average, more capital-abundant countries will export in more capital-intensive sectors. Second, intermediate input usage will also differ across sectors. There will be variation in the overall intensity of intermediate input usage relative to value added. In addition, the pattern of intermediate input usage across sectors will be governed by an input–output matrix taken from the data. Third, there are extensive input–output linkages into and out of the non-tradable sector: tradables use non-tradable inputs, and vice versa. And fourth, because the input varieties are traded internationally, our model features the complex international production linkages that have become so prominent in global trade in recent years: a good in sector X may be initially produced in country A, exported to country B, where it is used as an intermediate in the production of sector Y, and the output of sector Y can then be exported back to country A (or some other country C), either for final consumption or further processing. Our model thus features the complete global production and consumption chain.

Appendix Table A2 lists the sectors along with the key production function parameter values for each sector: labour intensity (α_j), intermediate input intensity (β_j), the share of non-tradable inputs in total inputs ($\gamma_{J+1,j}$), and the taste parameter in the utility function (ω_j).

In equilibrium, given all the exogenous parameter values, prices adjust so that all goods and factor markets clear. Importantly, factor market clearing involves optimal allocation of capital and labour across sectors (in Section 4 we explore a specific-factors variant of the model in which factors cannot move across sectors). Goods market clearing is obtained by imposing balanced trade.

The model has two principal uses. The first is to estimate sectoral productivity (denoted by T^j_n for country n in sector j from now on) for a large set of countries. The technology parameters in the tradable sectors relative to a reference country (the US) are estimated using data on sectoral output and bilateral trade. The procedure relies on fitting a structural gravity equation implied by the model. Intuitively, if controlling for the typical gravity determinants of trade, a country spends relatively more on domestically produced goods in a particular sector, it is revealed to have either a high relative productivity or a low relative unit cost in that sector. The procedure then uses data on factor and intermediate input prices to net out the role of factor costs, yielding an estimate of relative productivity. This step also produces estimates of bilateral, sector-level trade costs (denoted by d^j_{ni} for shipping from country i to country n in sector j). The next step is to estimate the technology parameters in the tradable sectors for the US. This procedure requires directly measuring TFP at the sectoral level using data on real output and inputs, and then correcting measured TFP for selection due to trade. Third, we calibrate the non-tradable technology for all countries using the first-order condition of the model and the relative prices of non-tradables observed in the data. The detailed procedures for all three steps are described in Levchenko and Zhang (2011) and reproduced in Web Appendix B.

The second use of the quantitative model is to perform welfare analysis. Given the estimated sectoral productivities, factor endowments, trade costs, and model parameters, we solve the system of equations defining the equilibrium under the baseline values, as well as under counterfactual scenarios, and compare welfare. The algorithm for solving the model is described in Levchenko and Zhang (2011).

3. THE WELFARE IMPACT OF EUROPEAN INTEGRATION

3.1. Basic patterns

Table 1 reports the matrix of correlations of T^j_n in the tradable sectors $j = 1,\ldots,J$ between all pairs of East and West European countries. In order to focus on differences in comparative rather than absolute advantage, we compute the correlations on the vectors of T^j_n demeaned by each country's geometric average T^j_n. It is clear that the differences in sectoral similarities between country pairs are pronounced. In East-

Table 1. Country-pair correlations

	BGR	CZE	EST	HUN	KAZ	LTU	LVA	MKD	POL	ROM	RUS	SVK	SVN	UKR	Mean
AUT	0.761	0.795	0.584	0.594	0.530	0.846	0.907	0.918	0.902	0.829	0.735	0.902	0.912	0.719	0.757
BLX	0.559	0.582	0.371	0.357	0.273	0.683	0.745	0.765	0.766	0.725	0.580	0.738	0.760	0.488	0.585
CHE	0.985	0.973	0.720	0.796	0.795	0.867	0.965	0.951	0.975	0.901	0.926	0.980	0.987	0.975	0.928
DEU	0.903	0.832	0.474	0.544	0.524	0.745	0.901	0.889	0.984	0.976	0.933	0.923	0.959	0.830	0.880
DNK	0.869	0.895	0.674	0.704	0.660	0.898	0.967	0.970	0.960	0.878	0.824	0.968	0.973	0.841	0.845
ESP	0.946	0.884	0.545	0.619	0.609	0.783	0.931	0.916	0.997	0.978	0.955	0.952	0.979	0.888	0.912
FIN	0.969	0.928	0.622	0.697	0.689	0.828	0.956	0.941	0.998	0.956	0.950	0.974	0.993	0.930	0.926
FRA	0.861	0.827	0.512	0.562	0.525	0.789	0.912	0.908	0.968	0.939	0.875	0.927	0.955	0.797	0.846
GBR	0.715	0.770	0.593	0.592	0.519	0.846	0.883	0.901	0.864	0.776	0.677	0.876	0.881	0.680	0.714
GRC	0.959	0.989	0.798	0.852	0.840	0.929	0.991	0.984	0.959	0.857	0.870	0.994	0.986	0.966	0.905
IRL	0.377	0.458	0.357	0.306	0.201	0.638	0.636	0.669	0.608	0.537	0.372	0.614	0.621	0.328	0.417
ISL	0.684	0.576	0.178	0.228	0.187	0.531	0.711	0.707	0.848	0.898	0.791	0.736	0.795	0.562	0.698
ITA	0.937	0.862	0.502	0.581	0.571	0.752	0.911	0.896	0.993	0.984	0.959	0.936	0.969	0.870	0.905
NLD	0.246	0.426	0.506	0.412	0.296	0.685	0.582	0.628	0.454	0.315	0.159	0.539	0.507	0.256	0.282
NOR	0.737	0.711	0.411	0.437	0.380	0.725	0.838	0.842	0.897	0.879	0.773	0.848	0.879	0.658	0.744
PRT	0.847	0.968	0.956	0.982	0.971	0.957	0.922	0.921	0.792	0.622	0.670	0.908	0.860	0.922	0.779
SWE	0.801	0.761	0.439	0.480	0.434	0.742	0.870	0.869	0.937	0.921	0.834	0.884	0.917	0.724	0.798
Mean	0.823	0.807	0.533	0.575	0.537	0.782	0.886	0.884	0.921	0.879	0.820	0.895	0.916	0.772	

Notes: This table reports the correlations in sectoral technological similarities between each West European-East European country pair. The correlations are between T_n^j's demeaned by the country-specific geometric average $\bar{T}_n$. The last column and last row report GDP-weighted average correlations.
Source: Authors' calculations.

ern Europe, countries most similar to the West are Poland, Slovenia and Slovakia, while Estonia and Kazakhstan are most different from the West. Among the West European countries, Finland and Switzerland have the most similar comparative advantage to Eastern Europe, while the Netherlands and Ireland are the most different.

3.2. Model fit

Our model matches quite closely the relative incomes of countries as well as bilateral and overall trade flows observed in the data. Table 2 compares the wages, returns to capital, and the trade shares in the baseline model solution and in the data. The top panel shows that mean and median wages implied by the model are very close to the data. The correlation coefficient between model-implied wages and those in the data is above 0.99. The second panel performs the same comparison for the return to capital. Since it is difficult to observe the return to capital in the data, we follow the approach adopted in the estimation of $T^j{}_n$, and impute return to capital r_n from an aggregate factor market clearing condition: $r_n/w_n = (1 - \alpha)\, L_n /(\alpha\, K_n)$, where α is the aggregate share of labour in GDP, assumed to be 2/3, w_n is the wage rate, K_n is the capital endowment, and L_n is the labour endowment. Once again, the average levels of r_n are very similar in the model and the data, and the correlation between the two is 0.95.

Next, we compare the trade shares implied by the model to those in the data. The third panel of Table 2 reports the spending on domestically produced goods as a

Table 2. The fit of the baseline model with the data

	Model	Data
Wages		
Mean	0.390	0.351
Median	0.133	0.150
Corr (model, data)	*0.994*	
Return to capital		
Mean	0.896	0.939
Median	0.674	0.698
Corr (model, data)	*0.950*	
$\pi^j{}_{nn}$		
Mean	0.614	0.569
Median	0.676	0.609
Corr (model, data)	*0.922*	
$\pi^j{}_{ni},\ i \neq n$		
Mean	0.005	0.006
Median	0.000	0.000
Corr (model, data)	*0.910*	

Notes: This table reports the means and medians of wages relative to the US (top panel); return to capital relative to the US (second panel), share of domestically produced goods in overall spending (third panel), and share of goods from country *i* in overall spending (bottom panel) in the model and in the data. Wages and return to capital in the data are calculated as described in Web Appendix B.
Source: Authors' calculations.

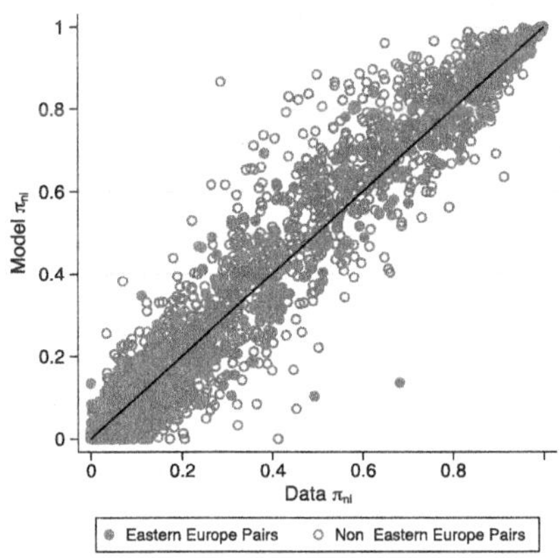

Figure 2. Benchmark Model vs. Data: p^j_{ni} for Eastern Europe and the Rest of the Sample

Notes This figure displays the model-implied values of p^j_{ni} on the y-axis against the values of p^j_{ni} in the data on the x-axis, where p^j_{ni} is defined as the share of spending on goods produced in country i in total sector j spending in country n. Solid dots depict p^j_{ni} in which either n or i is an East European country. Hollow dots represent the non-Eastern Europe p^j_{ni} 's. The line through the points is the 45-degree line

share of overall spending in country *n* and sector *j*, denoted by π^j_{nn}. These values reflect the overall trade openness, with lower values implying higher international trade as a share of absorption. Though we under-predict overall trade slightly (model π^j_{nn} tend to be higher), the averages are quite similar, and the correlation between the model and data values is 0.92. Finally, the bottom panel compares the international trade flows in the model and the data. The averages are very close, and the correlation between the model and data values is 0.91.

Figure 2 presents the comparison of trade flows graphically, by depicting the model-implied trade values against the data, along with a 45-degree line. Solid dots indicate cross-border trade shares (π^j_{ni}) that involve Eastern Europe, that is, trade flows in which an East European country is either an exporter or an importer. All in all the fit of the model to trade flows is quite good. Eastern Europe is unexceptional when it comes to the fit of the model, with East European trade flows clustered together with the rest of the observations.

3.3. Welfare analysis

This section evaluates the welfare gains from trade integration of Eastern Europe. To do so, we first compute welfare in the baseline model under the actual trade costs d^j_{ni}

estimated on data for the 2000s. We next compute the welfare in a counterfactual scenario in which all East European countries are in autarky.[5]

It is worth emphasizing precisely what our counterfactual exercises do, and correspondingly what effects would be missing from the welfare calculations presented in this paper. In the main counterfactual scenario, capital and labour endowments and all parameters characterizing technology are fixed at their baseline values, and only trade costs change (going from infinite to estimated values in Eastern Europe). This welfare comparison captures the static gains from goods trade for the countries involved. It does not, however, capture the possibility that this reduction in trade costs also caused endogenous cross-border movements of capital or labour, or endogenous changes in technology in the countries involved, for instance through technology transfer from West to East. Our counterfactuals also do not incorporate the possibility that trade opening caused changes in institutions for the countries involved. Section 4 will present some results on the welfare impact of technology and capital accumulation in Eastern Europe, that can be used to shed some light on the possible welfare impact of those types of changes as well, but a comprehensive assessment of the indirect effects of trade opening through factor endowment, technology or institutional changes remains outside the scope of this paper. Note also that while the precise numerical values for the welfare changes reported below may be the subject of some scepticism, the ranking of gains across countries and across sectors is both equally important, and probably more robust than the absolute numbers.

Table 3 reports, for each West and East European country, the percentage welfare gain from European integration (that is, the proportional difference in welfare between the benchmark model for the 2000s and the counterfactual model in which all East European countries are in autarky). All throughout, welfare is defined as the indirect utility function. Straightforward steps using the CES functional form can be used to show that indirect utility in each country n is equal to total income divided by the price level. Since the model is competitive, total income equals the total returns to factors of production. Expressed in per capita terms welfare is thus:

$$\frac{w_n + r_n k_n}{P_n} \tag{1}$$

where $k_n = K_n/L_n$ is capital per worker, and the consumption price level P_n comes from Equation (A.3) in the Web Appendix.

The gains to Western Europe are not large: the mean welfare increase is 0.16%, and the range is between essentially zero for Portugal and 0.4% for Austria. This

[5] In the counterfactual, each individual East European country is in autarky, that is, it does not trade with other Eastern bloc countries. Assuming complete autarky in this counterfactual may over-estimate the gains, since there was some trade among the Eastern bloc countries, as well as between those countries and the rest of the world. Our model is not suited to evaluate the welfare gains from trade among the communist bloc countries, since those were command economies in which all international exchange was centrally planned rather than driven by market forces.

Table 3. Welfare gains in Western and Eastern Europe

West	Δ Welfare (%)	East	Δ Welfare (%)
Austria	0.400	Bulgaria	12.571
Belgium–Luxembourg	0.131	Czech Republic	6.152
Denmark	0.202	Estonia	19.858
Finland	0.273	Hungary	8.117
France	0.074	Kazakhstan	9.654
Germany	0.226	Latvia	15.396
Greece	0.150	Lithuania	10.725
Iceland	0.211	Macedonia, FYR	10.914
Ireland	0.154	Poland	4.078
Italy	0.134	Romania	7.580
Netherlands	0.154	Russian Federation	2.855
Norway	0.116	Slovak Republic	8.220
Portugal	0.027	Slovenia	7.308
Spain	0.063	Ukraine	5.792
Sweden	0.177		
Switzerland	0.078		
United Kingdom	0.075		
Mean	0.156	Mean	9.230

Notes: This table reports the percentage changes in welfare due to the trade integration of Eastern Europe. It compares welfare in the baselines scenario under the estimated trade costs in the 2000s to a counterfactuals scenario in which each and every East European country is in autarky.
Source: Authors' calculations.

result is not surprising. First, in the 2000s imports from Eastern Europe were only about 22% of overall West European imports from outside Western Europe, and only 8% of total West European imports (including from within the region). In addition, our counterfactual takes into account the fact that in the absence of Eastern Europe, the total West European imports would not fall by 8%: Western Europe will increase imports from all other regions to partially substitute for East European imports. In fact, as we discuss in detail in Section 3.4, in the complete absence of Eastern Europe, total West European imports would only fall by 4.7%.

For Eastern Europe, gains are much greater, since in this case we are comparing complete autarky to trade. The median change in welfare is 9.23%, ranging from 2.85% for Russia to nearly 20% for Estonia. Not surprisingly, larger and farther away countries (Russia, Ukraine) tend to gain much less than smaller ones, such as the Baltic countries, FYR Macedonia and Bulgaria. Note that the gains are from trade with the entire world, not just with Western Europe.

How much does comparative advantage affect the magnitude of these gains? To account for the variation in the gains from East European trade, we regress the total welfare change on the average d^j_{ni}, the correlation between the Ts, as well as total GDP to control for the well-known role of country size. Note that we do not seek any kind of causal interpretation of these regressions. Rather, we only want to see which variables correlate with the variation in the welfare gains, and can 'explain' it in the least-squares sense. Table 4 reports the results, for three ways of weighting d^j_{ni} and correlations of T: equal-weighted, GDP-weighted and population-weighted. That is, when the regression is carried out on the

Table 4. Welfare gains, technological similarity, and trade costs

	(1) Equal-weighted	(2) Population-weighted	(3) GDP-weighted
Panel A: Western Europe			
Dep. Var.: Change in Welfare			
Technological similarity	−0.244	−0.060	−0.065
	(0.617)	(0.371)	(0.378)
Trade costs	−6.047***	−5.643***	−5.551***
	(1.386)	(1.536)	(1.503)
Real GDP	−0.456***	−0.500***	−0.491***
	(0.075)	(0.094)	(0.092)
Constant	12.080***	12.581***	12.276***
	(2.574)	(3.052)	(2.972)
Observations	17	17	17
R^2	0.704	0.653	0.650
Panel B: Eastern Europe			
Technological similarity	−0.968***	−0.858***	−0.845***
	(0.262)	(0.256)	(0.251)
Trade costs	−0.182	−0.105	−0.108
	(0.373)	(0.395)	(0.392)
Real GDP	−0.347***	−0.335***	−0.336***
	(0.035)	(0.037)	(0.036)
Constant	8.390***	8.160***	8.173***
	(0.694)	(0.726)	(0.719)
Observations	14	14	14
R^2	0.889	0.880	0.881

Notes: Robust standard errors in parentheses; *** significant at 1%. All left-hand side and right-hand side variables are in natural logs. The sample is of West European countries in Panel A, and of East European countries in Panel B. 'Equal-weighted', 'Population-weighted' and 'GDP-weighted' refers to how Technological similarity and Trade cost variables are averaged for each country across its trading partners in the other region. Variable definitions and sources are described in detail in the text.
Source: Authors' calculations.

sample of West European countries, we compute, for each country, the (weighted) average of its trade cost to each East European country, and the (weighted) average of its technological similarity to each East European country. When the regression is run on the sample of East European countries, these averages are computed across West European countries. All the left-hand side variables and the regressors are in logs throughout.[6]

Panel A reports the results for the 17 West European countries. The R^2 of these regressions is between 0.65 and 0.7, indicating that the three regressors account for the bulk of the cross-country variation in welfare gains. Trade costs and country size are significant at the 1% level in all specifications. By contrast, sectoral similarity has the 'right' sign but the coefficient is close to zero and insignificant.

Panel B reports the results for the 14 East European countries. The same three variables do a better job in absorbing the variation in the welfare gains for Eastern Europe: the R^2 is above 0.88 in all three specifications. Here, by contrast, technolo-

[6] None of the average correlations or welfare gains are negative, so taking logs does not lead to dropped observations. Estimating these relationships in levels delivers similar results.

gical similarity to Western Europe matters a great deal. Even in such a small sample, the coefficients on similarity are significant at the 1% level, with robust *t*-statistics of about 3.5. The coefficients are also large in magnitude. A one-standard deviation change in GDP-weighted technological similarity increases welfare gains from trade integration by 2.43 percentage points. On the other hand, trade costs do not seem to matter much in accounting for the gains from trade in Eastern Europe, in spite of the fact that the variation in trade costs is very similar in the West and East European samples.

Figure 3 presents the contrast between Western and Eastern Europe graphically. It plots the partial correlations between the welfare gain from East European integration and the GDP-weighted technological similarity (left side), and the GDP-weighted d^{ij}_{ni} (right side), after netting out the other variables in Table 4. The

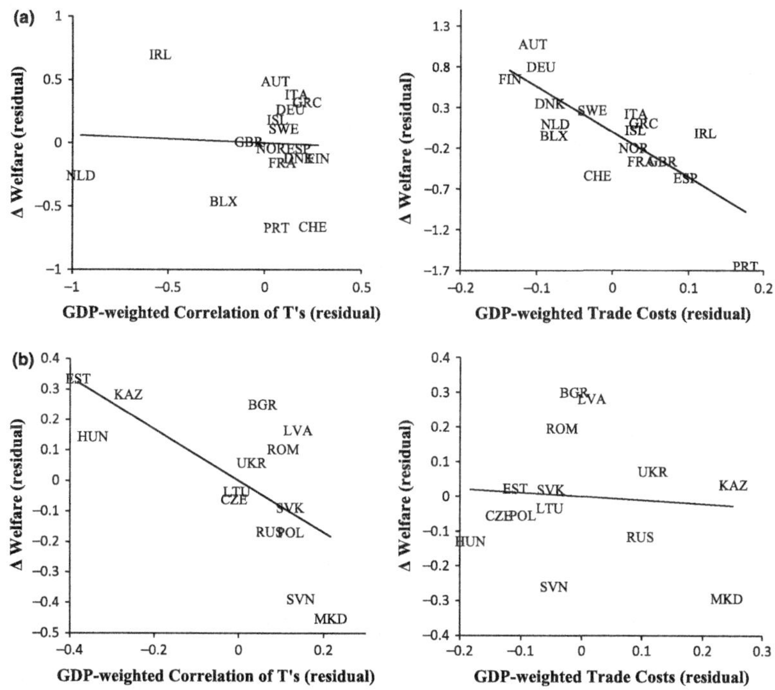

Figure 3. Welfare gains, similarity, and trade costs (a) Western Europe, (b) Eastern Europe

Notes: This figure plots the partial correlations between log welfare gains from European integration and the log GDP-weighted sectoral similarity (left graph), after netting out trade costs and total country GDP, and the partial correlation between log welfare gains from European integration and the log GDP-weighted trade costs, after netting out sectoral similarity and total country GDP (right graph). The top panel depicts these relationships for Western Europe, the bottom panel for Eastern Europe.

Source: Authors' calculations.

top panel reports the results for Western Europe, the bottom panel for Eastern Europe. As shown by the regression estimates, for Western Europe trade costs explain the variation in welfare gains remarkably well, while there is virtually no relationship with technological similarity. For Eastern Europe, trade costs do not do as well, but there is a pronounced negative relationship between similarity and the welfare gains.

This difference in outcomes between Western and Eastern Europe is due to the difference in relative importance of the two groups in each other's total trade. In the period we consider, 72% of Eastern Europe's imports come from Western Europe. Thus, technological similarity with Western Europe is an important determinant of the gains from trade relative to autarky. However, East European countries remain relatively small trade partners for Western Europe, accounting for about 22% of its imports from the rest of the world on average in the 2000s. Thus, for Western Europe, East European trade and technological similarity has to be evaluated in the context of its broader international trade relationships. That is, for Western Europe what should matter is not so much its similarity to Eastern Europe *per se*, but the relative similarity of Eastern Europe to the average country with which Western Europe already trades (see di Giovanni *et al.*, 2012 for a closely related result).

To that end, we compute the average productivity of East European countries in a sector, and correlate it to the average productivity of all the other trade partners of Western Europe (the Americas, Asia, the Pacific, Middle East and North Africa, and sub-Saharan Africa). It turns out that from the perspective of Western Europe, Eastern Europe looks very much like the rest of the world with which it trades. The correlation between the average sectoral productivity in Eastern Europe and in the rest of the world is a remarkable 0.91. Figure 4 presents this result graphically, with average productivities expressed as a fraction of the world frontier (this regularity holds for population- and GDP-weighted averages as well). Of course, individual

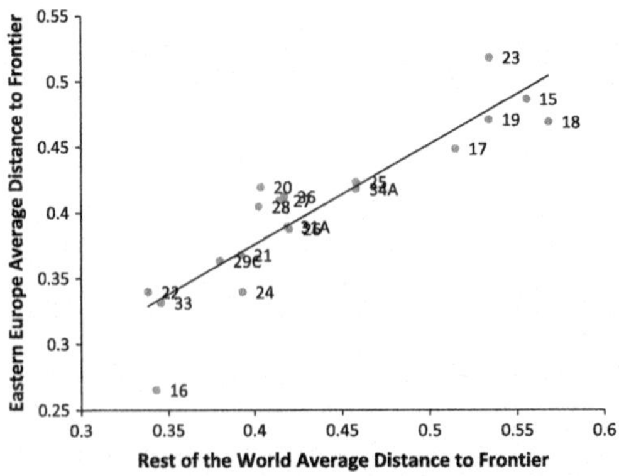

Figure 4. Eastern Europe and rest of world average comparative advantage

East European countries often have a comparative advantage that is very different from the rest of the world. But Eastern Europe contains many diverse countries, and as a group they look much like the rest of the world economy in terms of their relative technology.

Thus, the gains to Western Europe from East European trade come not primarily from trading with technologically different countries, but from the expansion of markets. As a result, trade costs explain very well the variation in the gains from trade for Western Europe, while technological similarity to Eastern Europe does not matter much.

3.4. Global trade volumes

We next explore how East European integration changes the pattern of global trade. By construction, when Eastern Europe opens to trade, exports from Eastern Europe to all other countries rise. But what happens to exports from other regions, in particular to Western Europe? As Eastern Europe takes up a substantial share of West European imports, do imports to Western Europe from other regions fall, and if yes, by how much?

Before describing the comparison between the counterfactual and the benchmark, we check how well the model reproduces the cross-regional trade shares. To do so, we compute, in both the data and the benchmark model, the shares of total extra-regional imports going to each region. That is, we take the total imports from the rest of the world to, say, Western Europe, and compute the share of those imports captured by Eastern Europe, as well as every other region. The regions we consider are non-Europe OECD countries (which for us are the United States, Canada, Japan, Australia and New Zealand); Latin America and the Caribbean; Middle East and North Africa; East and South Asia; and sub-Saharan Africa. Figure 5 presents the scatterplot of those shares in the data (on the x-axis) against the model, along with a 45-degree line. All in all, the model matches the cross-regional import shares remarkably well. The correlation between model and data shares is 0.98, and the Spearman rank correlation is 0.98 as well.

Next, Table 5 presents the matrix of percentage changes in cross-regional trade volumes from the counterfactual to the benchmark. The table omits Eastern Europe from both the rows and the columns of the table because in the counterfactual Eastern Europe is in autarky, and thus percentage changes between the counterfactual and the benchmark are infinity. Of particular interest is the top row that shows imports into Western Europe. As Eastern Europe opens to trade, imports from all other regions fall, by between −1.45% from non-Europe OECD and −4.09% from the Middle East/North Africa region. As a result, total West European imports – inclusive of Eastern Europe – increase by only 4.7%. This modest change is an illustration of why the gains to Western Europe from the opening up of Eastern Europe are so modest: if Eastern Europe were not there, the Western countries would substitute imports from other world regions for East European imports. The pattern looks similar

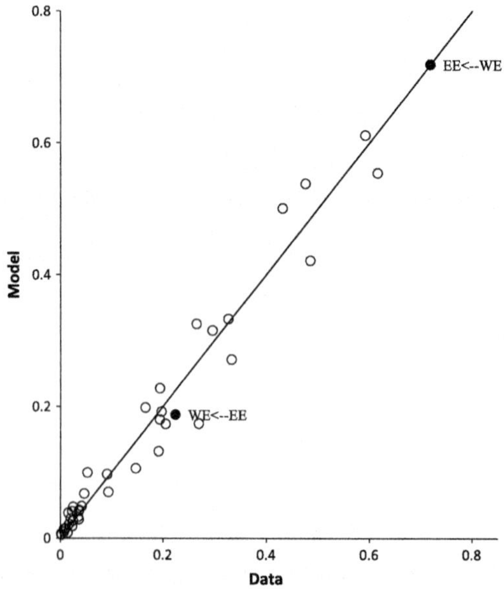

Figure 5. Shares of manufacturing imports: model vs data

Notes: This figure displays the scatterplot of the share of manufacturing imports from each region to each region in the data (*x*-axis) against the model (*y*-axis). For convenience, a 45-degree line is added to the plot. Data labels: WE = Western Europe, EE = Eastern Europe. The first label represents the importing region, the second label the exporting region (thus, WE<–EE is the share of West European imports coming from Eastern Europe).

Source: Authors' calculations.

elsewhere in the world. Total imports rise, but by less than in Western Europe. Imports from regions other than Eastern Europe fall modestly.

3.5. Changes in sectoral structure

A closely related question is what happens to industrial structure in Western Europe as a result of European integration. In this subsection, we compare sectoral structure implied by the baseline model to the counterfactual sectoral structure that would have prevailed had Eastern Europe not been integrated.

Figure 6(a) presents the absolute changes in shares of value added in each sector and each country as Eastern Europe opens to trade. The most striking result is just how little change in sectoral structure takes place. Aside from the non-tradable sector, in which shares usually decrease and sometimes by as much as 0.0025 (or a quarter of a percentage point), one hardly observes changes in value added shares in excess of 0.0005, or 0.05 percentage points. By and large, industrial structure remains the same as Western Europe opens to trade with Eastern Europe. This lack of effect is in part

Table 5. Percentage changes in cross-regional trade volumes

	Source country groups						
	Western Europe	Non-Europe OECD	Latin America/ Caribbean	Middle East/ North Africa	East and South Asia	Sub-Saharan Africa	Total
Destination country groups							
Western Europe	–	−1.45	−2.85	−4.09	−2.91	−1.95	4.67
Non-Europe OECD	−0.89	–	−0.25	0.3	−0.15	0.34	0.91
Latin America/ Caribbean	−0.83	−0.2	–	−0.06	−0.21	−0.79	0.36
Middle East/ North Africa	−3.63	−1.79	−4.88	–	−2.04	−8.36	3.9
East and South Asia	−1.41	−0.52	−1.84	−0.48	–	−1.84	1.32
Sub-Saharan Africa	−3.59	−1.79	−8.4	−7.92	−2.1	–	0.45

Notes: This table reports the percentage changes in imports from regions in the columns to regions in the rows. The last column reports the percentage changes in total imports for each region in the row. That value includes the East European imports.
Source: Authors' calculations.

because, as mentioned above, Eastern Europe represents only 22% of all West European imports from outside the region, and in part because Eastern Europe has similar technology to the rest of Western Europe's trading partners. Thus, trade liberalization of Eastern Europe does not represent a significant change in West European comparative advantage vis-à-vis the rest of the world with which it trades.

This lack of change in Western sectoral structure is in sharp contrast with Eastern Europe, depicted in Figure 6(b). Note the difference in scale of the y-axis: while for Western Europe, changes in the tradable sector range from –0.0005 to 0.0015, with the non-tradable share falling by less than 0.0025 in all cases, for Eastern Europe the changes in tradable sector shares range from about –0.005 to 0.02, and as much as –0.05 in the non-tradable sector. This is a difference in sectoral share changes of an order of magnitude. Not surprisingly, welfare changes in Eastern Europe are much greater.

4. BENCHMARKING THE GAINS AND POLICY IMPLICATIONS

Are the gains from East European integration produced by our model large or small? Comparing the main welfare results to alternative policy experiments will shed light on where integration of Eastern Europe falls in the ranking of different changes that occurred, or might occur, in the European economy. These differences in impact will then inform the policy priorities, by highlighting economic changes that have relatively large or small welfare pay-offs. This section develops a number of alternative counterfactuals, with an eye on comparing the welfare impact of these alternative changes to the welfare impact of the integration of Eastern Europe.

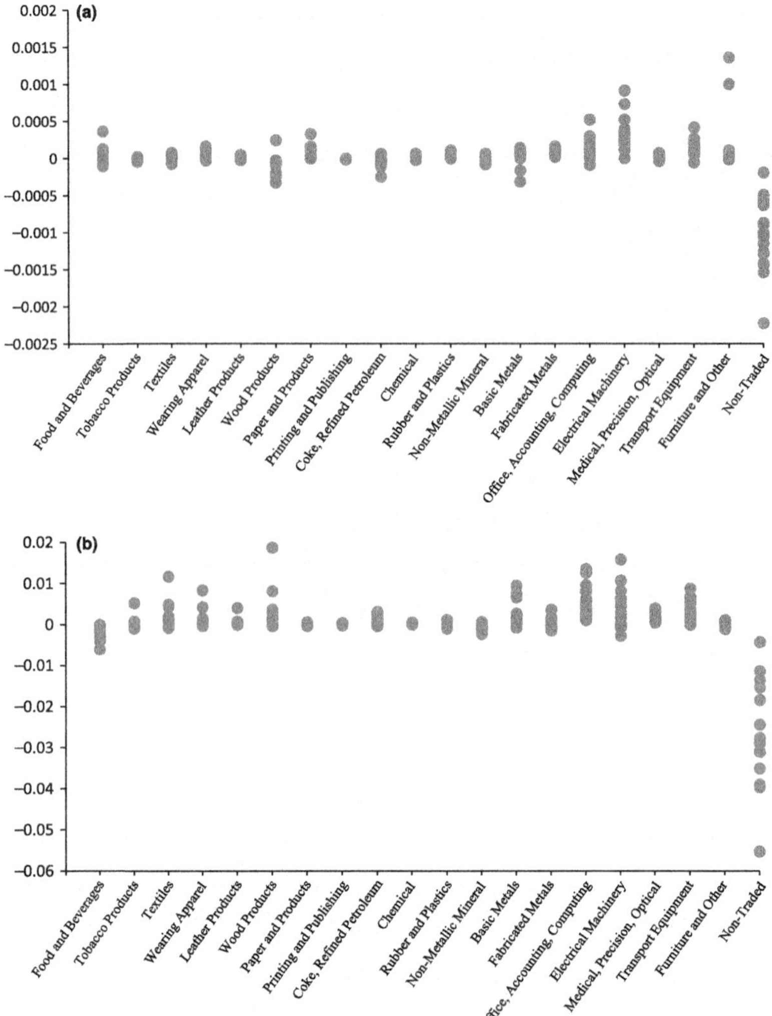

Figure 6. Changes in sectoral composition: shares of value added (a) Western Europe, (b) Eastern Europe

Notes: This figure displays the absolute changes in the shares of value-added when Eastern Europe opens to trade, for each sector and each West European country (top panel) and each East European country (bottom panel).

Source: Authors' calculations.

4.1. West European integration

The obvious comparison for East European integration is the earlier integration within Western Europe. Unlike the fall of the Iron Curtain that brought about an abrupt integration of Eastern Europe, West European integration has been a much more gradual and continuous process. Starting with the Treaty establishing the European Coal and Steel Community among the original six members that went into effect in 1952, integration both broadened by expanding the EU to 15 West European members, and deepened over time. The major treaties are the Treaty of Rome (went into effect 1958), Single European Act (1987), the Treaty on European Union (also known as the Maastricht Treaty, 1993), and up to the Treaty of Lisbon (signed 2007). In between these major milestones, there were more minor treaties as well. Thus, the basic difficulty in simulating the welfare impact of West European integration is that there is no single year, or even decade, during which integration occurred.

To take the broadest view of this process, we simulate a counterfactual scenario in which trade costs d_{ni}^{j} between West European trade partners are rolled back to their 1960s values. Our estimates for the 1960s show that trade costs within Western Europe are 45% higher in the 1960s compared to today, and this is the change in trade costs that we simulate. This exercise in effect attributes all of the fall in iceberg trade costs within Western Europe from the 1960s to the 2000s to policy measures relating to West European integration, and thus may over-estimate the total impact of policy measures. On the other hand, a great deal of policy barriers to cross-border trade in particular were dismantled prior to 1962 (the earliest year in our data) among the original six members. The fact that we start in the 1960s may thus under-estimate the total sweep of the EU's impact. A fall in trade costs of this magnitude appears to be in a reasonable ballpark for assessing the impact of deep economic integration on trade flows.

The first column of Table 6 presents the results. Precisely, we report the change in West European welfare due to a reduction in intra-West-European trade costs by 45%, the end point of this reduction being today's trade costs. This counterfactual assumes that Eastern Europe stays in autarky throughout, in order to mimic, albeit in a very rough way, historical developments. Western Europe was well on its way towards deep integration within the region when Eastern Europe was integrated. The mean welfare gains to Western Europe from observed within-region integration are 2.53%. These gains are on average 16 times larger than the gains from opening to Eastern Europe. This finding is not surprising, since West European trade partners are far more important for a typical West European country than East European partners.

To probe further, column 2 of Table 6 presents the West European countries' gains from trade relative to complete autarky.[7] The model implies that the mean gains from

[7] In this calculation, gains are computed with respect to the baseline scenario, that is, each West European country goes from trading with no one to trading with everyone including Eastern Europe.

Table 6. Welfare gains in Western Europe, alternative scenarios

	(1) West European integration (%)	(2) Gains from trade (%)	(3) Gains from EU Eastern Europe (%)	(4) Gains from non-EU Eastern Europe (%)	(5) Gains from growth in Eastern Europe (%)
Austria	2.728	4.430	0.329	0.070	0.055
Belgium–Luxembourg	4.551	7.597	0.097	0.034	0.025
Denmark	3.369	5.612	0.150	0.052	0.016
Finland	2.133	3.586	0.156	0.118	0.019
France	1.229	1.950	0.050	0.024	0.021
Germany	1.388	2.680	0.168	0.058	0.045
Greece	1.600	2.727	0.030	0.120	0.067
Iceland	3.766	8.453	0.163	0.047	0.002
Ireland	3.923	9.327	0.096	0.058	0.054
Italy	1.333	2.155	0.080	0.054	0.025
Netherlands	3.874	7.051	0.092	0.061	0.040
Norway	2.181	3.513	0.110	0.006	0.016
Portugal	2.963	3.810	0.018	0.009	0.015
Spain	1.450	2.085	0.040	0.023	0.021
Sweden	2.415	3.741	0.137	0.040	0.023
Switzerland	3.061	5.164	0.051	0.026	0.018
United Kingdom	1.114	3.257	0.044	0.032	0.013
Mean	2.534	4.538	0.107	0.049	0.028

Notes: This table reports the percentage welfare changes. Column 1 reports the welfare impact of reducing the iceberg trade costs between West European countries from their 1960s levels to their 2000s levels. Column 2 reports the welfare gains from trade relative to complete autarky. Column 3 reports the welfare gains from trading with EU East European countries. Column 4 reports the gains from trading with non-EU East European countries, conditional on already trading with EU East European countries. Column 5 reports the welfare impact of observed productivity growth and capital accumulation in Eastern Europe between the 1990s and 2000s.
Source: Authors' calculations.

trade in Western Europe are 4.54%. Strikingly, just a 45% reduction in trade costs with only fellow West European countries accounts for more than half of the total gains from trade for Western Europe. These results speak to the policy trade-off between the benefits of continued 'deep' integration within Western Europe, and the 'shallow' but broad integration with other regions, such as Eastern Europe and beyond. West European economies are relatively large, productive and close to each other. Thus, quantitatively the gains from reductions in trade barriers within that group of countries are an order of magnitude larger than even the gains from integration of large economic blocs such as Eastern Europe, China or India.[8] These results point to a potentially much greater benefit of deeper, rather than broader, integration.

[8] Elsewhere (di Giovanni *et al.*, 2012) we computed the worldwide gains from the trade integration of China. For West European countries, the mean gains from trade with China are 0.09%, with the maximum gain of 0.162%.

The gains from trade relative to autarky in Western Europe can also be compared to the gains for Eastern Europe in Table 3. East European gains from trade are two times larger than Western Europe's gains. Not surprisingly, since East European countries tend to be both smaller in size and less productive, they derive greater benefits from international exchange. From a policy perspective, this suggests that further trade integration in Eastern Europe, especially with its West European neighbours, is likely to have an even larger welfare impact than reductions in West European trade barriers. Thus, policies that improve the links between the two groups of countries, such as investment in infrastructure, are likely to have a larger pay-off in Eastern Europe compared to the West.

4.2. East European integration and productivity growth

Another facet of the trade-off between deeper and broader integration relates to the differing degrees of integration of East European countries with the West. Does Western Europe gain more from deeper integration with the Central European countries currently in the European Union, or from a more arm's-length trade relationship with non-EU countries? The answer is not clear *ex ante*: non-EU countries such as Russia, Ukraine and Kazakhstan are both larger in size, and more technologically different, than the EU-25 countries of Central Europe. Columns 3 and 4 of Table 6 report the gains from integration of EU-member East European countries, and the gains from integration of non-EU East European countries respectively. Of the total mean gains from East European integration, 0.156%, two-thirds (0.107%) are due to integration of the EU East European countries. The remaining one-third (0.049%) is due to non-EU Eastern Europe.[9] Once again, these results are suggestive that economic policies should aim at deeper integration of current EU member countries, rather than broader integration of countries farther afield.

The previous exercises compare our main results to the impact of other types of reductions in trade costs, whether within Western Europe, or for different sets of East European countries. Next, we benchmark the results against another drastic change that took place in the East European economy, namely economic growth. Has Western Europe benefited more from a fall in trade costs with Eastern Europe *per se*, or from the dramatic productivity growth (and the somewhat less dramatic capital accumulation) that took place in Eastern Europe since the fall of the Iron Curtain? To answer this question, we simulate the welfare benefit to Western Europe from the productivity growth and capital accumulation that actually occurred in the East

[9] The EU East European countries are Czech Republic, Estonia, Hungary, Latvia, Lithuania, Poland, Slovak Republic and Slovenia. All of these joined the EU in 2004, in the middle of our sample of years. Bulgaria and Romania joined in 2007, the last year of our sample, and thus we put them in the non-EU group. Adding them to the EU group will make the difference between the welfare impact of EU and non-EU integration even more pronounced.

European countries from the 1990s to the 2000s. Over this period, these economies grew dramatically, with productivity rising 33% over a decade (2.9% growth per annum).[10] Note that, as is well known in the trade literature, a trading partner's productivity growth need not improve a country's welfare (see, e.g., Hicks, 1953; Samuelson, 2004). In addition, quantitative assessments in other contexts have found that the overwhelming majority of welfare benefits from productivity growth accrue to the growing country itself rather than to other countries through trade (Hsieh and Ossa, 2011; di Giovanni *et al.*, 2012).

Column 5 of Table 6 reports the welfare gains to Western Europe from the observed growth in Eastern Europe from the 1990s to the 2000s. These gains are virtually nil: 0.028% (i.e. 0.00028), with a maximum of 0.067%. Thus, it appears that the modest welfare gains to Western Europe from trade integration with the East are still larger than the gains from productivity growth in those countries, even though that productivity growth has been dramatic. This finding suggests that policies favouring eastward technology transfer and foreign direct investment do not have a large aggregate welfare pay-off for the West, even relative to reductions in trade costs with East European countries. Of course, those policies will have a much greater positive welfare impact on the East European countries themselves.

4.3. Importance of factor reallocation

The preceding counterfactuals assumed that the factors of production reallocate optimally in response to each change in trade costs, and thus labour and capital markets clear within each country. A frequently expressed concern with greater integration – be it with Eastern Europe or other regions – is that reallocation of production factors within a country is difficult. Barriers to factor reallocation will both reduce the magnitude of the gains from trade, and create winners and losers even when aggregate gains are positive. To the extent that factor reallocation is required for reaping the benefits of trade, policies that impede that reallocation, such as rigid labour market institutions, may also reduce the gains from trade.

To assess the importance of factor reallocation quantitatively, we compute the welfare gains from East European integration under the assumption that capital and labour in each broad sector are fixed, and when Eastern Europe opens to trade factors cannot move from one sector to another in response. In this exercise, capital and labour can still reallocate between varieties within each sector. That is, we assume that while capital and workers in, say, the Wearing Apparel sector cannot move to the

[10] To be precise, we compare welfare in Western Europe under the 2000s baseline to a counterfactual scenario in which Eastern Europe's trade costs are the same as in the baseline, but East European productivities and capital–labour ratios are as they were in the 1990s. Thus, the counterfactual scenario is a world in which trade integration with Eastern Europe took place, but there was no growth in those countries from the 1990s to today.

Table 7. Welfare gains in Western and Eastern Europe, no factor reallocation

West	Δ Welfare (%)	East	Δ Welfare (%)
Austria	0.388	Bulgaria	10.566
Belgium–Luxembourg	0.119	Czech Republic	6.033
Denmark	0.170	Estonia	17.251
Finland	0.240	Hungary	7.860
France	0.074	Kazakhstan	6.777
Germany	0.213	Latvia	11.931
Greece	0.136	Lithuania	8.911
Iceland	0.180	Macedonia, FYR	8.733
Ireland	0.157	Poland	3.891
Italy	0.126	Romania	6.848
Netherlands	0.120	Russian Federation	2.349
Norway	0.100	Slovak Republic	8.053
Portugal	0.024	Slovenia	6.702
Spain	0.058	Ukraine	5.263
Sweden	0.170		
Switzerland	0.079		
United Kingdom	0.066		
Mean	0.142	Mean	7.941

Notes: This table reports the percentage changes in welfare due to the trade integration of Eastern Europe, under the assumption that factors of production cannot reallocate across sectors. It starts with the counterfactual scenario in which each and every East European country is in autarky, and lowers the trade costs to their levels as of the 2000s, but assuming that factors cannot reallocate across sectors from their counterfactual values.
Source: Authors' calculations.

Precision and Medical Machinery sector, they are free to switch between infinitesimal varieties within the Apparel sector, for instance switch from making shirts to making pants. Table 7 reports the welfare changes in that experiment. As expected, the welfare gains from East European integration are smaller for every country if factors are not mobile across sectors. For Western Europe, the difference is not large in absolute terms: the mean gains are 0.142% instead of 0.156% in the main analysis. For Eastern Europe, however, the welfare gains without sectoral reallocation are significantly smaller in both absolute and relative terms. The mean gain from trade drops to 7.94%, which is 14% less than the 9.23% welfare gain when factors are mobile. The pronounced difference between the two groups of countries in the impact of factor reallocation on welfare gains is not surprising in light of the results in Section 3.5. As Figure 6 makes clear, East European integration induced only small changes in sectoral structure in Western Europe, whereas in Eastern Europe sectoral composition changed much more dramatically.

A distinct but related question is how large are the distributional consequences of trade opening. Understanding the magnitudes of the distributional effects is important in designing the social safety net programmes to cushion the negative consequences of trade opening for import-competing sectors. To address this question exhaustively, one would require a model with explicit frictions in the mobility of factors across sectors. The exercise here represents an extreme case in which factors are

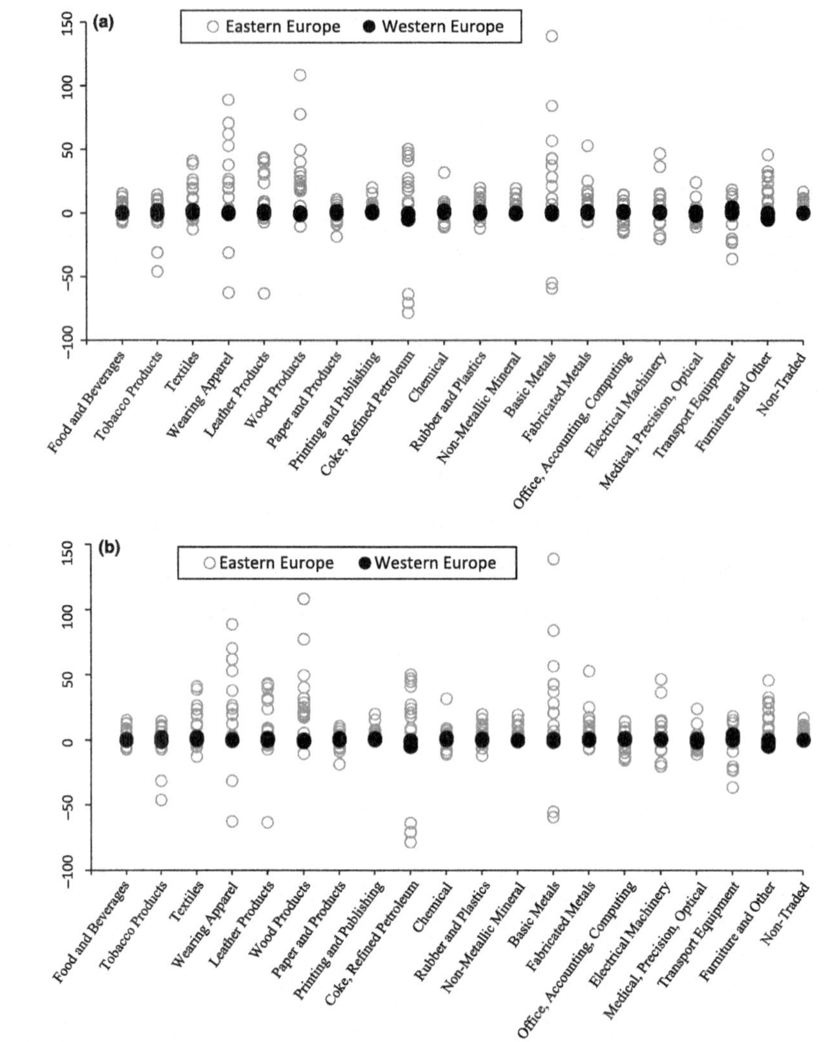

Figure 7. Changes in (a) real wages and (b) real returns to capital, no factor reallocation

Notes: This figure displays the scatterplots of the changes in real wages (top panel) and real returns to capital (bottom panel) in each sector and each country when Eastern Europe opens to trade but factors cannot reallocate across sectors.

Source: Authors' calculations.

not allowed to move at all between sectors. In addition, we do not take an explicit stand on who owns the capital in each sector, and thus we can only compute changes in wages and returns to capital in each sector, rather than in individuals' overall incomes. Nonetheless, analysing the factor price changes can give us a rough sense of the distributional impact of trade opening when factors are immobile across sectors.

Figure 7 presents, for each sector, the distribution of percentage changes in sector-specific real wage (top panel) and real return to capital (bottom panel) when Eastern Europe opens to trade. The solid dots represent Western Europe, and hollow dots Eastern Europe. Two conclusions emerge. First, the variation in real factor returns across sectors dwarfs the magnitude of the aggregate impact. For Western Europe, as we saw above the mean welfare change is 0.142%. By contrast, the changes in real wage and the real return to capital range across sectors from about −1% to 1% in every country, and as much as from −5% to 5% in smaller countries such as Iceland and Ireland. Second, the cross-sectoral dispersion in wage and return to capital changes is far larger in Eastern Europe. It is not uncommon to observe 50% reductions, or 100% increases in the real returns to factors in individual industries.

These results further inform policy priorities. First, in order to both reap the full gains from trade, and to limit the distributional consequences, trade liberalization should be accompanied by efforts to promote smooth functioning of labour and capital markets, especially in trade liberalization episodes that are expected to produce large cross-sectoral reallocations. This may mean policies that allow for flexible hiring and firing of workers. Since human capital is often sector-specific and difficult to redeploy elsewhere at least in the short run, investment in education and programmes that facilitate acquisition of new and more advanced skills are especially important.

At the same time, the finding that the distributional impacts of trade liberalization can be an order of magnitude higher than the aggregate gains points to the primary importance of social safety net programmes. In Western Europe, the absolute welfare changes even in the most import-competing sectors are small, rarely more than 1%. Thus, East European integration is unlikely to have led to a large amount of dislocation in the West. By contrast, East European workers and capital owners in particular sectors can experience very large swings (from halving to doubling of real wages or capital returns). Thus, social safety nets are especially needed in those countries as they open to trade.

Finally, we stress an important complementarity between policies that promote smooth and efficient factor markets and the social safety net programmes. The distributional impacts of trade liberalization will be limited when factors can reallocate easily across sectors. This in turn will place less strain on the redistributive social safety net policies. This suggests that there may be important interactions between rigid labour market policies, social safety nets (and therefore government budgets), and globalization. To the extent that globalization increases the need for reallocation of resources, rigid factor markets will both reduce the gains from trade, and place additional strain on the social safety net programmes.

5. CONCLUSION

Ever since the original formulation of the Ricardian model in the nineteenth century, it has been understood that the magnitude of the relative differences in technology – 'the strength of comparative advantage' – matters for the size of the gains from trade. Broadly speaking, stronger comparative advantage leads to larger gains from trade. However, the importance of this effect has not been assessed quantitatively.

This paper uses the trade integration of Eastern Europe after the fall of the Iron Curtain as a laboratory for evaluating the role of comparative advantage in the gains from trade. We estimate sector-level productivities for 19 sectors in 79 countries, and document that differences in relative technology do indeed vary a great deal among the Western and East European country pairs. Using a multi-sector, multi-factor quantitative model of trade and these sectoral productivity estimates, we evaluate the gains from European integration for each country.

The variation in gains to West European countries is mainly accounted for by trade costs, with technological similarity playing little or no role. By contrast, the dispersion in gains to Eastern Europe is well explained by technological similarity to Western Europe. This difference is due to the asymmetry in the relative importance of the two country groups as trade partners. The large majority of East European trade is with Western Europe. For Western Europe, however, Eastern Europe is still a minor trade partner. Furthermore, a comparison of sectoral productivities reveals that as a group, Eastern Europe has a similar comparative advantage as the rest of Western Europe's trade partners. Thus, the gains to Western Europe come mainly from expansion of markets, rather than from technological differences with Eastern Europe.

Placing the East European trade opening episode within a broader context of West European integration allows us to draw out a number of policy implications. Deeper within-Europe integration appears to confer greater welfare benefits than shallower but broader trade integration. Technology transfer from Western to Eastern Europe will benefit East European countries, but have virtually no positive welfare impact on the West. Eastern Europe has likely experienced large distributional effects due to trade opening. Thus, it is imperative that trade integration is accompanied by policies that promote optimal reallocation of factors of production, and ensure a minimum safety net for those displaced by import competition.

We conclude by reiterating that the results presented in the paper, with limited exceptions, reveal the static gains from goods trade. When evaluating the impact of reductions in trade costs, we keep factor endowments and technology constant. Thus, if trade opening in turn caused capital and labour to move across borders, or if it caused technology of the trading countries to change, there will be additional – positive or negative – effects of reductions in trade costs that are not captured by our analysis. Comprehensive quantitative evaluations of the indirect benefits of trade liberalization remains a fruitful avenue for future research.

Discussion

Chiara Fumagalli

Università Bocconi

This paper performs a rigorous and thoughtful quantitative assessment of the welfare gains produced by trade integration, and improves our understanding of the role played by comparative advantage. There is a lot that we can learn from this paper as the topic is extremely relevant and the analysis is both accurate and sound. Of course, in order to make the quantitative exercise tractable, some factors have been omitted from the analysis. These limitations have been mentioned throughout the paper and do not undermine the validity of the analysis. However, in order to give an appropriate interpretation to the results of the paper, I believe it is important to keep these limitations into proper consideration. My discussion will elaborate on them.

First, sectoral productivities are kept constant when comparing the actual scenario to the counterfactual scenario where Eastern Europe is in autarky. However, trade integration is likely to make competition in the market more intense and, through this channel, to foster incentives to innovate, thereby changing sectoral productivities and shaping the pattern of comparative advantage. The welfare gains associated with trade integration are likely to be larger when one accounts for this effect. For instance, Italy – given the present structure of comparative advantage – is likely to suffer substantially from trade integration with China. However, Italian firms facing tougher competition from Chinese products might be forced to invest in order to produce superior quality/innovation intensive products, thereby making Italian industrial structure more differentiated from the Chinese one and eventually benefiting from trade integration.

This consideration highlights that trade integration needs to go hand in hand with policy intervention aimed at facilitating innovation. Policy intervention may consist of specific policies, such as subsidies to innovation investment or patent policy reforms; it may also consist of broader policies such as financial markets/corporate governance reforms that alleviate financial constraints innovative firms are particularly vulnerable to, or reforms of the education system that increases the supply of high-skilled workers. This consideration also highlights the second limitation of the analysis, that is, the fact that the quality of institutions is kept constant across the actual and counterfactual scenario. More intense competition associated with trade integration may instead prompt governments to undertake reforms that improve the quality of institutions, thereby shaping the pattern of comparative advantage also through this channel.

Third, the model does not incorporate worker heterogeneity and does not allow for factors to move across countries. As a consequence it is not the appropriate model to account for distributional issues. (Still, distributional issues are partially addressed by considering the case where factors cannot reallocate across sectors.) Distributional effects associated with trade integration may be sizeable. After integration with Eastern Europe many West European firms, especially the ones active in labour-intensive sectors, have relocated their activity to Eastern Europe, attracted by cheap labour. At the same time, West European countries have experienced flows of workers from Eastern Europe, attracted by high wages. Both phenomena have represented a serious threat for low-skilled workers in Western Europe, and have generated opposition against trade liberalization. This makes even more compelling the implementation of active labour market policies, such as policies that assist workers in acquiring more advanced skills, of investment programmes in education and, more generally, of social safety net programmes.

My last comment concerns the conclusions drawn from the comparison between a counterfactual scenario where trade costs between West European countries are increased by 45% (rolled back to 1960s values) and a baseline scenario where trade costs are the present ones. Both in the counterfactual and in the base-line scenario Eastern Europe remains in autarky. The (mean) welfare gain for Western European countries is 2.53% (16 times larger than gains from trade opening of Eastern Europe). The authors conclude: 'These results speak to the policy trade-off between the benefits of *continued* "deep" integration within Western Europe and the "shallow" but broad integration with other regions such as Eastern Europe and beyond.' I am not sure that such a conclusion can be inferred from the analysis of the paper. The analysis shows that decreasing trade costs from their value in the 1960s to their present value has benefitted Western Europe. We cannot conclude that decreasing trade costs by the same amount from the present value generates the same welfare gains, unless one assumes linearity in the relationship between trade costs and welfare. On top of this, integration with emerging blocs is to some extent inevitable and the priority of Western Europe should be perhaps to find the proper tools to benefit as much as possible from it.

Panel discussion

Thorsten Beck asked if the authors had to assume that the countries were in steady state in the year 2000 and whether this was a reasonable assumption for some of the transition economies. Second, he enquired if it would be possible to relate differences in welfare gains from trade liberalization in CEE economies to the size of initial distortions (inherited from socialist times). Andrea Ichino wondered if estimates of the losses suffered by non-European countries from the shift in trade by Western Europe could be provided. Next, he asked what the assumption on the movement of labour is in the paper. Lastly, he wanted to know if the authors' calculations also include the indirect gains from trade (demand size effects). Peter Egger noted that the model employed for estimation may not be the most appropriate for disaggregated data (sectoral level) as the number of bilateral trade zeros may matter significantly in this case. He was also surprised by the size of the estimated welfare gains given the bigger gains reported in some of the previous studies, such as that of Anderson and van Wincoop (2001). Egger noted that if one were to examine the preferential integration of markets, for instance, much larger welfare gains would be observed. Given the relatively small welfare gains, Refet Gürkaynak felt that either countries were already managing to achieve optimal allocations or that the general approach to welfare analysis is fundamentally flawed. Giancarlo Corsetti asked if the aggregate effects of integration are an order of magnitude lower than the distributional effects. Second, referring to Sturm's analysis of the paper, he doubted the increasing role of distance. On the computation of technological similarities, Thierry Tressel raised the point that some sectors across countries may be involved in the same production chain and therefore higher correlations in sectoral productivities may just reflect higher correlations in trade between countries. He wondered how the authors accounted for this in their study.

Andrei Levchenko first stressed that the paper is measuring the gains from trade rather than integration. However, he acknowledged that what is completely missing from the paper is some notion that the opening of trade itself produced productivity improvements, additional investment and movements of orders. He noted that in a reduced form manner they are also measuring any movements in labour and capital and technology transfers to the extent that the data are capturing these flows. Nonetheless, Levchenko added that they do not have a good way of linking these flows directly to trade *per se*. He further explained that to the extent that trade stimulated FDI to Eastern Europe and productivity advances in the region, they can confidently say that the impact of this on Western Europe was almost zero (upper bound in fact) in the context of the model. Conversely, the effect in Eastern Europe was large but more precise estimates would require specifying the connection between trade and the different flows. Levchenko stated that the gains from trade in their paper are much larger than the gains from financial integration and that ultimately what constitutes a large or small gain is in the eye of the beholder. Moreover, he pointed out that the size of the welfare gains can vary greatly depending on which element of the model is tweaked (different policy experiments).

APPENDIX

Table A1. Country coverage

Western–Europe		Eastern Europe	
Austria	Italy	Bulgaria	Macedonia, FYR
Belgium-Luxembourg	Netherlands	Czech Republic	Poland
Denmark	Norway	Estonia	Romania
Finland	Portugal	Hungary	Russian Federation
France	Spain	Kazakhstan	Slovak Republic
Germany	Sweden	Latvia	Slovenia
Greece	Switzerland	Lithuania	Ukraine
Iceland	United Kingdom		
Ireland			
Rest of world			
Argentina	El Salvador	Kenya	Senegal
Australia	Ethiopia	Korea, Rep.	South Africa
Bangladesh	Fiji	Kuwait	Sri Lanka
Bolivia	Ghana	Malaysia	Taiwan Province of China
Brazil	Guatemala	Mauritius	Tanzania
Canada	Honduras	Mexico	Thailand
Chile	India	New Zealand	Trinidad and Tobago
China	Indonesia	Nigeria	Turkey
Colombia	Iran, Islamic Rep.	Pakistan	United States
Costa Rica	Israel	Peru	Uruguay
Ecuador	Japan	Philippines	Venezuela, RB
Egypt, Arab Rep.	Jordan	Saudi Arabia	Vietnam

Table A2. Sectors

ISIC code	Sector name	α_j	β_j	$\gamma_{J+1,j}$	ω_j
15	Food and Beverages	0.290	0.290	0.303	0.166
16	Tobacco Products	0.272	0.490	0.527	0.014
17	Textiles	0.444	0.368	0.295	0.019
18	Wearing Apparel, Fur	0.468	0.369	0.320	0.105
19	Leather, Leather Products, Footwear	0.469	0.350	0.330	0.014
20	Wood Products (Excl. Furniture)	0.455	0.368	0.288	0.008
21	Paper and Paper Products	0.351	0.341	0.407	0.012
22	Printing and Publishing	0.484	0.453	0.407	0.004
23	Coke, Refined Petroleum Products, Nuclear Fuel	0.248	0.246	0.246	0.175
24	Chemical and Chemical Products	0.297	0.368	0.479	0.009
25	Rubber and Plastics Products	0.366	0.375	0.350	0.013
26	Non-Metallic Mineral Products	0.350	0.448	0.499	0.070
27	Basic Metals	0.345	0.298	0.451	0.002
28	Fabricated Metal Products	0.424	0.387	0.364	0.012
29C	Office, Accounting, Computing, and Other Machinery	0.481	0.381	0.388	0.062
31A	Electrical Machinery, Communication Equipment	0.369	0.368	0.416	0.028
33	Medical, Precision, and Optical Instruments	0.451	0.428	0.441	0.041
34A	Transport Equipment	0.437	0.329	0.286	0.179
36	Furniture and Other Manufacturing	0.447	0.396	0.397	0.066
4A	Non-tradables	0.561	0.651	0.788	
	Mean	0.414	0.393	0.399	0.053

Table A2. (Continued)

ISIC code	Sector name	α_j	β_j	$\gamma_{J+1,j}$	ω_j
	Min	0.244	0.243	0.246	0.002
	Max	0.561	0.651	0.788	0.209

Notes: This table reports the sectors used in the analysis. The classification corresponds to the ISIC Revision3 2-digit, aggregated further due to data availability. α_j is the value-added based labour intensity; β_j is the share of value added in total output; $\gamma_{J+1,j}$ is the share of non-tradable inputs in total intermediate inputs; ω_j is the taste parameter for tradable sector j, estimated using the procedure described in Web Appendix Section B.3. Variable definitions and sources are described in detail in the text.
Source: Authors' calculations.

REFERENCES

Alvarez, F. and R.E. Lucas (2007). 'General equilibrium analysis of the Eaton–Kortum model of international trade', *Journal of Monetary Economics*, 54(6), 1726–68.

Anderson, James E. and Eric van Wincoop (2001). 'Borders, trade, and welfare', in Susan M. Collins and Dani Rodrik (eds.), *Brookings Trade Forum*, *Brookings*, Institution Press, Washington, DC.

Arkolakis, C., A. Costinot and A. Rodríguez-Clare (2012). 'New trade models, same old gains?, *American Economic Review*, 102(1), 94–130.

Baldwin, R.E. and A. Venables (1995). 'Regional economic integration', in G. Grossman and K. Rogoff (eds.), *Handbook of International Economics*, Vol. III, Elsevier Science, Amsterdam, pp. 1597–644.

Baldwin, R.E., J. Francois and R. Portes (1997). 'The costs and benefits of Eastern enlargement: the impact on the EU and Central Europe', *Economic Policy*, 12(24), 125–76.

Baourakis, G., C. Lakatos and A. Xepapadeas (2008). 'Economic implications of the EU accession of Bulgaria and Romania: a CGE approach', TradeAg – Agricultural Trade Agreements Working Paper Series 08/1.

Brown, D., A. Deardorff, S. Djankov and R.M. Stern (1997). 'An economic assessment of the integration of Czechoslovakia, Hungary, and Poland into the European Union', in Stanley W. Black (eds.), *Europe's Economy Looks East: Implications for Germany and the European Union*, Cambridge University Press, New York.

Caliendo, L. and F. Parro (2010). 'Estimates of the trade and welfare effects of NAFTA', mimeo, University of Chicago.

Chor, D. (2010). 'Unpacking sources of comparative advantage: a quantitative approach', *Journal of International Economics*, 82(2), 152–67.

Corcos, G., M. Del Gatto, G. Mion and G. Ottaviano (2012). 'Productivity and firm selection: quantifying the "new" gains from trade', *Economic Journal*, 122(561), 754–98.

Costinot, A., D. Donaldson and I. Komunjer (2012). 'What goods do countries trade? A quantitative exploration of Ricardo's ideas', *Review of Economic Studies*, 79(2), 581–608.

di Giovanni, J., A. Levchenko and J. Zhang (2012). 'The global welfare impact of China: trade integration and technological change', RSIE Discussion Paper 625.

Eaton, J. and S. Kortum (2002). 'Technology, geography, and trade', *Econometrica*, 70(5), 1741–79.

Hertel, T., M. Brockmeier and P. Swaminathan (1997). 'Sectoral and economy-wide analysis of integrating Central and Eastern European countries into the EU: implications of alternative strategies', *European Review of Agricultural Economics*, 24(3-4), 359–86.

Hicks, J. (1953). 'An inaugural lecture', *Oxford Economic Papers*, 5(2), 117–35.

Hsieh, C. and R. Ossa (2011). 'A global view of productivity growth in China', NBER Working Paper No. 16778.

Levchenko, A. and J. Zhang (2011). 'The evolution of comparative advantage: measurement and welfare implications', NBER Working Paper No. 16806.

Ottaviano, G., D. Taglioni and F. di Mauro (2009). 'The euro and the competitiveness of European firms', *Economic Policy*, 24, 5–53.

Samuelson, P. (2004). 'Where Ricardo and Mill rebut and confirm arguments of mainstream economists supporting globalization', *Journal of Economic Perspectives*, 18(3), 135–46.

Shikher, S. (2011). 'Capital, technology, and specialization in the neoclassical model', *Journal of International Economics*, 83(2), 229–42.

Smith, A. and A. Venables (1988). 'Completing the internal market in the European Community: some industry simulations', *European Economic Review*, 32(7), 1501–25.

IMF Economic Review
Vol. 61, No. 3

The Global Labor Market Impact of Emerging Giants: A Quantitative Assessment

ANDREI A. LEVCHENKO AND JING ZHANG*

This paper investigates both aggregate and distributional impacts of the trade integration of China, India, and Central and Eastern Europe in a quantitative multicountry multisector model, comparing outcomes with and without factor market frictions. Under perfect within-country factor mobility, the gains to the rest of the world from trade integration of emerging giants are 0.37 percent, ranging from −0.37 percent for Honduras to 2.28 percent for Sri Lanka. Reallocation of factors across sectors contributes relatively little to the aggregate gains, but has large distributional effects. The aggregate gains to the rest of the world are only 0.065 percentage points lower when neither capital nor labor can move across sectors within a country. On the other hand, the distributional effects of the emerging giants' trade integration are an order of magnitude larger, with changes in real factor returns ranging from −5 percent to 5 percent across sectors in most countries. The workers and capital owners in emerging giants' comparative advantage sectors such as Textiles and Wearing Apparel experience greatest losses, whereas factor owners in Printing and Medical, Precision and Optical Instruments normally gain the most. [JEL F11; F15; F16]
IMF Economic Review (2013) **61,** 479–519. doi:10.1057/imfer.2013.16

*Andrei A. Levchenko is an associate professor of Economics at the University of Michigan. Jing Zhang is a Senior Economist at the Federal Reserve Bank of Chicago. The authors are grateful to the editors (Pierre-Olivier Gourinchas, Ayhan Kose, and Prakash Loungani), Rafael Dix-Carneiro, two anonymous referees, and conference participants at the IMF Jacques Polak Annual Research Conference, CEPR ESSIM, and Barcelona GSE Summer Forum for helpful suggestions.

Andrei A. Levchenko and Jing Zhang

The biggest event in world trade in the last 20 years is the rapid integration of emerging giants: China, India, and Central and Eastern European countries (CEECs). Their export growth since 1990 has been nothing short of spectacular: 12-fold in China, 8-fold in CEECs, and 6-fold in India. Together, these countries now account for 20 percent of world trade, up from 6 percent in 1990 (Figure 1). The rise of emerging giants raises two important questions. First, what is the aggregate welfare impact of emerging giants' trade integration on economies around the world, and what are the distributional impacts across sectors within a country? And second, how do factor market frictions affect these outcomes?

Although the increased global trade integration should benefit the world as a whole, the gains to individual countries and sectors are likely to vary. When it comes to the aggregate gains, some countries—those with comparative advantages similar to the emerging giants—may lose from the giants' integration

Figure 1. Emerging Giants' Trade, 1962–2007: (a) Exports, Index Number 1990 = 100; (b) Share of Emerging Giants in Global Imports

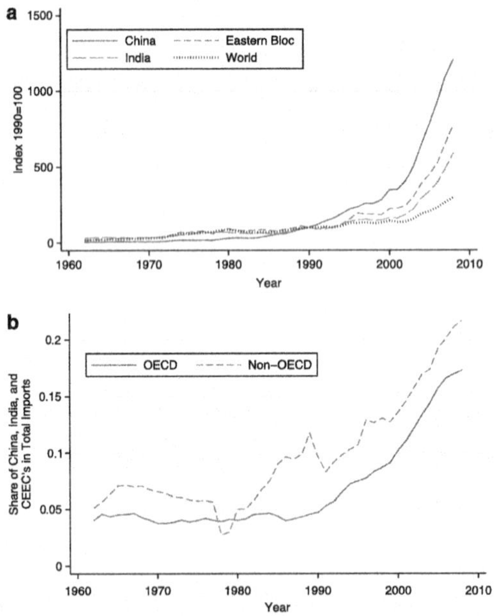

Notes: Figure 1(a) plots the total real (inflation-adjusted) exports from China, India, the CEECs, and the world for the period 1962–2007. All series are normalized such that the 1990 value equals 100. Figure 1 (b) plots the share of imports coming from these countries in the total imports of the OECD and the non-OECD countries, 1962–2007.

into global trade. For instance, there is some evidence that the growing importance of China has reduced export demand for a number of emerging market countries (Hanson and Robertson, 2010), and it has been conjectured that the rise of China has been partly responsible for slower than expected economic growth in Mexico (Hanson, 2010).

At the same time, trade integration of emerging giants will create both winners and losers within a country even if the aggregate gains are positive. There is a great deal of evidence that factor market reallocations in response to trade liberalization are far from frictionless (Artuç, 2009; Artuç, Chaudhuri, and McLaren, 2010; Dix-Carneiro, 2011). OECD (2005) provides evidence that developed country workers displaced by import competition experienced longer unemployment spells and larger income losses compared with workers losing jobs for other reasons. Autor, Dorn, and Hanson (2012a) and Autor and others (2012b) find a large differential impact of Chinese imports to the United States across local labor markets and individual workers. Relatedly, International Monetary Fund (2005) shows that the rise of emerging market exports contributed to the fall in the labor share of GDP in the OECD countries.

Not surprisingly, these developments led to a great deal of discussion about the optimal policies to address trade-induced labor market adjustments (OECD, 2005 and 2012), as well as concrete policy responses. In the United States, the Trade Adjustment Assistance program was expanded significantly in 2009 (GAO, 2012). At the same time, there were legislative proposals to raise tariffs on Chinese imports in retaliation for China's alleged currency manipulation (*New York Times*, 2011).

This paper develops the first comprehensive global-scale quantitative welfare assessment of both aggregate and distributional effects of the emerging giants' trade integration. A model-based assessment is crucial for the following reasons. First and foremost, evaluating the impact of emerging giants on other countries requires finding the counterfactual equilibrium that would obtain in the absence of trade with the emerging giants. If a country cannot trade with the emerging giants, its trade with all of its other trading partners will change, which would in turn change the trade of its trading partners with other partners, and so on. The impact of emerging giants on each country depends on the magnitude and nature of that adjustment. A fully specified model allows us to calculate the counterfactual production allocations and trade flows, and the resulting counterfactual welfare. A regression estimation-based exercise cannot adequately capture the notion of a general equilibrium counterfactual and the associated complex changes in production and trade flows. Second, a fully specified model enables us to make statements about welfare. Computing welfare changes requires accounting for changes not just in (relative) factor prices, but goods prices as well, as gains from trade will be reaped partly through reductions in the latter. Although our approach takes those into account, doing so is generally inaccessible to empirical work, in which relative factor prices or relative incomes are normally the objects of analysis. And third, we adopt an explicitly global perspective and analyze the impact of emerging giants on a wide variety of countries. In contrast to one-country studies such as Autor, Dorn, and Hanson (2012a), this allows us to detect and quantify some general patterns in the worldwide results.

Our analysis extends the large-scale quantitative model of the world economy recently developed by Levchenko and Zhang (2011 and 2012). We build a multisector Ricardian-Heckscher-Ohlin model that incorporates a number of realistic features, such as multiple factors of production, an explicit nontraded sector, the full specification of input-output linkages between the sectors, and both inter- and intraindustry trade. The model is estimated using data on production and trade to yield sector-level productivities for 19 manufacturing sectors and a sample of 75 countries that includes China, India, all major CEECs, as well as virtually all of the other important economies in the world. Having estimated and solved for the long-run equilibrium of the model, we simulate the trade opening of the emerging giants under two extreme sets of assumptions: perfect within-country factor mobility and no factor mobility across sectors. This exercise allows us to isolate the impact of factor market frictions. In addition, we focus separately on frictions in the labor and capital markets, to identify which ones are more important for reaping the full gains from trade.

The main results can be summarized as follows. First, the gains to the rest of the world from integration of emerging giants under perfect factor mobility are 0.37 percent, ranging from –0.37 percent for Honduras to 2.28 percent for Sri Lanka. Second, reallocation of factors across sectors contributes relatively little to these gains: the welfare gains to the rest of the world are only about 0.065 percentage points lower in the fixed-factors version of the model in which neither capital nor labor can move across sectors within a country. Thus the aggregate gains from trade with emerging giants come largely from intraindustry trade.

Third, there are strong complementarities between reallocation of labor and capital across sectors. Versions of the model with immobile labor but mobile capital, or with immobile capital but mobile labor produce welfare changes that are quite close to the outcome when both factors are immobile. This suggests that to reap the full benefits of sectoral reallocation due to globalization, it is essential that both labor and capital markets function smoothly. Just one inflexible factor market, be it rigid labor markets (as in continental Europe), or poor capital markets (as in much of the developing world) will, quantitatively, negate the benefits of reallocation in the other factor markets.

Fourth, with imperfect factor mobility the distributional consequences of the emerging giants' integration are an order of magnitude greater than the aggregate consequences. Although the aggregate gains to the rest of the world tend to amount to a fraction of a percent, in a typical country changes in real wages and returns to capital range from –5 percent to 5 percent across sectors. As a group, emerging giants' comparative advantage is in light manufacturing industries such as Textiles and Wearing Apparel, and their comparative disadvantage is in high-tech manufacturing industries such as Printing and Medical, Precision and Optical Instruments. Not surprisingly, in the rest of the world the workers and capital owners in light manufacturing experience greatest losses, whereas factor owners in high-tech sectors normally gain the most. Controlling for country and sector fixed effects, sectors with higher productivity tend to benefit the most/lose the least from trade opening.

Methodologically, our work builds on recent quantitative welfare assessments of trade integration in multisector Ricardian models (Caliendo and Parro, 2010; Shikher, 2011; Costinot, Donaldson, and Komunjer, 2012). A number of studies analyze the long-run aggregate impact of some of the emerging giant countries on welfare around the world (Coleman, 2007; Hsieh and Ossa, 2011; Levchenko and Zhang, 2012; di Giovanni, Levchenko, and Zhang, 2013). This paper is the first to quantitatively explore the consequences of factor market frictions in this type of framework. In addition, because the trade integration of these emerging giant countries has been concurrent, we consider their joint global welfare impact.

Our work is also related to the Computable General Equilibrium (CGE) assessments of trade integration of the major emerging markets: see, for example, Francois and Wignaraja (2008) and Ghosh and Rao (2010) for China, and Baldwin, Francois, and Portes (1997), Brown and others (1997); Hertel, Brockmeier, and Swaminathan (1997), and Baourakis, Lakatos, and Xepapadeas (2008) for Eastern Europe. Unlike the traditional CGE approach, our quantitative framework is based on Eaton and Kortum's (2002) Ricardian model of trade with endogenous specialization both within and across sectors, which enables us to relate our findings to comparative advantage. Our global general equilibrium approach complements recent microlevel studies of the impact of trade with emerging markets in developed countries, such as Autor, Dorn, and Hanson (2012a), Bloom, Draca, and Van Reenen (2011), and Hummels and others (2011).

Before moving on to the description of the model and the results, we outline some limitations of our analysis. Our model features fixed labor supply, and thus cannot be used to explore the role of emerging giants in the phenomenon of workers permanently leaving the labor force and the resulting reduction in aggregate employment. We conjecture that allowing for the possibility of workers leaving the labor force would reduce the labor supply in the import-competing industries, which would mitigate the adverse wage impact on the active workers. On the other hand, the welfare impact on those leaving the labor force would then depend on their utility from not working. Similarly for capital, our analysis ignores the endogenous response of either domestic capital accumulation or cross-border capital flows to the opening of emerging giants. We do not have a working model of cross-border capital mobility that can be adapted to a large-scale cross-sectional quantitative model like ours, and developing such a model is beyond the scope of the paper. Our current framework also cannot be used to evaluate the role emerging giants may have played in the permanent de-industrialization process observed in a number of advanced economies. To capture this effect, the model would need to be augmented to incorporate tradable services. Unfortunately, the data required for estimating the model with tradable services are not currently available.

Finally, any exploration of the distributional effects of trade liberalization will depend on the level of sectoral disaggregation used in the analysis. In the immobile-factor equilibrium, our exercise by construction assumes that factors are specific to the sector at the level of disaggregation we employ (19 tradable sectors and 1 nontradable).[1] Outcomes would differ if in reality factors were specific to much more narrowly defined activities. For instance, one of the sectors in our analysis is textiles, and thus our assumption is that a textile worker's skills are deployable in all types of textiles. However, if the skills of workers in cotton textiles were very different from the skills of workers in wool textiles, and cotton and wool sectors experienced very different trade shocks, then our analysis would likely understate the distributional impact of the trade shocks.

The rest of the paper is organized as follows. Section I lays out the quantitative framework and discusses the details of calibration and estimation. Section II discusses the main results, and Section III concludes.

I. Quantitative Framework

The Environment

The world is comprised of N countries, indexed by n and i. There are J tradable sectors, plus one nontradable sector J+1. Utility over these sectors in country n is given by:

$$U_n = \left(\sum_{j=1}^{J} \omega_j^{\frac{1}{\eta}} \left(Y_n^j\right)^{\frac{\eta-1}{\eta}} \right)^{\frac{\eta}{\eta-1}\xi_n} \left(Y_n^{J+1}\right)^{1-\xi_n}, \tag{1}$$

where ξ_n denotes the Cobb-Douglas weight for the tradable sector composite good, η is the elasticity of substitution between the tradable sectors, ω_j is the taste parameter for tradable sector j, Y_n^{J+1} is the nontradable-sector composite good, and Y_n^j is the composite good in tradable sector j.

Each sector j aggregates a continuum of varieties $q \in [0,1]$ unique to each sector using a CES production function:

$$Q_n^j = \left[\int_0^1 Q_n^j(q)^{\frac{\varepsilon-1}{\varepsilon}} dq \right]^{\frac{\varepsilon}{\varepsilon-1}},$$

where ε denotes the elasticity of substitution across varieties q, Q_n^j is the total output of sector j in country n, and $Q_n^j(q)$ is the amount of variety q that is used in production in sector j and country n. Producing one unit of good q in sector j in country n requires $1/(z_n^j(q))$ input bundles.

[1]Our choice of the level of disaggregation is dictated by two considerations. The first is data availability: we require domestic output data, which are not available at much finer levels of disaggregation for as large a sample of countries as we would like. The second is conceptual: to make our framework tractable, we impose an Eaton and Kortum (2002) structure within each sector. That is, within each sector there is a continuum of varieties that can be produced in all countries but with different productivities. This ensures interior trade shares in each country and sector, and makes a large-scale quantitative analysis possible. Making sectors much more disaggregated will strain the assumption that there is still a continuum of varieties in each sector and all trade shares are interior.

THE GLOBAL LABOR MARKET IMPACT OF EMERGING GIANTS

Production uses labor (L), capital (K), and intermediate inputs from other sectors. The cost of an input bundle is:

$$c_n^j = \left((w_n^j)^{\alpha_j}(r_n^j)^{1-\alpha_j}\right)^{\beta_j}\left(\prod_{k=1}^{J+1}(p_n^k)^{\gamma_{k,j}}\right)^{1-\beta_j},$$

where w_n^j is the wage of workers in sector j, r_n^j is the return to capital installed in sector j, and p_n^k is the price of intermediate input from sector k. The value-added-based labor intensity is given by α_j, and the share of value added in total output by β_j. Both vary by sector. The shares of inputs from other sectors, $\gamma_{k,j}$ vary by output industry j as well as input industry k.

Following Eaton and Kortum (2002, henceforth EK), productivity $z_n^j(q)$ for each $q \in [0,1]$ in each sector j is random, and drawn from the Fréchet distribution with cdf:

$$F_n^j(z) = e^{-T_n^j z^{-\theta}}.$$

In this distribution, the absolute advantage term T_n^j varies by both country and sector, with higher values of T_n^j implying higher average productivity draws in sector j in country n. The parameter θ captures dispersion, with larger values of θ implying smaller dispersion in draws.

The production cost of one unit of good q in sector j and country n is thus equal to $c_n^j/z_n^j(q)$. Each country can produce each good in each sector, and international trade is subject to iceberg costs: $d_{ni}^j>1$ units of good q produced in sector j in country i must be shipped to country n in order for one unit to be available for consumption there. The trade costs need not be symmetric—d_{ni}^j need not equal d_{in}^j—and will vary by sector. We normalize $d_{nn}^j = 1$ for any n and j.

All the product and factor markets are perfectly competitive, and thus the price at which country i supplies tradable good q in sector j to country n is:

$$p_{ni}^j(q) = \left(\frac{c_i^j}{z_i^j(q)}\right)d_{ni}^j.$$

Buyers of each good q in tradable sector j in country n will only buy from the cheapest source country, and thus the price actually paid for this good in country n will be:

$$p_n^j(q) = \min_{i=1,\dots,N}\left\{p_{ni}^j(q)\right\}.$$

Characterization of Equilibrium

The *competitive equilibrium* of this model world economy consists of a set of prices, allocation rules, and trade shares such that (i) given the prices, all firms' inputs satisfy the first-order conditions, and their output is given by the production function; (ii) given the prices, the consumers' demand satisfies the first-order conditions; (iii) the prices ensure the market clearing conditions for labor, capital, tradable goods, and nontradable goods; (iv) trade shares ensure balanced trade for each country.

The set of prices includes the wage rates $\{w_n^j\}_{j=1}^{J+1}$, the rental rates $\{r_n^j\}_{j=1}^{J+1}$, the sectoral prices $\{p_n^j\}_{j=1}^{J+1}$, and the aggregate price P_n in each country n. The allocation rules include final consumption demand $\{Y_n^j\}_{j=1}^{J+1}$, total demand $\{Q_n^j\}_{j=1}^{J+1}$ (both final and intermediate goods) for each sector, and potentially the capital and labor allocation across sectors $\{K_n^j, L_n^j\}_{j=1}^{J+1}$. The trade shares include the expenditure share π_{ni}^j in country n on goods coming from country i in sector j.

We distinguish between four types of equilibria, that differ in the assumptions on factor market frictions: (i) flexible-factors equilibrium, in which both capital and labor are free to move across sectors; (ii) fixed-factors equilibrium, in which both capital and labor belong to a particular sector and cannot move across sectors; (iii) flexible-labor, fixed-capital equilibrium, in which capital cannot move across sectors but labor can do so frictionlessly, and (iv) flexible-capital, fixed-labor equilibrium, in which labor cannot move across sectors but capital can do so frictionlessly. All throughout, both capital are labor are immobile across countries.

Demand and Prices

The four equilibria have identical goods market clearing conditions. It can be easily shown that the price of sector j's output will be given by:

$$p_n^j = \left[\int_0^1 p_n^j(q)^{1-\varepsilon} dq\right]^{\frac{1}{1-\varepsilon}}.$$

Following the standard EK approach, it is helpful to define

$$\Phi_n^j = \sum_{i=1}^{N} T_i^j \left(c_i^j d_{ni}^j\right)^{-\theta}.$$

This value summarizes, for country n, the access to production technologies in sector j. Its value will be higher if in sector j, country n's trading partners have high productivity (T_i^j) or low cost (c_i^j). It will also be higher if the trade costs that country n faces in this sector are low. Standard steps lead to the familiar result that the price of good j in country n is simply

$$p_n^j = \Gamma\left(\Phi_n^j\right)^{-\frac{1}{\theta}}, \tag{2}$$

where $\Gamma = [\Gamma((\theta+1-\varepsilon)/\theta)]^{1/1-\varepsilon}$, with Γ the Gamma function. The consumption price index in country n is then:

$$P_n = B_n \left(\sum_{j=1}^{J} \omega_j (p_n^j)^{1-\eta}\right)^{\frac{1}{1-\eta}\xi_n} (p_n^{J+1})^{1-\xi_n}, \tag{3}$$

where $B_n = \xi_n^{-\xi_n}(1-\xi_n)^{-(1-\xi_n)}$.

The budget constraint (or the resource constraint) of the consumer is thus given by:

$$\sum_{j=1}^{J+1} p_n^j Y_n^j = \sum_{j=1}^{J+1} w_n^j L_n^j + \sum_{j=1}^{J+1} r_n^j K_n^j, \tag{4}$$

where K_n^j and L_n^j are the amounts of capital and labor, respectively, in country n, sector j.

Given the set of prices $\{\{w_n^j\}_{j=1}^{J+1}, \{r_n^j\}_{j=1}^{J+1}, P_n, \{p_n^j\}_{j=1}^{J+1}\}_{n=1}^N$, we first characterize the optimal allocations from final demand. Consumers maximize utility (1) subject to the budget constraint (4). The first-order conditions associated with this optimization problem imply the following final demand:

$$p_n^j Y_n^j = \xi_n \left(\sum_{j=1}^{J+1} w_n^j L_n^j + \sum_{j=1}^{J+1} r_n^j K_n^j \right) \frac{\omega_j (p_n^j)^{1-\eta}}{\sum_{k=1}^{J} \omega_k (p_n^k)^{1-\eta}},$$
$$\text{for all } j = \{1, \ldots, J\} \tag{5}$$

and

$$p_n^{J+1} Y_n^{J+1} = (1-\xi_n) \left(\sum_{j=1}^{J+1} w_n^j L_n^j + \sum_{j=1}^{J+1} r_n^j K_n^j \right).$$

Production Allocation and Goods Market Clearing

Let Q_n^j denote the total sectoral demand in country n and sector j. Q_n^j is used for both final consumption and as intermediate inputs in domestic production of all sectors. Denote by $X_n^j = p_n^j Q_n^j$ the total *spending* on the sector j goods in country n, and by X_{ni}^j country n's total spending on sector j goods coming from country i, that is, n's imports of j from country i. The EK structure in each sector j delivers the standard result that the probability of importing good q from country i, π_{ni}^j is equal to the share of total spending on goods coming from country i, X_{ni}^j / X_n^j, and is given by:

$$\frac{X_{ni}^j}{X_n^j} = \pi_{ni}^j = \frac{T_i^j \left(c_i^j d_{ni}^j \right)^{-\theta}}{\Phi_n^j}. \tag{6}$$

The market clearing condition for expenditure on sector j in country n is:

$$p_n^j Q_n^j = p_n^j Y_n^j + \sum_{k=1}^{J} (1-\beta_k) \gamma_{j,k} \left(\sum_{i=1}^{N} \pi_{in}^k p_i^k Q_i^k \right)$$
$$+ (1-\beta_{J+1}) \gamma_{j,J+1} p_n^{J+1} Q_n^{J+1}.$$

Total expenditure in sector j of country n, $p_n^j Q_n^j$, is the sum of (i) domestic final consumption expenditure $p_n^j Y_n^j$; (ii) expenditure on sector j goods as intermediate inputs in all the traded sectors $\sum_{k=1}^{J} (1-\beta_k) \gamma_{j,k} (\sum_{i=1}^{N} \pi_{in}^k p_i^k Q_i^k)$, and (iii) expenditure on the j's sector intermediate inputs in the domestic nontraded sector

$(1-\beta_{J+1})\gamma_{j,J+1}p_n^{J+1}Q_n^{J+1}$. These market clearing conditions summarize two important features of the world economy captured by our model: complex international production linkages, as much of world trade is in intermediate inputs, and a good crosses borders multiple times before being consumed (Hummels, Ishii, and Yi, 2001); and two-way input linkages between the tradable and the nontradable sectors.

In each tradable sector j, some goods q are imported from abroad and some goods q are exported to the rest of the world. Country n's exports in sector j are given by $EX_n^j = \sum_{i=1}^N I_{i\neq n}\pi_{in}^j p_i^j Q_i^j$, and its imports in sector j are given by $IM_n^j = \sum_{i=1}^N I_{i\neq n}\pi_{ni}^j p_n^j Q_n^j$, where $I_{i\neq n}$ is the indicator function. The total exports of country n are then $EX_n = \sum_{j=1}^j EX_n^j$, and total imports are $IM_n = \sum_{j=1}^j IM_n^j$. Trade balance requires that for any country n, $EX_n - IM_n = 0$.

Factor Market Clearing in the Four Equilibria

Given the total production revenue in tradable sector j in country n, $\sum_{i=1}^N \pi_{in}^j p_i^j Q_i^j$, the sectoral factor allocations and factor prices must satisfy

$$\sum_{i=1}^{N} \pi_{in}^j p_i^j Q_i^j = \frac{w_n^j L_n^j}{\alpha_j \beta_j} = \frac{r_n^j K_n^j}{(1-\alpha_j)\beta_j}. \tag{7}$$

For the nontradable sector J+1, the optimal factor allocations in country n are simply given by:

$$p_n^{J+1} Q_n^{J+1} = \frac{w_n^{J+1} L_n^{J+1}}{\alpha_{J+1}\beta_{J+1}} = \frac{r_n^{J+1} K_n^{J+1}}{(1-\alpha_{J+1})\beta_{J+1}}. \tag{8}$$

Finally, the feasibility conditions for factors are given by, for every n,

$$\sum_{j=1}^{J+1} L_n^j = L_n \quad \text{and} \quad \sum_{j=1}^{J+1} K_n^j = K_n, \tag{9}$$

where L_n and K_n are aggregate country endowments of labor and capital.

In the *flexible-factors equilibrium*, both factors can move, so that wages and returns to capital must be equalized across sectors in each country: $w_n^j = w_n$ and $r_n^j = r_n$ for all j. Correspondingly, sectoral factor allocations L_n^j and K_n^j are equilibrium outcomes that will adjust to satisfy equality of factor returns in all sectors. Equilibrium w_n, r_n, and $\{K_n^j, L_n^j\}_{j=1}^{J+1}$ are the solutions to the systems of equations (7)–(9).

In the *fixed-factors equilibrium*, $\{K_n^j, L_n^j\}_{j=1}^{J+1}$ are instead fixed endowments in each country and sector. Once we take a stand on what those endowments are, the set of conditions (9) becomes vacuous, and the systems of equations (7)-(8) are instead solved for sectoral factor prices $\{w_n^j, r_n^j\}_{j=1}^{J+1}$ given sectoral factor endowments.

The *flexible-labor, fixed-capital* and *flexible-capital, fixed-labor* equilibria are intermediate cases. In the former, $\{L_n^j\}_{j=1}^{J+1}$ are endogenous equilibrium outcomes that ensure equality of wages across sectors within a country, $w_n^j = w_n$

for all j, but $\{K_n^j\}_{j=1}^{J+1}$ are exogenous endowments used to compute sector-specific rates of return $\{r_n^j\}_{j=1}^{J+1}$. In the latter, assumptions on which factors are fixed and flexible are reversed.

The fixed-factor equilibria are in effect modern versions of the Specific-Factors Model (Jones, 1971; Mussa, 1974). Although all of the models in our analysis are formally static, the implicit assumption is that the fixed-factor models are in some sense short-run, whereas the long-run outcome is captured by the flexible-factor equilibrium. An extreme opposite approach to factor market frictions is adopted by Święcki (2013) (following Haberler, 1950; Hagen, 1958; Bhagwati and Ramaswami, 1963). In that framework, wage disparities across sectors arise due to institutional frictions and persist even under perfect cross-sectoral factor mobility. By assumption, the size of those wage disparities is fixed, and thus trade shocks have no effect on cross-sectoral wage distributions.

One limitation of our analysis is that we do not model the transition between the fixed-factors ("short-run") and the flexible-factors ("long-run") equilibria, and thus cannot provide a unified intertemporal welfare assessment that cumulates welfare changes for workers along the transition path. To do so would require a model of frictional unemployment, since a typical finding in the literature is that workers in import-competing industries suffer unemployment spells and only find new jobs with some delay (Menezes-Filho and Muendler, 2011; Autor, Dorn, and Hanson, 2012a). Combining a multisector frictional unemployment model with a global general equilibrium production and trade framework is a substantial modeling and computational challenge that is left to future work.

The model has two principal uses. The first is to estimate the sector-level technology parameters T_n^j for a large set of countries. The technology parameters in the tradable sectors relative to a reference country (the United States) are estimated using data on sectoral output and bilateral trade. The procedure relies on fitting a structural gravity equation implied by the model. Intuitively, if controlling for the typical gravity determinants of trade, a country spends relatively more on domestically produced goods in a particular sector, it is revealed to have either a high relative productivity or a low relative unit cost in that sector. The procedure then uses data on factor and intermediate input prices to net out the role of factor costs, yielding an estimate of relative productivity. This step also produces estimates of bilateral, sector-level trade costs d_{ni}^j. The next step is to estimate the technology parameters in the tradable sectors for the United States. This procedure requires directly measuring TFP at the sectoral level using data on real output and inputs, and then correcting measured TFP for selection due to trade. Third, we calibrate the nontradable technology for all countries using the first-order condition of the model and the relative prices of nontradables observed in the data. The detailed procedures for all three steps are described in Levchenko and Zhang (2011) and reproduced in Appendix.

The second use of the quantitative model is to perform welfare analysis. Given the estimated sectoral productivities, factor endowments, trade costs, and model parameters, we solve the system of equations defining the equilibrium under the baseline values, as well as under counterfactual scenarios, and compare welfare. The algorithm for solving the model is described in Levchenko and Zhang (2011).

Welfare

Welfare in this framework corresponds to the indirect utility function. The functional form of the utility function and homothetic preferences imply that welfare of any agent in the economy equals his/her total income divided by the price level. As both goods and factor markets are competitive, total income equals the total returns to factors of production. Total welfare in the economy is given by:

$$\frac{\sum_{j=1}^{J+1} w_n^j L_n^j + \sum_{j=1}^{J+1} r_n^j K_n^j}{P_n}, \tag{10}$$

where the consumption price level P_n comes from Equation (3). This expression is the metric of aggregate welfare in all counterfactual exercises below. Of course, in the flexible market equilibrium, when all factor returns are the same, the expression above simplifies to, in per capita terms, the more familiar expression $(w_n+r_nk_n)/P_n$, where $k_n = K_n/L_n$ is capital per worker.

When (some) factor markets are not flexible, workers and units of capital employed in the different sectors will earn different wages and returns. Without making assumptions about individuals' capital asset holdings, we cannot make statements about individuals' welfare. Thus, when discussing distributional impacts in our counterfactual exercises, we will present results with respect to the real wage and the real returns to capital across sectors, w_n^j/P_n and r_n^j/P_n.

Calibration

In order to implement the model numerically, we must calibrate the following sets of parameters: (i) moments of the productivity distributions T_n^j and θ; (ii) trade costs d_{ni}^j; (iii) production function parameters α_j, β_j, $\gamma_{k,j}$, and ε; (iv) country factor endowments L_n and K_n; and (v) preference parameters ξ_n, ω_j, and η. We discuss the calibration of each in turn.

Estimation of sectoral productivity parameters T_n^j and trade costs d_{ni}^j requires data on total output by sector, as well as sectoral data on bilateral trade. For 52 countries in the sample, information on output comes from the 2009 UNIDO Industrial Statistics Database. For the European Union countries, the EUROSTAT database contains data of superior quality, and thus for those countries we use EUROSTAT production data. The two output data sources are merged at the roughly 2-digit ISIC Revision 3 level of disaggregation, yielding 19 manufacturing sectors. Bilateral trade data were collected from the UN COMTRADE database, and concorded to the same sectoral classification. The baseline analysis assumes that the dispersion parameter θ does not vary across sectors. We pick the value of $\theta = 8.28$, which is the preferred estimate of EK. To check whether our conclusions are sensitive to this restriction, Section "Additional Exercises" reports the results of implementing the model with sector-specific values of θ_j sourced from Caliendo and Parro (2010).[2]

[2]It may also be important to assess how the results below are affected by the level of θ. One may be especially concerned about how the results change under lower values of θ. Lower θ implies greater

The production function parameters α_j and β_j are estimated using the UNIDO and EUROSTAT production data, which contain information on output, value added, employment, and wage bills. To compute α_j for each sector, we calculate the share of the total wage bill in value added, and take a simple median across countries (taking the mean yields essentially the same results). To compute β_j, we take the median of value added divided by total output.

The intermediate input coefficients $\gamma_{k,j}$ are obtained from the Direct Requirements Table for the United States. We use the 1997 Benchmark Detailed Make and Use Tables (covering approximately 500 distinct sectors), as well as a concordance to the ISIC Revision 3 classification to build a Direct Requirements Table at the 2-digit ISIC level. The Direct Requirements Table gives the value of the intermediate input in row k required to produce one dollar of final output in column j. Thus, it is the direct counterpart to the input coefficients $\gamma_{k,j}$. Note that we assume these to be the same in all countries.[3] In addition, we use the U.S. Input-Output (I-O) matrix to obtain α_{J+1} and β_{J+1} in the nontradable sector, which cannot be obtained from UNIDO.[4] The elasticity of substitution between varieties within each tradable sector, ε, is set to 4 (as is well known, in the EK model this elasticity plays no role, entering only the constant Γ).

The total labor force in each country, L_n, and the total capital stock, K_n, are obtained from the Penn World Tables 6.3. Following the standard approach in the literature (see, for example, Hall and Jones, 1999; Bernanke and Gurkaynak, 2001; Caselli, 2005), the total labor force is calculated from the data on the total GDP per capita and per worker.[5] The total capital is calculated using the perpetual inventory method that assumes a depreciation rate of 6 percent: $K_{n,t} = (1-0.06)K_{n,t-1}+I_{n,t}$, where $I_{n,t}$ is total investment in country n in period t. For most countries, investment data start in 1950, and the initial value of K_n is set equal to $I_{n,0}/(\gamma+0.06)$, where γ is the average growth rate of investment in the first 10 years for which data are available.

---

within-sector heterogeneity in the random productivity draws. Thus, trade flows become less sensitive to the costs of the input bundles (c_i^j), and the gains from intrasectoral trade become larger relative to the gains from intersectoral trade. Elsewhere (Levchenko and Zhang, 2011) we re-estimated all the technology parameters using instead a value of $\theta = 4$, which has been advocated by Simonovska and Waugh (2011) and is at or near the bottom of the range that has been used in the literature. Overall, the outcome was remarkably similar. The correlation between estimated T_i^j's under $\theta = 4$ and the baseline is above 0.95, and there is actually somewhat greater variability in T_i^j's under $\theta = 4$.

[3]di Giovanni and Levchenko (2010) provide suggestive evidence that at such a coarse level of aggregation, Input-Output matrices are indeed similar across countries. To check robustness of the results, we collected country-specific I-O matrices from the GTAP database. Productivities computed based on country-specific I-O matrices were very similar to the baseline values. In our sample of countries, the median correlation was 0.98, with all but 3 out of 75 countries having a correlation of 0.93 or above, and the minimum correlation of 0.65.

[4]The U.S. I-O matrix provides an alternative way of computing α_j and β_j. These parameters calculated based on the U.S. I-O table are very similar to those obtained from UNIDO, with the correlation coefficients between them above 0.85 in each case. The U.S. I-O table implies greater variability in α_j's and β_j's across sectors than does UNIDO.

[5]Using the variable name conventions in the Penn World Tables, $L_n = 1000 \times pop \times rgdpch/rgdpwok$.

The share of expenditure on traded goods, ξ_n in each country is sourced from Yi and Zhang (2010), who compile this information for 36 developed and developing countries. For countries unavailable in the Yi and Zhang data, values of ξ_n are imputed based on their level of development. We fit a simple linear relationship between ξ_n and log PPP-adjusted per capita GDP from the Penn World Tables on the countries in the Yi and Zhang (2010) data set. The fit of this simple bivariate linear relationship is quite good, with an R^2 of 0.55. For the remaining countries, we then set ξ_n to the value predicted by this bivariate regression at their level of income. The taste parameters for tradable sectors ω_j were estimated by combining the model structure above with data on final consumption expenditure shares in the United States sourced from the U.S. I-O matrix, as described in the Appendix. The elasticity of substitution between broad sectors within the tradable bundle, η, is set to 2. As these are very large product categories, it is sensible that this elasticity would be relatively low. It is higher, however, than the elasticity of substitution between tradable and nontradable goods, which is set to 1 by the Cobb-Douglas assumption.

Summary of the Estimates and Basic Patterns

All of the variables that vary over time are averaged over the period 2005–2007 (the latest available year), which is the time period on which we carry out the analysis. Table A1 lists the 75 countries used in the analysis, separating them into the major country groups and regions. Table A2 lists the 20 sectors along with the key parameter values for each sector: α_j, β_j, the share of nontradable inputs in total inputs $\gamma_{J+1,j}$, and the taste parameter ω_j.

What do the data tell us about the emerging giants' comparative advantage? Figure 2 reports the population-weighted average sectoral productivities of emerging giant countries, expressed as a ratio to the world frontier. To be precise, we compute the world frontier productivity in each sector as the geometric average

Figure 2. Productivity in Emerging Giants, Population-Weighted

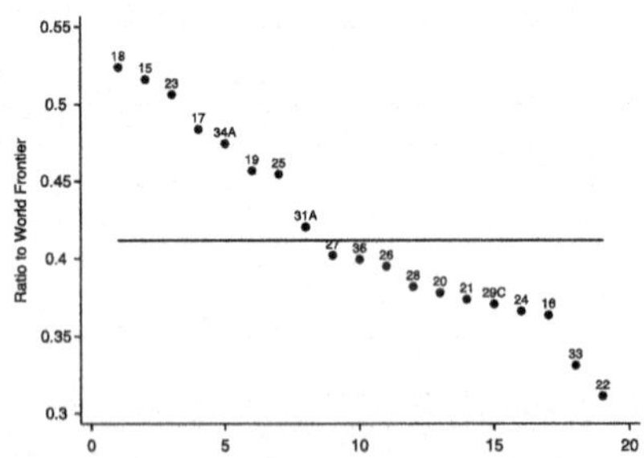

Notes: This figure displays the emerging giants' population-weighted productivity $((T_n^j)^{1/\theta})$, as a ratio to the world frontier in each sector. The horizontal line is the geometric average emerging giants' productivity across sectors. The key for sector labels is reported in Table A2.

of the top two productivities in the sample of all countries. As average sectoral productivity scales with $(T_n^j)^{1/\theta}$ rather than T_n^j, we report the (population-weighted) ratio of $(T_n^j)^{1/\theta}$ to the world frontier $(T_F^j)^{1/\theta}$.

Even taken as a group, emerging giants do indeed have pronounced comparative advantage. The top four sectors are Wearing Apparel (ISIC 18), Food and Beverages (15), Fuels (23), and Textiles (15). In these sectors, emerging giants' productivity is about 0.50–0.55 of the world frontier. By contrast, the least productive sectors are Printing and Publishing (22) and Medical, Precision, and Optical Instruments (33), with productivity in the range of 0.3–0.35 of the world frontier.

II. Welfare Analysis

This section analyzes the global welfare impact of emerging giants' trade integration under the different assumptions on factor market reallocation. We proceed by first solving the model under the baseline values of all the estimated parameters, and present a number of checks on the model fit with respect to observed data. The baseline estimation and solution is carried out under the assumption of flexible factor markets. This approach in effect assumes that by the mid-2000s, factor market adjustment to the trade opening of these countries had already (largely) occurred.

Then, we compute counterfactual welfare and sectoral factor allocations under the assumption that the emerging giants are in autarky, and factor markets are flexible. This is the "long-run" state of the world economy in the hypothetical absence of trade with emerging giants. The welfare change because of the opening of emerging giants under flexible factor markets is then given by the comparison of baseline welfare to welfare when emerging giants are in autarky.

Then, we solve the model under three additional scenarios with inflexible factor markets. In the fixed-factors equilibrium, emerging giants are open to trade, but all factors must remain in sectors where they were *when the emerging giants were in autarky.* The comparison between this counterfactual and the equilibrium with emerging giants in autarky thus captures the welfare change that occurs when emerging giants open to trade, but factors cannot move to optimally adjust to this trade integration. In the fixed-labor equilibrium, only labor cannot move from its allocation when emerging giants were in autarky, whereas in the fixed-capital equilibrium, only capital cannot.

Model Fit

Table 1 compares the wages, returns to capital, and trade shares in the baseline model and in the data. The top panel shows that mean and median wages implied by the model are very close to the data. The correlation coefficient between model-implied wages and those in the data is above 0.99. The second panel performs the same comparison for the return to capital. As it is difficult to observe the return to capital in the data, we follow the approach adopted in the estimation of T_n^j's and impute r_n from an aggregate factor market clearing condition: $r_n/w_n = (1-\alpha)L_n/(\alpha K_n)$, where α is the aggregate share of labor in GDP, assumed to be

Table 1. The Fit of the Baseline Model with the Data

	Model		Data
Wages			
mean	0.463		0.413
median	0.149		0.154
corr(model, data)		*0.994*	
Return to capital			
mean	1.035		1.074
median	0.767		0.758
corr(model, data)		*0.938*	
Sectoral labor shares			
corr(model, data)		*0.711*	
π^j_{nn}			
mean	0.620		0.565
median	0.678		0.607
corr(model, data)		*0.914*	
$\pi^j_{ni}, i \neq n$			
mean	0.0055		0.0059
median	0.0002		0.0002
corr(model, data)		*0.886*	

Notes: This table reports the means and medians of wages relative to the United States (top panel); return to capital relative to the United States (second panel); correlations between model and data sectoral employment shares (third panel); share of domestically produced goods in overall spending (fourth panel); and share of goods from country i in overall spending (bottom panel) in the model and in the data. Wages and return to capital in the data are calculated as described in the Appendix.

2/3. Once again, the average levels of r_n are very similar in the model and the data, and the correlation between the two is about 0.94.

Because much of the paper is concerned with the cross-sectoral distributional effects, it is important to check how well the baseline model solution reproduces observed sectoral labor shares. For most (but not all) countries in the sample, sectoral employment data for manufacturing are available in the EUROSTAT and UNIDO databases. We correlate those observed sectoral employment shares with those implied by the model. The correlation, reported in Table 1, is quite high at 0.711.[6] It is important to emphasize that there are many reasons why the model would not reproduce sectoral labor shares perfectly, beyond the fact that our match of relative factor prices and trade shares is not exact. For instance, taste parameters (ω_j's), I-O matrices, and factor intensities (α_j's) may differ across countries, whereas our model assumes those to be the same. Nonetheless, it is quite

[6]We do not report model and data averages for sectoral trade shares, as the mean sectoral employment share is by construction equal to $1/J$.

reassuring that the model employment shares are actually close to the data. To flesh out country detail, Appendix Table A3 summarizes country-specific employment share correlations by region.[7] We can see that by and large the fit of the model to observed employment shares in individual countries is quite good. In many regions, mean/median country-level correlations of sectoral employment shares between the model and the data are around 0.8. Even looking at the minimum values of those correlations, we can see that these are still quite high in most regions. The exception is Saudi Arabia, for which sectoral labor shares in the model and data are virtually uncorrelated. Saudi Arabia is very special in its extreme reliance on oil exports. As our model does not include the raw mining sectors, it is not surprising that the model fit to Saudi Arabia is poor. As will become clear below, none of the results are driven by what happens in this particular country.[8]

Next, we compare the trade shares implied by the model with those in the data. The fourth panel of Table 1 reports the spending on domestically produced goods as a share of overall spending, π^j_{nn}. These values reflect the overall trade openness, with lower values implying higher international trade as a share of absorption. Though we underpredict overall trade slightly (model π^j_{nn}'s tend to be higher), the averages are quite similar, and the correlation between the model and data values is 0.91. Finally, the bottom panel compares the international trade flows in the model and the data. The averages are very close, and the correlation between model and data is nearly 0.9.

Figure 3 presents the comparison of trade flows graphically, by depicting the model-implied trade values against the data, along with a 45-degree line. Red/solid dots indicate π^j_{ni}'s that involve one of the emerging giants, that is, trade flows in which an emerging giant is either an exporter or an importer. All in all the fit of the model to trade flows is quite good. Emerging giants are unexceptional, with their trade flows clustered together with the rest of the observations.

We conclude from this exercise that our model matches quite closely with the relative incomes of countries, sectoral employment shares, as well as bilateral and overall trade flows observed in the data. We now use the model to carry out a number of counterfactual scenarios to assess the emerging giants' global welfare impact.

Gains under Flexible Factor Markets

Panel A of Table 2 reports the gains from trade with the emerging giants around the world under the assumption of flexible factor markets. To compute these, we

[7]Note that not all countries have data on sectoral labor shares. In addition, we impose a cutoff that to compute a country-specific correlation of employment shares, the country must have data for at least 17 out of 19 possible tradable sectors. Varying this data availability cutoff between 2 and 19 produces quite similar results.

[8]We cannot compare model and data sectoral allocations of capital, because we do not have comprehensive data on sectoral capital stocks. To construct sectoral capital stocks in our data would require cumulating sectoral investment series. However, these investment series are not as reliable as we would like, have patchy coverage, and for many countries start too late to make the perpetual inventory method applicable.

Figure 3. Benchmark Model vs. Data: π^j_{ni} for Emerging Giants and the Rest of the Sample

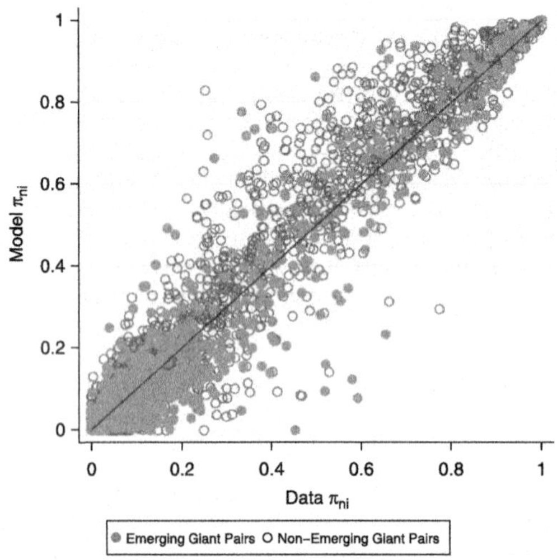

Notes: This figure displays the model-implied values of π^j_{ni} on the y-axis against the values of π^j_{ni} in the data on the x-axis. Solid red dots depict π^j_{ni} in which either n or i is one of the emerging giants. Hollow dots represent the nonemerging giant π^j_{ni}'s. The line through the points is the 45-degree line.

compare the welfare of each country in the baseline (current levels of trade costs and productivities as we estimate them in the world today) against a counterfactual scenario in which emerging giants are in autarky. The table reports the change in welfare for emerging giants themselves, as well as the summary statistics for each region and country group. China's gains from trade relative to complete autarky are 3.48 percent, India's 1.63 percent, and CEECs' gains range from 2.75 percent for Russia to 13.26 percent for Bulgaria, with an average of 7.26 percent. Elsewhere in the world, the gains range from –0.37 percent to 2.28 percent, with the mean of 0.37 percent.[9] The gains for the rest of the world from emerging giants' trade integration are smaller than for emerging giants themselves because these gains are relative to the counterfactual that preserves all the global trade relationships other than with the emerging giants.

The countries gaining the most tend to be close to the emerging giants geographically. The top three are Sri Lanka (2.28 percent), Senegal (1.21 percent), and Malaysia (1.16 percent). Of the top 10, six are in Asia, the other four being Senegal,

[9]This is the unweighted mean across the 63 rest-of-the-world countries. The population-weighted mean is similar at 0.33 percent.

Table 2. Welfare Gains from Trade with Emerging Giants

	Mean	Median	Min.	Max.	Countries
Panel A: Flexible factors					
China	3.48				
India	1.63				
CEECs	7.26	7.18	2.75	13.36	10
OECD	0.28	0.30	–0.01	0.57	22
East and South Asia	0.70	0.58	–0.05	2.28	11
Latin America and Caribbean	0.16	0.15	–0.38	0.54	15
Middle East and North Africa	0.44	0.49	0.25	0.60	7
Sub-Saharan Africa	0.48	0.29	0.12	1.21	8
Panel B: Fixed factors					
China	3.13				
India	1.40				
CEECs	6.48	6.17	2.09	11.76	10
OECD	0.23	0.25	–0.09	0.52	22
East and South Asia	0.67	0.53	–0.08	2.33	11
Latin America and Caribbean	0.11	0.13	–0.53	0.50	15
Middle East and North Africa	0.29	0.28	0.04	0.48	7
Sub-Saharan Africa	0.40	0.22	0.07	1.17	8

Notes: Units are in percentage points. This table reports the changes in welfare from two counterfactual scenarios. Panel A presents the welfare gains in the benchmark for 2005–07, relative to the scenario in which emerging giants are in autarky, under the assumption that factor markets are flexible. Panel B presents the changes in welfare relative to the scenario in which emerging giants are in autarky, under the assumption that factors are fixed in their respective sectors, at the equilibrium values pre-opening of emerging giants to trade.

Ethiopia, Kuwait, and Austria. As a region, East and South Asia gains the most (0.7 percent average), whereas Latin America and the Caribbean gain the least (0.16 percent). Table 2 also reveals that in several major country groups, the welfare changes range from negative to positive. A total of four countries lose in absolute terms from entry of emerging giants into world trade: Honduras (–0.37 percent), El Salvador (–0.13 percent), Pakistan (–0.05 percent), and Portugal (–0.01 percent).

Sectoral Reallocation and Reaping the Aggregate Gains

The preceding counterfactual assumed that factor markets are fully flexible within countries, and thus the welfare changes computed in that scenario corresponded to the long-run, complete gains from trade integration with the emerging giants. Next, we assess the importance of cross-sectoral reallocation in reaping the full magnitude of those gains.

Panel B of Table 2 reports the welfare gains from trade with emerging giants under the assumption of all factors fixed. It is immediate that gains are smaller. For China, for instance, the gains from trade are now 3.13 percent,

Table 3. Differences in Welfare Changes, Alternative Factor Market Equilibria

	Difference with Respect to Flexible Factors			
	Fixed factors	Fixed labor	Fixed capital	Countries
China	–0.35	–0.25	–0.28	
India	–0.23	–0.15	–0.19	
CEECs	–0.78	–0.50	–0.65	10
OECD	–0.05	–0.04	–0.05	22
East and South Asia	–0.03	–0.02	–0.04	11
Latin America and Caribbean	–0.06	–0.04	–0.05	15
Middle East and North Africa	–0.15	–0.10	–0.13	7
Sub-Saharan Africa	–0.08	–0.05	–0.07	8

Notes: Units are in percentage points. This table reports the correlations between the welfare gains from trade integration of emerging giants under the different assumptions on the factor market equilibrium.

compared with 3.48 percent under flexible factors. It is also clear that the broad patterns in the data as to which regions gain the most and least are the same.

Table 3 reports the differences between the percentage changes in welfare from the opening up of emerging giants under the assumption of fixed factor(s) and the welfare changes under flexible markets. Negative numbers imply that gains under the fixed factors are (unsurprisingly) smaller than under flexible factors. The first column presents the difference under both factors fixed. China gains 0.35 percentage points less when both factors are fixed compared with the flexible case (3.13 percent vs. 3.48 percent). India gains 0.23 percent less, whereas in the CEECs the effect is somewhat larger in absolute terms, 0.78 percent. Elsewhere in the world, the mean difference amounts to 0.03–0.16 percent. By and large, perfect factor reallocation between sectors contributes 10–15 percent of the total gains from trade with these countries.

Is there a factor of production that is especially crucial for reaping the benefits of factor reallocation? To answer this question, we evaluated the gains from trade with the emerging giants under two additional sets of assumptions: fixed-labor and fixed-capital, with the corresponding other factor being mobile. The results are reported in the second and third columns of Table 3. Several conclusions stand out. As expected, the differences with respect to the flexible-factor case tend to be smaller under these two scenarios: gains tend to be larger when one of the factors can reallocate optimally than when none of the factors can. However, the difference is quite minor quantitatively. For all intents and purposes, the scenarios with one factor fixed produce very similar results to the case in which both factors are fixed. This result points to a strong complementarity between reallocation of labor and capital. Both are required to reap the full gains from reallocation, and just one immobile factor prevents the large majority of total gains from factor reallocation.

We explore further the relationship between the welfare gains under the different factor (im)mobilities in Table 4 and Figure 4. The table presents the correlations between the welfare changes implied by the four scenarios. It is clear

Table 4. Correlations in Welfare Gains across Factor Market Equilibria

	Flexible	Fixed Factors	Fixed Labor
Panel A: Emerging giants ($n = 12$)			
Fixed factors	0.981		
Fixed labor	0.991	0.998	
Fixed capital	0.987	0.999	0.999
Panel B: Rest of the world ($n = 63$)			
Fixed factors	0.977		
Fixed labor	0.989	0.997	
Fixed capital	0.984	0.999	0.999

Notes: This table reports the correlations between the gains from trade with emerging giants across the different assumptions on factor market frictions.

Figure 4. Welfare Gains Under Flexible and Fixed Factors

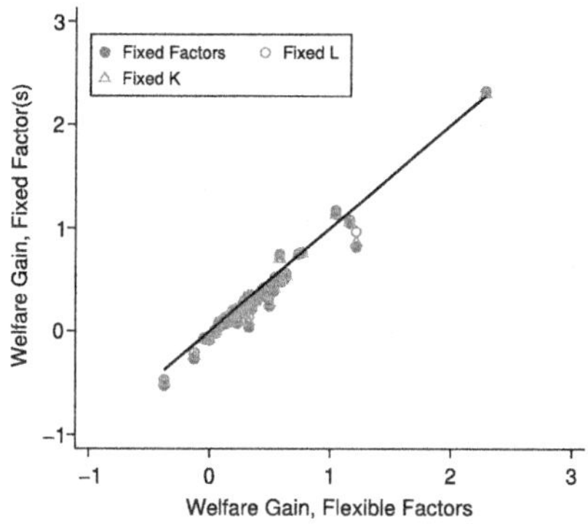

Notes: This figure displays the welfare gains to the rest of the world under flexible factor markets (on the x-axis) against the gains to the rest of the world under the three alternative assumptions on the factor markets (all factors fixed, L only fixed, and K only fixed), along with the 45-degree line.

that all four are extremely highly correlated, with correlation coefficients in excess of 0.98 in nearly all cases, and above 0.99 between the three fixed-factors equilibria. The figure presents the scatterplot of the welfare changes in the three inflexible equilibria on the y-axis against the welfare change in the flexible case on the x-axis, along with the 45-degree line. By and large, the observations are slightly below the 45-degree line. The different inflexible equilibria are different from each other, but only very slightly.

Why does the cross-sectoral factor reallocation contribute relatively little to reaping the aggregate gains from trade with emerging giants? A proximate explanation for this outcome is that even with fully flexible factor markets, the cross-sectoral reallocation that occurs in response to emerging giants' opening is minor. In the rest of the world, when emerging giants open to trade absolute changes in sectoral employment shares range from −1.5 to 1.9 percent (that is, in the entire sample of the rest of the world country-sectors, an individual sector's share of total employment rises by a maximum of 1.9 percentage points). In most countries this range is much smaller. For instance, in the United States, the most hard-hit sector contracts its share of aggregate employment by 0.03 percentage points, whereas the sector with the largest expansion lifts its share of total employment by 0.06 percentage points. Thus, the absolute factor reallocation required to adjust to the emerging giants' trade opening is not that large in most countries. As a result, cross-sectoral reallocation contributes relatively little to aggregate gains. However, as we will see below, the lack of factor reallocation does produce more substantial distributional effects.

Additional Exercises

Before moving on to the distributional effects, we discuss two sets of additional experiments. A number of recent papers have called attention to the differences in trade elasticities across sectors (Caliendo and Parro, 2010; Chen and Novy, 2011; Imbs and Mejean, 2011). To check how our results change if we instead assume that the trade elasticities differ across sectors, we re-implement the model using Caliendo and Parro's (2010) estimates of sector-specific θ_j. Note that this alternative approach requires us to re-estimate the entire model, starting with the sectoral productivity parameters T_n^j and trade costs d_{ni}^j.

Table 5 reports the results. The gains from the emerging giants' integration do appear somewhat larger than under the baseline assumption of identical θ across sectors. Under flexible factor markets (Panel A), the mean gains to the rest of the world are 0.87 percent, with a median of 0.53 percent. The range is similar to the baseline, from –0.25 to 3.94 percent. The relative importance of cross-sectoral reallocation for aggregate gains is also close to the baseline. The mean gains to the rest of the world under immobile factors (Panel B) are 0.78 percent, or about 0.09 percent lower than under flexible factor markets.

Next, rather than evaluating the impact of emerging giants by placing them in autarky, we consider two intermediate experiments. First, we simulate a less drastic change in trade costs. Ideally, one would look at how emerging giants' estimated trade costs changed between some pre-trade liberalization period and the present, and evaluate the welfare impact of that change. Unfortunately, for most of the emerging giants we only have data starting in the mid-1990s, and our estimates for that period indicate that by then the reduction in d_{ni}^j had already largely occurred (that is, the subsequent change in d_{ni}^j between mid-1990s and the 2005–07 period has been minor). To simulate a substantial change in trade costs, we evaluate the welfare impact of a uniform 45 percent reduction in trade costs of all emerging giants down to their present level. That is, we compare the baseline level of welfare to the welfare that would obtain if all emerging giants' trade costs were 45 percent higher. The value of 45 percent is motivated by the size of the drop in d_{ni}^j between the 1970s and 2005–07 for India, the one emerging giant for

Table 5. Welfare Gains from Trade with Emerging Giants: Sector-Specific θ_j

	Mean	Median	Min.	Max.	Countries
Panel A: Flexible factors					
China	3.10				
India	1.81				
CEECs	10.76	11.04	3.54	18.26	10
OECD	0.45	0.44	0.04	0.87	22
East and South Asia	1.69	1.01	0.50	3.94	11
Latin America and Caribbean	0.52	0.40	−0.25	2.27	15
Middle East and North Africa	0.77	0.87	0.37	1.35	7
Sub-Saharan Africa	1.69	1.73	0.41	3.33	8
Panel B: Fixed factors					
China	2.95				
India	1.72				
CEECs	9.72	9.37	2.92	16.90	10
OECD	0.41	0.39	−0.01	0.88	22
East and South Asia	1.61	0.93	0.48	3.80	11
Latin America and Caribbean	0.46	0.28	−0.34	2.34	15
Middle East and North Africa	0.51	0.52	0.09	0.83	7
Sub-Saharan Africa	1.52	1.49	0.35	3.37	8

Notes: Units are in percentage points. This table reports the changes in welfare from two counterfactual scenarios, under sector-specific θ_j's sourced from Caliendo and Parro (2010). Panel A presents the welfare gains in the benchmark for 2005–07, relative to the scenario in which emerging giants are in autarky, under the assumption that factor markets are flexible. Panel B presents the changes in welfare relative to the scenario in which emerging giants are in autarky, under the assumption that factors are fixed in their respective sectors, at the equilibrium values preopening of emerging giants to trade.

which we have pre-1980 data. Panel A of Table 6 presents the results. On average, the gains to the rest of the world from a 45 percent reduction in trade costs are 0.16 percent, or nearly half of the total gains from trade with emerging giants.

A closely related question is whether the gains to the rest of the world come from the reductions in trade costs or from the rapid productivity growth in emerging giants over this period. Note that in a multisector environment, it is well known that productivity growth in one trading partner need not improve the welfare of another (Hicks, 1953; Dornbusch, Fischer, and Samuelson, 1977; Samuelson, 2004; Ju and Yang, 2009), and the outcomes become even more nuanced when there are more than two countries (di Giovanni, Levchenko, and Zhang, 2013). To assess the global welfare impact of emerging giants' growth, we simulate the effect of the productivity growth in those countries between the 1995–99 and 2005–07 periods. To be precise, we compare welfare in the baseline with the counterfactual in which trade costs are unchanged, but the emerging giants' productivity in each sector is reduced to the 1995–99 estimated value.

Panel B of Table 6 presents the results. Not surprisingly, the welfare changes from productivity growth are smaller than the full welfare impact of trade integration. The mean gains to the rest of the world from emerging giants'

Table 6. Welfare Gains: Intermediate Experiments

	Mean	Median	Min.	Max.	Countries
Panel A: 45 percent drop in d^j_{ni} of emerging giants					
China	1.06				
India	0.78				
CEECs	2.31	2.36	1.18	3.76	10
OECD	0.11	0.10	0.04	0.19	22
Eastand South Asia	0.29	0.20	0.10	0.90	11
Latin America and Caribbean	0.10	0.09	−0.12	0.34	15
Middle East and North Africa	0.18	0.17	0.13	0.25	7
Sub-Saharan Africa	0.21	0.15	0.05	0.46	8
Panel B: Productivity growth of emerging giants					
China	102.94				
India	13.44				
CEECs	92.65	77.75	2.81	218.61	10
OECD	−0.05	−0.04	−0.16	0.09	22
East and South Asia	0.25	0.10	−0.34	1.58	11
Latin America and Caribbean	0.15	0.01	−0.29	1.43	15
Middle East and North Africa	0.34	0.14	−0.16	1.28	7
Sub-Saharan Africa	0.14	0.01	−0.05	1.04	8

Notes: Units are in percentage points. This table reports the changes in welfare from two counterfactual scenarios. Panel A presents the welfare gains in the benchmark for 2005–07, relative to the scenario in which emerging giants' trade costs d^j_{ni} are uniformly 45 percent higher. Panel B presents the changes in welfare relative to the scenario in which emerging giants' productivities in all sectors are set to the 1995–99 values.

productivity growth are 0.12 percent, or about one-third of the full gains from their integration relative to autarky. There is some interesting variation across regions as well. The OECD countries experience on average a 0.05 percent welfare loss from observed productivity growth in emerging giants, equivalent in absolute value to about one-sixth of their average gains from trade with those countries. Other regions show gains that are higher than the global average. In the Middle East-North Africa region, the average gains from the emerging giants' productivity growth, 0.34 percent, are more than three-quarters of the total gains from trade with emerging giants, which are 0.44 percent in this group.

All in all, though there is no reason to expect the impacts of reductions in trade costs and productivity growth to be additive, the combined average gains to the rest of the world from these two experiments are 0.28 percent, equivalent to three-quarters of the total average gains from trade with emerging giants, which are 0.37 percent.

Distributional Effects

The key feature of the fixed-factors equilibrium is that the changes in real wages and returns to capital brought about by the opening of emerging giants will differ across sectors. This allows us to examine the distributional effects of this episode. Tables A4 and A5 report the summary statistics for the distribution of sectoral real wage changes (w_n^j/P_n's) for the emerging giant and the rest of the world samples, respectively.[10]

The first important conclusion is that the distributional effects are an order of magnitude larger than the average/aggregate effects. We saw above that for emerging giants, aggregate welfare gains were on the order of a few percentage points, ranging from about 1.7 percent to about 14 percent in this set of countries. The cross-sectoral standard deviation of real wage changes, by contrast, ranges from 7.24 percent in Poland to 31.96 percent for Kazakhstan, with an average of 15.76 percent. The range of outcomes is very wide, from large losses (more than halving of the real wage) to large gains (such as a doubling of the real wage). For the rest of the world, both the aggregate gains (as we saw above), and the dispersion are smaller, but it is still the case that the distributional consequences are far larger than the aggregate changes.

We now document the patterns found in these sectoral real wage changes. The first question we ask is, are there particular sectors that bore the brunt of the adjustment, and others that on average benefited the most? Table 7 reports the cross-country medians of the real wage changes in each sector, separately for the emerging giants and the rest of the world. The beneficiary sectors for emerging giants are Wood Products, Leather and Footwear, Basic Metals, and Wearing Apparel. By contrast, Medical, Precision, and Optical Instruments and Paper and Paper Products experience net losses, on average. For the Rest of the World, the sectors with the largest losses are Wearing Apparel, Textiles, Furniture, and Leather and Footwear, all experiencing absolute losses between 1.5 and 3.5 percent.

There is a striking (though not surprising) regularity that the sectoral gains and losses are negatively correlated across the two groups. Figure 5 presents a scatterplot of sectoral wage changes in the rest of the world on the y-axis against sectoral wage changes in emerging giants, along with the least squares fit line. The negative relationship is quite pronounced, with the correlation of -0.63. Sectors that tend to gain in emerging giant countries tend to lose in the rest of the world, and vice versa. By and large, the opening of emerging giants benefited light manufacturing in the emerging giants (Textiles, Apparel, Footwear), and hurt workers in those sectors elsewhere. By contrast, in the rest of the world workers in high-tech manufacturing sectors (Medical and Precision Machinery, Office and Computing Equipment) tend to gain.

This pronounced global pattern at sector level hides a fair amount of heterogeneity across countries and regions. Figure 6 plots, for each sector, the median real wage change in each region. For emerging giants, we separate China, India, and the median for the CEECs. For the rest of the world, we report medians

[10]Owing to the Cobb-Douglas assumption in production, the changes in real returns to capital are very close to the changes in real wages, both in terms of the overall magnitudes, and in terms of correlations between changes in real wages and real returns to capital across country-sectors. Thus, the focus on real wages is in some sense without loss of generality.

Table 7. Sectoral Real Wage Changes, Medians

ISIC code	Sector Name	Emerging Giants	Rest of World
15	Food and Beverages	0.57	0.67
16	Tobacco Products	0.92	–0.40
17	Textiles	9.97	–2.27
18	Wearing Apparel, Fur	10.81	–3.64
19	Leather, Leather Products, Footwear	16.67	–1.29
20	Wood Products (Excl. Furniture)	18.35	–0.65
21	Paper and Paper Products	–0.99	1.30
22	Printing and Publishing	2.12	0.15
23	Coke, Refined Petroleum Products, Nuclear Fuel	10.61	–0.53
24	Chemical and Chemical Products	0.86	0.56
25	Rubber and Plastics Products	9.91	–0.91
26	Nonmetallic Mineral Products	6.83	–0.82
27	Basic Metals	13.91	0.37
28	Fabricated Metal Products	3.79	–0.30
29C	Office, Accounting, Computing, and Other Machinery	0.53	1.52
31A	Electrical Machinery, Communication Equipment	5.89	–0.19
33	Medical, Precision, and Optical Instruments	–2.56	1.55
34A	Transport Equipment	2.22	0.85
36	Furniture and Other Manufacturing	7.45	–1.43
4A	Nontradables	6.03	0.28

Notes: This table reports the median percentage changes in real wages (w_n^j/P_n) in each sector, separating emerging giants and the rest of the world.

Figure 5. Changes in Real Factor Returns by Sector: Emerging Giants vs. Rest of World

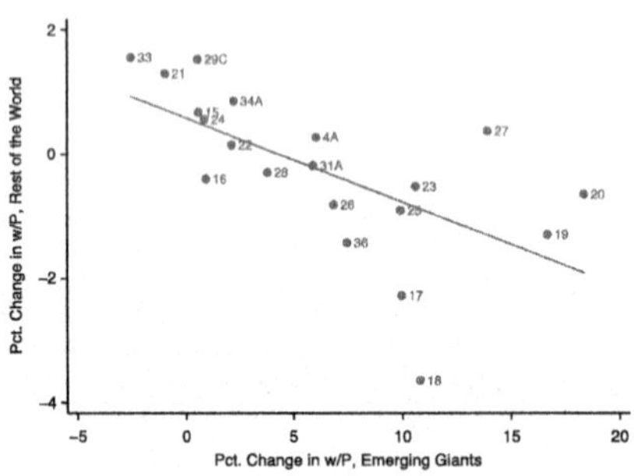

Notes: This figure displays the median percentage change in the real wage in the rest of the world (y-axis) against the median percentage change in the real wage in the emerging giants in each sector. The key for sector labels is reported in Table A2.

for each major region/country group. (The numbers used to build this figure are reported in Table A6.) The cross-regional heterogeneity is apparent. For instance, the rest of the world loses on average in Wearing Apparel. We see from the figure

Figure 6. Changes in Real Wages, Fixed Factors, by Sector and Region: (a) Rest of World; (b) Emerging Giants

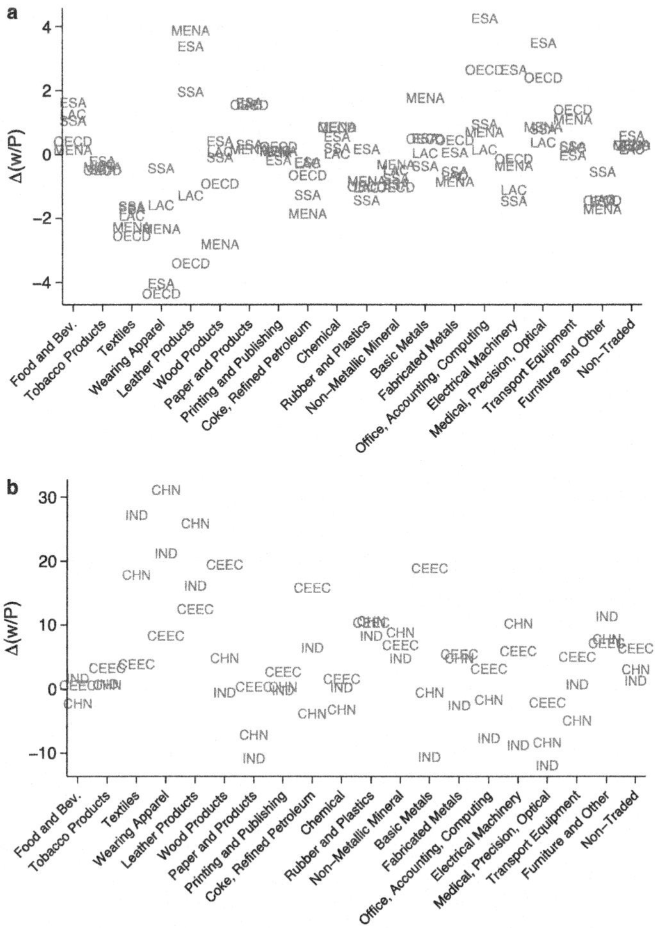

Notes: This figure displays the scatterplots of the median percentage changes in real wages in the rest of the world (top panel) and in emerging giants (bottom panel) in each sector and each region when emerging giants open to trade but factors cannot reallocate across sectors. Region label key: CHN = China, IND = India, CEEC = CEECs, OECD = OECD, ESA = East and South Asia, LAC = Latin America and Caribbean, MENA = Middle East and North Africa, SSA = sub-Saharan Africa.

Figure 7. Changes in Real Wages and Sectoral Productivity: Partial Correlations: (a) Rest of World; (b) Emerging Giants

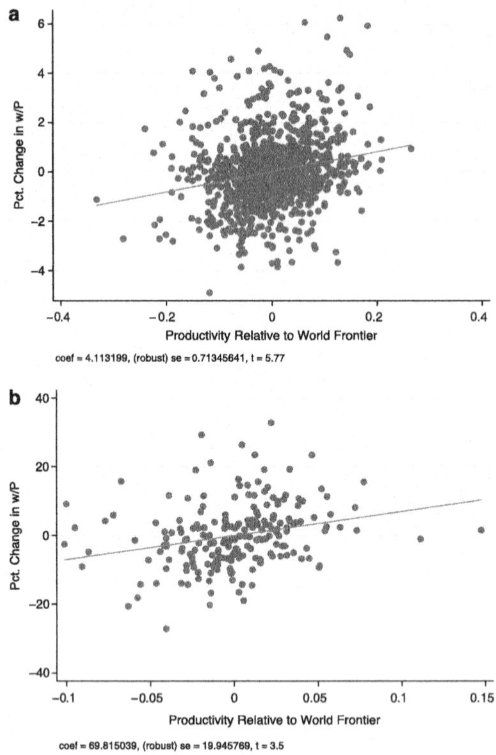

Notes: This figure displays the partial correlations between changes in sectoral real wages and the productivity relative to the world frontier in a sector, after partialling out the full set of country and sector effects. The top panel represents the rest of the world, the bottom panel emerging giants.

that the highest losses in that sector were in the OECD and East and South Asia. For Leather and Footwear, the gains across regions actually range from large negative for the OECD to large positive for the Middle East/North Africa and East and South Asia. On average we found that the high-tech manufacturing sectors in the rest of the world tend to benefit. It is clear from the figure that the main beneficiaries are the OECD and East and South Asian countries.

For the emerging giants, we see a great deal of dispersion within each sector as well. In the light manufacturing sectors, the gains to China and India are much larger than to the CEECs, whereas the losses in Paper and Products and high-tech manufacturing are also larger for China and India. There are sectors, notably Basic Metals, for which the regions diverge dramatically, some exhibiting largest losses, some largest gains.

Finally, we disaggregate further to the country level and exploit the role of sectoral productivity (T_n^j) in driving the real wage changes. Although import competition should lower real wages on average, it should still be the case that the losses are smaller (or gains are larger) in countries in which a sector is more productive. To assess the importance of this effect, we regress the percent change in the real wage on the full set of country and sector effects, as well as sectoral productivity expressed as a ratio to world frontier, $(T_n^j/T_F^j)^{1/\theta}$. The partial correlation plots are presented in Figure 7, broken down into two country groups. In both the rest of the world and the emerging giants, relatively more productive sectors gain more/lose less. The effect is highly statistically significant (we use robust standard errors), and economically large.[11] In the rest of the world one standard deviation change in T relative to the frontier (a change 0.24, for example, a move from 0.2 to 0.44 of the world frontier productivity) leads to a 1 percentage point higher real wage due to the opening of emerging giants. Given that average real wage changes are for the most part less than 1 percent, this is a large effect. In other words, although import-competing sectors such as Wearing Apparel, Textiles, and Footwear do lose from the opening of emerging giants on average, for individual sectors in individual countries higher productivity can still play a major role in mitigating the losses.

III. Conclusion

The rapid trade integration of the major emerging markets has been the major development in world trade over the past 20 years. This paper carries out a quantitative assessment of both aggregate and distributional consequences of the emerging giants' trade opening. Our findings can be summarized as follows. First, the aggregate welfare gains from the integration of emerging giants to the rest of the world are 0.37 percent on average, with a range from modest absolute losses in a small number of countries to gains of 1–2 percentage points. Second, cross-sectoral reallocation of labor and capital contributes only modestly (0.065 percentage points) to the overall aggregate gains. This is because there is a great deal of room for within-sector reallocation of production to reap the gains from trade with these countries. Third, there are strong complementarities between cross-sectoral mobility of factors. Fixing one of the factors to its initial sectors results in very similar welfare losses to the case in which both factors cannot move. This suggests that policies promoting smooth functioning of labor and capital markets will have the largest effect when implemented together. Fourth, the distributional consequences of this episode of trade opening are an order of magnitude larger than aggregate consequences. Although aggregate gains to a

[11]These figures are presented dropping the top 2.5 percent and bottom 2.5 percent of the sample in terms of percentage changes in the real wage. Keeping outliers does not change the size or significance of the coefficients.

typical country are a fraction of a percent, the real wage changes across sectors typically range from −5 to 5 percent. There are pronounced patterns in the distributional impact of emerging giants. Light manufacturing industries tend to gain the most in emerging giants, and lose the most in the rest of the world, and the opposite is true for high-tech manufacturing. Controlling for sectoral and country average changes, more productive sectors gain more.

APPENDIX

Procedure for Estimating T^j_n, d^j_{ni}, and ω_j

This appendix reproduces from Levchenko and Zhang (2011) the details of the procedure for estimating technology, trade costs, and taste parameters required to implement the model. Interested readers should consult that paper for further details on estimation steps and data sources.

Tradable Sector Relative Technology

We now focus on the tradable sectors. Following the standard EK approach, first divide trade shares by their domestic counterpart:

$$\frac{\pi^j_{ni}}{\pi^j_{nn}} = \frac{X^j_{ni}}{X^j_{nn}} = \frac{T^j_i\left(c^j_i d^j_{ni}\right)^{-\theta}}{T^j_n\left(c^j_n\right)^{-\theta}},$$

which in logs becomes:

$$\ln\left(\frac{X^j_{ni}}{X^j_{nn}}\right) = \ln\left(T^j_i(c^j_i)^{-\theta}\right) - \ln\left(T^j_n(c^j_n)^{-\theta}\right) - \theta \ln d^j_{ni}.$$

Let the (log) iceberg costs be given by the following expression:

$$\ln d^j_{ni} = d^j_k + b^j_{ni} + CU^j_{ni} + RTA^j_{ni} + ex^j_i + \nu^j_{ni},$$

where d^j_k is an indicator variable for a distance interval. Following EK, we set the distance intervals, in miles, to [0, 350], [350, 750], [750, 1500], [1500, 3000], [3000, 6000], [6000, maximum). Additional variables are whether the two countries share a common border (b^j_{ni}), belong to a currency union (CU^j_{ni}), or to a regional trade agreement (RTA^j_{ni}). Following the arguments in Waugh (2010), we include an exporter fixed effect ex^j_i. Finally, there is an error term ν^j_{ni}. Note that all the variables have a sector superscript j: we allow all the trade cost proxy variables to affect true iceberg trade costs d^j_{ni} differentially across sectors. There is a range of evidence that trade volumes at sector level vary in their sensitivity to distance or common border (see, among many others, Do and Levchenko, 2007; Berthelon and Freund, 2008).

This leads to the following final estimating equation:

$$\ln\left(\frac{X_{ni}^j}{X_{nn}^j}\right) = \underbrace{\ln\left(T_i^j(c_i^j)^{-\theta}\right) - \theta ex_i^j}_{\text{Exporter Fixed Effect}} \underbrace{- \ln\left(T_n^j(c_n^j)^{-\theta}\right)}_{\text{Importer Fixed Effect}}$$

$$\underbrace{-\theta d_k^j - \theta b_{ni}^j - \theta CU_{ni}^j - \theta RTA_{ni}^j}_{\text{Bilateral Observables}} \underbrace{-\theta \nu_{ni}^j}_{\text{Error Term}} .$$

This equation is estimated for each tradable sector $j = 1,\ldots J$. Estimating this relationship will thus yield, for each country, an estimate of its technology-cum-unit-cost term in each sector j, $T_n^j(c_n^j)^{-\theta}$, which is obtained by exponentiating the importer fixed effect. The available degrees of freedom imply that these estimates are of each country's $T_n^j(c_n^j)^{-\theta}$ relative to a reference country, which in our estimation is the United States. We denote this estimated value by S_n^j:

$$S_n^j = \frac{T_n^j}{T_{us}^j}\left(\frac{c_n^j}{c_{us}^j}\right)^{-\theta},$$

where the subscript us denotes the United States. It is immediate from this expression that estimation delivers a convolution of technology parameters T_n^j and cost parameters c_n^j. Both will of course affect trade volumes, but we would like to extract technology T_n^j from these estimates. In order to do that, we follow the approach of Shikher (2012). In particular, for each country n, the share of total spending going to home-produced goods is given by:

$$\frac{X_{nn}^j}{X_n^j} = T_n^j\left(\frac{\Gamma c_n^j}{p_n^j}\right)^{-\theta}.$$

Dividing by its U.S. counterpart yields:

$$\frac{X_{nn}^j/X_n^j}{X_{us,us}^j/X_{us}^j} = \frac{T_n^j}{T_{us}^j}\left(\frac{c_n^j}{c_{us}^j}\frac{p_{us}^j}{p_n^j}\right)^{-\theta} = S_n^j\left(\frac{p_{us}^j}{p_n^j}\right)^{-\theta},$$

and thus the ratio of price levels in sector j relative to the United States becomes:

$$\frac{p_n^j}{p_{us}^j} = \left(\frac{X_{nn}^j/X_n^j}{X_{us,us}^j/X_{us}^j}\frac{1}{S_n^j}\right)^{\frac{1}{\theta}}. \qquad \text{(A.1)}$$

The entire right-hand side of this expression is either observable or estimated. Thus, we can impute the price levels relative to the United States in each country and each tradable sector.

The cost of the input bundles relative to the United States can be written as:

$$\frac{c_n^j}{c_{us}^j} = \left(\frac{w_n}{w_{us}}\right)^{\alpha_j\beta_j}\left(\frac{r_n}{r_{us}}\right)^{(1-\alpha_j)\beta_j}\left(\prod_{k=1}^{J}\left(\frac{p_n^k}{p_{us}^k}\right)^{\gamma_{kj}}\right)^{1-\beta_j}\left(\frac{p_n^{J+1}}{p_{us}^{J+1}}\right)^{\gamma_{J+1,j}(1-\beta_j)}.$$

Using information on relative wages, returns to capital, price in each tradable sector from Equation (A.1), and the nontradable sector price relative to the United States, we can thus impute the costs of the input bundles relative to the United States. in each country and each sector. Armed with those values, it is straightforward to back out the relative technology parameters:

$$\frac{T_n^j}{T_{us}^j} = S_n^j\left(\frac{c_n^j}{c_{us}^j}\right)^{\theta}.$$

Trade Costs

The bilateral, directional, sector-level trade costs of shipping from country i to country n in sector j are then computed based on the estimated coefficients as:

$$\ln \hat{d}^j_{ni} = \theta \hat{d}^j_k + \theta \hat{b}^j_{ni} + \theta \widehat{CU}^j_{ni} + \theta \widehat{RTA}^j_{ni} + \theta \widehat{ex}^j_i + \theta \hat{\nu}^j_{ni},$$

for an assumed value of θ. Note that the estimate of the trade costs includes the residual from the gravity regression $\theta \hat{\nu}^j_{ni}$. Thus, the trade costs computed as above will fit bilateral sectoral trade flows exactly, given the estimated fixed effects. Note also that the exporter component of the trade costs $\widehat{ex}^j_i$ is part of the exporter fixed effect. As each country in the sample appears as both an exporter and an importer, the exporter and importer estimated fixed effects are combined to extract an estimate of $\theta \widehat{ex}^j_i$.

Complete Estimation

So far we have estimated the levels of technology of the tradable sectors relative to the United States. To complete our estimation, we still need to find (i) the levels of T for the tradable sectors in the United States; (ii) the taste parameters ω_j, and (iii) the nontradable technology levels for all countries.

To obtain (i), we use the NBER-CES Manufacturing Industry Database for the United States (Bartelsman and Gray, 1996). We start by measuring the observed TFP levels for the tradable sectors in the United States. The form of the production function gives

$$\ln Z^j_{us} = \ln \Lambda^j_{us} + \beta_j \alpha_j \ln L^j_{us} + \beta_j (1 - \alpha_j) \ln K^j_{us} + (1 - \beta_j) \sum_{k=1}^{J+1} \gamma_{k,j} \ln M^{k,j}_{us}, \qquad \text{(A.2)}$$

where Λ^j denotes the measured TFP in sector j, Z^j denotes the output, L^j denotes the labor input, K^j denotes the capital input, and $M^{k,j}$ denotes the intermediate input from sector k. The NBER-CES Manufacturing Industry Database offers information on output, and inputs of labor, capital, and intermediates, along with deflators for each. Thus, we can estimate the observed TFP level for each manufacturing tradable sector using the above equation.

If the United States were a closed economy, the observed TFP level for sector j would be given by $\Lambda^j_{us} = (T^j_{us})^{\frac{1}{\theta}}$. In the open economies, the goods with inefficient domestic productivity draws will not be produced and will be imported instead. Thus, international trade and competition introduce selection in the observed TFP level, as demonstrated by Finicelli, Pagano, and Sbracia (2013). We thus use the model to back out the true level of T^j_{us} of each tradable sector in the United States. Here we follow Finicelli, Pagano, and Sbracia (2013) and use the following relationship:

$$(\Lambda^j_{us})^{\theta} = T^j_{us} + \sum_{i \neq us} T^j_i \left(\frac{c^j_i d^j_{us,i}}{c^j_{us}} \right)^{-\theta}.$$

Thus, we have

$$(\Lambda^j_{us})^{\theta} = T^j_{us} \left[1 + \sum_{i \neq us} \frac{T^j_i}{T^j_{us}} \left(\frac{c^j_i d^j_{us,i}}{c^j_{us}} \right)^{-\theta} \right] = T^j_{us} \left[1 + \sum_{i \neq us} S^j_i \left(d^j_{us,i} \right)^{-\theta} \right]. \qquad \text{(A.3)}$$

This equation can be solved for underlying technology parameters T^j_{us} in the United States, given estimated observed TFP Λ^j_{us}, and all the S^j_i's and $d^j_{us,i}$'s estimated in the previous subsection.

To estimate the taste parameters $\{\omega_j\}_{j=1}^{j}$, we use information on final consumption shares in the tradable sectors in the United States. We start with a guess of $\{\omega_j\}_{j=1}^{j}$ and find sectoral prices p_n^k as follows. For an initial guess of sectoral prices, we compute the tradable sector aggregate price and the nontradable sector price using the data on the relative prices of nontradables to tradables. Using these prices, we calculate sectoral unit costs and Φ_n^j's, and update prices according to Equation (2), iterating until the prices converge. We then update the taste parameters according to Equation (5), using the data on final sectoral expenditure shares in the United States. We normalize the vector of ω_j's to have a sum of one, and repeat the above procedure until the values for the taste parameters converge.

Finally, we estimate the nontradable sector TFP using the relative prices. In the model, the nontradable sector price is given by:

$$p_n^{J+1} = \Gamma(T_n^{J+1})^{-\frac{1}{\theta}} c_n^{J+1}.$$

As we know the aggregate price level in the tradable sector p_n^T, c_n^{j+1}, and the relative price of nontradables (which we take from the data), we can back out T_n^{j+1} from the equation above for all countries (see Tables A1–A6).

Table A1. Country Coverage

Emerging Giants
Bulgaria
China
Czech Republic
Hungary
India
Kazakhstan
Poland
Romania
Russian Federation
Slovak Republic
Slovenia
Ukraine

OECD
Australia
Austria
Belgium-Luxembourg
Canada
Denmark
Finland
France
Germany
Greece
Iceland
Ireland
Italy
Japan
Netherlands
New Zealand
Norway
Portugal
Spain
Sweden
Switzerland
United Kingdom
United States

East and South Asia
Bangladesh
Fiji
Indonesia
Korea, Rep.
Malaysia
Pakistan
Philippines
Sri Lanka
Taiwan Province of China
Thailand
Vietnam

Latin America and Caribbean
Argentina
Bolivia
Brazil
Chile
Colombia
Costa Rica
Ecuador
El Salvador
Guatemala
Honduras
Mexico
Peru
Trinidad and Tobago
Uruguay
Venezuela, RB

Middle East and North Africa
Egypt, Arab Rep.
Iran, Islamic Rep.
Israel
Jordan
Kuwait
Saudi Arabia
Turkey

Sub-Saharan Africa
Ethiopia
Ghana
Kenya
Mauritius
Nigeria
Senegal
South Africa
Tanzania

Notes: This table reports the countries in the sample.

Table A2. Sectors

ISIC code	Sector Name	α_j	β_j	$\gamma_{J+1,j}$	ω_j
15	Food and Beverages	0.290	0.290	0.303	0.169
16	Tobacco Products	0.272	0.490	0.527	0.014
17	Textiles	0.444	0.368	0.295	0.019
18	Wearing Apparel, Fur	0.468	0.369	0.320	0.109
19	Leather, Leather Products, Footwear	0.469	0.350	0.330	0.015
20	Wood Products (Excl. Furniture)	0.455	0.368	0.288	0.008
21	Paper and Paper Products	0.351	0.341	0.407	0.012
22	Printing and Publishing	0.484	0.453	0.407	0.005
23	Coke, Refined Petroleum Products, Nuclear Fuel	0.248	0.246	0.246	0.141
24	Chemical and Chemical Products	0.297	0.368	0.479	0.009
25	Rubber and Plastics Products	0.366	0.375	0.350	0.014
26	Nonmetallic Mineral Products	0.350	0.448	0.499	0.073
27	Basic Metals	0.345	0.298	0.451	0.002
28	Fabricated Metal Products	0.424	0.387	0.364	0.013
29C	Office, Accounting, Computing, and Other Machinery	0.481	0.381	0.388	0.051
31A	Electrical Machinery, Communication Equipment	0.369	0.368	0.416	0.022
33	Medical, Precision, and Optical Instruments	0.451	0.428	0.441	0.038
34A	Transport Equipment	0.437	0.329	0.286	0.220
36	Furniture and Other Manufacturing	0.447	0.396	0.397	0.065
4A	Nontradables	0.561	0.651	0.788	
	Mean	0.400	0.385	0.399	0.053
	Min	0.248	0.246	0.246	0.002
	Max	0.561	0.651	0.788	0.220

Notes: This table reports the sectors used in the analysis. The classification corresponds to the ISIC Revision 3 2-digit, aggregated further because of data availability. α_j is the value-added-based labor intensity; β_j is the share of value added in total output; $\gamma_{J+1,j}$ is the share of nontradable inputs in total intermediate inputs; ω_j is the taste parameter for tradable sector j, estimated using the procedure described in the Appendix. Variable definitions and sources are described in detail in the text.

Table A3. Sectoral Labor Shares: Correlations of Model and Data, by Region

	Mean	Median	Min.	Max.	Countries
Emerging giants	0.627	0.704	0.202	0.861	8
OECD	0.764	0.790	0.479	0.927	18
East and South Asia	0.792	0.800	0.675	0.878	8
Latin America and Caribbean	0.717	0.743	0.351	0.957	9
Middle East and North Africa	0.514	0.581	–0.001	0.766	6
Sub-Saharan Africa	0.833	0.864	0.638	0.997	3

Notes: This table summarizes the country-specific correlations between sectoral labor shares between the model and the data, by region and country group.

Table A4. Emerging Giants: Sectoral Real Wage Changes, Summary Statistics by Country

	Mean	Median	St. Dev.	Min.	Max.
Bulgaria	14.275	11.207	20.058	−23.994	75.773
China	4.668	1.846	10.511	−8.390	31.037
Czech Republic	4.332	5.107	8.689	−8.219	19.624
Hungary	5.360	3.527	10.618	−10.231	39.865
India	2.327	0.753	10.555	−11.946	27.139
Kazakhstan	7.426	3.662	31.958	−34.266	123.651
Poland	4.436	4.259	7.235	−7.215	20.095
Romania	7.179	7.746	22.622	−74.360	42.703
Russian Federation	4.663	−1.635	18.307	−17.603	50.224
Slovak Republic	7.661	8.968	11.834	−16.095	28.412
Slovenia	6.539	13.353	21.790	−67.104	24.555
Ukraine	7.637	4.163	14.923	−11.734	52.387

Notes: This table reports the median percentage changes in real wages (w_n^j/P_n) in each sector, by region.

Table A5. Rest of the World: Sectoral Real Wage Changes, Summary Statistics by Country

	Mean	Median	St. Dev.	Min.	Max.
Argentina	−0.334	−0.783	2.224	−2.594	7.252
Australia	0.303	0.151	3.512	−6.771	11.827
Austria	0.250	0.150	1.878	−4.146	4.242
Bangladesh	0.256	0.322	2.948	−6.767	9.380
Belgium-Luxembourg	−0.065	0.231	2.374	−4.476	5.089
Bolivia	0.008	−0.116	1.496	−2.747	3.127
Brazil	−0.201	−0.223	1.029	−2.033	1.931
Canada	−0.310	−0.116	1.956	−4.632	2.872
Chile	−0.663	−0.479	1.917	−4.623	3.937
Colombia	−0.059	0.003	0.975	−1.788	1.551
Costa Rica	−0.966	−1.122	2.025	−4.237	5.585
Denmark	0.076	−0.062	1.720	−3.280	3.619
Ecuador	−0.116	−0.159	0.875	−1.889	1.581
Egypt, Arab Rep.	0.347	0.270	1.867	−2.199	5.533
El Salvador	0.241	0.385	1.324	−2.423	2.170
Ethiopia	0.064	−0.193	2.367	−3.505	7.021
Fiji	0.447	0.602	2.992	−8.515	4.412
Finland	−0.309	0.130	1.935	−5.253	3.358
France	−0.385	−0.174	1.847	−4.419	2.463
Germany	−0.328	−0.328	2.028	−4.236	3.595
Ghana	−0.189	−0.202	1.704	−2.642	5.536
Greece	0.237	0.592	1.338	−2.633	1.779
Guatemala	−0.360	−0.357	1.693	−2.774	3.818
Honduras	0.404	0.493	1.093	−1.808	2.066
Iceland	−0.290	0.189	1.682	−4.470	2.523
Indonesia	0.782	0.478	3.241	−4.043	11.343
Iran, Islamic Rep.	0.191	0.066	2.473	−4.148	6.275
Ireland	−1.089	−0.751	2.249	−5.708	1.758

Table A5: *(Continued)*

	Mean	Median	St. Dev.	Min.	Max.
Israel	−0.557	−0.056	2.256	−4.720	3.820
Italy	−0.051	0.014	1.508	−3.343	3.261
Japan	−0.718	−0.095	3.412	−11.567	4.694
Jordan	0.791	0.097	3.850	−4.144	15.753
Kenya	0.123	−0.198	1.988	−1.912	7.247
Korea, Rep.	0.720	0.440	3.030	−3.644	8.232
Kuwait	−0.056	−2.073	6.553	−5.760	23.051
Malaysia	0.374	0.025	2.338	−4.391	4.135
Mauritius	0.188	0.320	2.022	−4.833	3.681
Mexico	−0.109	0.094	1.588	−3.712	2.350
Netherlands	0.114	0.105	2.107	−4.062	4.787
New Zealand	−0.222	−0.100	2.345	−5.841	4.689
Nigeria	−0.069	−0.042	0.900	−2.962	1.322
Norway	−0.394	−0.036	2.189	−6.104	2.980
Pakistan	0.314	−0.005	2.391	−5.770	5.428
Peru	−0.784	−0.934	2.173	−3.761	6.576
Philippines	−0.321	−1.196	4.462	−5.153	14.520
Portugal	0.090	0.154	1.818	−3.881	3.513
Saudi Arabia	0.271	−0.751	5.187	−4.966	20.942
Senegal	0.637	−0.707	9.954	−8.199	41.274
South Africa	0.190	0.202	1.938	−2.506	5.390
Spain	−0.212	−0.083	1.479	−3.239	2.062
Sri Lanka	6.247	3.430	10.383	−8.741	43.442
Sweden	−0.435	0.063	1.917	−4.825	2.805
Switzerland	−0.703	−0.610	1.973	−4.807	2.839
Taiwan Province of China	0.523	−0.554	4.875	−6.972	17.459
Tanzania	0.231	0.320	2.257	−3.455	5.690
Thailand	0.185	0.063	2.735	−5.015	7.553
Trinidad and Tobago	−0.262	0.051	1.429	−3.008	1.633
Turkey	0.799	0.415	1.958	−2.479	4.586
United Kingdom	−0.233	−0.108	1.774	−4.315	3.094
United States	−0.400	−0.127	1.924	−4.944	3.207
Uruguay	−0.184	−0.221	1.031	−1.905	1.977
Venezuela, RB	−0.270	−0.167	0.795	−1.532	1.353
Vietnam	0.971	0.578	2.015	−2.917	4.580

Notes: This table reports the median percentage changes in real wages (w_n^j/P_n) in each sector, by region.

Table A6. Sectoral Real Wage Changes, Medians by Region

ISIC code	Sector Name	China	India	East. Europe and Cent. Asia	OECD	East and South Asia	Latin America and Carib.	Middle East and N. Africa	Sub-Saharan Africa
15	Food and Beverages	−2.256	1.629	0.565	0.410	1.623	1.255	0.146	1.057
16	Tobacco Products	0.638	0.786	3.254	−0.507	−0.219	−0.326	−0.405	−0.479
17	Textiles	17.772	27.139	3.851	−2.557	−1.716	−1.927	−2.275	−1.632
18	Wearing Apparel, Fur	31.037	21.166	8.269	−4.367	−4.043	−1.597	−2.339	−0.445
19	Leather, Leather Products, Footwear	25.836	16.074	12.427	−3.411	3.375	−1.294	3.868	1.954
20	Wood Products (Excl. Furniture)	4.805	−0.558	19.416	−0.928	0.413	0.079	−2.810	−0.103
21	Paper and Paper Products	−7.188	−10.870	0.344	1.545	1.613	1.551	0.162	0.304
22	Printing and Publishing	0.319	−0.197	2.652	0.236	−0.189	0.110	0.099	0.068
23	Coke, Refined Petroleum, Fuel	−3.882	6.416	15.740	−0.664	−0.258	−0.290	−1.863	−1.280
24	Chemical and Chemical Products	−3.225	0.241	1.565	0.845	0.558	0.013	0.861	0.195
25	Rubber and Plastics Products	10.546	8.264	10.332	−1.014	0.170	−1.045	−0.844	−1.443
26	Nonmetallic Mineral Products	8.794	4.764	6.834	−1.034	−0.951	−0.505	−0.327	−0.754
27	Basic Metals	−0.545	−10.630	18.824	0.492	0.511	0.035	1.771	−0.372
28	Fabricated Metal Products	4.787	−2.590	5.417	0.449	0.058	−0.660	−0.865	−0.545
29C	Office, Accounting, Computing Mach.	−1.694	−7.685	3.136	2.641	4.254	0.154	0.699	0.946
31A	Electrical Machinery, Comm. Equip.	10.178	−8.782	5.894	−0.143	2.644	−1.118	−0.363	−1.465
33	Medical, Precision, and Optical Instr.	−8.390	−11.946	−2.124	2.397	3.486	0.375	0.858	0.791
34A	Transport Equipment	−4.972	0.719	4.988	1.398	−0.039	0.208	1.092	0.254
36	Furniture and Other Manufacturing	7.745	11.293	7.120	−1.446	−1.488	−1.426	−1.726	−0.554
4A	Nontradables	3.053	1.303	6.322	0.275	0.580	0.160	0.300	0.247

Notes: This table reports the median percentage changes in real wages (w_n^j/P_n) in each sector, by region.

REFERENCES

Artuç, Erhan, 2009, "Intergenerational Effects of Trade Liberalization," December 2009. TUSYAD-Koç University Economic Research Forum Working Paper 0913.

Artuç, Erhan, Shubham Chaudhuri and John McLaren, 2010, "Trade Shocks and Labor Adjustment: A Structural Empirical Approach," *American Economic Review*, Vol. 100, No. 3, pp. 1008–45.

Autor, David, David Dorn and Gordon Hanson, 2012a, "The China Syndrome: Local Labor Market Effects of Import Competition in the United States," May. mimeo, MIT, CEMFI, and UC San Diego.

Autor, David H., David Dorn, Gordon H. Hanson and Jae Song, 2012b, "Trade Adjustment: Worker Level Evidence," July 2012. mimeo, MIT, CEMFI, UC San Diego, and SSA.

Baldwin, Richard E., Joseph F. Francois and Richard Portes, 1997, "The Costs and Benefits of Eastern Enlargement: The Impact on the EU and Central Europe," *Economic Policy*, Vol. 12, No. 24, pp. 125–176.

Baourakis, George, Csilla Lakatos and Anastasios Xepapadeas, 2008, "Economic Implications of the EU Accession of Bulgaria and Romania: A CGE Approach," TradeAg —Agricultural Trade Agreements Working Paper Series 08/1.

Bartelsman, Eric J. and Wayne Gray, 1996, "The NBER Manufacturing Productivity Database," October. NBER Technical Working Paper 205.

Bernanke, Ben and Refet Gürkaynak, 2001, "Is Growth Exogenous? Taking Mankiw, Romer, and Weil Seriously," *NBER Macroeconomics Annual*, Vol. 16, No. 1, pp. 11–57.

Berthelon, Matias and Caroline Freund, 2008, "On the Conservation of Distance in International Trade," *Journal of International Economics*, Vol. 75, No. 2, pp. 310–320.

Bhagwati, Jagdish and V.K. Ramaswami, 1963, "Domestic Distortions, Tariffs and the Theory of Optimum Subsidy," *Journal of Political Economy*, Vol. 71, No. 1, pp. 44–50.

Bloom, Nicholas, Mirko Draca and John Van Reenen, 2011, "Trade Induced Technical Change: The Impact of Chinese Imports on Innovation, Diffusion and Productivity," January 2011, NBER WP 16717.

Brown, Drusilla K., Alan V. Deardoroff, Simeon Djankov and Robert M. Stern, 1997, "An Economic Assessment of the Integration of Czechoslovakia, Hungary, and Poland into the European Union," in *Europe's Economy Looks East: Implications for Germany and the European Union*, ed. by Stanley W. Black (New York: Cambridge University Press).

Caliendo, Lorenzo and Fernando Parro, 2010, "Estimates of the Trade and Welfare Effects of NAFTA," January 2010, mimeo, University of Chicago.

Caselli, Francesco, 2005, "Accounting for Cross-Country Income Differences," in *Handbook of Economic Growth* Vol. 1, ed. by Steven Durlauf Philippe Aghion (Amsterdam: Elsevier-North Holland) Chapter 9, pp. 679–741.

Chen, Natalie and Dennis Novy, 2011, "Gravity, Trade Integration, and Heterogeneity across Industries," *Journal of International Economics*, Vol. 85, No. 2, pp. 206–221.

Coleman, Wilbur John, 2007, "Accommodating Emerging Giants," November 2007, mimeo, Duke University.

Costinot, Arnaud, Dave Donaldson and Ivana Komunjer, 2012, "What Goods Do Countries Trade? A Quantitative Exploration of Ricardo's Ideas," *Review of Economic Studies*, Vol. 79, No. 2, pp. 581–608.

di Giovanni, Julian and Andrei A. Levchenko, 2010, "Putting the Parts Together: Trade, Vertical Linkages, and Business Cycle Comovement," *American Economic Journal: Macroeconomics*, Vol. 2, No. 2, pp. 95–124.

di Giovanni, Julian, Andrei A. Levchenko and Jing Zhang, 2013, "The Global Welfare Impact of China: Trade Integration and Technological Change," *American Economic Journal: Macroeconomics*, May, Forthcoming.

Dix-Carneiro, Raphael, 2011, "Trade Liberalization and Labor Market Dynamics," December 2011, mimeo, University of Maryland.

Do, Quy-Toan and Andrei A. Levchenko, 2007, "Comparative Advantage, Demand for External Finance, and Financial Development," *Journal of Financial Economics*, Vol. 86, No. 3, pp. 796–834.

Dornbusch, Rudiger, Stanley Fischer and Paul Samuelson, 1977, "Comparative Advantage, Trade, and Payments in a Ricardian Model with a Continuum of Goods," *American Economic Review*, Vol. 67, No. 5, pp. 823–39.

Eaton, Jonathan and Samuel Kortum, 2002, "Technology, Geography, and Trade," *Econometrica*, Vol. 70, No. 5, pp. 1741–1779.

Finicelli, Andrea, Patrizio Pagano and Massimo Sbracia, 2013, "Ricardian Selection," *Journal of International Economics*, Vol. 89, No. 1, pp. 96–109.

Francois, Joseph F. and Ganeshan Wignaraja, 2008, "Economic Implications of Asian Integration," *Global Economy Journal*, Vol. 8, No. 3, Article 1.

GAO. 2012, "TRADE ADJUSTMENT ASSISTANCE Commerce Program Has Helped Manufacturing and Services Firms, but Measures, Data, and Funding Formula Could Improve," September 2012. Report to Congressional Committees.

Ghosh, Madanmohan and Someshwar Rao, 2010, "Chinese Accession to the WTO: Economic Implications for China, Other Asian and North American Economies," *Journal of Policy Modeling*, Vol. 32, No. 3, pp. 389–98.

Haberler, Gottfried, 1950, "Some Problems in the Pure Theory of International Trade," *Economic Journal*, Vol. 60, No. 238, pp. 223–240.

Hagen, Everett E., 1958, "An Economic Justification of Protectionism," *The Quarterly Journal of Economics*, Vol. 72, No. 4, pp. 496–514.

Hall, Robert and Charles Jones, 1999, "Why Do Some Countries Produce So Much More Output per Worker then Others," *Quarterly Journal of Economics*, Vol. 114, No. 1, pp. 83–116.

Hanson, Gordan H., 2010, "Why Isn't Mexico Rich?," *Journal of Economic Literature*, Vol. 48, No. 4, pp. 987–1004.

Hanson, Gordan H. and Raymond Robertson, 2010, "China and the Manufacturing Exports of Other Developing Countries," in *China's Growing Role in World Trade*, ed. by Robert Feenstra and Shang-Jin Wei (Chicago: University of Chicago Press and the NBER) pp. 137–159.

Hertel, Thomas W., Martina Brockmeier and Padma V. Swaminathan, 1997, "Sectoral and Economy-wide Analysis of Integrating Central and Eastern European Countries into the EU: Implications of Alternative Strategies," *European Review of Agricultural Economics*, Vol. 24, No. 3–4, pp. 359–386.

Hicks, John, 1953, "An Inaugural Lecture," *Oxford Economic Papers*, Vol. 5, No. 2, pp. 117–135.

Hsieh, Chang-Tai and Ralph Ossa, 2011, "A Global View of Productivity Growth in China," February 2011, NBER Working Paper No. 16778.

Hummels, David, Jun Ishii and Kei-Mu Yi, 2001, "The Nature and Growth of Vertical Specialization in World Trade," *Journal of International Economics*, Vol. 54, No. 1, pp. 75–96.

Hummels, David, Rasmus Jorgensen, Jakob Munch and Chong Xiang, 2011, "The Wage Effects of Offshoring: Evidence from Danish Matched Worker-Firm Data," October 2011, NBER Working Paper No. 17496.

Imbs, Jean and Isabelle Mejean, 2011, "Trade Elasticities," August 2011, mimeo, Paris School of Economics and Ecole Polytechnique.

International Monetary Fund (IMF). 2005, *World Economic Outlook*, World Economic and Financial Surveys (Washington, September).

Jones, Ronald, 1971, "A Three-Factor Model in Theory, Trade, and History," in *Trade, Balance of Payments, and Growth: Papers in International Economics in Honor of Charles P. Kindleberger*, ed. by Jagdish Bhagwati (Amsterdam: North-Holland).

Ju, Jiandong and Xuebing Yang, 2009, "Hicks Theorem: Effects of Technological Improvement in the Ricardian Model," *International Review of Economics and Finance*, Vol. 18, No. 2, pp. 239–247.

Levchenko, Andrei A. and Jing Zhang, 2011, "The Evolution of Comparative Advantage: Measurement and Welfare Implications," February 2011, NBER Working Paper No. 16806.

———, 2012, "Comparative Advantage and the Welfare Impact of European Integration," *Economic Policy*, Vol. 27, No. 72, pp. 567–602.

Menezes-Filho, Naércio Aquino and Marc-Andreas Muendler, 2011, "Labor Reallocation in Response to Trade Reform," August 2011, NBER Working Paper No. 17372.

Mussa, Michael, 1974, "Tariffs and the Distribution of Income: The Importance of Factor Specificity, Substitutability, an Intensity in the Short and Long Run," *Journal of Political Economy*, Vol. 82, No. 6, pp. 1191–1203.

New York Times. 2011, "U.S. Senate Backs Tough China Trade Moves," October 3.

OECD. 2005, OECD Employment Outlook OECD Publishing. http://www.dx.doi.org/10.1787/empl_outlook-2012-en.

OECD. 2012, OECD Employment Outlook OECD Publishing. http://www.dx.doi.org/10.1787/empl_outlook-2005-en.

Samuelson, Paul A., 2004, "Where Ricardo and Mill Rebut and Confirm Arguments of Mainstream Economists Supporting Globalization," *Journal of Economic Perspectives*, Vol. 18, No. 3, pp. 135–146.

Shikher, Serge, 2011, "Capital, Technology, and Specialization in the Neoclassical Model," *Journal of International Economics*, Vol. 83, No. 2, pp. 229–242.

———, 2012, "Putting Industries into the Eaton-Kortum Model," *Journal of International Trade and Economic Development*, Vol. 21, No. 6, pp. 807–837.

Simonovska, Ina and Michael E. Waugh, 2011, "The Elasticity of Trade: Estimates and Evidence," February 2011, UC Davis Working Paper No. 11-2.

Święcki, Tomasz, 2013, "Intersectoral Distortions, Structural Change and the Welfare Gains from Trade," April 2013, mimeo, Princeton University.

Waugh, Michael, 2010, "International Trade and Income Differences," *American Economic Review*, Vol. 100, No. 5, pp. 2093–2124.

Yi, Kei-Mu and Jing Zhang, 2010, "Structural Change in an Open Economy," mimeo, Federal Reserve Bank of Philadelphia and University of Michigan.

Journal of Economic Behavior & Organization 94 (2013) 314–329

Contents lists available at ScienceDirect

Journal of Economic Behavior & Organization

journal homepage: www.elsevier.com/locate/jebo

Comparative advantage, complexity, and volatility☆

Pravin Krishna[a,*], Andrei A. Levchenko[b]

[a] Johns Hopkins University and NBER, United States
[b] University of Michigan and NBER, United States

ARTICLE INFO

Article history:
Received 7 November 2011
Received in revised form 3 October 2012
Accepted 13 November 2012
Available online 23 November 2012

JEL classification:
F40

Keywords:
Product complexity
Comparative advantage
Volatility

ABSTRACT

Less developed countries tend to experience higher output volatility, a fact that is in part explained by their specialization in more volatile sectors. This paper proposes theoretical explanations for this pattern of specialization – with the complexity of the goods playing a central role. Specifically, less developed countries with lower institutional ability to enforce contracts, or alternately, with low levels of human capital will specialize in less complex goods which are also characterized by higher levels of output volatility. We provide novel empirical evidence that less complex industries are indeed more volatile.

1. Introduction

Understanding the sources of volatility is an important quest in economics. In a seminal paper, Lucas (1988) observed that, over long horizons, fluctuations in rates of growth are likely to be more substantial in less developed countries, suggesting a link between a country's level of economic development and its volatility. Indeed, as Fig. 1 illustrates, the negative relationship between a country's level of development and aggregate volatility is quite pronounced. Analyzing the sources of this differential aggregate volatility across countries, Koren and Tenreyro (2007) and Tapia (2012) show that an important proximate explanation for the higher output volatility in developing countries is their production specialization in more volatile sectors. Fig. 2 depicts the weighted average volatility of the sectors in which a country specializes against the level of development. More developed countries tend to specialize, on average, in less volatile sectors.

At the same time, several recent empirical studies have suggested that openness to international trade plays an important role in determining economic volatility (see, e.g., Rodrik, 1998; Krebs et al., 2010; di Giovanni and Levchenko, 2009, 2012). While the empirical literature has variously suggested links between a country's level of development, pattern of production specialization, trade, and economic volatility, the reasons for these patterns are not well understood – that is, a coherent theoretical explanation linking these factors is, as yet, lacking.

This paper develops a theoretical framework in which openness to international trade leads to specialization in more volatile sectors in poorer countries – consistent with the empirical findings of Koren and Tenreyro (2007) mentioned above. In our framework, the central concept driving the linkage between trade openness, specialization, and volatility is the complexity of goods being produced. Complexity is defined as the number of different inputs required for the production of

☆ We are grateful to the editor (Pol Antràs), two anonymous referees, Arnaud Costinot, Miklós Koren, and workshop participants at the University of Michigan, the 2009 AEA Meetings, and the 2009 European Trade Study Group for helpful suggestions.

* Corresponding author.
E-mail addresses: Pravin_Krishna@jhu.edu (P. Krishna), alev@umich.edu (A.A. Levchenko).

0167-2681/$ – see front matter © 2012 Elsevier B.V. All rights reserved.
http://dx.doi.org/10.1016/j.jebo.2012.11.004

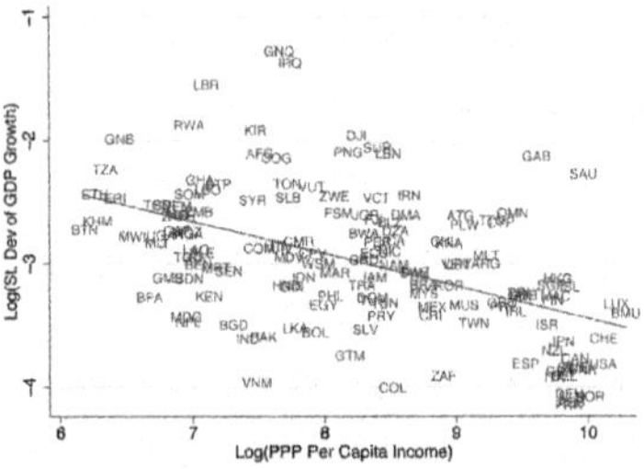

Notes: This figure displays the relationship between per capita income and the standard deviation of per capita GDP growth, in natural logs. Source: Penn World Tables.

Fig. 1. Volatility and development, 1970–2000.

one unit of the good (as in Becker and Murphy, 1992). We show that sectoral output volatility depends on the complexity of goods produced in that sector. This is because when individual inputs to production are subject to shocks, the volatility of output will depend on how many such inputs there are. In particular, the more complex goods are less volatile, as the production in a sector that uses many inputs will be less affected, on average, by shocks to any particular input (a point also emphasized by Koren and Tenreyro, forthcoming). By contrast, the volatility of a good that uses very few inputs will be more affected by the shocks to each individual input.

Starting from this technological characterization of industries in terms of their product complexity, we model two mechanisms through which less developed countries come to exhibit comparative advantage in the less complex – and therefore more volatile – goods. The first, building on Blanchard and Kremer (1997) and Levchenko (2007), relies on differences in the quality of contract enforcement. The more complex the production process, the greater is the number of parties to production, and the greater is the number of contracts that it requires. This implies that the relative loss of output due to imperfect contract enforcement is greater in the more complex sectors in countries with worse institutions, generating comparative advantage.

The second approach, building on Costinot (2009), relies on the differences in human capital endowments across countries and the optimal division of labor in production. In this second mechanism, the scope of the division of labor in production is determined endogenously as a function of the complexity of goods. Countries with higher levels of human capital per worker have a comparative advantage in the more complex goods because higher human capital allows each worker to learn more of the necessary production tasks (as we discuss in detail below). While we use the theoretical frameworks of Blanchard and Kremer (1997) and Costinot (2009) as building blocks of our analysis, neither of these important papers is concerned with the question of economic volatility, which is the focus of the present analysis.

Thus, openness to international trade moves less developed countries toward the production of less complex and more volatile goods. This is the main theoretical result obtained in the paper. The relationship between economic development and volatility in our framework is then driven by two mechanisms: the specialization in less complex goods by less developed countries and the greater volatility of goods with lower complexity. The first theoretical prediction – that less developed economies will specialize in less complex goods – is supported by several recent empirical studies. For instance, Levchenko

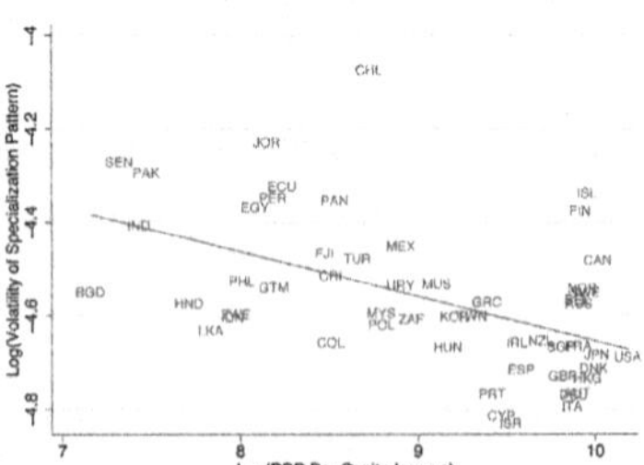

Notes: This figure displays the relationship between per capita income and the weighted average variance of the specialization pattern constructed following the methodology of Koren and Tenreyro (2007), in natural logs. Source: Penn World Tables and UNIDO.

Fig. 2. Level of development and specialization in volatile sectors, 1970–2000.

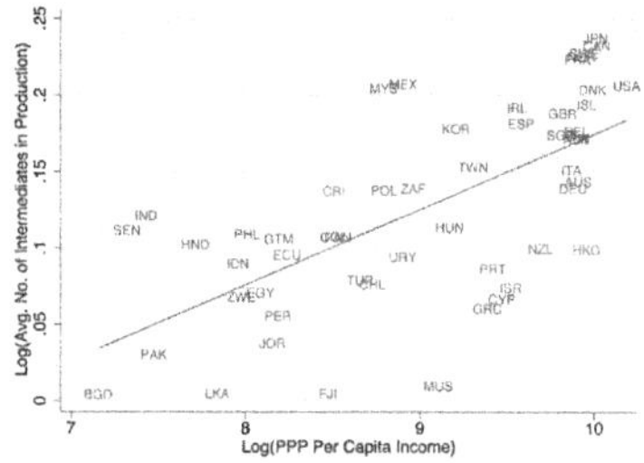

Notes: This figure displays the relationship between per capita income and the weighted average number of intermediates used in production, with the weights equal to output shares. Source: Penn World Tables and UNIDO.

Fig. 3. Level of development and specialization in complex sectors, 1970–2000.

(2007) has shown that countries with worse institutions have relatively higher export shares in goods with low product complexity – with complexity measured as the number of intermediates required for production in each sector. Similarly, Costinot (2009) has found that less developed countries specialize in less complex goods, with complexity measured as the average learning cost that a worker must pay in each sector before becoming productive. Finally, Nunn (2007) has demonstrated that less developed countries specialize in industries requiring less "relationship-specific" investments in their production – which could also be interpreted as industries with a lower degree of product complexity. Chor (2010) carries out a comprehensive empirical investigation by including these and other determinants of comparative advantage jointly in the analysis, and shows that they are all relevant for explaining trade patterns. By way of illustration of these results, Fig. 3 shows that there is a pronounced positive relationship between the average complexity of a country's specialization pattern and the level of development: richer countries tend to specialize in more complex goods.

The second theoretical mechanism on which our paper relies – that less complex goods are characterized by greater volatility – has not previously been analyzed empirically in the literature. In this paper, we provide the first evidence regarding this relationship. Using U.S. sectoral production data from the NBER Productivity Database, we calculate industry-level volatility measures for some 460 4-digit SIC87 sectors over the period 1970–1997. Consistent with the theoretical results, we focus on the volatility of physical output rather than total sales or value added. We combine the volatility data with empirical measures of product complexity computed from the U.S. Input–Output Tables. Our results demonstrate that there is a strong negative relationship between complexity and volatility, with complexity alone explaining some 18% of the variation in the actual volatility found in the data. The results are robust to a number of additional controls (such as factor intensity and sector-level elasticity of substitution), detrending methods, time periods, complexity measures, and removing outliers.

In sum, this paper contributes to the literature on economic development and international trade, by linking the patterns of comparative advantage with volatility. In our framework, production specialization in more volatile sectors takes place in poorer countries and emerges naturally from differences in complexity of goods and in the productivity of input factors across countries. The theoretical predictions are consistent with stylized empirical facts.

The rest of the paper is organized as follows. Section 2 describes the theoretical framework and derives the main results. Section 3 provides empirical evidence on the complexity-volatility link. Section 4 concludes.

2. Modeling complexity, volatility, and comparative advantage

We present below two theoretical mechanisms through which less developed countries come to exhibit comparative advantage in the less complex – and therefore more volatile – goods. The first, building on Blanchard and Kremer (1997) and Levchenko (2007), relies on differences in the quality of contract enforcement. The second approach, building on Costinot (2009), relies on the differences in human capital endowments across countries and the optimal division of labor. We now consider each of these mechanisms in turn.

2.1. Intermediate inputs and the contracting environment

Consider an economy with a large number of industries, each characterized by the number of intermediates z required for production, $z \in (0, \bar{z}]$. For simplicity, we assume that the final output in industry z is produced with a Leontief production function

$$q_z = \min(q(1), \ldots, q(s), \ldots, q(z)), \tag{1}$$

where $q(s)$ is the quantity of intermediate good s that goes into production of the final good, $s = 1, \ldots, z$. There is one factor of production, L, and a large number of ex-ante identical potential intermediate goods producers. These hire labor to produce intermediates with a linear production function $q(s) = l$. Both the intermediate and the final goods sectors are competitive.

Final good producers in a sector requiring z inputs contract with z intermediate goods producers to deliver the inputs. The country's contracting environment is imperfect. In particular, after the intermediates have been contracted for by the final goods producer, each intermediates producer reneges on the project with some probability $1 - \rho$. When this happens, the entire project yields the output of zero. The value of ρ captures the level of institutional quality in the country. The higher it is, the more unlikely an intermediate input producer is to renege. As a result, for a given level of investment into each intermediate good production, the final output is given by

$$\min(l(1), \ldots, l(z)). \tag{2}$$

with probability ρ^z, and zero with probability $1 - \rho^z$.

Since all intermediate goods producers are ex ante identical and enter symmetrically into the production function, the final goods producer contracts for the same level of investment/employment for each intermediate. Therefore, the expected final output per worker is given by ρ^z/z in industry z. Thus, output per worker depends on the complexity, z, of the good, and the quality of institutions ρ. Note that expected output per worker decreases in z at any level of institutional quality ρ. This is a result in the spirit of the O-ring theory of Kremer (1993) and the complementarity model of Jones (2011): the more steps the good requires, the higher is the chance that something will go wrong. If the inputs are "essential" as they are with a Leontief production function, the lower is the expected output. Note that in a model with multiple goods, this also implies that more complex goods command higher prices. While we are not aware of empirical studies of such a relationship in the data, the prediction appears *prima facie* sensible and intuitive.[1]

In this setting, less complex goods – that is, goods with lower z – are more volatile. The overall output per worker is $1/z$ with probability ρ^z and zero with probability $1 - \rho^z$. Therefore, the variance of output per worker is given by $(1/z^2)\rho^z(1 - \rho^z)$. We state the following Lemma, proved formally in Appendix B:

Lemma 1 (Complexity and volatility in the imperfect contracting model). *The variance of output per worker decreases in z:* $(d/dz)\mathrm{Var}(\rho^z/z) < 0$.

This result is intuitive: the fewer inputs to production there are, the greater is the (marginal) impact of an individual input on the overall output. Thus, the behavior of an individual input more closely approximates the behavior of the total output. By contrast, with a large number of inputs, the total output is determined by a combination of a large number of uncorrelated shocks, and is thus less volatile.[2,3]

2.2. Imperfect contracting and comparative advantage

Now suppose there are two countries, North and South. While we do not model contract enforcement explicitly, we assume that a better contracting environment in a country implies that the probability that someone reneges $(1 - \rho)$ is lower there. Without loss of generality, let us assume that the North has a more efficient contracting environment. Thus, $\rho_N > \rho_S$.

We can map this setting into the Ricardian model of Dornbusch et al. (1977). Denote by $a^N(z) = z/\rho_N^z$ the unit labor requirement for good z in the North, and similarly in the South. Then, the relative unit labor requirement for good z in the two countries is:

$$A(z) = \frac{a^S(z)}{a^N(z)} = \left(\frac{\rho_N}{\rho_S}\right)^z. \tag{3}$$

Does an efficient contracting environment create comparative advantage? That is, is the North relatively more productive in goods with higher z? The derivative of this ratio of productivities with respect to z is:

$$\left(\frac{\rho_N}{\rho_S}\right)^z \log\left(\frac{\rho_N}{\rho_S}\right) > 0. \tag{4}$$

We have just proved the following result:

---

1 It is well documented that more developed countries export goods with higher unit values. Since both in the theoretical model and in the data more developed countries export the more complex goods, in this respect the model appears consistent with the data.

2 Note that the assumption of zero output in case of default is not important for the results. Alternatively, we could assume that even when the supplier reneges successfully, the final goods producer can force it to deliver a fraction δ of the contracted quantity of the intermediate good. In that case, the total output per worker is δ/z when no supplier defaults, and the variance of output is simply $(1/z^2)\rho^z(1 - \rho^z)(1 - \delta)^2$. It is clear that all the results carry over to this case.

3 Note that the only shock, and thus the only volatility in this model comes from the possibility that an input supplier reneges on the delivery of the good. This assumption is not crucial: the result above extends to the case in which there is both a reneging shock and a genuine productivity shock, as long as the two are uncorrelated for each supplier.

Lemma 2 (Comparative advantage in the imperfect contracting model). *The North has comparative advantage in goods with higher z: $dA(z)/dz > 0$.*

The North is indeed relatively more productive in high-z goods.

The preceding theoretical framework, while admittedly highly stylized, serves to illustrate two key ideas. First, output volatility is driven by product complexity. And second, better (worse) contracting environments can therefore generate comparative advantage in less (more) volatile goods. If we expect the efficiency of the contracting environment to improve with development, we obtain specialization in more volatile goods in less developed countries – consistent with the empirical findings of Koren and Tenreyro (2007) discussed above.

What is the role of the Leontief production function assumption for these results? Lemma 1 – volatility decreasing with the number of inputs – is clearly much more general, in the sense that it applies under other elasticities of substitution between inputs. It is present, for instance, in the opposite extreme case with perfect substitute inputs, as well as intermediate elasticities of substitution. Koren and Tenreyro (forthcoming) develop this idea further. Indeed, assuming extreme complementarity actually stacks the cards against finding this relationship: more substitutable inputs imply possibilities for diversification across inputs (in the extreme case of perfect substitutability this simply becomes the law of large numbers), which makes the result that more inputs means lower volatility even more straightforward.

Where the Leontief-type structure is really necessary is to generate comparative advantage: contractual frictions have to compound with complexity, so that not only is the country with better institutions more productive in every good, but it is *relatively* more productive in the more complex goods. It is this aspect of the model that relies on the Leontief assumption. This type of physical environment is quite typical in models with incomplete contracts (Blanchard and Kremer, 1997; Caballero and Hammour, 1998; Levchenko, 2007). The strict Leontief structure could be relaxed somewhat by adopting a more general production function for the total output conditional on delivery of all the inputs, but assuming that if just one input supplier reneges, the total output is still zero.

2.3. Human capital and the division of labor

Our second modeling approach, based on Costinot (2009), relies on the differences in human capital endowments across countries and the optimal division of labor in the production of final goods. As in the previous section, more complex final goods require a larger number of intermediate inputs to be supplied or, as interpreted here, a larger number of different tasks to be performed. It is assumed that each of the tasks necessary for the production of the final good requires some fixed labor costs to be incurred. As in Costinot (2009), dividing up the tasks among a larger number of workers generates gains from specialization – fewer tasks taken on by a single worker implies lower fixed costs incurred per worker, thereby raising output per worker. On the other hand, since workers are subject to random productivity shocks, complementarity in production implies that the expected level of output is lower with a larger number of workers.[4] In the analysis that follows, we see how the trade-off between these two forces determines optimal team size used in production (and thus unit production costs) as a function of complexity. Then we will examine how, in this context, countries with high human capital workers have comparative advantage in the production of more complex goods.

Once again, consider an economy with many goods indexed by $z \in (0, \bar{z}]$. Each good is produced with a Leontief technology requiring z tasks to be performed. Let $s \in (0, z]$ denote a particular task that must be performed in order to produce good z, and let $q(s)$ be the quantity of task s. Then, the total output of good z, q_z, is given by

$$q_z = \min_{s \in (0,z)} q(s). \tag{5}$$

The economy is populated by L workers, each with productivity h. There are fixed costs associated with performing each task s. In particular, a worker must first spend 1 unit of labor learning to perform each task. Let N be the team size that characterizes production of a good with complexity z. The first question we ask is what is the team size that maximizes output per worker in sector z.

With a team of size N, each team member specializes in z/N tasks, and allocates her endowment of labor equally to each of them. Therefore, after paying the fixed cost to learn these tasks, each worker has $h - (z/N)$ units of labor to spend on production. Hence, each worker is able to dedicate $(h - (z/N))/(z/N)$ units of labor to each task.

After paying the fixed costs, each worker receives a productivity shock ε, affecting her performance of each task equally. Therefore, the worker's actual output is

$$q(s) = \left(\frac{hN}{z} - 1\right)\varepsilon \tag{6}$$

[4] This point has been emphasized recently by Jones (2011).

of each task s. Plugging Eq. (6) into (5), it is immediate that the total output of this team is $q_z = ((hN/z) - 1)\min_{n=1,\ldots,N}\varepsilon_n$, while the output per worker is

$$\frac{q_z}{N} = \left(\frac{h}{z} - \frac{1}{N}\right)\min_{n=1,\ldots,N}\varepsilon_n. \tag{7}$$

Note that, holding team size fixed, output per worker is higher, the greater the human capital level h and the lower the complexity of the good being produced z. This is as is expected. Furthermore, output per worker is a function of the random productivity shocks faced by workers. What is the team size that maximizes output per worker in this setting? Assume that the shocks are uncorrelated across workers. The expected output per worker is then equal to

$$E\left(\frac{q_z}{N}\right) = \left(\frac{h}{z} - \frac{1}{N}\right)E(\varepsilon_{(1)}), \tag{8}$$

where $\varepsilon_{(1)} \equiv \min_{n=1,\ldots,N}\varepsilon_n$ is the first order statistic associated with the sample of N outcomes of a random variable ε_n across the workers in a team (see Appendix A).

For the sake of tractability, assume for now that the shocks to workers are distributed $\varepsilon \sim \text{Uniform}(0, 1)$. This assumption has the advantage of leading to a simple closed-form solution for the optimal team size. In particular, the expected output per worker with team size N is equal to (see Eq. (A.4)): $((h/z) - 1/N)(1/(N+1))$. Following Costinot (2009), this expression can be used to find the optimal team size N_z in a sector with complexity z:

$$N_z = \text{argmax}_N \left(\frac{h}{z} - \frac{1}{N}\right)\frac{1}{N+1}. \tag{9}$$

The first-order condition is given by:

$$\frac{1}{N^2}\frac{1}{N+1} + \left(\frac{h}{z} - \frac{1}{N}\right)\left(\frac{1}{(N+1)^2}\right) = 0. \tag{10}$$

Straightforward manipulation gives the optimal team size in sector z of:

$$N_z = \frac{z}{h}\left(1 + \sqrt{1 + \frac{h}{z}}\right). \tag{11}$$

The optimal team size increases in the complexity of the good, z, and decreases in the worker productivity h. Optimal team size increases with complexity due to the gains from specialization that are obtained when the necessary tasks are divided up among a larger number of workers. The higher is the level of human capital, the costlier a low productivity draw becomes, and thus optimal team size falls in h. As we will see, the relationship we have established between optimal team size, complexity and human capital will be important in determining the pattern of comparative advantage.

Though the model of the division of labor and team size follows Costinot (2009), the key tension that pins down the optimal team size is different in our paper. In Costinot (2009), the tension is between greater division of labor and the resulting higher per worker productivity on the one hand, and imperfect contract enforcement: the more workers are in a team, the greater is the probability that at least one of them reneges. In our setup, the tension is between division of labor and the greater possibility of an adverse productivity shock that an individual worker may experience, in a production setting characterized by strong complementarities, a mechanism inspired by Jones (2011). Note also that though we choose to follow Costinot's terminology and call the team members "workers," the model will not change if we think of N as intermediate inputs suppliers instead.

The first result we would like to establish is that in this setting more complex goods are also less volatile. Going back to the expression for output per worker (7), it is immediate that the volatility of output per worker is given by:

$$\text{Var}\left(\frac{q_z}{N}\right) = \left(\frac{h}{z} - \frac{1}{N}\right)^2\text{Var}(\varepsilon_{(1)}). \tag{12}$$

We state the counterpart of Lemma 1 for this model:

Lemma 3 (Complexity and volatility in the division of labor model). *The variance of output per worker decreases in z:* $(d/dz)\text{Var}(q_z/N) < 0$.

The proof is provided in Appendix B. We should note that the result in Lemma 3 depends in an important way on the property that the variance of the first order statistic (the minimum of a random sample) decreases in the sample size. Though this property appears intuitive, there are no finite sample general results in statistics about how the variance of the first order statistic behaves as the sample size increases. However, it can be confirmed using direct calculation that this variance indeed decreases in the sample size for some important distributions such as the uniform (as in this paper), exponential, Pareto, and Fréchet. This gives us some confidence that our main results are not excessively driven by the particular distributional assumptions that we adopt.

A related result is that *in each sector z*, a country with lower productivity of workers experiences lower volatility. This is because higher productivity implies lower team size, which in turn increases the volatility of output.

2.4. Human capital differences and comparative advantage

Suppose now that there are two countries, North and South. The only difference between them is that the North's workers are more productive: $h^N > h^S$. Following Costinot (2009), we map this model into the Ricardian framework of Dornbusch et al. (1977), by considering the unit labor requirements in each good z in the two countries. The average labor requirement of a unit of the good z in the North is:

$$a^N(z) = \frac{h^N}{((h^N/z) - (1/N_z^N))(1/N_z^N + 1)} = \frac{zh^N N_z^N (N_z^N + 1)}{(h^N N_z^N - z)}, \tag{13}$$

and similarly in the South. Therefore, the ratio of relative unit labor requirements is given by:

$$A(z) = \frac{a^S(z)}{a^N(z)} = \frac{h^S N_z^S (N_z^S + 1)(h^N N_z^N - z)}{h^N N_z^N (N_z^N + 1)(h^S N_z^S - z)}. \tag{14}$$

In order to establish the direction of comparative advantage, we must ascertain whether the schedule $A(z)$ is increasing or decreasing. Taking the derivative with respect to z, and applying the envelope theorem, we obtain:

$$A'(z) = \frac{(\partial a^S/\partial z)a^N - a^S(\partial a^N/\partial z)}{(a^N)^2}. \tag{15}$$

Evaluating the partial derivatives with respect to z based on Eq. (13) and simplifying, $A'(z)$ becomes:

$$A'(z) = \frac{h^S N^S (N^S + 1)}{(h^S N^S - z)^2 h^N N^N (N^N + 1)} (h^N N^N - h^S N^S). \tag{16}$$

Therefore, the sign of this derivative is the same as the sign of $(h^N N^N - h^S N^S)$. Using Eq. (11), it is immediate that $(h^N N^N - h^S N^S) > 0$, and therefore the North has a comparative advantage in the more complex goods, as expected. We summarize the discussion above in the following Lemma:

Lemma 4 (Comparative advantage in the division of labor model). *The North has comparative advantage in goods with higher z: $dA(z)/dz > 0$.*

The intuition for this result is straightforward: When workers have higher human capital, they spend a smaller fraction of their time learning, and so unit labor requirements are lower. Importantly, this reduction is not uniform across goods. In the more complex sectors, learning costs are more important and the decrease in unit labor requirements is larger. As a result, the country with workers with greater human capital is relatively more efficient in the more complex industries.

2.5. Trade equilibrium

We now specified the pattern of comparative advantage $A(z)$ in two ways: by relying on contract enforcement (Eq. (3)), and human capital differences (Eq. (14)). In order to close the model, we must specify agents' preferences. Assume, following Dornbusch et al. (1977), that all agents have identical Cobb-Douglas preferences, so that each good receives a constant share of expenditure. Let $\omega = w^N/w^S$ be the relative wage between the two countries. There exists a cutoff $\tilde{z}$, such that

$$\omega = A(\tilde{z}). \tag{17}$$

Let $S(\tilde{z})$ be the share of income spent on Southern goods. Then, the trade balance condition is given by

$$\omega = \frac{h^S L^S [1 - S(\tilde{z})]}{h^N L^N S(\tilde{z})}. \tag{18}$$

The equilibrium specialization pattern is illustrated in Fig. 4. Eqs. (17) and (18) jointly determine the equilibrium pair $(\omega, \tilde{z})$. It is immediate that the South produces goods $(0, \tilde{z})$, while the North produces goods $(\tilde{z}, \bar{z})$. As such, the South ends up in the less complex industries in which production is the most volatile for each firm.

Though these models are of course much too stylized to explain the observed differences in per capita income across countries, we can circle back to the empirical facts motivating the paper, which are about how specialization in volatile and complex sectors is related to per capita income. The relative per capita incomes in equilibrium are given by Eq. (17), and since the price levels are the same in the two countries, Eq. (17) also gives the ratio of the real per capita incomes. Thus, a necessary condition for the country with better institutions or higher human capital to have higher per capita income is that at the cutoff value $\tilde{z}$, $A(\tilde{z}) > 1$. A sufficient condition is that at every z, $A(z) > 1$, that is, the country with better institutions or higher human capital has an absolute advantage in every good. This sufficient condition is easily verified in both models, and thus it is indeed the case that the higher-income country exports more complex and less volatile goods.[5]

[5] It is immediate from (3) that the imperfect contracting model satisfies the sufficient condition. The easiest way to see that the human capital model satisfies the sufficient condition is to differentiate the expression for $a(z)$ in (13) (dropping the N-superscript) with respect to h, applying the envelope theorem.

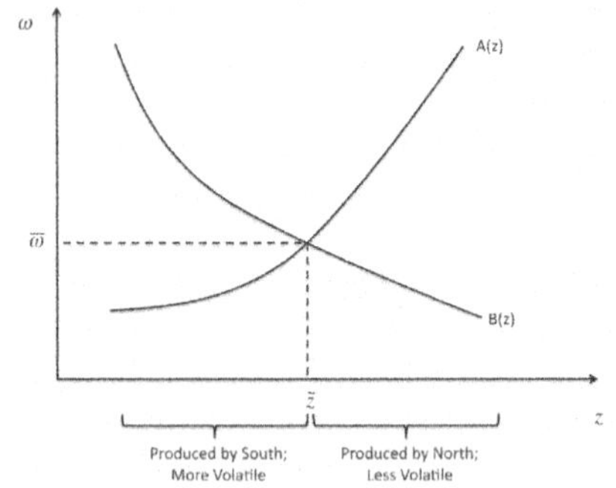

Fig. 4. Pattern of production and trade.

3. Empirical evidence

There are two crucial pieces of evidence that we must bring to bear to support the theory proposed above. The first is that poorer countries do indeed specialize in less complex goods. This result has been established recently in a series of studies. Levchenko (2007) shows that countries with worse institutions – which are essentially the less developed countries – have relatively higher export shares in goods with low product complexity. In that study, measures of product complexity at sector level are constructed using the Input–Output Tables for the United States, and by examining how many intermediates each sector requires to produce. Costinot (2009) provides similar results using an alternative measure, which is the average learning cost that a worker must pay in each sector before she becomes productive. Nunn (2007) constructs a measure of contract intensity by combining the U.S. Input–Output Table data with a classification of intermediate goods industries into those that require relationship-specific investments and those that do not. Nunn finds that less developed countries specialize in industries that do not rely on relationship-specific investments, which could be another way of capturing industries with a low z in the model above. Finally, Chor (2010) includes these and other determinants of comparative advantage jointly in the analysis, and shows that they are all relevant for explaining trade patterns. Since the finding that less developed countries specialize in less complex goods is well established in the literature, we do not revisit it in this paper (beyond depicting this pronounced pattern in Fig. 3), and refer the reader to the papers above.

The second crucial element is the negative relationship between complexity and volatility at sector level. On this score, we are not aware of any existing empirical evidence. In this section, we use data on the actual complexity and volatility of the U.S. manufacturing sectors to demonstrate that complexity is a robust and highly significant predictor of volatility. The empirical strategy is focused on testing the predictions of the model for physical output, rather than total sales as is typical in the literature. This is important because predictions of the model regarding total sales would depend more heavily on assumptions on preferences.

In order to demonstrate the conditional correlation between product complexity and output volatility while controlling for other industry characteristics, we fit the following relationship on the cross-section of sectors using OLS:

$$\text{StDev}_i = \alpha + \beta \text{ImpliedStDev}(z)_i + \gamma \mathbf{X}_i + \varepsilon_i,$$

where i indexes sectors, StDev_i is the standard deviation of output in sector i, $\text{ImpliedStDev}(z)_i$ is the standard deviation of that sector's output implied by its complexity z, and X_i is a vector of other sectoral characteristics used as controls.

3.1. Data

Industry-level data on volatility come from the NBER Productivity Database that reports information on 459 manufacturing sectors in the U.S. at the 4-digit SIC87 classification. We compute output per worker using data on total shipments and employment in each sector. Total output is deflated using sector-specific deflators provided in the database, ensuring that we capture the volatility of quantities. Because the level of real output per worker exhibits a trend, we compute the time series of the growth rate of output per worker for each sector, and take the standard deviation over time for the period 1970–1997. Taking growth rates is the simplest way of detrending the data. To check robustness of the results, we also HP-filter the output per worker series in each sector, and compute the volatility of the deviations from the HP-filtered trend. Following the recommendation of Ravn and Uhlig (2002), we set the HP filter parameter to 6.25, since the data are at the annual frequency. Output per worker data may be contaminated by the time variation in the use of inputs or other factors of production. Thus, we compute the volatility of two alternative series: value added per worker, and Total Factor Productivity

Table 1
Summary statistics.

Variable	Mean	Std. dev.	Min	Max	Obs.
Complexity (z)	77.0	25.2	16	160	459
Actual volatility	0.080	0.040	0.027	0.339	459

Notes: Complexity is the number of intermediates used in production, calculated based on the U.S. I–O matrix. Actual volatility is the standard deviation of real output per worker growth, 1970–1997, calculated based on the NBER Productivity Database.

Table 2
Most and least complex sectors.

SIC code	Sector name	Number of intermediates
Least complex sectors		
2429	Special product sawmills, n.e.c.	16
3263	Semivitreous table and kitchenware	17
3151	Leather gloves and mittens	17
3131	Footwear cut stock	21
3292	Asbestos products	22
3142	House slippers	24
2397	Schiffli machine embroideries	24
3259	Structural clay products, n.e.c.	28
2441	Nailed wood boxes and shook	29
2121	Cigars	29
Most complex sectors		
3728	Aircraft parts and equipment, n.e.c.	120
2865	Cyclic crudes and intermediates	122
281	Industrial inorganic chemicals	122
3585	Refrigeration and heating equipment	122
3731	Ship building and repairing	125
3812	Search and navigation equipment	136
3721	Aircraft	138
308	Miscellaneous plastics products	139
3714	Motor vehicle parts and accessories	148
3711	Motor vehicles and car bodies	160

Notes: This table reports the most and least complex sectors, with complexity measured by the number of intermediates used in production, calculated based on the U.S. I–O matrix.

(TFP). The sector-specific TFP series is available in the same database. For both of these, we compute the standard deviation of the growth rate of the series, though the HP-filtering procedure delivers the same results.

Data on product complexity come from the U.S. Input–Output Tables for 1992, and have been previously used by Cowan and Neut (2007) and Levchenko (2007). In particular, in this exercise we use the total number of intermediates in production as a proxy for product complexity z in the model above. It turns out that the number of intermediates ranges from 16 to 160, a tenfold difference. Table 1 reports the summary statistics for both complexity and the actual volatility (standard deviation of output per worker growth) of the sectors in our data. Table 2 reports the top 10 most and least complex sectors, according to the total number of intermediates used.

Using the variation in actual product complexity in place of z in the model, we can compute the optimal team size N from Eq. (11), and as a result the volatility in each sector from Eq. (B.2). The resulting standard deviation of output as a function of product complexity z is depicted in Fig. 5. Volatility is decreasing in complexity.[6]

3.2. Results

Is the standard deviation of a sector as implied by its complexity a robust predictor of the actual volatility in that sector? Fig. 6 presents the scatter plot of the standard deviation of output per worker growth against the implied volatility of output per worker constructed based on our model. There is a robust positive relationship between the two variables.

Table 3 presents the regression results. All throughout, we report the standardized beta coefficients, obtained by first demeaning all the variables and normalizing each to have a standard deviation of 1. Thus, the regression coefficients correspond to the number of standard deviations change in the left-hand side variable that would be due to a one standard deviation change in the corresponding independent variable. The four panels differ only in the measure of actual volatility used on the left-hand side. Panel A uses standard deviation of output per worker growth; Panel B, the volatility of deviations

[6] The relationship between complexity and volatility would be similar if we instead computed implied volatility using the imperfect contracting model of Section 2.1. All of the results are virtually unchanged under this alternative approach, so we do not report the full set of results based on the imperfect contracting model to avoid unnecessary repetition. To compute the variance, we choose the value of $h = 20$. We checked the robustness using all values of h between 1 and 200, and while h affects the level of the implied variance of output, the statistical significance of the results is unchanged.

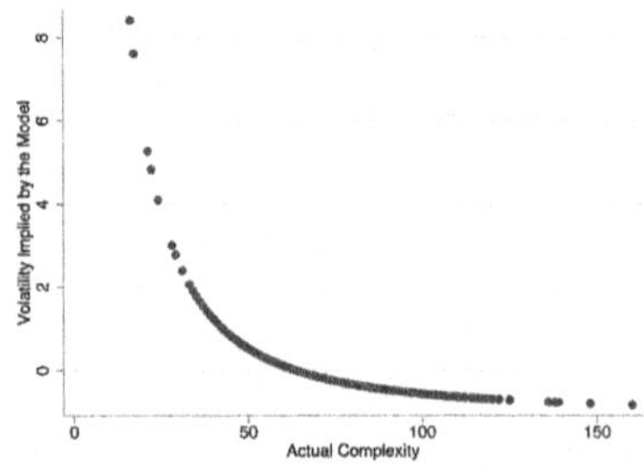

Notes: This figure displays the relationship between the number of intermediate inputs in production (z) and volatility of output per worker, as implied by theory. *Actual Complexity* is the number of intermediate inputs used in a 4-digit SIC sector, calculated from the 1992 U.S. Input-Output Tables. It ranges from 16 to 160.

Fig. 5. Volatility as a function of product complexity: model.

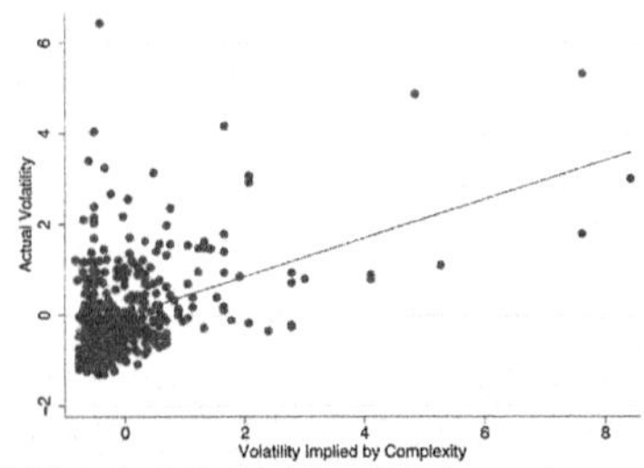

Notes: *Actual Volatility* is the standard deviation of output per worker growth of a 4-digit SIC manufacturing sector in the United States over the period 1970-1997, sourced from the NBER Productivity database. *Volatility Implied by Complexity* is the standard deviation of output per worker implied by the theory, given the number of intermediate inputs used in that sector. The number of intermediates used in each 4-digit SIC sector is computed using the 1992 U.S. Input-Output Tables.

Fig. 6. Actual volatility and volatility implied by product complexity.

from HP trend; Panel C, volatility of value added per worker; Panel D, standard deviation of TFP growth. Column 1 reports the results of a bivariate regression of the actual on the implied volatility. The positive relationship is very pronounced: with the exception of the deviations from the HP trend series, the t-statistics on the coefficient on the implied volatility are in the range of 5–7, and the R^2's of the bivariate regressions are as high as 0.18.

Column 2 controls for other sector characteristics, such as raw materials intensity, capital intensity, and skill intensity, constructed based on Romalis (2004). As we can see, after controlling for other sector characteristics, the coefficient of interest in Panel B goes from being insignificant to significant at the 1% level, while the rest of the results are virtually unchanged. Finally, column 3 removes the outliers in terms of actual volatility, and still finds that the relationship of interest is quite strong and statistically significant.[7] Finally, it may be that what we are picking up are differences in the elasticity of substitution across goods. For instance, Kraay and Ventura (2007) argue that developing countries are more volatile because they specialize in goods that have a higher elasticity of substitution. We use data from Broda and Weinstein (2006) to check whether sectoral volatility is systematically correlated with elasticity. Column 4 in each panel reports the results. Because the Broda–Weinstein data are in a different industrial classification, we lose 10 of the the sectors due to an imperfect concordance. Controlling for the elasticity of substitution leaves the main results completely unchanged.

The control variables tend to come in with the expected sign. Sectors with the higher raw material intensity and with higher capital intensity tend to be more volatile. The coefficient on the elasticity of substitution is positive, and significant in two out of four specifications. Plausibly, sectors with higher elasticity of substitution are also more volatile. Perhaps a bit

[7] More precisely, we drop the top 5% most volatile sectors, according to each corresponding measure of volatility. Alternatively, we also dropped the top 5% of most volatile sectors according to the implied volatility (i.e., the RHS variable), and the results were fully robust.

Table 3
Actual and implied volatility.

	(1)	(2)	(3)	(4)	(1)	(2)	(3)	(4)
	Panel A: Dep. Var.: standard deviation of output per worker growth				*Panel B: Dep. Var.: standard deviation of output per worker deviation from HP trend*			
Implied volatility	0.426*** (0.064)	0.447*** (0.071)	0.343*** (0.044)	0.445*** (0.071)	0.043 (0.040)	0.145*** (0.039)	0.092*** (0.024)	0.143*** (0.039)
Raw materials intensity		0.261*** (0.100)	0.243*** (0.067)	0.219** (0.102)		1.105*** (0.114)	0.631*** (0.052)	1.071*** (0.118)
Capital intensity		0.084 (0.071)	0.116** (0.052)	0.069 (0.072)		0.661*** (0.076)	0.438*** (0.043)	0.650*** (0.076)
Skill intensity		0.118* (0.069)	0.045 (0.051)	0.088 (0.069)		0.336*** (0.074)	0.139*** (0.028)	0.306*** (0.079)
Elasticity				0.085* (0.047)				0.096** (0.044)
Observations	459	459	436	449	459	459	436	449
R^2	0.18	0.2	0.16	0.21	0.00	0.32	0.41	0.33
Sample	Full	Full	No outliers	Full	Full	Full	No outliers	Full
	Panel C: Dep. Var.: standard deviation of value added per worker growth				*Panel D: Dep. Var.: standard deviation of TFP growth*			
Implied volatility	0.300*** (0.059)	0.330*** (0.072)	0.234*** (0.029)	0.328*** (0.072)	0.426*** (0.084)	0.489*** (0.092)	0.316*** (0.049)	0.489*** (0.093)
Raw materials intensity		0.642*** (0.111)	0.366*** (0.051)	0.622*** (0.119)		0.466*** (0.103)	0.197*** (0.065)	0.448*** (0.106)
Capital intensity		0.184*** (0.055)	0.138*** (0.037)	0.175*** (0.055)		0.303*** (0.070)	0.178*** (0.050)	0.302*** (0.073)
Skill intensity		0.181*** (0.053)	0.097** (0.041)	0.165*** (0.055)		0.245*** (0.072)	0.091* (0.051)	0.226*** (0.066)
Elasticity				0.039 (0.039)				0.063 (0.055)
Observations	459	459	436	449	459	459	436	449
R^2	0.09	0.26	0.26	0.26	0.18	0.23	0.15	0.24
Sample	Full	Full	No outliers	Full	Full	Full	No outliers	Full

Notes: Standardized beta coefficients reported throughout. Robust standard errors in parentheses. The dependent variables are standard deviations computed over the period 1970–1997. *Implied volatility* is the standard deviation of a sector implied by its complexity as in Eq. (12), where complexity is measured as the number of intermediates used by a sector, from the U.S. Input–Output matrix. *raw material intensity* = (value of raw material inputs)/(value of raw material inputs + value added); *capital intensity* = [1 − (total compensation)/(value added)] × (1 − raw material intensity); *skill intensity* = [(nonproduction workers)/(total employment)] × (1 − capital intensity) × (1 − raw material intensity), all computed based on the NBER Productivity Database. *Elasticity* is the elasticity of substitution between varieties in a given SIC sector (source: Broda and Weinstein, 2006).

* Significant at 10%.

** Significant at 5%.

*** Significant at 1%.

more surprisingly, sectors with higher skill intensity also tend to be more volatile. Two points are worth noting in this respect. First, the model is silent on this issue, since all the workers are the same and all the sectors in the theoretical model have the same "skill intensity." Second, the coefficient on skill intensity represents the conditional correlation, after controlling for complexity and other covariates. Indeed, it turns out that when omitting implied volatility from the right-hand side, skill intensity is actually negatively (but insignificantly) correlated with volatility. There is no strong *prima facie* case to expect a particular sign, especially after conditioning on the other correlates of sectoral volatility.

We now assess whether this relationship is robust to a number of additional alternative left- and right-hand side measures and samples. As mentioned above, the results are robust to constructing the implied volatility based on the imperfect contracting model instead. Column 1 of Table 4 presents the results, computing implied volatility under the assumption that $\rho = 0.9$ (i.e., the probability a supplier reneges is 10%). The coefficient magnitude and the explanatory power of the implied volatility measure is virtually identical.[8] In constructing the implied volatility, in the baseline procedure we use the total number of intermediate inputs in each industry. However, it could be that some inputs in some industries have minuscule usage, and thus should not really be counted as adding to complexity. We thus computed an alternative measure for the number of intermediates, that only counts inputs whose share in the total input usage is at least at the 10th percentile of all the non-zero entries in the IO matrix. This truncating procedure in effect drops the bottom 10% of all input usages. Predictably, the range of the number of inputs across industries shrinks somewhat: while the unrestricted measure ranges from 16 to 160, the restricted measure ranges from 16 to 109. The two have a correlation of 0.8. Column 2 of Table 4 presents the main result while using the restricted measure of the number of inputs to construct implied volatility. The results are fully robust to this alternative approach.

Rather than use the data on the number of intermediate inputs to compute sectoral volatility as implied by the model, we can also assess whether actual volatility is positively correlated with measures of product complexity directly. The rest of Table 4 presents the results of estimating the relationship between actual volatility and various indicators of product complexity. Following Cowan and Neut (2007) and Levchenko (2007), we use a number of variables, all constructed using the 1992 Benchmark Input–Output Table for the United States. Column 1 regresses volatility on the number of intermediates used in production. Column 2 used the Herfindahl index of intermediate goods shares; Column 3, the Gini coefficient of intermediate use, columns 4 and 5 the shares of the 10 and 20 largest intermediate inputs in the total input use. These variables have been used in the literature to measure product complexity. They may be preferable to simply using the number of intermediates if intermediate input use is dominated by one or two inputs (high concentration) and all the other intermediates are used very little. In that case what really matters to the final good producer is the relationship it has with the largest one or two suppliers. The scope for and consequences of reneging by suppliers of minor inputs is probably much smaller than by important suppliers. Thus, simply taking the number of intermediates may give excessive weight to insignificant input suppliers and overestimate the effective product complexity. Note that complexity increases in the number of intermediates, but decreases in all the other indicators. Thus, in columns 4 through 7 we should expect positive coefficients. We can see that with the exception of column 4, all the coefficients are significant at the 1% level. The coefficient on the Herfindahl index is not significant, but nonetheless enters with the expected sign.

We next check whether the main result is sensitive to the sample period and the detrending method, and whether it is confined to the U.S. data. Columns 1 and 2 of Table 5 compute sectoral volatility on the pre- and post-1984 periods respectively. This may be important because 1984 is widely seen as the onset of the Great Moderation, with lower volatility throughout the economy for the following 2 decades. It is clear that the relationship between complexity and volatility is equally significant and possesses a similar magnitude in both periods. In the baseline results, when HP-detrending the data we used a parameter of 6.5, recommended for annual data by Ravn and Uhlig (2002). To see whether the results are sensitive to this choice, we used the parameter of 100 instead. Column 3 of Table 5 presents the results. It is clear that the basic relationship is not driven by the HP-detrending parameter.

Finally, it remains an open question whether the relationship between complexity and volatility we demonstrated thus far in the U.S. data holds in a large set of other countries. Unfortunately, data availability does not permit us to carry out an analysis in a cross-section of countries at the same level of disaggregation (~450 sectors). However, we can carry out this exercise based on the UNIDO sectoral production database, which reports data at the 3-digit ISIC level of disaggregation (28 sectors) over the period 1970–1999 for about 60 countries. The data and specification come from di Giovanni and Levchenko (2009), which can be consulted for further details. Implied volatility and factor intensity measures are concorded from the SIC to the ISIC classification. The results are reported in column 4 of Table 5. It is clear that the basic relationship between product complexity and sectoral volatility holds even in this large sample of countries, and even at the much coarser level of sectoral disaggregation. An additional question is whether this relationship holds in both high- and low-income countries. We estimated the specification in column 4 for the OECD and non-OECD samples separately, and the relationship is quite similar in both groups of countries, both in the size of the coefficient and in the level of significance. Those results are not reported in order to conserve space, but are available upon request.

We conclude that in a large sample of sectors, variation in complexity does play a significant role in explaining sectoral volatility, which is a key building block of our theory.

[8] The results are robust to a wide variety of values of ρ, from $\rho = 0.1$ (90% probability of reneging) to $\rho = 0.99$ (1% probability of reneging).

Table 4
Robustness: alternative measures of implied volatility or complexity.

	(1)	(2)	(3)	(4)	(5)	(6)	(7)
Dep. var.: standard deviation of output per worker growth							
Implied volatility (contract enforcement model)	0.432^{***} (0.077)						
Implied volatility (min input usage cutoff)		0.473^{***} (0.071)					
Number of intermediates			-0.300^{***} (0.056)				
Herfindahl index				0.121 (0.087)			
Gini coefficient					0.319^{***} (0.057)		
Share of 10 largest intermediates						0.253^{***} (0.056)	
Share of 20 largest intermediates							0.358^{***} (0.065)
Raw materials intensity	0.247^{**} (0.099)	0.247^{**} (0.098)	0.161 (0.116)	−0.009 (0.141)	−0.04 (0.125)	−0.045 (0.128)	−0.039 (0.123)
Capital intensity	0.068 (0.069)	0.092 (0.068)	0.012 (0.081)	−0.083 (0.083)	−0.079 (0.082)	−0.089 (0.084)	−0.082 (0.080)
Skill intensity	0.092 (0.069)	0.137^{**} (0.068)	0.073 (0.072)	−0.025 (0.073)	0.075 (0.068)	0.037 (0.071)	0.098 (0.067)
Observations	459	459	459	459	459	459	459
R^2	0.20	0.22	0.10	0.03	0.09	0.06	0.11

Notes: Standardized beta coefficients reported throughout. Robust standard errors in parentheses. The dependent variables are standard deviations computed over the period 1970–1997. *Implied volatility (contract enforcement model)* is the standard deviation of a sector implied by its complexity in the contract enforcement model. *Implied volatility (min input usage cutoff)* is the standard deviation of a sector implied by its complexity as in Eq. (12), but imposing a minimum usage cutoff before being counted as an intermediate. *Number of intermediates* is the number of intermediates used in production; Herfindahl index is the Herfindahl index of intermediate input use; Gini coefficient is the Gini coefficient of the intermediate input use. Share of 10 and 20 Largest intermediates are shares in of the top 10 or 20 intermediate inputs in the total intermediate input use. *raw material intensity* = (value of raw material inputs)/(value of raw material inputs + value added); *capital intensity* = [1 − (total compensation)/(value added)] × (1 − raw material intensity); *skill intensity* = [(nonproduction workers)/(total employment)] × (1 − capital intensity) × (1 − raw material intensity), all computed based on the NBER Productivity Database.

* Significant at 10%.

** Significant at 5%.

*** Significant at 1%.

Table 5
Robustness: alternative samples, detrending procedures, and datasets.

	(1)	(2)	(3)	(4)
Implied volatility	0.313*** (0.053)	0.437*** (0.095)	0.101*** (0.029)	0.123*** (0.021)
Raw materials intensity	0.443*** (0.093)	0.086 (0.106)	0.954*** (0.117)	0.131** (0.061)
Capital intensity	0.124* (0.065)	0.055 (0.076)	0.586*** (0.082)	-0.009 (0.036)
Skill intensity	0.099* (0.056)	0.113 (0.076)	0.337*** (0.091)	0.059* (0.030)
Log (trade/output)				0.223*** (0.029)
Log (initial output)				0.189*** (0.035)
Country FE				Yes
Observations	459	459	459	1579
R^2	0.18	0.18	0.23	0.50
Sample	Pre-1984	Post-1984	Full, HP(100)	UNIDO

Notes: Standardized beta coefficients reported throughout. Robust standard errors in parentheses. The dependent variables are standard deviations computed over the period 1970–1997. *Implied volatility* is the standard deviation of a sector implied by its complexity as in Eq. (12), where complexity is measured as the number of intermediates used by a sector, from the U.S. Input–Output matrix. *raw material intensity* = (value of raw material inputs)/(value of raw material inputs + value added); *capital intensity* = [1 − (total compensation)/(value added)] × (1 − raw material intensity); *skill intensity* = [(nonproduction workers)/(total employment)] × (1 − capital intensity) × (1 − raw material intensity), all computed based on the NBER Productivity Database. *Log (trade/output)* is the log of the ratio of imports plus exports to total output in a sector. *Log (initial output)* is the log of the beginning-of-period output in a sector. The last column reports estimates based on a multi-country sample of the 3-digit ISIC manufacturing data from UNIDO.

* Significant at 10%.
** Significant at 5%.
*** Significant at 1%.

4. Conclusion

Recent literature has made important advances in understanding the patterns of macroeconomic volatility across countries. It is well known that poorer countries experience higher volatility. Koren and Tenreyro (2007) and Tapia (2012) demonstrate that part of the higher volatility in developing countries can be accounted for by the fact that they produce on average in more volatile sectors.

What can explain this puzzling observation? In this paper, we argue that international trade plays an important role. In particular, recent literature emphasized that poorer countries tend to export goods that are less complex (Levchenko, 2007; Costinot, 2009). Since these goods use fewer intermediates, shocks to each intermediate input are more important for production (a point also emphasized by Koren and Tenreyro, forthcoming). Therefore, less complex goods tend to be more volatile. Comparative advantage in less complex goods, that could arise from institutional quality or productivity differences, drives specialization in more volatile industries by developing countries.

There is one aspect of our argument for which there is no extant empirical evidence. Namely, it has not been demonstrated previously that less complex goods are indeed more volatile. In the last section of the paper we use data on the actual complexity of sectors in the United States to construct the volatility of each industry based on our model. We then relate this implied volatility to the actual volatilities of sectors observed in the data, and show that there is a robustly significant relationship: less complex industries are indeed more volatile.

Appendix A. Order statistics

Suppose that $\varepsilon_1, \ldots, \varepsilon_N$ is a random sample of size N drawn from a distribution with pdf f_ε and cdf F_ε. The first order statistic is defined as $\varepsilon_{(1)} \equiv \min_{n=1\ldots,N} \varepsilon_n$, that is, it is the minimum value in this random sample. The distribution of $\varepsilon_{(1)}$ can be derived as follows. The cdf of this variable is given by:

$$F_{\varepsilon_{(1)}}(x) = P(\min_{n=1,\ldots,N} \varepsilon_n < x) = 1 - P(\min_{n=1,\ldots,N} \varepsilon_n > x) = 1 - (1 - F_\varepsilon(x))^N. \tag{A.1}$$

Correspondingly, the pdf of $\varepsilon_{(1)}$ is obtained by differentiating the cdf:

$$f_{\varepsilon_{(1)}}(x) = N(1 - F_\varepsilon(x))^{N-1} f_\varepsilon(x). \tag{A.2}$$

As an example, suppose that $\varepsilon \sim$ Uniform (0, 1). The pdf of ε is $f_\varepsilon(x) = 1$, and the cdf is $F_\varepsilon(x) = x$. Then, the pdf of the first order statistic is

$$f_{\varepsilon_{(1)}}(x) = N(1 - x)^{N-1}. \tag{A.3}$$

Using integration by parts, it is straightforward to establish that in this case, the expectation and the variance of $\varepsilon_{(1)}$ are given by:

$$E(\varepsilon_{(1)}) = \frac{1}{N+1} \tag{A.4}$$

$$\mathrm{Var}(\varepsilon_{(1)}) = \frac{N}{(N+1)^2(N+2)}. \tag{A.5}$$

These results will be useful in the main text.

Appendix B. Proofs

B.1. Proof of Lemma 1

Proof. Taking this derivative directly,

$$\frac{d}{dz}\mathrm{Var}\left(\frac{1}{z}\rho^z\right) = -\frac{2}{z^3}\rho^z(1-\rho^z) + \rho^z(1-2\rho^z)\ln\rho\frac{1}{z^2} = \frac{\rho^z}{z^2}\left[\ln\rho(1-2\rho^z) - \frac{2}{z}(1-\rho^z)\right].$$

Rearranging, the Lemma holds if and only if:

$$\frac{1-2\rho^z}{1-\rho^z}\ln\rho^z < 2.$$

When $\rho \in (0,1)$ and $z \geq 1$, it is always the case that $\rho^z \in (0,1)$. Therefore, the result necessary for the proposition obtains if

$$\frac{1-2\rho}{1-\rho}\ln\rho < 2 \quad \forall\rho\in(0,1).$$

We now show that this condition holds by proceeding in two steps. First, we show that the function $f(\rho) = ((1-2\rho)/(1-\rho))\ln\rho$ is monotonically increasing throughout the interval $\rho \in (0,1)$. And second, we show that the supremum of this function, which obtains when $\rho \to 1$ is less than 2, satisfying this required condition.

Differentiating $f(\rho)$:

$$\frac{d}{d\rho}\left[\frac{1-2\rho}{1-\rho}\ln\rho\right] = \frac{1-2\rho}{1-\rho}\frac{1}{\rho} + \ln\rho\left[\frac{-2(1-\rho)-(-1)(1-\rho)}{(1-\rho)^2}\right] = \frac{1-2\rho}{1-\rho}\frac{1}{\rho} + \frac{\ln\rho}{(1-\rho)^2} = \frac{(1-2\rho)(1-\rho)-\rho\ln\rho}{(1-\rho)^2\rho}$$

$$= \frac{(1-\rho)^2-\rho(1-\rho)-\rho\ln\rho}{(1-\rho)^2\rho} = \frac{1}{\rho} - \frac{(1-\rho)+\ln\rho}{(1-\rho)^2}.$$

Thus, this derivative is positive if $(1-\rho)+\ln\rho < 0$. It is immediate that $\lim_{\rho\to 0}(1-\rho+\ln\rho) = -\infty$ and $\lim_{\rho\to 0}(1-\rho+\ln\rho) = 0$. Therefore, if this function is monotonic for $\rho\in(0,1)$, it is everywhere less than 0, as required. Taking the derivative of this function,

$$\frac{d}{d\rho}[1-\rho+\ln\rho] = -1+\frac{1}{\rho} > 0 \quad \forall\rho\in(0,1).$$

This establishes that $f(\rho) = ((1-2\rho)/(1-\rho))\ln\rho$ is monotonically increasing in the interval $(0, 1)$. We now show that its supremum is less than 2. The supremum obtains as $\rho \to 1$.

$$\lim_{\rho\to 1}\left[\frac{1-2\rho}{1-\rho}\ln\rho\right] = \lim_{\rho\to 1}(1-2\rho)\lim_{\rho\to 1}\left[\frac{\ln\rho}{1-\rho}\right] = (-1)\lim_{\rho\to 1}\frac{\ln\rho}{1-\rho} = -\lim_{\rho\to 1}\frac{1/\rho}{-1} = 1 < 2,$$

where the last equality comes from applying l'Hôpital's Rule. This completes the proof. □

B.2. Proof of Lemma 3

Proof. Using the optimal value of N in Eq. (11), the term in parentheses simplifies to:

$$\left(\frac{h}{z} - \frac{1}{N}\right)^2 = \frac{1+(h/z)}{N^2}. \tag{B.1}$$

Using Eq. (A.5) from Appendix, the variance becomes:

$$\mathrm{Var}\left(\frac{q_z}{N}\right) = \left(1+\frac{h}{z}\right)\frac{1}{N(N+1)^2(N+2)}. \tag{B.2}$$

To establish that the variance decreases in good complexity z, evaluate its derivative with respect to z:

$$\frac{d}{dz}\mathrm{Var}\left(\frac{q_z}{N}\right) = \frac{\partial}{\partial z}\mathrm{Var}\left(\frac{q_z}{N}\right) + \frac{\partial}{\partial N}\mathrm{Var}\left(\frac{q_z}{N}\right)\frac{dN}{dz}. \tag{B.3}$$

Evaluating each of these subcomponents separately, it is indeed the case that $(d/dz)\mathrm{Var}(q_z/N) < 0$. □

References

Becker, G., Murphy, K., 1992. The division of labor, coordination costs, and knowledge. Quarterly Journal of Economics 107, 1137–1160.
Blanchard, O., Kremer, M., 1997. Disorganization. Quarterly Journal of Economics 112, 1091–1126.
Broda, C., Weinstein, D., 2006. Globalization and the gains from variety. Quarterly Journal of Economics 121 (2), 541–585.
Caballero, R., Hammour, M., 1998. The macroeconomics of specificity. Journal of Political Economy 106, 724–767.
Chor, D., 2010. Unpacking sources of comparative advantage: a quantitative approach. Journal of International Economics 82 (2), 152–167.
Costinot, A., 2009. On the origins of comparative advantage. Journal of International Economics 77 (2), 255–264.
Cowan, K., Neut, A., 2007. Intermediate Goods, Institutions, and Output Per Worker. Central Bank of Chile Working Paper No. 420.
di Giovanni, J., Levchenko, A.A., 2009. Trade openness and volatility. Review of Economics and Statistics 91 (3), 558–585.
di Giovanni, J., Levchenko, A.A., 2012. The risk content of exports: a portfolio view of international trade. NBER International Seminar on Macroeconomics 8 (1), 97–151.
Dornbusch, R., Fischer, S., Samuelson, P., 1977. Comparative advantage, trade, and payments in a ricardian model with a continuum of goods. American Economic Review 67, 823–839.
Jones, C., 2011. Intermediate goods and weak links in the theory of economic development. American Economic Journal: Macroeconomics 3 (2), 1–28.
Koren, M., Tenreyro, S., 2007. Volatility and development. Quarterly Journal of Economics 122 (1), 243–287.
Koren, M., Tenreyro, S. Technological diversification. American Economic Review, forthcoming.
Kraay, A., Ventura, J., 2007. Comparative advantage and the cross-section of business cycles. Journal of European Economic Association 5 (6), 1300–1333.
Krebs, T., Krishna, P., Maloney, W., 2010. Trade policy, income risk, and welfare. Review of Economics and Statistics 92 (3), 467–481.
Kremer, M., 1993. The O-ring theory of economic development. Quarterly Journal of Economics 108 (3), 551–575.
Levchenko, A.A., 2007. Institutional quality and international trade. Review of Economic Studies 74 (3), 791–819.
Lucas Jr., R.E., 1988. On the mechanics of economic development. Journal of Monetary Economics 22, 3–42.
Nunn, N., 2007. Relationship-specificity, incomplete contracts and the pattern of trade. Quarterly Journal of Economics 122, 569–600.
Ravn, M.O., Uhlig, H., 2002. On adjusting the hodrick-prescott filter for the frequency of observations. Review of Economics and Statistics 84 (2), 371–376.
Rodrik, D., 1998. Why do more open economies have bigger governments? Journal of Political Economy 106 (5), 997–1032.
Romalis, J., 2004. Factor proportions and the structure of commodity trade. American Economic Review 94, 67–97.
Tapia, H., 2012. Volatility and Wealth. mimeo, Columbia University.

Part II

Firm Heterogeneity

Journal of International Economics 85 (2011) 42–52

Contents lists available at ScienceDirect

Journal of International Economics

journal homepage: www.elsevier.com/locate/jie

Power laws in firm size and openness to trade: Measurement and implications☆

Julian di Giovanni [a], Andrei A. Levchenko [b,c,*], Romain Rancière [d,e,f]

[a] Research Department, International Monetary Fund, 700 19th Street NW, Washington, DC, 20431, USA
[b] Department of Economics, University of Michigan, 611 Tappan Street, Ann Arbor, MI 48109, USA
[c] National Bureau of Economic Research, Cambridge, MA, USA
[d] Paris School of Economics, 48 Boulevard Jourdan, F-75014 Paris, France
[e] Research Department, International Monetary Fund, 700 19th Street NW, Washington, DC, 20431, USA
[f] Center for Economic Policy and Research, London, UK

ARTICLE INFO

Article history:
Received 9 April 2010
Received in revised form 6 May 2011
Accepted 9 May 2011
Available online 19 May 2011

JEL classification:
F12
F15

Keywords:
Firm size distribution
International trade
Power laws

ABSTRACT

Existing estimates of power laws in firm size typically ignore the impact of international trade. Using a simple theoretical framework, we show that international trade systematically affects the distribution of firm size: the power law exponent among exporting firms should be strictly lower in absolute value than the power law exponent among non-exporting firms. We use a dataset of French firms to demonstrate that this prediction is strongly supported by the data, both for the economy as a whole and at the industry level. Furthermore, the differences between power law coefficients for exporters and non-exporters are larger in sectors that are more open to trade. While estimates of power law exponents have been used to pin down parameters in theoretical and quantitative models, our analysis implies that the existing estimates are systematically lower than the true values. We propose two simple ways of estimating power law parameters that take explicit account of exporting behavior.

1. Introduction

Many relationships in economics appear to be governed by power laws. A distributional power law is a relationship of the type: $Pr(X>x)=Cx^{-\zeta}$ where $Pr(X>x)$ is the probability that a random variable X is greater than x, and C and ζ are constants. Power laws arise in a variety of contexts, such as the distribution city size (Zipf, 1949), income (Champernowne, 1953), firm size (Axtell, 2001), and sectoral trade flows (Hinloopen and van Marrewijk, 2006; Easterly et al., 2009).

The literature has emphasized the importance of the precise value of the power law exponent, ζ. For instance, for the distribution of firm size in the U.S., Axtell, (2001) reports a range of estimates between 0.996 and 1.059, very precisely estimated with standard errors between 0.054 and 0.064. The literature has sought to both explain why ζ is close to 1 (a phenomenon known as Zipf's Law) and to explore its implications in a variety of contexts. It has been argued that Zipf's Law will arise when the variable of interest, be it city, or firm size, follows a geometric Brownian motion (Gabaix, 1999; Luttmer, 2007; Rossi-Hansberg and Wright, 2007). At the same time, the precise magnitude of the power law exponent has been shown to matter for such different phenomena as macroeconomic fluctuations (Gabaix, 2011; di Giovanni and Levchenko, 2010a), regulation of entry (di Giovanni and Levchenko, 2010b), and executive compensation (Gabaix and Landier, 2007).

This paper revisits the power law in the distribution of firm size in the context of international trade. We first set up a simple version of the Melitz (2003) model of production and trade, adopting the common assumption that the distribution of firm productivities is Pareto. This model is naturally suited to studying the firm size distribution because of its emphasis on heterogeneous firms. The Melitz–Pareto framework delivers a power law in firm size. However, it also predicts that in the presence of international trade, the power law exponent in the distribution of firm size is not constant. Because larger firms are more likely to export, and the more productive the firm, the more markets it serves, we would expect the estimated power law exponent to be lower in absolute value among exporting firms compared to the non-exporting ones. In other words, in the presence of international trade, power law estimates that do not take

☆ We are grateful to Xavier Gabaix, the editor (Jonathan Eaton), and an anonymous referee for detailed suggestions, and Michael Aubourg for superb research assistance. This paper was completed while Romain Rancière was visiting INSEE whose hospitality – and in particular the help of Pauline Givord – is gratefully acknowledged. Romain Rancière thanks CEPREMAP for financial support. The views expressed in this paper are those of the authors and should not be attributed to the International Monetary Fund, its Executive Board, or its management.

* Corresponding author at: Department of Economics, University of Michigan, 611 Tappan Street, Ann Arbor, MI 48109, USA. Tel.: +1 734 764 3296; fax: +1 734 764 2769.

E-mail addresses: JdiGiovanni@imf.org (J. di Giovanni), alev@umich.edu (A.A. Levchenko), ranciere@pse.ens.fr (R. Rancière).

URLs: http://julian.digiovanni.ca (J. di Giovanni), http://alevchenko.com (A.A. Levchenko), http://romainranciere.com (R. Rancière).

[1] See Gabaix (2009) for a recent survey.

0022-1996/$ – see front matter © 2011 Elsevier B.V. All rights reserved.
doi:10.1016/j.jinteco.2011.05.003

into account international trade could be misleading regarding the deep parameters of the economy.[2]

We evaluate these predictions of the Melitz–Pareto model using the data on production and exports for a large sample of French firms. In the full sample that includes all firms, the power law in firm size is strikingly similar to what Axtell (2001) found for the census of U.S. firms. The estimated power law exponent and the fit of the relationship are both nearly identical. However, when we separate the firms into exporting and non-exporting ones, it turns out that in the exporting sample, the power law coefficient is consistently lower, while in the non-exporting sample, consistently higher than in the full sample of firms. This difference is present across all estimators, and is highly statistically significant. In addition, we show that, as predicted by theory, the power law exponent for exporting firms converges to the power law exponent for domestic firms as we restrict the sample to larger and larger exporters.

Results based on the economy as a whole are not conclusive evidence that exporting behavior *per se* generates the difference in power law coefficients between exporters and non-exporters. For instance, it is well known that exporters tend to be larger than non-exporters, and thus the findings could be driven by a departure from an exact power law for larger firms. We address this concern in two ways. First, to focus specifically on the role of international trade, we estimate power law coefficients for exporting and non-exporting firms by sector. At the disaggregated industry level, the estimates exhibit the same pattern: power law coefficients for exporters are systematically lower than for non-exporters. More tellingly, the differences between power law coefficients are larger in industries that are more open to trade, a striking regularity consistent with the theoretical intuition developed in the paper. Second, we re-estimate the power laws on sub-samples of exporters and non-exporters of the same mean size, confirming the main result. All of these pieces of evidence lend empirical support to the main idea of the paper: international trade systematically changes the distribution of firm size, and inference that does not take that into account will likely lead to biased estimates.

One of the reasons empirical power law estimates are important is that they are used to pin down crucial parameters in calibrated heterogeneous firm models (see, among many others, Helpman et al., 2004; Chaney, 2008; Buera and Shin, 2010; di Giovanni and Levchenko, 2010a). At the same time, quantitative results often depend very sharply on the precise parameter values that govern the distribution of firm size. di Giovanni and Levchenko (2010b) show that welfare gains from reductions in fixed costs are an order of magnitude lower, and gains from reductions in variable costs an order of magnitude higher in a model calibrated to Zipf's Law compared to the counterfactual case in which $\zeta=2$ instead. We return to the Melitz–Pareto model, and propose two alternative ways of estimating the power law parameters that are internally consistent with the canonical heterogeneous firm model of trade. The first is to use a sample of only non-exporting firms. The second is to use only domestic sales to estimate the power law parameter.

We are not the first to provide parameter estimates for the firm size distribution that explicitly account for international trade. Eaton et al. (forthcoming) set up a multi-country heterogeneous firms model and estimate a set of model parameters with Simulated Method of Moments using the data on French firms.[3] The advantage of our approach is simplicity. The alternative estimation strategies proposed here are very easy to implement and do not require any additional modeling or estimation techniques. All they rely on is an appropriate modification of the sample or variables used in estimation. Our approach thus substantially lowers the barriers to obtaining reliable power law estimates, and can be applied easily in many contexts.

The rest of the paper is organized as follows. Section 2 presents the theoretical framework. Section 3 describes the dataset used in the analysis and the methodology for estimating power laws. Section 4 describes the results. Section 5 concludes.

2. Theoretical framework

This section describes the firm size distribution in the canonical heterogeneous firms model, and in particular how it is affected by international trade. Throughout this section, sales are the measure of firm size, though all the empirical results are reported below for both sales and employment as an alternative size variable. Firm sales, S_i, in the economy are said to follow a power law if their distribution is described by[4]:

$$Pr(S_i > s) = Cs^{-\zeta}. \quad (1)$$

The canonical monopolistic competition model with CES demand and heterogeneous firms implies that domestic sales of firm i in market n are given by

$$D_i = M_n \times B_i,$$

where M_n is a measure of the size of domestic demand, which is the same for all firms, and $B_i \equiv a_i^{1-\varepsilon}$ is the firm-specific (but not market-specific) productivity-cum-sales term. In this expression, a_i is the marginal cost of firm i, and ε is the elasticity of substitution between CES varieties.[5]

We postulate that B_i follows a Pareto distribution with exponent ζ. Under some conditions (e.g., Gabaix, 1999; Luttmer, 2007), B_i comes from a random growth model, which yields a value of ζ close to 1. It turns out that in the canonical heterogeneous firms model this is equivalent to assuming that firm productivity is Pareto, but with a different exponent. To see this, suppose that firm productivity has the Pareto cdf: $\Pr(1/a<y) = 1-\left(\frac{b}{y}\right)^{\theta}$. In the autarkic economy, where $S_i = D_i$, the power law follows:

$$Pr(S_i > s) = Pr(M_n B_i > s) = Pr\left(a_i^{1-\varepsilon} > \frac{s}{M_n}\right) = \left(b^{\varepsilon-1} M_n\right)^{\frac{\theta}{\varepsilon-1}} s^{-\frac{\theta}{\varepsilon-1}}, \quad (2)$$

satisfying Eq. (1) for $C = (b^{\varepsilon-1}M_n)^{\frac{\theta}{\varepsilon-1}}$ and $\zeta = \frac{\theta}{\varepsilon-1}$. The model-implied distribution of sales is depicted in Fig. 1. In addition, this calculation shows that $S_i \sim \text{Pareto}(b^{\varepsilon-1}M_n, \frac{\theta}{\varepsilon-1})$.

The result that the power law exponent is constant and equal to $\frac{\theta}{\varepsilon-1}$ holds true in autarky, and also among non-exporting firms in the trade equilibrium. But how does exporting behavior change the firm size distribution? We describe two mechanisms by which exporting tilts the power law relationship systematically to make it flatter (more right-skewed). The first relies on entry into progressively more foreign markets. The second, on stochastic export market entry costs that vary by firm. In the second case, it is possible to obtain a number of analytical results about the distribution of firm sales, and show that it is systematically affected by international trade.

To start exporting from country n to country m, firm i must pay the fixed cost κ_{mni} that potentially varies by firm, and an iceberg per-unit cost of $\tau_{mn}>1$. It is easy to verify that export sales by firm i to market m can be expressed as $M_m^* B_i$, where M_m^* is m's market size *from the*

[2] This paper focuses on power law estimation because power laws appear to be the best description of observed firm size distributions (Luttmer, 2007). However, the qualitative mechanisms we highlight apply to any other underlying distribution of firm size.

[3] See Arkolakis (2009, 2010) for related theoretical treatments.

[4] Unless otherwise noted, in the discussion below all parameter values are nonnegative.

[5] $M_n = \frac{Y_n}{P_n^{1-\varepsilon}} \left(\frac{\varepsilon}{\varepsilon-1}\omega_n\right)^{1-\varepsilon}$, where Y_n is total expenditure, P_n is the price level, and ω_n is the cost of the input bundle. For details of this type of model, see, e.g., di Giovanni and Levchenko (2010b).

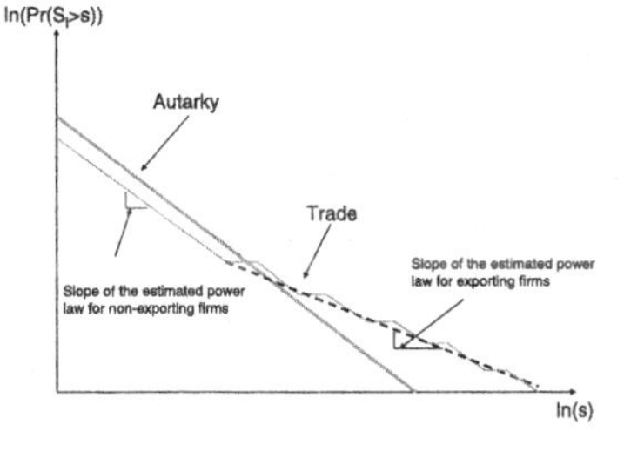

Fig. 1. The analytical power law in the Melitz–Pareto model: multiple export markets.

perspective of the firm that exports there from n, and B_i is defined above. As is well known, variable profits from exporting to m are equal to $M_m^* B_i/\varepsilon$, and firm i exports to that market only if

$$\frac{M_m^* B_i}{\varepsilon} \geq \kappa_{mni}. \tag{3}$$

Consider first the case of multiple export markets. For simplicity, let $\kappa_{mni} = \kappa_{mn}\ \forall\ i$. In the presence of firm heterogeneity and fixed costs of entering export markets, there is a hierarchy of firms in their export market participation. Eq. (3) defines a partition of firms according to how many markets m the firm serves. A greater range of firms will serve markets with higher M_m^*. We can order potential export destinations according to how productive a firm needs to be in order to export there. This is illustrated in Fig. 2, which orders firms according to marginal cost, with more productive firms closer to the origin. Since each firm in the home country faces the same aggregate conditions and trade costs in each trading partner, if a firm exports to any market, it also exports to all markets served by the less productive firms.

What this implies for the distribution of firm sales is illustrated in Fig. 1. For all the firms that only sell to the domestic market, the power law is still a straight line with the same slope as what we derived for autarky, $\frac{\theta}{\varepsilon-1}$. However, participation in export markets results in a series of parallel shifts in this cumulative distribution function, one for each additional export market that firms might enter. Because the more productive a firm is, the more markets it sells to, the distribution of firm size becomes more fat-tailed.

The second mechanism that tilts the power law in firm size is the stochastic fixed costs of exporting that vary across firms, as in Eaton et al. (forthcoming). In this case, there will not be a single "exporting cutoff," above which all firms export, and below which none do. Instead, there will be both exporting and non-exporting firms with the same exact productivity, or equivalently, domestic sales. To obtain a number of analytical results, we assume that there is only one export market m. Clearly, this should be thought of as a composite of the potential for global sales of the company. This framework would thus apply particularly well if there is a considerable fixed cost common to entering any and all foreign markets, but once a firm exports to one country, it finds it much easier to export to others.[6]

[6] Hanson and Xiang (2011) use U.S. motion picture exports to provide empirical evidence that fixed exporting costs are global rather market-specific.

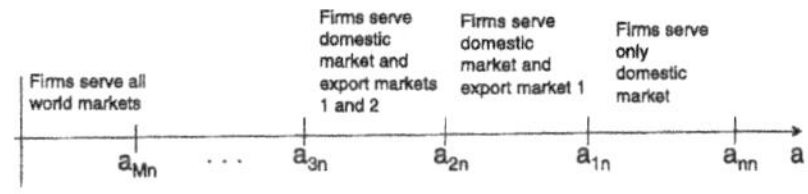

Fig. 2. Partition of firms.

Defining $\phi \equiv \frac{M_m^*}{M_n}$ to be the ratio of the foreign market size relative to the domestic one, the exporting decision condition (3) can be written as a function of domestic sales:

$$\frac{\phi D_i}{\varepsilon} \geq \kappa_i,$$

where to streamline notation we omit the mn-subscripts: $\kappa_i = \kappa_{mni}$. Denote by H the pdf of $\kappa / \left(\frac{\phi}{\varepsilon}\right)$:

$$H(x) = Pr\left(\kappa_i \leq \frac{\phi x}{\varepsilon}\right).$$

We will call $H(x)$ the "export probability function": a firm with domestic size D_i exports with probability $H(D_i)$, which is weakly increasing in D_i. If the firm exports, the exports are $X_i = M_n^* B_i = \phi D_i$, and its total sales, $S_i = D_i + X_i = (1+\phi)D_i$. The distributions of domestic sales, export sales, and total sales are described in the following proposition. The proof is presented in Appendix A.

Proposition 1. *The densities of domestic sales D_i, exports X_i (when they are nonzero), and worldwide sales S_i are:*

$$p_D(x) = kx^{-\zeta-1} 1_{x > \underline{D}} \tag{4}$$

$$p_X(x) = Kx^{-\zeta-1} H\left(\frac{x}{\phi}\right) 1_{x > \phi\underline{D}} \tag{5}$$

$$p_S(x) = kx^{-\zeta-1}\left[1 - H(x) + H\left(\frac{x}{1+\phi}\right)(1+\phi)^{\zeta}\right] 1_{x > (1+\phi)\underline{D}} + kx^{-\zeta-1} 1_{\underline{D} < x < (1+\phi)\underline{D}}, \tag{6}$$

where $k = \zeta \underline{D}^{\zeta}$, K is a constant ensuring $\int p_X(x)\, dx = 1$, and $1_{\{.\}}$ is the indicator function.

In other words, when the underlying distribution of productivity, and therefore domestic sales, is Pareto, the presence of exporting behavior implies that the distribution of total sales, as well as export sales, is systematically different. Thus, the standard practice of estimating power laws in firm size based on total firm sales will not yield reliable estimates of the underlying power law parameter, ζ, which is in turn often used to calibrate the model parameter combination, $\theta/(\varepsilon-1)$. As is evident from Eq. (6) that describes the distribution of total sales, fitting instead the simple power law relationship (1) will not yield the correct estimate of the power law exponent.

As an example, suppose that the distribution of fixed exporting cost κ_i is itself Pareto, with some upper truncation: $H(x/\phi) = k'' x^{\alpha}$, for $x < x^*$ and some $k'' > 0$ and $\alpha > 0$, and $H(x/\phi) = k''(x^*)^{\alpha}$ for $x > x^*$. Then, Eq. (5) implies that the distribution of export sales is given by:

$$p_X(x) \propto \begin{cases} x^{-\zeta-1+\alpha} & \text{for} \quad x < x^* \\ x^{-\zeta-1} & \text{for} \quad x \geq x^* \end{cases},$$

and thus the power law exponent of X is $\zeta - \alpha$ for $x < x^*$, and ζ for $x \geq x^*$. When H has a high slope, the Pareto exponent of X is lower than that of domestic sales: there are fewer small exporters, due to the selection effect coming from the fixed cost of exporting. However, in the region where the H function "saturates," the local Pareto exponent

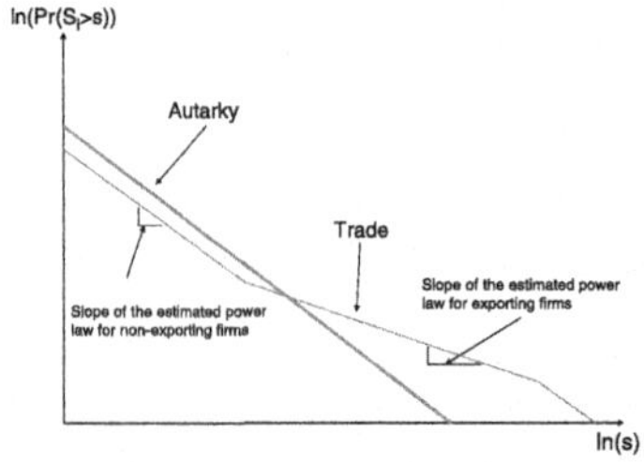

Fig. 3. The analytical power law in the Melitz–Pareto model: stochastic export entry costs.

of exports converges to the exponent of domestic sales. Such a possibility is depicted in Fig. 3. We will provide evidence consistent with this auxiliary prediction of the model in Section 4.1 below.

In summary, we have now described two mechanisms by which the estimated slope of the power law among exporting firms is systematically lower in absolute value than the slope among the firms that sell only to the domestic market, at least in some regions. The preceding discussion also identifies two ways of estimating the power law parameter that take explicit account of exporting behavior. The first, suggested by Figs. 1 and 3, is to use only non-exporting firms in the estimation of ζ. The second, suggested by Eq. (2) and Proposition 1, is to estimate the power law exponent on the firms' domestic sales only. We now test the theoretical predictions using a comprehensive dataset on sales and exports of French firms, and present the results of implementing the two simple alternative ways of estimating ζ that correct for the exporting behavior.

3. Data and empirical methodology

3.1. Data and estimation sample

To carry out the empirical analysis, we start with a comprehensive dataset that covers the entire universe of French firms for 2006. The data are based on the mandatory reporting of firms' income statements to tax authorities. What is crucial for our analysis is that each firm has to report the breakdown of its total sales between domestic sales and exports. In total, the dataset includes 2,182,571 firms, of which 194,444 (roughly 9%) are exporters.

The exhaustive nature of the dataset implies that there are many observations for very small firms, whose economic activity is practically nil, and are thus both uninformative and uninteresting to the researcher. For our purposes, this is important because it is widely recognized that many power laws fit the data well only above a certain minimum size threshold (Axtell, 2001; Luttmer, 2007). Thus, a power law may not be a good description of the size distribution of very small firms. To address this problem, we follow the common practice in the literature and pick the lower cutoff based on visual inspection (Gabaix, 2009). The minimum sales cutoff we select is Euro 750,000 of annual sales.[7] This cutoff is quite low: though it results in the removal of a large number of firms from the dataset, the dropped firms account for only 7.7% of total sales. Our results are robust to a variety of cutoffs, including sales cutoffs as low as Euro 100,000.

Since the focus of the paper is on how exporting behavior changes the firm size distribution, we also omit non-tradeable sectors. The conventional approach to isolate the tradeable sector is to focus exclusively on manufacturing. However, many sectors in agriculture, mining, and services report non-trivial export sales as well. To broaden the definition of the tradeable sector, we only drop industries for which total exports are less than 5% of total sales.[8] The remaining sample (of industries with exports of at least 5% of total sales) includes all of the manufacturing, agricultural, and natural resource sectors, as well as some services such as consulting and wholesale trade. The non-tradeable sector accounts for 51% of the total sales in the universe of French firms, so this is a large reduction in the sample. However, all of our main results are robust to including the non-traded sector in the estimation.

Appendix Table A1 provides descriptive statistics for the final sample of domestic sales and exports. The final sample includes 157,084 firms, 67,078 of which are exporters (42.7%). An average exporter's total sales are approximately four times larger than those of an average non-exporter (Euro 24.2 million vs. Euro 6.4 million). We also consider the number of employees as an alternative measure of firm size. Appendix Table A1 reports the summary statistics for the number of employees in each panel (all firms, non-exporting, and exporting firms). When measured by employees, the average exporter is approximately three times larger than the average non-exporter (69.8 vs. 25.4 workers).

3.2. Empirical methodology

In order to obtain reliable estimates, this paper uses three standard methods of estimating the slope of the power law ζ. We now describe each in turn. The first method, based on Axtell (2001), makes direct use of the definition of the power law (1), which in natural logs becomes:

$$ln(Pr(S_i > s)) = ln(C) - \zeta ln(s). \tag{7}$$

For a grid of values of sales s, the estimated probability $Pr(S_i > s)$ is simply the number of firms in the sample with sales greater than s divided by the total number of firms. We then regress the natural log of this probability on $ln(s)$ to obtain our first estimate of ζ. Following the typical approach in the literature, we do this for the values of s that are equidistant from each other on a log scale. This implies that in absolute terms, the intervals containing low values of s are narrower than the intervals at high values of s. This is done to get a greater precision of the estimates: since there are fewer large firms, observations in small intervals for very high values of s would be more noisy.

The second approach starts with the observation that the cdf in Eq. (1) has a probability density function

$$f(s) = C\zeta s^{-(\zeta + 1)}. \tag{8}$$

To estimate this pdf, we divide the values of firm sales into bins of equal size on the log scale, and compute the frequency as the number of firms in each bin divided by the width of the bin. Since in absolute terms the bins are of unequal size, we regress the resulting frequency observations on the value of s which is the geometric mean of the

[7] This value also has an institutional justification: below this sales threshold, firms have the option of filing their information according to simplified reporting requirements, while above it the firms must provide comprehensive accounting data to tax authorities.

[8] This leads to dropping of Construction, Retail Trade, Real Estate, Financial Services, Post and Telecommunications, Business Services, Hotels and Restaurants, Recreational, Cultural, and Athletic Activities, Health and Social Action, Public Administration, and Unions and Extra-Territorial Activities, most of which are plausibly non-tradeable sectors.

endpoints of the bin (this approach follows Axtell, 2001). Note that the resulting coefficient is an estimate of $-(\zeta+1)$, so when reporting the results we subtract 1 from the estimate to recover a value of ζ.

Alternatively, we simply regress the natural log of ($\text{Rank}_i - 1/2$) of each firm in the sales distribution on log of its sales:

$$ln\left(\text{Rank}_i - \frac{1}{2}\right) = \text{Constant} + \widehat{\zeta}_{LR}\, ln\, S_i + \varepsilon_i,$$

where i indexes firms, and S_i are sales. This is the estimator suggested by Gabaix and Ibragimov (2011). The power law coefficient $\widehat{\zeta}_{LR}$ has a standard error of $|\widehat{\zeta}_{LR}|(N/2)^{-1/2}$, where N is the sample size. This standard error is reported throughout for this estimator. As we show below, in practice the three estimators deliver remarkably similar results.

4. Results

We begin by replicating the conventional results in the literature that pool all firms and do not consider exporting behavior. Table 1 reports estimates of the power law in firm size using the three methods outlined above. Panel I uses total sales as the measure of firm size. We can see that the fit of the data for sales is quite similar to that reported in existing studies: the R^2's are all 99% or above. The point estimates of ζ are close to what Axtell (2001) finds for the U.S. Fig. 4 presents the results graphically for sales. The two panels show the cdf and pdf of the power law in firm size. For convenience, each plot also reports the regression equation, the fit, and the number of firms underlying the estimation. It is clear that in these data on French firms, the power law holds about as well as in the existing studies. Panel II reports estimates on the number of employees instead. The fit is again quite good and the point estimates are similar to those for sales.

We now present the main results of the paper, which show that the power law in fact differs significantly between exporting and non-exporting firms as implied by theory. Table 2 reports estimates of the power law for exporting and non-exporting firms separately. Once again, Panel I uses sales as the measure of firm size, while Panel II uses employees. Columns (1), (3), and (5) present the results of estimating power laws on exporting firms only, while columns (2), (4), and (6) for non-exporting firms only. Once again, we report the estimate, standard error, R^2, and the number of firms for each estimate. Comparing the columns for exporters and non-exporters, we can see the main result clearly. In every case, the exponent of the power law

Table 1
Power law in firm size, all firms: sales and employees.

	(1) CDF	(2) PDF	(3) ln(Rank − 0.5)
I. Sales			
ζ	1.017	1.019	0.825
	(0.032)	(0.031)	(0.004)
R^2	0.990	0.998	0.991
No. of firms	157,084	157,084	157,084
II. Employees			
ζ	1.078	1.093	0.790
	(0.072)	(0.083)	(0.003)
R^2	0.958	0.985	0.906
No. of firms	152,429	152,429	152,429

Notes: This table reports the estimates of power laws in firm size (total sales or employees), using the three methods described in the text. Column (1) estimates the CDF of the power law specified in Eq. (7). Column (2) estimates the PDF of the power law specified in Eq. (8). Column 3 regresses ln(Rank − 0.5) of the firm in the size distribution on the natural logarithm of its size (Gabaix and Ibragimov, 2011).

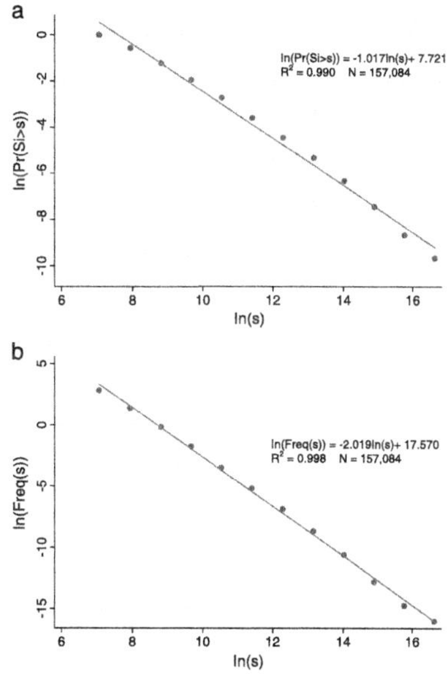

Fig. 4. Power laws in the distribution of firm size, all firms. Notes: This figure reports the estimated power laws in firm size based on total sales and all firms. The power laws are estimated with two different methods, the cdf (panel a) and the pdf (panel b).

among exporting firms is lower than that for non-exporting firms. In other words, the size distribution for exporting firms is systematically more fat-tailed than the size distribution of the non-exporting ones. The difference is highly statistically significant. Column (7) reports the t-statistic for the difference between the coefficients in columns (5) and (6), and shows that they are in fact significantly different.[9] As we argue above, while this is exactly what theory predicts, this aspect of the firm size distribution has until now been ignored in the empirical literature.

Fig. 5 presents the sales results graphically. Panels (a) and (b) report the cdf and the pdf, respectively. The cdf for exporting firms is everywhere flatter and above the cdf for non-exporting ones. At each size cutoff, there are more large firms that export than those that do not. The pdf plot conveys the same message.

A couple of other features of the results are worth noting. First, for all estimation methods, the full-sample coefficient from Table 1 is always between the exporting and the non-exporting sample coefficients in Table 2. This is exactly what we would expect. Second, we can see that the fit of the power law relationships in both subsamples

[9] We do not report the t-tests for whether the CDF and PDF coefficients are statistically significantly different from each other, as those are "heuristic" estimators without a well-developed statistical model of standard errors. Nonetheless, a simple t-test based on the coefficients and standard errors reported in Table 2 always rejects equality between the CDF and PDF coefficients in Columns (1) compared to (2) and (3) compared to (4).

Table 2
Power laws in firm size, non-exporting and exporting firms: sales and employees.

	CDF		PDF		ln(Rank − 0.5)		
	(1) Exporters	(2) Non-exporters	(3) Exporters	(4) Non-exporters	(5) Exporters	(6) Non-exporters	(7) t-stat
I. Sales							
ζ	0.964	1.055	0.967	1.095	0.738	1.029	37.03**
	(0.042)	(0.011)	(0.041)	(0.044)	(0.006)	(0.005)	
R^2	0.981	0.999	0.996	0.996	0.972	0.998	
No. of firms	67,078	90,006	67,078	90,006	67,078	90,006	
II. Employees							
ζ	0.967	1.251	0.949	1.111	0.724	0.891	28.54**
	(0.078)	(0.074)	(0.100)	(0.041)	(0.004)	(0.004)	
R^2	0.939	0.967	0.974	0.991	0.906	0.870	
No. of firms	66,040	86,389	66,040	86,389	66,040	86,389	

Notes: This table reports the estimates of power laws in firm size (total sales or employees) for non-exporting and exporting firms separately, using the three methods described in the text. Columns (1)–(2) estimate the CDF of the power law specified in Eq. (7). Columns (3)–(4) estimate the PDF of the power law specified in Eq. (8). Columns (5)–(6) regress ln (Rank − 0.5) of the firm in the size distribution on the natural logarithm of its size (Gabaix and Ibragimov, 2011). The last column reports the *t*-statistic for the test of the difference between the coefficients in columns (5) and (6).

** Significant at the 1% level.

is still quite good. The range of the R^2's is 0.972 to 0.999 for sales, and 0.870 to 0.991 for employees.

It could be that the results are driven by the fact that exporters are on average larger than non-exporters. To check robustness of the results, we therefore compare the exporters' group to a non-exporters' group while dropping smallest non-exporting firms so that the mean sales of the two groups is equal. This way, the power laws for exporters and non-exporters are estimated on the samples with identical mean firm size. The results, reported in Appendix Table A3, are robust to matching up the mean size of non-exporters and exporters.

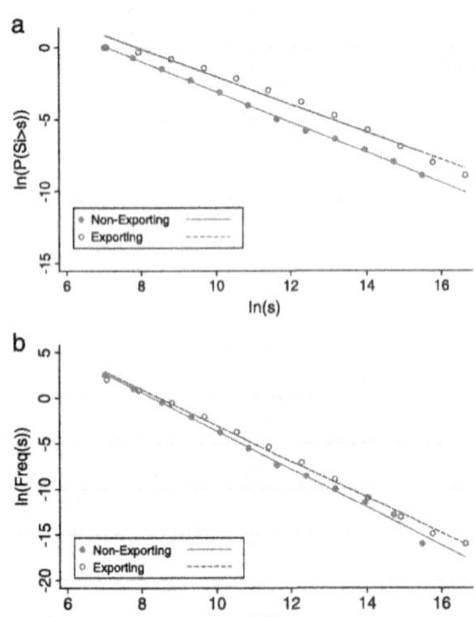

Fig. 5. Power laws in the distribution of firm size, exporting and non-exporting firms. Notes: This figure reports the estimated power laws in firm size for exporting and non-exporting firms separately. The power laws are estimated with two different methods, the CDF (panel a) and the pdf (panel b).

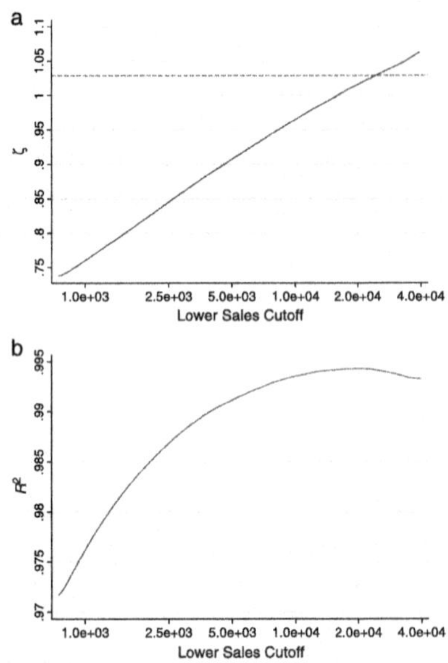

Fig. 6. Power law coefficient for exporting firms. Notes: The top panel of this Figure depicts the power law coefficient estimated on exporting firms on the vertical axis, plotted against the minimum sales cutoff on the horizontal axis. The dashed horizontal line in the top panel is the power law coefficient for domestic firms. The bottom panel depicts the concomitant evolution in the R^2's of the estimates.

Table 3
Power laws in firm size by sector, non-exporting and exporting firms: sales.

Sector	Exporting firms (1) ζ	(2) Std. error	(3) R^2	(4) No. of firms	Non-exporting firms (5) ζ	(6) Std. error	(7) R^2	(8) No. of firms	(9) t-stat
Agriculture, Forestry, and Fishing	1.010	0.046	0.985	982	1.418	0.037	0.997	2967	6.98^{**}
Food Products	0.609	0.016	0.908	2876	0.937	0.021	0.984	4155	12.57^{**}
Apparel and Leather Products	0.818	0.034	0.958	1135	1.287	0.092	0.990	394	4.79^{**}
Printing and Publishing	0.808	0.025	0.971	2136	1.127	0.035	0.997	2056	7.44^{**}
Pharmaceuticals, Perfumes, and Beauty Products	0.512	0.029	0.903	605	0.604	0.071	0.975	145	1.19
Furniture, Household Goods	0.755	0.027	0.969	1540	1.490	0.068	0.993	971	10.08^{**}
Automotive	0.531	0.030	0.958	608	0.651	0.049	0.903	347	2.07^{*}
Transport Equipment	0.554	0.040	0.975	393	0.877	0.084	0.991	218	3.48^{**}
Non-electrical Machinery	0.785	0.017	0.967	4166	1.338	0.028	0.984	4556	16.81^{**}
Electrical Machinery	0.710	0.027	0.979	1394	1.437	0.059	0.991	1179	11.18^{**}
Mineral Products	0.656	0.031	0.948	919	0.979	0.031	0.948	2062	7.49^{**}
Textiles	0.844	0.038	0.919	1008	1.194	0.091	0.992	346	3.56^{**}
Wood and Paper Products	0.765	0.026	0.958	1695	1.234	0.045	0.982	1511	9.01^{**}
Chemicals, Plastic, and Rubber	0.662	0.018	0.935	2613	0.888	0.039	0.976	1046	5.27^{**}
Metals	0.793	0.017	0.976	4574	1.241	0.031	0.993	3244	12.79^{**}
Electrical and Electronic Components	0.648	0.029	0.958	977	1.181	0.077	0.992	473	6.48^{**}
Fuels	0.378	0.076	0.955	49	0.470	0.077	0.924	75	0.85
Water, Gas, Electricity	0.362	0.081	0.944	40	0.622	0.038	0.967	529	2.90^{**}
Automotive Sales and Repair	0.737	0.016	0.947	4516	1.029	0.012	0.981	14,648	14.84^{**}
Wholesale Trade, Intermediaries	0.760	0.008	0.967	20,216	0.923	0.009	0.994	20,265	13.70^{**}
Transport	0.856	0.017	0.970	5339	1.014	0.016	0.995	8293	6.91^{**}
Professional Services	0.814	0.012	0.987	8687	1.155	0.012	1.000	18,165	19.72^{**}
Research and Development	0.751	0.072	0.983	219	0.832	0.093	0.976	159	0.69
Personal and Domestic Services	1.011	0.116	0.967	153	1.663	0.078	0.997	898	4.66^{**}
Education	0.989	0.091	0.971	238	1.387	0.054	0.995	1304	3.77^{**}

Notes: This table reports the estimates of power laws in firm size (total sales) for non-exporting and exporting firms separately, for each individual sector, estimated using the log–rank–log–size estimator. The last column reports the *t*-statistic for the test of the difference between the coefficients in columns (1) and (5).
** Significant at the 1% level.
* Significant at the 5% level.

4.1. Size distribution for exporting firms: nonlinearity and saturation

One of the predictions of the two trade mechanisms outlined above is that for big enough exporting firms, the power law coefficient will converge back to the "true" ζ. This would be the case either because eventually all the big firms will have entered all markets, as in the lower right-hand corner of Fig. 1, or because the stochastic fixed exporting costs have some upper bound, so that (nearly) every firm above a certain productivity cutoff finds it profitable to export. To check for this possibility, we re-estimated the power law in total sales for exporting firms while moving the lower cutoff. Theory predicts that as we constrain the sample to bigger and bigger exporting firms, the power law coefficient will get larger and larger in absolute value, converging eventually to ζ, the coefficient for domestic firms. Fig. 6 depicts the estimates of the power law in firm size for exporting firms as a function of the lower sales cutoff. That is, as we move to the right on the horizontal axis, the power law is estimated on subsamples of bigger and bigger exporting firms.

In line with theory, as we move the cutoff upwards, the power law coefficient becomes larger and larger in absolute value, converging to 1.029, the non-exporting firms coefficient. The bottom panel of the figure reports the R^2 of the power law fit. In the sample of exporting firms, as the estimated coefficient converges to the conceptually correct value, the fit of the power law estimate improves as well, from 0.97 to more than 0.99. This is once again consistent with theory: because exporting behavior induces deviations from a precise power law in the sample of exporting firms, the fit is less tight initially. However, a power law becomes a better and better description of the exporters' size distribution as we constrain the sample to larger and larger firms.

4.2. Sector-level evidence

The model in Section 2 can be interpreted as describing an individual sector rather than the whole economy. Thus, at sector level we should expect to see the same patterns as found above for the aggregate. Examining the predictions of the heterogeneous firm model at the industry level is important for at least two reasons. First, estimates for the economy as a whole are not conclusive evidence that exporting behavior per se generates the differences in power law coefficients. For instance, it is well known that exporters tend to be larger than non-exporters, and thus the findings could be driven by a departure from an exact power law for larger firms. Some of this concern can be assuaged by constraining the sample of exporters and non-exporters to have the same mean size, as we do above. A more convincing approach is to exploit differences in trade openness by sector to provide further evidence for the role of exporting in generating these results. In addition, looking at sector-level data can also reassure us that the results are not driven by compositional effects.

Table 3 reports the results of estimating the power laws in firm size for exporters and non-exporters by sector, the industry-level equivalent of Table 2.[10] For compactness, we only report the log–rank–log–size estimates, though the PDF and the CDF estimators deliver virtually identical results. It is clear that the effects we illustrate in the economy-wide data are present at the sector level. In every one of the 25 tradeable sectors, the power law coefficient for non-exporting firms is larger in absolute value than the coefficient for exporting firms. In 22 out of 25 of these sectors, this difference is statistically significant. In fact, if anything the difference between the two coefficients is slightly more pronounced at the sector level: while in the aggregate results of Table 2 the difference between the two coefficients is 0.29, at sector level the mean difference between these coefficients is 0.35.

An auxiliary prediction of theory is that the exporting behavior will induce greater deviations in the value of power law exponents in

[10] Appendix Table A4 presents the sector-level estimates for employees rather than total sales for size. The results are the same.

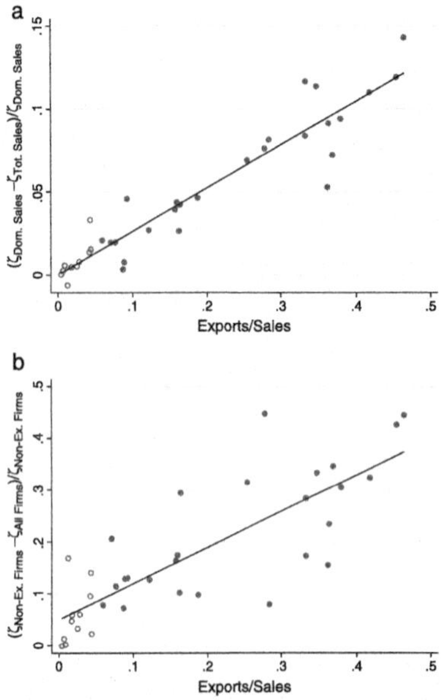

Fig. 7. Deviations in power law estimates and openness at sector level. Notes: The Figure plots the differences between the power law coefficients at sector level against trade openness. In both panels, sector-level exports relative to total sales are on the horizontal axis. In the top panel, on the vertical axis is the percentage difference between the power law exponent estimated on domestic sales only and the power law exponent estimated on total sales: $\frac{\zeta_{dom}-\zeta_{total}}{\zeta_{dom}}$. In the bottom panel, on the vertical axis is the percentage difference between the power law exponent estimated on sales of non-exporting firms only and the power law exponent estimated on total sales of all firms: $\frac{\zeta_{nonex}-\zeta_{total}}{\zeta_{nonex}}$. The non-tradeable sectors are denoted by hollow dots, and the tradeable sectors by solid dots. The straight line is the OLS fit through the data.

sectors that are more open to trade. Fig. 7(a) investigates this prediction. On the vertical axis is the percentage difference between the power law coefficient for domestic sales and the traditional power law coefficient as estimated on the total sales of all firms in the sector: $\frac{\zeta_{dom}-\zeta_{total}}{\zeta_{dom}}$, where ζ_{dom} is the coefficient obtained from fitting a power law on domestic sales only, and ζ_{total} is the exponent of the power law for total sales. On the horizontal axis is the overall sector openness: the ratio of exports to total sales in the sector. For ease of comparison, the non-tradeable sectors are denoted by hollow dots, and the tradeable sectors by solid dots. The figure also reports the OLS fit through the data. The underlying power law coefficients and exports to sales ratios are reported in Appendix Table A2.

The relationship is striking: the more open the sector, the greater is the difference between the conventional power law coefficient estimated on total sales and the power law coefficient estimated on domestic sales only. The simple bivariate correlation between these two variables is a remarkable 0.92. Similarly, Fig. 7(b) plots the relationship between sector openness and the difference between the conventional power law coefficient and the coefficient estimated on non-exporting firms only: $\frac{\zeta_{nonex}-\zeta_{total}}{\zeta_{nonex}}$, where ζ_{nonex} is the power law coefficient estimated on the sales of non-exporting firms only, reported in column 5 of Table 3. Once again, the positive and significant relationship is quite pronounced: the correlation between the two variables is 0.72.

The variation in the impact of exporting behavior on power law coefficients across sectors thus provides remarkable supporting evidence that international trade changes the distribution of firm size in systematic and predictable ways.

4.3. Corrections and quantitative implications

What is the economic significance of these differences? In Section 2, we show analytically that the power law exponent in firm size, ζ, is related to $\frac{\theta}{\varepsilon-1}$, where θ is the parameter in the distribution of productivities, and ε is the elasticity of substitution between goods. As such, estimates of ζ have been used in empirical and quantitative analyses to pin down this combination of parameters (see, e.g. Helpman et al., 2004; Chaney, 2008). Above, we showed that estimating power laws without regard for exporting behavior implies that the estimated ζ does not actually equal $\frac{\theta}{\varepsilon-1}$.

However, it is still possible to recover a reliable estimate of $\frac{\theta}{\varepsilon-1}$ in two simple ways suggested by theory. The first relies on the observation that in the sample of non-exporting firms only, ζ does in fact correspond to $\frac{\theta}{\varepsilon-1}$. Thus, in any dataset that contains explicit information on whether or not a firm exports (without necessarily reporting the value of exports), $\frac{\theta}{\varepsilon-1}$ can be estimated by restricting attention to non-exporting firms.

The non-exporters estimates of Table 2 do precisely that. Comparing the conventional estimates of ζ that are based on all firms in the economy (Table 1) with the estimates based on the non-exporting sample (columns 2, 4, and 6 of Table 2) thus allows us to get a sense of how far off are the conventional estimates of $\frac{\theta}{\varepsilon-1}$. In practice, for the CDF and PDF estimators, this does not turn out to be a large difference: Table 1 coefficients for all firms are only about 3.6% off from the "true" estimates of $\frac{\theta}{\varepsilon-1}$, that are based on the non-exporting firms only. For the log-rank–log-size estimator, this difference is larger, 20%.

The second correction suggested by theory is that for all firms, the domestic sales will obey the power law with exponent $\frac{\theta}{\varepsilon-1}$. Thus, another conceptually correct way of estimating this combination of parameters is to fit a power law on domestic sales for all firms, non-exporting and exporting. Table 4 reports the results. Several things are worth noting. First, as predicted by theory, the power law estimates in Table 4 are higher in absolute value than in Table 1 for total sales. Once again, we see that ignoring exporting behavior leads to power law estimates that are too low. Second, the coefficients in Table 4 are quite similar to the non-exporter coefficients of Table 2, suggesting that the two different corrections we propose deliver mutually consistent

Table 4
Power law in firm size, all firms, domestic sales only.

	(1) CDF	(2) PDF	(3) ln(Rank − 0.5)
ζ	1.048	1.055	0.869
	(0.030)	(0.027)	(0.004)
R^2	0.992	0.998	0.992
No. of firms	157,084	157,084	157,084

Notes: This table reports the estimates of power laws in firm size (domestic sales), using the three methods described in the text. Column (1) estimates the CDF of the power law specified in Eq. (7). Column (2) estimates the PDF of the power law specified in Eq. (8). Column 3 regresses ln(Rank − 0.5) of the firm in the size distribution on the natural logarithm of its size (Gabaix and Ibragimov, 2011).

results. Of course, this correction cannot be implemented using employment instead of sales, since employment data cannot be broken down into workers producing for domestic market and those producing for exports.

5. Conclusion

It has been known since at least the 1940s and the 1950s that the probability distributions for many economic variables can be described by power laws. Fifty years on, renewed interest in the causes and consequences of these phenomena coincides with the advancement and application of theoretical frameworks that model heterogeneous firms. This paper argues that theories of heterogeneous firms can fruitfully inform the empirics of estimating power laws in firm size. We set up a simple version of such a model, and show that international trade affects the distribution of firm size systematically: the exponent of the power law among exporting firms is lower than among the non-exporting firms. We then use a comprehensive dataset of French firms to demonstrate that this prediction holds very strongly in the data.

Two corrections can be implemented to obtain power law estimates consistent with theory. The main advantage of the methods proposed here is simplicity: all they require is an appropriate modification of either the estimation sample, or the variable to be used. In practice, it turns out that at the economy-wide level, the estimated corrected coefficients do not differ much from the traditional, unadjusted ones. One possible conclusion from this exercise is that if one is interested in a ballpark estimate of the extent of firm size heterogeneity, systematic biases introduced by exporting behavior are not that large. However, we would caution against generalizing this conclusion to other countries and settings. For instance, the impact of exporting behavior could be much greater in smaller countries, or in developing ones, or in individual industries. Thus, a more general approach to obtaining reliable estimates would be to implement the corrections suggested in this paper.

Appendix A. Proof of Proposition 1

Proof. The firm's export sales are given by:

$$X_i = \begin{cases} 0 & \text{if } \frac{\phi D_i}{\varepsilon} < \kappa_i; \text{ probability } 1-H(D_i) \\ \phi D_i & \text{if } \frac{\phi D_i}{\varepsilon} \geq \kappa_i; \text{ probability } H(D_i). \end{cases} \quad \text{A.1}$$

The total (worldwide) sales of the firms are $S_i = D_i + X_i$, which implies that

$$S_i = \begin{cases} D_i & \text{if } \frac{\phi D_i}{\varepsilon} < \kappa_i; \text{ probability } 1-H(D_i) \\ (1+\phi)\ D_i & \text{if } \frac{\phi D_i}{\varepsilon} \geq \kappa_i; \text{ probability } H(D_i). \end{cases} \quad \text{A.2}$$

From Eq. (A.1), the probability of exports, conditioning on domestic size is:

$$P(X_i > 0 \mid D_i) = H(D_i).$$

Call p_Y the density of a generic variable Y. We start from the postulate (e.g., coming from random growth) that the distribution of baseline sizes is:

$$p_D(x) = kx^{-\zeta-1} 1_{x > \underline{D}}, \quad \text{(A.3)}$$

where k is an integration constant, $k = \zeta \underline{D}^{\zeta}$.

We next calculate the distribution of exports. To do that, we consider an arbitrary "test function" g (continuous and non-zero over on a compact set), and calculate the expected value of a test function $g(X)$. First, given (A.1),

$$E[g(X_i) \mid D_i] = (1-H(D_i)\ )\ g(0) + H(D_i)\ g(\phi D_i).$$

Therefore,

$$\begin{aligned} E[g(X_i)\ ] &= E[E[g(X_i) \mid D_i]] \\ &= E[(1-H(D_i))\ g(0) + H(D_i)\ g(\phi D_i)] \\ &= \int_D (1-H(D))\ g(0) p_D(D) + H(D)\ g(\phi D)\ p_D(D)\ dD \\ E[g(X_i)\ ] &= \left(\int_D (1-H(D))\ p_D(D)\right) g(0) + \int_{x>0} \left(H\left(\frac{x}{\phi}\right) p_D\left(\frac{x}{\phi}\right) \frac{1}{\phi}\right) g(x)\ dx. \end{aligned} \quad \text{(A.4)}$$

Eq. (A.4) implies that the probability measure associated with x has a point mass $\int_D (1-H(D))p_D(D)$ on $X=0$, and a density $H\left(\frac{x}{\phi}\right) p_D\left(\frac{x}{\phi}\right) \frac{1}{\phi}$ for $x>0$. Hence, the density associated with the restriction of the exports to $X>0$ is

$$p_X(x) = k' p_D\left(\frac{x}{\phi}\right) H\left(\frac{x}{\phi}\right) \frac{1}{\phi}$$

for a constant k' such that $\int_{x>0} p_X(x) dx = 1$. With the Pareto density of baseline sizes (A.3),

$$p_X(x) = Kx^{-\zeta-1} H\left(\frac{x}{\phi}\right) 1_{x > \phi \underline{D}}$$

for a constant $K = k' \phi^{\zeta} k$.

We can calculate the distribution of S_i using a similar approach. From Eq. (A.2), a reasoning analogous to the one used for exports shows:

$$p_S(x) = p_D(x)\ (1-H(x)) + p_D\left(\frac{x}{1+\phi}\right) H\left(\frac{x}{1+\phi}\right) \frac{1}{1+\phi}.$$

Thus, with the Pareto specification for D:

$$p_S(x) = kx^{-\zeta-1}\left[1-H(x) + H\left(\frac{x}{1+\phi}\right) (1+\phi)^{\zeta}\right] 1_{x > (1+\phi)\underline{D}} + kx^{-\zeta-1} 1_{\underline{D} < x < (1+\phi)\underline{D}}. \quad \text{(A.5)}$$

We see a Pareto shape in the tails, but modulated by the export probability function H. □

Table A1
Summary statistics.

	No. of firms	Mean	St. dev.	Min	Max
All firms					
Total Sales	157,084	14,024	254,450	751	6.16E+07
Export Sales	157,084	2894	89,232	0	1.95E+07
Employees	152,429	44.64	626	1	168,386
Correlation (Sales, Employees) = 0.67					
Non-exporting firms					
Total Sales	90,006	6434	86,009	751	1.67E+07
Employees	86,389	25.42	583	1	168,386
Correlation (Sales, Employees) = 0.77					
Exporting firms					
Total Sales	67,078	24,208	376,185	752	6.16E+07
Export Sales	67,078	6777	136,456	1	1.95E+07
Employees	66,040	69.79	678	1	96,856
Correlation (Sales, Employees) = 0.79					

Notes: This table presents the summary statistics for the variables used in the estimation. Sales figures are in thousands of Euros.

Table A2
Power laws in firm size by sector, all sales and domestic sales.

	All sales			Domestic sales				
	(1) ζ	(2) Std. error	(3) R^2	(4) ζ	(5) Std. error	(6) R^2	(7) No. of firms	(8) Exports/sales
Tradeable sectors								
Agriculture, Forestry, and Fishing	−1.233	0.028	0.997	−1.292	0.029	0.998	3949	0.092
Food Products	−0.661	0.011	0.962	−0.691	0.012	0.964	7031	0.164
Apparel and Leather Products	−0.842	0.030	0.970	−0.908	0.033	0.968	1529	0.368
Printing and Publishing	−0.895	0.020	0.988	−0.913	0.020	0.989	4192	0.071
Pharmaceuticals, Perfumes, and Beauty Products	−0.510	0.026	0.912	−0.539	0.028	0.927	750	0.362
Furniture, Household Goods	−0.824	0.023	0.989	−0.892	0.025	0.992	2511	0.278
Automotive	−0.538	0.025	0.987	−0.588	0.027	0.993	955	0.333
Transport Equipment	−0.593	0.034	0.987	−0.667	0.038	0.994	611	0.418
Non-electrical Machinery	−0.893	0.014	0.989	−1.007	0.015	0.986	8722	0.347
Electrical Machinery	−0.798	0.022	0.995	−0.931	0.026	0.996	2573	0.464
Mineral Products	−0.809	0.021	0.972	−0.845	0.022	0.971	2981	0.159
Textiles	−0.855	0.033	0.938	−0.968	0.037	0.949	1354	0.333
Wood and Paper Products	−0.845	0.021	0.981	−0.908	0.023	0.979	3206	0.254
Chemicals, Plastic, and Rubber	−0.680	0.016	0.949	−0.748	0.017	0.955	3659	0.363
Metals	−0.863	0.014	0.989	−0.952	0.015	0.988	7818	0.379
Electrical and Electronic Components	−0.678	0.025	0.976	−0.770	0.029	0.978	1450	0.454
Fuels	−0.422	0.054	0.957	−0.434	0.055	0.957	124	0.162
Water, Gas, Electricity	−0.577	0.034	0.979	−0.579	0.034	0.978	569	0.087
Automotive Sales and Repair	−1.146	0.008	0.996	−1.152	0.008	0.996	38,100	0.089
Wholesale Trade, Intermediaries	−0.896	0.009	0.980	−0.903	0.009	0.979	19,164	0.122
Transport	−0.806	0.006	0.982	−0.828	0.006	0.985	40,481	0.187
Professional Services	−1.107	0.007	0.996	−1.112	0.007	0.996	52,780	0.157
Research and Development	−0.915	0.011	0.987	−0.959	0.012	0.988	13,632	0.284
Personal and Domestic Services	−0.545	0.011	0.984	−0.548	0.011	0.984	4632	0.077
Education	−0.959	0.011	0.986	−0.959	0.011	0.986	15,329	0.059
Non-tradeable sectors								
Construction	−0.548	0.037	0.994	−0.567	0.038	0.995	439	0.017
Retail Trade	−0.966	0.008	0.998	−1.006	0.009	0.999	26,852	0.018
Real Estate	−0.892	0.012	0.990	−0.899	0.012	0.991	11,183	0.004
Financial Services	−0.766	0.056	0.983	−0.834	0.061	0.988	378	0.009
Post and Telecommunications	−1.367	0.018	0.991	−1.374	0.018	0.991	12,152	0.043
Business Services	−0.928	0.021	0.994	−0.941	0.021	0.994	3888	0.028
Hotels and Restaurants	−1.473	0.064	0.989	−1.503	0.066	0.993	1051	0.025
Recreational, Cultural, and Athletic Activities	−1.279	0.046	0.996	−1.306	0.047	0.996	1542	0.042
Health and Social Action	−1.111	0.021	0.978	−1.114	0.021	0.978	5853	0.007
Public Administration	−0.901	0.157	0.990	−0.896	0.156	0.989	66	0.013
Unions and Extra-Territorial Activities	−1.012	0.055	0.993	−1.027	0.055	0.993	687	0.044

Notes: This table reports the estimates of power laws in firm size, for total sales (Columns 1–3), and for domestic sales (Columns 4–6), for each individual sector, estimated using the log-rank–log-size estimator. The last column reports the exports/total sales ratio in each sector.

Table A3
Power laws in firm size, non-exporting and exporting firms: robustness to size distribution.

	CDF		PDF		ln(Rank −0.5)		
	(1) Exporters	(2) Non-exporters	(3) Exporters	(4) Non-exporters	(5) Exporters	(6) Non-exporters	(7) t-stat
I. Sales							
ζ	0.964	1.112	0.967	1.116	0.738	1.106	30.88**
	(0.042)	(0.025)	(0.041)	(0.040)	(0.004)	(0.011)	
R^2	0.981	0.995	0.996	0.997	0.972	0.998	
No. of firms	67,078	19,447	67,078	19,447	67,078	19,447	

Notes: This table reports the estimates of power laws in firm size (total sales) for non-exporting and exporting firms separately, using the three methods described in the text. The non-exporting sample has been trimmed of small firms, such that the mean of sales for non-exporting firms equals the mean of sales for exporting firms. Columns (1)–(2) estimate the CDF of the power law specified in Eq. (7). Columns (3)–(4) estimate the PDF of the power law specified in Eq. (8). Columns (5)–(6) regress ln(Rank − 0.5) of the firm in the size distribution on the natural logarithm of its size (Gabaix and Ibragimov, 2011). The last column reports the t-statistic for the test of the difference between the coefficients in columns (5) and (6).

** Significant at the 1% level.

Table A4
Power laws in firm size by sector, non-exporting and exporting firms: employees.

	Exporting firms				Non-exporting firms				
Sector	(1) ζ	(2) Std. error	(3) R^2	(4) No. of firms	(5) ζ	(6) Std. error	(7) R^2	(8) No. of firms	(9) t-stat
Agriculture, Forestry, and Fishing	0.850	0.039	0.869	952	0.975	0.026	0.806	2868	2.66**
Food Products	0.698	0.018	0.889	2850	0.994	0.022	0.878	4082	10.28**
Apparel and Leather Products	0.778	0.033	0.900	1128	0.819	0.059	0.791	390	0.62
Printing and Publishing	0.808	0.025	0.905	2105	0.986	0.031	0.894	2013	4.48**
Pharmaceuticals, Perfumes, and Beauty Products	0.555	0.032	0.841	597	0.626	0.076	0.921	137	0.86
Furniture, Household Goods	0.789	0.028	0.923	1536	1.205	0.055	0.899	964	6.72**
Automotive	0.598	0.034	0.924	602	1.045	0.081	0.905	336	5.10**
Transport Equipment	0.553	0.040	0.940	389	0.730	0.071	0.925	212	2.18*
Non-electrical Machinery	0.809	0.018	0.918	4154	1.158	0.024	0.872	4534	11.59**
Electrical Machinery	0.756	0.029	0.947	1391	1.191	0.049	0.891	1174	7.65**
Mineral Products	0.727	0.034	0.927	917	0.960	0.031	0.855	1928	5.08**
Textiles	0.850	0.038	0.858	1004	0.995	0.076	0.861	344	1.71+
Wood and Paper Products	0.835	0.029	0.911	1693	1.131	0.041	0.880	1504	5.90**
Chemicals, Plastic, and Rubber	0.733	0.020	0.893	2601	0.903	0.040	0.889	1019	3.80**
Metals	0.875	0.018	0.929	4566	1.129	0.028	0.872	3213	7.55**
Electrical and Electronic Components	0.667	0.030	0.920	972	0.975	0.063	0.877	472	4.38**
Fuels	0.507	0.105	0.884	47	0.473	0.087	0.888	59	−0.25
Water, Gas, Electricity	0.382	0.091	0.970	35	0.523	0.044	0.892	286	1.40
Automotive Sales and Repair	0.795	0.017	0.882	4436	0.953	0.011	0.859	14,204	7.78**
Wholesale Trade, Intermediaries	0.793	0.008	0.907	19,651	0.894	0.009	0.883	19,154	8.28**
Transport	0.815	0.016	0.906	5312	0.854	0.014	0.898	7965	1.87+
Professional Services	0.760	0.012	0.925	8508	0.914	0.010	0.876	17,230	10.11**
Research and Development	0.738	0.072	0.900	210	0.648	0.076	0.888	147	−0.86
Personal and Domestic Services	0.920	0.105	0.953	153	1.142	0.054	0.877	887	1.88+
Education	0.889	0.083	0.873	231	1.041	0.041	0.875	1267	1.64+

Notes: This table reports the estimates of power laws in firm size (employees) for non-exporting and exporting firms separately, for each individual sector, estimated using the log-rank-log-size estimator. The last column reports the *t*-statistic for the test of the difference between the coefficients in Columns (1) and (5).
** Significant at the 1% level.
* Significant at the 5% level.
+ Significant at the 10% level.

References

Arkolakis, C., May 2009. A unified theory of firm selection and growth, mimeo, Yale University.

Arkolakis, C., 2010. Market penetration costs and the new consumers margin in international trade. Journal of Political Economy 118 (6), 1151–1199 December.

Axtell, R.L., 2001. Zipf distribution of U.S. firm sizes. Science 293 (5536), 1818–1820 September.

Buera, F., Shin, Y., 2010. Financial Frictions and the Persistence of History: A Quantitative Exploration, NBER Working Paper No. 16400. September.

Champernowne, D., 1953. A model of income distribution. Economic Journal 83, 318–351.

Chaney, T., 2008. Distorted gravity: the intensive and extensive margins of international trade. American Economic Review 98 (4), 1707–1721 September.

di Giovanni, J., Levchenko, A.A., 2010a. Country Size, International Trade and Aggregate Fluctuations in Granular Economies, RSIE Discussion Paper 585. November.

di Giovanni, J., Levchenko, A.A., 2010b. Firm Entry, Trade, and Welfare in Zipf's World, NBER Working Paper No. 16313. August.

Easterly, W., Reshef, A., Schwenkenberg, J., 2009. The Power of Exports, World Bank Policy Research Working Paper 5081. October.

Eaton, J., Kortum, S., Kramarz, F., December forthcoming. An anatomy of international trade: evidence from French firms. Econometrica.

Gabaix, X., 1999. Zipf's law for cities: an explanation. Quarterly Journal of Economics 114, 739–767.

Gabaix, X., 2009. Power laws in economics and finance. Annual Reviews of Economics 1, 255–293.

Gabaix, X., 2011. The granular origins of aggregate fluctuations. Econometrica 79 (3), 733–772 May.

Gabaix, X., Ibragimov, R., 2011. Rank-1/2: a simple way to improve the OLS estimation of tail exponents. Journal of Business and Economic Statistics 29 (1), 24–39 January.

Gabaix, X., Landier, A., 2007. Why has CEO pay increased so much? Quarterly Journal of Economics 123, 49–100.

Hanson, G.H., Xiang, C., 2011. Trade barriers and trade flows with product heterogeneity: an application to U.S. motion picture exports. Journal of International Economics 83 (1), 14–26 January.

Helpman, E., Melitz, M.J., Yeaple, S.R., 2004. Export versus FDI with heterogeneous firms. American Economic Review 94 (1), 300–316 March.

Hinloopen, J., van Marrewijk, C., 2006. Comparative Advantage, the Rank–Size Rule, and Zipf's Law, Tinbergen Institute Discussion Paper 06-100/1.

Luttmer, E., 2007. Selection, growth, and the size distribution of firms. Quarterly Journal of Economics 122, 1103–1144.

Melitz, M.J., 2003. The impact of trade on intra-industry reallocations and aggregate industry productivity. Econometrica 71 (6), 1695–1725 November.

Rossi-Hansberg, E., Wright, M., 2007. Urban structure and growth. Review of Economic Studies 74, 597–624.

Zipf, G., 1949. Human Behavior and the Principle of Least Effort. Addison-Wesley, Cambridge, Mass.

Journal of International Economics 89 (2013) 283–296

Contents lists available at SciVerse ScienceDirect

Journal of International Economics

journal homepage: www.elsevier.com/locate/jie

Firm entry, trade, and welfare in Zipf's world☆

Julian di Giovanni [a], Andrei A. Levchenko [b,c,]*

[a] International Monetary Fund, United States
[b] University of Michigan, United States
[c] NBER, United States

ARTICLE INFO

Article history:
Received 31 August 2011
Received in revised form 30 June 2012
Accepted 6 August 2012
Available online 21 August 2012

JEL classification:
F12
F15

Keywords:
Zipf's Law
Welfare
Entry costs
Trade barriers

ABSTRACT

Firm size follows Zipf's Law, a very fat-tailed distribution that implies a few large firms account for a disproportionate share of overall economic activity. This distribution of firm size is crucial for evaluating the welfare impact of economic policies such as barriers to entry or trade liberalization. Using a multi-country model of production and trade calibrated to the observed distribution of firm size, we show that the welfare impact of high entry costs is small. In the sample of the 50 largest economies in the world, a reduction in entry costs all the way to the U.S. level leads to an average increase in welfare of only 3.25%. In addition, when the firm size distribution follows Zipf's Law, the welfare impact of the extensive margin of trade – newly imported goods at or near the exporting cutoff – is negligible. The extensive margin of imports accounts for only about 5.2% of the total gains from a 10% reduction in trade barriers in our model. This is because under Zipf's Law, the large, infra-marginal firms have a far greater welfare impact than the much smaller firms that comprise the extensive margin in these policy experiments. The distribution of firm size matters for these results: in a counterfactual model economy that does not exhibit Zipf's Law the gains from a reduction in fixed entry barriers are an order of magnitude larger, while the gains from a reduction in variable trade costs are an order of magnitude smaller.

1. Introduction

An influential recent literature combines fixed costs of production and exporting with firm heterogeneity to study firm-level participation in international trade. Naturally, when the unit of the analysis is the firm, much of the emphasis has been placed on the entry decision into export markets — the so-called "extensive margin." This literature is closely related to the research agenda in economic growth that documents the existence of large impediments to entry and cross-border trade, especially in developing countries.

This paper evaluates the importance of fixed costs of production and trade and the extensive margin of imports for welfare.[1] The key ingredient of our study is the observation that firm size follows Zipf's Law, a very fat-tailed distribution that implies a few large firms account for a disproportionate share of overall economic activity.[2] Our main result is that once Zipf's Law in firm size is accounted for, the impact of fixed costs and the extensive margin on welfare is vanishingly small.

The analysis is based on the workhorse multi-country model of international trade in the spirit of Melitz (2003) and Eaton et al. (2011). We show how this model can be calibrated to match Zipf's Law in firm size, and illustrate analytically how the shape of the firm size distribution affects the importance of fixed costs and the extensive

☆ We are grateful to the editor (Pol Antràs), two anonymous referees, Roc Armenter, Jonathan Eaton, Stefania Garetto, Chris House, Amit Khandelwal, Francesc Ortega, Romain Rancière, David Romer, Matthew Shapiro, Linda Tesar, and seminar participants at the University of Michigan, Trinity College Dublin, International Monetary Fund, University of Houston, Boston University, Vanderbilt University, Tufts University, Tsinghua University,Hong Kong University of Science and Technology, CUNY-Queens College, 2009 NBER ITI Spring Meetings, 2009 CEPR ESSIM, the 2009 Philadelphia Area International Trade Workshop, and the 2011 AEA Meetings for helpful suggestions, and to Aaron Flaaen forexpert research assistance. Levchenko thanks the National Science Foundation for financial support under grant SES-0921971. The views expressed in this paper are those of the authors and should not be attributed to the International Monetary Fund, its Executive Board, or its management.
* Corresponding author.
URL's: JdiGiovanni@imf.org, http://julian.digiovanni.ca (J. di Giovanni), alev@umich.edu, http://www.alevchenko.com (A.A. Levchenko).

0022-1996/$ – see front matter © 2012 Elsevier B.V. All rights reserved.
http://dx.doi.org/10.1016/j.jinteco.2012.08.002

[1] As will become clear below, we analyze the extensive margin defined as the (dis) appearance of firms and exporters due to the changes in the production and exporting productivity cutoffs. This extensive margin is the focus of Chaney (2008), Arkolakis (2010), and Eaton et al. (2011), among many others. The longer NBER WP version of our paper (di Giovanni and Levchenko, 2010) also discusses the impact of the extensive margin coming from changes in the mass of potential firms in the economy, as in Krugman (1980) and Melitz (2003).

[2] This has been documented by Axtell (2001) for the census of U.S. firms, and by di Giovanni et al. (2011) for the census of French firms. Similar findings obtain for several European countries (Fujiwara et al., 2004) and Japan (Okuyama et al., 1999). Other phenomena known to follow power laws include city size, income and wealth, and CEO compensation (Gabaix, 2009).

margin of trade. Then, we calibrate the model to the 50 largest economies in the world, paying special attention to the observed variation in the fixed costs of starting a business or trading internationally. Paradoxically, when the canonical heterogeneous firm framework ideally suited to study the extensive margin of trade is actually calibrated to the observed degree of firm heterogeneity, the extensive margin ceases to matter.

In the quantitative exercise, we first simulate the welfare impact of a world-wide reduction in the fixed costs of entry and exporting all the way to the U.S. level — a 6-fold fall in fixed costs for the average country in the sample. Even such a sizeable improvement leads to an average increase in welfare of only 3.25%. Second, we reduce the variable ("iceberg") trade costs by 10%, and decompose the welfare impact of this change into the intensive margin – existing exporters selling more at lower prices – and the extensive margin – new exporters entering markets. The results are striking: the extensive margin of foreign varieties accounts for only 5.2% of the total welfare gains in this policy experiment. By contrast, the intensive margin is responsible for 98% of the total welfare impact of the fall in the iceberg costs.[3] Finally, we show that Zipf's Law matters a great deal quantitatively. We carry out a counterfactual calibration in which the firm size distribution is instead not fat-tailed. Under this alternative, gains from a reduction in fixed costs are about 12 times *higher*, while total gains from the reduction in iceberg trade costs are 15 times *lower*. Predictably, in this counterfactual calibration the extensive margin of trade is also more important, accounting for 14.7% of the total welfare impact of a 10% fall in variable trade costs. Thus, the distribution of firm size matters a great deal for whether fixed or variable costs have a larger welfare impact. In fact, depending on whether the firm size distribution is fat-tailed, the conclusions are reversed: in Zipf's world fixed costs matter little, while variable costs a great deal; the opposite is true in the counterfactual alternative calibration.

What is the intuition for these results? Changes in fixed costs affect only the behavior of marginal firms; similarly, the welfare impact of the extensive margin of international trade comes by definition from new, marginal exporters. The distribution of firm size contains information about the relative importance of the marginal compared to the infra-marginal firms for welfare. It is especially important to take this into account because Zipf's Law – a power law with an exponent close to -1 – is a very fat-tailed distribution.[4] Economically, Zipf's Law implies that the marginal producers and exporters are far less productive, and therefore are much smaller and sell much less. As a result, their weight in the price index (this index corresponding roughly to the inverse of welfare) is extremely low. By contrast, the infra-marginal, extremely large firms sell a lot and carry a large weight in the price index. Therefore, what happens to the large firms has a first-order impact on welfare. Our calibration exercise allows us to make this mechanism quantitatively precise. In fact, we show analytically that in the limit as the model parameters approach Zipf's Law, the welfare impact of the extensive margin of foreign trade goes to zero.

Ever since the influential work of Djankov et al. (2002), it has been known that cross-country differences in the cost of entry by firms are pronounced. These authors assemble data on the entry regulations in 85 countries, and document that the amount of time, the number of procedures, and the costs – in either dollar terms or as a percentage of per capita income – required to start a business vary widely between countries. The World Bank's Doing Business Initiative collected data on regulations regarding obtaining licenses, registering property, hiring workers, getting credit, and more. Almost invariably, the data show that the variation in these regulations across countries is considerable. In addition, in a cross section of countries entry barriers are robustly negatively correlated with per-capita income and other measures of welfare. However, using cross-country econometric models to quantify the size of the impact is difficult, if not impossible. Our paper presents an alternative approach to welfare analysis. We use the World Bank's Doing Business Indicators database to calibrate the observed variation in fixed costs across countries, and show that a model-based welfare assessment reaches very different conclusions.

Parallel to the research on entry barriers, recent advances in international trade have focused attention on the role of individual firms, both in theory and empirics. Many stylized facts have emerged: most firms do not export, most exporters sell only small amounts abroad, while the bulk of exports at any one point in time is accounted for by a relatively small number of firms (see, e.g. Bernard et al., 2007). The very same model we analyze in this paper has been used in dozens of studies to examine the firm's decision whether to export (e.g., Chaney, 2008), or how much to export (e.g., Arkolakis, 2010). Our analysis suggests that this literature's emphasis on the marginal firms may have been misplaced, at least when it comes to aggregate welfare.

Arkolakis et al. (2008) and Arkolakis et al. (2012) show that in several classes of models, including the standard model of monopolistic competition with endogenous variety adopted in this paper, gains from trade are summarized by the overall trade volume relative to domestic absorption. These authors argue that the overall trade volume is a "sufficient statistic," and thus information on the extensive margin is not necessary to estimate the total gains from trade. Atkeson and Burstein (2010) and Feenstra (2010) show that in two-country heterogeneous firm models with free entry and international trade, the welfare impact of newly imported varieties and existing firms' productivity upgrading decisions is largely offset by the impact of changes in net entry, resulting in virtually no net welfare gains from variety.

Relative to these two results, our paper's substantive point is complementary and distinct. In the sufficient statistic literature, the extensive margin "doesn't matter" only in the sense that one need not observe it to estimate the gains from trade. The sufficient statistic analysis is silent on whether observed changes in the overall trade volumes, and therefore welfare, are due to the extensive or intensive margins. Thus, it cannot be used to determine which policy instruments – for instance, fixed or variable costs – have the greatest welfare impact. In our analysis, the extensive margin doesn't matter for a very different, economic reason: the marginal firms are small. It is thus informative about the role of fixed versus variable costs in welfare. Our results complement Atkeson and Burstein's (2010) and Feenstra's (2010) by demonstrating that under Zipf's Law, the welfare impact of not only the "net extensive margin" – foreign plus domestic – but also of the "gross extensive margin" – foreign and domestic individually – vanishes. In a sense, this is a stronger result as it does not depend on the two gross margins canceling out perfectly. Instead we show that they are both vanishingly small in absolute value. Finally, an additional contribution of this paper is quantitative: we present a systematic assessment of the role of both fixed entry costs and variable trade barriers for welfare in a calibrated multi-country model.

Neary (2010) and Bekkers and Francois (2008) depart from the monopolistic competition paradigm, and develop heterogeneous firm models that feature strategic interactions between the large firms. Since we show that under the empirically observed distribution of firm size the small firms are unimportant, our results are complementary to the research agenda that seeks a richer model of the interaction between the largest firms.

Before moving on to the description of the model, a caveat is in order for interpreting the results. Our quantitative exercise does not strictly speaking tell us that the extensive margin does not matter

[3] The disappearing domestic varieties (the domestic extensive margin) have a correspondingly negative welfare impact.

[4] A random variable generating a power law with an exponent between -1 and -2 has infinite variance. When the power law exponent is less than 1 in absolute value, the mean becomes infinite as well.

for welfare. As such, it is not in direct contradiction with the empirical studies that find a welfare impact of increased varieties (Broda and Weinstein, 2006; Goldberg et al., 2009, 2010). First, the extensive margin in the model need not coincide with the extensive margin measured in the data. For instance, the extensive margin as measured in the data corresponds to new varieties at any point of the distribution, rather than at the cutoff as in our baseline model. Second, our counterfactual scenario of a 10% reduction in iceberg trade costs need not be a good approximation of the shocks that affected the number of varieties in the existing empirical studies. What our results demonstrate is that if the extensive margin is to matter for welfare, it would be through channels not captured by the standard model in this paper. This is important because the literature so far has predominantly used this type of model for the study of the extensive margin.

The rest of the paper is organized as follows. Section 2 presents the theoretical framework. We show how the parameters of the model govern the distribution of firm size, and how they can be mapped into the empirical firm size distribution. We then derive a number of analytical results that foreshadow the conclusions from the quantitative exercise. Section 3 solves the model economy numerically and presents the quantitative results. Section 4 concludes.

2. Theoretical framework

The world is composed of N countries, indexed by $i,j=1,\ldots,N$. In country i, buyers (who could be final consumers or firms buying intermediate inputs) solve

$$\max\left[\int_{J_i} Q_i(k)^{\frac{\varepsilon-1}{\varepsilon}} dk\right]^{\frac{\varepsilon}{\varepsilon-1}}$$
$$s.t.$$
$$\int_{J_i} p_i(k) Q_i(k) dk = X_i,$$

where $Q_i(k)$ is the quantity sold of good k in country i, $p_i(k)$ is the price of this good, X_i is total expenditure in the economy, and J_i is the mass of varieties consumed in country i, coming from all countries. It is well known that demand for variety k in country i is equal to

$$Q_i(k) = \frac{X_i}{P_i^{1-\varepsilon}} p_i(k)^{-\varepsilon}, \tag{1}$$

where P_i is the ideal price index in this economy,

$$P_i = \left[\int_{J_i} p_i(k)^{1-\varepsilon} dk\right]^{\frac{1}{1-\varepsilon}}. \tag{2}$$

Each country has a fixed number of potential (but not actual) entrepreneurs n_i, as in Chaney (2008), Arkolakis (2010), and Eaton et al. (2011).[5] Each potential entrepreneur can produce a unique variety k, and faces downward-sloping demand given by Eq. (1). There are both fixed and variable costs of production and trade. Each entrepreneur's type is given by the unit input requirement $a(k)$. On the basis $a(k)$, each entrepreneur in country j decides which, if any, markets to serve. A firm based in country j that decides to sell to market i must pay a fixed cost f_{ij}, and an iceberg per-unit cost of $\tau_{ij} > 1$, with the iceberg cost of domestic sales normalized to one: $\tau_{jj} = 1$.

There is one factor of production, labor, with country endowments given by L_j, $j=1,\ldots,N$. Production uses both labor and intermediate inputs. In particular, the entrepreneur with unit input requirement $a(k)$ must use this many input bundles to produce one unit of output. An input bundle has a cost $c_j = w_j^{\beta} P_j^{1-\beta}$, where w_j is the wage of workers in country j, and P_j is, as above, the ideal price index of all varieties available in j. Firm k from country j thus has a marginal cost $\tau_{ij} c_j a(k)$ of serving this market i. As is well known, the profit-maximizing price is a constant markup over marginal cost, $p_i(k) = \frac{\varepsilon}{\varepsilon-1}\tau_{ij} c_j a(k)$, the revenue is equal to $\frac{X_i}{P_i^{1-\varepsilon}}\left(\frac{\varepsilon}{\varepsilon-1}\tau_{ij} c_j a(k)\right)^{1-\varepsilon}$, and the variable profits are a constant multiple $1/\varepsilon$ of revenue.

The production structure of the economy is pinned down by the number of firms from each country that enter each market. In particular, there is a cutoff unit input requirement a_{ij}, above which firms in country j do not serve market i. The cutoff a_{ij} characterizes the entrepreneur in j who earns zero profits from shipping to country i:

$$a_{ij} = \frac{\varepsilon-1}{\varepsilon}\frac{P_i}{\tau_{ij} c_j}\left(\frac{X_i}{\varepsilon c_j f_{ij}}\right)^{\frac{1}{\varepsilon-1}}. \tag{3}$$

Closing the model involves finding expressions for a_{ij}, P_i, and w_i for all $i,j=1,\ldots,N$.

We make the standard assumption that productivity, $1/a$, is Pareto(b,θ), where b is the minimum value productivity can take, and θ regulates dispersion[6]:

$$\Pr(1/a < x) = 1 - \left(\frac{b}{x}\right)^{\theta}.$$

It is then straightforward to show that the unit input requirement, a, has a distribution function $G(a) = (ba)^{\theta}$. The price level then becomes, after plugging in the expressions for a_{ij} in Eq. (3):

$$\begin{aligned} P_i &= \left\{\sum_{j=1}^{N}\int_{J_{ij}}\left[\frac{\varepsilon}{\varepsilon-1}\tau_{ij} c_j a(k)\right]^{1-\varepsilon} dk\right\}^{\frac{1}{1-\varepsilon}} \\ &= \left(\sum_{j=1}^{N} n_j \int_0^{a_{ij}}\left[\frac{\varepsilon}{\varepsilon-1}\tau_{ij} c_j a\right]^{1-\varepsilon} dG(a)\right)^{\frac{1}{1-\varepsilon}} \end{aligned} \tag{4}$$

$$= \frac{1}{b}\left[\frac{\theta}{\theta-(\varepsilon-1)}\right]^{-\frac{1}{\theta}}\frac{\varepsilon}{\varepsilon-1}\left(\frac{X_i}{\varepsilon}\right)^{-\frac{\theta-(\varepsilon-1)}{\theta(\varepsilon-1)}}\left(\sum_{j=1}^{N} n_j\left(\tau_{ij} c_j\right)^{-\theta}\left(c_j f_{ij}\right)^{-\frac{\theta-(\varepsilon-1)}{\varepsilon-1}}\right)^{-\frac{1}{\theta}}. \tag{5}$$

We impose balanced trade for each country, and use the convenient property (originally noted by Eaton and Kortum, 2005) that total profits in the economy are a constant multiple of X_i: $\Pi_i = \frac{\varepsilon-1}{\theta\varepsilon}X_i$.[7] Since total sales in the economy are equal to X_i, and the total profits are $\frac{\varepsilon-1}{\theta\varepsilon}X_i$, the total spending on inputs is $(1-\frac{\varepsilon-1}{\theta\varepsilon})X_i$. Labor receives a constant fraction β of the spending on inputs. Thus, total spending in country i is a constant multiple of its total labor income:

$$X_i = \frac{1}{\beta(1-\frac{\varepsilon-1}{\theta\varepsilon})} w_i L_i. \tag{6}$$

The value of exports from country i to country j can be written as:

$$X_{ji} = \frac{X_j}{P_j^{1-\varepsilon}}\left(\frac{\varepsilon}{\varepsilon-1}\tau_{ji} c_i\right)^{1-\varepsilon} n_i \frac{b^{\theta}\theta}{\theta-(\varepsilon-1)} a_{ji}^{\theta-(\varepsilon-1)}.$$

---

[5] This is an appropriate description of the economy at a given point in time, and thus the comparative statics based on this model should be interpreted as short- to medium-run. The NBER WP version of this paper (di Giovanni and Levchenko, 2010) presents a model in which the mass of potential entrepreneurs can adjust, as in Krugman (1980) and Melitz (2003). The main quantitative results are similar.

[6] The Pareto assumption is by far the most common distributional assumption made in the heterogeneous firm models. As we show below, it leads to a power law relationship in firm size. An alternative would be to assume a lognormal distribution with a high enough variance. However, Luttmer (2007) argues thata power law relationship fits the distribution of firm size significantly better than the lognormal distribution.

[7] The NBER WP version of this paper (di Giovanni and Levchenko, 2010) presents the proof.

Using the expression for a_{ji} in Eq. (3), and P_j in Eq. (5), total exports from i to j become:

$$X_{ji} = \frac{n_i\left(\tau_{ji}c_i\right)^{-\theta}\left(c_i f_{ji}\right)^{-\frac{\theta-(\varepsilon-1)}{\varepsilon-1}}}{\sum_{l=1}^{N} n_l\left(\tau_{jl}c_l\right)^{-\theta}\left(c_l f_{jl}\right)^{-\frac{\theta-(\varepsilon-1)}{\varepsilon-1}}} X_j. \tag{7}$$

Using the trade balance conditions, $X_i = \sum_{j=1}^{N} X_{ji}$ for each $i = 1,\ldots,N$, the expression for X_i in Eq. (6), and the definition of c_i leads to the following system of equations in w_i:

$$w_i L_i = \sum_{j=1}^{N} \frac{n_i\left(\tau_{ji}w_i^{\beta}P_i^{1-\beta}\right)^{-\theta}\left(w_i^{\beta}P_i^{1-\beta}f_{ji}\right)^{-\frac{\theta-(\varepsilon-1)}{\varepsilon-1}}}{\sum_{l=1}^{N} n_l\left(\tau_{jl}w_l^{\beta}P_l^{1-\beta}\right)^{-\theta}\left(w_l^{\beta}P_l^{1-\beta}f_{jl}\right)^{-\frac{\theta-(\varepsilon-1)}{\varepsilon-1}}} w_j L_j, \tag{8}$$

$i = 1,\ldots,N$. There are $N-1$ independent equations in this system, which can be solved for wages in $N-1$ countries given a numéraire wage in the remaining country. The wages and the price levels in all countries are determined jointly by Eq. (8) for wages and Eq. (5) for prices. We will solve these numerically in order to carry out the main quantitative exercise in this paper.

2.1. The distribution of firm size: model and data

Denote the sales of an individual firm k by $x(a(k))$. Firm sales x follow a power law if

$$\Pr(x > s) = cs^{-\zeta}. \tag{9}$$

When the exponent ζ is close to 1 in absolute value, the distribution is known as Zipf's Law. It has been argued that in the data, the firm sales distribution is quite well approximated by Zipf's Law. Thus, the empirical firm size distribution places a key restriction on important parameter values in models with heterogeneous firms.

Calibrating a trade model in which not all firms export to the firm size data requires some care. The conventional estimation approach is to fit a power law relationship in Eq. (9) to total firm sales (see, e.g. Axtell, 2001, for a prominent example). As argued at length by di Giovanni et al. (2011), in a model with selection into exporting total firm sales will not follow a power law, and thus there is no simple combination of parameters that can be set equal to the conventional empirical power law estimate. However, di Giovanni et al. (2011) also provide a solution to this problem, by suggesting two alternative approaches to calibrate heterogeneous firm models to the firm size data. The key is to notice that while in the model *total* sales do not follow a power law, *domestic* sales do. To see this, note that in the model, the domestic sales of a firm as a function of its unit input requirement are: $x(a) = Ca^{1-\varepsilon}$, where the constant C reflects market size, and we drop the country subscripts. Under the assumption that $1/a \sim Pareto(b,\theta)$, the power law follows:

$$\Pr(x > s) = \Pr\left(Ca^{1-\varepsilon} > s\right) = \Pr\left(\frac{1}{a} > \left(\frac{s}{C}\right)^{\frac{1}{\varepsilon-1}}\right) = \left(\frac{b^{\varepsilon-1}C}{s}\right)^{\frac{\theta}{\varepsilon-1}},$$

satisfying Eq. (9) for $c = \left(b^{\varepsilon-1}C\right)^{\frac{\theta}{\varepsilon-1}}$ and $\zeta = \frac{\theta}{\varepsilon-1}$.

The key point for connecting the model to the data is that in the model, *domestic sales* follow a power law with the slope of $\frac{\theta}{\varepsilon-1}$. Since this exponent can also be estimated in the data, what we observe in the data is informative about this combination of parameters. What do the data tell us about the domestic sales ζ? Di Giovanni et al. (2011) report a range of estimates of the power laws in domestic sales, all of which are quite close to 1. The mid-range estimate in di Giovanni et al. (2011) is 1.06, which is the value used throughout this paper.[8]

The question remains whether Zipf's Law obtains in the domestic sales distributions of many countries. Currently, no comprehensive set of results exists. Axtell (2001) estimates a power law for firm size in the U.S., and reports a range of estimates of ζ between 0.996 and 1.059, very precisely estimated with standard errors between 0.054 and 0.064. Evidence for a limited set of European countries is presented by Fujiwara et al. (2004) and for Japan by Okuyama et al. (1999). In Appendix B, we use ORBIS – the largest publicly available firm-level dataset covering a large number of countries – to show that firm size distributions are well approximated by a power law, with exponents quite close to -1 in most countries.[9] In addition to the paucity of estimates based on total sales, there are no existing results that take explicit account of selection into exporting, and report estimates based on domestic rather than total sales. However, by comparing the power law estimates based on total and domestic sales, di Giovanni et al. (2011) show that the bias introduced by selection into exporting is typically not large for France, and thus empirical power law estimates based on total sales probably give a reasonably accurate ballpark estimate of the degree of dispersion in domestic sales as well.

To summarize, empirical estimates of the distribution of firm size put discipline on the parameters of the Melitz–Pareto model. In particular, existing estimates suggest that $\frac{\theta}{\varepsilon-1}$ is very close to 1. As we show in a series of exercises below, this has striking implications regarding gains from reductions in entry barriers and trade costs and the relative importance of intensive and extensive margins.

2.2. Entry costs, trade openness, and the magnitude of gains from trade

We now present a number of analytical results about the relative importance of fixed costs, trade openness, and the extensive margin for welfare. Real income per capita in country i is proportional to w_i/P_i, which is also a measure of welfare.[10] It is possible to use trade shares to simplify the expression for the price level. Define $\pi_{ij} \equiv X_{ij}/X_i$ to be the share of total spending in country i on goods from country

[8] Crozet and Koenig (2010, henceforth CK) use French firm-level export data and within-France geographical location to provide structural estimates of θ and ε at sector level, and find values that imply $\theta/(\varepsilon-1)$ much higher than 1. However, (i) their structural estimates are most likely inconsistent with other relationships implied by their own model, namely sales distributions; and (ii) there are important reasons to suspect the validity of these estimates because of inconsistencies in their estimation procedures. The structural model adopted by CK implies export sales to an individual destination follow a power law with exponent $\theta/(\varepsilon-1)$. The sector-level estimates of $\theta/(\varepsilon-1)$ based on the sales distributions in di Giovanni et al. (2011) reveal values close to 1. In our view the estimates reported in di Giovanni et al. (2011) paper are more reliable, because while CK's procedure is based on estimating three structural equations, and thus relies fully on three model-implied relationships, estimates in di Giovanni et al. (2011) are much more parsimonious, based on just one equation. In addition, the third estimating equation in CK is not internally consistent. It backs out the $\theta-(\varepsilon-1)$ combination of parameters based on the cumulative sales of all firms with marginal cost less than a. To proxy for a, they use Olley–Pakes TFP estimates, which are revenue-based, whereas a is physical productivity. Revenue-based TFP, unlike true physical marginal cost a, is not distributed Pareto(θ), since more productive firms will charge lower prices. Thus, CK's third estimating equation is not precisely specified, and the coefficient in that equation should not be thought of as $\theta-(\varepsilon-1)$. Indeed, it is clear that this equation is responsible for the divergence between di Giovanni et al.'s (2011) estimates and CK's results: Zipf's Law implies that $\theta-(\varepsilon-1)$ is close to zero, whereas CK's coefficients in the third equation are between about 1.5 and 3.

[9] Other related results also shed light on how fat-tailed size distributions are. For instance, it turns out that measures of Balassa revealed comparative advantage (Hinloopen and van Marrewijk, 2006) and highly disaggregated trade flows (Easterly et al., 2009) also follow power laws with an exponent close to -1.

[10] Welfare is proportional to the real wage even though in this economy there are profits. At noted above, profits are a constant multiple of the total expenditure, while due to the Cobb–Douglas functional form of the input bundle, the wage bill $w_i L_i$ is a constant multiple of total expenditure as well. Hence, the total profits in the economy are a constant multiple of the wage bill, making the total welfare proportional to the real wage. See Eq. (6).

j. Using Eq. (7), setting $i=j$ and rearranging yields the following relationship:

$$\sum_{l=1}^{N} n_l(\tau_{il}c_l)^{-\theta}(c_i f_{il})^{-1} = \frac{1}{\pi_{ii}} n_i(c_i)^{-\theta}(c_i f_{ii})^{-\frac{\theta-(\varepsilon-1)}{\varepsilon-1}}.$$

Plugging this expression into the price level (Eq. (5)) and rearranging, welfare in this economy can be written as:

$$\frac{w_i}{P_i} = \left\{\frac{1}{b}\left[\frac{\theta}{\theta-(\varepsilon-1)}\right]^{-\frac{1}{\theta}} \frac{\varepsilon}{\varepsilon-1} n_i^{-\frac{1}{\theta}} \left(\frac{L_i}{f_{ii}\varepsilon\beta(1-\frac{\varepsilon-1}{\varepsilon\theta})}\right)^{-\frac{\theta-(\varepsilon-1)}{\theta(\varepsilon-1)}} \pi_{ii}^{\frac{1}{\theta}}\right\}^{-\frac{1}{B}} \tag{10}$$

where $B \equiv \beta-(1-\beta)\frac{\theta-(\varepsilon-1)}{\theta(\varepsilon-1)}$. This allows us to represent real income per capita in each country relative to the U.S. as a product of several components:

$$\frac{w_i/P_i}{w_{US}/P_{US}} = \left(\frac{n_i}{n_{US}}\right)^{\frac{1}{\theta B}} \left(\frac{L_i}{L_{US}}\right)^{\frac{\theta-(\varepsilon-1)}{\theta(\varepsilon-1)B}} \left(\frac{f_{ii}}{f_{US,US}}\right)^{\frac{\theta-(\varepsilon-1)}{\theta(\varepsilon-1)B}} \left(\frac{\pi_{ii}}{\pi_{US,US}}\right)^{\frac{1}{\theta B}}.$$

A special case of this expression is obtained if we adopt the assumption in Alvarez and Lucas (2007) and Chaney (2008) that the number of productivity draws in each country is proportional to its size: $n_i = \gamma L_i$, where γ is a constant. In that case, income differences can be decomposed as:

$$\frac{w_i/P_i}{w_{US}/P_{US}} = \left(\frac{L_i}{L_{US}}\right)^{\frac{1}{(\varepsilon-1)B}} \left(\frac{f_{ii}}{f_{US,US}}\right)^{-\frac{\theta-(\varepsilon-1)}{\theta(\varepsilon-1)B}} \left(\frac{\pi_{ii}}{\pi_{US,US}}\right)^{-\frac{1}{\theta B}}.$$

This expression is similar in spirit to Waugh (2010), with some key differences. The similarity is in the contribution of trade to income differences, which is summarized simply by the relative openness ($\pi_{ii}/\pi_{US,US}$). The difference is that in our model entry costs also matter (the $f_{ii}/f_{US,US}$ term), and there is a market size effect such that larger countries have lower price levels and higher real per-capita incomes, all else equal.

We can get a sense of the magnitudes involved by examining both the variation in the relative fixed costs and openness, as well as the exponents. We choose the parameter values as follows: $\beta=0.5$ from Jones (2011), $\varepsilon=6$ (Anderson and van Wincoop, 2004), and $\theta=5.3$, designed to match the power law exponent in domestic sales, $\frac{\theta}{\varepsilon-1}=1.06$ (di Giovanni et al., 2011). Then, the exponents in the expression above become:

$$\frac{w_i/P_i}{w_{US}/P_{US}} = \left(\frac{L_i}{L_{US}}\right)^{0.40} \left(\frac{f_{ii}}{f_{US,US}}\right)^{-0.02} \left(\frac{\pi_{ii}}{\pi_{US,US}}\right)^{-0.38}.$$

It is immediate that the relative fixed costs will matter far less than the other two terms. In a Zipf economy, what is really important for welfare is the presence of the large, very productive firms, which are inframarginal and not affected much by the level of fixed costs.

To make this more precise, we use the World Bank's Doing Business Indicators to measure variation in $f_{ii}/f_{US,US}$ present in the data, and compute how much per-capita income variation those can generate. It turns out that the country at the 95th percentile of the fixed cost distribution has an f_{ii} that is between 16 and 658 times the U.S. value, depending on the precise indicator we use. Plugging those ratios into the equation above, we get that the country at the 95th percentile of fixed entry costs has an income level between 0.86 and 0.94 that of the U.S., all else equal. In a Zipf economy, differences in fixed costs of entry cannot generate large per-capita income – and welfare – differences.

What about trade? In the sample of the 49 largest economies by total GDP, the ratio $\pi_{ii}/\pi_{US,US}$ for the economy in the 95th percentile of openness is 0.577. Taking that to the correct exponent implies that this country has an income level 1.23 times that of the U.S. While the absolute variation in $\pi_{ii}/\pi_{US,US}$ in the data is far lower than the variation in fixed costs, the impact of trade openness on welfare is larger.

The distribution of firm size matters for these magnitudes. To see what happens when we depart from Zipf's Law, we set $\frac{\theta}{\varepsilon-1}$ equal to 2 (implying a value of $\theta=10$ given our chosen elasticity of substitution). When the exponent on the power law in firm size is greater than or equal to 2, the distribution of firm size has finite variance. Thus, in this alternative calibration we set the exponent on the power law in firm size to be the smallest such that the distribution still has a finite variance.

In a non-Zipf economy, the exponents change dramatically: on the $f_{ii}/f_{US,US}$ term, the exponent goes up from 0.02 to 0.22 in absolute value, a tenfold increase. By contrast, the exponent on the $\pi_{ii}/\pi_{US,US}$ term drops by almost half, from 0.38 to 0.22. This implies that the importance of fixed costs rises: now, a country in the 95th percentile of the f_{ii} distribution has an income level between 0.23 and 0.54 that of the U.S. By contrast, the contribution of trade drops by half: the country in the 95th percentile of trade openness has income per capita only about 1.12 times the U.S. level.

As a related point, the shape of the firm size distribution matters a great deal for the magnitude of gains from trade. In this model, gains from trade are equal to[11]:

$$\pi_{ii}^{-\frac{1}{\theta B}}. \tag{11}$$

At a given π_{ii}, gains from trade are decreasing in $\frac{\theta}{\varepsilon-1}$ as long as $\beta\varepsilon>1$.[12] In other words, the closer is the economy to Zipf's Law, the larger are the gains from trade. This is intuitive: in the world dominated by ultra-productive firms, the big gains from trade come from having access to those extremely productive foreign varieties. Using the values of β, ε, and θ described above, in the sample of 50 largest economies in the world, average gains from trade are 13%, with a standard deviation of 11% across countries. Assuming instead that $\frac{\theta}{\varepsilon-1}=2$ (the firm size distribution is not fat-tailed) reduces the estimated mean gains almost in half (to 7%), and the variation across countries in half as well (standard deviation of 6%).

We note the connections between our results and others in the literature. Bernard et al. (2003) also use firm/plant data to calibrate a quantitative trade model with firm-level heterogeneity. Although they use a different framework, by calibrating to firm-level data they also obtain a lower value of θ than what is implied by alternative estimation procedures, and in turn, larger overall welfare gains from trade. Something similar is taking place in our analysis: when calibrating the model using firm-level data, we find a value of θ close to 5, which is at the lower end of the estimates from the gravity literature. On a related note, the choice of $\varepsilon=6$ and $\frac{\theta}{\varepsilon-1}$ ranging from 1 to 2 corresponds to θ between 5 and 10, which is the same range of θs considered in Arkolakis et al. (2012).

2.3. Extensive vs. intensive margins

The Zipf economy is one dominated by few large producers, that are not likely to be "marginal" exporters. Intuitively, this suggests that the distribution of firm size will also affect the relative importance of intensive versus extensive margins for welfare. In this subsection we examine analytically the importance of the two margins. The conclusion is striking: as the firm-size distribution converges to Zipf's Law, the welfare impact of the extensive margin of exports (or indeed domestic production) goes to zero.

---

[11] The gains from trade can be calculated by observing that autarky welfare is given by Eq. (10) when $\pi_{ii}=1$.

[12] This latter condition is likely to be satisfied in the data. Typical estimates of ε range from 3 to 10, while β is on the order of 0.5 (Jones, 2011).

The price level, Eq. (4), can be rewritten as a function of the extensive margin as follows:

$$P_i = \left(\frac{\varepsilon}{\varepsilon-1} b^{\varepsilon-1} \frac{\theta}{\theta-(\varepsilon-1)} \sum_{j=1}^{N} n_j \left(\tau_{ij} c_j\right)^{1-\varepsilon} G\left(a_{ij}\right)^{\frac{\theta-(\varepsilon-1)}{\theta}}\right)^{\frac{1}{1-\varepsilon}}. \quad (12)$$

Here, the price level is expressed in terms of the share of firms from country j supplying country i, $G(a_{ij})$, which is precisely the extensive margin: a change in $G(a_{ij})$ is exactly the increase in the number (mass) of firms supplying market i. To derive the analytical result in the simplest way, let us assume that the countries are symmetric: $L_i = L$, $n_i = n$, $f_{ii} = f\ \forall i$, and $\tau_{ij} = \tau$, $f_{ij} = f_X\ \forall i,j,\ j \neq i$. In that case, wages are the same in all countries, and we normalize them to 1. The price levels are the same in all countries as well, and thus dropping the country subscripts we obtain:

$$P = \left\{\frac{\varepsilon}{\varepsilon-1} b^{\varepsilon-1} \frac{\theta}{\theta-(\varepsilon-1)} n \left(G(a_D)^{\frac{\theta-(\varepsilon-1)}{\theta}} + (N-1)\tau^{1-\varepsilon} G(a_X)^{\frac{\theta-(\varepsilon-1)}{\theta}}\right)\right\}^{\frac{1}{\beta(1-\varepsilon)}}, \quad (13)$$

where a_D is the cutoff for domestic production, and a_X is the cutoff for exporting. These are of course the same across all countries as well.

Note that since wages are normalized to 1, the total welfare in this economy is simply $W = 1/P$. We are now ready to evaluate the relative importance of the extensive and intensive margins. Imagine that there is a reduction in trade costs τ. This reduction will affect both the prices that existing exporters charge in the domestic market, given by $p(k) = \frac{\varepsilon}{\varepsilon-1}\tau c a(k)$, and the mass of firms serving the market, $G(a_X)$. The elasticity of welfare with respect to the extensive and the intensive margins is described in the following proposition.

Proposition 1. *With symmetric countries,*

$$\lim_{\frac{\theta}{\varepsilon-1}\to 1} \frac{d \log W}{d \log G(a_X)} = 0$$

and

$$\lim_{\frac{\theta}{\varepsilon-1}\to 1} \frac{d \log W}{d \log p} > 0.$$

Proof. From the expression for the price level (Eq. (13)), it is immediate that the elasticity of welfare with respect to the extensive margin is equal to:

$$\frac{d \log W}{d \log G(a_X)} = \frac{1}{\beta} \frac{\theta-(\varepsilon-1)}{\theta} \frac{(N-1)\tau^{1-\varepsilon} G(a_X)^{\frac{\theta-(\varepsilon-1)}{\theta}}}{G(a_D)^{\frac{\theta-(\varepsilon-1)}{\theta}} + (N-1)\tau^{1-\varepsilon} G(a_X)^{\frac{\theta-(\varepsilon-1)}{\theta}}}.$$

As the economy approaches Zipf's Law – $\theta \to (\varepsilon - 1)$ – the welfare impact of the extensive margin goes to zero: $\frac{d \log W}{d \log G(a_X)} \to 0$.

The same is not true for the intensive margin. The price p that each exporter charges in the domestic market is proportional to τ. Therefore, the elasticity of welfare with respect to the intensive margin equals:

$$\frac{d \log W}{d \log p} = \frac{1}{\beta} \frac{(N-1)\tau^{1-\varepsilon} G(a_X)^{\frac{\theta-(\varepsilon-1)}{\theta}}}{G(a_D)^{\frac{\theta-(\varepsilon-1)}{\theta}} + (N-1)\tau^{1-\varepsilon} G(a_X)^{\frac{\theta-(\varepsilon-1)}{\theta}}}.$$

The welfare impact of the intensive margin clearly does not converge to zero as $\theta \to (\varepsilon - 1)$. □

What is the intuition for these results? In a Zipf economy the most productive firms are vastly better than the marginal firms. As a result, most of the welfare impact of trade is driven by what happens to these best firms, rather than by whether trade liberalization leads to new entry. That is, a reduction in trade costs impacts welfare mainly because the "major brands" – Sony, Panasonic, etc. – become cheaper, rather than because many additional inferior brands of television sets become available.

The statement of the proposition may be somewhat unconventional in the sense that the comparative statics are with respect to the extensive margin of imports $G(a_X)$, which is itself an endogenous object and a function of model parameters. This is done for expositional simplicity, in order to convey the point that the welfare impact *through the extensive margin* of any parameter change that we could consider is negligible in the limit. To be completely rigorous, we could have stated the results with respect to the impact of each parameter in the model ξ (which could be fixed or variable trade costs, L, n, etc.) on welfare through the extensive margin, $\frac{d \log W}{d \log G(a_X)} \frac{d \log G(a_X)}{d \log \xi}$. It is easily verified that for any exogenous parameter, $\frac{d \log G(a_X)}{d \log \xi}$ is finite.[13] Thus, the proposition that the derivative $\frac{d \log W}{d \log G(a_X)} \frac{d \log G(a_X)}{d \log \xi}$ goes to zero in the limit as $\theta \to (\varepsilon - 1)$ holds.

This discussion shows that the conclusions about the impact of entry barriers, international trade, and the extensive margin are very sensitive to the assumption about the shape of the firm size distribution. All else equal, the fixed costs of production and exporting and the extensive margin matter less as the economy approaches Zipf's Law.

Before proceeding to the quantitative assessment of the importance of entry costs and the intensive and extensive margins of trade in a multi-country calibrated model, it is worth making two additional remarks regarding our modeling approach to fixed costs. Arkolakis (2010) develops a framework in which the fixed costs of entry are replaced by smoother market penetration costs, and firms choose not just whether to enter markets, but also what share of consumers to serve in each market. Appendix A.1 presents the model with market penetration costs, and shows that proportional changes in welfare obtained in that model are identical to those in a simple fixed costs model of the main text. This result holds for all parameter values that govern the distribution of firm size and the curvature of market penetration costs. In addition, we show that as the distribution of firm size converges to Zipf's Law, the *level* of welfare in that model also becomes identical to the baseline model. This is because under Zipf's Law, what matters most for welfare are the very large firms, which are least affected by the introduction of the market penetration margin. The large firms choose to penetrate markets fully, making their sales nearly the same as what they would be in a simple fixed cost model.

Second, as pointed out by Eaton et al. (2011) among others, there is evidence that not all exporters face the same fixed costs of entering foreign markets. Appendix A.2 develops an extension of the model with heterogeneous export entry costs, and shows that the results are unchanged by that alternative modeling approach as well. For these reasons, we choose to adopt the standard formulation of fixed costs of entry in our analysis.

3. Quantitative assessment

In order to implement the model numerically, we find the wages and price levels for each country, w_i and P_i that satisfy the system of equations given by Eqs. (5) and (8). To solve this system, we calibrate the values of L_i, n_i, τ_{ij}, and f_{ij} for each country and country pair, as well as the parameters common to all countries.

[13] The closed-form expression for the extensive margin in terms of exogenous parameters is: $G(a_X) = \left(\frac{\varepsilon-1}{\varepsilon} b\right)^{(1-\Omega)\theta} \left(\frac{\theta-(\varepsilon-1)}{\theta}\right)^{\Omega} \left(\tau f_X^{\frac{1}{\varepsilon-1}}\right)^{-\theta} n^{-\Omega} \left[\beta\varepsilon\left(1-\frac{\varepsilon-1}{\varepsilon\theta}\right)L\right]^{\frac{\theta}{\varepsilon-1}-\left(\frac{\theta}{\varepsilon-1}-1\right)\Omega} \left[f^{-\frac{\theta-(\varepsilon-1)}{\varepsilon-1}} + (N-1)\tau^{-\theta} f_X^{-\frac{\theta-(\varepsilon-1)}{\varepsilon-1}}\right]^{-\Omega}$, where $\Omega \equiv \frac{\theta(\beta\varepsilon-1)}{\theta(\beta\varepsilon-1)+(1-\beta)(\varepsilon-1)}$.

3.1. Calibration

The elasticity of substitution is $\varepsilon = 6$. Anderson and van Wincoop (2004) report available estimates of this elasticity to be in the range of 3 to 10, and we pick a value close to the middle of the range. The key parameter is θ, as it governs the slope of the power law. As described above, in this model domestic sales follow a power law with the exponent equal to $\frac{\theta}{\varepsilon-1}$. In the data, domestic sales follow a power law with the exponent close to 1. Di Giovanni et al. (2011) report the value of 1.06, which we use to find θ given our preferred value of ε: $\theta = 1.06 \times (\varepsilon - 1) = 5.3$. As mentioned above, we set the share of intermediates $\beta = 0.5$, following Jones (2011).

For finding the values of L_i, we follow the approach of Alvarez and Lucas (2007). First, we would like to think of L not as population per se, but as "equipped labor," to take explicit account of TFP and capital endowment differences between countries. To obtain the values of L that are internally consistent in the model, we start with an initial guess for L_i for all $i = 1,\ldots,N$, and use it to solve the model. Given the vector of equilibrium wages, we update our guess for L_i for each country in order to match the ratio of total GDPs between each country i and the U.S. Using the resulting values of L_i, we solve for the new set of wages, and iterate to convergence (for more on this approach, see Alvarez and Lucas, 2007). Thus, our procedure generates vectors w_i and L_i in such a way as to match exactly the relative total GDPs of the countries in the sample. In practice, the results are close to simply equating L_i to the relative GDPs of the countries. In this procedure, we must normalize the population of one of the countries. We thus set L_{US} to its actual value of 291 million as of 2003, and compute L_i of every other country relative to this U.S. value. Finally, we set n_i in proportion to L_i. That is, the country's endowment of entrepreneurs is simply proportional to its "equipped labor" endowment. An important consequence of this assumption is that countries with higher TFP and capital abundance will have a greater number of potential productivity draws, all else equal. This is an assumption adopted by Alvarez and Lucas (2007) and Chaney (2008). We set $n_{US} = 10{,}000{,}000$, that is, there are ten million potential firms in the U.S. In this calibration it implies that there are about 9,500,000 operating firms there. According to the 2002 U.S. Economic Census, there were 6,773,632 establishments with a payroll in the United States. There are an additional 17,646,062 business entities that are not employers, but they account for less than 3.5% of total shipments. Thus, choosing $n_{US} = 10{,}000{,}000$ gets the correct order of magnitude for the number of firms.

Next, we must calibrate the values of τ_{ij} for each pair of countries. To do that we use the set of gravity estimates from the empirical model of Helpman et al. (2008). That is, we combine geographical characteristics such as bilateral distance, common border, common language, whether the two countries are in a currency union and others, with the coefficient estimates reported by Helpman et al. (2008) to calculate values of τ_{ij} for each country pair. Note that in this formulation, $\tau_{ij} = \tau_{ji}$ for all i and j.

Finally, we must take a stand on the values of f_{ii} and f_{ij}. The Doing Business Indicators database (The World Bank, 2007a) collects information on the administrative costs of setting up a firm – the time it takes, the number of procedures, and the monetary cost – in a large sample of countries in the world. The particular variable we use is the amount of time required to set up a business. We favor this indicator compared to others that measure entry costs either in dollars or in units of per capita income, because in our model f_{ii} is a quantity of inputs rather than value. As we must normalize f_{ii} for one country, we set the absolute level of $f_{US,US}$ to ensure an interior solution for the domestic production cutoff.[14] Then, if according to the Doing Business Indicators database it takes 10 times longer to register a business in country i than in the U.S., $f_{ii} = 10 \times f_{US,US}$.[15]

To measure the fixed costs of international trade, we use the Trading Across Borders module of the Doing Business Indicators. This module provides the costs of exporting a 20-foot dry-cargo container out of each country, as well as the costs of importing the same kind of container into each country. Parallel to our approach to setting the domestic cost f_{ii}, the indicators we choose are the amount of time required to carry out these transactions. This ensures that f_{ii} and f_{ij} are measured in the same units. We take the bilateral fixed cost f_{ij} to be the sum of the two: the cost of exporting from country j plus the cost of importing into country i.[16] The foreign trade costs f_{ij} are on average about 40% of the domestic entry costsf_{ii}. This is sensible, as it presumably is more difficult to set up production than to set up a capacity to export.

We carry out the analysis on the sample of the largest 49 countries by total GDP, plus the 50th that represents the rest of the world.[17] These 49 countries together cover 97% of world GDP. We exclude entrepôt economies of Hong Kong and Singapore, both of which have total trade well in excess of their GDP, due to significant re-exporting activity. Thus, our model is not intended to fit these countries. (We do place them into the rest-of-the-world category.) The country sample, sorted by total GDP, is reported in Table A1.

3.2. Model fit

As described above, our iterative procedure ensures that the ratio of total GDPs in the model for any two countries matches exactly the ratio of the total GDPs in the data. Since one of the goals of the paper is to examine the role of trade openness in welfare, it is also important that the model produces bilateral and overall trade volumes that are close to the data.

Fig. 1a reports the scatterplot of bilateral trade ratios $\pi_{ij} = X_{ij}/X_i$. On the horizontal axis is the natural log of π_{ij} that comes from the model, while on the vertical axis is the corresponding value of that bilateral trade flow in the data. Hollow dots represent exports from one country to another, π_{ij}, $i \neq j$. Solid dots, at the top of the scatterplot, represent sales of domestic firms as a share of domestic absorption, π_{ii}. For convenience, we added a 45-degree line. It is clear that the trade volumes implied by the model match the actual data well.

[14] That is, we set $f_{US,US}$ to a level just high enough that $a_{ji} < 1/b$ for all $i,j = 1,\ldots,N$ in all the baseline and counterfactual exercises, with $1/b$ being the upper limit of the distribution of $a(k)$.

[15] In our calibration, individuals differ across countries in their efficiency units of labor. Taking the Doing Business Indicator data literally in light of differences in efficiency units of labor would compress the variation in f_{ii} and f_{ij} across countries, and lead to an even smaller welfare impact of the reductions in f's, making our results even more dramatic. This is because countries with low efficiency units of labor are also the countries with high f_{ii}'s. As an example, suppose that the Doing Business Indicators database says that it takes 10 days to start a business in Mexico, and 1 day in the U.S. And suppose that when we calibrate efficiency units of labor, we find that one U.S. worker (workday) is 10 times as productive as one Mexican worker (workday). In that case, it takes the same amount of efficiency units of labor – one U.S. worker/workday – to start a business in the U.S. as in Mexico. Thus, the patterns in the data are such that accounting for differences in efficiency units of labor will only reduce the variation in f_{ij}'s across countries. The variation in efficiency units of labor observed in the data does not apply as much to the values in the Doing Business Indicators. While for a variety of reasons – adoption of technologies, quantity and quality of capital, etc. – workers in different countries have very different efficiencies in production of output, it is much less clear that efficiency differences should be equally large for the activities that the Doing Business Indicators measure, such as visiting government offices, filling out forms, and getting permits.

[16] An earlier version of the paper carried out the analysis setting the bilateral fixed cost to be the sum of domestic costs of starting a business in the source and destination countries: $f_{ij} = f_{ii} + f_{jj}$. This approach may be preferred if fixed costs of exporting involved more than just shipping, and required, for instance, the exporting firm to create a subsidiary for the distribution in the destination country. The results were virtually identical.

[17] We set the parameters, such as τ_{ij} and f_{ij}, for the rest-of-the-world category as the average values among the remaining countries in the world.

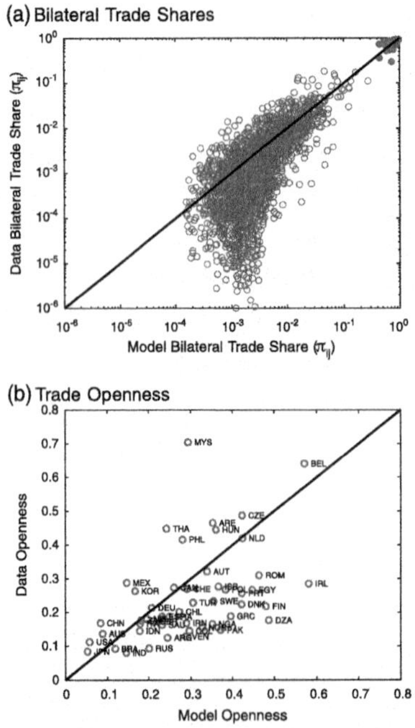

Fig. 1. Bilateral trade shares and trade openness: data and model predictions. Notes: Figure (a) reports the scatterplot of domestic output (π_{ii}) and bilateral trade (π_{ij}), both as a share of domestic absorption. Solid dots represent observations of π_{ii}, while hollow dots represent bilateral trade observations (π_{ij}). Both axes are in log scale. Figure (b) reports the scatterplot of total imports as a share of domestic absorption ($1-\pi_{ii}$). In both figures, the values implied by the model are on the horizontal axis; actual values are on the vertical axis, and the line through the data is the 45-degree line. Source: International Monetary Fund (2007).

Most observations are quite close to the 45-degree line. It is especially important that we get the overall trade openness ($1-\pi_{ii}$) right, since that will drive the gains from trade in each country. Fig. 1b plots the actual values of ($1-\pi_{ii}$) against those implied by the model, along with a 45-degree line. We can see that though the relationship is not perfect, it is close.

Table 1 compares the means and medians of π_{ii} and π_{ij}'s for the model and the data, and reports the correlations between the two. The correlation between domestic shares π_{ii} in the model and in the data for this sample of countries is around 0.49. The means and the medians look very similar as well, with the countries in the model slightly more open on average than the data. The correlation between export shares, π_{ij}, is actually higher at 0.72.

Overall, the model fits bilateral trade data well. This is of course not surprising, as the Helpman et al. (2008) coefficient estimates are based on the gravity relationship, which is well known to fit trade data quite well. Nonetheless, since our calibration procedure does not use explicit information on actual trade flows, we must

Table 1
Bilateral trade shares: data and model predictions for the 50-country sample.
Source: International Monetary Fund (2007).

	Model	Data
Domestic sales as a share of domestic absorption (π_{ii})		
Mean	0.7070	0.7555
Median	0.7086	0.7982
Corr(model, data)	0.4900	
Export sales as a share of domestic absorption (π_{ij})		
Mean	0.0060	0.0047
Median	0.0027	0.0011
Corr(model, data)	0.7171	

Notes: This table reports the means and medians of domestic output (top panel), and bilateral trade (bottom panel), both as a share of domestic absorption, in the model and in the data.

check the fit to actual trade. We now turn to the analysis of welfare gains from reduction in entry costs and trade barriers implied by the model.

3.3. Counterfactual I: reduction in entry costs

Using the calibrated model above, the first counterfactual we perform is a reduction in the fixed costs of entry f_{ii} and f_{ij}. We simulate a complete harmonization of entry costs across the world, such that entry costs everywhere are the same as in the U.S.[18] This is a substantial improvement. As first shown by Djankov et al. (2002), the differences in these fixed costs are substantial across countries. In our sample of the world's 49 largest economies, it takes on average 6 times longer to start a business compared to the U.S. For a country at the 75th percentile of the distribution, it takes almost 8 times longer, and the country with the highest entry costs in this sample – Brazil – it takes 25 times longer than in the U.S. This experiment also entails a substantial drop in the fixed costs of cross-border trade. The average exporting cost in this sample is 3 times higher than in the U.S., and the average importing cost is 4 times higher.

Table 2 reports the associated welfare gains. The top panel presents the baseline calibration, in which the firm-size distribution is set to match Zipf's Law. The welfare gains are small. Even a dramatic drop (6-fold on average) in the fixed costs of production and exporting improves welfare by only 3.26% on average. It could be that this average number is hiding a lot of heterogeneity, since different countries are experiencing a different size reduction in trade costs. In parentheses below the average value, we report the range of welfare gains in the entire sample. We can see that even in the country that gains the most from this institutional improvement, the gain is only about double the average, at 7.32%.[19] Zipf's Law matters a great deal for this conclusion. The bottom panel reports the alternative counterfactual calibration, in which $\theta/(\varepsilon-1)=2$. The welfare gain from the same reduction in entry barriers is on average 40.87% in the non-Zipf world, 12 times higher than in the Zipf's Law

[18] To be precise, we set the cost of setting up a firm, $f_{ii}=f_{US,US}$, and then we set the cost of importing to any country i to the cost of importing to the U.S., and set the cost of exporting from any country i to the cost of exporting from the U.S. Thus the fixed cost of exporting between any two countries f_{ij} in the counterfactual becomes equal to the fixed cost of exporting from the U.S. plus the fixed cost of importing into the U.S.

[19] Without input linkages ($c_i=w_i$), since by construction f_{ij} affects entry but not the variable costs of existing firms, we can think of these welfare gains as coming from the extensive margin. In the presence of input–output linkages, this is not strictly speaking correct because of general equilibrium effects: entry affects the price levels in each country, which in turn enter the marginal costs of each operating firm, and thus can have an impact through the intensive margin as well. Separating out the positive intensive margin effect would leave an even smaller direct extensive margin effect of reductions in entry costs.

Table 2
Welfare gains.

Counterfactual	Total change in welfare	Intensive margin	Extensive margin	
			Foreign	Domestic
$\frac{\theta}{\varepsilon-1} = 1.06$ (Zipf's world)				
Complete harmonization of entry costs	3.26 (0.03, 7.32)			
10% reduction in τ	4.33 (0.28, 8.26)	4.23 (0.28, 8.06) **0.980**	0.21 (0.02, 0.34) **0.052**	−0.11 (−0.14, −0.03) **−0.032**
$\frac{\theta}{\varepsilon-1} = 2$				
Complete harmonization of entry costs	40.87 (0.00, 104.78)			
10% reduction in τ	0.28 (0.01, 1.72)	0.27 (0.01, 1.64) **0.968**	0.038 (0.000, 0.194) **0.147**	−0.025 (−0.114, −0.001) **−0.115**

Notes: This table reports the welfare changes, in percentage points, due to each counterfactual experiment. The numbers in parentheses indicate the range across the 50 countries in the sample. The numbers in bold give the share of each margin (intensive, foreign extensive, and domestic extensive) in the total welfare impact.

calibration. The range is also greater: the country gaining the most more than doubles its welfare.[20]

The intuition for this result is that the distribution of firm size contains information on the relative importance of the marginal and the inframarginal varieties. Under Zipf's Law, the inframarginal varieties – the very large firms – are overwhelmingly more important than the marginal varieties. Thus, since the high entry costs do not affect the entry decision of the very large firms, they do not have much impact on welfare. As our quantitative exercise demonstrates, this is true even in a model with a substantial intermediate input multiplier. As we move away from Zipf's Law, the distribution of firm size becomes flatter. As a result, entry of the marginal firms, and consequently the fixed costs of entry, become more important for welfare.

3.4. Counterfactual II: reduction in variable trade barriers

Consider a global reduction in trade costs τ_{ij}. How will it affect welfare, and what will be the relative importance of the intensive and the extensive margins? We know that welfare in this model is proportional to real income, $W_i = w_i/P_i$. From Eq. (12), welfare can be expressed, up to a constant that is the same in all countries and trade regimes, as follows:

$$W_i = \left[\sum_{j=1}^{N} n_j \left(\tau_{ij}\frac{c_j}{c_i}\right)^{1-\varepsilon} G\left(a_{ij}\right)^{\frac{\theta-(\varepsilon-1)}{\theta}}\right]^{\frac{1}{\beta(\varepsilon-1)}}. \tag{14}$$

A reduction in trade costs will impact the intensive margin, by making existing goods cheaper. That is captured by the $\tau_{ij}\frac{c_j}{c_i}$ term. Additionally, welfare will increase due to the extensive margin, by leading to a greater number of varieties. This is captured by the $G(a_{ij})$ term. Using a Taylor expansion, we can write the proportional increase in welfare as a function of the two margins:

$$\frac{\Delta W_i}{W_i} \approx \frac{1}{\beta}\sum_{j=1}^{N}\varphi_{ij}\left[\underbrace{-\frac{\Delta\left(\tau_{ij}\frac{c_j}{c_i}\right)}{\tau_{ij}\frac{c_j}{c_i}}}_{\text{Intensive Margin}} + \underbrace{\frac{\theta-(\varepsilon-1)}{\theta(\varepsilon-1)}\frac{\Delta G\left(a_{ij}\right)}{G\left(a_{ij}\right)}}_{\text{Extensive Margin}}\right], \tag{15}$$

where φ_{ij} is the weight of country j in country i's price level:

$$\varphi_{ij} \equiv \frac{n_j\left(\tau_{ij}c_j\right)^{1-\varepsilon}G\left(a_{ij}\right)^{\frac{\theta-(\varepsilon-1)}{\theta}}}{\sum_{l=1}^{N} n_l(\tau_{il}c_l)^{1-\varepsilon}G(a_{il})^{\frac{\theta-(\varepsilon-1)}{\theta}}}.$$

It is immediate from Eq. (15) that the extensive margin does not have much of a chance to impact welfare. Any given change in the mass of new firms, $\frac{\Delta G(a_{ij})}{G(a_{ij})}$, while it may be large, is pre-multiplied by the term $\frac{\theta-(\varepsilon-1)}{\theta(\varepsilon-1)}$, which goes to zero as the economy approaches Zipf's Law. The calibrated value of this combination of parameters is about 0.01.

Table 2 reports the quantitative results for our sample of countries. A 10% reduction in trade barriers leads to an average increase in welfare of about 4.3%, with a range between 0.28% and 8.26%. Notably, this is somewhat higher than welfare gain we saw following a complete harmonization of entry barriers across countries. It turns out that the intensive margin accounts for 98% of the overall welfare gain. The table breaks down the extensive margin into the component coming from the new foreign varieties, and the component due to the disappearance of some domestic ones. The foreign extensive margin contributes 5.2% of the total welfare gain. It is partially undone by the domestic extensive margin, whose welfare impact is negative. As we can see, in Zipf's world, the extensive margin plays a minimal role relative to the intensive one.

It is important to emphasize that this result is not due to a small increase in the number of foreign varieties. In this experiment, the 10% reduction in τ_{ij} leads to an average 28% increase in the number of imported foreign varieties in this set of countries. The extensive margin, as measured by the number of varieties, is quantitatively important. However, its contribution to welfare is not.

The bottom panel reports these results with the alternative, non-fat-tailed calibration. Two features are most striking. First, the overall gains from a 10% reduction in τ_{ij} are tiny compared to the baseline calibration. The average gains are only 0.28% (less than one third of 1%), with a maximum of 1.7%. This is 15 times lower than the same reduction in trade costs in the baseline calibration. Second, the overall importance of the intensive margin is almost the same as in the baseline calibration, 96.8%. At first glance this is surprising. But it turns out that the welfare impact of the foreign extensive margin is indeed much bigger than in the baseline calibration, as expected. The foreign extensive margin contributes 14.7% of the total welfare gain, almost 3 times greater than in the baseline calibration. However, the domestic extensive margin is also more important for welfare, contributing −11.5% of the total impact. That is, the disappearance of existing domestic varieties that accompanies the drop in trade costs also has a greater (negative) welfare impact compared to the Zipf case. The two partially cancel out, leaving the relative importance of the intensive margin roughly unchanged.

The main results are presented graphically in Fig. 2. On the x-axis is the power law exponent in firm size, $\theta/(\varepsilon-1)$, which varies from 1.06 (Zipf's Law calibration) to 2. The lines display the welfare impact of the two counterfactual experiments we consider: a 10% reduction in τ_{ij} (solid line) and the complete harmonization in f_{ij} to their U.S. level. The figure illustrates the importance of the firm size distribution for our conclusions about welfare. In particular, it is clear that changes in

[20] An interesting question is how large is the role of international trade in generating this welfare gain. To get a sense of this, we calculated the gains from the same reduction in fixed costs of entry under the assumption that each country is in autarky. It turns out that the magnitude of the autarky gains is very similar. For instance, in the Zipf calibration the autarky gain is 3.47%, compared to 3.26% in the baseline open economy case. We conjecture that the average autarky percentage gain is slightly higher because in the absence of the possibility of importing, it is more important to have access to the most domestic varieties.

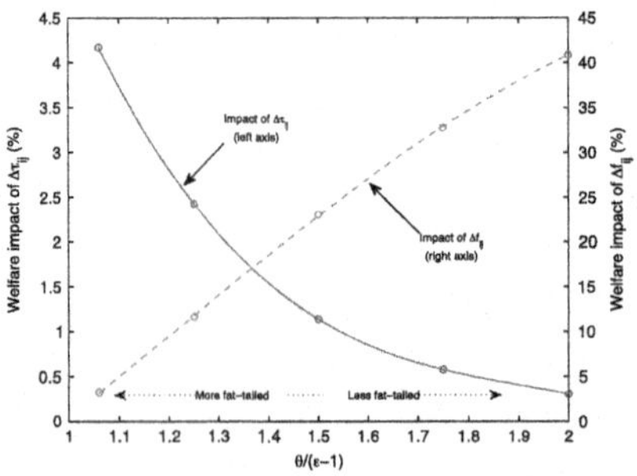

Fig. 2. The welfare impact of reductions in fixed and variable costs and the size distribution of firms. Notes: This figure reports the percentage changes in welfare due to a reduction in iceberg trade costs (solid line, left axis) and a reduction in fixed costs of entry (dashed line, right axis), as a function of the distribution of firm size.

variable costs matter *more* for welfare as the economy approaches Zipf's Law, while changes in fixed costs matter *less*.

3.5. Robustness

This section assesses the robustness of the main results in several dimensions: (i) alternative calibration of iceberg trade costs; (ii) alternative values of the elasticity of substitution; and (iii) the importance of the continuum of goods assumption.

The baseline calibration uses estimates of τ_{ij} from Helpman et al. (2008), and does not match bilateral or overall trade flows perfectly. A natural question is whether the results are affected by this approach. To check for this possibility, we implement an alternative solution procedure, that instead of matching relative country GDPs, picks values of τ_{ij} to match perfectly all bilateral trade flows. To be precise, given the values of L_i implied by our baseline procedure, we find values of w_i, P_i, and $\tau_{ij} \forall i,j$ such that the equilibrium market clearing conditions (5) and (8) hold and all the trade shares (7) in the model match perfectly the data values.[21]

The results are presented in the first row of Table 3. The change in welfare due to the fall in f_{ij} of 3.24% is virtually the same as the baseline value of 3.26%. The welfare impact of a 10% reduction in τ_{ij} is somewhat lower, at 2.57%, but the extensive margin of exports contributes 0.13% to welfare, or 5% of the total. This share of the extensive margin is virtually identical to the baseline finding.

Next, we assess the sensitivity of the results to our choice of ε, by implementing the model under two alternative values, while keeping the calibration to Zipf's law, that is, $\theta/(\varepsilon-1)=1.06$ throughout. We try a lower value of $\varepsilon=4$ (and thus $\theta=3.18$), and then a higher value of $\varepsilon=8$ (and thus $\theta=7.42$). Table 3 presents the results. As expected, the gains under a lower ε are higher, and vice versa, but the main conclusions are unchanged. With respect to the harmonization in entry costs, the gains are 2.42% under $\varepsilon=8$ and 4.86% under $\varepsilon=4$, compared to the baseline of 3.26%. The range of gains from a 10% reduction in τ_{ij} is somewhat larger, from 0.9% to 10.55%, but in either case the contribution of the extensive margin of exports is small, 0.08% and 0.2% respectively (compared to the baseline of 0.21%).

Finally, we check how important the continuum of firms assumption is for the results. The main mechanism in our paper is that under Zipf's Law, the largest firms are extremely large, and thus matter much more for welfare than the marginal firms. Under the continuum of firms assumption and the Pareto distribution, the upper support of firm productivity is infinite. However, in the real world of course no actual firm has infinite productivity, instead there is a discrete and finite number of firms in each country (the implications of this for international trade flows have recently been explored by Eaton et al., 2012). To assess how this affects the results, we simulate the model under a discrete number of firms. That is, we randomly draw n_i productivities for each country i, and given the model solution for the cutoffs a_{ij}, check whether each discrete firm produces domestically and serves each export market. For each set of global productivity draws we perform the main experiments of lowering f_{ij} and lowering τ_{ij}. We compute the price indices directly as the discrete equivalents of Eq. (2), and changes in the extensive margin $\frac{\Delta G(a_{ij})}{G(a_{ij})}$ in Eq. (15) directly as the proportional changes in the numbers of active firms from each market j in each i. We draw a worldwide set of random productivities 1001 times, and take the median welfare change in each country for each counterfactual experiment.[22]

The results, reported in Table 3, are very similar to the baseline. As expected, the impact of reductions in f_{ij} and τ_{ij} is slightly higher than under the continuum of firms. The discrete simulation effectively cuts out the infinitely productive upper tail, thus making the marginal firms slightly more important. The difference is not large, however. The impact of the extensive margin of exports, in both the absolute terms and relative to the total increase in welfare, is virtually identical. We conclude from this exercise that the assumption of a continuum of firms does not drive the quantitative results.

Table 3
Robustness.

	Complete harmonization of entry costs	10% reduction in τ	
		Total	Foreign extensive
Perfect match to trade flows	3.24	2.57	0.13
$\varepsilon=4$	4.86	10.55	0.20
$\varepsilon=8$	2.42	0.91	0.08
Discrete number of firms	5.00	4.61	0.22

Notes: This table reports the welfare changes, in percentage points, under alternative calibration approaches.

4. Conclusion

The world economy and world trade flows are dominated by very large firms. This paper studies the implications of this stylized fact for two related aspects of the economy: entry costs and the extensive margin of exports. The conclusions about the welfare impact of higher entry barriers and the extensive margin of trade are very sensitive to

[21] We cannot match both relative country sizes (as in the baseline calibration) and trade flows perfectly at the same time. We conjecture that this is because the model is too simple: it has one factor of production, no explicit non-traded sector, and no aggregate trade imbalances. The calibration that matches trade flows perfectly produces relative country sizes that are very close to the data, with the correlation in country size between the model and the data of 0.92. Among the 2500 possible unidirectional bilateral trade flows, 18 are zeros. Since the model solution cannot handle zero trade flows, in the matching procedure we replace each data zero trade share with the value of the smallest non-zero trade share found in the sample, which has order of magnitude 10^{-6}.

[22] See di Giovanni and Levchenko (2011) for a more detailed description of the model and simulation with a discrete number of firms. Note that this procedure does not represent a complete solution to the model under each individual set of random productivity draws, because we do not re-calculate the cutoffs a_{ij} and relative wages w_i for each draw. Finding the complete solution to the model under a discrete number of firms would not be feasible, as it would require for each vector of random productivity draws to solve for a fixed point in all the cutoffs, prices, and aggregate expenditures. Since we draw 10 million productivities just for the U.S., and thus dozens of millions of productivity draws for the world overall, looking for the fixed point in a_{ij}'s, w's and X's for the 50 countries would be impractical. Thus, our simulation uses values of a_{ij}'s computed in the solution of the model with a continuum of firms. This procedure is clearly an approximation, but nonetheless it can give us a sense of how the continuum assumption affects the main mechanisms of the model.

the assumptions on the size distribution of firms. In a model calibrated to match the observed firm-size distribution, the welfare costs of entry barriers are low, and the extensive margin accounts for only 5% of the overall gains from a reduction in iceberg trade costs.

What should we take away from this exercise? Quantitative evidence cannot be used to argue that entry costs and the extensive margin of trade are not important for welfare. We can establish, however, that the canonical model of production and trade with endogenous variety cannot generate a significant welfare impact of entry barriers and the extensive margin, while at the same time matching both the empirically observed distribution of firm size and trade volumes. If these matter, it must be through some other channel. Uncovering the conditions under which the costs of entry into domestic and foreign markets matter more remains a fruitful avenue for future research.

Appendix A. Alternative specifications of fixed costs

A.1. Market penetration costs

A recent contribution by Arkolakis (2010) emphasizes that the model with simple fixed costs of accessing markets is too stark. Instead, Arkolakis (2010) proposes a model in which firms choose not only whether to enter a particular market, but what share of the consumers in that market to serve. Arkolakis (2010) and Eaton et al. (2011) demonstrate that modeling entry costs in this more continuous way is important to account for the empirical regularity that many firms export only small amounts abroad.

In this appendix, we extend the baseline model to feature market penetration costs instead of fixed entry costs, and demonstrate that the total welfare in such a model differs from the baseline only by a constant. As a result, in any policy experiment the market penetration costs model produces welfare changes that are identical to the baseline fixed costs model.

Our functional form assumption follows Eaton et al. (2011). Assume that rather than paying the fixed cost $f_{ij}c_j$ to gain access to all consumers in market i, a firm in country j incurs a cost

$$f_{ij}c_j\frac{1-(1-s)^{1-\frac{1}{\lambda}}}{1-\frac{1}{\lambda}}$$

to reach a share s of consumers in that market. Given the demand for its variety by the consumer reached in country i, the firm with unit input requirement $a(k)$ from country j maximizes its profits by choosing both its price and market penetration $s_i(k)$ optimally. The profits are given by:

$$\pi_i(k) = \left[p_i(k)-\tau_{ij}c_ja(k)\right]\left(\frac{p_i(k)}{P_i}\right)^{-\varepsilon}s_i(k)X_i-f_{ij}c_j\frac{1-(1-s)^{1-\frac{1}{\lambda}}}{1-\frac{1}{\lambda}},$$

where the price index, P_i, now aggregates over the prices of varieties available to a typical consumer in i, and not over all the varieties that are sold in that country. It is easily verified that the price is still a constant markup over the marginal cost. Optimal market penetration for a firm with unit input requirement $a(k)$ is given by:

$$s_i(k) = 1-\left[\frac{X_i}{\varepsilon c_j f_{ij}}\left(\frac{\frac{\varepsilon}{\varepsilon-1}\tau_{ij}c_ja(k)}{P_i}\right)^{1-\varepsilon}\right]^{-\lambda}. \tag{A.1}$$

Finally, the firm will only enter market i if at zero market penetration, profits are increasing in s: $\frac{\partial\pi_i(k)}{\partial s}|_{s=0} > 0$. It turns out that the cutoff a_{ij} for positive sales from j to i has the exact same form as in the baseline model, and is given by Eq. (3). That expression can be combined with Eq. (A.1) to write the sales of a firm with unit input requirement $a(k)$ from country j to country i as:

$$\left[1-\left(\frac{a(k)}{a_{ij}}\right)^{\lambda(\varepsilon-1)}\right]\left(\frac{\frac{\varepsilon}{\varepsilon-1}\tau_{ij}c_ja(k)}{P_i}\right)^{1-\varepsilon}X_i.$$

As first observed by Arkolakis (2010), the baseline model with simple fixed costs provides the best approximation to the sales of the largest firms: as the unit input requirement $a(k)$ decreases, $s_i(k) = \left[1-\left(\frac{a(k)}{a_{ij}}\right)^{\lambda(\varepsilon-1)}\right]$ approaches 1 and the firm penetrates the entire market. This result does not rely on the Zipf's Law assumption: the market penetration ratio $s_i(k)$ does not depend on the combination of parameters $\frac{\theta}{\varepsilon-1}$. As we argue at the end of this section, Zipf's Law does imply that the large firms are the ones most important for welfare, and thus the assumption of simple fixed costs adopted in the main text will not substantially affect our conclusions.

Under the Pareto distribution of productivity draws, the expression for the price level in country i is given by:

$$\begin{aligned}P_i^{mp} &= \left(\sum_{j=1}^{N}n_j\int_0^{a_{ij}}\left[\frac{\varepsilon}{\varepsilon-1}\tau_{ij}c_ja(k)\right]^{1-\varepsilon}s_j(k)dG(a(k))\right)^{\frac{1}{1-\varepsilon}}\\ &= \frac{1}{b}\left[\frac{\theta}{\theta-(\varepsilon-1)}-\frac{\theta}{\theta-(\varepsilon-1)(1-\lambda)}\right]^{-\frac{1}{\theta}}\frac{\varepsilon}{\varepsilon-1}\left(\frac{X_i}{\varepsilon}\right)^{-\frac{\theta-(\varepsilon-1)}{\theta(\varepsilon-1)}}\\ &\quad\times\left(\sum_{j=1}^{N}n_j\left(\tau_{ij}c_j\right)^{-\theta}\left(c_jf_{ij}\right)^{-\frac{\theta-(\varepsilon-1)}{\varepsilon-1}}\right).\end{aligned} \tag{A.2}$$

Comparing Eqs. (5) and (A.2), it is clear that the price levels in the baseline model and the market penetration cost model differ only by a constant. The rest of the solution is unchanged. In particular, it is straightforward to show that total profits in each economy are still a constant multiple of X_i, and that the wages are still determined by Eq. (8). Thus, the solution to the market penetration costs model proceeds to find w_i^{mp} and P_i^{mp} for all $i = 1,\ldots,N$ that solve the system of equations given by Eqs. (8) and (A.2). We now state the main result of this section.

Proposition 2. *Let the vectors $[w_1,\ldots,w_N]$ and $[P_1,\ldots,P_N]$ jointly be a solution to the system of equations defining the equilibrium in the baseline fixed costs model, Eqs.(5) and (8). Then, the vectors*

$$\left[w_1^{mp},\ldots,w_N^{mp}\right] = \left[w_1,\ldots,w_N\right] \tag{A.3}$$

and

$$\left[P_1^{mp},\ldots,P_N^{mp}\right] = \delta\left[P_1,\ldots,P_N\right] \tag{A.4}$$

are a solution to the system of Eqs.(A.2) and (8) that define the equilibrium in the market penetration costs model.

Proof. It is immediate from examining Eq. (8) that the vector $[w_1,\ldots,w_N]$ that solves Eq. (8) is the same under $[P_1,\ldots,P_N]$ and $[P_1^{mp},\ldots,P_N^{mp}]$ when the latter is defined by Eq. (A.4), since δ cancels out from the numerator and the denominator. We now show that as long as Eq. (A.3) is satisfied, Eq. (A.4) holds as well for some constant δ. The vector $[P_1^{mp},\ldots,P_N^{mp}]$ provides a solution to the market penetration costs model if $\forall i$, Eq. (A.2) holds. We check directly whether the vector $\delta[P_1,\ldots,P_N]$ satisfies that condition:

$$\begin{aligned}P_i^{mp} = \delta P_i &= \frac{1}{b}\left[\frac{\theta}{\theta-(\varepsilon-1)}-\frac{\theta}{\theta-(\varepsilon-1)(1-\lambda)}\right]^{-\frac{1}{\theta}}\frac{\varepsilon}{\varepsilon-1}\left(\frac{w_iL_i}{\varepsilon\beta\left(1-\frac{\varepsilon-1}{\theta\varepsilon}\right)}\right)^{-\frac{\theta-(\varepsilon-1)}{\theta(\varepsilon-1)}}\\ &\quad\times\left(\sum_{j=1}^{N}n_j\left(\tau_{ij}w_j^{\beta}\left(\delta P_j\right)^{1-\beta}\right)^{-\theta}\left(w_j^{\beta}\left(\delta P_j\right)^{1-\beta}f_{ij}\right)^{-\frac{\theta-(\varepsilon-1)}{\varepsilon-1}}\right)^{-\frac{1}{\theta}}.\end{aligned} \tag{A.5}$$

294 J. di Giovanni, A.A. Levchenko / Journal of International Economics 89 (2013) 283–296

After rearranging it becomes:

$$\delta^{\beta-(1-\beta)\frac{\theta-(\varepsilon-1)}{\theta(\varepsilon-1)}}P_i=\frac{1}{b}\left[\frac{\theta}{\theta-(\varepsilon-1)}-\frac{\theta}{\theta-(\varepsilon-1)(1-\lambda)}\right]^{-\frac{1}{\theta}}\frac{\varepsilon}{\varepsilon-1}\left(\frac{w_iL_i}{\varepsilon\beta\left(1-\frac{\varepsilon-1}{\theta\varepsilon}\right)}\right)^{-\frac{\theta-(\varepsilon-1)}{\theta(\varepsilon-1)}}$$
$$\times\left(\sum_{j=1}^{N}n_j\left(\tau_{ij}w_j^{\beta}P_j^{1-\beta}\right)^{-\theta}\left(w_j^{\beta}P_j^{1-\beta}f_{ij}\right)^{-\frac{\theta-(\varepsilon-1)}{\varepsilon-1}}\right)^{-\frac{1}{\theta}},$$

which is the same as Eq. (5) for δ satisfying $\left[\frac{\theta}{\theta-(\varepsilon-1)}\right]^{-\frac{1}{\theta}}=\left[\frac{\theta}{\theta-(\varepsilon-1)}-\frac{\theta}{\theta-(\varepsilon-1)(1-\lambda)}\right]^{-\frac{1}{\theta}}\delta^{-\left(\beta-(1-\beta)\frac{\theta-(\varepsilon-1)}{\theta(\varepsilon-1)}\right)}$. Since the vector $[P_1,\ldots,P_N]$ satisfies Eq. (5), we have shown that $\delta[P_1,\ldots,P_N]$ satisfies Eq. (A.5), which completes the proof. □

The main consequence of Proposition 2 is that the total welfare in the market penetration costs model differs from the welfare in the basic fixed costs model only by a constant: $w_i^{mp}/P_i^{mp}=(1/\delta)w_i/P_i$. This implies that any percentage change in welfare calculated in this model will be identical to the baseline in the main text.

One additional remark is worth making on the relationship between the market penetration costs model and this paper. Straightforward rearranging yields the following expression for δ:

$$\delta=\left[\frac{\lambda(\varepsilon-1)}{\theta-(\varepsilon-1)(1-\lambda)}\right]^{-\frac{1}{\theta}\frac{1}{\beta-(1-\beta)\frac{\theta-(\varepsilon-1)}{\theta(\varepsilon-1)}}}.$$

Setting $\lambda=1$ the expression in the square brackets becomes $(\varepsilon-1)/\theta$.[23] Therefore, it is immediate that as we approach Zipf's Law, $\delta\rightarrow1$ and the welfare *level* in the market penetration cost model converges exactly to the welfare level in the simple fixed costs model. This is intuitive: under Zipf's Law, what matters the most for welfare are the biggest firms, for which the market penetration margin matters the least, since they choose to serve the entire market.

A.2. Stochastic fixed costs

Another concern with respect to fixed costs is that they may not be the same for all firms. For instance, the model with non-stochastic fixed costs implies a strict hierarchy of entry into markets, which is known not to hold perfectly (Eaton et al., 2011). This section presents an extension of the model with stochastic export entry costs, and shows that it is largely isomorphic to the basic model in the main text.

Suppose that a firm in market j faces a fixed cost $f_{ij}\eta$ to enter market $i\neq j$, where f_{ij} is the component common across firms and $\eta>0$ is a random firm-specific shock. Following standard practice (see, e.g. Eaton et al., 2011), we assume that η is distributed independently of firm unit input requirement a. The cutoff for entering market i by market j firms is now contingent on the realization of η:

$$a_{ij}(\eta)=\frac{\varepsilon-1}{\varepsilon}\frac{P_i}{\tau_{ij}c_j}\left(\frac{X_i}{\varepsilon c_jf_{ij}\eta}\right)^{\frac{1}{\varepsilon-1}}. \tag{A.6}$$

The price level then becomes

$$P_i=\left(\sum_{j=1}^{N}n_j\int_\eta\int_0^{a_{ij}}\left[\frac{\varepsilon}{\varepsilon-1}\tau_{ij}c_ja\right]^{1-\varepsilon}dG(a)dF_{ij}(\eta)\right)^{\frac{1}{1-\varepsilon}}$$
$$=\frac{1}{b}\left[\frac{\theta}{\theta-(\varepsilon-1)}\right]^{-\frac{1}{\theta}}\frac{\varepsilon}{\varepsilon-1}\left(\frac{X_i}{\varepsilon}\right)^{-\frac{\theta-(\varepsilon-1)}{\theta(\varepsilon-1)}}\left(\sum_{j=1}^{N}n_j\tilde{\eta}_{ij}\left(\tau_{ij}c_j\right)^{-\theta}\left(c_jf_{ij}\right)^{-\frac{\theta-(\varepsilon-1)}{\varepsilon-1}}\right)^{-\frac{1}{\theta}},$$

where $F_{ij}(\eta)$ is the CDF of η that can vary by both source and destination, and $\tilde{\eta}_{ij}\equiv\int_\eta\eta^{-\frac{\theta-(\varepsilon-1)}{\varepsilon-1}}dF_{ij}(\eta)$. Since we assume that the costs of entering the domestic market are non-stochastic, trivially $\tilde{\eta}_{ij}=1\forall i$.

It is immediate that the expression for welfare in Eq. (10), and the analysis in Section 2.2 is unchanged. When it comes to the analysis of the impact of the extensive margin on trade in Section 2.3, straightforward steps lead to the following modified expression for the price level, and hence welfare:

$$P=\left\{\frac{\varepsilon}{\varepsilon-1}b^{\varepsilon-1}\frac{\theta}{\theta-(\varepsilon-1)}n\left(G(a_D)^{\frac{\theta-(\varepsilon-1)}{\theta}}+(N-1)\tau^{1-\varepsilon}\int_\eta G(a_X(\eta))^{\frac{\theta-(\varepsilon-1)}{\theta}}dF(\eta)\right)\right\}^{\frac{1}{\beta(1-\varepsilon)}}, \tag{A.8}$$

where now $a_X(\eta)$ is the cutoff unit input requirement necessary for exporting for firms that drew the entry cost disturbance equal to η. Differentiating inside the integral, the elasticity of welfare with respect to the extensive margin $G(a_X(\eta))$ for each level of η is equal to:

$$\frac{d\log W}{d\log G(a_X(\eta))}=\frac{1}{\beta}\frac{\theta-(\varepsilon-1)}{\theta}\frac{(N-1)\tau^{1-\varepsilon}G(a_X(\eta))^{\frac{\theta-(\varepsilon-1)}{\theta}}}{G(a_D)^{\frac{\theta-(\varepsilon-1)}{\theta}}+(N-1)\tau^{1-\varepsilon}\int_\eta G(a_X(\eta))^{\frac{\theta-(\varepsilon-1)}{\theta}}dF(\eta)}.$$

As the economy approaches Zipf's Law – $\theta\rightarrow(\varepsilon-1)$ – the welfare impact of the extensive margin at each level of η goes to zero: $\frac{d\log W}{d\log G(a_X(\eta))}\rightarrow0$.

Introducing stochastic fixed exporting costs has virtually no impact on the results because our main mechanism operates at each level of fixed costs. That is, as long as the distribution of sales is fat-tailed *conditional on any realization of entry costs $f_{ij}\eta$*, it is still the case that the inframarginal exporters among that set of firms are much more productive than the marginal ones. To build intuition, suppose that for some exporter j, η can take only two values, η_H and η_L. This setup is roughly equivalent to facing two exporting countries each with non-stochastic fixed exporting costs, one with $f_{ij}\eta_H$, the other with $f_{ij}\eta_L$, and all of the results in the main text apply.[24] Assuming a continuum of η's instead of two discrete values leaves the basic intuition unchanged.

Appendix B. Power laws in firm size in the ORBIS database

This appendix uses a large cross-country firm-level database to assess whether Zipf's Law approximates well the distribution of firm size in a large sample of countries. Though we use the largest available non-proprietary firm-level database in this analysis, the results should be interpreted with caution: coverage is quite uneven across countries and years, implying that power law estimates may not be reliable or comparable across countries. Nonetheless, as we describe below, Zipf's Law provides a good approximation for the firm size distribution in most countries in this sample.

---

[23] This is the value of λ preferred by Arkolakis (2010). Using Simulated Method of Moments, Eaton et al. (2011) indeed estimate a value of $\lambda=0.91$ with a standard error of 0.12. This type of value for λ implies a fair amount of curvature to the market penetration costs, and thus many firms that choose to penetrate only a small share of the export market. The fixed cost model obtains instead when $\lambda=\infty$.

[24] The reason this setup is not exactly equivalent to having two countries is that labor markets have to clear and a single wage has to prevail in exporter j. This general equilibrium effect does not appreciably affect the heuristic argument here.

ORBIS is a multi-country database published by Bureau van Dijk that contains information on more than 50 million companies worldwide.[25] The data come from a variety of sources, including, but not limited to, registered filings and annual reports. Coverage varies by world region: there are data on some 17 million companies in the U.S. and Canada, 22 million companies in the 46 European countries, 6.2 million companies from Central and South America, 5.3 million from Asia, but only 260,000 from Africa and 45,000 from the Middle East. Importantly, the database includes both publicly traded and privately held firms. While in principle data are available going back to mid-1990s for some countries, coverage improves dramatically for more recent years. Thus, for each country we use the year with the largest number of firms to generate power law estimates. In practice, this implies using more recent years, 2006 to 2008. The main variable used in the analysis is total sales. It has been observed that in some instances a power law is only a good fit for the size distribution above a certain minimum cutoff. This is potentially an even more serious problem in this database, as the likely undersampling of smaller firms will bias the power law estimates towards zero. Following standard practice (Gabaix, 2009), we plot the data for all firms for each country, and select the minimum size cutoff by looking for a "kink" in the distribution above which the relationship between log rank and log size is approximately linear.[26] We restrict our empirical analysis to countries that have sales figures for at least 1000 firms. The final sample includes 44 countries.

In order to obtain reliable estimates, this paper uses three standard methods of estimating the slope of the power law ζ. The first method, based on Axtell (2001), makes direct use of the definition of the power law (Eq. (9)), which in natural logs becomes:

$$\log(\Pr(x > s)) = \log(c) - \zeta \log(s). \tag{B.1}$$

For a grid of values of sales s, the estimated probability $\Pr(x > s)$ is simply the number of firms in the sample with sales greater than s divided by the total number of firms. We then regress the natural log of this probability on $\log(s)$ to obtain our first estimate of ζ. Following the typical approach in the literature, we do this for the values of s that are equidistant from each other on log scale. This implies that in absolute terms, the intervals containing low values of s are narrower than the intervals at high values of s. This is done to get a greater precision of the estimates: since there are fewer large firms, observations in small intervals for very high values of s would be more noisy.

The second approach starts with the observation that the cdf in Eq. (9) has a probability density function

$$f(s) = c\zeta s^{-(\zeta+1)}. \tag{B.2}$$

To estimate this pdf, we divide the values of firm sales into bins of equal size on the log scale, and compute the frequency as the number of firms in each bin divided by the width of the bin. Since in absolute terms the bins are of unequal size, we regress the resulting frequency observations on the value of s which is the geometric mean of the endpoints of the bin (this approach follows Axtell, 2001). Note that the resulting coefficient is an estimate of $-(\zeta+1)$.[27]

[25] The well-known AMADEUS database of European firms is the precursor of ORBIS, which contains all of AMADEUS plus information on non-European countries. Thus, AMADEUS is a strict subset of ORBIS.

[26] This is a conservative approach. The estimates obtained without imposing the minimum size cutoff yield power law coefficients even lower in absolute value, implying an even more fat-tailed distribution of firm size.

[27] Finally, we also regressed $\log(rank - 1/2)$ of each firm in the sales distribution on log of its sales. This is the estimator suggested by Gabaix and Ibragimov (2011), which delivers very similar results. If anything, the power law exponents implied by this estimator are even lower in absolute value than those reported in this appendix.

Table A2 reports the results. The left panel reports estimates of Eq. (B.1), the right panel, Eq. (B.2). (Note that the right panel's estimates are of $-(\zeta+1)$, thus they should differ from the right panel by about -1.) The columns report the power law coefficient, the R^2, and the p-value of the test that the coefficient differs from -1 (-2 in the right panel). Several things are worth noting about these results. First, the power law approximates the data well: the median R^2 is 0.99, with the minimum R^2 of 0.95. Second, most of the power law coefficients are very close to -1 in absolute terms, and many are not statistically different from -1. Those that are statistically different from -1 tend to be *lower* in absolute value, implying that if the firm size distribution follows a power law in those countries, it is even more fat-failed than Zipf. The least fat-tailed country, Serbia, has the power law exponent of about -1.18 or -1.16, still quite far from -2 and thus comfortably within the Zipf's Law range. Finally, the country sample is diverse: it includes major European economies (France, Germany, Netherlands), smaller E.U. accession countries (Czech Republic, Estonia), major middle income countries (Brazil, Argentina), as well as the two largest emerging markets (India and China). All in all, in this sample of 44 countries with very different characteristics, the distributions of firm size are remarkably consistent with Zipf's Law.

It is important to note that these results do not establish that the distribution of firm size in these countries follows a power law, as opposed to some other distribution. Indeed, as noted by Gabaix (2009), with more parameters (allowing for more curvature), one will always fit the data better. Rather, Gabaix (2009) suggests that what is important is whether a power law provides a good fit to the data, which appears to be the case in our results.

Table A1
Top 49 countries and the rest of the world in terms of 2004 GDP.
Source: The World Bank (2007b).

Country	GDP/world GDP	Country	GDP/world GDP
United States	0.300	Indonesia	0.006
Japan	0.124	South Africa	0.006
Germany	0.076	Norway	0.006
France	0.054	Poland	0.005
United Kingdom	0.044	Finland	0.005
Italy	0.041	Greece	0.004
China	0.028	Venezuela, RB	0.004
Canada	0.026	Thailand	0.004
Brazil	0.021	Portugal	0.003
Spain	0.020	Colombia	0.003
India	0.017	Nigeria	0.003
Australia	0.016	Algeria	0.003
Russian Federation	0.015	Israel	0.003
Mexico	0.015	Philippines	0.003
Netherlands	0.015	Malaysia	0.002
Korea, Rep.	0.011	Ireland	0.002
Sweden	0.010	Egypt, Arab Rep.	0.002
Switzerland	0.010	Pakistan	0.002
Belgium	0.009	Chile	0.002
Argentina	0.008	New Zealand	0.002
Saudi Arabia	0.007	Czech Republic	0.002
Austria	0.007	United Arab Emirates	0.002
Iran, Islamic Rep.	0.007	Hungary	0.002
Turkey	0.007	Romania	0.002
Denmark	0.006	Rest of the world	0.027

Notes: Ranking of top 49 countries and the rest of the world in terms of 2004 U.S.$ GDP. We include Hong Kong, POC, and Singapore in Rest of the world.

Table A2
Country-by-country estimates of power laws in firm size.

Country	CDF estimation			PDF estimation		
	PL coef.	R^2	*p*-Value	PL coef.	R^2	*p*-Value
Argentina	−1.046**	0.988	0.243	−2.039**	0.994	0.466
Australia	−0.992**	0.986	0.838	−1.905**	0.994	0.076
Austria	−0.695**	0.963	0.000	−1.677**	0.989	0.000
Belgium	−0.972**	0.999	0.011	−1.956**	0.998	0.150
Bosnia and Herzegovina	−1.022**	0.990	0.508	−2.036**	0.992	0.550
Brazil	−0.918**	0.966	0.162	−1.892**	0.991	0.096
Bulgaria	−0.981**	0.979	0.686	−2.007**	0.992	0.908
Canada	−0.888**	0.989	0.004	−1.913**	0.995	0.069
China	−1.117**	0.976	0.060	−2.091**	0.996	0.061
Croatia	−1.094**	0.988	0.034	−2.120**	0.992	0.074
Czech Republic	−1.083**	0.992	0.020	−2.072**	0.998	0.031
Denmark	−0.776**	0.950	0.003	−1.684**	0.987	0.001
Estonia	−1.017**	0.986	0.674	−2.067**	0.987	0.389
Finland	−0.869**	0.989	0.001	−1.879**	0.997	0.006
France	−0.886**	0.999	0.000	−1.894**	1.000	0.000
Germany	−0.853**	0.999	0.000	−1.960**	0.981	0.653
Greece	−0.992**	0.997	0.620	−1.951**	0.998	0.089
Hungary	−0.953**	0.995	0.050	−1.987**	0.996	0.741
India	−0.975**	0.988	0.476	−1.954**	0.995	0.319
Ireland	−0.761**	0.998	0.000	−1.718**	0.999	0.000
Italy	−1.030**	0.996	0.172	−2.037**	0.999	0.093
Japan	−0.955**	0.990	0.177	−1.985**	0.996	0.716
Latvia	−1.118**	0.989	0.011	−2.054**	0.995	0.281
Lithuania	−1.153**	0.992	0.001	−2.151**	0.996	0.009
Macedonia	−1.109**	0.999	0.000	−2.095**	0.990	0.176
Netherlands	−0.906**	0.994	0.002	−1.917**	0.995	0.082
Norway	−1.045**	0.970	0.454	−1.975**	0.997	0.516
Poland	−1.086**	0.987	0.051	−2.125**	0.995	0.028
Portugal	−0.919**	0.996	0.001	−1.924**	0.999	0.001
Korea	−0.880**	0.999	0.000	−1.860**	1.000	0.000
Romania	−1.002**	0.990	0.956	−2.047**	0.995	0.349
Russia	−1.039**	0.996	0.086	−2.027**	0.998	0.384
Serbia	−1.181**	0.989	0.001	−2.163**	0.996	0.004
Singapore	−0.888**	0.979	0.021	−1.825**	0.995	0.002
Slovakia	−1.139**	0.990	0.003	−2.124**	0.996	0.018
Slovenia	−0.993**	0.986	0.846	−1.998**	0.989	0.981
Spain	−0.978**	1.000	0.005	−2.011**	0.997	0.769
Sweden	−0.884**	0.997	0.000	−1.895**	0.998	0.002
Switzerland	−0.791**	0.990	0.000	−1.760**	0.996	0.000
Taiwan POC	−0.889**	0.989	0.003	−1.863**	0.991	0.031
Thailand	−0.956**	0.976	0.381	−1.953**	0.994	0.358
Ukraine	−1.058**	0.991	0.102	−2.007**	0.999	0.802
United Kingdom	−1.010**	0.975	0.856	−2.017**	0.992	0.775

Notes: This table reports the estimated of power laws in firm size across countries. Column "PL coef." reports the coefficient on the power law for each country, the second column reports the R^2, the third column reports the *p*-value of the test that the power law coefficient is statistically different from −1 (−2 in the right panel). The estimates are based on firm-level sales data from ORBIS. Variable definitions, sources, and estimation techniques are described in detail in the text.

** Significant at the 1% level.

References

Alvarez, Fernando, Lucas Jr., Robert E., 2007. General equilibrium analysis of the Eaton–Kortum model of international trade. Journal of Monetary Economics 54 (6), 1726–1768 (September).

Anderson, James, van Wincoop, Eric, 2004. Trade costs. Journal of Economic Literature 42 (3), 691–751.

Arkolakis, Costas, 2010. Market penetration costs and the new consumers margin in international trade. Journal of Political Economy 118 (6), 1151–1199 (December).

Arkolakis, Costas, Demidova, Svetlana, Klenow, Peter J., Rodríguez-Clare, Andrés, 2008. Endogenous variety and the gains from trade. American Economic Review Papers and Proceedings 98 (2), 444–450 (May).

Arkolakis, Costas, Costinot, Arnaud, Rodríguez-Clare, Andrés, 2012. New trade models, same old gains? American Economic Review 102 (1), 94–130 (February).

Atkeson, Andrew, Burstein, Ariel, 2010. Innovation, firm dynamics, and international trade. Journal of Political Economy 3, 433–484 (June).

Axtell, Robert L., 2001. Zipf distribution of U.S. firm sizes. Science 293 (5536), 1818–1820 (September).

Bekkers, Eddy, Francois, Joseph, 2008. Heterogeneous firms, the structure of industry, and trade under oligopoly. Working Paper 0811. Department of Economics, Johannes Kepler University of Linz. August.

Bernard, Andrew B., Eaton, Jonathan, Bradford Jensen, J., Kortum, Samuel, 2003. Plants and productivity in international trade. American Economic Review 93 (4), 1268–1290 (September).

Bernard, Andrew, Bradford Jensen, J., Redding, Stephen, Schott, Peter, 2007. Firms in international trade. Journal of Economic Perspectives 21, 105–130.

Broda, Christian, Weinstein, David, 2006. Globalization and the gains from variety. Quarterly Journal of Economics 121 (2), 541–585 (May).

Chaney, Thomas, 2008. Distorted gravity: the intensive and extensive margins of international trade. American Economic Review 4, 1707–1721 (September).

Crozet, Matthieu, Koenig, Pamina, 2010. Structural gravity equation with extensive and intensive margins. Canadian Journal of Economics 43 (1), 41–62 (February).

di Giovanni, Julian, Levchenko, Andrei A., 2010. Firm entry, trade, and welfare in Zipf's world. NBER Working Paper No. 16313. August.

di Giovanni, Julian, Levchenko, Andrei A., 2011. Country size, international trade, and aggregate fluctuations in granular economies. NBER Working Paper No. 17335. August.

di Giovanni, Julian, Levchenko, Andrei A., Rancière, Romain, 2011. Power laws in firm size and openness to trade: measurement and implications. Journal of International Economics 85 (1), 42–52 (September).

Djankov, Simeon, La Porta, Rafael, Lopez-de-Silanes, Florencio, Shleifer, Andrei, 2002. The regulation of entry. Quarterly Journal of Economics 117 (1), 1–37.

Easterly, William, Reshef, Ariell, Schwenkenberg, Julia, 2009. The power of exports. World Bank Policy Research Working Paper 5081. October.

Eaton, Jonathan, Kortum, Samuel S., 2005. Technology in the global economy: a framework for quantitative analysis. Book Manuscript. New York University and University of Chicago.

Eaton, Jonathan, Kortum, Samuel S., Kramarz, Francis, 2011. An anatomy of international trade: evidence from French firms. Econometrica 5, 1453–1498 (September).

Eaton, Jonathan, Kortum, Samuel S., Sotelo, Sebastian, 2012. International trade: linking micro and macro. NBER Working Paper No. 17864. February.

Feenstra, Robert C., 2010. Measuring the gains from trade under monopolistic competition. Canadian Journal of Economics 43 (1), 1–28 (February).

Fujiwara, Yoshi, Aoyama, Hideaki, Di Guilmi, Corrado, Souma, Wataru, Gallegati, Mauro, 2004. Gibrat and Pareto–Zipf Revisited with European firms. Physica A: Statistical Mechanics and its Applications 344 (1–2), 112–116.

Gabaix, Xavier, 2009. Power laws in economics and finance. Annual Reviews of Economics 1, 255–293.

Gabaix, Xavier, Ibragimov, Rustam, 2011. Rank-1/2: a simple way to improve the OLS estimation of tail exponents. Journal of Business and Economic Statistics 29 (1), 24–39 (January).

Goldberg, Pinelopi, Khandelwal, Amit, Pavcnik, Nina, Topalova, Petia, 2009. Trade liberalization and new imported inputs. American Economic Review Papers and Proceedings 99 (2), 494–500 (May).

Goldberg, Pinelopi, Khandelwal, Amit, Pavcnik, Nina, Topalova, Petia, 2010. Imported intermediate inputs and domestic product growth: evidence from India. Quarterly Journal of Economics 125 (4), 1727–1767 (November).

Helpman, Elhanan, Melitz, Marc, Rubinstein, Yona, 2008. Estimating trade flows: trading partners and trading volumes. Quarterly Journal of Economics 123 (2), 441–487 (May).

Hinloopen, Jeroen, van Marrewijk, Charles, 2006. Comparative advantage, the rank-size rule, and Zipf's law. Tinbergen Institute Discussion Paper 06-100/1.

International Monetary Fund, 2007. Directions of Trade Statistics.

Jones, Charles, 2011. Intermediate goods and weak links in the theory of economic development. American Economic Journal: Macroeconomics 3 (2), 1–28 (April).

Krugman, Paul, 1980. Scale economies, product differentiation, and the pattern of trade. American Economic Review 70 (5), 950–959.

Luttmer, Erzo, 2007. Selection, growth, and the size distribution of firms. Quarterly Journal of Economics 122, 1103–1144.

Melitz, Marc J., 2003. The impact of trade on intra-industry reallocations and aggregate industry productivity. Econometrica 6, 1695–1725 (November).

Neary, J. Peter, 2010. Two and a half theories of trade. The World Economy 33 (1), 1–19 (January).

Okuyama, K., Takayasu, M., Takayasu, H., 1999. Zipf's law in income distribution of companies. Physica A: Statistical Mechanics and its Applications 269 (1), 125–131.

The World Bank, 2007a. Doing Business Indicators.

The World Bank, 2007b. World Development Indicators.

Waugh, Michael, 2010. International trade and income differences. American Economic Review 100 (5), 2093–2124 (December).

Country Size, International Trade, and Aggregate Fluctuations in Granular Economies

Julian di Giovanni

International Monetary Fund

Andrei A. Levchenko

University of Michigan and National Bureau of Economic Research

This paper proposes a new mechanism by which country size and international trade affect macroeconomic volatility. We study a model with heterogeneous firms that are subject to idiosyncratic firm-specific shocks, calibrated to data for the 50 largest economies in the world. When the firm size distribution follows a power law with an exponent close to minus one, idiosyncratic shocks to large firms have an impact on aggregate volatility. Smaller countries have fewer firms and, thus, higher volatility. Trade opening makes the large firms more important, thus raising macroeconomic volatility. Trade can increase aggregate volatility by 15–20 percent in some small open economies.

I. Introduction

Output volatility varies substantially across economies: over the past 35 years, the standard deviation of annual real per capita GDP growth has been two and a half times higher in non-OECD countries compared to

We are grateful to the editor (Sam Kortum), two anonymous referees, Michael Alexeev, Stijn Claessens, Aaron Flaaen, Fabio Ghironi, Gordon Hanson, Chris House, Marc Melitz, Andy Rose, Matthew Shapiro, Linda Tesar, and workshop participants at various institutions for helpful suggestions and to Edith Laget, Lin Ma, and Ryan Monarch for expert research assistance. Levchenko thanks the National Science Foundation for financial support under grant SES-0921971. The views expressed in this paper are those of the authors and should

[*Journal of Political Economy*, 2012, vol. 120, no. 6]

the OECD countries. Understanding the sources of these differences is important, as aggregate volatility itself has an impact on a wide variety of economic outcomes.[1]

This paper investigates the role of large firms in explaining cross-country differences in aggregate volatility. We show that the impact of shocks to large firms on aggregate volatility can help account for two robust empirical regularities: (i) smaller countries are more volatile, and (ii) more open countries are more volatile. The key ingredient of our study is that the distribution of firm size is very fat tailed: the typical economy is dominated by a few very large firms (Axtell 2001). In a recent contribution, Gabaix (2011) demonstrates that under these conditions idiosyncratic shocks to individual firms do not cancel out and can instead generate aggregate fluctuations (see also Delli Gatti et al. 2005). Gabaix provides both statistical and anecdotal evidence that even in the largest and most diversified economy in the world—the United States—shocks to the biggest firms can appreciably affect macroeconomic fluctuations. The economy is "granular" rather than smooth.

We develop a theoretical and quantitative framework to study the consequences of this phenomenon in a large cross section of countries. The analysis is based on the canonical multicountry model with heterogeneous firms in the spirit of Melitz (2003) and Eaton, Kortum, and Kramarz (2011), implemented on the 50 largest economies in the world. In order to study the impact of large firms on aggregate fluctuations, the equilibrium total number of firms is determined endogenously in the model, and the parameters are calibrated to match the observed firm size distribution. The solution procedure targets the key aggregate country characteristics—GDPs and average trade volumes—and successfully reproduces a number of nontargeted features of the micro data, such as the share of firms that export and the relative size of the largest firms across countries.

Our main results can be summarized as follows. First, the model endogenously generates a negative relationship between country size and aggregate volatility. The reason is that smaller countries will have a smaller equilibrium number of firms (as implied by many models since at least Krugman [1980]), and thus shocks to the largest firms will matter more for aggregate volatility. In effect, smaller economies are less diversified when diversification is measured at the firm level. The model matches this relationship not only qualitatively but also quantitatively: the rate at

not be attributed to the International Monetary Fund, its Executive Board, or its management. The Supplementary Web Appendix to this paper is available at http://alevchenko.com/diGiovanni_Levchenko_granular_web_appendix.pdf.

[1] Numerous studies identify its effects on long-run growth (Ramey and Ramey 1995), welfare (Pallage and Robe 2003; Barlevy 2004), and inequality and poverty (Gavin and Hausmann 1998; Laursen and Mahajan 2005).

which volatility decreases in country size in the model is very similar to what is observed in the data. Both in the model and in the data, a typical country that accounts for 0.5 percent of world GDP (such as Poland or South Africa) has aggregate volatility that is two times higher than that of the largest economy in the world—the United States.

Second, trade openness increases volatility by making the economy more granular. When a country opens to trade, only the largest and most productive firms export, while smaller firms shrink or disappear (Melitz 2003). This effect implies that after opening, the biggest firms become even larger relative to the size of the economy, thus contributing more to aggregate output fluctuations. In the counterfactual exercise, we compute what aggregate volatility would be for each country in autarky and compare it to the volatility under the current trade costs. It turns out that at the levels of trade openness observed today, international trade increases volatility relative to autarky in every country. The importance of trade for aggregate volatility varies greatly depending on country characteristics. In the largest economies such as Japan or the United States, aggregate volatility is only 1.5–3.5 percent higher than it would have been in complete autarky. In small, remote economies such as South Africa or New Zealand, trade raises volatility by about 10 percent compared to autarky. Finally, in small, highly integrated economies such as Denmark or Romania, international trade raises aggregate volatility by some 15–20 percent.

The theoretical link between country size, trade openness, and volatility we explore in this paper has not previously been proposed. Head (1995) and Crucini (1997) examine the relationship between country size and volatility in a two-country international real business cycle (IRBC) model. In those papers, the smaller country has higher volatility because the world interest rate is less sensitive to shocks occurring in that country. Thus, following a positive shock, it can expand investment without much of an impact on interest rates.[2] Our explanation for the size-volatility relationship is qualitatively different and relies instead on the notion that smaller countries have fewer firms. When it comes to the relationship between trade openness and volatility, existing explanations have focused on the propagation of global demand or supply shocks (Newbery and Stiglitz 1984; Kraay and Ventura 2007). We show that trade can increase volatility even if the nature of shocks affecting the firms is

[2] The Supplementary Web Appendix implements the canonical IRBC model of Backus, Kehoe, and Kydland (1995) and examines the relationship between country size and volatility, and between trade openness and volatility, in that model. It turns out that while the calibrated IRBC model can produce higher volatility in smaller countries, the relationship between country size and volatility in that model is two orders of magnitude flatter than what is observed in the data. The relationship between trade openness and volatility in the IRBC model is ambiguous, its sign depending crucially on the elasticity of substitution between domestic and foreign goods.

unchanged upon opening. Finally, the mechanism in our model resembles the traditional arguments that smaller countries, and more open countries, will have a less diversified sectoral production structure and thus exhibit higher volatility (see Katzenstein [1985], OECD [2006], and Blattman, Hwang, and Williamson [2007], among many others). Our analysis shows that this argument applies to individual firms as well as to sectors and makes this point quantitatively precise by calibrating the model to the observed firm size distribution.

Our work is also related to the empirical literature that studies macroeconomic volatility using disaggregated data. Koren and Tenreyro (2007) explore the importance of sector-specific shocks in explaining the relationship between a country's level of development and its aggregate volatility, while di Giovanni and Levchenko (2009, 2012) use sector-level data to study the openness-volatility relationship. Canals et al. (2007) analyze sector- and firm-level export data and demonstrate that exports are highly undiversified across both firms and sectors and across destinations. Furthermore, they show that this feature of export baskets can explain why aggregate macroeconomic variables cannot account for much of the movements in the current account.[3]

The rest of the paper is organized as follows. Section II presents the empirical regularities that motivate our study, as well as some novel stylized facts about firm size distributions in a large cross section of countries. Section III develops a simple theoretical framework and illustrates analytically the mechanisms behind the key results of the paper. Section IV presents the quantitative results based on a calibrated model of the world economy. Section V discusses robustness checks and results based on model perturbations. Section VI presents conclusions.

II. Basic Facts

Figure 1 presents a scatter plot of log macroeconomic volatility against log country size for a sample of 143 countries. Volatility is the standard deviation of the yearly growth rate of real per capita GDP, while country size is the share of the country in world GDP.[4] The figure depicts the

[3] Our work is complementary to the research agenda that studies the impact of firm dynamics on macroeconomic outcomes in two-country IRBC models. Ghironi and Melitz (2005) use the heterogeneous firms model to help account for the persistence of deviations from purchasing power parity (PPP), while Alessandria and Choi (2007) and Ruhl (2008) evaluate the quantitative importance of firm entry and exit for aggregate trade dynamics. An important difference between these papers and our work is that these contributions examine consequences of aggregate shocks, while in our paper all the shocks are at the firm level. In addition, our work features multiple countries and explains cross-sectional differences in volatility between countries.

[4] Detailed variable definitions and sources for all the data in this section are described in App. A.

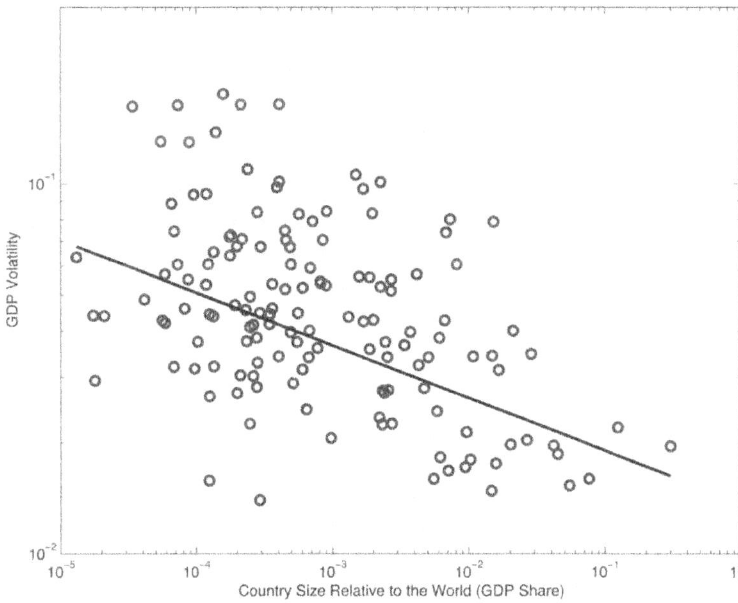

FIG. 1.—Country size and aggregate volatility. This figure reports the partial correlation plot of aggregate volatility, measured as the standard deviation of the annual growth rate of per capita GDP over 1970–2006, on the *y*-axis against country size on the *x*-axis, after netting out the impact of per capita income. Both axes are in log scale. Source: World Bank World Development Indicators.

partial correlation between these two variables after netting out per capita income, as it has been shown that high-income countries tend to experience lower volatility. As established by Canning et al. (1998) and Furceri and Karras (2007), among others, smaller countries are more volatile. The elasticity of volatility with respect to country size is about -0.14 in this set of countries, and the relationship is highly significant, with a *t*-statistic of 6.2.

At the same time, it has been argued that countries that trade more tend to be more volatile. This empirical regularity has been demonstrated in a cross section of countries by Easterly, Islam, and Stiglitz (2001) and Kose, Prasad, and Terrones (2003). The cross-country evidence is likely to be affected by reverse causality and omitted variables problems. In addition, in a cross section of countries one does not typically have enough power to distinguish between trade openness and other correlates of macroeconomic volatility (such as, most relevant here, country size). Di Giovanni and Levchenko (2009) investigate the openness-volatility relationship in great detail using industry-level data, which makes it possible to overcome these econometric estimation concerns. They confirm that the relationship between trade openness and macroeconomic volatility is indeed positive and economically significant, even after controlling for the size of both countries and sectors using fixed effects. Below we follow an alternative and complementary strategy to isolate the impact of openness on volatility. We develop a quantitative model that captures a particular channel for this relationship and evaluate the impact of trade using counterfactual scenarios.

The analysis below focuses on the role of large firms in explaining these cross-country patterns. Anecdotal evidence on the importance of large firms for aggregate fluctuations abounds. Here, we describe two examples in which the roles of country size and international trade are especially evident. In New Zealand a single firm, Fonterra, is responsible for a full one-third of global dairy exports (it is the world's single-largest exporter of dairy products). Such a large exporter from such a small country clearly matters for the macroeconomy. Indeed, Fonterra's sales (95 percent of which are exports) account for 20 percent of New Zealand's overall exports and 7 percent of its GDP.[5] Two points about this firm are worth noting. First, international trade clearly plays a prominent role in making Fonterra as large as it is. And second, the distribution of firm size in the dairy sector is indeed highly skewed. The second-largest producer of dairy products in New Zealand is 1.3 percent the size of Fonterra. This phenomenon is not confined to commodity-exporting countries. In Korea, a larger manufacturing-based economy, the 10 biggest business groups account for 54 percent of GDP and 51 percent of total exports. Even among the top 10, the distribution of firm size and total exports is extremely skewed. The largest one, Samsung, is responsible for 23 percent of exports and 14 percent of GDP (see fig. 2).[6]

There is a growing body of additional evidence on the predominance of the largest firms, especially in total exports. Eaton, Kortum, and Sotelo (2012) report that in France the top 10 exporters account for nearly 25 percent of total exports. According to Canals et al. (2007), in Japan the top 10 exporters account for about 30 percent and the top 50 exporters for more than half of total exports. Cebeci et al. (2012) report that in a sample of 45 developed and developing countries, the top 1 percent of exporters account for 55 percent of total exports on average. In a number of countries (Chile, Peru, South Africa) the top 1 percent of exporters are responsible for 80 percent or so of total exports.

[5] It is important to note that GDP represents value added, and thus Fonterra's total sales are less than 7 percent of the total sales of all firms in New Zealand. However, because exports are recorded as total sales, Fonterra's export sales are directly comparable to New Zealand's total exports. The same caveat applies to the example that follows.

[6] It turns out that the size distribution of firms is quite skewed even within business groups. For instance, breaking Samsung down into its constituent firms reveals that the sales of Samsung Electronics alone accounted for 7 percent of GDP and 15.5 percent of Korea's exports in 2006.

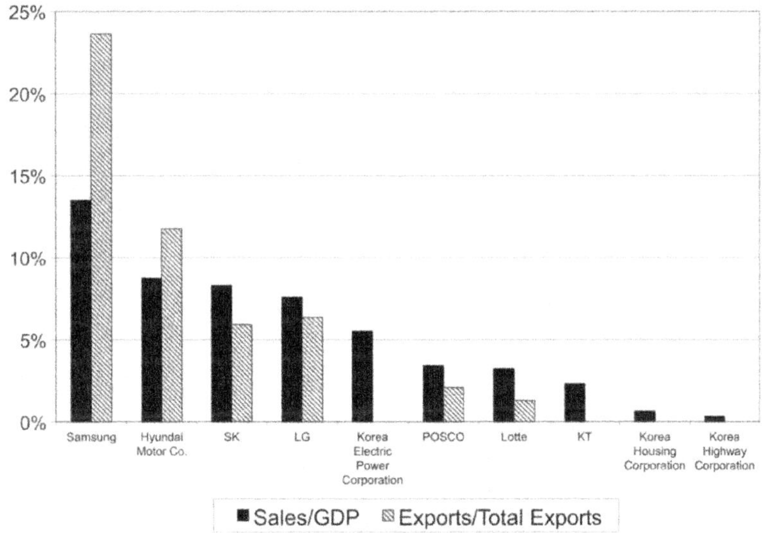

FIG. 2.—Korean business groups' sales as a share of GDP and total exports. This figure reports the 2006 sales of the top 10 Korean business groups, as a share of Korean GDP (dark bars) and total Korean exports (light bars). Source: Korean Development Institute.

Gabaix (2011) shows that aggregate volatility due to the idiosyncratic shocks to firms is an increasing function of the Herfindahl index of the firms' output shares. To produce the country size-volatility relationship in figure 1 through the shocks to large firms, it must be the case that smaller countries have higher Herfindahl indices of firm output: they are less diversified. Figure 3*A* presents the partial correlations between the Herfindahl index of firm sales and country size, after netting out the impact of per capita income, with all variables in natural logs.[7] The figure also plots the ordinary least squares best fit through the data, along with the slope coefficients, standard errors, and the R^2's. The firm-level data used to compute the Herfindahl indices come from the ORBIS database described in Appendix A. Because the number of firms covered by ORBIS varies substantially across countries, we present the results for three samples: (i) all 134 countries for which it is possible to calculate the Herfindahl index in ORBIS data, (ii) the 81 countries with sales data for at least 100 firms, and (iii) the 52 countries with sales data for at least

[7] The Herfindahl index is defined as the sum of squared shares of firm sales in total sales, $h = \sum_k h(k)^2$, where k indexes firms, and $h(k)$ is the share of firm k in total sales by all firms.

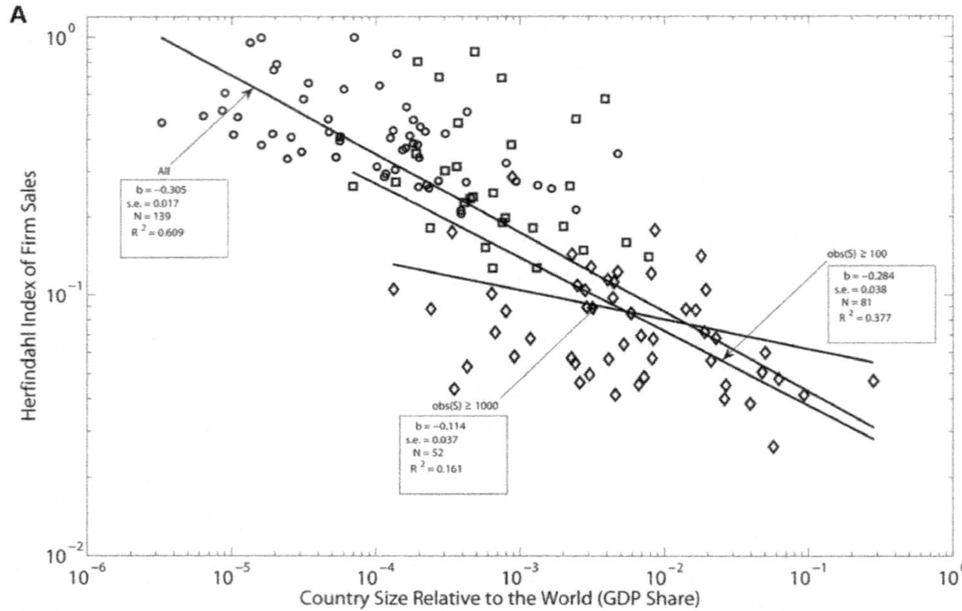

FIG. 3.—Country size, firm sales concentration, and size of large firms. These figures present the scatter plots of log country size and (*A*) the log Herfindahl index of firm sales, (*B*) the log size of the 10 largest firms, and (*C*) the log size of the largest firm, in all cases after netting out per capita GDP. The countries with more than 1,000 firms with sales data are labeled with diamonds, the countries with between 100 and 1,000 firms with sales data are labeled with squares, and the countries with fewer than 100 firms with sales data are labeled with circles. The regression lines through the samples of (i) all countries, (ii) countries with ≥100 firms, and (iii) countries with ≥1,000 firms are plotted through the data. Both axes are in log scale. Sources: ORBIS and World Bank World Development Indicators.

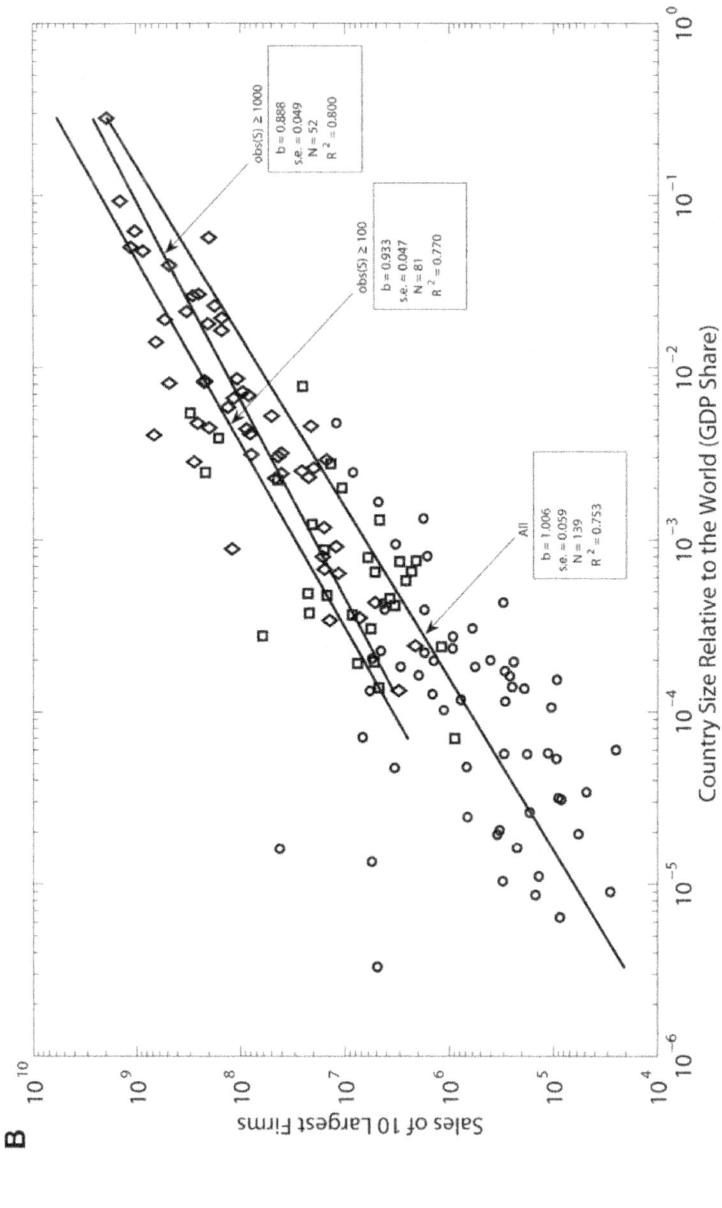

Fig. 3.—(*Continued*)

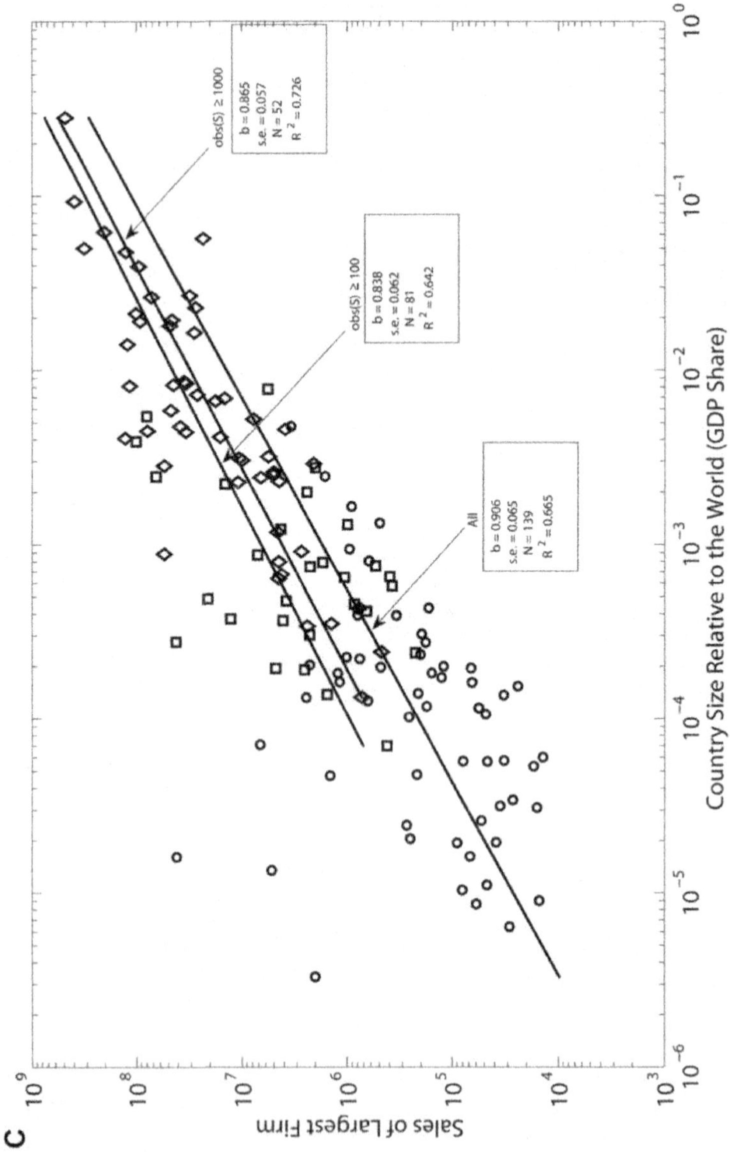

FIG. 3.—(*Continued*)

1,000 firms. The countries with different numbers of firms are labeled with different symbols. Figure 3*A* shows that the relationship between the Herfindahl index and country size is negative as expected and highly statistically significant in all three samples.

The Herfindahl index is the variable most directly relevant to the quantitative results in the paper. However, because ideally it requires information on the entire firm size distribution, the Herfindahl index may also be most heavily influenced by differences in coverage in the ORBIS database. Because of this, we also present the relationship of country size to two other indicators of firm size: the combined sales of the 10 largest firms in the country and the size of the single-largest firm. These indicators focus on the very largest firms that are measured more reliably in the data, and thus the problems of coverage are less severe. In addition, these empirical relationships capture a related feature of the data that is crucial for evaluating the role of large firms for the country size–volatility relationship. A bigger country could either have larger firms or have more firms than a smaller country. There are two extreme cases that can be useful benchmarks. The first is that the largest firms in big countries are no bigger than the large firms in small countries. That is, what makes a country larger is that it has more firms, not bigger firms. This hypothetical possibility would manifest itself as a slope of zero in figures 3*B* and 3*C* and would have important implications for the relationship between country size and (granular) volatility. In particular, a slope of zero would imply that volatility declines very rapidly in country size. The other benchmark is a slope of one. When the slope is one, the largest firms are no bigger relative to the size of the economy in small countries compared to large ones. That would suggest that larger countries have larger firms but not more firms and that the size-volatility relationship is perfectly flat: (granular) volatility in the larger countries is no lower than in small countries.[8] Since these two possibilities have very different implications for how aggregate volatility changes with country size, it is important for our model to match the relative size of the largest firms in countries of different sizes.

Figure 3*B* depicts the partial correlation between the log size of the 10 largest firms and log country size, once again after netting out log per capita income. The results are reported for all three ORBIS samples, as above. There is a significant positive relationship between the absolute size of the largest 10 firms and country size: not surprisingly, larger countries have bigger firms, with an elasticity of around 0.9. The slope coefficient and the fit are both quite stable across the samples. Figure 3*C* reports the analogous relationship for the size of the single-largest firm

[8] This discussion is of course only suggestive because the precise outcomes will depend on the details of the rest of the firm size distribution and because we do not have closed-form results with respect to the size of the top one or 10 largest firms.

in each country, with quite similar conclusions. The fact that the slope is much higher than zero, and indeed only slightly below one, is suggestive that volatility will decrease with country size, but at a much slower rate than the zero slope benchmark. As we discuss in Section IV.C, our model matches these slope coefficients quite closely.

III. Theoretical Framework

This section lays out a simplified analytical framework to illustrate the main mechanisms behind the results. The quantitative investigation based on an extended model follows in Section IV. The full description of the equations defining the extended model is presented in Appendix B.

The minimalist framework that can be used to model the role of firms in the relationship between country size and volatility has to feature (i) a firm size distribution that can be matched to the data, (ii) endogenous determination of the set of firms operating in equilibrium, and (iii) idiosyncratic shocks to firms. In addition, to investigate the role of international trade, the model must have (iv) an export participation decision by firms.

A. *The Environment*

Consider a model in the spirit of Melitz (2003), but with a discrete number of goods as in Krugman (1980). The world is made up of C countries, indexed by $i, j = 1, \ldots, C$. In country i, buyers (who could be final consumers or firms purchasing intermediate inputs) maximize a standard constant elasticity of substitution (CES) objective over the set of J_i varieties available in country i. It is well known that in country i demand for an individual variety k is equal to

$$x_i(k) = \frac{X_i}{P_i^{1-\varepsilon}} p_i(k)^{1-\varepsilon}, \tag{1}$$

where ε is the elasticity of substitution between varieties, $x_i(k)$ is the total expenditure on good k at price $p_i(k)$, X_i is total expenditure in the economy, and P_i is the ideal price index:

$$P_i = \left[\sum_{k=1}^{J_i} p_i(k)^{1-\varepsilon}\right]^{1/(1-\varepsilon)}. \tag{2}$$

There is one factor of production, labor, with country endowments given by $L_j, j = 1, \ldots, C$, and wages denoted by w_j. Production uses both labor and intermediate inputs. In particular, a firm with unit input requirement a must use a input bundles to produce one unit of output. An input bundle in country j has a cost

$$c_j = w_j^{\beta} P_j^{1-\beta}.$$

There are both fixed and variable costs of production and trade. The timing in the economy is depicted in figure 4. At the beginning of the period each potential producer of variety $k = 1, \ldots, \bar{I}_j$ in each $j = 1, \ldots, C$ must pay an "exploration" cost f_e in order to become an entrepreneur. Upon paying this cost, entrepreneur k discovers her productivity, indexed by a unit input requirement $a(k)$, and faces downward-sloping demand for her unique variety given by (1). On the basis of this draw, each entrepreneur in country j decides whether to operate and which markets to serve. To start serving market i from country j, a firm must pay a fixed cost f_{ij} and an iceberg per-unit cost of $\tau_{ij} > 1$ (with τ_{jj} normalized to one). Having paid the fixed costs of entering these markets, the firm learns the realization of a transitory shock $z(k)$, independently and identically distributed (i.i.d.) across firms. Once all of the uncertainty has been realized, each firm produces with a unit input requirement $a(k)z(k)$, markets clear, and consumption takes place.[9]

If a firm from country j decides to sell to country i, its profit-maximizing price is a constant markup over marginal cost

$$p_i(k) = \frac{\varepsilon}{\varepsilon - 1} \tau_{ij} c_j a(k) z(k),$$

the quantity supplied is equal to

$$\frac{X_i}{P_i^{1-\varepsilon}} \left[\frac{\varepsilon}{\varepsilon - 1} \tau_{ij} c_j a(k) z(k) \right]^{-\varepsilon},$$

and its expected profits from serving i are

$$\mathrm{E}\left[\frac{X_i}{\varepsilon P_i^{1-\varepsilon}} \left[\frac{\varepsilon}{\varepsilon - 1} \tau_{ij} c_j a(k) z(k) \right]^{1-\varepsilon} - c_j f_{ij} \,\middle|\, a(k) \right]. \tag{3}$$

[9] Note that the assumption on the timing of events, namely, that the decision to enter markets takes place before $z(k)$ is realized, implies that the realization of the firm-specific transitory shock does not affect the equilibrium number of firms in each market. This simplification lets us analyze the equilibrium production allocation as an approximation around a case in which the variance of z is zero. That is, we abstract from the extensive margin of exports and entry and exit of firms in response to transitory shocks. This simplification delivers substantial analytical convenience, while it is unlikely to affect the results. The reason is that the focus of the paper is on the role of the largest firms in generating aggregate volatility, and the largest firms are inframarginal: their entry decision will be unaffected by the realization of the transitory shock. Note also that this timing assumption implies that our analytical approach is akin to the common one of analyzing the response to shocks in deviations from a nonstochastic steady state.

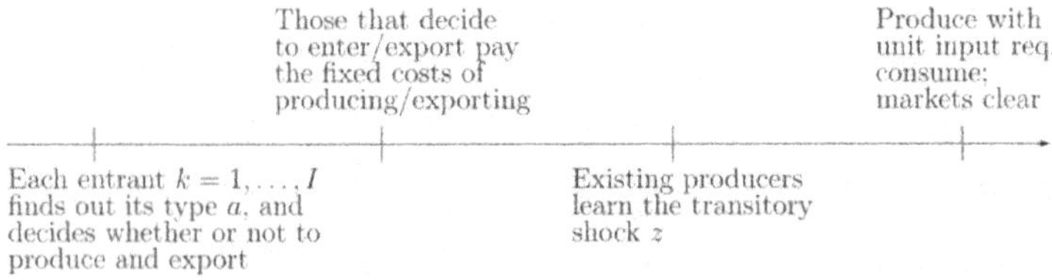

FIG. 4.—The timing of the economy

Because of fixed costs of serving a market, there is a cutoff unit input requirement a_{ij} above which firms in country j do not serve market i, defined as the level of $a(k) = a_{ij}$ such that the expected profits in equation (3) equal zero. To go forward with the analysis, we make the following two assumptions.

ASSUMPTION 1. The marginal firm is small enough that it ignores the impact of its own realization of $z(k)$ on the total expenditure X_i and the price level P_i in all potential destination markets $i = 1, \ldots, \mathcal{C}$.

ASSUMPTION 2. The marginal firm treats X_i and P_i as fixed (nonstochastic).

The first assumption is not controversial and has been made in the literature since Dixit and Stiglitz (1977) and Krugman (1980). The second assumption allows us to take X_i and P_i outside of the expectation operator. It amounts to assuming that the marginal entrepreneur ignores the volatility of aggregate output and the price level when deciding to enter a market.[10] Under these two assumptions, when we set (3) to zero and take the expectation over z, the zero-profit cutoff condition for serving market i from country j reduces to

[10] It is important to emphasize that these are assumptions placed on the behavior of the marginal entrepreneur. They allow us to compute the cutoffs for production and exporting a_{ij} as if the model were nonstochastic. This delivers substantial analytical and computational simplicity without affecting any of the main conclusions since in our model the economy is dominated by very large firms, and thus the marginal ones are not important for the aggregate outcomes. On the other hand, one may question our assumption about the behavior of the largest firms, namely, that markups are a constant multiple of marginal cost. If the largest firms in the economy are so large that their pricing decisions can affect the price level, their profit-maximizing prices will depart from the simple Dixit-Stiglitz constant markup benchmark. Note that, qualitatively, this critique applies to all implementations of the Dixit-Stiglitz framework and their extensions to heterogeneous firms. It is ultimately a quantitative question how much this force matters (Dixit and Stiglitz 1993; Yang and Heijdra 1993). While the full solution of our model under flexible markups would be impractical, and to our knowledge has not yet been implemented in this type of large-scale setting, we can perform a simple simulation that assesses the quantitative importance of allowing for variable markups in this setting. The Supplementary Web Appendix describes the exercise in detail and shows that, quantitatively, the deviations of flexible-markup prices from the constant-markup benchmark are very small even for the largest firms in small countries.

$$a_{ij} = \frac{\varepsilon - 1}{\varepsilon} \frac{P_i}{\tau_{ij} c_j} \left(\frac{X_i}{\varepsilon c_j f_{ij}} \right)^{1/(\varepsilon - 1)} \tag{4}$$

after normalizing the transitory shocks z such that $E_z(z^{1-\varepsilon}) = 1$.

The equilibrium number of potential entrepreneurs $\bar{I}_j$ is pinned down by the familiar free-entry condition in each country. Entrepreneurs will enter until the expected profit equals the cost of finding out one's type:

$$E\left[\sum_{i=1}^{C} \mathbf{1}[a(k) \le a_{ij}] \left\{ \frac{X_i}{\varepsilon P_i^{1-\varepsilon}} \left[\frac{\varepsilon}{\varepsilon - 1} \tau_{ij} c_j a(k) z(k) \right]^{1-\varepsilon} - c_j f_{ij} \right\} \right] = c_j f_e \tag{5}$$

for each country j, where $\mathbf{1}[\cdot]$ is the indicator function.

Closing the model involves finding expressions for a_{ij}, P_i, w_i, and $\bar{I}_i$ for all $i, j = 1, \ldots, C$. As an approximation, we solve for the equilibrium production allocation and price levels ignoring firm-specific transitory shocks. When we take the expectations over $a(k)$ and $z(k)$ and use the fact that $E_z(z^{1-\varepsilon}) = 1$, the price levels become[11]

$$P_i = \left[\sum_{j=1}^{C} \left(\frac{\varepsilon}{\varepsilon - 1} \tau_{ij} c_j \right)^{1-\varepsilon} \bar{I}_j \Pr(a < a_{ij}) E(a^{1-\varepsilon} | a < a_{ij}) \right]^{1/(1-\varepsilon)}. \tag{6}$$

We make the standard distributional assumption on productivity.

Assumption 3. Firm productivity $1/a$ follows a Pareto(b, θ) distribution: $\Pr(1/a < y) = 1 - (b/y)^\theta$, where b is the minimum value productivity can take, and θ regulates dispersion.

When we use the distributional assumption to compute the cumulative density functions (cdfs) and conditional expectations over a and plug in the expressions for a_{ij} in (4), the price levels become

$$\begin{aligned} P_i = {} & \frac{1}{b} \left[\frac{\theta}{\theta - (\varepsilon - 1)} \right]^{-1/\theta} \frac{\varepsilon}{\varepsilon - 1} \left(\frac{X_i}{\varepsilon} \right)^{-[\theta - (\varepsilon - 1)]/[\theta(\varepsilon - 1)]} \\ & \times \left[\sum_{j=1}^{C} \bar{I}_j \left(\frac{1}{\tau_{ij} c_j} \right)^{\theta} \left(\frac{1}{c_j f_{ij}} \right)^{[\theta - (\varepsilon - 1)]/(\varepsilon - 1)} \right]^{-1/\theta}. \end{aligned} \tag{7}$$

The model is closed by assuming balanced trade in each country, which delivers a system of equations defining the vector of equilibrium wages w_i. The definition of equilibrium and the set of equilibrium conditions

[11] When the expressions for the price levels in (2) and (6) are compared, the set of varieties J_i available in country i comprise varieties coming from all countries serving market i. Thus, the expected number of varieties available in country i is equal to $\sum_{j=1}^{C} \bar{I}_j \Pr(a < a_{ij})$.

for the complete two-sector model are laid out in Appendix B. In the remainder of this section, we use the relationships implied by the simple model above to illustrate the main mechanisms behind our results.

B. *Power Law in Firm Size and Aggregate Volatility in the Model and the Data*

Total sales in the economy is defined by

$$X = \sum_{k=1}^{I} x(a(k), z(k)), \tag{8}$$

where I is the total number of operating firms, $x(a(k), z(k))$ is the sales of firm k, and we omit the country subscripts. Appendix C shows that the standard deviation of the growth rate of aggregate sales, or more precisely of the deviation from the expected aggregate sales, is equal to

$$\mathrm{SD}_z\left[\frac{\Delta X}{\mathrm{E}_z(X)}\right] = \sigma\sqrt{h}, \tag{9}$$

where $h = \sum_{k=1}^{I} h(k)^2$ is the Herfindahl index of production shares of firms in this economy, and σ is the standard deviation of the growth rate of sales of an individual firm. This is the familiar expression for the standard deviation of a weighted sum of random variables and is the same as the one used by Gabaix (2011).[12]

This economy is granular, that is, idiosyncratic shocks to firms result in aggregate fluctuations, if the distribution of firm size follows a power law with an exponent sufficiently close to one in absolute value. In other words, firm sales x in the economy must conform to

$$\Pr(x > q) = \delta q^{-\zeta}, \tag{10}$$

where ζ is close to one. Gabaix (2011, proposition 2) shows that when the firm size distribution follows a power law with an exponent $-\zeta$, the economy is populated by $\mathcal{N}$ firms, and each firm has a standard deviation of sales growth equal to σ, the aggregate volatility given by (9) is proportional to $\sigma/\mathcal{N}^{1-1/\zeta}$ for $1 < \zeta < 2$ and to $\sigma/\log\mathcal{N}$ when $\zeta = 1$. This result means that when $\zeta < 2$ and thus the distribution of firm size has infinite variance, the conventional law of large numbers does not apply, and aggregate volatility decays in the number of firms $\mathcal{N}$ only very slowly. In other words, under finite variance in the firm size distribution, aggregate volatility decays at rate $\sqrt{\mathcal{N}}$ in the number of firms. But under Zipf's law—defined as $\zeta \approx 1$—it decays only at rate $\log\mathcal{N}$.

[12] Note that there are no aggregate shocks in the model, only the firm-specific idiosyncratic shocks.

In this paper, we take this statistical result for granted. This section relates it to our theoretical framework by first demonstrating how the parameters of the model can be calibrated to the observed distribution of firm size. Then we discuss the two key comparative statics: the role of country size and the role of trade openness in aggregate volatility.

It turns out that the baseline Melitz-Pareto model delivers a power law in firm size. We demonstrate the power law in an autarkic economy and then discuss how the distribution of firm size is affected by international trade. In our model, the expected sales of a firm as a function of its unit input requirement are $x(a) = Da^{1-\varepsilon}$, where the constant D reflects the size of domestic demand. Under the assumption that $1/a \sim \text{Pareto}(b, \theta)$, the power law follows

$$\begin{aligned} \Pr(x > q) &= \Pr(Da^{1-\varepsilon} > q) \\ &= \Pr\left(\frac{1}{a} > \left(\frac{q}{D}\right)^{1/(\varepsilon-1)}\right) \\ &= \left(\frac{b^{\varepsilon-1}D}{q}\right)^{\theta/(\varepsilon-1)}, \end{aligned}$$

satisfying (10) for $\delta = (b^{\varepsilon-1}D)^{\theta/(\varepsilon-1)}$ and $\zeta = \theta/(\varepsilon - 1)$. This relationship is depicted in figure 5. Thus, our model economy will be granular if $\theta/(\varepsilon - 1)$ is close enough to one—the power law exponent in the data (see, e.g., Axtell 2001; di Giovanni, Levchenko, and Rancière 2011; di Giovanni and Levchenko 2013).

Gabaix (2011) shows that although aggregate volatility decays in the number of firms much more slowly than under the conventional law of large numbers, countries with a greater number of firms $\mathcal{N}$ will nonetheless have lower aggregate volatility. This forms the basis of the relationship between country size and aggregate volatility. Larger countries—those with higher L in our model—will feature a larger number of firms in equilibrium. Thus, they can be expected to have lower aggregate volatility. This can be demonstrated most transparently in the autarky equilibrium. When the number of countries is set to $C = 1$ and the Pareto distributional assumption is used, equation (5) can be used to compute the production cutoff a_{aut} consistent with free entry. With zero net aggregate profits, the total expenditure in the economy is equal to $X = L/\beta$, where we set the wage to be the numeraire. Equations (4) and (7) then imply that the equilibrium number of entrants $\bar{I}_{\text{aut}}$ is proportional to

$$\bar{I}_{\text{aut}} \sim L^{1/\{1-[(1-\beta)/\beta][1/(\varepsilon-1)]\}}. \tag{11}$$

This is the well-known result that the number of firms increases in country size, measured by L. It is immediate that without input-output

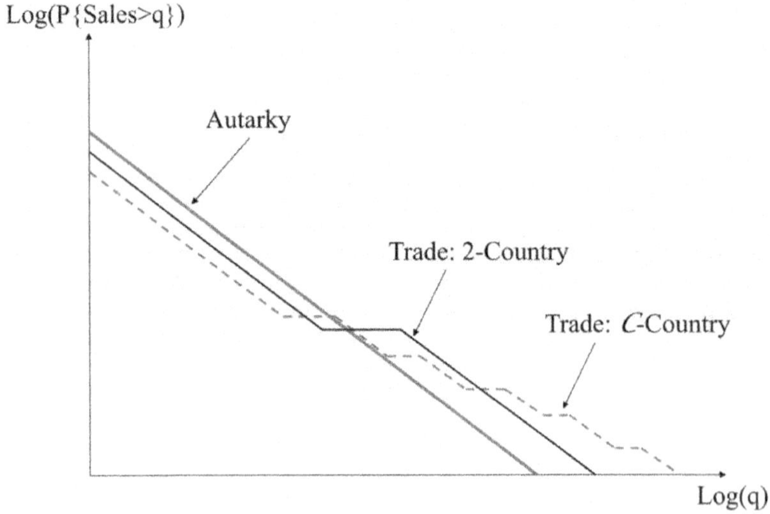

FIG. 5.—The analytical power law in the Melitz-Pareto model. This figure depicts the distribution of firm size, measured by sales, and how it changes as it moves from autarky to a two-country trade equilibrium and finally to a *C*-country trade equilibrium. In the two-country case, there is a single productivity cutoff, above which firms export abroad. Compared to autarky, there is a higher probability of finding larger firms above this cutoff. In the *C*-country case, with multiple export markets there will be cutoffs for each market, with progressively more productive firms exporting to more and more markets and growing larger and larger relative to domestic GDP.

linkages ($\beta = 1$), the relationship is simply proportional.[13] The presence of input-output linkages actually tends to raise this elasticity above one: as long as $\beta\varepsilon > 1$, the number of firms responds more than proportionately to the increase in market size. The condition that $\beta\varepsilon > 1$ is akin to the "no black hole" assumption (Fujita, Krugman, and Venables 2001). Otherwise, if $\beta\varepsilon < 1$, increasing returns are so strong that countries with higher L actually have a smaller number of entrants.[14] We impose the restriction that $\beta\varepsilon > 1$ throughout. It is likely to be comfortably satisfied in the data, as available estimates put β in the range of 0.5, while ε is typically assumed to be around six (see Sec. IV.A for details).[15] The

[13] In that case, the solution for the equilibrium number of entrants has the particularly simple form

$$\bar{I}_{\text{aut}} = \frac{L}{\varepsilon f_e}\frac{\varepsilon - 1}{\theta}.$$

[14] The model does not have a solution when $\beta\varepsilon = 1$, and the equilibrium $\bar{I}_{\text{aut}}$ is discontinuous in $\beta\varepsilon$ in the neighborhood of $\beta\varepsilon = 1$: as $\beta\varepsilon \to 1$ from below, $\bar{I}_{\text{aut}}$ goes to zero; but as $\beta\varepsilon \to 1$ from above, $\bar{I}_{\text{aut}}$ goes to infinity.

[15] One may wonder whether the larger number of entrants $\bar{I}$ actually translates into a larger number of operating firms, since not all entrants decide to produce. The number of

equilibrium relationship (11) combined with Zipf's law in firm size thus forms the basis for the first main result of the paper: smaller countries will have fewer firms and, thus, higher aggregate volatility.

C. *International Trade and Aggregate Volatility*

How does international trade affect the distribution of firm size and therefore aggregate volatility? As first demonstrated by Melitz (2003), the distribution of firm size becomes more unequal under trade: compared to autarky, the least productive firms exit, and only the most productive firms export abroad. Owing to competition from foreign varieties, domestic sales and profits decrease. Thus, as a country opens to trade, sales of most firms shrink, while the largest firms grow larger as a result of exporting.[16] Figure 5 depicts this effect. In the two-country case, there is a single productivity cutoff, above which firms export abroad. Compared to autarky, there is a higher probability of finding larger firms above this cutoff. In the C-country case with multiple export markets, there will be cutoffs for each market, with progressively more productive firms exporting to more and more markets and growing larger and larger relative to domestic GDP. Thus, if the distribution of firm sales follows a power law and the economy is granular, international trade has the potential to increase the size of the largest firms, in effect creating a "hypergranular" economy, with clear implications for the relationship between trade openness and aggregate volatility. All else equal, this "selection into exporting" effect implies that after trade opening, aggregate volatility increases.

operating firms is given by $\bar{I}_{\text{aut}} G(a_{\text{aut}})$, where $G(\cdot)$ is the cdf of a. The solution to a_{aut} does not depend on L in this model, and thus the number of actual operating firms is proportional to $\bar{I}_{\text{aut}}$.

[16] Firm-level studies of dynamic adjustment to trade liberalization appear to find empirical support for these predictions. Pavcnik (2002) provides evidence that trade liberalization led to a shift in resources from the least to the most productive firms in Chile. Bernard, Jensen, and Schott (2003) show that a fall in trade costs leads to both exit by the least productive firms and entry by firms into export markets. In addition, existing exporters ship more abroad. A recent contribution by Holmes and Stevens (2010) shows that in the United States, in some sectors the large firms are the ones suffering the most from foreign competition, because smaller firms are highly specialized boutique operations that are less affected by imports than the large factories producing standardized products with close foreign substitutes. The point made by Holmes and Stevens is a very important one, but it can be thought of as one about industrial classification: large factories and boutique ones produce different types of goods, which face very different market structures—competitive environments, trade costs, and so on. This comes through most clearly in the modeling approach adopted in that paper, in which it classifies the small boutique producers as nontradable. Thus, the Holmes and Stevens finding can be easily reconciled with our complete two-sector model, described in App. B and used in the quantitative analysis, by assuming that the standardized producers are part of the tradable sector, while the boutique producers are part of the nontradable sector. Indeed, this is very close to the assumption that Holmes and Stevens actually adopt in their model.

Before moving on to the quantitative assessment of the relationships between country size, international trade, and volatility illustrated above, we allude to another mechanism through which trade can affect volatility in a model with free entry. When a country opens to trade, the possibility of getting a sufficiently high productivity draw and becoming an exporter induces more potential entrepreneurs to enter and draw their productivity: $\bar{I}$ rises. Because aggregate volatility decreases in the number of firms, this "net entry" effect will tend to decrease volatility when a country opens to trade. As Section V demonstrates, however, this effect is quite small quantitatively: the impact of international trade on aggregate volatility is virtually the same whether we allow new net entry after opening or not.[17]

IV. Quantitative Assessment

Though the analytical results obtained in a one-sector model are informative, we would like to evaluate quantitatively the importance of these mechanisms and exploit the rich heterogeneity among the countries in the world. In order to do this, we numerically implement a multicountry model that extends the framework in Section III to include a nontraded sector with intermediate input linkages both within and between sectors. Since only the minority of economic activity takes place in sectors with substantial cross-border trade, including an explicitly nontraded sector in the quantitative exercise is especially important for evaluating the impact of international trade on volatility.

In particular, suppose that in each country there are two broad sectors, the tradable T and the nontradable N. Consumer preferences are Cobb-Douglas in CES aggregates of N and T, with the share of N in

[17] We can use a back-of-the-envelope calculation to illustrate why quantitatively free entry plays such a minor role for the impact of trade. When countries are symmetric ($L_i = L$, $f_{ii} = f$ for all i, and $\tau_{ij} = \tau$, $f_{ij} = f^X$ for all i, j), the number of entrants under trade is

$$\bar{I}_{\text{trade}} = [1 + (C-1)\tau^{-\theta}(f/f^X)^{[\theta-(\varepsilon-1)]/(\varepsilon-1)}]^{[(1-\beta)/\beta\theta](1/\{1-[(1-\beta)/\beta][1/(\varepsilon-1)]\})}\bar{I}_{\text{aut}}.$$

Trade opening thus increases the number of entrants relative to autarky under the maintained assumption that $\beta\varepsilon > 1$, since the term in brackets is larger than one. At reasonable parameter values, the exponent on the bracket in the equation above is quite small, and thus the change in $\bar{I}$ from autarky to trade is modest. Furthermore, even if the number of operating firms increases by as much as the difference between $\bar{I}_{\text{aut}}$ and $\bar{I}_{\text{trade}}$, this effect alone would amount to a proportional reduction in volatility of only $1 - (\bar{I}_{\text{trade}}/\bar{I}_{\text{aut}})^{1-1/\zeta}$, which is very small if ζ is close to one. To get a sense of the magnitudes, we plug in the parameter values for τ, f, f_X, θ, ε, and β from the quantitative model below (see Sec. IV.A and table 1). It turns out that with 100 symmetric countries (each thus accounting for 1 percent of world GDP), $\bar{I}_{\text{trade}}/\bar{I}_{\text{aut}} = 1.21$, which alone would imply a reduction in aggregate volatility of only 0.9 percent compared to autarky. With 200 countries (each 0.5 percent of world GDP), the reduction is 1.4 percent. These are upper bounds because the number of actual operating firms will increase by less than the term in brackets above, as the production cutoffs will also become more stringent under trade.

final expenditure equal to α. Intermediate inputs are also Cobb-Douglas in the N and T aggregates, with the share of N equal to η_s in sector $s = N, T$. The share of labor in total spending on inputs, β_s, will also now vary by sector. The rest of the model remains unchanged. Appendix B presents the complete description of the equations defining the equilibrium in the two-sector model.

A. *Calibration*

We numerically implement the economy under the following parameter values (see table 1 for a summary). The elasticity of substitution is $\varepsilon_s = 6$. Anderson and van Wincoop (2004) report available estimates of this elasticity to be in the range of 3–10, and we pick a value close to the middle of the range. The key parameter is θ_s, as it governs the slope of the power law. As described above, in this model firm sales follow a power law with the exponent equal to $\theta_s/(\varepsilon_s - 1)$. In the data, firm sales follow a power law with the exponent close to one. Axtell (2001) reports the value of 1.06, which we use to find θ_s given our preferred value of ε_s: $\theta_s = 1.06 \times (\varepsilon_s - 1) = 5.3$. We set both the elasticity of substitution and the Pareto exponent to be the same in the N and the T sectors. Appendix B justifies in detail the calibration of the two-sector model parameters to the observed firm size distributions.

We set the share of nontradables in consumption $\alpha = 0.65$. This is the mean value of services value added in total value added in the database

TABLE 1
PARAMETER VALUES FOR THE CALIBRATED MODEL

Parameter	Baseline	Source
ε	6	Anderson and van Wincoop (2004)
θ	5.3	Axtell (2001): $\theta/(\varepsilon - 1) = 1.06$
α	.65	Yi and Zhang (2010)
$\{\beta_N, \beta_T\}$	{.65, .35}	1997 US Benchmark Input-Output Table
$\{\eta_N, \eta_T\}$	{.77, .35}	1997 US Benchmark Input-Output Table
τ_{ij}	2.30	Helpman et al. (2008)
f_{ii}	14.24	World Bank Doing Business Indicators: normalizing $f_{US,US}$ so that nearly all firms in the United States produce
f_{ij}	7.20	World Bank Doing Business Indicators: normalizing $f_{US,US}$ so that nearly all firms in the United States produce
f	34.0	To match 7 million firms in the United States (US Economic Census)
σ	.1	Standard deviation of sales growth of the top 100 firms in Compustat

NOTE.—For ε, robustness checks include $\varepsilon = 4$ and $\varepsilon = 8$. For θ, robustness checks include $\theta/(\varepsilon - 1) = 1.5$ and $\varepsilon = 6$, so that $\theta = 6.5$. For τ_{ij}, f_{ii}, and f_{ij} the table reports the average in our sample of 50 countries. For τ_{ij}, $\tau_{ij} = \tau_{ji}$. Trade costs are adjusted by a constant ratio to match the median level of openness across the 50-country sample. Robustness checks include σ varying with firm sales: $\sigma = Ax^{-\xi}$, where $\xi = 1/6$.

compiled by the Groningen Growth and Development Center and extended to additional countries by Yi and Zhang (2010). It is the value also adopted by Alvarez and Lucas (2007). The values of β_N and β_T—share of labor/value added in total output—are calibrated using the 1997 US Benchmark Input-Output Table. We take the Detailed Make and Use tables, featuring more than 400 distinct sectors, and aggregate them into a two-sector Direct Requirements Table. This table gives the amount of N, T, and factor inputs required to produce a unit of final output. Thus, β_s is equal to the share of total sector s output that is not used to pay for intermediate inputs, that is, the payments to factors of production. According to the US Input-Output Matrix, $\beta_N = 0.65$ and $\beta_T = 0.35$: the traded sector is considerably more input-intensive than the nontraded sector. The shares of nontraded and traded inputs in both sectors are also calibrated from the US Input-Output Table. According to the data, more than 75 percent of the inputs used in the N sector come from the N sector itself ($\eta_N = 0.77$), while only 35 percent of T-sector inputs are nontradable ($\eta_T = 0.35$). Nonetheless, these values still leave substantial room for cross-sectoral input-output linkages.

To calibrate the values of τ_{ij} for each pair of countries, we use the gravity estimates from the empirical model of Helpman, Melitz, and Rubinstein (2008). To take a stand on the values of f_{ii}^s and f_{ij}^s, we follow di Giovanni and Levchenko (2013) and use the information on entry costs from the World Bank's Doing Business Indicators database. The data sources and the details of the calibration of τ_{ij} and f_{ij}^s are described in Appendix A.

Finally, we set the value of the "exploration cost" f_e such that the equilibrium number of operating firms in the United States is about 7 million. According to the 2002 US Economic Census, there were 6,773,632 establishments with a payroll in the United States. There are an additional 17,646,062 business entities that are not employers, but they account for less than 3.5 percent of total shipments. Thus, while the United States may have many more legal entities than what we assume here, 7 million is a number sufficiently high as to let us consider consequences of granularity. Since we do not have information on the total number of firms in other countries, we choose to set f_e to be the same in all countries. In the absence of data, this is the most agnostic approach we could take. In addition, since f_e represents the cost of finding out one's abilities, we do not expect it to be affected by policies and thus differ across countries. The resulting value of f_e is 15 times higher than $f_{\text{US,US}}^s$ and 2.4 times higher than the average f_{ii}^s in the rest of the sample. The finding that the ex ante fixed cost of learning one's type is much higher than the ex post fixed cost of production is common in the quantitative models of this type (see, e.g., Ghironi and Melitz 2005).

We carry out the analysis on the sample of the largest 49 countries by total GDP plus the fiftieth that represents the rest of the world. These 49 countries together cover 97 percent of world GDP. We exclude the entrepôt economies of Hong Kong and Singapore, both of which have total trade well in excess of their GDP because of significant reexporting activity. Thus, our model is not intended to fit these countries. (We do place them into the rest-of-the-world category.) The country sample, sorted by total GDP, is reported in table 2.

B. *Model Solution and Simulation Method*

In order to solve the model numerically, we must find the wages and price indices for each country, w_i, P_i^N, and P_i^T, that satisfy equations (B1), (B2), and (B3) jointly with the values of $\bar{I}_i^N$ and $\bar{I}_i^T$ that satisfy equations (5) for each sector. The system is nonreducible such that all of the prices and numbers of entrants must be solved simultaneously. Note that in this step the equilibrium values are computed under the assumption that the

TABLE 2
TOP 49 COUNTRIES AND THE REST OF THE WORLD IN TERMS OF TOTAL GDP

Country	GDP/World GDP	Country	GDP/World GDP
United States	.300	Indonesia	.006
Japan	.124	South Africa	.006
Germany	.076	Norway	.006
France	.054	Poland	.005
United Kingdom	.044	Finland	.005
Italy	.041	Greece	.004
China	.028	Venezuela, RB	.004
Canada	.026	Thailand	.004
Brazil	.021	Portugal	.003
Spain	.020	Colombia	.003
India	.017	Nigeria	.003
Australia	.016	Algeria	.003
Russian Federation	.015	Israel	.003
Mexico	.015	Philippines	.003
Netherlands	.015	Malaysia	.002
Korea, Republic	.011	Ireland	.002
Sweden	.010	Egypt, Arab Republic	.002
Switzerland	.010	Pakistan	.002
Belgium	.009	Chile	.002
Argentina	.008	New Zealand	.002
Saudi Arabia	.007	Czech Republic	.002
Austria	.007	United Arab Emirates	.002
Iran, Islamic Republic	.007	Hungary	.002
Turkey	.007	Romania	.002
Denmark	.006	Rest of the world	.027

NOTE.—Ranking of top 49 countries and the rest of the world in terms of total US$ GDP, with the average share in world GDP over 1970–2006. Source: World Bank World Development Indicators.

model aggregates take on their expected values. That is, this step ignores any variation in P_i^s's, $\bar{I}_i^s$'s, and a_{ij}^s's that would arise from one random draw of a vector of a's to another—a common approach in monopolistic competition models.

Using the equilibrium equations and the chosen parameter values, we can solve the full model for a given vector of L_i. For finding the values of L_i, we follow the approach of Alvarez and Lucas (2007). First, we would like to think of L_i not as population per se but as "equipped labor," to take explicit account of total factor productivity (TFP) and capital endowment differences between countries. To obtain the values of L_i that are internally consistent in the model, we start with an initial guess for L_i for all $i = 1, \ldots, \mathcal{C}$ and use it to solve the full model. Given the solution for wages, we update our guess for L_i for each country in order to match the GDP ratio between each country i and the United States. Using the resulting values of L_i, we solve the model again to obtain the new set of wages and iterate to convergence (Alvarez and Lucas 2007). Thus, our procedure generates vectors w_i and L_i in such a way as to match exactly the relative total GDPs of the countries in the sample. In practice, the results are close to simply equating L_i to the relative GDPs. In this procedure, we must normalize the population of one of the countries. We thus set L_{US} to its actual value of 291 million as of 2003 and compute L_i of every other country relative to this US value. An important consequence of this approach is that countries with higher TFP and capital abundance will tend to have a greater number of potential productivity draws $\bar{I}_i^s$, all else equal, since our procedure will effectively give them a higher L_i. This is akin to the assumption adopted by Alvarez and Lucas (2007) and Chaney (2008) that the number of productivity draws is a constant multiple of equipped labor L_i. The difference in our approach is that though we take labor-cum-productivity to be the measure of market size, we solve for $\bar{I}_i^N$ and $\bar{I}_i^T$ endogenously within the model.

Having solved the model given the data on country GDPs and trade costs, we now simulate it using random productivity draws for each firm in each economy. Namely, in each country i and sector s we draw $\bar{I}_i^s$ productivities from a Pareto(b_s, θ_s) distribution. For each firm, we use the cutoffs a_{ji}^s for serving each market j (including its own market $j = i$) given by equation (4) to determine whether the firm operates and which, if any, foreign markets it serves. We next calculate the total sales of each firm as the sum of its sales in each market it serves and compute the Herfindahl index of firm sales in country i. Since the distribution of firm productivities gives rise to a highly skewed distribution of firm sales, there is variation in the Herfindahl index from simulation to simulation, even though we draw as many as 7 million operating firms in a given country; note that this number is the total for the N and T sectors, where we take independent draws for each sector. We thus repeat the exercise 1,001 times and take the median values of the Herfindahl index in each country. In parallel, we also compute the Herfindahl index of firm sales in autarky for each country, which will allow us to gauge the contribution of international trade to aggregate volatility. Given these values of the Herfindahl index h, we can then construct each country's aggregate volatility under trade and in autarky using the formula for the standard deviation of aggregate output growth (9) and a realistic value of σ. Following Gabaix (2011), we set $\sigma = 0.1$, although since in this paper we will not exploit any variation in σ across countries, none of the results will be driven by this choice.

It is worth making a comparison between our procedure and the one adopted by Eaton et al. (2012). The authors simulate the firm behavior first, starting with the lowest cost and working their way up. That procedure makes it easier to then calculate entry cutoffs and price indices for each country conditional on the firm-level draws. The advantage of this approach is that in calculating the price index, the issue of an exploding integral does not arise even if $\theta_s < \varepsilon_s - 1$. A disadvantage is that, to keep the procedure tractable, Eaton et al. need to impose additional assumptions so that the total spending in each country and the wage can be taken as exogenous. This would be problematic in our setting since for us the equilibrium number of entrants is an endogenous, and central, outcome driving the results on the cross-country variation in volatility.

C. *Model Fit*

We assess the model fit along three dimensions: (i) overall and bilateral trade volumes, (ii) the relationship between country size and the size of the largest firms in each country, and (iii) the share of exporting firms in the economy.

Figure 6*A* reports the scatter plot of bilateral trade ratios, $\pi_{ij} = X_{ij}/w_i L_i$. Note that since in the data we have bilateral trade only as a share of GDP, not of total sales, we compute the same object in the model. This captures both the distinction between trade, which is recorded as total value, and GDP, which is recorded as value added, as well as the fact that there is a large nontraded sector in both the model and the data. On the horizontal axis is the natural logarithm of π_{ij} that comes from the model, while on the vertical axis is the corresponding value of that bilateral trade flow in the data. Hollow dots represent exports from one country to another, π_{ij}, $i \neq j$. Solid dots, at the top of the scatter plot, represent sales of domestic firms as a share of domestic absorption, π_{ii}. It is especially important that we reproduce the variation in the overall trade openness $(1 - \pi_{ii})$ since that will drive the contribution of trade to the aggregate volatility in each country. Figure 6*B* plots the actual values of $1 - \pi_{ii}$ against those implied by the model. For convenience, we add a 45-degree line to both plots.

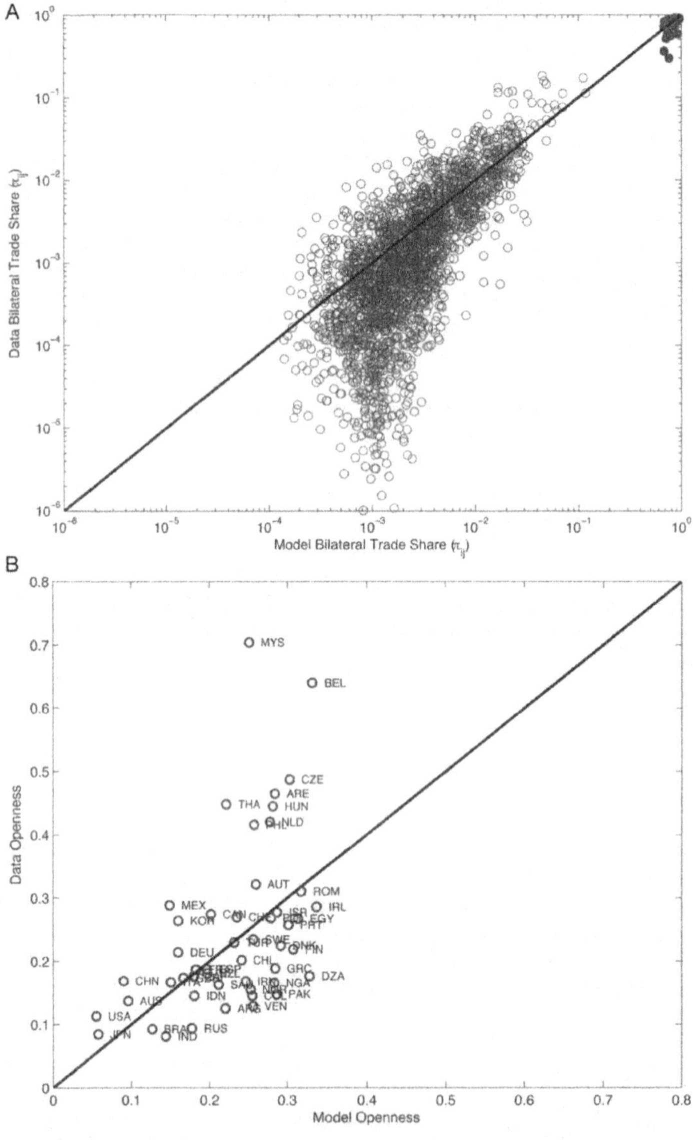

FIG. 6.—Bilateral trade shares and trade openness: data and model predictions. Panel *A* reports the scatter plot of domestic output (π_{ii}) and bilateral trade (π_{ij}), both as a share of country *i* GDP. Solid dots represent observations of π_{ii}, and hollow dots represent bilateral trade observations (π_{ij}). Both axes are in log scale. Panel *B* reports the scatter plot of total imports as a share of GDP. In both panels, the values implied by the model are on the horizontal axis; actual values are on the vertical axis, and the line through the data is the 45-degree line. Source: International Monetary Fund's Direction of Trade Statistics.

Table 3 compares the means and medians of π_{ii} and π_{ij}'s for the model and the data and reports the correlations between the two. The correlation between domestic shares π_{ii} calculated from the model and those in the data for this sample of countries is around .48. The correlation between export shares, π_{ij}, is actually higher at .78.[18] Since we use estimated gravity coefficients together with the actual data on bilateral country characteristics to compute trade costs, it is not surprising that bilateral trade flows implied by our model are closely correlated to those in the data given the success of the empirical gravity relationship. Nonetheless, since the gravity estimates we use come from outside of our calibration procedure, it is important to check that our model delivers outcomes similar to observed trade volumes.

We next assess whether the model reproduces the relationships between country size and the relevant features of the firm size distributions demonstrated in figure 3. In the data, log country size is negatively and significantly related to the log Herfindahl index of firm sales and positively and significantly related to the size of the 10 largest firms and the size of the largest firm in the economy. We can compare the data to the same relationships inside our model. It turns out that in the model the elasticity of the Herfindahl index with respect to country size is -0.135, which is right in between the Herfindahl–country size elasticity of -0.114 (sample of countries with more than 1,000 firms) and -0.284 (sample of countries with more than 100 firms) in figure 3*A*. Turning to the size of the largest firms, our model produces an elasticity of the 10 largest firms to country size of 0.903 and of the single-largest firm to country size of 0.908. These are close to the range of elasticities produced by the data: 0.888–1.006 for the 10 largest firms (fig. 3*B*) and 0.838–0.906 (fig. 3*C*) for the single-largest firm.

Finally, we use the model solution to calculate the percentage of firms that export in the total economy as well as in the tradable sector. In particular, the total number of exporters in country i equals $\bar{I}_i^T \times (b_T \max_{j \neq i}\{a_{ji}^T\})^{\theta_T}$. The total number of firms operating in the tradable sector equals $\bar{I}_i^T \times (b_T \max_j\{a_{ji}^T\})^{\theta_T}$ and in the nontradable sector $\bar{I}_i^N \times (b_N a_{ii}^N)^{\theta_N}$. We would like to compare the export participation shares in the model to what is found in the data. Unfortunately, there is no systematic empirical evidence on these shares across countries (and time). However, we have examined available data and existing literature and found these shares for eight countries: United States, Germany, France, Argentina, Colombia, Ireland, Chile, and New Zealand. Table 4 compares

[18] We also experimented with increasing the number of countries in the simulation to 60. The model fits the data well, but there are more zeros in bilateral trade data in the 60-country sample compared to the 50-country one. (With 50 countries, among the 2,500 possible unidirectional bilateral trade flows, only 18 are zeros.) Since our model does not generate zero bilateral trade outcomes, we stick with the largest 49 countries in our analysis.

TABLE 3
BILATERAL TRADE SHARES: DATA AND MODEL PREDICTIONS

	Model		Data
Domestic sales as a share of GDP (π_{ii}):			
Mean	.7900		.7520
Median	.7717		.7921
Corr(model, data)		.4783	
Imports as a share of GDP (π_{ij}):			
Mean	.0043		.0047
Median	.0021		.0047
Corr(model, data)		.7799	

NOTE.—This table reports the means and medians of domestic output (top panel) and bilateral trade (bottom panel), both as a share of domestic GDP, in the model and in the data. Source: International Monetary Fund's Direction of Trade Statistics.

TABLE 4
EXPORT PARTICIPATION: DATA AND MODEL PREDICTIONS FOR THE WHOLE ECONOMY AND THE TRADABLE SECTOR

	MODEL		DATA	
COUNTRY	Total (1)	Tradable (2)	Total (3)	Tradable (4)
United States	.010	.018	.040	.150
Germany	.111	.238	.100	. . .
France	.029	.065	.040	.090
Argentina	.112	.352	. . .	.422
Colombia	.148	.548	. . .	.363
Ireland	.332	1.000	. . .	.740
Chile	.095	.335	.105	. . .
New Zealand	.062	.189	.051	.135

SOURCE.—For the United States, data are imputed on the basis of publicly available US Economic Census data on the numbers of firms by sector, together with the summary statistics for the numbers of exporters reported in Bernard et al. (2007). Data for France are based on authors' calculations using the French census data in di Giovanni et al. (2011). Data for Germany are from Arndt, Buch, and Mattes (2009, table A2). Data for Argentina come from Bustos (2011, table D.1). For New Zealand, data come from Fabling and Sanderson (2008, table 4). Data on Ireland come from Fitzgerald and Haller (2010, table 1). Data for Chile come from private communication with Miguel Fuentes at the Central Bank of Chile. Data for Colombia come from private communication with Jorge Tovar at the Universidad de los Andes.

NOTE.—This table compares, for selected countries, the share of exporters among all firms in the model (col. 1) and the share of exporters among the tradable sector firms in the model (col. 2) with available estimates of corresponding shares in existing literature. Since for some countries data are reported relative to all the firms in the economy while for other countries they are reported relative to all the firms in the traded sector, col. 3 (data) should be compared to col. 1 (model) and col. 4 (data) should be compared to col. 2 (model).

the export participation shares produced by the model to those found in the data in this subset of countries. Columns 1 and 2 report the values in the model, with the shares of exporters relative to all the firms in the economy in column 1 and in the tradable sector only in column 2. Data sources differ across countries; in particular, the shares of exporting firms are sometimes reported relative only to all firms in the economy (which we record in col. 3) and sometimes relative to all the firms in the tradable sector (which we record in col. 4). Thus, data in column 3 should be compared to model outcomes in column 1, while data in column 4 should be compared to model outcomes in column 2.

In both the data and the model, larger countries tend to have fewer exporters relative to the overall number of firms (compare the United States to Colombia); countries closer to large markets tend to have higher shares of exporters compared to faraway countries (compare Ireland to New Zealand). In most cases the model-implied value is close to the data. We should note that by making ad hoc adjustments to trade costs in individual countries, we can match each and every one of these numbers exactly. We do not do so because this information is not available systematically for every country in our sample and because the available firm-level data themselves are noisy. Instead, we take trade costs as implied by a basic gravity model and the variation in fixed costs as implied by the Doing Business Indicators, an approach that is rather straightforward and does not involve any manual second-guessing.

D. *Main Results: Country Size and Trade Openness*

As would be expected, the level of aggregate volatility in the model is lower than what is observed in the data, since in the model all volatility comes from idiosyncratic shocks to firms. Column 1 of table 5 reports the ratio of the aggregate volatility implied by the model to the actual GDP volatility found in the data. It ranges between 0.14 and 0.72, with a value of 0.377 for the United States, almost identical to what Gabaix (2011) finds using a very different methodology. Note that the variation in aggregate volatility in the model across countries is generated by differences in country size as well as variation in bilateral trade costs.

How well can the model reproduce the empirical relationship between aggregate volatility and country size? Figure 7 plots volatility as a function of country size in the data and the model. Note that since the level of aggregate volatility in the model does not match up with the level in the data, this graph is informative about the comparison of only slopes, not intercepts. In the data the elasticity of GDP volatility with respect to country size is -0.139 (σ_{GDP}) in this sample of countries. Appendix table D1 reports the results of estimating the volatility-size relationship in the data for various country samples and with and without controls. The

TABLE 5
INTERNATIONAL TRADE AND AGGREGATE VOLATILITY

Country	Trade/ Actual (1)	Trade/ Autarky (2)	Country	Trade/ Actual (1)	Trade/ Autarky (2)
United States	.377	1.035	Indonesia	.376	1.060
Japan	.405	1.014	South Africa	.535	1.109
Germany	.582	1.080	Norway	.716	1.137
France	.559	1.098	Poland	.377	1.114
United Kingdom	.476	1.076	Finland	.437	1.109
Italy	.463	1.098	Greece	.414	1.116
China	.280	1.024	Venezuela, RB	.285	1.070
Canada	.446	1.077	Thailand	.337	1.099
Brazil	.311	1.045	Portugal	.379	1.068
Spain	.550	1.061	Colombia	.646	1.118
India	.371	1.064	Nigeria	.274	1.172
Australia	.513	1.051	Algeria	.271	1.156
Russian Federation	.144	1.099	Israel	.513	1.131
Mexico	.329	1.052	Philippines	.439	1.107
Netherlands	.693	1.104	Malaysia	.371	1.095
Korea, Republic	.296	1.059	Ireland	.457	1.087
Sweden	.634	1.099	Egypt, Arab Republic	.513	1.192
Switzerland	.548	1.107	Pakistan	.630	1.165
Belgium	.713	1.072	Chile	.262	1.119
Argentina	.219	1.091	New Zealand	.531	1.114
Saudi Arabia	.168	1.069	Czech Republic	.330	1.095
Austria	.716	1.066	United Arab Emirates	.178	1.089
Iran, Islamic Republic	.189	1.097	Hungary	.399	1.114
Turkey	.254	1.157	Romania	.242	1.218
Denmark	.612	1.156			

NOTE.—Trade/Actual reports the ratio of aggregate volatility implied by the model under trade to the actual volatility of per capita GDP growth. In calculating volatility in the model, this column assumes that the standard deviation of firm-level sales growth rate is equal to $\sigma = 0.1$. Trade/Autarky reports the ratio of volatility in the model under trade to the volatility under autarky for each country. Aggregate volatility referring to either the model or the data stands for the standard deviation of the aggregate growth rate.

baseline coefficient used in figure 7 comes from the 50-country sample and controlling for income per capita. Our calibrated model produces an elasticity of -0.135 (σ_T), which is extremely close to the one in the data though slightly below it in absolute terms.

We now assess the contribution of international trade to aggregate volatility in our sample of countries. Our model yields not only the aggregate volatility in the simulated trade equilibrium but also the aggregate volatility in autarky. As a preview of the results on the impact of trade openness, figure 7 reports the volatility-size relationship in autarky. Without trade this relationship is somewhat flatter: the elasticity of volatility with respect to country size in autarky is -0.115 (σ_A), lower than the -0.139 in the data. Thus, it appears that openness helps the model match the slope of the size-volatility relationship: without trade, smaller countries would be relatively less volatile than they actually are.

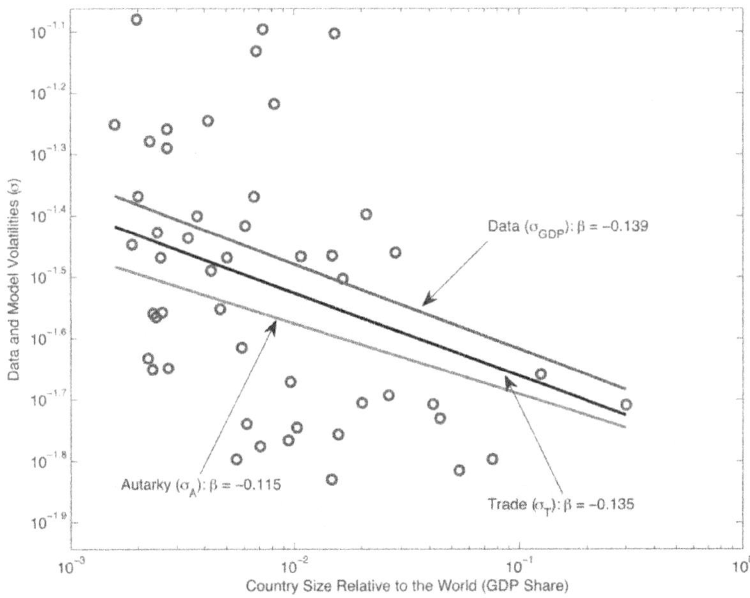

FIG. 7.—Volatility and country size: data and model predictions. This figure plots the relationship between country size and aggregate volatility implied by the data (conditioning on per capita GDP), the model under trade, and the model in autarky. The dots represent actual observations of volatility. Note that the data points and regression line are shifted by a constant for ease of visual comparability with the model regressions lines. Source: World Bank World Development Indicators.

Column 2 of table 5 reports the ratio of the volatility under the current trade regime to the volatility in autarky in each country in the sample. In the table, countries are ranked by size in descending order. We can see that international trade contributes very little to overall GDP volatility in the United States. The country is so large and trade volumes are so low (relative to total output) that its volatility under trade is only 1.035 times higher than it would be in a complete absence of trade. Similar results obtain for other very large economies, such as Japan and China. By contrast, smaller, centrally located countries experience substantially higher volatility compared to autarky. For instance, in a country such as Romania, the volatility under trade is some 22 percent higher than it would be in autarky, and in Turkey, Denmark, and Norway, it is 14–16 percent higher. In between are small but remote countries. South Africa, Argentina, and New Zealand experience aggregate volatility that is about 10 percent higher than it would have been in autarky.

Finally, we investigate how well the model predicts the actual GDP volatility found in the data. Table 6 presents regressions of actual vola-

TABLE 6
AGGREGATE VOLATILITY: DATA AND MODEL PREDICTIONS

	DEPENDENT VARIABLE: Log(GDP Volatility)			
	(1)	(2)	(3)	(4)
Log(σ_T)	1.578**	1.365**	1.099**	.765**
	(.244)	(.321)	(.287)	(.274)
Log(GDP per capita)		−.093	−.098	−.146*
		(.073)	(.065)	(.060)
Log(risk content of exports)			.100$^+$	−.064
			(.053)	(.052)
Log(Herfindahl of production)				−.134
				(.217)
Constant	3.490**	3.417**	2.994**	.282
	(1.092)	(1.145)	(1.079)	(1.045)
Observations	49	49	47	35
R^2	.353	.378	.477	.450

NOTE.—The dependent variable is the standard deviation of per capita GDP growth over the period 1970–2006. The term σ_T is the aggregate volatility implied by the simulated model. GDP per capita is the PPP-adjusted per capita GDP. Risk content of exports is the measure of the volatility of a country's export pattern taken from di Giovanni and Levchenko (2012). Herfindahl of production is the Herfindahl index of industry-level production shares, taken from di Giovanni and Levchenko (2009). Robust standard errors are in parentheses.

$^+$ Significant at 10 percent.
* Significant at 5 percent.
** Significant at 1 percent.

tility of per capita GDP growth over the period 1970–2006 against the one predicted by the model (σ_T), with all variables in natural logs. Column 1 includes no controls. The relationship is positive and highly significant. The fit of this simple bivariate relationship is remarkably high (R^2 = .353), given that in the model variation in σ_T is driven only by country size, trade barriers, and fixed costs. The model uses no information on any type of aggregate shocks (TFP, monetary, or fiscal policy) or any other country characteristics that have been shown to correlate with macroeconomic volatility, such as per capita income, institutions, or industrial specialization. Column 2 includes GDP per capita. The fit of the model improves slightly, and though the coefficient on the model volatility is somewhat smaller, it remains significant at the 1 percent level. The next two columns include measures of export structure volatility and sectoral specialization, since di Giovanni and Levchenko (2009, 2012) show that opening to trade can affect aggregate volatility through changes in these variables. Column 3 adds the risk content of exports, which captures the overall riskiness of a country's export structure.[19] The

[19] This measure is taken from di Giovanni and Levchenko (2012). A country's export structure can be volatile because of a lack of diversification and/or exporting in sectors that are more volatile.

model volatility remains significant, and the R^2 of the regression is now .477. Finally, column 4 adds a measure of production specialization for the manufacturing sector (Herfindahl of sectoral production shares).[20] The number of observations drops to 35 because of limited data availability, but the model volatility still remains significant.

V. Robustness Checks and Model Perturbations

A. *Free Entry and Intermediate Inputs*

The assumption that the number of potential projects is determined by a free-entry condition may not be realistic. We thus simulate the quantitative model under the assumption that the numbers of potential entrepreneurs $\bar{I}_i^s$ are fixed in every country and sector.[21] Table 7 reports the results of this robustness check. For ease of comparison, the top row presents the two main results from the baseline analysis. The first is that the model generates higher volatility in smaller countries, with the elasticity of volatility with respect to country size of -0.135. (As reported above, in the data this elasticity is very close, -0.139.) The second key result of the paper is the contribution of trade openness to aggregate volatility. Column 2 reports the mean ratio of aggregate volatility under the current level of trade openness relative to complete autarky.

Row 2 of table 7 reports these two main results of the paper under the alternative assumption that $\bar{I}_i^s$ is fixed. Not surprisingly, the elasticity of volatility with respect to country size is virtually identical. Less obviously, the fixed-$\bar{I}_i^s$ model delivers very similar changes in volatility due to trade openness: the mean impact is 9.0 percent, compared to 9.7 percent with free entry.

A somewhat related question involves the role of intermediate input linkages. With intermediate inputs, trade opening reduces the costs of the input bundle faced by firms, making it easier to enter markets, all else equal. To assess the importance of this effect, we implement the baseline model with free entry but without intermediate input linkages: $\beta_T = \beta_N = 1$. The two main results are presented in the third row of table 7. The elasticity of volatility with respect to country size is only slightly larger than in the baseline, at -0.145. The impact of trade on volatility is much larger, at 23.8 percent.

[20] This measure is calculated using the UNIDO database of sectoral production and is taken from di Giovanni and Levchenko (2009).

[21] We set the values of $\bar{I}_i^s$ to be the same as in the free-entry baseline and adjust f_{ii} to match the 7 million operating firms in the United States in the trade equilibrium; the results are virtually the same if we instead adopt the common ad hoc assumption that $\bar{I}_i^s$ are some constant fraction of L_i, as in Chaney (2008), for instance.

TABLE 7
SENSITIVITY CHECKS: THE IMPACT OF COUNTRY SIZE AND TRADE ON VOLATILITY

	β_{Size} (1)	Trade/ Autarky (2)
Baseline	−.135	1.097
Fixed $\bar{I}_i^s$	−.133	1.090
$\beta_T = \beta_N = 1$	−.145	1.238
$\sigma = Ax^{-\xi}$	−.286	1.291
$\zeta = 1.5$	−.123	1.116
$\varepsilon = 4$	−.119	1.099
$\varepsilon = 8$	−.138	1.111

NOTE.—This table reports (1) the coefficient of regressing the log of aggregate volatility on the log of country size (β_{Size}) in the trade equilibrium and (2) the contribution of international trade to aggregate volatility (the mean ratio of volatility under trade to the volatility in autarky) under alternative assumptions. Row 1 reports the results for the baseline trade equilibrium simulation. Row 2 reports the results of a simulation without free entry. Row 3 reports the results of a simulation without intermediates. Row 4 reports the results of a simulation in which the firm-specific volatility decreases in firm size. Row 5 reports the results of applying a power law coefficient of 1.5 rather than the baseline of 1.06. Rows 6 and 7 report the results when using an elasticity of substitution of 4 or 8, respectively.

B. *Volatility Varying with Firm Size*

An assumption that simplifies the analysis above is that the volatility of the proportional change in sales, σ, does not change in firm size x. If the volatility of sales decreases sufficiently fast in firm size, larger firms will be so much less volatile that they will not affect aggregate volatility. In fact, an economy in which larger firms are just agglomerations of smaller units each subject to i.i.d. shocks is not granular: shocks to firms cannot generate aggregate fluctuations.

In practice, however, the negative relationship between firm size and its sales volatility is not very strong. Several papers estimate the relationship between size and volatility of the type $\sigma = Ax^{-\xi}$ using Compustat data (see, e.g., Stanley et al. 1996; Sutton 2002). The benchmark case in which larger firms are simply collections of independent smaller firms would imply a value of $\xi = 1/2$ and the absence of granular fluctuations. Instead, the typical estimate of this parameter is about 1/6, implying that larger firms are not substantially less volatile than smaller ones.[22] Gabaix

[22] A related point concerns multiproduct firms: if large firms sell multiple imperfectly correlated products, then the volatility of the total sales for multiproduct firms will be lower than the volatility of single-product firms. Evidence suggests, however, that even in multiproduct firms the bulk of sales and exports is accounted for by a single product line. Sutton (2002) provides evidence that in large corporations, the constituent business units themselves follow a power law, with just a few very large business units and many much smaller ones. Along similar lines, Adalet (2009) shows that in the census of New Zealand firms, only

(2011) argues that these estimates may not be reliable since they are obtained using only data on the largest listed firms. In addition, it is not clear whether estimates based on the United States accurately reflect the experience of other countries. Hence, our baseline analysis sets $\xi = 0$ and a value of σ based on the largest 100 listed firms in the United States. In other words, we assume that all firms in the economy experience volatility as low as the largest firms in the economy.

To check robustness of our results, we allow the firm-specific volatility to decrease in firm size at the rate estimated in the literature. In that case, aggregate volatility is given by

$$\mathrm{SD}_z\left[\frac{\Delta X}{\mathrm{E}_z(X)}\right] = \sqrt{\sum_{k=1}^{I}\left[Ax(k)^{-\xi}h(k)\right]^2},$$

where, once again, $x(k)$ is sales of firm k, and $h(k)$ is the share of firm k's sales in total output in the economy.

The rest of the simulation remains unchanged. Since we are not matching the level of aggregate volatility, just the role of country size and trade, we do not need to posit a value of the constant A. However, it would be easy to calibrate to match the volatility of the top 100 firms in the United States as reported by Gabaix (2011), for example. Note that compared to the baseline simulation, modeling a decreasing relationship between firm size and volatility is a double-edged sword: while larger firms may be less volatile as a result, smaller firms are actually more volatile. This implies that the impact of either country size or international trade will not necessarily be more muted when we make this modification to the basic model.

Row 4 of table 7 reports the two main results of the paper under the alternative assumption that firm volatility decreases with firm size. In turns out that in this case, smaller countries are even more volatile relative to large ones (the size-volatility elasticity doubles to −0.286), and the contribution of trade is also larger, with trade leading to an average 29 percent increase in volatility compared to 9.7 percent in the baseline. Somewhat surprisingly, therefore, allowing volatility to decrease in firm size implies a larger contribution of trade to aggregate volatility, not a smaller one. In fact, this is the case in every country in the sample except the United States.[23]

about 6.5–9.5 percent of sales variation is explained by the extensive margin (more products per firm), with the rest explained by the intensive margin (greater sales per product).

[23] Another possible determinant of firm volatility that would be relevant to our analysis is exporting. The baseline model assumes that the volatility of a firm's sales growth does not change when it becomes an exporter. If exporters became systematically more or less volatile than nonexporters, the quantitative results could be affected. To check for this possibility, we used the Compustat quarterly database of listed US firms together with information on whether a firm is an exporter from the Compustat segments database. Appendix table D2 estimates the relationship between firm-level volatility—based on either

C. *Alternative Parameter Values*

We assess the sensitivity of the results in two additional ways. The first is an alternative assumption on the curvature of the firm size distribution. Eaton et al. (2011) estimate a range of values for $\theta/(\varepsilon-1)$ between 1.5 and 2.5. Though Gabaix (2011) shows that the shocks to large firms can still generate aggregate volatility when the power law exponent is less than two, it is important to check whether the main results of our paper survive under alternative values of $\theta/(\varepsilon-1)$. Row 5 of table 7 presents the two main results of the paper under the assumption that the slope of the power law in firm size is 1.5 instead of 1.06. Though in each case the numbers are slightly smaller in absolute value, the main qualitative and quantitative results remain unchanged: smaller countries still have lower volatility, with an elasticity of −0.123, and trade contributes slightly more to aggregate volatility, with an average increase of 11.6 percent.

Second, we recalibrate the model under two alternative values of ε, 4 and 8. In these exercises, we continue to assume that the economy is characterized by Zipf's law, so that $\theta/(\varepsilon-1)$ is still equal to our baseline value of 1.06. Thus, as we change ε, we change θ along with it. The results are presented in the last two rows of table 7. The size-volatility relationship is robust to these alternative assumptions. The elasticity of volatility with respect to country size is similar to the baseline, though slightly lower when $\varepsilon = 4$. The contribution of trade is quite similar as well, with 9.9 percent and 11.1 percent for $\varepsilon = 4$ and $\varepsilon = 8$, respectively.

Although for all of the robustness checks table 7 reports only the average impact of trade, it turns out that all of these alternative implementations preserve the basic patterns found in the baseline: trade raises volatility relative to autarky in all countries; larger countries and countries farther away from major trading partners tend to experience smaller changes in volatility due to trade.

D. *Further Reductions in Trade Costs*

The analysis above compares aggregate volatility under today's trade costs and in autarky and finds that the impact of trade on volatility has been robustly positive. We now evaluate how volatility would change if trade costs decreased further from their current levels. Table 8 presents the distribution of changes in aggregate volatility relative to its current

the growth rate of sales or a measure of the "granular residual" following Gabaix (2011)—and its export status and size. When we control for size, export status is always insignificant, and even the magnitude of the coefficient is exceedingly small, implying that volatility of exporters is between 96 and 99 percent of the volatility of nonexporters. Furthermore, the estimated elasticity of volatility with respect to firm size is similar to what is reported in the literature and used in the sensitivity check.

TABLE 8
THE IMPACT OF FURTHER REDUCTIONS IN TRADE COSTS ON AGGREGATE VOLATILITY

	REDUCTION IN TRADE COSTS			
	10% (1)	25% (2)	50% (3)	75% (4)
Percentile:				
5th	.998	.994	.984	1.003
10th	.998	.998	.991	1.006
25th	1.001	1.003	1.001	1.017
50th	1.004	1.011	1.011	1.034
75th	1.011	1.022	1.036	1.075
95th	1.019	1.036	1.055	1.129
Minimum	.995	.988	.973	.990
Maximum	1.030	1.050	1.084	1.167

NOTE.—This table reports percentiles and the minimum and maximum of the ratio of aggregate volatility under four reductions in iceberg trade costs τ_{ij} to the aggregate volatility as implied by the model under current trade costs.

level for various magnitudes of trade cost reductions, from 10 percent to 75 percent. Strikingly, a further reduction in trade costs leads to practically no change in volatility on average. For the median country, a 50 percent reduction in trade costs increases volatility by only 1.1 percent relative to the baseline. Furthermore, while the median volatility does rise slightly as trade costs fall, the impact always ranges from positive to negative.

What can explain this nonmonotonicity? Starting from autarky, as trade costs fall, only the largest firms export, and the distribution of firm size becomes more right-skewed. This is the main mechanism responsible for the positive effect of trade openness on volatility. However, as trade costs fall further, the exporting cutoff falls, and more and more firms begin exporting. Eventually, this process will make the firm size distribution less fat tailed: when trade costs are so low that everyone exports, there is no selection into exporting, and the power law in firm size exponent is the same as it was in autarky. Consistent with this intuition, we find that the change in aggregate volatility when trade costs fall is closely correlated with the concomitant change in the share of exporters. Smaller countries tend to experience the largest increases in the share of exporters and the greatest decreases in volatility in this counterfactual. The opposite is true for the biggest countries.

Two additional points are worth making about the impact of further reductions in trade costs. First, the nonmonotonicity is not due to the assumption of free entry: the results are virtually the same if we assume fixed $\bar{I}_i^s$ instead. Second, in the model without intermediates the nonmonotonicity disappears: reductions in trade costs always increase volatility in that model. The source of the difference is that without intermediates, a given fall in trade costs leads to a far smaller change in the exporting cutoffs than in the model with intermediates. Many fewer firms enter the export markets, and thus the selection into exporting effect is not reversed as it is in the baseline. What is the intuition for this difference? In both models, a global fall in τ_{ij} has the direct effect of lowering the firms' marginal cost of serving the export markets and thus makes the firm more likely to start selling abroad. In a model with intermediates, there is an additional effect that the fall in τ_{ij} lowers the cost of the input bundle c_j^s, since that input bundle includes foreign varieties and those are now cheaper. This indirect effect further lowers the exporting cutoffs, over and above the direct effect of τ_{ij}. In the model without intermediates the indirect effect is absent since the input bundle is just the wage. It turns out that quantitatively this makes a large difference for the results of a reduction in trade costs.

We conclude from these exercises that while the impact of openness on volatility at the current levels of trade costs is robustly positive in all the models we consider, the outcomes of further reductions in trade costs are sensitive to modeling assumptions about intermediate input linkages.

VI. Conclusion

Recent literature in both macroeconomics and international trade has focused attention on the role of large firms. Gabaix (2011) demonstrates that if the distribution of firm size follows a power law with an exponent close to negative one—which appears to be the case in the data—the economy is granular: shocks to the largest firms can lead to aggregate fluctuations.

This paper argues that the preponderance of large firms and their role in aggregate volatility can help explain two empirical regularities: (i) smaller countries are more volatile, and (ii) more open countries are more volatile. We calibrate and simulate a multicountry model of firm-level production and trade that can generate granular fluctuations. The model matches quite well a number of features of the data, such as observed bilateral and overall trade volumes, export participation ratios, and the relative size of the largest firms in different countries. We show that the model reproduces the elasticity of GDP volatility with respect to country size found in the data. The contribution of international trade to aggregate volatility varies a great deal depending on country characteristics. While it is minimal in large, relatively closed economies such as the United States or Japan, trade increases volatility by up to 15–20 percent in small open economies such as Denmark or Romania.

Recent research incorporates heterogeneous firms into fully dynamic general equilibrium macroeconomic models, focusing on the impact of persistent aggregate shocks and firm entry and exit (Ghironi and Melitz

2005; Alessandria and Choi 2007; Ruhl 2008). The importance of firm-specific idiosyncratic shocks for macroeconomic volatility via the granular channel emphasized in this paper should be viewed as complementary to this work. Future research incorporating these different mechanisms, as well as bringing disaggregated data to the models, will help provide an even more complete picture of the macroeconomic impact of trade integration.

Appendix A

Data Description and Sources

Data on total GDP, per capita income, and trade openness come from the World Bank's World Development Indicators database. Aggregate volatility is the standard deviation of the yearly growth rates of per capita GDP in constant local currency units over the period 1970–2006. Country size is the average share of the country's nominal US dollar GDP in the world US dollar GDP. Per capita income is the average real PPP-adjusted per capita GDP. All the averages are taken over the same period over which the volatility is computed, 1970–2006.

The figures on Fonterra are obtained from http://www.maf.govt.nz/mafnet/rural-nz/profitability-and-economics/contribution-of-land-based-industries-nz-economic-growth/contribution07.htm and http://tvnz.co.nz/view/page/423466/146647. The data on the 10 largest Korean business groups come from the Korean Development Institute courtesy of Wonhyuk Lim and are for the year 2006.

The data on the Herfindahl indices of firm sales and the size of the 10 largest and the single-largest firm come from ORBIS, a large multicountry database published by Bureau van Dijk that contains information on more than 50 million companies worldwide. The data come from a variety of sources, including, but not limited to, registered filings and annual reports. Importantly, the database includes both publicly traded and privately held firms. The main variable used in the analysis is total sales. For each country, we use the year with the most observations available, which is always between 2006 and 2008. ORBIS is the largest available nonproprietary firm-level database. Nonetheless, coverage is quite uneven across countries and years, implying that measures of concentration may not be reliable or comparable across countries. We alleviate this concern by restricting the sample of countries to those with a certain minimum number of firms and by using indices that are less prone to coverage-related biases. Di Giovanni and Levchenko (2013) present a more complete description of the ORBIS database and further evidence based on these data that firm size distributions in a large number of countries are extremely fat tailed.

To obtain values of τ_{ij}, we use the gravity estimates from the empirical model of Helpman et al. (2008). Combining geographical characteristics such as bilateral distance, common border, common language, whether the two countries are in a currency union, and others with the coefficient estimates reported by Helpman et al. yields, up to a multiplicative constant, the values of τ_{ij} for each country pair. We vary the multiplicative constant so as to match the mean and median imports/GDP ratios observed in the data in our sample of countries. Data on bilateral distance, common border, whether the country is an island or is land-locked, common language, and colonial ties are from Centre d'Etudes Prospectives et Informations Internationales. Data on legal origins come from La Porta et al. (1998). Finally, information on currency unions and free-trade areas come from Rose (2004), supplemented by Internet searches whenever needed. The advantage of the Helpman et al. estimates is that they are obtained in an empirical model that accounts explicitly for both fixed and variable costs of exporting and thus correspond most closely to the theoretical structure in our paper. Note that in this formulation, $\tau_{ij} = \tau_{ji}$ for all i and j.[24]

The values of f_{ii}^s and f_{ij}^s are calibrated following di Giovanni and Levchenko (2013). The World Bank's Doing Business Indicators database collects information on the administrative costs of setting up a firm—the time it takes, the number of procedures, and the monetary cost—in a large sample of countries in the world. The particular variable we use is the amount of time required to set up a business. We favor this indicator compared to others that measure entry costs either in dollars or in units of per capita income because in our model f_{ii}^s is a quantity of inputs rather than a value. We must normalize f_{ii}^s for one country. Thus, we proceed by setting $f_{\text{US,US}}^s$ to a level just high enough to ensure an interior solution for production cutoffs.[25] Then, for every other country f_{ii}^s is set relative to the United States. To be precise, if, according to the Doing Business Indicators database, it takes 10 times longer to register a business in country i than in the United States, then $f_{ii}^s = 10 \times f_{\text{US,US}}^s$. Since we do not have data on fixed costs of operating a business that vary by sector, we set f_{ii}^s to be equal in the N and T sectors.

To measure the fixed costs of international trade, we use the Trading across Borders module of the Doing Business Indicators. This module provides the costs of exporting a 20-foot dry-cargo container out of each country, as well as the costs of importing the same kind of container into each country. Parallel to our approach to setting the domestic cost f_{ii}^s, the indicators we choose are the amount of time required to carry out these transactions. This ensures that f_{ii}^T and f_{ij}^T are measured in the same units. We take the bilateral fixed cost f_{ij}^T to be the sum of the cost of exporting from country j and the cost of importing into country i. The foreign trade costs f_{ij}^T are on average about 40 percent of the domestic entry costs f_{ii}^T.[26]

[24] An earlier version of the paper also computed τ_{ij} using the estimates of Eaton and Kortum (2002) as a robustness check. The results were very similar.

[25] That is, we set $f_{\text{US,US}}^s$ to a level just high enough that $a_{ji}^s < 1/b_s$ for all $i, j = 1, \ldots, C$ in all the baseline and counterfactual exercises, with $1/b_s$ being the upper limit of the distribution of a.

[26] An earlier version of the paper was more agnostic about the nature of domestic fixed costs f_{ii}^T and assumed instead that they are equal (and low) in every country. The results were very similar. In addition, we carried out the analysis setting the bilateral fixed cost to be the sum of domestic costs of starting a business in the source and destination countries: $f_{ij}^T = f_{ii}^T + f_{jj}^T$. This approach may be preferred if fixed costs of exporting involved more than just shipping and required, for instance, the exporting firm to create a subsidiary for the distribution in the destination country. The results were virtually identical.

The bilateral and overall trade volumes as a share of GDP used for comparison to the model come from the International Monetary Fund's Direction of Trade Statistics.

Appendix B

The Complete Two-Sector Model

In country i, consumers maximize

$$\max_{\{y_i^N(k),y_i^T(k)\}} \left[\sum_{k=1}^{J_i^N} y_i^N(k)^{(\varepsilon_N-1)/\varepsilon_N}\right]^{\alpha\varepsilon_N/(\varepsilon_N-1)} \left[\sum_{k=1}^{J_i^T} y_i^T(k)^{(\varepsilon_T-1)/\varepsilon_T}\right]^{(1-\alpha)\varepsilon_T/(\varepsilon_T-1)}$$

subject to

$$\sum_{k=1}^{J_i^N} p_i^N(k)y_i^N(k) + \sum_{k=1}^{J_i^T} p_i^T(k)y_i^T(k) = Y_i,$$

where $y_i^s(k)$ is final consumption of good k belonging to sector $s = N, T$ in country i; $p_i^s(k)$ is the price of this good; Y_i is total final consumption expenditure in the economy; and J_i^s is the number of varieties available in sector s in country i coming from all countries. Since consumer preferences are Cobb-Douglas in CES aggregates of N and T, final consumption expenditure on sector N is equal to αY_i and on the T sector, $(1-\alpha)Y_i$.

The CES composites of both N and T are used both as consumption and as intermediate inputs in production. Let X_i^s denote the total spending—final and intermediate—on sector $s = N, T$ in country i. Given this total expenditure, it is well known that expenditure on an individual variety k in country i is equal to

$$x_i^s(k) = \frac{X_i^s}{(P_i^s)^{1-\varepsilon_s}} p_i^s(k)^{1-\varepsilon_s},$$

where P_i^s is the ideal price index of sector s in this economy, (2), augmented with the appropriate sector superscripts.

Production in both sectors uses both labor and CES composites of N and T as intermediate inputs. An input bundle in country j and sector s has a cost

$$c_j^s = w_j^{\beta_s}[(P_j^N)^{\eta_s}(P_j^T)^{1-\eta_s}]^{1-\beta_s}.$$

That is, production in sector $s = N, T$ requires labor, inputs of N, and inputs of T. The share of labor in value added, β_s, and the share of nontradable inputs in total input usage, η_s, both vary by sector.

Entrepreneurs can pay the exploration cost f_e to enter either sector. Each entrepreneur that entered sector s in country j decides whether or not to pay the fixed cost of production f_{jj}^s and which, if any, export markets to serve. In the N sector, we assume that trade costs are infinite, and thus a firm in country j may serve only its own market.

The expressions defining the input requirement cutoffs a_{ij}^s, (3) and (4), and the free-entry conditions (5) have the same form (up to the appropriate sector superscripts) and will hold in each sector. Following similar steps, we derive the expressions for the price levels in the two sectors:

$$P_i^N = \frac{1}{b_N}\left[\frac{\theta_N}{\theta_N-(\varepsilon_N-1)}\right]^{-1/\theta_N}\frac{\varepsilon_N}{\varepsilon_N-1}\left(\frac{X_i^N}{\varepsilon_N}\right)^{-[\theta_N-(\varepsilon_N-1)]/[\theta_N(\varepsilon_N-1)]} \times\left\{\bar{I}_i^N\left(\frac{1}{c_i^N}\right)^{\theta_N}\left(\frac{1}{c_i^N f_{ii}^N}\right)^{[\theta_N-(\varepsilon_N-1)]/(\varepsilon_N-1)}\right\}^{-1/\theta_N} \tag{B1}$$

and

$$P_i^T = \frac{1}{b_T}\left[\frac{\theta_T}{\theta_T-(\varepsilon_T-1)}\right]^{-1/\theta_T}\frac{\varepsilon_T}{\varepsilon_T-1}\left(\frac{X_i^T}{\varepsilon_T}\right)^{-[\theta_T-(\varepsilon_T-1)]/[\theta_T(\varepsilon_T-1)]} \times\left\{\sum_{j=1}^{C}\bar{I}_j^T\left(\frac{1}{\tau_{ij}c_j^T}\right)^{\theta_T}\left(\frac{1}{c_j^T f_{ij}^T}\right)^{[\theta_T-(\varepsilon_T-1)]/(\varepsilon_T-1)}\right\}^{-1/\theta_T}. \tag{B2}$$

Having expressed P_i^s and a_{ij}^s in terms of X_i^s and c_i^s for all $i, j = 1, \ldots, C$, it remains to close the model by solving for the X_i^s's and w_i's. To do this, we impose balanced trade for each country and the market-clearing conditions in each sector and country. Free entry implies that the total profits are zero, and thus final expenditure in country i simply equals labor income: $Y_i = w_i L_i$. Total expenditure X_i^N and X_i^T equal final spending plus expenditure on sector s as intermediate inputs in both sectors:

$$X_i^N = \alpha w_i L_i + (1-\beta_N)\eta_N X_i^N + (1-\beta_T)\eta_T X_i^T,$$

$$X_i^T = (1-\alpha)w_i L_i + (1-\beta_N)(1-\eta_N)X_i^N + (1-\beta_T)(1-\eta_T)X_i^T.$$

Note that even though the T sector has both imports and exports, the assumption that only T-sector goods can be traded amounts to imposing balanced trade within the T sector, and thus the second condition must be satisfied in equilibrium as written. These two conditions imply that total spending in each sector is a constant multiple of labor income $w_i L_i$.

Total sales from country i to country j can be written as

$$X_{ji}^T = \frac{X_j^T}{(P_j^T)^{1-\varepsilon_T}}\left(\frac{\varepsilon_T}{\varepsilon_T-1}\tau_{ji}c_i^T\right)^{1-\varepsilon_T}\bar{I}_i^T\frac{b_T^{\theta_T}\theta_T}{\theta_T-(\varepsilon_T-1)}(a_{ji}^T)^{\theta_T-(\varepsilon_T-1)}.$$

Using expressions for a_{ji}^T in (4) and P_j^T in (B2), total exports from i to j become

$$X_{ji}^T = \frac{\bar{I}_i^T (\tau_{ji} c_i^T)^{-\theta_T} (f_{ji}^T c_i^T)^{-[\theta_T - (\varepsilon_T - 1)]/(\varepsilon_T - 1)}}{\sum_{l=1}^{C} \bar{I}_l^T (\tau_{jl} c_l^T)^{-\theta_T} (f_{jl}^T c_l^T)^{-[\theta_T - (\varepsilon_T - 1)]/(\varepsilon_T - 1)}} X_j^T.$$

Using the trade balance conditions, $X_i^T = \sum_{j=1}^{C} X_{ji}^T$ for each $i = 1, \ldots, C$ as well as the property that total spending X_i^T is a constant multiple of $w_i L_i$ leads to the following system of equations in w_i:

$$\begin{aligned} w_i L_i = \sum_{j=1}^{C} \Bigg[\Bigg(& \bar{I}_i^T \tau_{ji}^{-\theta_T} (f_{ji}^T)^{-[\theta_T - (\varepsilon_T - 1)]/(\varepsilon_T - 1)} \\ & \times \{ w_i^{\beta_T} [(P_i^N)^{\eta_T} (P_i^T)^{1-\eta_T}]^{1-\beta_T} \}^{-\theta_T - [\theta_T - (\varepsilon_T - 1)]/(\varepsilon_T - 1)} \Bigg) \\ & \div \Bigg(\sum_{l=1}^{C} \bar{I}_l^T \tau_{jl}^{-\theta_T} (f_{jl}^T)^{-[\theta_T - (\varepsilon_T - 1)]/(\varepsilon_T - 1)} \\ & \times \{ w_l^{\beta_T} [(P_l^N)^{\eta_T} (P_l^T)^{1-\eta_T}]^{1-\beta_T} \}^{-\theta_T - [\theta_T - (\varepsilon_T - 1)]/(\varepsilon_T - 1)} \Bigg) \Bigg] w_j L_j, \end{aligned} \tag{B3}$$

$i = 1, \ldots, C$. There are $C - 1$ independent equations in this system, with wage in one of the countries as the numeraire.

A monopolistically competitive equilibrium is a set of prices $\{w_i, P_i^N, P_i^T\}_{i=1}^{C}$ and factor allocations such that (i) consumers maximize utility, (ii) firms maximize profits, and (iii) all goods and factor markets clear. The equilibrium is obtained as a solution to $(C - 1) + 2 \times C + 2 \times C$ equations in w_i, P_i^N, P_i^T, $\bar{I}_i^N$, and $\bar{I}_i^T$ that satisfies equations (5) for both $s = N, T$, (B1), (B2), and (B3) for each $i = 1, \ldots, C$. We solve these equations numerically in order to carry out the main quantitative exercise in this paper.

Calibrating to Zipf's law in firm size in a two-sector model with trade.—While Section III.B argues that, in a one-sector Melitz-Pareto economy, steady-state firm size follows a power law with exponent $\theta/(\varepsilon - 1)$, our quantitative model features two sectors, idiosyncratic shocks to firm sales and selection into exporting. Here we show that the aggregate model economy with these additional features will still exhibit Zipf's law in firm size.

Deriving an aggregate power law in an economy with two sectors involves computing the (counter-)cdf of the following mixture of distributions. Let Q be a random variable that follows a power law with exponent ζ_1 with probability p and with exponent ζ_2 with probability $1 - p$. It is straightforward to show that the counter-cdf of Q is equal to $\Pr(Q > q) = pD_1 q^{-\zeta_1} + (1 - p) D_2 q^{-\zeta_2}$. Importantly, when $\zeta_1 = \zeta_2 = \zeta$, Q is itself a power law with exponent ζ. This means that a two-sector economy in which both sectors follow a power law with the same exponent will, in aggregate, also exhibit a power law with that exponent. Our quantitative exercise adopts the assumption that both the N and T sectors follow Zipf's law. Though we are not aware of any comprehensive set of estimates of power law exponents in both traded and nontraded sectors, di Giovanni et al. (2011) estimate power law exponents for a wide range of both traded and nontraded industries using a census of French firms and find that power law exponents do not differ systematically between traded and nontraded sectors. It still could be the case that while the reduced-form exponents—which correspond to $\theta_T/(\varepsilon_T - 1)$ and $\theta_N/(\varepsilon_N - 1)$—are the same, the actual values of θ_s and ε_s differ. Since we do not have reliable information about how these two individual parameters differ across sectors, we adopt the most agnostic and neutral assumption that both θ_s and ε_s are the same in the two sectors.

Another concern is that even if steady-state firm size in the aggregate economy follows Zipf's law, when firms are hit by idiosyncratic shocks z, the resulting distribution would be something else. It turns out, however, that power laws are preserved under multiplication by a random variable with finite variance. That is, if firm sales are driven by a random productivity that generates Zipf's law ($1/a$ in our notation) and a finite variance shock (z), the resulting distribution of sales is still Zipf (Gabaix 2009, 258–59).

Another point regarding the calibration of power law parameters is that, strictly speaking, when not all firms export, selection into exporting implies that the power law exponent estimated on total sales—domestic plus exporting—is lower than $\theta/(\varepsilon - 1)$. Di Giovanni et al. (2011) explore this bias in detail using the census of French firms and suggest several corrections to the estimating procedure that can be used to estimate $\theta/(\varepsilon - 1)$ in an internally consistent way. Their analysis shows that the bias introduced by selection into exporting is not large. Corrected estimates obtained by di Giovanni et al. show that $\theta/(\varepsilon - 1)$ is about 1.05, roughly the same as the value used in the quantitative exercise.

Thus, even though the model is enriched with these additional features, the resulting distribution of firm size that the model produces still follows Zipf's law.

Appendix C

Aggregate Volatility Derivation

Firm k in country i with unit input requirement $a(k)$ and realization of transitory shock $z(k)$ has sales of

$$\begin{aligned} x^s(a(k), z(k)) &= \sum_{j=1}^{C} \mathbf{1}[a(k) \le a_{ij}] \frac{X_j^s}{(P_j^s)^{1-\varepsilon_s}} \left[\frac{\varepsilon_s}{\varepsilon_s - 1} \tau_{ji} c_i^s a(k) z(k) \right]^{1-\varepsilon_s} \\ &= \left\{ \sum_{j=1}^{C} \mathbf{1}[a(k) \le a_{ij}] \frac{X_j^s}{(P_j^s)^{1-\varepsilon_s}} \left[\frac{\varepsilon_s}{\varepsilon_s - 1} \tau_{ji} c_i^s a(k) \right]^{1-\varepsilon_s} \right\} \tilde{z}, \end{aligned} \tag{C1}$$

where $\mathbf{1}[\cdot]$ is the indicator function that captures whether firm k serves market j, and $\tilde{z} \equiv z^{1-\varepsilon_s}$. We already assumed that $E_z(\tilde{z}) = 1$, and now we further suppose that $\mathrm{Var}_z(\tilde{z}) = \sigma^2$. Expected sales for the firm with productivity $a(k)$ are

$$E_z[x^s(a(k), z(k))] = \sum_{j=1}^{C} \mathbf{1}[a(k) \le a_{ij}] \frac{X_j^s}{(P_j^s)^{1-\varepsilon_s}} \left[\frac{\varepsilon_s}{\varepsilon_s - 1} \tau_{ji} c_i^s a(k) \right]^{1-\varepsilon_s}. \tag{C2}$$

Given the expression for the actual sales of the firm with a transitory shock $z(k)$ in (C1) and the expected sales of the firm with productivity $a(k)$ in (C2), the actual sales as an approximation around $\mathrm{E}_z[x^s(a(k), z(k))]$ are

$$x^s(a(k), z(k)) \approx \mathrm{E}_z[x^s(a(k), z(k))] + \left.\frac{dx}{d\tilde{z}}\right|_{\tilde{z}=1} \Delta\tilde{z}.$$

Therefore, the proportional change in $x^s(a(k), z(k))$, or the growth rate, is given by

$$\frac{\Delta x^s(a(k), z(k))}{\mathrm{E}_z[x^s(a(k), z(k))]} = \tilde{z} - 1,$$

and the variance of this growth rate is

$$\mathrm{Var}_z \left\{ \frac{\Delta x^s(a(k), z(k))}{\mathrm{E}_z[x^s(a(k), z(k))]} \right\} = \sigma^2,$$

which we assume for simplicity is the same in the two sectors $s = N, T$. When we drop the sector superscripts, the total sales in the economy are given by (8); thus the change in the total sales relative to the nonstochastic steady state (the growth rate) is

$$\begin{aligned}\frac{\Delta X}{\mathrm{E}_z X} &= \frac{\sum_{k=1}^{I} \Delta x(a(k), z(k))}{\mathrm{E}_z X} \\ &= \sum_{k=1}^{I} \frac{\Delta x(a(k), z(k))}{\mathrm{E}_z[x(a(k), z(k))]} \frac{\mathrm{E}_z[x(a(k), z(k))]}{\mathrm{E}_z X}.\end{aligned}$$

This means that the aggregate volatility is

$$\begin{aligned}\mathrm{Var}_z\left(\frac{\Delta X}{\mathrm{E}_z X}\right) &= \mathrm{Var}_z \left\{ \sum_{k=1}^{I} \frac{\Delta x(a(k), z(k))}{\mathrm{E}_z[x(a(k), z(k))]} \frac{\mathrm{E}_z[x(a(k), z(k))]}{\mathrm{E}_z X} \right\} \\ &= \sum_{k=1}^{I} \mathrm{Var}_z \left\{ \frac{\Delta x(a(k), z(k))}{\mathrm{E}_z[x(a(k), z(k))]} \right\} \left\{ \frac{\mathrm{E}_z[x(a(k), z(k))]}{\mathrm{E}_z X} \right\}^2 \\ &= \sigma^2 \sum_{k=1}^{I} \left\{ \frac{\mathrm{E}_z[x(a(k), z(k))]}{\mathrm{E}_z X} \right\}^2 \\ &= \sigma^2 \sum_{k=1}^{I} h(k)^2,\end{aligned}$$

where $h(k)$ is the share of the firm k's expected sales in total expected sales in the economy. As expected, the volatility of total output in the economy is equal to the volatility of an individual firm's output times the Herfindahl index of production shares.

Appendix D

TABLE D1
AGGREGATE VOLATILITY AND COUNTRY SIZE REGRESSIONS

	DEPENDENT VARIABLE: Log(GDP Volatility)					
	(1)	(2)	(3)	(4)	(5)	(6)
Log(size)	−.177**	−.139**	−.090$^+$	−.209**	−.180**	−.142**
	(.038)	(.044)	(.045)	(.035)	(.027)	(.023)
Log(GDP per capita)		−.157*	−.261**	−.049	−.019	.018
		(.069)	(.070)	(.057)	(.045)	(.037)
Constant	−4.352**	−2.696**	−1.533$^+$	−4.010**	−4.154**	−4.291**
	(.190)	(.763)	(.773)	(.601)	(.473)	(.410)
Observations	49	49	30	75	100	143
R^2	.192	.273	.337	.328	.296	.225

NOTE.—The dependent variable is the log of the standard deviation of per capita GDP growth over the period 1970–2006. Size is a country's GDP as a share of world GDP; GDP per capita is PPP-adjusted per capita income. All right-hand-side variables are averages over 1970–2006. Robust standard errors are in parentheses.

$^+$ Significant at 10 percent.

* Significant at 5 percent.

** Significant at 1 percent.

TABLE D2
US EVIDENCE ON RELATIONSHIP BETWEEN FIRM-LEVEL VOLATILITY AND EXPORTER STATUS AND SIZE

	GROWTH		GRANULAR	
	All (1)	Restricted (2)	All (3)	Restricted (4)
	A. Sample Period: 1980–2007			
Exporter	−.022	−.014	−.024	−.017
	(.021)	(.022)	(.021)	(.023)
Log(sales)	−.129**	−.135**	−.128**	−.133**
	(.005)	(.005)	(.005)	(.004)
Observations	15,901	14,597	15,859	14,558
Number of SIC	440	415	427	403
R^2	.181	.183	.198	.201
	B. Sample Period: 1980–89			
Exporter	−.020	−.013	−.010	−.013
	(.021)	(.023)	(.020)	(.023)
Log(sales)	−.128**	−.133**	−.126**	−.133**
	(.005)	(.006)	(.004)	(.006)
Observations	8,529	7,693	8,509	7,693
Number of SIC	435	410	422	410
R^2	.171	.170	.181	.170
	C. Sample Period: 1990–2007			
Exporter	−.025	−.021	−.041	−.036
	(.029)	(.031)	(.029)	(.031)
Log(sales)	−.136**	−.140**	−.134**	−.140**
	(.008)	(.008)	(.008)	(.007)

TABLE D2 (*Continued*)

	Growth		Granular	
	All (1)	Restricted (2)	All (3)	Restricted (4)
Observations	6,881	6,467	6,857	6,443
Number of SIC	409	386	398	375
R^2	.149	.151	.165	.174

NOTE.—This table presents the results from regressing a measure of firm-level sales volatility on measures of its export status (exporter) and size (sales). Columns 1 and 2 (growth) take the natural logarithm of the standard deviation of firm real sales as the dependent variable. Columns 3 and 4 (granular) use a granular volatility measure, calculated as the standard deviation of the estimated residuals, $\hat{\varepsilon}_{ist}$, from the following firm-level panel regression: $\Delta\log(\text{sales}_{ist}) = \alpha_i + \alpha_{st} + \varepsilon_{ist}$, where i is a firm, s is a sector, and t is a quarter, so that α_i is a firm-level effect and α_{st} is a sector × time effect. Standard deviations are calculated over the given sample period, while export status and measures of firm size are averaged over the period. Regressions include sector-level fixed effects at the four-digit Standard Industrial Classification. All includes all firms, while restricted excludes firms in the commodity, energy, and public sectors. Data are taken from the Compustat Quarterly database of listed US firms together with information on whether a firm is an exporter from the Compustat Segments database. Robust standard errors are in parentheses.

$^+$ Significant at 10 percent.
* Significant at 5 percent.
** significant at 1 percent.

References

Adalet, Müge. 2009. "Multi-product Exporters and Product Turnover Behaviour of New Zealand Firms." Working Paper no. 09/01, New Zealand Treasury, Wellington.

Alessandria, George, and Horag Choi. 2007. "Do Sunk Costs of Exporting Matter for Net Export Dynamics?" *Q.J.E.* 122 (1): 289–336.

Alvarez, Fernando, and Robert E. Lucas Jr. 2007. "General Equilibrium Analysis of the Eaton-Kortum Model of International Trade." *J. Monetary Econ.* 54 (6): 1726–68.

Anderson, James, and Eric van Wincoop. 2004. "Trade Costs." *J. Econ. Literature* 42 (3): 691–751.

Arndt, Christian, Claudia Buch, and Anselm Mattes. 2009. "Barriers to Internationalization: Firm-Level Evidence from Germany." IAW Discussion Paper no. 52, Inst. Angewandte Wirtschaftsforschung, Tubingen.

Axtell, Robert L. 2001. "Zipf Distribution of U.S. Firm Sizes." *Science* 293 (5536): 1818–20.

Backus, David K., Patrick J. Kehoe, and Finn E. Kydland. 1995. "International Business Cycles: Theory and Evidence." In *Frontiers of Business Cycle Research*, edited by Thomas Cooley, 331–56. Princeton, NJ: Princeton Univ. Press.

Barlevy, Gadi. 2004. "The Costs of Business Cycles under Endogenous Growth." *A.E.R.* 94 (4): 964–90.

Bernard, Andrew B., J. Bradford Jensen, Stephen Redding, and Peter Schott. 2007. "Firms in International Trade." *J. Econ. Perspectives* 21:105–30.

Bernard, Andrew B., J. Bradford Jensen, and Peter Schott. 2003. "Falling Trade Costs, Heterogeneous Firms, and Industry Dynamics." Working Paper no. 9639, NBER, Cambridge, MA.

Blattman, Christopher, Jason Hwang, and Jeffrey G. Williamson. 2007. "Winners and Losers in the Commodity Lottery: The Impact of Terms of Trade Growth and Volatility in the Periphery 1870–1939." *J. Development Econ.* 82 (1): 156–79.

Bustos, Paula. 2011. "Trade Liberalization, Exports and Technology Upgrading: Evidence on the Impact of MERCOSUR on Argentinean Firms." *A.E.R.* 101 (1): 304–40.

Canals, Claudia, Xavier Gabaix, Josep M. Vilarrubia, and David E. Weinstein. 2007. "Trade Patterns, Trade Balances, and Idiosyncratic Shocks." Working Paper no. 02/2007, la Caixa, Barcelona.

Canning, D., L. A. N. Amaral, Y. Lee, M. Meyer, and H. E. Stanley. 1998. "Scaling the Volatility of GDP Growth Rates." *Econ. Letters* 60:335–41.

Cebeci, Tolga, Ana M. Fernandes, Caroline Freund, and Martha Denisse Pierola. 2012. "Exporter Dynamics Database." Manuscript, World Bank, Washington, DC.

Chaney, Thomas. 2008. "Distorted Gravity: The Intensive and Extensive Margins of International Trade." *A.E.R.* 98 (4): 1707–21.

Crucini, Mario J. 1997. "Country Size and Economic Fluctuations." *Rev. Internat. Econ.* 5 (2): 204–20.

Delli Gatti, Domenico, Corrado Di Guilmi, Edoardo Gaffeo, Gianfranco Giulioni, Mauro Gallegati, and Antonio Palestrini. 2005. "A New Approach to Business Fluctuations: Heterogeneous Interacting Agents, Scaling Laws and Financial Fragility." *J. Econ. Behavior and Org.* 56 (4): 489–512.

di Giovanni, Julian, and Andrei A. Levchenko. 2009. "Trade Openness and Volatility." *Rev. Econ. and Statis.* 91 (3): 558–85.

———. 2012. "The Risk Content of Exports: A Portfolio View of International Trade." *NBER Internat. Seminar Macroeconomics* 8:97–151.

———. 2013. "Firm Entry, Trade, and Welfare in Zipf's World." *J. Internat. Econ.*, forthcoming.

di Giovanni, Julian, Andrei A. Levchenko, and Romain Rancière. 2011. "Power Laws in Firm Size and Openness to Trade: Measurement and Implications." *J. Internat. Econ.* 85 (1): 42–52.

Dixit, Avinash K., and Joseph E. Stiglitz. 1977. "Monopolistic Competition and Optimum Product Diversity." *A.E.R.* 67 (3): 297–308.

———. 1993. "Monopolistic Competition and Optimum Product Diversity: Reply." *A.E.R.* 83 (1): 302–4.

Easterly, William, Roumeen Islam, and Joseph E. Stiglitz. 2001. "Shaken and Stirred: Explaining Growth Volatility." In *Annual World Bank Conference on Development Economics*, edited by B. Pleskovic and N. Stern. Washington, DC: World Bank.

Eaton, Jonathan, and Samuel S. Kortum. 2002. "Technology, Geography, and Trade." *Econometrica* 70 (5): 1741–79.

Eaton, Jonathan, Samuel S. Kortum, and Francis Kramarz. 2011. "An Anatomy of International Trade: Evidence from French Firms." *Econometrica* 79 (5): 1453–98.

Eaton, Jonathan, Samuel S. Kortum, and Sebastian Sotelo. 2012. "International Trade: Linking Micro and Macro." Working Paper no. 17864, NBER, Cambridge, MA.

Fabling, Richard, and Lynda Sanderson. 2008. "Firm Level Patterns in Merchandise Trade." Occasional Paper no. 08/03, New Zealand Ministry Econ. Development, Wellington.

Fitzgerald, Doireann, and Stefanie Haller. 2010. "Pricing-to-Market: Evidence from Plant-Level Prices." Manuscript, Stanford Univ. and Econ. and Soc. Res. Inst., Dublin.

Fujita, Masahisa, Paul Krugman, and Anthony J. Venables. 2001. *The Spatial Economy: Cities, Regions, and International Trade.* Cambridge, MA: MIT Press.

Furceri, Davide, and Georgios Karras. 2007. "Country Size and Business Cycle Volatility: Scale Really Matters." *J. Japanese and Internat. Econ.* 21 (4): 424–34.

Gabaix, Xavier. 2009. "Power Laws in Economics and Finance." *Ann. Revs. Econ.* 1:255–93.

———. 2011. "The Granular Origins of Aggregate Fluctuations." *Econometrica* 79 (3): 733–72.

Gavin, Michael, and Ricardo Hausmann. 1998. "Growth with Equity: The Volatility Connection." In *Beyond Tradeoffs: Market Reforms and Equitable Growth in Latin America*, edited by Nancy Birdsall, Carol Graham, and Richard H. Sabot, 91–109. Washington, DC: Inter-American Development Bank and Brookings Inst.

Ghironi, Fabio, and Marc J. Melitz. 2005. "International Trade and Macroeconomic Dynamics with Heterogeneous Firms." *Q.J.E.* 120 (3): 865–915.

Head, Allen C. 1995. "Country Size, Aggregate Fluctuations, and International Risk Sharing." *Canadian J. Econ.* 28 (4b): 1096–1119.

Helpman, Elhanan, Marc J. Melitz, and Yona Rubinstein. 2008. "Estimating Trade Flows: Trading Partners and Trading Volumes." *Q.J.E.* 123 (2): 441–87.

Holmes, Thomas J., and John J. Stevens. 2010. "An Alternative Theory of the Plant Size Distribution with an Application to Trade." Manuscript, Univ. Minnesota and Fed. Reserve Bd. Governors.

Katzenstein, Peter J. 1985. *Small States in World Markets: Industrial Policy in Europe.* Ithaca, NY: Cornell Univ. Press.

Koren, Miklós, and Silvana Tenreyro. 2007. "Volatility and Development." *Q.J.E.* 122 (1): 243–87.

Kose, M. Ayhan, Eswar S. Prasad, and Marco E. Terrones. 2003. "Financial Integration and Macroeconomic Volatility." *IMF Staff Papers* 50 (special issue): 119–41.

Kraay, Aart, and Jaume Ventura. 2007. "Comparative Advantage and the Cross-Section of Business Cycles." *J. European Econ. Assoc.* 5 (6): 1300–1333.

Krugman, Paul. 1980. "Scale Economies, Product Differentiation, and the Pattern of Trade." *A.E.R.* 70 (5): 950–59.

La Porta, Rafael, Florencio Lopez de Silanes, Andrei Shleifer, and Robert W. Vishny. 1998. "Law and Finance." *J.P.E.* 106 (6): 1113–55.

Laursen, Thomas, and Sandeep Mahajan. 2005. "Volatility, Income Distribution, and Poverty." In *Managing Economic Volatility and Crises: A Practitioner's Guide*, edited by Joshua Aizenman and Brian Pinto, 101–36. New York: Cambridge Univ. Press.

Melitz, Marc J. 2003. "The Impact of Trade on Intra-industry Reallocations and Aggregate Industry Productivity." *Econometrica* 71 (6): 1695–1725.

Newbery, David M. G., and Joseph E. Stiglitz. 1984. "Pareto Inferior Trade." *Rev. Econ. Studies* 51 (1): 1–12.

OECD. 2006. "The Rise of China and India: What's in It for Africa?" Tech. report, Development Centre Studies, OECD, Paris.

Pallage, Stéphane, and Michel A. Robe. 2003. "On the Welfare Cost of Economic Fluctuations in Developing Countries." *Internat. Econ. Rev.* 44 (2): 677–98.

Pavcnik, Nina. 2002. "Trade Liberalization, Exit, and Productivity Improvements: Evidence from Chilean Plants." *Rev. Econ. Studies* 69 (1): 245–76.

Ramey, Garey, and Valerie A. Ramey. 1995. "Cross-Country Evidence on the Link between Volatility and Growth." *A.E.R.* 85 (5): 1138–51.
Rose, Andrew K. 2004. "Do We Really Know That the WTO Increases Trade?" *A.E.R.* 94 (1): 98–114.
Ruhl, Kim J. 2008. "The International Elasticity Puzzle." Manuscript, Stern School Bus., New York Univ.
Stanley, Michael H. R., et al. 1996. "Scaling Behaviour in the Growth of Companies." *Nature* 379:804–6.
Sutton, John. 2002. "The Variance of Firm Growth Rates: The 'Scaling' Puzzle." *Physica A* 312:577–90.
Yang, Xiaokai, and Ben J. Heijdra. 1993. "Monopolistic Competition and Optimum Product Diversity: Comment." *A.E.R.* 83 (1): 295–301.
Yi, Kei-Mu, and Jing Zhang. 2010. "Structural Change in an Open Economy." Manuscript, Fed. Reserve Bank Philadelphia and Univ. Michigan.

Econometrica, Vol. 82, No. 4 (July, 2014), 1303–1340

FIRMS, DESTINATIONS, AND AGGREGATE FLUCTUATIONS

BY JULIAN DI GIOVANNI, ANDREI A. LEVCHENKO, AND ISABELLE MEJEAN[1]

This paper uses a data base covering the universe of French firms for the period 1990–2007 to provide a forensic account of the role of individual firms in generating aggregate fluctuations. We set up a simple multisector model of heterogeneous firms selling to multiple markets to motivate a theoretically founded decomposition of firms' annual sales growth rate into different components. We find that the firm-specific component contributes substantially to aggregate sales volatility, mattering about as much as the components capturing shocks that are common across firms within a sector or country. We then decompose the firm-specific component to provide evidence on two mechanisms that generate aggregate fluctuations from microeconomic shocks highlighted in the recent literature: (i) when the firm size distribution is fat-tailed, idiosyncratic shocks to large firms directly contribute to aggregate fluctuations, and (ii) aggregate fluctuations can arise from idiosyncratic shocks due to input–output linkages across the economy. Firm linkages are approximately three times as important as the direct effect of firm shocks in driving aggregate fluctuations.

KEYWORDS: Aggregate fluctuations, firm-level shocks, large firms, linkages.

1. INTRODUCTION

A LONG TRADITION IN MACROECONOMICS SEEKS to understand the microeconomic underpinnings of aggregate fluctuations. Starting with the seminal work of Long and Plosser (1983), an important line of research explores the role of sectoral shocks in generating aggregate fluctuations (see, e.g., Stockman (1988), Foerster, Sarte, and Watson (2011), Carvalho and Gabaix (2013), among many others). A running theme in this literature is that idiosyncratic shocks to a single sector can have sizeable aggregate effects if the sector is strongly interconnected with others in the economy through input linkages (Horvath (1998, 2000), Dupor (1999), Shea (2002), Conley and Dupor (2003), Acemoglu, Carvalho, Ozdaglar, and Tahbaz-Salehi (2012)). The role of individual firms in the aggregate business cycle has received comparatively less attention. Gabaix (2011) argues that because the firm size distribution is extremely fat-tailed (the economy is "granular"), idiosyncratic shocks to individual (large) firms will not average out and, instead, lead to movements in the

[1]We would like to thank a co-editor, two anonymous referees, George Akerlof, Gilles Duranton, Jonathan Eaton, Chris House, Ayhan Kose, Kory Kroft, Julien Martin, Akito Matsumoto, Ryan Monarch, Peter Morrow, Sophie Osotimehin, Tiago Ribeiro, Matthew Shapiro, Rishi Sharma, and seminar participants at various institutions for helpful suggestions. We are especially grateful to Matias Cattaneo for extensive input that greatly improved the paper. Di Giovanni thanks the Marie Curie International Incoming Fellowship FP7-PEOPLE-2013-IIF for financial support under Grant Agreement 622959. This research is supported by a public grant overseen by the French National Research Agency (ANR) as part of the "Investissements d'Avenir" program (Idex Grant Agreement ANR-11-IDEX-0003-02/Labex ECODEC ANR-11-LABEX-0047). All remaining errors are our own.

 DOI: 10.3982/ECTA11041

aggregates. However, there is currently little empirical evidence on the role of individual firms and firm-to-firm linkages in aggregate fluctuations.

This paper constructs a novel data base covering the universe of French firms' domestic sales and destination-specific exports for the period 1990–2007, and uses it to provide a forensic account of the contribution of individual firms to aggregate fluctuations. To guide the empirical exercise, we set up a simple multisector model of heterogeneous firms in the spirit of Melitz (2003) and Eaton, Kortum, and Kramarz (2011). The model implies that the growth rate of sales of an individual firm to a single destination market can be decomposed additively into a macroeconomic shock (defined as the component common to all firms), a sectoral shock (defined as the component common to all firms in a particular sector), and a firm-level shock.

Relative to standard empirical assessments of the role of sectoral or firm-specific shocks, a novel aspect of our approach is that it accounts explicitly for the sector- and firm-level participation in export markets. When firms sell to multiple, imperfectly correlated markets, total firm sales do not admit an exact decomposition into macroeconomic, sectoral, and firm-specific shocks, whereas sales to an individual destination do. Thus, in our analysis macroeconomic, sectoral, and firm-specific shocks are defined for each destination market. The heterogeneity across markets also allows us to distinguish the firm-specific shocks affecting a firm's sales to all markets it serves from shocks particular to individual markets.

We compute macroeconomic, sectoral, and firm-specific shocks using data on the annual firm–destination sales growth rates. The firm-specific component accounts for the overwhelming majority (98.7%) of the variation in sales growth rates across firms.[2] In addition, about half of the variation in the firm-specific component is explained by variation in that component across destinations, which can be interpreted as destination-specific demand shocks in our conceptual framework.

We extract the time series of the macroeconomic, sectoral, and firm-specific shocks for each destination served by each firm. We use these realizations of shocks to assess whether *microeconomic* shocks contribute significantly to *aggregate* volatility, and if yes, through which channels. We derive a decomposition of aggregate volatility in the economy into the contributions of macroeconomic/sectoral and firm-specific shocks, and quantify the importance of the latter for aggregate volatility.

Our main finding is that the firm-specific components contribute substantially to aggregate fluctuations. The standard deviation of the firm-specific shocks' contribution to aggregate sales growth amounts to 80% of the standard deviation of aggregate sales growth in the whole economy and to 69%

[2]This number is the share of the variance in the firm–destination growth rates that is not accounted for by the macro and sectoral components. Using the same metric, Haltiwanger (1997) and Castro, Clementi, and Lee (2013) find that idiosyncratic shocks account for more than 90% of the variation in firm growth rates in the U.S. Census' Longitudinal Research Database.

in the manufacturing sector. This contribution is similar in magnitude to the combined effect of all sectoral and macroeconomic shocks. The standard deviation of the sectoral and macroeconomic shocks' contribution to aggregate sales growth is 53% of the standard deviation of aggregate sales growth for the overall economy and 64% for the manufacturing sector.[3] To investigate whether exports differ systematically from domestic sales, we then carry out the aggregate volatility decomposition for domestic and export sales separately.[4] The firm-specific component contributes more to the volatility of exports than that of overall sales both in the economy as a whole and in the manufacturing sector, where exporting is more prevalent. Nonetheless, firm-specific shocks contribute substantially to the volatility of aggregate domestic sales as well.

The overall contribution of firm-specific shocks to aggregate volatility can be decomposed additively into terms that capture two proximate explanations for why firm-specific shocks matter: (i) a weighted sum of all the variances of firm-specific shocks and (ii) a weighted sum of all the covariances between the firm-specific shocks. We refer to the first as the *direct* effect, since this is the aggregate variance that would obtain directly from shocks to individual firms and would be there even in the complete absence of interconnectedness between the firms. Gabaix (2011) shows that firm-specific idiosyncratic shocks do not average out because of the presence of very large firms. The second term collects cross-firm covariances and can thus be thought of as arising at least in part from interconnectedness between firms (sector-level versions of this argument are explored in Horvath (1998, 2000), Dupor (1999), Shea (2002), Conley and Dupor (2003), Acemoglu et al. (2012), among others).[5] We refer to this as the *linkages* effect. Though both channels matter quantitatively, the majority of the contribution of firm-specific shocks to the aggregate variance is accounted for by the linkages term—the covariances of the firm-specific components of the sales growth rates.

We then exploit cross-sectoral heterogeneity to provide further evidence on the direct and linkages mechanisms. Gabaix (2011) shows that the direct effect of shocks to individual firms on aggregate fluctuations will be more pronounced the larger is the Herfindahl index of firm sales—a common measure of concentration. Confirming this result, firm-specific shocks in more concentrated industries, such as transport, petroleum, and motor vehicles, contribute

[3]These numbers add up to more than 1 because they have been converted to standard deviations. Since the aggregate variance is additive in the firm-specific and macro-sectoral variance components, the aggregate standard deviation is smaller than the sum of the standard deviations of the components.

[4]The analysis of the export subsample is motivated by two well known facts: (i) aggregate exports are more volatile than gross domestic product (GDP) and (ii) the largest firms tend to be exporters. Canals, Gabaix, Vilarrubia, and Weinstein (2007) show that international trade is very granular, both at the firm- and sector-destination level.

[5]Note that in this literature, the structural shocks are uncorrelated but generate positive covariances in firm sales.

more to aggregate volatility than firm-specific shocks in less concentrated sectors such as metal products or publishing. We also compare the covariances of the firm-specific shocks aggregated to the sector level to a measure of sectoral linkages taken from the input–output tables.[6] Sectors with stronger input–output linkages tend to exhibit significantly greater correlation of firm-specific shocks. We thus find direct corroboration in the data for the mechanisms behind both the direct and the linkages effects.

The results are robust in a number of dimensions. First and foremost, we continue to find a large contribution of firm-specific shocks to aggregate fluctuations when we allow for heterogeneous responses of firm sales growth to common shocks. In the baseline model, all firms have the same elasticity of sales with respect to the macroeconomic and sectoral shocks. While our framework shares this feature with the large majority of quantitative models in both macroeconomics and international trade, it is important to check whether the results are driven by this feature. In an alternative approach, we thus allow for the impact of sector–destination shocks on the growth rate of sales to vary by a wide variety of firm characteristics, such as size, age, access to capital markets, research and development (R&D) intensity, or export orientation. As additional checks, we also implement the model under several alternative definitions of the sales growth rates, accounting for local geographical area effects, different levels of sectoral disaggregation, and using multi-year growth rates instead of yearly ones. The results are robust to all of these alternative implementations.

Our paper draws on, and contributes to, three key themes in macroeconomics. The first is the quest to understand how aggregate fluctuations can arise from microeconomic sources. This literature dates back to Long and Plosser (1983) and has traditionally focused on shocks at the sectoral level (see, e.g., Jovanovic (1987), Stockman (1988), Carvalho and Gabaix (2013), among many others). The second theme is that input–output linkages are the key mechanism through which microeconomic shocks propagate and lead to aggregate fluctuations. Once again, this literature has predominantly focused on sector-level linkages (see, e.g., Horvath (1998, 2000), Dupor (1999), Shea (2002), Conley and Dupor (2003), Foerster, Sarte, and Watson (2011), Acemoglu et al. (2012)).[7]

The third theme is that studying firm- and plant-level behavior is essential for understanding aggregate fluctuations. For instance, evidence on large gross employment flows at the micro level has stimulated a line of research

[6]Ideally, we would relate the covariance of firm-specific shocks to a measure of linkages at the firm level. However, currently firm-to-firm input–output tables do not exist for France, and thus we must look for these relationships at the sector level.

[7]Important exceptions are Cohen and Frazzini (2008), Hertzel, Li, Officer, and Rodgers (2008), and Kelly and Lustig (2013), who relate the supplier relationships among U.S. listed firms to movements in their stock prices and sales volatility.

into their aggregate implications (Davis and Haltiwanger (1992), Davis, Haltiwanger, and Schuh (1996), Caballero, Engel, and Haltiwanger (1997), Davis, Faberman, and Haltiwanger (2006)). Similarly, plant-level investment is dominated by infrequent and large spikes, and an active literature has explored whether these micro-level patterns affect the behavior of aggregate investment (see, among many others, Doms and Dunne (1998), Cooper, Haltiwanger, and Power (1999), Cooper and Haltiwanger (2006), Gourio and Kashyap (2007)). Also closely related are studies of firm-level volatility (see, e.g., Comín and Philippon (2005), Davis, Haltiwanger, Jarmin, and Miranda (2007), Castro, Clementi, and Lee (2013), Thesmar and Thoenig (2011), Moscarini and Postel-Vinay (2012), Yoonsoo and Mukoyama (2012)). These research agendas have tended to emphasize that studying micro behavior is important as a way to learn what are the salient frictions in the economy. By and large, this literature has not pursued the idea that shocks to *individual* firms can impact aggregate fluctuations. A landmark recent exception is Gabaix (2011), who shows how idiosyncratic shocks to firms can lead to aggregate fluctuations in an economy dominated by very large firms and provides empirical evidence for this phenomenon using U.S. data. di Giovanni and Levchenko (2012a) extend this model to a multicountry framework and argue that it can help rationalize cross-country differences in the magnitude of aggregate fluctuations.

In line with the first two themes, our analysis emphasizes the role of both individual shocks and input–output linkages. In line with the third theme, but in contrast to the earlier literature, we shift the focus from sectors to firms. Our paper is the first to provide comprehensive empirical evidence on firms' contribution to aggregate fluctuations using the population of firms in a particular country. In addition, we incorporate the international dimension and show that it is important for a reliable computation of shocks. Finally, our data enable us to examine in detail the mechanisms behind the role of individual firms in generating aggregate volatility.

The rest of the paper is organized as follows. Section 2 presents a simple heterogeneous firms model and derives a theoretically founded decomposition of firm sales growth in each market into firm-specific, sector-level, and macroeconomic components. The section then derives a procedure to compute each component's contribution to aggregate volatility. Section 3 describes the data. Section 4 presents the main results. Section 5 concludes. The Supplemental Material (di Giovanni, Levchenko, and Mejean (2014)) contains the Appendixes and data and programs.

2. CONCEPTUAL FRAMEWORK

Total aggregate sales X_t by all French firms to all destinations in year t are by definition given by $X_t \equiv \sum_{f,n \in I_t} x_{fnt}$, where x_{fnt} is defined as the sales of firm f

to market n in year t, and I_t is the set of firms f *and* destinations n being served at t. Thus, the unit of observation is a firm–destination pair, rather than a firm.[8] The growth rate of aggregate sales is then defined simply as $\gamma_{At} = X_t/X_{t-1} - 1$, where we assume that X_{t-1} and X_t are the aggregate sales of all firms that exist both at $t-1$ and t, that is, we restrict attention to the *intensive margin* of aggregate sales growth. The choice to focus on the intensive margin is motivated in part by the difficulty of measuring the extensive margin reliably. Appendix A develops a complete decomposition of the total sales growth into extensive and intensive margins, and presents the results for the relative contributions of the extensive (as best as we can measure it) and intensive margins to aggregate volatility. The main result is that the large majority of the variance of aggregate sales is accounted for by the volatility of the intensive margin, with the extensive margin playing only a minor role.[9] Section 4.4.2 demonstrates the robustness of the results to an alternative definition of firm sales growth rates that treats entries and exits symmetrically with other sales.[10]

2.1. *A Motivating Model of Firm Sales Growth*

To motivate the decomposition of the growth of firm sales in a given year into (i) firm–destination and (ii) sector and country components, we set up a multisector heterogeneous firms model in the spirit of Melitz (2003) and Eaton, Kortum, and Kramarz (2011). While the model is largely illustrative and we will not use its full structure for estimation purposes, it serves to illustrate three main points. First, the sales decomposition adopted in our paper follows naturally from the workhorse heterogeneous firms model used in the literature. Second, the decomposition works only when applied to firm sales to an individual destination, rather than total (domestic plus export) sales. This result motivates our approach of extracting macro, sectoral, and idiosyncratic components for each individual destination market. And third, the model provides a simple and natural economic interpretation of the shocks as combinations of the demand and cost shocks that affect (sets of) firm–destinations.

There is a large number of countries indexed by n and J sectors indexed by j. In country n, consumer within-period utility is Cobb–Douglas in the sec-

[8]That is, suppose that there are two firms $f \in$ {Renault, Peugeot} and two markets, $n \in$ {France, Germany}, and both firms sell to both markets. Then I_t = {{Renault, France}, {Renault, Germany}, {Peugeot, France}, {Peugeot, Germany}} and X_t is simply a summation over the sales of each firm to each destination.

[9]These results are consistent with other work on the role of the extensive margin in short-run aggregate fluctuations in the French economy. For instance, Osotimehin (2013) finds that entry and exit contribute little to the year-on-year variability of French aggregate productivity.

[10]Recent work focuses on the importance of the extensive adjustment at the *product* level, potentially within a firm (e.g., Bernard, Redding, and Schott (2010), Bilbiie, Ghironi, and Melitz (2012)), whereas in our data, it is only possible to measure the extensive margin at the firm level.

tors $1, \ldots, J$,

$$(1) \qquad U_{nt} = \prod_{j=1}^{J} (C_{jnt})^{\varphi_{jnt}},$$

where C_{jnt} is consumption of sector j in country n at time t, and φ_{jnt} is a time-varying demand shock for sector j in country n (as in Eaton, Kortum, Neiman, and Romalis (2011)). The Cobb–Douglas functional form for the utility function leads to the well known property that expenditure on sector j is a fraction φ_{jnt} of the total expenditure in the economy, $Y_{jnt} = \varphi_{jnt} Y_{nt}$, where Y_{nt} is aggregate expenditure in country n at time t and Y_{jnt} is the expenditure in sector j.

Each sector j is a constant elasticity of substitution (CES) aggregate of Ω_{jnt} varieties available in country n at time t, indexed by f,

$$(2) \qquad C_{jnt} = \left[\sum_{f \in \Omega_{jnt}} (\omega_{fnt})^{1/\theta} C_{fnt}^{(\theta-1)/\theta} \right]^{\theta/(\theta-1)},$$

where ω_{fnt} is a time-varying demand shock for variety f in market n.

Every firm belongs to exactly one sector. Sector j in the producing country (d = France) is populated by I_{jdt} firms. Each of these firms sells a unique variety and, thus, has some market power. Firms also differ in productivity, with firm f characterized by a time-varying unit input requirement a_{fdt}. Firm f takes a_{fdt} input bundles to produce one unit of its good in period t. The input bundle in sector j in country d and period t has a cost c_{jdt}. Note that it can vary by sector, but not across firms within a sector. This input bundle can include, for instance, labor costs and the cost of capital. It is well known that these firms will price at a constant markup over their marginal cost, and conditional on selling to market n, sales by a French firm f (i.e., residing in country d) to market n in period t are given by

$$(3) \qquad x_{fnt} = \omega_{fnt} \frac{\varphi_{jnt} Y_{nt}}{(P_{jnt})^{1-\theta}} \left(\frac{\theta}{\theta - 1} \kappa_{jnd} c_{jdt} a_{fdt} \right)^{1-\theta},$$

where P_{jnt} is the price level in sector j in country n at time t and κ_{jnd} is the iceberg cost of selling from France to country n in sector j. This equation assumes that (i) κ_{jnd} is sector-specific, but does not vary over time (though that assumption can easily be relaxed, in which case the time variation in κ_{jnd} will be absorbed in the sector–destination shock), and (ii) the cost bundle c_{jdt} and the marginal cost a_{fdt} may vary over time, but are not destination-specific.

Sales to a single destination are then multiplicative in the macroeconomic, sectoral, and firm-specific components. The sales growth rate γ_{fnt} of firm f in sector j to market n between time $t-1$ and time t is approximated by a log difference,

$$(4) \qquad \gamma_{fnt} = \tilde{\delta}_{nt} + \tilde{\delta}_{jnt} + \varepsilon_{fnt},$$

where $\tilde{\delta}_{nt} = \Delta \log Y_{nt}$ is the aggregate ("macroeconomic") shock to the destination demand (to France if $n = d$), $\tilde{\delta}_{jnt} = \Delta \log \varphi_{jnt} + (1 - \theta)(\Delta \log c_{jdt} - \Delta \log P_{jnt})$ captures the sectoral (country n-specific) demand and cost shock, and $\varepsilon_{fnt} = \Delta \log \omega_{fnt} + (1 - \theta)\Delta \log a_{fdt}$ is the firm-specific demand and cost shock. Equation (4) characterizes firm sales growth to the domestic French market and to every foreign market.

While the theoretical framework distinguishes between macroeconomic shocks that are common to all firms selling goods in the same market and sectoral shocks in that market, in practice the macroeconomic shock and all of the sectoral shocks cannot be computed separately without further restrictions on the form they can take. However, since we are ultimately interested in the firm-specific component and its contribution to aggregate fluctuations, this does not pose a problem. In what follows, we work with the simpler model

$$\gamma_{fnt} = \delta_{jnt} + \varepsilon_{fnt} \tag{5}$$

that decomposes sales growth into a firm-specific shock ε_{fnt} and a sector–destination shock $\delta_{jnt} = \tilde{\delta}_{nt} + \tilde{\delta}_{jnt}$ encompassing the macroeconomic and sectoral shocks.

2.2. *Econometric Model*

The analysis below views the ε_{fnt}'s and δ_{jnt}'s as a set of stochastic processes that are (potentially) both cross-sectionally and serially correlated. Our ultimate goal is to assess the impact of firm-specific shocks ε_{fnt} on aggregate fluctuations. Under the log-difference approximation (5) to the growth rates of individual firms, the growth rate γ_{At} of aggregate sales between $t-1$ and t can be written as

$$\gamma_{At} = \sum_{j,n} w_{jnt-1}\delta_{jnt} + \sum_{f,n} w_{fnt-1}\varepsilon_{fnt}, \tag{6}$$

where w_{jnt-1} is the share of sector j's sales to market n in total sales of French firms to all sectors and destinations, and w_{fnt-1} is the share of firm f's sales to destination n in total sales. Unfortunately, working with equation (6) directly to produce a variance decomposition is impractical because time-varying weights w_{fnt-1} make the stochastic process (6) difficult to analyze.

Instead, we work with a closely related set of stochastic processes:

$$\gamma_{At|\tau} = \sum_{j,n} w_{jn\tau-1}\delta_{jnt} + \sum_{f,n} w_{fn\tau-1}\varepsilon_{fnt}. \tag{7}$$

For a given τ, $\gamma_{At|\tau}$ is a stochastic process in which weights $w_{fn\tau-1}$ are fixed over time at their $\tau - 1$ values and are combined with shocks from period t.

Naturally, when $\tau = t$, the "synthetic" aggregate growth rate $\gamma_{At|\tau}$ coincides with the actual aggregate growth rate γ_{At}. The last term in (7), $\sum_{f,n} w_{fn\tau-1}\varepsilon_{fnt}$, is none other than Gabaix's (2011) "granular residual," with the key difference that we build it with the ε_{fnt}'s of all firms in the economy, rather than the top 100 firms as in Gabaix (2011).

Denote by $\sigma^2_{A\tau}$ the variance of $\gamma_{At|\tau}$.[11] Using (7), it can be written as

$$\sigma^2_{A\tau} = \sigma^2_{JN\tau} + \sigma^2_{F\tau} + \mathrm{COV}_\tau, \tag{8}$$

where

$$\sigma^2_{JN\tau} = \mathrm{Var}\left(\sum_{j,n} w_{jn\tau-1}\delta_{jnt}\right) \quad \text{(sector–destination volatility)},$$

$$\sigma^2_{F\tau} = \mathrm{Var}\left(\sum_{f,n} w_{fn\tau-1}\varepsilon_{fnt}\right) \quad \text{(firm-specific volatility)},$$

$$\mathrm{COV}_\tau = \mathrm{Cov}\left(\sum_{j,n} w_{jn\tau-1}\delta_{jt}, \sum_{f,n} w_{fn\tau-1}\varepsilon_{fnt}\right)$$

(covariance of the shocks from different levels of aggregation).

The intuition for this procedure can be conveyed as follows. Since δ_{jnt} and ε_{fnt} are random variables, the growth rate of aggregate sales at time τ in (7) is itself a random variable and its variance is given by (8). The estimate of $\sigma^2_{A\tau}$ for a particular year can thus be thought of as the estimated variance of the aggregate growth rate in year τ. We are interested in exploiting the form of $\gamma_{At|\tau}$ to decompose the overall variance of $\gamma_{At|\tau}$ into firm-specific and other components, so as to assess the importance of firm-specific shocks for aggregate fluctuations.

In practice, we will be reporting estimates of $\sigma^2_{A\tau}$ and its components for each $\tau = 1991, \ldots, 2007$, as well as their averages over this period. The approach of constructing aggregate variances under weights that are fixed period-by-period follows Carvalho and Gabaix (2013), who perform a related exercise using sectoral data.

2.3. *Estimation*

The main goal of the paper is to provide estimates for $\sigma^2_{A\tau}$, $\sigma^2_{JN\tau}$, and $\sigma^2_{F\tau}$. Using sales data γ_{fnt}, the macro-sectoral shock δ_{jnt} is computed as the average growth rate of sales of all firms selling in sector j to market n. The firm-specific shock ε_{fnt} is computed as the deviation of γ_{fnt} from δ_{jnt}. This approach to iden-

[11] Appendix B presents further discussion of how our $\sigma^2_{A\tau}$'s relate to the variances of actual aggregate growth rate γ_{At} and its components.

tifying firm-specific shocks is adopted by Gabaix (2011) and Castro, Clementi, and Lee (2013), and follows in the tradition of Stockman (1988), who applied it at the sector level.

Our estimator for $\sigma^2_{F\tau}$ is simply the sample variance of the T realizations of the scalar-valued time series $\sum_{f,n} w_{fn\tau-1}\varepsilon_{fnt}$. Similarly, the estimators for $\sigma^2_{A\tau}$ and $\sigma^2_{JN\tau}$ are the sample variances of the realizations of $\gamma_{At|\tau}$ and $\sum_{j,n} w_{jnt-1}\delta_{jnt}$, respectively. Our sample consists of the realizations of the stochastic processes δ_{jnt} and ε_{fnt} for $T = 17$ years. Our framework allows for both cross-sectional and time dependence in the data-generating process. That is, ε_{fnt} for firm f can be correlated with another firm's ε_{gnt} as well as with its own past values. However, we do assume that the stochastic process for ε_{fnt} and δ_{jnt} is jointly stationary, that its degree of time dependence is not too high, and that $\gamma_{At|\tau}$ as well as its constituent parts have enough finite moments. Since both ε_{fnt} and δ_{jnt} describe growth rates, stationarity and limited time dependence are plausible assumptions. In practice, in our sample the autocorrelation in the series for $\gamma_{At|\tau}$ and its constituent parts is minimal. Appendix C states these conditions precisely, and proves the consistency and asymptotic normality of the estimators as T grows large. The appendix also gives formulas for the analytical standard errors of these estimators that we use below to construct confidence intervals. For robustness, we also report confidence intervals based on bootstrapping procedures.

We follow the convention in the literature and use the standard deviation as our measure of volatility. Therefore, when discussing contributions to aggregate volatility, we will present the results in terms of *relative standard deviations*, such as $\sigma_{F\tau}/\sigma_{A\tau}$.

2.4. *Discussion*

The first term in (8) measures the volatility of sector–destination shocks, which affect all firms in a sector selling to a particular destination market. It can be expressed as $\sigma^2_{JN\tau} = \sum_{k,m}\sum_{j,n} w_{jn\tau-1}w_{km\tau-1}\,\mathrm{Cov}(\delta_{jnt}, \delta_{kmt})$, making it clear that it is driven by the volatility of the sector–destination shocks ($\mathrm{Var}(\delta_{jnt})$) and their covariance across countries and sectors ($\mathrm{Cov}(\delta_{jnt}, \delta_{kmt})$). Obviously, the importance of any country- or sector-specific shock in explaining aggregate volatility is increasing in the relative size of that market (measured by $w_{jn\tau-1}$). Thus, French shocks have a larger impact on aggregate volatility than shocks affecting French firms' sales to, say, Japan. Likewise, a country specializing in highly volatile sectors is likely to display larger aggregate fluctuations (Koren and Tenreyro (2007), di Giovanni and Levchenko (2012b)). In that sense, diversification of sales across markets and sectors helps reduce aggregate fluctuations. In the meantime, comovement across countries or sectors tends to amplify aggregate fluctuations. For instance, an increased synchronization of business cycles among Economic and Monetary Union (EMU) members might drive up French volatility. Cross-sector correlations, created for example by input–output linkages, will also increase aggregate volatility (see, e.g., di Giovanni and Levchenko (2010)).

The second term in (8), $\sigma^2_{F_T}$, is the variance of the granular residual. It measures the contribution of firm-specific shocks to aggregate fluctuations. As in Gabaix (2011), the firm-specific contribution to aggregate volatility is likely to be larger, everything else equal, the more fat-tailed is the distribution of sales across firms. Furthermore, volatility also increases if the larger firms face more volatile shocks. Finally, a positive correlation of shocks across firms, for instance, driven by input–output linkages, will increase firms' contribution to aggregate fluctuations. Section 4.3 discusses in more detail the microeconomic underpinnings of $\sigma^2_{F_T}$, both in theory and in our data.

The firm-specific shocks ε_{fnt} need not be uncorrelated with each other as in Gabaix (2011). For example, these shocks may covary among firms if their activity is interconnected, say through input–output linkages (e.g., Foerster, Sarte, and Watson (2011), Acemoglu et al. (2012)) or other potential firm interactions. To illustrate this possibility, Appendix E presents a simple extension of the model that includes intermediate inputs specific to the firm. These intermediate linkages lead to positive comovement of firm-specific shocks through the propagation of productivity shocks from input providers to downstream firms. To assess the relevance of this channel, below we develop a decomposition of the firm-specific variance and covariance contributions to aggregate volatility, and provide evidence that industry structure and other proxies for linkages matter.

We have argued that from a theoretical perspective, it is important to compute shocks for each market separately. In our theoretical framework, the firm-specific shock $\varepsilon_{fnt} = \Delta \log \omega_{fnt} + (1-\theta)\Delta \log a_{fdt}$ contains a component common across all destination markets and a component that is destination-specific. Thus, it can be further decomposed as

$$\varepsilon_{fnt} = \varepsilon^1_{ft} + \varepsilon^2_{fnt}, \tag{9}$$

where ε^1_{ft} is the firm-specific shock common to all destinations and ε^2_{fnt} captures the destination-specific demand shock. Specifically, we compute ε^1_{ft} as the time t average of ε_{fnt} for each firm that serves multiple destinations (including the domestic market). Note that this procedure does not allow us to separate demand shocks from cost shocks cleanly, because ε^1_{ft} captures not only the productivity shock $(1-\theta)\Delta \log a_{fdt}$, but also other firm-level shocks that are common across destinations, for instance, common taste shocks. Nonetheless, we can get a sense of the relative importance of the firmwide versus destination-specific shocks by computing the share of variation in ε_{fnt} that is absorbed by ε^1_{ft}.

3. DATA AND SUMMARY STATISTICS

The analysis employs firm-level data containing the universe of domestic and export sales of French firms over the 1990–2007 period. Even though the time dimension is somewhat limited, we are still able to pick up cycles of the French economy, including the 1992–1993 and 2000–2001 recessions, and the acceleration of growth at the end of the nineties. The firm-level information is sourced from two rich data sets provided to us by the French administration. The first data set, obtained from the fiscal administration, contains balance-sheet information collected from the firms' tax forms, most importantly total firm sales. The second data set is the firm-level export data from the French customs authorities. This data base gives the (free on board) value of each French firm's exports to each of its foreign destination markets in a given fiscal year.

Appendix D contains a detailed description of the data. Our final data set covers 1,577,039 firms undertaking activities in 52 NAF (Nomenclature d'Activités Française) sectors, representing around 30% of industrial and service firms but more than 90% of aggregate sales. Of those firms, 208,596 belong to the manufacturing sector (22 NAF industries), which accounts for around 30% of aggregate sales. In our sample, 18% of all firms (and 42% of manufacturing firms) export at some point in time. The total sales and export sales in this sample of firms mimic aggregate activity quite well: the growth rate of total sales tracks the growth rate of GDP (Figure 1), while the growth of total export sales moves with the growth of country exports over time (Figure 2).

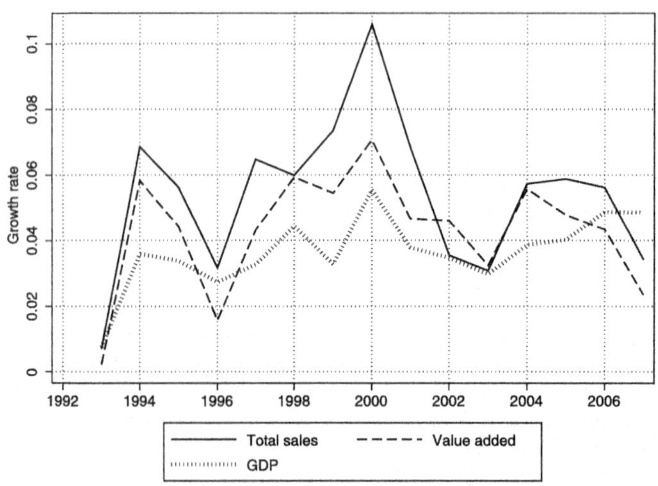

FIGURE 1.—Growth of aggregate sales, aggregate value added, and GDP. This figure presents the time series of the growth rates of total sales and before-tax value added in our data and GDP sourced from the International Monetary Fund (IMF) International Financial Statistics.

FIGURE 2.—Growth of aggregate exports. This figure presents the time series of the growth rates of total exports in our data and total French exports sourced from the IMF International Financial Statistics.

Table I presents summary statistics for firm-level growth rates for the whole economy and the manufacturing sector. The average growth rate of aggregate sales, 0.0369 for the whole economy and 0.0290 for manufacturing, is lower than the (unweighted) average growth rate of individual firm–destinations, which is 0.0465 for the whole economy and 0.0537 for manufacturing. This is to be expected, as smaller firms tend to grow faster than larger firms, conditional on survival. The average firm–destination has a standard deviation of sales growth of 0.23 in the whole economy and 0.28 in manufacturing. The table also reports averages of firm sales volatility by quintile. Smaller firms are more volatile than large ones. The very top firms, however, are even less volatile than the top quintile firms. While the top 20% of firm–destinations by size have an average standard deviation of sales growth of almost 20%, the top 100 firm–destinations have an average standard deviation of 13% and the top 10 firms slightly lower still. Finally, the table also reports the square root of the firm–destination Herfindahl index of sales shares as well as the square root of the overall firm sales Herfindahl index. The Herfindahl indices have an order of magnitude consistent with what has been conjectured by Gabaix (2011) and show that the economy is "granular": shocks to the large firms have the potential to lead to aggregate fluctuations. All in all, the patterns for the manufacturing sector are quite similar to the whole economy.

Table II presents the average standard deviations of firm–destination growth rates across sectors, along with the shares of each sector in total sales. The raw volatility of sales growth varies across sectors, with the standard deviation rang-

TABLE I

SUMMARY STATISTICS[a]

	Whole Economy	Manufacturing Sector
Average aggregate growth rate	0.0369	0.0290
Mean of individual growth rates	0.0465	0.0537
Standard deviation of sales growth rate		
Average	0.2342	0.2829
0–20 size percentile	0.3011	0.3550
21–40 size percentile	0.2425	0.3252
41–60 size percentile	0.2163	0.2654
61–80 size percentile	0.2043	0.2409
81–100 size percentile	0.2069	0.2278
Top 100	0.1319	0.1816
Top 10	0.1269	0.1364
Average $\sqrt{\text{Herf}(f, n)}$	0.0301	0.0447
Average $\sqrt{\text{Herf}(f)}$	0.0332	0.0592

[a]This table presents the summary statistics for the whole economy and manufacturing firms over 1991–2007. $\text{Herf}(f, n)$ is the Herfindahl index of the firm–destination sales shares. $\text{Herf}(f)$ is the Herfindahl index of the total firm sales shares.

ing from a low of 0.1489 (Health and social work) to a high of 0.3248 (Coke, refined petroleum, and nuclear fuel), and a cross-sectoral mean standard deviation of 0.2593. The wholesale and retail trade sector has by far the highest share in aggregate sales, at nearly 37% of the total. While the standard deviation of sales growth, at 0.2188, is quite typical of the rest of the economy, clearly wholesale and retail trade is quite special in other ways. To establish the robustness of the results, all of the analysis below is carried out both on the whole economy and on the manufacturing sector.

The analysis in the paper uses the growth rates of firm–destination sales. Other related work focuses on measures of firm productivity such as value added per worker (e.g., Gabaix (2011), Castro, Clementi, and Lee (2013)) or total factor productivity (TFP) (Carvalho and Gabaix (2013)), or employment (e.g., Moscarini and Postel-Vinay (2012)). Unfortunately, neither employment nor value added per worker data can be broken down into destinations—it is of course impossible to know which workers in the firm are producing for exports and which for domestic sales—whereas we show above that to carry out our analysis, the destination-by-destination breakdown is essential. This is the reason we use sales growth in the baseline analysis. As a robustness check, Section 4.2 presents the results for value added growth, under the (nontrivial) assumption that a firm's value added has the same breakdown across markets as its sales do. We cannot compute the firms' TFP process for the additional reason that we do not have firm-specific input and output deflators (Klette and Griliches (1996), among others, discuss the serious shortcomings of firm-level

TABLE II

FIRM-LEVEL VOLATILITY BY SECTOR[a]

NAF	Sector	St. Dev.	Share	NAF	Sector	St. Dev.	Share
01–05	Agriculture, forestry, and fishing	0.2389	0.0049	35	Other transport equipment	0.3232	0.0113
10–14	Mining and quarrying	0.2533	0.0037	36–37	Manufacturing n.e.c.	0.2853	0.0096
15–16	Food and tobacco	0.2340	0.0635	40–41	Electricity, gas, and water supply	0.2103	0.0292
17–19	Textile, wearing apparel, and leather	0.3118	0.0150	45	Construction	0.2314	0.0495
20	Wood products	0.2606	0.0049	50	Wholesale and retail trade	0.2188	0.3689
21–22	Paper products, publishing	0.2558	0.0235	55	Hotels and restaurants	0.1614	0.0141
23	Coke, refined petroleum, and nuclear fuel	0.3255	0.0241	60–63	Transport	0.2033	0.0399
24	Chemical industry	0.3193	0.0421	64	Post and telecommunications	0.2425	0.0226
25	Rubber and plastics	0.3066	0.0145	70	Real estate activities	0.2102	0.0235
26	Mineral products	0.2689	0.0114	71	Rental without operator	0.2158	0.0070
27	Basic metals	0.3189	0.0129	72	Computer services	0.2695	0.0114
28	Metal products	0.2715	0.0207	73	Research and development	0.2915	0.0015
29	Machinery and equipment	0.3122	0.0203	74	Other business services	0.2384	0.0578
30	Office machinery	0.3241	0.0051	75	Public administration	0.1734	0.0003
31	Electrical equipment	0.3096	0.0111	80	Education	0.2283	0.0014
32	Radio, TV, and communication	0.3161	0.0100	85	Health and social work	0.1490	0.0069
33	Medical and optical instruments	0.3017	0.0079	90–93	Personal services	0.1986	0.0164
34	Motor vehicles	0.2950	0.0332				

[a]This table presents the standard deviations of firm–destination growth rates broken down by sector over 1991–2007. “Share” is the share of the sector in total sales. The manufacturing sector covers NAF sectors 15–37. “N.e.c.” stands for “not elsewhere classified.”

TFP estimation that does not employ firm-specific price data). We can also calculate the means and standard deviations of employment and value added per worker growth rates, and compare them to firm–destination sales growth rates. It turns out that these series have very similar first and second moments. For the whole economy, employment growth is 0.0345 at the mean, with an average standard deviation of 0.2437; value added per worker growth is 0.0400, with an average standard deviation of 0.2586. All of these are quite close to the corresponding numbers for sales growth in Table I.[12]

4. EMPIRICAL RESULTS

4.1. *Properties of Shocks*

Before assessing the impact of firm-specific shocks on aggregate volatility, we present the importance of the different components in explaining the variation in sales growth at the firm–destination level. The top panels of Table III and Table IV report the relative standard deviations of the firm–destination components and the sector–destination shocks for the whole economy and the manufacturing sector, respectively. The last column reports the correlation of each component with the actual firm sales growth. The bottom two panels report the same statistics for domestic and export firm sales.

It is clear that at the level of an individual firm–destination, variation in sales growth is dominated by the firm-specific component, rather than the sector–destination shocks. The standard deviation of the firm-specific component is nearly the same as the standard deviation of actual sales growth and the correlation is almost perfect. By contrast, the estimated sector–destination shocks are much less volatile and have much lower correlation with actual sales growth. These results are of course not surprising and confirm the conventional wisdom that most shocks hitting firms are firm-specific (Haltiwanger (1997), Castro, Clementi, and Lee (2013)).[13] Examining the bottom two panels, it is clear that the importance of the firm-specific component is similar for both domestic and export sales.

It has been less well understood whether the firm-specific shocks are mostly common to all destination markets served by the firm or mostly destination-specific. Table V presents the results of extracting the common firm component from firm–destination effects as in equation (9), for both the whole econ-

[12]Average sales growth reported in the table is lower than the sum of average value added per worker growth and average employment growth. Value added is defined as total sales minus input purchases (taking into account changes in the value of input inventories) plus changes in inventories plus subsidies minus taxes. Thus, sales would grow slower than value added if these other categories had slower growth rates than value added. This appears to be the case in our data, reconciling the seeming discrepancy.

[13]A variance decomposition of the firm-level growth rates indicates that 98.7% is accounted for by the firm-specific component for the whole economy (98.2% for the manufacturing sector).

TABLE III

SUMMARY STATISTICS AND CORRELATIONS OF ACTUAL FIRM–DESTINATION-LEVEL GROWTH AND FIRM-SPECIFIC VERSUS SECTOR–DESTINATION-SPECIFIC COMPONENTS: WHOLE ECONOMY[a]

	Obs. (1)	Mean (2)	St. Dev. (3)	Correlation (4)
		A. Total Sales		
Actual	9,856,891	0.0467	0.2601	1.0000
Firm-specific	9,856,891	0.0000	0.2584	0.9935
Sector–destination	16,235	0.0762	0.1209	0.1140
		B. Domestic Sales		
Actual	8,031,453	0.0410	0.2266	1.0000
Firm-specific	8,031,453	0.0000	0.2255	0.9954
Sector–destination	595	0.0453	0.0297	0.0957
		C. Export Sales		
Actual	1,825,438	0.0718	0.3723	1.0000
Firm-specific	1,825,438	0.0000	0.3697	0.9931
Sector–destination	15,640	0.0774	0.1229	0.1171

[a]"Actual" refers to γ_{fnt}, "Firm-specific" to ε_{fnt}, and "Sector–destination" to δ_{jnt} (equation (5)). Column (2) reports the average γ_{fnt}, ε_{fnt}, and δ_{jnt} in the sample of firm–destinations and years. Column (3) reports the average sample standard deviation of γ_{fnt}, ε_{fnt}, and δ_{jnt}. Column (4) presents the correlation between γ_{fnt} and γ_{fnt}, ε_{fnt}, and δ_{jnt}.

TABLE IV

SUMMARY STATISTICS AND CORRELATIONS OF ACTUAL FIRM–DESTINATION-LEVEL GROWTH AND FIRM-SPECIFIC VERSUS SECTOR–DESTINATION-SPECIFIC COMPONENTS: MANUFACTURING SECTOR[a]

	Obs. (1)	Mean (2)	St. Dev. (3)	Correlation (4)
		A. Total Sales		
Actual	2,436,013	0.0542	0.3038	1.0000
Firm-specific	2,436,013	0.0000	0.3011	0.9909
Sector–destination	10,269	0.0727	0.0885	0.1342
		B. Domestic Sales		
Actual	1,233,902	0.0378	0.2233	1.0000
Firm-specific	1,233,902	0.0000	0.2214	0.9917
Sector–destination	306	0.0416	0.0313	0.1285
		C. Export Sales		
Actual	1,202,111	0.0709	0.3679	1.0000
Firm-specific	1,202,111	0.0000	0.3652	0.9927
Sector–destination	9,963	0.0737	0.0895	0.1207

[a]"Actual" refers to γ_{fnt}, "Firm-specific" to ε_{fnt}, and "Sector–destination" to δ_{jnt}. Column (2) reports the average γ_{fnt}, ε_{fnt}, and δ_{jnt} in the sample of firm–destinations and years. Column (3) reports the average sample standard deviation of γ_{fnt}, ε_{fnt}, and δ_{jnt}. Column (4) presents the correlation between γ_{fnt} and γ_{fnt}, ε_{fnt}, and δ_{jnt}.

TABLE V

SUMMARY STATISTICS AND CORRELATIONS OF FIRM-SPECIFIC GROWTH AND COMPONENTS[a]

	Obs. (1)	Mean (2)	St. Dev. (3)	Correlation (4)
		A. Whole Economy		
Firm	2,273,943	0.0009	0.3450	1.0000
Firm–dest.	2,273,943	0.0000	0.3011	0.8728
Firm–com.	479,101	0.0020	0.1949	0.4881
		B. Manufacturing Sector		
Firm	1,448,234	−0.0003	0.3436	1.0000
Firm–dest.	1,448,234	0.0000	0.3052	0.8880
Firm–com.	258,530	0.0007	0.1854	0.4598

[a]"Firm" refers to ε_{fnt}, "Firm–dest." to ε^2_{fnt}, and "Firm–com." to ε^1_{ft} (equation (9)). This table presents the average growth rates and standard deviations of ε_{fnt}, ε^2_{fnt}, and ε^1_{ft} in the sample, as well as the correlations between ε_{fnt} and ε_{fnt}, ε^2_{fnt}, and ε^1_{ft}. The set of firm–destinations is restricted to firms that serve at least two markets.

omy and the manufacturing sector.[14] Looking at the data through the lens of the model in Section 2, this decomposition is suggestive of whether supply or demand shocks are driving firms' sales growth. Since the firm's marginal cost of serving each market (modulo iceberg trade costs) is the same, productivity shocks will be part of the component of the firm-specific shock that is common to all destinations. In addition, the common component will also include the part of the taste shock ω_{fnt} for firm f that is common across locations n. The destination-specific component of the firm shock is then interpreted as a demand shock idiosyncratic to a particular location.

Results are similar for the two sets of firms. For the economy as a whole, the destination-specific component has a higher relative standard deviation than the common factor (0.30 vs. 0.19). It is also more correlated with the total estimated firm-specific component (correlation coefficient of 0.87 compared to 0.49 for the common component). For the manufacturing sector, the relative standard deviation of the destination-specific shock is 0.31, whereas that of the common shocks is 0.19. Similarly, the correlation with the overall firm-specific component is higher for the destination-specific component than for the common component (0.89 vs. 0.46). We conclude from this exercise that destination-specific shocks at the firm level are more important than the shocks common to all destinations.[15]

[14]Note that this decomposition can only be done for firms that serve at least two markets. Therefore, the number of firm–destination and firm-common observations will be smaller than the total number of firm-specific shocks in Tables III and IV.

[15]This result is consistent with the findings of Eaton, Kortum, and Kramarz (2011), who estimate a structural trade model on French export data and find that a firm–destination specific

4.2. *The Aggregate Impact of Firm-Specific Shocks*

The fact that most of the variation in the growth rate of sales is accounted for by firm-specific shocks does not mean that firm-specific shocks manifest themselves in aggregate fluctuations. To assess the importance of the different types of shocks for the aggregate, we must take into account the distribution of firm size by decomposing the aggregate sales volatility as in Section 2.2.

Figure 3 and Table VI report the main results of the paper. Figure 3 depicts the estimates of σ_{A_T} and its main components: firm-specific (σ_{F_T}) and sector–destination (σ_{JN_T}) for the whole economy (panel A) and the manufacturing sector (panel B). The figure also displays two kinds of 95% confidence intervals: analytical and bootstrapped. Table VI reports the averages of our estimates of σ_{A_T}, σ_{JN_T}, and σ_{F_T}, as well as their ratios, over the sample period. The results for the whole economy are in the first two columns, and for the manufacturing sector in the next two columns.

Not surprisingly, the firm–destination component matters much less for the aggregate sales volatility than for the volatility of individual firm sales. However, its importance is nonnegligible: for the whole economy the relative standard deviation of the firm-specific component of aggregate sales is 0.8 relative to that of actual sales volatility. In fact, our results show that the firm-specific component is more important for aggregate fluctuations than the contribution of sector–destination shocks, which has a relative standard deviation of 0.53.

The standard deviation of the firm-specific component comoves with the standard deviation of aggregate sales over time, whereas the standard deviation of sector–destination shocks is nearly constant over time. Recalling how the different components are calculated from (8), note that the time variation in sales' share (at the firm and sector–destination levels) will drive the time variation in the different volatility measures. These shares do not change dramatically at the sector–country level. More interestingly, the firm-specific shocks increase in importance over time. For the whole economy, the relative standard deviation of the firm-specific to total sales is about 0.5 at the beginning of the sample and about 0.85 at the end. These results are a first glimpse of the importance of large firms and firm linkages on aggregate fluctuations. We discuss further what drives these findings in Section 4.3.

The contributions of firm-specific and macro-sector shocks are both statistically significant throughout the sample. In spite of computing the sample variance on a time series of only 17 observations for each σ_{F_T} and σ_{JN_T}, we always have enough power to reject the null that the contribution of σ_{F_T} and σ_{JN_T} is nil. The analytical standard errors are computed as detailed in Appendix C. These standard errors may not capture the full extent of estimation uncertainty in

shock has to be added for the model to fit the data. This suggests that firm-specific shocks common across destinations are not sufficient for explaining aggregate exports.

A. Whole Economy

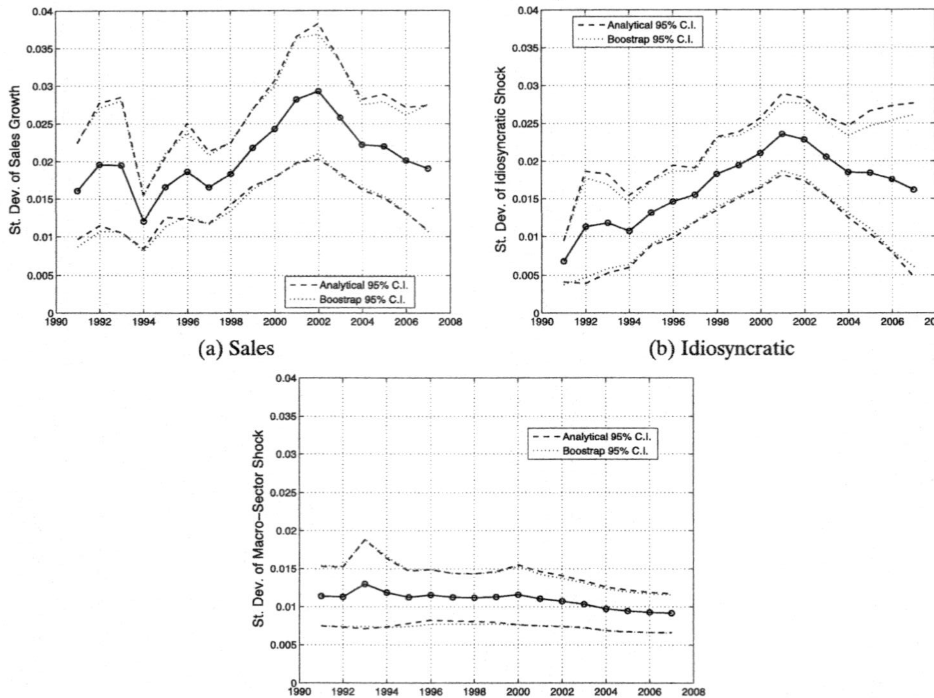

(a) Sales

(b) Idiosyncratic

(c) Macroeconomic

FIGURE 3.—Volatility of sales growth and its components. *Notes*: This figure presents the estimates of $\sigma_{A\tau}$, $\sigma_{F\tau}$, and $\sigma_{JN\tau}$ for the whole economy (panel A) and the manufacturing sector (panel B), along with both analytical and bootstrap 95% confidence intervals.

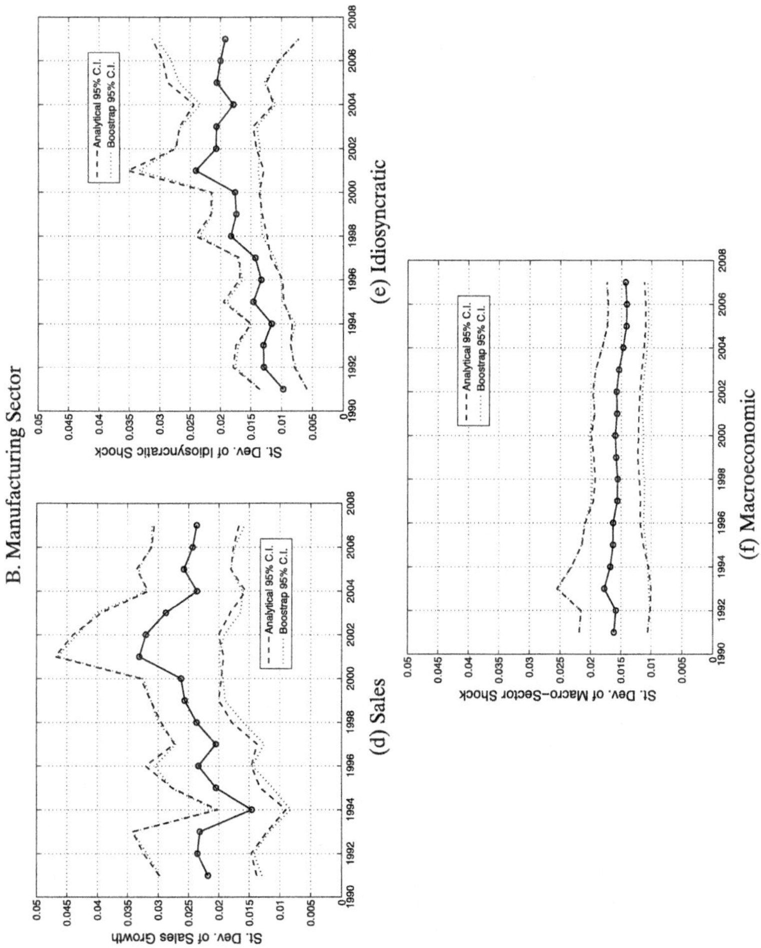

FIGURE 3.—*Continued.*

TABLE VI

THE AGGREGATE IMPACT OF FIRM-SPECIFIC SHOCKS ON AGGREGATE VOLATILITY: WHOLE ECONOMY AND MANUFACTURING SECTOR[a]

	Whole Economy		Manufacturing Sector	
	St. Dev. (1)	Relative SD (2)	St. Dev. (3)	Relative SD (4)
		A. Total Sales		
Actual	0.0206	1.0000	0.0244	1.0000
Firm-specific	0.0165	0.8010	0.0168	0.6885
Sector–destination	0.0109	0.5291	0.0157	0.6434
		B. Domestic Sales		
Actual	0.0196	1.0000	0.0231	1.0000
Firm-specific	0.0154	0.7857	0.0151	0.6537
Sector–destination	0.0112	0.5714	0.0167	0.7229
		C. Export Sales		
Actual	0.0361	1.0000	0.0374	1.0000
Firm-specific	0.0304	0.8421	0.0287	0.7674
Sector–destination	0.0129	0.3573	0.0153	0.4091
		D. Value Added		
Actual	0.0210	1.0000	0.0215	1.0000
Firm-specific	0.0190	0.9048	0.0184	0.8558
Sector–destination	0.0107	0.5095	0.0123	0.5721

[a]This table presents the averages of $\sigma_{A\tau}$ ("Actual"), $\sigma_{F\tau}$ ("Firm-specific"), and $\sigma_{JN\tau}$ ("Sector–destination") over the sample period—$\frac{1}{T}\sum_{\tau=1991}^{2007}\sigma_{A\tau}$, $\frac{1}{T}\sum_{\tau=1991}^{2007}\sigma_{F\tau}$, $\frac{1}{T}\sum_{\tau=1991}^{2007}\sigma_{JN\tau}$—and in relative terms with respect to the actual—$\frac{1}{T}\sum_{\tau=1991}^{2007}\frac{\sigma_{Ft}}{\sigma_{A\tau}}$, $\frac{1}{T}\sum_{\tau=1991}^{2007}\frac{\sigma_{JNt}}{\sigma_{A\tau}}$.

such a small sample. To explore robustness of the results further, we also use a block bootstrapping procedure in which, for each τ, we sample 10,001 draws of 17 observations with replacement from the time series of $\gamma_{At|\tau}$, $\sum_{j,n} w_{jn\tau-1}\delta_{jnt}$, and $\sum_{f,n} w_{fn\tau-1}\varepsilon_{fnt}$. The results are robust to using bootstrapped rather than analytical confidence intervals.[16]

The results for the manufacturing sector largely mimic those of the economy as a whole. The relative standard deviation of the firm-specific component of aggregate sales is 0.69 of actual sales volatility. In this set of firms, the firm-specific component is about as important for aggregate fluctuations as the sector–destination shocks, which have a relative standard deviation of 0.64. The contribution of firms to aggregate fluctuations also increases over time in the manufacturing sector, from 0.45 in 1991 to 0.81 in 2007.

[16]To account for time dependence in the data, the bootstrap procedure samples (overlapping) blocks of one, two, and three observations. The figures report the confidence intervals under a block size of 1, but differences are minimal if we instead use blocks of size 2 or 3.

Panels B and C of Table VI check the results on domestic and export sales separately. Both panels confirm the importance of firm-specific shocks for aggregate fluctuations. Moreover, export sales are dominated by firm-specific shocks, while the relative weights of firm-specific and sector–destination components as a driver of aggregate fluctuations are roughly equal for domestic sales. The greater relative importance of firm shocks for exports compared to domestic sales is exactly as expected given that exports are more granular than overall sales (Canals et al. (2007)).

Since GDP is measured in value added, GDP fluctuations correspond more closely to fluctuations in firm value added. We thus repeat the analysis using firm value added instead of gross sales. This exercise entails a nontrivial assumption. Namely, our framework makes it clear that for proper identification of shocks, we must use data on each destination separately. Since both exports and domestic sales are recorded in gross terms, when we use sales, this is noncontroversial: total firm sales are the sum of sales to each destination market served by the firm. Indeed, this is the reason that we work with sales throughout the paper.

However, for value added, we do not have the right data, because value added exports are not recorded. The data we have are (i) gross domestic sales and exports, and (ii) total firm value added. The assumption we make to move forward is that the breakdown of value added across markets follows the same proportions as total sales. Thus, to compute a firm's value added exports to Germany, we multiply total firm value added by the share of exports to Germany in the firm's total gross sales. In the absence of value added export data, this is the best we can do. It amounts to the restriction that the input usage inside the firm is identical for each destination of its output. For an advanced economy like France, this appears to be a reasonable assumption.

With that caveat, Table VI reports the results. Shocks to firm value added explain, if anything, more of the fluctuations in aggregate value added. The results are similar if we break up value added into the domestic and export components, and thus we do not report them to conserve space.

4.3. *Channels for Firms' Contribution to Aggregate Fluctuations*

Having established the substantial contribution of the firm-specific component to aggregate fluctuations, we next examine the estimates in greater detail so as to disentangle the economic mechanisms at work. Aggregate firm-specific volatility $\sigma^2_{F\tau}$ can be written as

$$\sigma^2_{F\tau} = \mathrm{Var}\left(\sum_{f,n} w_{fn\tau-1}\varepsilon_{fnt}\right) = \sum_{g,m}\sum_{f,n} w_{gm\tau-1}w_{fn\tau-1}\,\mathrm{Cov}(\varepsilon_{gmt}, \varepsilon_{fnt}).$$

We decompose it following Carvalho and Gabaix (2013) into the contribution of individual variances and comovements between firms:

$$\sigma_{F_\tau}^2 = \underbrace{\sum_{f,n} w_{fn\tau-1}^2 \operatorname{Var}(\varepsilon_{fnt})}_{\text{DIRECT}_\tau} + \underbrace{\sum_{g\neq f, m\neq n} \sum_{f,n} w_{gm\tau-1} w_{fn\tau-1} \operatorname{Cov}(\varepsilon_{gmt}, \varepsilon_{fnt})}_{\text{LINK}_\tau}. \tag{10}$$

This decomposition emphasizes two potential proximate channels through which shocks to individual firms may lead to a large variance of the firm-specific component: (i) the variance of individual shocks, labelled DIRECT, and (ii) the covariance of shocks across firms, labelled LINK.

The first term in (10) captures the direct effect of shocks to firms on aggregate volatility, in the sense that it would obtain in the complete absence of firm-to-firm linkages. The predominant tradition in macroeconomics has been to assume that the DIRECT term is negligible due to the law of large numbers: when the distribution of firm size has finite variance, the impact of shocks to individual firms on aggregate volatility converges to zero at the rate $\sqrt{N}$, where N is the number of firms (or, more precisely in our context, firm–destination sales) in the economy. However, recent literature in macroeconomics (most notably Gabaix (2011)) challenges this view by arguing that the observed firm size distribution is so fat-tailed that the conventional law of large numbers does not apply and shocks to individual (large) firms do, in fact, translate into aggregate fluctuations.[17] The LINK component has also been ignored by most of the macroeconomics literature based on the argument that covariances between firms were, in fact, an artefact of firms being hit by common aggregate or sectoral shocks. This view has also been challenged in recent papers, such as Acemoglu et al. (2012) or Foerster, Sarte, and Watson (2011).

Figure 4 presents the decomposition graphically for the whole economy and the manufacturing sector. The LINK component explains the majority of total firm-specific volatility: $\sqrt{\text{LINK}_\tau}/\sigma_{F_\tau}$ is over 90% on average over the sample period for both the whole economy and the manufacturing sector. However, it is apparent from the figures that the DIRECT component is also nonnegligible. The ratio of $\sqrt{\text{DIRECT}_\tau}$ to σ_{F_τ} is 26% on average over this period for the whole economy and 40% for the manufacturing sector.

4.3.1. *The Contribution of the Direct Effect*

As shown by Gabaix (2011), when the distribution of firm size is sufficiently fat-tailed (i.e., the economy is "granular"), idiosyncratic shocks to individual

[17]Gabaix (2011) shows that when the distribution of firm size follows a power law with an exponent close to 1 in absolute value—a distribution known as Zipf's law—aggregate volatility declines at the rate $\log N$ and idiosyncratic shocks will not cancel out in aggregate under a realistic number of firms in the U.S. economy. di Giovanni, Levchenko, and Rancière (2011) use the census of French firms to show that the firm size distribution in France does indeed follow Zipf's law.

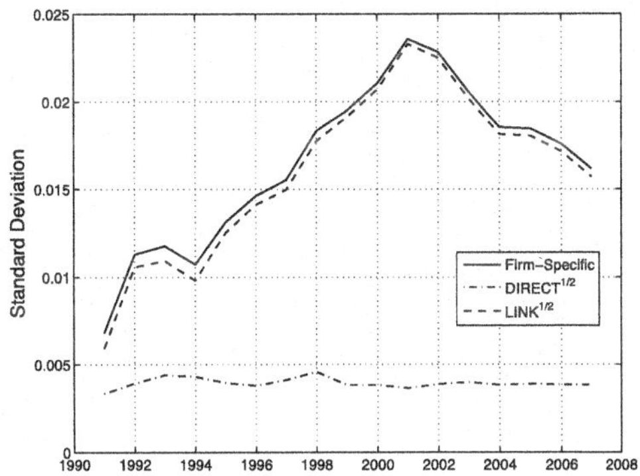

(a) Whole Economy

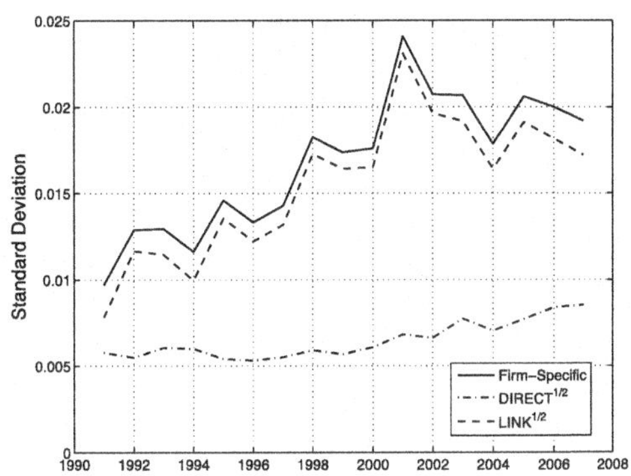

(b) Manufacturing Sector

FIGURE 4.—Contribution of individual volatilities and covariance terms to firm-specific fluctuations. *Notes*: This figure presents a decomposition of the firm-specific aggregate variance into two components that measure the contribution of firm-specific variances ($\sqrt{\text{DIRECT}_\tau}$) and of covariances across firms ($\sqrt{\text{LINK}_\tau}$). The decomposition is based on equation (10).

firms do not wash out at the aggregate level, because the idiosyncratic shocks to large firms do not cancel out with shocks to smaller units. This idea can be discussed most easily in the simplest case when shocks are uncorrelated across firms (i.e., $\text{Cov}(\varepsilon_{gmt}, \varepsilon_{fnt}) = 0 \; \forall (g, m) \neq (f, n)$) and across markets within a firm ($\text{Cov}(\varepsilon_{fmt}, \varepsilon_{fnt}) = 0, m \neq n$), and the variance of shocks is identical across firms ($\text{Var}(\varepsilon_{fnt}) = \sigma^2 \; \forall f, n$). Under these assumptions, aggregate firm-specific volatility (10) is

$$\sigma_{F_\tau}^2 = \sigma^2 \sum_{f,n} w_{fn\tau-1}^2 = \sigma^2 \times \text{Herf}_{\tau-1}, \tag{11}$$

where $\text{Herf}_{\tau-1} = \sum_{f,n} w^2_{fn\tau-1}$ denotes the Herfindahl index. The more fat-tailed is the distribution of firm size, the larger will be the Herfindahl index and the greater will be the aggregate volatility generated by firm-specific shocks. In the opposite extreme case, if all firm–destination sales are instead symmetric in size ($w_{fn\tau-1} = 1/N_{\tau-1}$, where $N_{\tau-1}$ is the number of firm–destination sales in the economy), $\sigma_{F\tau} = \sigma/\sqrt{N_{\tau-1}}$ and the contribution of firms to aggregate volatility decays rapidly with the number of firms in the economy.

The role of the firm size distribution emphasized by Gabaix (2011) can be illustrated using the following simple counterfactual. We calculate the DIRECT component under the assumption that all firms and markets are of equal weight (i.e., $w_{fn\tau-1} = 1/N_{\tau-1}\ \forall f, n$). When shocks are independent across firms, this "equal-weighted" aggregate variance is expected to be vanishingly small. Instead, the contribution of firms to aggregate volatility that takes into account the actual distribution of sales across firms is expected to be larger.

This is indeed what happens. For the whole economy, the $\sqrt{\text{DIRECT}}$ component implied by equal weights is 0.0003, or 13 times smaller than the average $\sqrt{\text{DIRECT}}$ component, which is equal to 0.004. For the manufacturing sector, the standard deviation implied by equal weights is 0.0008, an order of magnitude smaller than the $\sqrt{\text{DIRECT}}$ component of 0.0065. This comparison clearly shows that the firm size distribution does matter a great deal quantitatively for the contribution of individual firms' shocks to aggregate fluctuations.

Next, we exploit differences across sectors to evaluate the importance of the direct effect. To do so, we decompose the DIRECT component in equation (10) into sectors, where sector j's DIRECT component is defined as $\text{DIRECT}_{j\tau} \equiv \sum_{(f,n)\in j} w^2_{fn\tau-1}\,\text{Var}(\varepsilon_{fnt})$, and $\text{DIRECT}_\tau = \sum_{j=1}^{J} \text{DIRECT}_{j\tau}$. Again, if $\text{Var}(\varepsilon_{fnt}) = \sigma^2\ \forall f, n$, we would expect that more concentrated sectors would display larger volatilities.[18] Figure 5 evaluates this prediction, by plotting (the square root of the) mean sectoral $\text{DIRECT}_{j\tau}$ against the (square root of the) mean sectoral Herfindahl index for the whole economy and the manufacturing sector. In Figure 5, $\text{DIRECT}_{j\tau}$ and the Herfindahl are computed with weights normalized by the size of each sector in aggregate sales. Otherwise, they would mechanically be proportional to the contribution of each sector to overall sales. The correlation is strongly positive: sectors with higher sales concentration contribute more to the total DIRECT component, which is consistent with granularity. The correlation is lower for the whole economy (0.86) than for the manufacturing sector (0.93). The correlation is less than perfect because firm-level variances differ both across and within sectors. In the data, small firms tend to be more volatile on average (Table I). This heterogeneity

[18]The firm-specific volatilities do in fact vary by sector, to the same degree as the standard deviations of the raw growth rates in Table II—the correlation between the standard deviations of the actual growth rates and the firm-specific shocks is 0.996 across sectors.

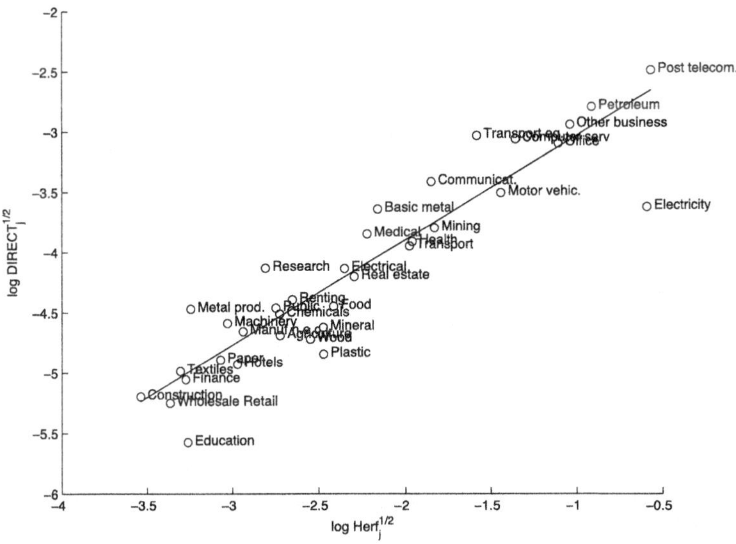

(a) Whole Economy

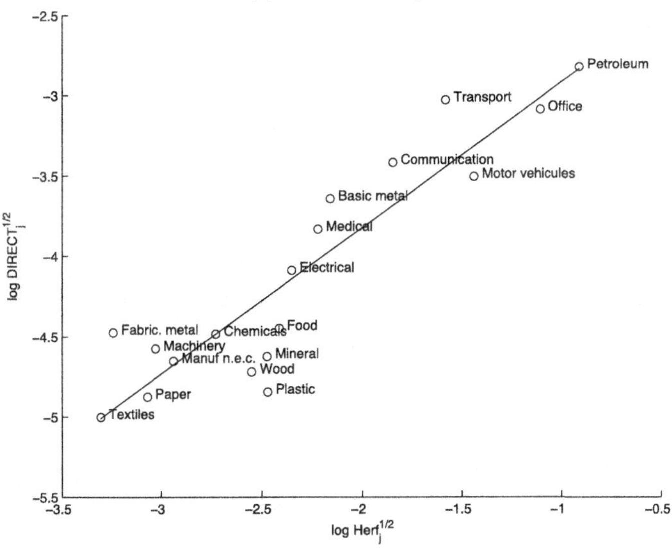

(b) Manufacturing Sector

FIGURE 5.—Firm-specific volatility aggregated at the sector level and the sectoral mean Herfindahl index. *Notes*: This figure plots the time average of the sectoral $\sqrt{\text{DIRECT}_{j\tau}}$ component against the square root of the sectoral mean Herfindahl index. The correlation between time average $\sqrt{\text{DIRECT}_{j\tau}}$ and $\sqrt{\text{Herf}_{j\tau}}$ is 0.86 for the whole economy and 0.93 for the manufacturing sector.

in firm-level volatilities counteracts the impact of sales concentration, thus reducing the overall size of the DIRECT component relative to what would be expected in a purely "granular" world with identical variances across firms.

4.3.2. *The Contribution of Firm Linkages*

The second explanation for why firm shocks can drive aggregate fluctuations is inspired by the literature on the role of sectoral input–output linkages in aggregate fluctuations (Horvath (1998, 2000), Dupor (1999), Shea (2002), Conley and Dupor (2003), Gabaix (2011), Acemoglu et al. (2012)), and is captured by the covariance term LINK in (10). The idea is that idiosyncratic shocks do not wash out at the aggregate level because they propagate across firms or sectors through "interconnections." If firms in the economy are connected, say through input–output linkages, shocks affecting upstream firms propagate to downstream firms via adjustments in the price of inputs. This propagation mechanism amplifies the initial impact of structural shocks. Moreover, it generates positive covariances in the residual growth rate of sales for firms that are connected.

Note that simply observing positive covariances in the firm-specific components (gathered in the LINK term) is not conclusive evidence that input–output linkages are responsible for the comovement, as there may be other reasons for cross-sectional dependence between firms, such as local labor market interactions. While we cannot identify the precise share of the LINK term that is due to input–output linkages per se, we provide direct, if suggestive, evidence that input–output linkages are at least partly responsible for the positive LINK term.

Appendix E lays out a simple model of such firm-level interconnections. Firms produce with a constant marginal cost using labor and intermediate inputs bought from other firms in the economy. Input–output linkages create a positive covariance of sales growth rates for any two firms that are connected. For instance, take firms f and g, and assume firm g sells inputs to firm f. If the only source of shocks is productivity shocks to firm g, then the covariance between the sales growth rates of those two firms is

$$\mathrm{Cov}(\varepsilon_{gmt}, \varepsilon_{fnt}) = (1-\theta)^2(1-\lambda_f)\rho_{fg}\,\mathrm{Var}(a_{gmt}),$$

where θ is the elasticity of substitution, $(1-\lambda_f)$ is the share of intermediate goods in firm f's total costs, ρ_{fg} is the share of those inputs that is sourced from firm g, and $\mathrm{Var}(a_{gmt})$ is the volatility of firm g's productivity. The covariance is positive and increasing in the strength of the connection between f and g, that is, in the share of inputs from g used in f's production, $(1-\lambda_f)\rho_{fg}$. In this setup, the propagation goes from upstream to downstream firms through the price of inputs. In a more general setting, one can also expect shocks to propagate from downstream to upstream firms through the demand of intermediates.[19]

Ideally, one would test the linkage hypothesis using firm-level measures of interconnections. Since information on firm-to-firm input linkages (ρ_{fg}) is not available, we instead proxy for production networks using sector-level data and use the input–output (IO) tables for France compiled by the Organization for Economic Cooperation and Development (OECD). Assuming that the share of intermediates in total costs is homogeneous across firms within a sector (i.e., $\lambda_f = \lambda_i\ \forall f \in i$) and that all firms within a sector interact with the same input providers (i.e., $\rho_{fg} = \rho_{ij}\tilde{w}_{g/j}\ \forall f \in i, g \in j$, where $\tilde{w}_{g/j}$ is the share of firm g in total sector j intermediate input sales to i), the structure of sectoral IO matrices can be used to approximate the intensity of IO linkages between firms from each pair of sectors. The intensity of IO linkages between a pair of sectors can then be related to the magnitude of covariances between firms in those sectors. We expect the weighted sum of covariances to be higher for sector pairs that display stronger IO linkages.[20]

Figure 6 examines this hypothesis. We decompose the LINK component in equation (10) across sector pairs, where the LINK term specific to the pair (i, j) is defined as $\text{LINK}_{ij\tau} \equiv \sum_{(f,n)\in i} \sum_{(g,m)\in j} w_{fn\tau-1} w_{gm\tau-1} \operatorname{Cov}(\varepsilon_{fnt}, \varepsilon_{gmt})$ and $\text{LINK}_\tau = \sum_{i=1}^{J} \sum_{j=1; j\neq i}^{J} \text{LINK}_{ij\tau}$. We then correlate the (square root of the) average $\text{LINK}_{ij\tau}$ of a pair of sectors to the mean intensity of IO linkages between them. $\text{LINK}_{ij\tau}$ is normalized by the size of each sector to control for the mechanical impact of sector sizes on the magnitude of the aggregated covariance terms. The mean intensity of IO linkages is defined as $0.5 \times [(1-\lambda_i)\rho_{ij} + (1-\lambda_j)\rho_{ji}]$, where λ_i is the share of value added in sector i's total output and ρ_{ij} is the share of inputs from j in sector i's spending on intermediates, both taken from the French IO tables for 1995. Input–output linkages are thus stronger if either one or both sectors intensively use intermediates from the other sector.

The correlation between the LINK term and the intensity of IO linkages is positive, both for the whole economy Figure 6(a) and the manufacturing sector Figure 6(b).[21] The relationship is marginally more pronounced for the manu-

[19]This is ruled out in the setting of Appendix E as well as in the model of Acemoglu et al. (2012) because of the Cobb–Douglas assumption on the production function. More flexible specifications of technology would allow downstream firms' productivity shocks to propagate upstream to input providers.

[20]See Appendix E for details.

[21]Note that Figure 6 drops negative bilateral covariance terms as well as zero input–output linkages, since we are taking log transformations. Input–output linkages would not explain negative covariances according to the model. Such negative numbers should instead reflect substitution effects across competing firms. Likewise, our stylized model is unable to explain a strictly positive LINK term between firms in sectors that do not interact through IO linkages. Fortunately, observations with negative covariance terms and/or zero input–output linkages are rare in our data, representing less than 6% of the total possible sector pairs.

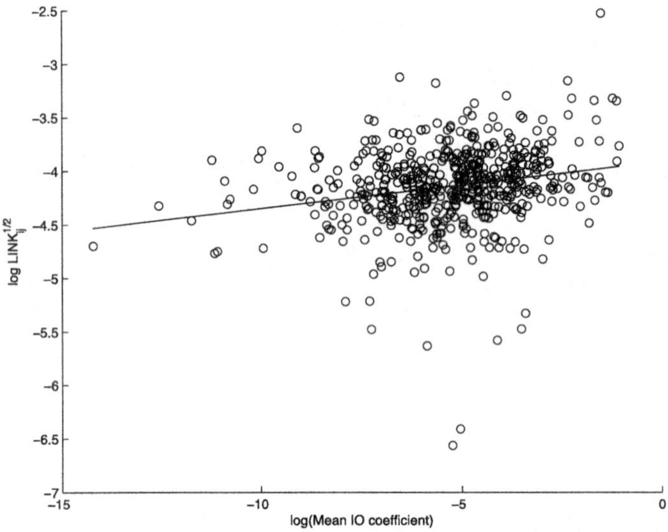

(a) Whole Economy

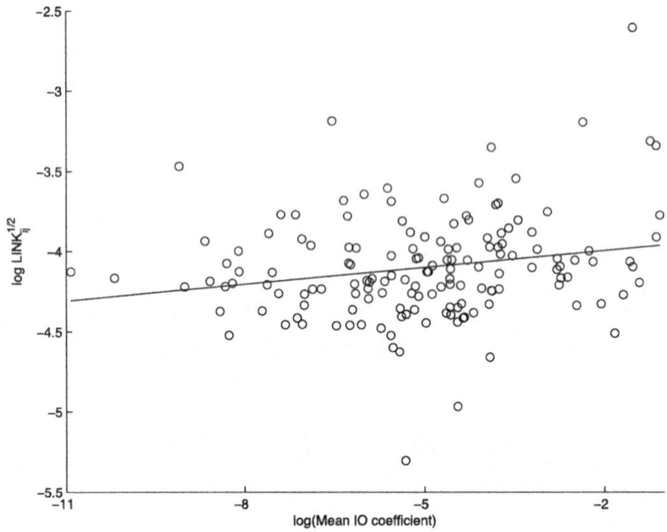

(b) Manufacturing Sector

FIGURE 6.—Covariances of firm-specific shocks across sectors and their input–output linkages. *Notes*: This figure plots the time average of the sector pair $\sqrt{\mathrm{LINK}_{ij\tau}}$ component against the mean IO linkage (share of intermediate inputs in total costs times the share of the upstream sector in intermediate consumption between sectors i and j). The correlation between the time average $\sqrt{\mathrm{LINK}_{ij\tau}}$ and the IO linkages is 0.29 for the whole economy and 0.34 for the manufacturing sector.

facturing sector, with a correlation coefficient of 0.34 compared to 0.29 for the whole economy. The results are direct empirical evidence that input–output linkages across firms are important in transmitting microeconomic shocks across the economy.

4.4. *Extensions and Robustness*

4.4.1. *Differences in Firm Sensitivity to Macro and Sectoral Shocks*

In the baseline model, the elasticity of firm sales with respect to aggregate and sectoral shocks is the same across firms. Our conceptual framework shares this feature with Dixit and Stiglitz (1977), Krugman (1980), Melitz (2003), and the enormous literature that followed in this tradition. However, it is possible that firms will systematically react differently to sector- and country-level shocks. In that case, the computed values of ε_{fnt} will be combinations of firm-specific shocks and the heterogeneous responses to the aggregate and sectoral shocks. There are several theoretical channels that would deliver a heterogeneous response. One example is a model laid out in Appendix F, in which firms react heterogeneously to sector–destination shocks because of variable markups. di Giovanni and Levchenko (2012a) argue that the impact of this channel on aggregate volatility is small. However, as a robustness check, we carry out alternative estimations in which we instead impose the augmented model

$$\gamma_{fnt} = \delta_{jnt} + \delta_{jnt} \times \text{CHAR}_{ft} + \beta\text{CHAR}_{ft} + \varepsilon_{fnt}, \tag{12}$$

where CHAR_{ft} is a particular observable firm characteristic. In this model, heterogeneity of firm responses to macroeconomic and sectoral shocks is thus systematically related to observable firm characteristics. We attempt a variety of different types of CHAR_{ft}: measures of (i) firm size (log sales or sales quintile dummy),[22] (ii) firm age (log years or dummy for whether the firm is less or more than 5 years old),[23] (iii) R&D intensity (dummy for whether R&D expenses are higher than 1% of value added),[24] (iv) patent intensity (dummy for whether patent expenses are more than 5% of value added), (v) export inten-

[22]Following the accepted practice in the literature, our preferred specification captures size differences using quintile dummies, since that allows for greater (nonparametric) flexibility in the functional form. See Fortin, Lemieux, and Firpo (2011) for an exhaustive survey on decomposition methods.

[23]Fort, Haltiwanger, Jarmin, and Miranda (2013) report that in the United States, young/small businesses are more sensitive to the cycle than older/larger businesses.

[24]Comín and Philippon (2005) report that in the United States, sectors with largest increases in R&D have become less correlated with the business cycle.

TABLE VII

THE IMPACT OF FIRM-SPECIFIC SHOCKS ON AGGREGATE VOLATILITY: DIFFERING FIRM SENSITIVITY TO SECTORAL AND MACROECONOMIC SHOCKS[a]

	Whole Economy		Manufacturing Sector	
	St. Dev. (1)	Relative SD (2)	St. Dev. (3)	Relative SD (4)
Actual	0.0206	1.0000	0.0244	1.0000
	Firm-Specific Component (Average $\sigma_{F\tau}$)			
Differing sensitivity				
By size	0.0169	0.8204	0.0172	0.7049
By age	0.0122	0.5922	0.0133	0.5451
By R&D intensity	0.0164	0.7961	0.0167	0.6844
By patenting intensity	0.0162	0.7864	0.0167	0.6844
By openness	0.0166	0.8058	0.0167	0.6844
By debt	0.0164	0.7961	0.0167	0.6844
By all of the above	0.0134	0.6505	0.0123	0.5041

[a]The row labelled "Actual" reports the average standard deviation of actual aggregate sales growth over 1991–2007: $\frac{1}{T}\sum_{\tau=1991}^{2007}\sigma_{A\tau}$. The rest of the table reports the average standard deviation of the firm-specific component, $\frac{1}{T}\sum_{\tau=1991}^{2007}\sigma_{F\tau}$, and its average value relative to the actual, $\frac{1}{T}\sum_{\tau=1991}^{2007}\frac{\sigma_{F\tau}}{\sigma_{A\tau}}$, under a series of augmented models (12) in which firms have heterogeneous sensitivity to sector–destination shocks. "Size" is the dummy for the firm's quintile in the sales distribution. "Age" is the dummy for whether the firm is more than 5 years old. "R&D intensity" is a dummy for whether R&D expenses are higher than 1% of value added. "Patent intensity" is a dummy for whether patent expenses are more than 5% of value added. "Openness" is the ratio of exports to total firm sales. "Debt" is the quintile dummy for the firm's debt to sales ratio.

sity (ratio of exports to total firm sales),[25] and (vi) debt to sales ratio.[26] We also implement a model in which all of these characteristics are included together.

Table VII reports the results. Allowing firm sensitivity to aggregate and sectoral shocks to differ by firm size leaves the conclusions unchanged. The table reports the implementation in which firm size is captured by sales quintile dummies. The results are unaffected if we instead use a continuous measure of size, such as log sales, or use employment or total assets as measures of size. If we allow a firm's sensitivity to shocks to differ by firm age, the contribution of firm shocks to aggregate fluctuations falls somewhat. Nonetheless, the relative importance of firm-specific shocks for aggregate volatility, $\sigma_{F\tau}/\sigma_{A\tau}$, is still nearly 0.6. The table reports the results of using a dummy for whether the firm is more than 5 years old. Using actual years of age instead leaves the results unchanged. Allowing sensitivity to differ by any of the other character-

[25]There is evidence that firms substitute domestic for foreign sales in response to demand shocks abroad (e.g., Blum, Claro, and Horstmann (2013)). Thus, it may be that exporters exhibit systematically different sensitivity to shocks in an individual market.

[26]There is evidence that access to capital markets affects firms' responses to aggregate shocks (Gertler and Gilchrist (1994), Kashyap, Lamont, and Stein (1994)).

istics we consider—R&D and patent intensity, overall export orientation, or debt structure—also leaves the results unchanged. While the table reports the results using the quintile dummies for the debt to total sales ratio of the firm, the results are unchanged if we instead use bond debt, bank debt, or ratio of bond to bank debt, each in both continuous and quintile dummy forms.

Finally, the last row of the table reports the results of allowing firm sensitivity to aggregate and sectoral shocks to depend on all of the above characteristics simultaneously. The importance of firm-specific shocks is somewhat lower than in the baseline, with $\sigma_{F_T}/\sigma_{A_T}$ equal to 0.65 for the whole economy and 0.5 for the manufacturing sector. Nonetheless, this contribution is still sizeable. We take this as evidence that our results are robust to allowing for firm–destination sales growth to react heterogeneously to macroeconomic and sectoral shocks.

4.4.2. *Entry and Exit*

The baseline analysis is carried out on the intensive margin, that is, sales growth rates for continuing firm–destinations. Appendix A presents an explicit decomposition of aggregate sales growth into extensive and intensive margins, and argues that the bulk of aggregate sales fluctuations is driven by the intensive margin. As an alternative approach, we report results for the growth rates adopted by Davis, Haltiwanger, and Schuh (1996) and the large literature that followed:

$$\gamma'_{fnt} \equiv \frac{x_{fnt} - x_{fnt-1}}{0.5(x_{fnt} + x_{fnt-1})}. \tag{13}$$

This growth rate, which we label DHS, has a number of attractive properties: it encompasses entries and exits (treating them in the same way as other observations), it ranges from -2 to 2 and thus limits the impact of outliers, and it lends itself to consistent aggregation. Under this definition of growth rates, the correct weights for aggregation are

$$w'_{fnt} \equiv \frac{(x_{fnt} + x_{fnt-1})}{\sum_{f,n}(x_{fnt} + x_{fnt-1})}$$

and the aggregate growth rate of x is

$$\gamma'_{At} \equiv \frac{X_t - X_{t-1}}{0.5(X_t + X_{t-1})} = \sum_{f,n} w'_{fnt}\gamma'_{fnt}.$$

Note, however, that a firm growth defined this way does not admit a log-difference decomposition (4) into macro, sectoral, and firm-specific components, and thus the results using these growth rates should be interpreted as approximations. The results are presented in Table VIII, panel A. Using these

TABLE VIII

THE IMPACT OF FIRM-SPECIFIC SHOCKS ON AGGREGATE VOLATILITY: ROBUSTNESS CHECKS[a]

	Whole Economy		Manufacturing Sector	
	St. Dev. (1)	Relative SD (2)	St. Dev. (3)	Relative SD (4)
		A. DHS Growth Rates		
Actual	0.1420	1.0000	0.1203	1.0000
Firm-specific	0.1014	0.7141	0.0833	0.6924
		B. Demeaned Growth Rates		
Actual	0.0206	1.0000	0.0244	1.0000
Firm-specific	0.0128	0.6214	0.0152	0.6230
		C. Additional Local Market Effects		
Actual	0.0206	1.0000	0.0244	1.0000
Firm-specific	0.0165	0.8010	0.0164	0.6721
		D. More Disaggregated Sectors		
Actual	0.0209	1.0000	0.0244	1.0000
Firm-specific	0.0169	0.8086	0.0156	0.6393
		E. Three-Year Growth Rates		
Actual	0.0290	1.0000	0.0323	1.0000
Firm-specific	0.0266	0.9140	0.0269	0.8885

[a]The rows labelled "Actual" report the average standard deviation of actual aggregate sales growth over 1991–2007: $\frac{1}{T}\sum_{\tau=1991}^{2007}\sigma_{A\tau}$. The rows labelled "Firm-specific" report the average standard deviation of the firm-specific component, $\frac{1}{T}\sum_{\tau=1991}^{2007}\sigma_{F\tau}$, and its average value relative to the actual, $\frac{1}{T}\sum_{\tau=1991}^{2007}\frac{\sigma_{F\tau}}{\sigma_{A\tau}}$, under a series of alternative models. Panel A implements the model under the firm growth rate defined as in (13). Panel B reports the results under first demeaning firm sales growth by the firm–destination specific average growth rate. Panel C reports the results of augmenting the model to include location-specific shocks. Panel D reports the results under defining sectors according to the five-digit NAF level of disaggregation (about 700 sectors in the whole economy). Panel E uses the baseline model, but takes the average firm–destination growth rates over s periods: 1990–1993, 1994–1997, 1998–2001, 2002–2005. Means of standard deviations and relative standard deviations are presented.

growth rates changes the sample of firms and produces lower aggregate volatility, but the share of the firm-specific contribution to the aggregate volatility remains very similar to the baseline at $\sigma_{F\tau}/\sigma_{A\tau}$ of about 0.7 for both the whole economy and the manufacturing sector.

4.4.3. *Other Robustness Checks*

One may be concerned about how differential trend growth rates across firms (especially of different sizes) can affect the calculation of the firms' contribution to aggregate volatility. To check if this matters, we demean each firm–destination growth rate by the average growth rate of that firm–destination. The results are presented in Table VIII, panel B. The contribution of the firm-specific component is still important.

It may be that firms in different regions of France are subject to shocks specific to their geographical location. This could be because factor (or goods) markets are local, for instance. To check for this possibility, we implement an augmented model in which we add a geographic location-specific shock that affects all firms located in a particular geographic area within France. The definition of geographic area corresponds to the "employment zone" (zone d'emploi), which is intended to capture the extent of the local labor market. It is larger than a city (at least when the city is small), but smaller than a county. There are about 300 zones d'emploi in France. The results are reported in Table VIII, panel C. Adding shocks specific to the local labor market leaves the basic results unchanged.

All of the above results use a particular level of disaggregation (about 50 sectors, among them 22 manufacturing). It could be that sectoral shocks take place at a more detailed level. To check for this possibility, panel D in Table VIII implements the model under more finely disaggregated sectors: five-digit NAF, or about 700 distinct sectors. The results are virtually unchanged from the baseline.

Finally, as a different robustness check, panel E in Table VIII presents results when implementing the baseline model on 3-year average firm–destination growth rates instead of yearly growth rates. The results are robust to time aggregation.[27]

5. CONCLUSION

Do firm-level dynamics have an impact on aggregate fluctuations? Recent contributions argue that idiosyncratic shocks to firms can indeed manifest themselves in aggregate fluctuations if the firm size distribution is sufficiently fat-tailed (Gabaix (2011)) or when linkages propagate microeconomic shocks across firms leading to positive endogenous comovement (e.g., Acemoglu et al. (2012)). However, the empirical evidence supporting these different theories has been limited. This paper constructs a novel data set that merges French domestic and export sales at the firm level over the period 1990–2007, and provides a forensic account of the role of individual firms in generating aggregate fluctuations.

We begin by proposing a simple model, in the spirit of Melitz (2003) and Eaton, Kortum, and Kramarz (2011), to motivate an estimation framework that allows us to extract the macroeconomic, sectoral, and firm-specific components of a firm's sales to a given destination. These estimates are then aggregated up to explain the relative contribution of each component to the volatility of aggregate sales. Our main results can be summarized as follows. First, the firm-specific component accounts for an important part of the fluctuations of

[27]We also ran specifications restricting the sample to firms that exist for at least 8 years. Results were similar to the baseline specification, and are available from the authors upon request.

aggregate sales growth. The standard deviation of the aggregated firm-specific shocks amounts to 80% of the standard deviation of aggregate sales in the whole economy and to 69% in the manufacturing sector. We interpret this as evidence for the relevance of firm-level shocks for aggregate fluctuations. Second, while the direct effect of firm shocks on aggregate volatility is quantitatively relevant, the majority of the contribution of firm shocks to aggregate fluctuations is accounted for by firm-to-firm covariance terms, which we interpret as evidence of linkages.

REFERENCES

ACEMOGLU, D., V. M. CARVALHO, A. OZDAGLAR, AND A. TAHBAZ-SALEHI (2012): "The Network Origins of Aggregate Fluctuations," *Econometrica*, 80 (5), 1977–2016. [1303,1305,1306,1313,1326,1330,1331,1337]

BERNARD, A. B., S. J. REDDING, AND P. K. SCHOTT (2010): "Multiple-Product Firms and Product Switching," *American Economic Review*, 100 (1), 70–97. [1308]

BILBIIE, F. O., F. GHIRONI, AND M. J. MELITZ (2012): "Endogenous Entry, Product Variety and Business Cycles," *Journal of Political Economy*, 120 (2), 304–345. [1308]

BLUM, B. S., S. CLARO, AND I. HORSTMANN (2013): "Occasional and Perennial Exporters," *Journal of International Economics*, 90 (1), 65–74. [1334]

CABALLERO, R. J., E. M. R. A. ENGEL, AND J. HALTIWANGER (1997): "Aggregate Employment Dynamics: Building From Microeconomic Evidence," *American Economic Review*, 87 (1), 115–137. [1307]

CANALS, C., X. GABAIX, J. M. VILARRUBIA, AND D. E. WEINSTEIN (2007): "Trade Patterns, Trade Balances, and Idiosyncratic Shocks," Working Paper 02/2007, la Caixa. [1305,1325]

CARVALHO, V. M., AND X. GABAIX (2013): "The Great Diversification and Its Undoing," *American Economic Review*, 103 (5), 1697–1727. [1303,1306,1311,1316,1326]

CASTRO, R., G. L. CLEMENTI, AND Y. LEE (2013): "Cross-Sectoral Variation in Plant-Level Idiosyncratic Risk," *Journal of Industrial Economics* (forthcoming). [1304,1307,1312,1316,1318]

COHEN, L., AND A. FRAZZINI (2008): "Economic Links and Predictable Returns," *Journal of Finance*, 63 (4), 1977–2011. [1306]

COMÍN, D., AND T. PHILIPPON (2006): "The Rise in Firm-Level Volatility: Causes and Consequences," in *NBER Macroeconomics Annual 2005*, Vol. 20, ed. by M. Gertler and K. S. Rogoff. Cambridge, MA: MIT Press, Chapter 1, 167–201. [1307,1333]

CONLEY, T. G., AND B. DUPOR (2003): "A Spatial Analysis of Sectoral Complementarity," *Journal of Political Economy*, 111 (2), 311–352. [1303,1305,1306,1330]

COOPER, R., J. HALTIWANGER, AND L. POWER (1999): "Machine Replacement and the Business Cycle: Lumps and Bumps," *American Economic Review*, 89 (4), 921–946. [1307]

COOPER, R. W., AND J. C. HALTIWANGER (2006): "On the Nature of Capital Adjustment Costs," *Review of Economic Studies*, 73 (256), 611–633. [1307]

DAVIS, S. J., AND J. C. HALTIWANGER (1992): "Gross Job Creation, Gross Job Destruction, and Employment Reallocation," *Quarterly Journal of Economics*, 107 (3), 819–863. [1307]

DAVIS, S. J., R. J. FABERMAN, AND J. HALTIWANGER (2006): "The Flow Approach to Labor Markets: New Data Sources and Micro-Macro Links," *Journal of Economic Perspectives*, 20 (3), 3–26. [1307]

DAVIS, S. J., J. C. HALTIWANGER, AND S. SCHUH (1996): *Job Creation and Destruction*. Cambridge, MA: MIT Press. [1307,1335]

DAVIS, S. J., J. HALTIWANGER, R. JARMIN, AND J. MIRANDA (2007): "Volatility and Dispersion in Business Growth Rates Publicly Traded versus Privately Held Firms," in *NBER Macroeconomics Annual 2006*, Vol. 21, ed. by D. Acemoglu, K. Rogoff, and M. Woodford. Cambridge, MA: MIT Press, Chapter 2, 107–180. [1307]

DI GIOVANNI, J., AND A. A. LEVCHENKO (2010): "Putting the Parts Together: Trade, Vertical Linkages, and Business Cycle Comovement," *American Economic Journal: Macroeconomics*, 2 (2), 95–124. [1313]

——— (2012a): "Country Size, International Trade, and Aggregate Fluctuations in Granular Economies," *Journal of Political Economy*, 120 (6), 1083–1132. [1307,1333]

——— (2012b): "The Risk Content of Exports: A Portfolio View of International Trade," in *NBER International Seminar on Macroeconomics*, Vol. 8, ed. by J. Frankel and C. Pissarides. Chicago, IL: University of Chicago Press, Chapter 3, 97–151. [1312]

DI GIOVANNI, J., A. A. LEVCHENKO, AND I. MEJEAN (2014): "Supplement to 'Firms, Destinations, and Aggregate Fluctuations'," *Econometrica Supplemental Material*, 82, http://www.econometricsociety.org/ecta/supmat/11041_miscellaneous.pdf; http://www.econometricsociety.org/ecta/supmat/11041_data_and_programs.zip. [1307]

DI GIOVANNI, J., A. A. LEVCHENKO, AND R. RANCIÈRE (2011): "Power Laws in Firm Size and Openness to Trade: Measurement and Implications," *Journal of International Economics*, 85 (1), 42–52. [1326]

DIXIT, A. K., AND J. E. STIGLITZ (1977): "Monopolistic Competition and Optimum Product Diversity," *American Economic Review*, 67 (3), 297–308. [1333]

DOMS, M. E., AND T. DUNNE (1998): "Capital Adjustment Patterns in Manufacturing Plants," *Review of Economic Dynamics*, 1 (2), 409–429. [1307]

DUPOR, B. (1999): "Aggregation and Irrelevance in Multi-Sector Models," *Journal of Monetary Economics*, 43 (2), 391–409. [1303,1305,1306,1330]

EATON, J., S. S. KORTUM, AND F. KRAMARZ (2011): "An Anatomy of International Trade: Evidence From French Firms," *Econometrica*, 79 (5), 1453–1498. [1304,1308,1320,1337]

EATON, J., S. S. KORTUM, B. NEIMAN, AND J. ROMALIS (2011): "Trade and the Global Recession," Working Paper 16666, NBER. [1309]

FIRPO, S., N. M. FORTIN, AND T. LEMIEUX (2011): "Decomposition Methods in Economics," in *Handbook of Labor Economics*, Vol. 4, ed. by O. Ashenfelter and D. E. Card. Amsterdam: Elsevier, 1–102. [1333]

FOERSTER, A. T., P.-D. G. SARTE, AND M. W. WATSON (2011): "Sectoral vs. Aggregate Shocks: A Structural Factor Analysis of Industrial Production," *Journal of Political Economy*, 119 (1), 1–38. [1303,1306,1313,1326]

FORT, T. C., J. HALTIWANGER, R. S. JARMIN, AND J. MIRANDA (2013): "How Firms Respond to Business Cycles: The Role of Firm Age and Firm Size," *IMF Economic Review*, 61 (3), 520–559. [1333]

GABAIX, X. (2011): "The Granular Origins of Aggregate Fluctuations," *Econometrica*, 79 (3), 733–772. [1303,1305,1307,1311-1313,1315,1316,1326,1328,1330,1337]

GERTLER, M., AND S. GILCHRIST (1994): "Monetary Policy, Business Cycles, and the Behavior of Small Manufacturing Firms," *Quarterly Journal of Economics*, 109 (2), 309–340. [1334]

GOURIO, F., AND A. K. KASHYAP (2007): "Investment Spikes: New Facts and a General Equilibrium Exploration," *Journal of Monetary Economics*, 54 (Supplement), 1–22. [1307]

HALTIWANGER, J. C. (1997): "Measuring and Analyzing Aggregate Fluctuations: The Importance of Building From Microeconomic Evidence," *Federal Reserve Bank of St. Louis Review*, 79 (3), 55–77. [1304,1318]

HERTZEL, M. G., Z. LI, M. S. OFFICER, AND K. J. RODGERS (2008): "Inter-Firm Linkages and the Wealth Effects of Financial Distress Along the Supply Chain," *Journal of Financial Economics*, 87 (2), 374–387. [1306]

HORVATH, M. (1998): "Cyclicality and Sectoral Linkages: Aggregate Fluctuations From Independent Sectoral Shocks," *Review of Economic Dynamics*, 1 (4), 781–808. [1303,1305,1306, 1330]

——— (2000): "Sectoral Shocks and Aggregate Fluctuations," *Journal of Monetary Economics*, 45 (1), 69–106. [1303,1305,1306,1330]

JOVANOVIC, B. (1987): "Micro Shocks and Aggregate Risk," *Quarterly Journal of Economics*, 102 (2), 395–410. [1306]

KASHYAP, A. K., O. A. LAMONT, AND J. C. STEIN (1994): "Credit Conditions and the Cyclical Behavior of Inventories," *Quarterly Journal of Economics*, 109 (3), 565–592. [1334]

KELLY, B., H. LUSTIG, AND S. VAN NIEUWERBURGH (2013): "Firm Volatility in Granular Networks," Report, University of Chicago, UCLA, and NYU. [1306]

KLETTE, T. J., AND Z. GRILICHES (1996): "The Inconsistency of Common Scale Estimators When Output Prices Are Unobserved and Endogenous," *Journal of Applied Econometrics*, 11 (4), 343–361. [1316]

KOREN, M., AND S. TENREYRO (2007): "Volatility and Development," *Quarterly Journal of Economics*, 122 (1), 243–287. [1312]

KRUGMAN, P. (1980): "Scale Economies, Product Differentiation, and the Pattern of Trade," *American Economic Review*, 70 (5), 950–959. [1333]

LEE, Y., AND T. MUKOYAMA (2012): "Entry, Exit, and Plant-Level Dynamics Over the Business Cycle," Report, Sogang University, Federal Reserve Bank of Cleveland, and University of Virginia. [1307]

LONG, J. B., AND C. I. PLOSSER (1983): "Real Business Cycles," *Journal of Political Economy*, 91 (1), 39–69. [1303,1306]

MELITZ, M. J. (2003): "The Impact of Trade on Intra-Industry Reallocations and Aggregate Industry Productivity," *Econometrica*, 71 (6), 1695–1725. [1304,1308,1333,1337]

MOSCARINI, G., AND F. POSTEL-VINAY (2012): "The Contribution of Large and Small Employers to Job Creation in Times of High and Low Unemployment," *American Economic Review*, 102 (6), 2509–2539. [1307,1316]

OSOTIMEHIN, S. (2013): "Aggregate Productivity and the Allocation of Resources Over the Business Cycle," Report, University of Virginia. [1308]

SHEA, J. (2002): "Complementarities and Comovements," *Journal of Money, Credit, and Banking*, 34 (2), 412–433. [1303,1305,1306,1330]

STOCKMAN, A. C. (1988): "Sectoral and National Aggregate Disturbances to Industrial Output in Seven European Countries," *Journal of Monetary Economics*, 21, 387–409. [1303,1306,1312]

THESMAR, D., AND M. THOENIG (2011): "Contrasting Trends in Firm Volatility," *American Economic Journal: Macroeconomics*, 3 (4), 143–180. [1307]

Dept. of Economics and Business, Universitat Pompeu Fabra, Ramon Trias Fargas 25-27, 08005 Barcelona, Spain, Barcelona GSE, CREI, and CEPR; julian.digiovanni@upf.edu,

Dept. of Economics, University of Michigan, 611 Tappan Street, Ann Arbor, MI 48104, U.S.A., NBER, and CEPR; alev@umich.edu,

and

Dept. of Economics, Ecole Polytechnique, Routed de Saclay, 91128 Palaiseau cedex, France and CEPR; isabelle.mejean@polytechnique.edu.

Manuscript received August, 2012; final revision received April, 2014.

A GLOBAL VIEW OF CROSS-BORDER MIGRATION

Julian di Giovanni
Universitat Pompeu Fabra
and Barcelona GSE

Andrei A. Levchenko
University of Michigan

Francesc Ortega
Queens College-CUNY

Abstract

This paper evaluates the global welfare impact of observed levels of migration using a quantitative multi-sector model of the world economy calibrated to aggregate and firm-level data. Our framework features cross-country labor productivity differences, international trade, remittances, and a heterogeneous workforce. We compare welfare under the observed levels of migration to a no-migration counterfactual. In the long run, natives in countries that received a lot of migration—such as Canada or Australia—are better off due to greater product variety available in consumption and as intermediate inputs. In the short run, the impact of migration on average welfare in these countries is close to zero, while the skilled and unskilled natives tend to experience welfare changes of opposite signs. The remaining natives in countries with large emigration flows—such as Jamaica or El Salvador—are also better off due to migration, but for a different reason: remittances. The welfare impact of observed levels of migration is substantial, at about 5% to 10% for the main receiving countries and about 10% in countries with large incoming remittances. (JEL: F12, F15, F22, F24)

1. Introduction

International migration has risen steadily over the last three decades. By the 2000s, substantial fractions of the total population in many receiving countries were foreign-born. For instance, immigrants account for 8%–12% of the population in several G7 countries such as the United States, the United Kingdom, and France, and some 20% of the population in other wealthy countries such as Australia, Canada, and New

The editor in charge of this paper was Fabrizio Zilibotti.

Acknowledgments: We are grateful to the editor, anonymous referees, Antonio Ciccone, Frédéric Docquier, Luca Opromolla, Giovanni Peri, and seminar and conference participants at various institutions for helpful suggestions, and to Lin Ma and Rishi Sharma for excellent research assistance. Di Giovanni is a Research Associate at CREI, and a Research Fellow of the CEPR. Levchenko is a Research Associate at NBER, and a Research Fellow of the CEPR.

E-mail: julian.digiovanni@upf.edu (di Giovanni); alev@umich.edu (Levchenko); fortega@qc.cuny.edu (Ortega)

Journal of the European Economic Association February 2015 13(1):168–202

DOI: 10.1111/jeea.12110

Zealand. By the same token, some developing countries have lost a substantial fraction of their population to emigration. Emigrants account for some 10% of the population of Mexico, and as much as 20%–30% in smaller countries such as El Salvador or Jamaica.

The sheer scale of the cross-border movements of people has led to a growing interest in understanding their welfare effects. However, compared to the attention paid to the welfare analysis of international trade, very few estimates of the welfare effects of international migration are available. This paper provides a quantitative assessment of the global welfare impact of the observed levels of migration on both origin and destination countries, taking explicitly into account the consequences of international trade and remittances. Our multi-country general equilibrium model is calibrated to match the world income distribution and world trade patterns. It incorporates several first-order features of the world economy that are important for obtaining reliable estimates of the welfare impact of migration. First, we calibrate labor productivity differences between and within countries. In order to develop reliable estimates of migrants' impact on the host economies, our framework accounts for a great deal of worker heterogeneity, with worker productivity varying by skill level, country of origin, and country of residence. In addition, we match the levels of remittances observed in the data. Remittances transfer some of the gains from the increased productivity of migrants back to the natives that remained in the home country.

Second, our model incorporates the insights of the recent literature on firm heterogeneity under monopolistic competition (e.g., Melitz 2003). In recent years, a great deal of evidence has shown that these models are highly successful at replicating both the key macro features (total trade flows, the gravity relationship) and key micro features (firm size distributions, systematically larger exporters) of the economy, making them especially suitable for quantitative analysis. Economically, the key mechanism linking migration and welfare in this framework is product variety. Inflows of immigrants increase market size, and thus the range of varieties available for consumption and as intermediate inputs. Importantly, in the presence of large labor productivity differences between countries, the impact of migration on equilibrium variety depends not only on changes in population, but also the size of the productivity gap between source and destination countries.

Third, we take explicit account of the role of goods trade in affecting the gains from migration. In our model an increase in a country's market size due to immigration will affect other countries through an increase in export variety. To capture the quantitative importance of this effect, the model features both traded and nontraded sectors with intermediate input linkages between the two, and matches the overall levels of goods trade relative to GDP. The model is solved on a sample of 60 developed and developing countries comprising some 98% of world GDP, taking into account all the multilateral trade relationships between them.

Finally, we distinguish between the short-run and the long-run impact of migration. In the short-run equilibrium, the set of potential varieties available in the economy is fixed, and thus it corresponds to the framework of Chaney (2008) and Eaton, Kortum, and Kramarz (2011). In this case, migration has an impact on product variety by affecting the entry and exit decisions of only the marginal firms (i.e., those near the productivity cutoff for operating a firm). Since these are the least productive firms in the economy, their economic impact is very limited. In the long-run equilibrium, the set of potential varieties will change in response to migration to dissipate net aggregate profits (free entry) as in Krugman (1980) and Melitz (2003). Because some of those new firms will be quite productive, they can have a large impact on welfare. Thus, the difference in the welfare impact of migration between the short and the long run depends crucially on the relative productivity of the marginal firms compared to the inframarginal ones. Our quantitative analysis calibrates the key parameters of the model that determine equilibrium variety in both the short and the long run: relative country size and the firm size distribution.[1]

The main use of our calibrated model is to compute welfare in the baseline under the observed levels of bilateral migration and in the counterfactual scenario in which global migration is undone. Our findings can be summarized as follows. In the long run, the average natives in practically every receiving country would have been worse off in the absence of migration, and this welfare loss increases in the observed share of the nonnative population. Natives in the countries with the largest stocks of immigrants relative to population (such as Australia, New Zealand, and Canada) have 5%–10% higher welfare under the current levels of migration compared to the no-migration counterfactual. This welfare effect is driven by the general equilibrium response of domestic variety. A lower population in the absence of migration implies a smaller equilibrium mass of varieties available in the home market, and thus lower per capita welfare.

In the short run, the welfare impact of immigration on the receiving countries is much smaller, at less than 0.5% on average, and not always positive. This is because the general equilibrium effect of increased variety is only of limited importance in the short run. At the same time, the welfare impacts of migration on the skilled and the unskilled are frequently of opposite signs, and tend to be an order of magnitude larger than the overall impact. Thus, in the short run, the main welfare impact of migration on receiving countries is distributional, and driven by the changes in the relative supply of skills associated with migration. This distributional impact is limited in the long run, as the increased variety effect predominates and the welfare changes of the two skill groups tend to be similar.

For the sending countries, the welfare impact on the staying natives depends on a tradeoff. Symmetrically to the main migration receiving countries, these source countries would ceteris paribus be better off without emigration because a larger labor force implies greater variety in production and consumption. However, absent emigration, there would be no remittances. For countries such as El Salvador or the

1. Our quantitative framework features a (long-run) scale effect. That is, other things equal, a larger labor force increases per capita welfare in the long run. Online Appendix B.3 presents a detailed treatment of both the relevance and the quantitative importance of the scale effect in our model. First, it reviews the existing empirical literature on the scale effect, and provides a comparison of the size and nature of the scale effect implied by our model to the available empirical estimates. Though our model is not calibrated to match the observed magnitude of the scale effect, the model-implied scale effect is in line with the existing empirical estimates. Second, it reports alternative welfare results under a weaker scale effect corresponding to the bottom of the range of estimates found in the literature.

Philippines, where remittances account for more than 10% of GDP, the latter effect dominates and the average native stayer is about 10% better off under the current levels of migration. Underlying these results is the fact that the typical migrant moves from a low to a high TFP region, leading to an overall increase in the efficiency units of labor worldwide. Part of the welfare benefit of that reallocation is enjoyed by the native stayers through remittances. However, the remittance effect is not always larger than the general equilibrium variety effect. Some important emigration countries, such as Mexico, Trinidad and Tobago, and Turkey, would actually be 1%–5% better off in the no-migration counterfactual.

For the sending countries, the short-run impact tends to be similar to the long-run impact. This is because for these countries welfare changes are driven primarily by the loss of remittances, which is the first-order effect in both the short and the long run. By the same token, the distributional impact of migration is also limited in the sending countries, as the impact of emigration on the skill premium is small compared to the remittance effect.

The finding that the receiving countries are better off with immigration may seem unappealing because it appears at odds with the widespread opposition to immigration in high-income countries. However, observed opposition to migration is not evidence against our approach. First of all, even within the model, the receiving countries are better off only in the long run. In the short run, there is nothing in our model that guarantees gains from immigration. Thus, it could be that political opposition is driven by the short-run considerations. Second, our framework features distributional effects, that are especially pronounced in the short run. In many countries, the unskilled experience short-run welfare losses due to immigration, and thus would be expected to oppose it.[2] Finally, the fact that restrictive migration policies are observed in the data is by no means evidence that those policies are welfare improving, much less optimal. Indeed, there is generally no presumption that observed economic policies are optimal, in any area of economic activity.

The seminal early treatment of the welfare consequences of migration is Berry and Soligo (1969). The existing literature on the quantitative welfare impact of migration has focused almost exclusively on the implications of cross-country labor productivity differences in a neoclassical framework with a fixed set of goods. Hamilton and Whalley (1984), Klein and Ventura (2007, 2009), Benhabib and Jovanovic (2012), and Docquier, Machado, and Sekkat (2012) develop analyses of this type in one-sector models without international trade. Davis and Weinstein (2002) and Kennan (2013) investigate the welfare effects of migration in the presence of labor-augmenting productivity differences in Ricardian and Heckscher–Ohlin models of trade, respectively. The key consequence of employing a neoclassical framework is that

2. For work on the determinants of immigration restrictions see Benhabib (1996), Ortega (2005, 2010), Facchini, Mayda, and Mishra (2011), or Facchini and Steinhardt (2011). For empirical work on individual attitudes toward immigration see Mayda (2006) and Facchini and Mayda (2009), and Ortega and Polavieja (2012) in the European context.

immigration always weakly reduces the welfare of the native workers (i.e., suppliers of the labor input) in the receiving countries.

Our framework incorporates the driving force in these studies—labor productivity differences. The main departure of our analysis from the neoclassical migration literature is endogenous product variety. This is the key feature qualitatively as well as quantitatively, because it opens the possibility that immigration may improve the native workers' welfare. To our knowledge, the only existing study of migration with endogenous product variety is by Iranzo and Peri (2009a), who explore migration between Eastern and Western Europe in a two-country model. Our paper shares with Iranzo and Peri (2009a) the emphasis on market size and endogenous variety, but differs from it in several important respects. First and foremost, our model features bilateral remittances, which we show to be crucial for evaluating the overall welfare effect of migration in a number of sending countries. While both studies find that welfare in the emigration country is higher in the migration equilibrium, the mechanism is different: in Iranzo and Peri (2009a) the main reason is the increase in imported varieties, in our analysis it is mainly due to remittances. Second, our framework is implemented on 60 countries, and incorporates many important aspects of the world economy, such as heterogeneous country-pair specific trade costs, a nontraded sector, and two-way input–output linkages, among others. This allows for both greater realism, as well as a range of outcomes on how migration affects a wide variety of countries depending on their characteristics. And third, our analysis distinguishes between the short-run and the long-run effects of migration.

More broadly, our paper complements the small but growing empirical literature on the firm-level responses to migration and remittances. Lewis (2011) finds that unskilled immigration led to significantly lower rates of adoption of new automation techniques that substitute for unskilled labor. Using data on the universe of German firms, Dustmann and Glitz (2014) find that migration led to an increase in the size of firms that use the abundant factor more intensively, to a greater adoption of production technologies that rely on the more abundant factor, and to firm entry. Yang (2008) finds a positive effect of remittances on the number of household entrepreneurs in the Philippines. Our analysis shares with these papers the emphasis on the interaction between migration and firm decisions, but focuses on the general equilibrium perspective in which migration affects firm entry and exit through changes in overall size of the market and the labor force.

The rest of the paper is organized as follows. Section 2 introduces the migration and remittance data sources, and describes the basic patterns. Section 3 presents the theoretical framework, while Section 4 discusses the quantitative implementation of the model economy. Section 5 presents counterfactual experiments and the main welfare results. Section 6 discusses extensions and sensitivity, and Section 7 concludes.

2. Migration and Remittances: Data Sources and Basic Patterns

To construct the labor force disaggregated by skill level, origin, and destination country we rely on two sources: the aggregate migration stocks for the year 2006 from the OECD International Migration Database and the data for the year 2000 on the labor force for each country in the world by education level, origin, and destination produced by Docquier, Lowell, and Marfouk (2009) and Docquier et al. (2010a). The OECD International Migration Database contains information on the stocks of immigrants by both destination and origin country. We use data for 2006, the most recent year these data are available with comprehensive coverage. An important feature of these data is that they only contain information on 26 OECD destination countries. Thus, while we have data on nearly all origin countries, we only have immigration information for rich country destinations. As a result, strictly speaking, our counterfactual exercise analyzes the consequences of undoing migration to developed countries. Any migration to developing countries will be left unchanged.[3]

The shares of skilled individuals among migrants in 2000 (for ages 25 and above) by origin and destination country are sourced from Docquier et al. (2010a), and the shares of skilled among the native stayers from Docquier, Lowell, and Marfouk (2009). These shares are then applied to the 2006 aggregate migration stocks for each origin–destination country pair. Skilled individuals are those that completed at least one year of college.[4] Remittances data are sourced from Ratha and Shaw (2007).

To calibrate the parameters governing the relative demand for skilled labor in production in each country we estimate skill premia following the approach of Docquier, Özden, and Peri (2010b). First, we use the Barro and Lee (2010) data to compute the average years of education in the two skill groups (individuals with some college education and individuals without) for each country in our sample for the year 2005.[5] Second, to compute the country skill premium we multiply the gap in average years of schooling between the two groups by the country-specific return to a year of schooling. Hendricks (2004) has collected Mincerian returns to schooling for a large set of countries that were estimated from micro data.[6] The median return per

3. The OECD DIOC-E database contains information on immigrants to both developing and developed countries. The disadvantage of these data is that they are only available up to the year 2000. We made the choice to use the most recent data, at the cost of not being able to evaluate migration into the non-OECD. The reason we took this route was the large migration inflows experienced by the European countries post-2000. For Europe in particular, using data for 2000 would mean that we are missing a large share of current migration. In the 2000 data, the receiving countries in our analysis account for 47% of the global stock of cross-border migrants. The new borders erected after the collapse of the Soviet Union are partly responsible for the high observed migration into the non-OECD. Excluding the former Soviet Union our receiving countries account for 55% of the global migrant stock.

4. There is a small discrepancy in how the two datasets define a skilled individual. Namely, a skilled native stayer is defined in Docquier, Lowell, and Marfouk (2009) as someone who completed college, rather than had some college. We do not believe this discrepancy to have a material impact on the results.

5. There is a great deal of variation in the average years of schooling among the unskilled workers across countries. In the United States the average years of schooling among individuals that did not attend college was 10.95. The cross-country variation in this variable is from 1.01 (Mali) to 12.80 years (Czech Republic). By contrast, among the skilled the cross-country variation in the years of schooling is much smaller, ranging from 14.15 to 15.94 in the Barro and Lee (2010) data.

6. We try to use estimates based on 1995 data, which is the most recent period reported by Hendricks (2004). If the Mincerian coefficient estimate is not available for a country we follow Docquier, Özden, and Peri (2010b) and impute that value on the basis of estimates from neighboring countries with similar levels of income per capita.

year of schooling in these data is 7.3%, and the 10th and 90th percentiles are 4.2% and 12.6%. The 10th, 50th, and 90th percentiles for the wage skill premium we obtain are 26%, 43%, and 106%.

We carry out the analysis on the sample of the largest 49 countries in the world by total GDP, plus a selection of eleven smaller countries that have experienced migration outflows of 10% or more of the native labor force. These 60 countries together cover 98% of world GDP. There is a 61st, rest-of-the-world category. We exclude the entrepôt economies of Hong Kong and Singapore, both of which have total trade well in excess of their GDP due to significant re-exporting activity, and place them into the rest-of-the-world category. The sources and details for the other data used in the quantitative exercise are described when we discuss the calibration.

Table 1 lists the OECD countries in the sample and reports the share of immigrants (foreign-born), the share of emigrants, the counterfactual population change, the size of net remittances relative to GDP, and the share of skilled workers among stayers, immigrants, and emigrants. These are the countries for which data on immigrant stocks for 2006 are available.[7] Table 2 reports the shares of emigrants and remittances as a share of GDP for the non-OECD countries. The population change in the counterfactual in the non-OECD coincides with the share of emigrants.

Several points are worth noting. First, the data reveal a great deal of dispersion in immigration and emigration shares. At one extreme there are countries such as Australia and New Zealand, where 25% of the population are foreign-born. At the other, El Salvador, Trinidad and Tobago, and Jamaica display emigration shares in the 20%–30% range.[8] Second, some of the OECD countries have large gross stocks of both immigrants and emigrants. As a result, if migration had never taken place their population would be roughly the same (the third column). Ireland is the clearest example: its share of immigrants is 13%, but the share of emigrants is 16%. In a world without migration, its population would only be 3% higher.

The table also reports the net remittances in each country as a share of GDP. Negative values mean that a country is a net sender of remittances. Clearly, most OECD countries send more remittances than they receive, but the total net remittances are only a small share of GDP, ranging from −1% (Australia) to +1% (Portugal). In contrast, remittances are large relative to GDP for several non-OECD countries. For instance, Colombia, India, Mexico, and Nigeria report remittances of 3% of GDP. However, these are small compared to Jamaica (20%), Serbia and Montenegro (19.1%), El Salvador (17.8%), the Philippines (15.5%) and the Dominican Republic (14.3%). Hence, for these countries it will be important to take remittances into account when evaluating the welfare impact of migration.

7. Throughout the paper we use the shorthand "OECD" to refer to the group of the 26 countries for which immigration data are available in our database, and "non-OECD" to describe the rest of the country sample. The "OECD" group is predominantly the wealthy, net immigration countries. Formally, the Organization for Economic Cooperation and Development has additional member countries, such as Mexico and Turkey.

8. Once again, for these countries we are reporting data on emigration to OECD countries only. In the counterfactual these countries only experience a return of their emigrants, but not the exit of the immigrants residing in these countries.

TABLE 1. OECD countries: migrant stocks, skill composition, and remittances.

Country	Share immigrants	Share emigrants	Pop. change in counterfactuals	Remittances /GDP	Share skilled stayers	Share skilled immigrants	Share skilled emigrants
Australia	0.242	0.015	−0.226	−0.009	0.29	0.45	0.55
Austria	0.108	0.046	−0.062	0.001	0.23	0.12	0.33
Belgium	0.108	0.030	−0.078	0.014	0.28	0.19	0.34
Canada	0.185	0.032	−0.154	−0.016	0.49	0.58	0.60
Czech Rep.	0.023	0.026	0.003	0.005	0.10	0.11	0.34
Denmark	0.058	0.038	−0.019	0.001	0.21	0.17	0.41
Finland	0.034	0.053	0.019	0.002	0.26	0.23	0.27
France	0.076	0.017	−0.060	−0.001	0.24	0.16	0.33
Germany	0.064	0.033	−0.031	−0.004	0.25	0.21	0.39
Greece	0.014	0.066	0.052	−0.002	0.15	0.15	0.20
Hungary	0.034	0.030	−0.005	−0.003	0.12	0.13	0.39
Ireland	0.129	0.156	0.026	−0.007	0.17	0.40	0.33
Italy	0.025	0.042	0.018	−0.002	0.18	0.15	0.16
Japan	0.015	0.005	−0.010	−0.001	0.23	0.28	0.61
Korea, Rep.	0.011	0.038	0.028	−0.001	0.25	0.37	0.50
Netherlands	0.101	0.047	−0.055	−0.002	0.21	0.22	0.43
New Zealand	0.251	0.128	−0.122	0.003	0.21	0.41	0.48
Norway	0.086	0.030	−0.056	−0.002	0.21	0.28	0.38
Poland	0.001	0.046	0.045	0.012	0.11	0.13	0.37
Portugal	0.023	0.134	0.111	0.010	0.12	0.18	0.10
Slovak Rep.	0.005	0.041	0.036	0.006	0.11	0.27	0.18
Spain	0.116	0.016	−0.100	−0.003	0.15	0.18	0.18
Sweden	0.106	0.022	−0.083	−0.005	0.17	0.25	0.46
Switzerland	0.137	0.035	−0.103	−0.007	0.20	0.21	0.40
United Kingdom	0.084	0.060	−0.024	−0.003	0.18	0.34	0.46
United States	0.119	0.003	−0.116	−0.008	0.52	0.42	0.58

Notes: This table presents the developed country sample, for which inward migration data are available for 2006. The first column presents the percentage of foreign-born in total population. The second column presents the share of emigrants from each country to the receiving countries in the sample, as a share of the remaining population. The third column presents the percentage change in the population if there were no migration. This is the percentage change in the population evaluated in the counterfactual. The remaining columns report remittances as a share of GDP (negative numbers signify net outflows of remittances), and the shares of skilled among the native stayers, immigrants, and emigrants. Data sources and variable definitions are described in detail in the text.

TABLE 2. Non-OECD countries: migrant stocks, skill composition, and remittances.

Country	Share emigrants	Remittances /GDP	Share skilled stayers	Share skilled emigrants
Algeria	0.025	0.023	0.062	0.147
Argentina	0.012	−0.004	0.201	0.408
Belarus	0.005	0.001	0.201	0.172
Brazil	0.005	0.005	0.084	0.328
Bulgaria	0.037	0.082	0.189	0.234
Chile	0.016	−0.002	0.158	0.403
China	0.003	0.012	0.026	0.281
Colombia	0.023	0.034	0.099	0.317
Croatia	0.103	0.020	0.094	0.199
Dominican Rep.	0.097	0.143	0.141	0.256
Ecuador	0.068	0.050	0.160	0.266
Egypt, Arab Rep.	0.004	0.042	0.104	0.271
El Salvador	0.190	0.178	0.107	0.198
India	0.003	0.030	0.047	0.318
Indonesia	0.002	0.007	0.050	0.182
Iran, Islamic Rep.	0.011	0.006	0.067	0.487
Israel	0.021	−0.023	0.241	0.235
Jamaica	0.317	0.200	0.040	0.420
Malaysia	0.010	−0.006	0.077	0.352
Mexico	0.107	0.031	0.111	0.148
Nigeria	0.003	0.031	0.028	0.313
Pakistan	0.005	0.044	0.025	0.231
Philippines	0.030	0.155	0.159	0.545
Romania	0.070	0.058	0.087	0.334
Russian Fed.	0.008	0.001	0.202	0.309
Saudi Arabia	0.004	−0.049	0.093	0.301
Serbia and Mont.	0.106	0.191	0.082	0.230
South Africa	0.011	0.001	0.098	0.510
Thailand	0.006	0.002	0.110	0.296
Trinidad and Tob.	0.179	0.006	0.099	0.494
Turkey	0.038	−0.001	0.081	0.092
Ukraine	0.019	−0.010	0.162	0.222
UAE	0.003	–	0.031	0.206
Venezuela	0.011	−0.004	0.185	0.521
Rest of World	0.011	0.021	0.095	0.118

Notes: This table presents the developing country sample, for which only outward migration data to the developed countries are available for 2006. Thus, the population change in the counterfactual coincides with the share of emigrants. The second column presents the share of emigrants from each country to the receiving countries in the sample relative the remaining population. The third column presents the percentage change in the population if there were no migration. This is the percentage change in the population evaluated in the counterfactual. The last column reports net remittances as a share of GDP (negative numbers signify net outflows of remittances). Data sources and variable definitions are described in detail in the text.

Across all origin–destination pairs, the share of skilled is 0.25, with a standard deviation of 0.24. There is large heterogeneity in the share of skilled among immigrants relative to the natives of the host country. For instance, US immigrants are relatively unskilled, by our measure of educational attainment: 52% of US-born stayers are skilled, compared to 42% of immigrants into the United States. By contrast, in Canada immigrants are relatively skilled (58%) compared to native stayers (49%).

3. Theoretical Framework

Our framework augments an otherwise standard multicountry heterogeneous firm model of production and trade with three elements that are crucial for a global quantitative assessment of the gains from migration: cross-country labor productivity differences, worker heterogeneity (across skills as well as between natives and immigrants), and remittances. We consider a monopolistically competitive setup with endogenous product variety and fixed costs of production and exporting. Production uses skilled and unskilled labor and intermediate inputs.

3.1. Preferences, Welfare, and Love for Variety

The world is comprised of C countries, indexed by $i, j = 1, \ldots, C$. In each country there are two broad sectors, the tradeable T and the nontradeable N. In country i, a consumer with income y_i maximizes

$$\max_{\{y_i^N(k), y_i^T(k)\}} \left(\int_{J_i^N} y_i^N(k)^{\frac{\varepsilon_N - 1}{\varepsilon_N}} dk \right)^{\alpha \frac{\varepsilon_N}{\varepsilon_N - 1}} \left(\int_{J_i^T} y_i^T(k)^{\frac{\varepsilon_T - 1}{\varepsilon_T}} dk \right)^{(1-\alpha) \frac{\varepsilon_T}{\varepsilon_T - 1}}$$

$$\text{subj. to: } \int_{J_i^N} p_i^N(k)\, y_i^N(k)\, dk + \int_{J_i^T} p_i^T(k)\, y_i^T(k)\, dk = y_i,$$

where $y_i^s(k)$ is consumption of good k belonging to sector $s = N, T$ in country i, $p_i^s(k)$ is the price of this good, J_i^s is the mass of varieties available in sector s in country i coming from all countries, and ε_s is the elasticity of substitution between varieties in s. Standard steps yield an expression for welfare—that is, the indirect utility function—of an individual with income y_i living in country i,

$$W_i(y_i) = \frac{y_i}{\left(P_i^N\right)^{\alpha} \left(P_i^T\right)^{1-\alpha}}, \tag{1}$$

where P_i^s is the ideal price index in sector $s = N, T$ in country i,

$$P_i^s = \left[\int_{J_i^s} p_i^s(k)^{1-\varepsilon_s} dk \right]^{\frac{1}{1-\varepsilon_s}}. \tag{2}$$

Welfare is thus simply equivalent to real income. In our model, an individual's nominal income y_i may be composed of (i) labor income, (ii) profits of firms, and (iii) remittances, though some of these may be zero in some cases. Thus migration will have an impact on welfare through nominal income to the extent that it affects any of these three terms for an individual, either directly or through general equilibrium effects.

Welfare falls in the consumption price level $(P_i^N)^\alpha (P_i^T)^{1-\alpha}$. We assume that $\varepsilon_s > 1, s = N, T$ (Dixit and Stiglitz 1977). The key consequence of this assumption is that preferences exhibit love for variety: holding nominal expenditure and individual goods prices fixed, the agent attains higher utility when the set of goods J_i^N and J_i^T available for consumption increases. Thus, to the extent that migration affects the equilibrium set of varieties available in economy i, it will have a welfare impact through that channel as well.

In our framework, incomes differ across individuals within each country. However, preferences are identical and homothetic, and thus admit a representative consumer. Total income Y_i in country i is the sum of labor income $w_i L_i$, net profits (if any) in the two sectors $\Pi_i^N + \Pi_i^T$, and net remittances received from abroad R_i: $Y_i = w_i L_i + \Pi_i^N + \Pi_i^T + R_i$. Since consumer preferences are Cobb–Douglas in the CES aggregates of N and T, it is well known that consumption expenditure on sector N is equal to αY_i, and on T sector, $(1-\alpha)Y_i$.

3.2. Migration, Productivity, and Labor Force Composition

Each country's labor force is composed of natives and immigrants, who can be unskilled or skilled, indexed by $e = \ell, h$ respectively. Denote by N_{ji}^e the number of workers with skill level e born in country i that live in country j (throughout the paper, we adopt the convention that the first subscript denotes the destination country, and the second subscript, the source). As in Trefler (1993, 1995), the effective labor endowment is a combination of the number of people that live in a country and their efficiency units. We build on this approach by taking explicit account of migration. Workers of skill level e born in country i and working in country j have A_{ji}^e efficiency units of labor. Skilled and unskilled labor are imperfect substitutes in production. Specifically, the total effective labor in country j, L_j, is given by the CES aggregate

$$L_j = \left[\left(\sum_{i=1}^{C} A_{ji}^\ell N_{ji}^\ell \right)^{\frac{\sigma-1}{\sigma}} + \zeta_j \left(\sum_{i=1}^{C} A_{ji}^h N_{ji}^h \right)^{\frac{\sigma-1}{\sigma}} \right]^{\frac{\sigma}{\sigma-1}}, \tag{3}$$

where σ is the elasticity of substitution between skilled and unskilled labor, ζ_j captures the relative importance of skilled labor in production, and, of course, the endowments of labor of each type include the native workers and their efficiency, $A_{jj}^e N_{jj}^e$, $e = \ell, h$.

This approach to modeling the labor force is flexible enough to capture a number of features that are important for evaluating the impact of migration. First and foremost, the framework accommodates the (large) observed cross-country labor productivity differences through differences in the A_{ji}^e. Second, skilled workers are more productive than unskilled workers. And third, conditional on skill level, immigrants may differ from native workers in how many efficiency units of labor they possess. To streamline notation and link the productivity parameters more transparently to observed wages, it is useful to denote the *skilled–unskilled productivity gap* among natives by

$$\frac{A_{jj}^{h}}{A_{jj}^{\ell}} \equiv \mu_j \geq 1, \tag{4}$$

and *native–immigrant productivity gaps* for immigrants of origin $i \neq j$ and skill level e by

$$\frac{A_{ji}^{e}}{A_{jj}^{e}} \equiv \varphi_{ji}^{e}. \tag{5}$$

The latter feature allows us to account for native–immigrant wage differences conditional on educational attainment. The quantitative implementation uses several empirically relevant parameterizations of the productivity differential φ_{ji}^{e}, that can capture a number of reasons for migrant–native productivity differences, such as imperfect skill transferability or selection into migration.

Combining (3), (4), and (5), L_j can be rewritten as

$$L_j = A_{jj}\left[\left(\sum_{i=1}^{C}\varphi_{ji}^{\ell}N_{ji}^{\ell}\right)^{\frac{\sigma-1}{\sigma}} + \zeta_j\left(\mu_j\sum_{i=1}^{C}\varphi_{ji}^{h}N_{ji}^{h}\right)^{\frac{\sigma-1}{\sigma}}\right]^{\frac{\sigma}{\sigma-1}}, \tag{6}$$

where to simplify notation we relabelled the unskilled native productivity as $A_{jj}^{\ell} = A_{jj}$, which can be interpreted as the economywide productivity level.

In this framework, immigrants are not the same as natives in two ways that will condition the impact of immigration. First, the share of skilled among immigrants can differ from the share of skilled among the natives. Since the skilled and the unskilled are imperfect substitutes in production, the skill composition of the immigrant population will have an effect on both the aggregate supply of labor, and on the relative wages of the skilled compared to the unskilled. Second, immigrants may have different productivity than the natives within the same skill category. This distinction has an impact on how much a given stock of foreign-born individuals changes the effective supply of labor of a particular skill level.

The baseline framework makes a number of simplifying assumptions, some of which will be relaxed in the extensions. First, immigrant and native labor of the same skill level are perfect substitutes. Online Appendix B.2 develops an extension in which immigrants and natives are imperfectly substitutable in production (Manacorda, Manning, and Wadsworth 2012; Ottaviano and Peri 2012), and shows that the main results are robust. Second, the productivity terms A_{ji}^{e}, while calibrated to data, are exogenous. Online Appendix B.4 relaxes this assumption and allows worker productivity to be a function of the share of skilled in the population (e.g., Jones 2002).

3.3. Technology

Importantly in our framework, the sets of available goods J_i^T and J_i^N will differ across countries due to trade costs, and will be affected by migration. The market structure is monopolistic competition as in Melitz (2003). Each country j is populated by a mass n_j^s of entrepreneurs in sector s. Each entrepreneur k in each sector $s = N, T$ and $j = 1, \ldots, C$ has the ability to produce a unique variety and thus has some market power. Productivity is heterogeneous: entrepreneur k needs $a(k)$ input bundles to produce one unit of its good (thus more productive firms have *lower* $a(k)$). Since each entrepreneur is able to produce only one good with a particular productivity, we use the terms "entrepreneur" and "project" interchangeably.

Each entrepreneur in country j and sector s must incur a fixed cost f_{jj}^s to start production, and as a result not all entrepreneurs decide to produce. We reserve the term "firm" for those entrepreneurs that actually undertake production. In sector T, to start exporting from country j to country i, a firm must pay a fixed cost f_{ij}, and an iceberg per-unit cost of $\tau_{ij} > 1$, with the iceberg cost of domestic sales normalized to one: $\tau_{jj} = 1$. We assume that trade costs are infinite in the nontraded sector, and thus firms in sector N only sell domestically.

Production uses skilled labor, unskilled labor, and intermediates from sectors N and T. The production function is Cobb–Douglas in the labor, T, and N composites. The labor composite is a CES aggregate of skilled and unskilled workers as in equation (3). The sector $s = N, T$ composites are CES aggregates of sector s varieties available in the country. The minimized cost of one unit of the input bundle in country j is given by

$$c_j^s = w_j^{\beta_s} \left[\left(P_j^N\right)^{\eta_s} \left(P_j^T\right)^{1-\eta_s} \right]^{1-\beta_s}, \tag{7}$$

where w_j is the composite wage (i.e., the price of one unit of L) in country j, and P_j^s is the price of sector s CES composite, given by equation (2). Parameters β_s and η_s correspond, respectively, to the share of labor in total sales and the share of nontradeable inputs in total input usage in each sector s.

Thus, firm k in sector s from country j has a marginal cost $\tau_{ij} c_j^s a(k)$ of serving market i. Firms and consumers in country i have a demand for an individual variety k from sector s that is given by

$$x_i^s(k) = \frac{X_i^s}{\left(P_i^s\right)^{1-\varepsilon_s}} p_i^s(k)^{-\varepsilon_s}, \tag{8}$$

where X_i^s denotes the total spending—final plus intermediate—on sector s in country i.

Productivity heterogeneity combined with fixed costs of production and trade imply that not all firms will decide to serve all markets. As is well known, profit maximization yields a price that is a constant markup $\varepsilon_s/(\varepsilon_s - 1)$ over marginal cost, and the total ex-post variable profits from selling to market i are a constant multiple $1/\varepsilon_s$ of revenue. Given the price level and total spending, there is a cutoff unit input requirement a_{ij}^s

above which firms in country j do not serve market i. This cutoff is found as the unit input requirement at which the firm obtains zero profits from serving market i, and is given by

$$a_{ij}^{s} = \frac{\varepsilon_s - 1}{\varepsilon_s} \frac{P_i^s}{\tau_{ij} c_j^s} \left(\frac{X_i^s}{\varepsilon_s c_j^s f_{ij}^s} \right)^{\frac{1}{\varepsilon_s - 1}}. \tag{9}$$

We adopt the standard assumption that firm productivity in sector s, $1/a$, follows a Pareto (b_s, θ_s) distribution: $\Pr(1/a < y) = 1 - (b_s/y)^{\theta_s}$, where b_s is the minimum value labor productivity can take, and θ_s regulates dispersion. It is then straightforward to show that the unit input requirement, a, has a distribution function $G(a) = (b_s a)^{\theta_s}$. Under this distributional assumption, we can combine equations (2) and (9) to derive expressions for the price indices:

$$\begin{aligned}
P_i^s &= \left\{ \sum_{j=1}^{C} \int_{J_{ij}^s} \left[\frac{\varepsilon_s}{\varepsilon_s - 1} \tau_{ij}^s c_j^s a(k) \right]^{1-\varepsilon_s} dk \right\}^{\frac{1}{1-\varepsilon_s}} \\
&= \left(\sum_{j=1}^{C} n_j^s \int_0^{a_{ij}^s} \left[\frac{\varepsilon_s}{\varepsilon_s - 1} \tau_{ij}^s c_j^s a \right]^{1-\varepsilon_s} dG(a) \right)^{\frac{1}{1-\varepsilon_s}} \\
&= \frac{1}{b_s} \left[\frac{\theta_s}{\theta_s - (\varepsilon_s - 1)} \right]^{-\frac{1}{\theta_s}} \frac{\varepsilon_s}{\varepsilon_s - 1} \left(\frac{X_i^s}{\varepsilon_s} \right)^{-\frac{\theta_s - (\varepsilon_s - 1)}{\theta_s(\varepsilon_s - 1)}} \\
&\quad \times \left(\sum_{j=1}^{C} n_j^s \left(\tau_{ij}^s c_j^s \right)^{-\theta_s} \left(c_j^s f_{ij}^s \right)^{-\frac{\theta_s - (\varepsilon_s - 1)}{\varepsilon_s - 1}} \right)^{-\frac{1}{\theta_s}},
\end{aligned} \tag{10}$$

where J_{ij}^s is the set of varieties from country j that gets exported to country i.[9]

Trade is not balanced because of remittances. Let R_i denote the net remittances *received* by country i, which can be positive (for countries receiving remittances), or negative (for countries sending them).[10] Remittance-receiving countries will be able to afford imports above the value of their exports, while the opposite will be true for countries with negative net remittances.

9. It is understood that in the nontraded sector $\tau_{ij}^N = \infty \; \forall i \neq j$, and thus the summations are in effect over one nonzero element, $j = i$.

10. Of course, for the world as a whole, remittances sum to zero: $\sum_i R_i = 0$. The data on remittances used in what follows to implement the model satisfy this requirement.

3.4. Short-Run and Long-Run Equilibria

In assessing the welfare impact of migration, we consider two types of equilibria. The two equilibria differ in their assumptions on the mass of projects n_i^s in each country and sector.

The short-run equilibrium assumes that the set of projects n_i^s is fixed in each country and sector, as in Chaney (2008) and Eaton, Kortum, and Kramarz (2011), and thus it cannot adjust to changes in the labor force. A *short-run monopolistically competitive equilibrium* is a set of prices $\{w_i, P_i^N, P_i^T\}_{i=1}^C$, and factor allocations such that (i) consumers maximize utility; (ii) firms maximize profits; and (iii) all goods and factor markets clear, given country endowments L_i and n_i^s.

In the long-run equilibrium, the set of projects n_i^s is an equilibrium outcome that responds to changing economic conditions, in our case migration. Each country has a potentially infinite number of entrepreneurs (projects) with zero outside option. In order to become an entrepreneur, an agent must pay an "exploration" cost f_E. Upon paying this cost, the entrepreneur k discovers her productivity, indexed by a unit input requirement $a(k)$, and develops an ability to produce a unique variety of N or T valued by consumers and other firms. The equilibrium number of projects n_i^s is then pinned down by the familiar free entry condition in each sector and each country, as in Krugman (1980) and Melitz (2003). A *long-run monopolistically competitive equilibrium* is a set of prices $\{w_i, P_i^N, P_i^T\}_{i=1}^C$, equilibrium masses of projects $\{n_i^N, n_i^T\}_{i=1}^C$, and factor allocations such that (i) consumers maximize utility; (ii) firms maximize profits; (iii) all goods and factor markets clear; and (iv) the net profits in the economy equal zero, given country endowments L_i $\forall i$.

Online Appendix A.1 presents the complete equations defining both types of equilibria.

3.5. Mechanisms

Immigration into country i increases L_i. In addition to its impact on nominal wages, immigration will affect the natives' welfare by changing equilibrium product variety. The vectors of n_j^s and the array of cutoffs (9) together determine the set of varieties offered in each country.[11] An increase in the set of varieties available in country i implies a lower price level and, other things equal, higher utility/real income. Consumers benefit directly from the variety-induced reduction in the price level, as well as indirectly through cheaper intermediate inputs available to firms.

However, in the presence of firm heterogeneity not all varieties are equally valuable: an unproductive variety (higher $a(k)$) raises welfare by less than a more productive one. Thus, changes in equilibrium variety due to movements in the a_{ij}^s have a smaller welfare impact than those coming from changes in the n_j^s. This is because movements

11. For instance, the measure of *domestic* varieties available in sector s in country i is equal to $n_i^s G(a_{ii}^s)$. Of course, the total variety in the T sector is the sum of domestic and imported varieties.

in the a^s_{ij} correspond to entry/exit of the least productive firms in the economy, whereas movements in the n^s_j result in entry/exit along the entire firm size distribution.

In this respect, the critical difference between the long run and the short run is that in the long run, the n^s_j will change in response to migration. In the short run, the set of projects n^s_j is fixed. However, even in the short run the set of *actual* firms that serve the market—and thus the equilibrium product variety in the economy—will still change due to migration. This is because generically, not all projects are implemented in equilibrium, and migration changes the cutoffs a^s_{ii}/a^s_{ij} for producing and exporting. Entry and exit do occur in the short run, but they are confined to the marginal firms, which are the least productive in the economy.

By contrast, in the long run entry/exit of firms will occur along the entire productivity distribution, rather than only among the least productive firms. A well-known property of monopolistic competition models with free entry is that n^s_i increases in L_i: larger countries have a greater set of projects.[12] Migration thus affects welfare in the long run by changing n^s_i. Natives in countries that end up with larger L_i because of immigration will be better off, all else equal, because immigration will lead to greater equilibrium variety (see the expressions for the price indices (10)).

International trade will mitigate this effect because changes in the availability of foreign varieties also have a welfare impact. For instance, suppose that country i loses workers to country j. As a result, product variety will fall in i and rise in j.[13] From equation (10), it is clear that an increase in foreign n^T_j will also have a positive impact on welfare in country i due to an increase in the set of varieties imported from j. However, due to trade costs increases in foreign n^T_j are less valuable for country i than increases in its own n^T_i and n^N_i. Thus, while greater imported variety will counteract the impact of migration on domestically available variety, it will not do so fully, and the size of this mitigation effect is ultimately a quantitative question. We answer it in what follows by calibrating the size of the nontraded sector and the trade costs in the traded sector, and by comparing the main results to an alternative counterfactual exercise in which the trade channel is turned off.

By contrast, input–output linkages embodied in the cost function (7) will raise the welfare impact of changes in domestically available varieties, and will thus amplify the welfare impact of migration. The magnitude of this effect is a quantitative question, and thus we calibrate the parameters β_s and η_s that regulate the strength of input–output linkages based on observed Input–Output tables.

Finally, though capital is not explicitly in the model, one can follow the interpretation suggested by Ghironi and Melitz (2005) and Bergin and Corsetti (2008) that the set of projects available to entrepreneurs is a form of the capital endowment.

12. While the full-fledged, multisector model with unbalanced trade in this paper cannot be used to show this relationship analytically, di Giovanni and Levchenko (2012, 2013) show the positive relationship between L_i and n^s_i in somewhat simpler models with symmetric countries.

13. The exact change in variety in each country will depend on the labor productivity parameters A_{ii} and A_{jj}. If we assume that the origin country has lower labor productivity than the destination—as is typically the case—then there may be a net increase in worldwide product variety.

TABLE 3. Calibrated parameter values.

Parameter	Baseline	Source
σ	3	Ottaviano and Peri (2012)
ε^s	6	Anderson and van Wincoop (2004)
θ^s	5.3	Axtell (2001): $\theta/(\varepsilon - 1) = 1.06$
α	0.65	Uy, Yi, and Zhang (2013)
$\{\beta_N, \beta_T\}$	$\{0.65, 0.35\}$	1997 US Benchmark Input–Output Table
$\{\eta_N, \eta_T\}$	$\{0.77, 0.35\}$	
τ_{ij}	2.30	Helpman, Melitz, and Rubinstein (2008)
f_{ii}^s	14.24	The World Bank (2007); normalizing $f_{US,US}$
f_{ij}	7.20	so that nearly all firms the US produce
f_E	34.0	To match 7,000,000 firms in the United States (US Economic Census)

Notes: The details of how these parameters are chosen are described in Online Appendix A.2.

Similarly, the creation of new firms is a form of capital investment. This interpretation is natural in the sense that these projects are in effect a factor of production without which workers cannot generate output. Thus, the short-run equilibrium corresponds to a case in which the other factors of production—n_j^s here—have not had a chance to adjust to the new endowment of labor, whereas the long-run equilibrium is the one that obtains after the adjustment of other factors.

4. Quantitative Implementation and Model Fit

We numerically implement the model laid out in Section 3. We use information on country sizes, fixed and variable trade costs, and bilateral migration flows and remittances to solve the model in the baseline scenario—that is, under the observed levels of migration and remittances. Then in Section 5 we simulate the effects of undoing the migration flows observed in the data. That is, we repatriate all immigrants in the OECD countries back to their countries of origin. Table 3 summarizes the calibrated parameter values of the model, and Online Appendix A.2 discusses the details of how the parameters are chosen.

4.1. Labor Productivity Parameters

To complete the implementation of the baseline scenario requires finding the values of L_j, or equivalently, A_{jj}. While we have actual data on the numbers of natives and immigrants N_{ji}^e in each origin and destination, L_j is not population per se, but a combination of the number of workers and the efficiency units—or labor productivity—possessed by workers in country j (Section 3.2).

To find L_j we follow the approach of Alvarez and Lucas (2007). Starting with an initial guess for L_j for all $j = 1, \ldots, C$, we solve the full model in the long-run equilibrium. Given the solution for w_j, we update our guess for L_j for each country in order to match the nominal US$ GDP ratio between each country j and the United States. Using the resulting values of L_j, we solve the model again to obtain the new set of wages, and iterate to convergence. Thus, our procedure generates vectors w_j and L_j in such a way as to match exactly the relative total GDPs of the countries in the sample while imposing that the model world economy is in the long-run equilibrium.

Having obtained the total efficiency-adjusted labor endowments L_j, and using the data on bilateral immigrant stocks by skill for each destination and origin country, we obtain country-specific productivity A_{jj} for every country j from equation (6):

$$A_{jj} = \frac{L_j}{\left[\left(\sum_{i=1}^{C} \varphi_{ji}^{\ell} N_{ji}^{\ell}\right)^{\frac{\sigma-1}{\sigma}} + \zeta_j \left(\mu_j \sum_{i=1}^{C} \varphi_{ji}^{h} N_{ji}^{h}\right)^{\frac{\sigma-1}{\sigma}}\right]^{\frac{\sigma}{\sigma-1}}}. \tag{11}$$

Intuitively, this procedure infers productivity from total country GDPs and the labor force composition of each country. Section 4.2 checks that the resulting productivity estimates are plausible. A notable consequence of this approach is that, controlling for population, countries with higher labor productivity A_{jj} will tend to have a greater number of entrepreneurs n_j^s, all else equal, since our procedure will give them a higher L_j.[14]

The previous calculation requires assigning values to (i) the term $\zeta_j \mu_j^{\sigma-1/\sigma}$, and (ii) φ_{ji}^e. We calibrate $\zeta_j \mu_j^{\sigma-1/\sigma}$ using skill premia. Optimal factor usage implies the following relationship:

$$\frac{w_j^h}{w_j^\ell} = \zeta_j \mu_j^{\frac{\sigma-1}{\sigma}} \left(\frac{\sum_{i=1}^{C} \varphi_{ji}^{h} N_{ji}^{h}}{\sum_{i=1}^{C} \varphi_{ji}^{\ell} N_{ji}^{\ell}}\right)^{-\frac{1}{\sigma}},$$

where w_j^e is the wage of the worker of skill level $e = \ell, h$. Using country-specific data on the skill premium w_j^h / w_j^ℓ described in Section 2 as well as the population composition by skill $\sum_{i=1}^{C} \varphi_{ji}^{h} N_{ji}^{h}$ and $\sum_{i=1}^{C} \varphi_{ji}^{\ell} N_{ji}^{\ell}$ allows us to back out the combination $\zeta_j \mu_j^{\sigma-1/\sigma}$ of the skill share parameter and the skilled worker's productivity advantage. This procedure ensures that the baseline equilibrium matches perfectly the observed skill premium in each country.

On φ_{ji}^e, we adopt three approaches. The first is to assume that $\varphi_{ji}^\ell = \varphi_{ji}^h = 1$, common across all countries. In this case, the average equilibrium wages of natives and immigrants with the same skill level will be equal within each country (although they will of course differ across countries). This will be our baseline scenario as we find it helpful in conveying the main mechanisms driving our results. It corresponds

14. That is, population and efficiency enter symmetrically and multiplicatively in determining market size, which in turn determines equilibrium variety. This approach is common in the literature. For instance, Alvarez and Lucas (2007) and Chaney (2008) assume that the number of productivity draws is a constant multiple of L_j.

TABLE 4. Bilateral trade shares: data and model predictions.

	Model		Data
Domestic sales as a share of domestic absorption (π_{ii})			
mean	0.7559		0.7286
median	0.7468		0.7697
corr(model,data)		0.5662	
Export sales as a share of domestic absorption (π_{ij})			
mean	0.0041		0.0042
median	0.0018		0.0042
corr(model,data)		0.7822	

Notes: This table reports the means and medians of domestic output (top panel), and bilateral trade (bottom panel), both as a share of domestic absorption, in the model and in the data.
Source: International Monetary Fund (2007) and model output.

to the broad pattern in the data that the wages of migrants are well approximated by the wages of the natives in the host country, and are often an order of magnitude larger than wages of similar workers in the source country (Pritchett 2006).

We check the robustness of the results to two alternative calibrations of $\{\varphi^e_{ji}\}$. The first captures a plausible amount of imperfect cross-border transferability of skills. The second allows for origin-specific native–immigrant productivity gaps that reflect migrant selection (positive or negative), or differences in the quality of education across countries. The results and a more detailed discussion are in Section 6 and Online Appendix B.1.

4.2. Model Fit

Before describing the counterfactual results, we assess the model fit on overall and bilateral trade, as well as on how the total labor productivities implied by the model compare to GDP per capita at the country level. The baseline is solved as the long-run equilibrium given the population compositions, total GDPs, and remittances in all countries as they are in the data in 2006.

Table 4 compares the bilateral and overall trade volumes in the model and in the data. Note that since in the data we only have bilateral trade as a share of GDP, not of total sales, we compute the same object in the model: $\pi_{ij} = X_{ij}/w_i L_i$.[15] This captures both the distinction between trade, which is recorded as total value, and GDP, which is recorded as value added—as well as the fact that there is a large nontraded sector in both the model and in the data.

The top panel of the table compares the share of domestically produced goods in GDP, π_{ii}, which is one minus imports/GDP, and can be thought of as the opposite of trade openness. It is clear that the overall trade volumes implied by the model match the actual data well. The means and medians are similar, and the correlation between

15. Since the baseline is solved as the long-run equilibrium, total profits are zero and GDP is simply labor income.

π_{ii} calculated from the model and those in the data for this sample of countries is around 0.57. The bottom panel compares bilateral trade shares π_{ij}, $i \neq j$. The average levels are quite similar, and the correlation between model and data bilateral trade shares is actually higher at 0.78. Since we use estimated gravity coefficients together with the actual data on bilateral country characteristics to compute trade costs, it is not surprising that our model fits bilateral trade data quite well given the success of the empirical gravity relationship. Nonetheless, since the gravity estimates we use come from outside of our calibration procedure, it is important to check that our model delivers outcomes similar to observed trade volumes.

The model delivers a vector of implied baseline labor productivities A_{jj} for each country, and we would like to compare these estimates to the data. Unfortunately, as a model object A_{jj} reflects the physical productivity of a worker, which we cannot measure in the data. In addition, in the model wages of a single efficiency unit of labor, w_j, will differ across countries to ensure global market clearing. To match the model precisely with the data, we calculate in the model the real PPP-adjusted per capita income for an individual living in j, which is given by

$$\frac{w_j L_j}{P_j \sum_i \sum_{e=\ell,h} N_{ji}^e},$$

with $P_j = (P_j^N)^\alpha (P_j^T)^{1-\alpha}$ the consumption price level, and $\sum_i \sum_{e=\ell,h} N_{ji}^e$ simply the total population of country j. This object is then directly comparable to income data from the Penn World Tables. Figure 1 presents the scatterplot of the real PPP-adjusted per capita income for 2006 from the Penn World Tables on the x-axis against the corresponding object in the model, along with the 45-degree line. The model matches the broad variation in per capita income in our sample of countries quite well. The countries line up along the 45-degree line, though it appears that the model tends to underpredict the relative income levels of poorer countries, and slightly overpredict the relative income levels of the richest countries. Overall, however, both the simple correlation and the Spearman rank correlation between the model and the data are 0.94.[16]

5. Counterfactuals

Our counterfactual experiments evaluate the welfare effects of sending all foreign-born individuals currently living in the OECD countries back to their countries of birth. In

16. The plots and the correlations are reported dropping the United Arab Emirates (UAE), for which the model underpredicts real per capita income by about a factor of 2. The UAE is a very small, special economy for which we do not have immigration data, and thus the poor performance of the model regarding the UAE is highly unlikely to affect any of the substantive results in the paper. Including the UAE, the simple correlation between the model and the data is 0.91, and the Spearman correlation is still 0.94.

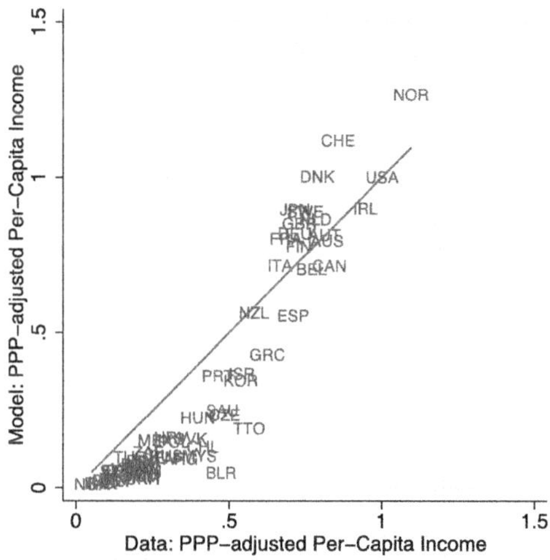

FIGURE 1. Real incomes: model versus data. This figure reports the scatterplot of the real PPP-adjusted per capita income from the Penn World Tables (x-axis) against the real PPP-adjusted per capita income implied by the model. Both are expressed relative to the United States.

the counterfactual scenario effective labor endowments of each country j will be

$$\widetilde{L}_j = A_{jj}\left[\left(\sum_{i=1}^{C} N_{ij}^{\ell}\right)^{\frac{\sigma-1}{\sigma}} + \zeta_j\left(\mu_j \sum_{i=1}^{C} N_{ij}^{h}\right)^{\frac{\sigma-1}{\sigma}}\right]^{\frac{\sigma}{\sigma-1}}. \tag{12}$$

That is, all the workers native to j that ever migrated to any destination country i are returned home. Their labor productivity is assumed to be the same as for their compatriots with the same skill, regardless of whether and where they migrated.[17]

Our main measure of welfare is the average utility of native stayers, taking into account the distribution of skill levels among them.[18] Individual welfare is given by equation (1). In the baseline equilibrium the welfare of the native stayers (born and residing in j) is given by

$$W_{jj} = \frac{(1-\omega_{jj})w_j^{\ell} + \omega_{jj}w_j^{h} + \left(\Pi_j^N + \Pi_j^T\right)/\sum_{e=\ell,h}\sum_{k=1}^{C} N_{jk}^{e} + R_j^{in}/N_{jj}}{\left(P_j^N\right)^{\alpha}\left(P_j^T\right)^{1-\alpha}},$$

17. In reality, return migrants may bring back skills learned at the destination country. However, there are very few estimates available for the rates of return to those skills. For more details see Dustmann (2003, 2008) and Dustmann, Fadlon, and Weiss (2011). See also Rauch and Trindade (2002, 2003) for estimates of the effects of migration on enhancing trade flows via the information conveyed through ethnic networks.

18. Online Appendix B.6 reports estimates of the welfare changes for the migrants themselves.

where, as previously, w_j^e is the wage of a native-born individual of skill level e, $\omega_{jj} \equiv N_{jj}^h/(N_{jj}^\ell + N_{jj}^h)$ is the share of skilled among the natives, $N_{jj} = N_{jj}^\ell + N_{jj}^h$ is the total population of natives, $\sum_{e=\ell,h} \sum_{k=1}^{C} N_{jk}^e$ is the total population of country j, and R_j^{in} is the total gross amount of remittances received by country j.[19]

This expression for welfare thus makes an assumption on remittances and an assumption on the distribution of firm profits. On remittances, we assume that (i) outgoing remittances are sent by the migrants only, that is, natives living in their home country are not transferring any of their income abroad; and that (ii) incoming remittances are received by the native stayers only, that is, remittances from abroad coming into the country go to natives, and not to immigrants living in that country.[20] On profits, we assume that all residents of a country have an equal number of shares in domestic profits, regardless of their skill level or country of birth.[21] This is a strong assumption, but it only matters in the short run. In the long run, profits are zero due to free entry.

In the counterfactual scenario each country's population is composed of the individuals that were born in that country, including both those that never left and returnees. The expressions for individual welfare in the counterfactual equilibrium are analogous to the previous expressions, with the proviso that there are no longer any remittances. Hence, the counterfactual individual welfare of a native stayer in country j is given by

$$\widetilde{W}_{jj} = \frac{(1-\omega_{jj})\tilde{w}_j^\ell + \omega_{jj}\tilde{w}_j^h + (\tilde{\Pi}_j^N + \tilde{\Pi}_j^T)/\sum_{k=1}^{C} N_{kj}}{(\tilde{P}_j^N)^\alpha (\tilde{P}_j^T)^{1-\alpha}}, \tag{13}$$

where the tilde denotes the counterfactual equilibrium values.

The change in the average welfare of natives between the baseline and the no-migration scenarios is closely related to the concept of the *immigration surplus*, defined as the change in the real average income of natives caused by an inflow

19. Recall that R_j was used to denote the total *net* remittances received by country j from the rest of the world, which can take both positive and negative values.

20. For example, remittances from Mexicans working in the United States are received by native Mexicans living in Mexico, and not by Guatemalan immigrants living in Mexico or by Mexicans living in Spain. We lack data to evaluate the plausibility of this assumption but it appears reasonable and unlikely to bias the results.

21. We are not aware of a good empirical benchmark that directly speaks to the question of the immigrants' share of a country's total profits. However, it is helpful to compare the entrepreneurship rates of natives and immigrants. Fairlie (2012) reports a higher business ownership rate among immigrants (10.5%) than among natives (9.3%) in the United States. Likewise the startup rate is also higher for immigrants than for non-immigrants (0.62% versus 0.28%). However, these figures are likely to overestimate the share of profits accruing to immigrants because immigrant-owned businesses tend to be smaller than native-owned ones. According to Fairlie (2012) immigrant-owned businesses have about 30% lower revenue. In light of these numbers it appears reasonable to allocate aggregate profits to natives and immigrants in proportion to their population shares.

of immigrants (Berry and Soligo 1969; Borjas 1995). Virtually all studies that quantify the immigration surplus employ a one-good framework and a standard neoclassical production function. In our framework each firm produces a different good and product variety is endogenous. In this context income is deflated by the ideal price index, which encapsulates the impact of changes in product variety on firms and consumers. But it is still the case that real income per native, our main welfare criterion, coincides with the immigration surplus also in per-native terms.

5.1. The Long Run

Table 5 reports our main results. For each country, we report the percent change in the real average income of native stayers (across the two skill levels) in the no-migration counterfactual relative to the benchmark scenario. Negative values thus represent welfare losses from undoing international migration. We break up the sample into the OECD and the non-OECD countries. Roughly, we can think of the OECD group (left panel) as the migrant-receiving countries and the non-OECD group (right panel) as the migrant-sending countries, though keeping in mind that there is substantial migration within the OECD as well.

The first important observation is that in the long run the large majority of OECD countries would be worse off in the absence of migration. The average OECD country would experience a welfare change of −2.38%, with substantial dispersion in outcomes (standard deviation of 3.07%). In this group, the largest losses are experienced by the natives of the countries with the largest observed shares of the foreign-born in the population: Australia (−11.63%), Canada (−7.07%), and New Zealand (−6.89%). However, it is worth noting that a handful of OECD countries would experience welfare gains: Greece, Korea, and Portugal would all be about 1.1%–1.4% better off in the no-migration counterfactual. As Table 1 shows, these are the OECD countries with noticeable net out-migration. In the no-migration counterfactual these countries' population would rise by 5.2%, 2.8%, and 11.1%, respectively.

Second, the majority of non-OECD countries also have lower welfare in the no-migration counterfactual, although dispersion in country outcomes is substantial. The average welfare change is −2.00% with an associated standard deviation of 3.55%. The highest welfare losses are to native stayers in El Salvador, the Dominican Republic, Jamaica, and the Philippines, at around −7% to −10%. Interestingly, a handful of non-OECD countries experience welfare gains: mainly, Trinidad and Tobago (5.70%), Mexico (1.32%), and Turkey (1.07%). A quick glance at Table 2 shows that these countries are characterized by substantial emigration rates but small incoming remittances relative to their GDP and to their emigration rates. For instance, while Mexico has an emigration rate over 10%, remittances amount to only 3.1% of its GDP. In contrast, the emigration rate of the Philippines is around 3% but the incoming remittances are equal to 15.5% of its GDP.[22]

22. However, it is also important to qualify the impact of cross-country variation in incoming remittances. In our framework remittances are exogenous and taken directly from the data. As such, our analysis is

TABLE 5. Percentage change in average welfare in the counterfactual relative to benchmark.

	OECD countries			Non-OECD countries	
Country	Long run	Short run	Country	Long run	Short run
Australia	−11.63	−0.68	Algeria	−1.55	−2.14
Austria	−3.06	−0.41	Argentina	0.07	−0.19
Belgium	−4.63	−1.36	Belarus	−1.25	−1.03
Canada	−7.07	0.25	Brazil	−0.27	−0.43
Czech Republic	−1.02	−0.85	Bulgaria	−5.68	−6.60
Denmark	−1.29	−0.31	Chile	0.34	−0.11
Finland	−0.13	−0.55	China	−0.75	−0.88
France	−3.12	−0.39	Colombia	−2.01	−2.75
Germany	−1.55	−0.09	Croatia	−0.35	−3.29
Greece	1.17	−0.59	Dominican Republic	−9.02	−11.55
Hungary	−0.46	−0.12	Ecuador	−2.26	−4.42
Ireland	−0.07	−0.54	Egypt, Arab Rep.	−3.47	−3.40
Italy	0.43	−0.15	El Salvador	−8.72	−14.08
Japan	−0.48	−0.01	India	−2.51	−2.53
Korea, Rep.	1.12	−0.01	Indonesia	−0.65	−0.63
Netherlands	−2.60	−0.12	Iran, Islamic Rep.	−0.15	−0.53
New Zealand	−6.89	−1.21	Israel	0.12	−0.04
Norway	−2.53	−0.05	Jamaica	−5.61	−14.89
Poland	0.16	−1.32	Malaysia	−0.39	−0.43
Portugal	1.37	−2.04	Mexico	1.32	−2.59
Slovak Republic	−0.10	−1.10	Nigeria	−2.74	−2.59
Spain	−4.91	−0.42	Pakistan	−3.45	−3.45
Sweden	−3.45	0.15	Philippines	−10.08	−11.27
Switzerland	−4.42	0.06	Romania	−2.73	4.89
United Kingdom	−1.46	−0.23	Russian Federation	−0.18	−0.38
United States	−5.37	0.14	Saudi Arabia	−0.26	0.66
			Serbia and Montenegro	−11.54	−14.46
			South Africa	−0.05	−0.31
			Thailand	−0.51	−0.56
			Trinidad and Tobago	5.70	−0.77
			Turkey	1.07	−0.30
			Ukraine	−0.34	−−0.58
			United Arab Emirates	−0.06	−0.07
			Venezuela, RB	0.10	−0.14
Mean	−2.38	−0.46	Mean	−2.00	−3.28
Std Dev.	3.07	0.56	Std Dev.	3.55	4.54

Notes: This table presents the percent change in welfare between baseline and counterfactual equilibria, assuming $\varphi_i^\ell = \varphi_i^h = 1$ for all countries. The measure of welfare employed here is the average real income of native stayers. The first column reports the welfare change in the long run, the second column in the short run.

silent on why remittances, conditional on emigrant stocks, vary across countries. It could be that in some countries entire families emigrate, while in others families are split and only one family member goes abroad. These patterns have clear implications for remittance flows (Merkle and Zimmermann 1992), but will also presumably have a direct and unmodeled impact on the disutility from emigration if people value living in the same location as their family.

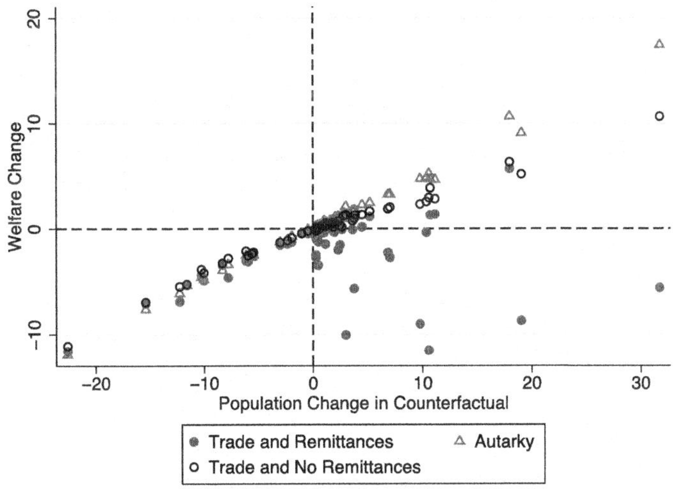

FIGURE 2. Change in average welfare in the long run: autarky, trade, and remittances. This figure reports the percentage change in welfare in the long-run counterfactual relative to the baseline (assuming $\varphi_i^{\ell} = \varphi_i^h = 1$ for all countries i) in three different scenarios. Solid dots depict the welfare change with both trade and remittances. Hollow dots depict the welfare change with international trade but keeping remittances constant at zero in the baseline and counterfactual equilibria. Hollow triangles depict the welfare changes under prohibitive trade costs and no remittances. The measure of welfare is the average real income of native stayers. On the y-axis is the percent change in the population in the counterfactual relative to the baseline.

Thus, both developed and developing countries tend to gain from the observed levels of migration. In the OECD, net immigration leads to a larger market size. In the presence of positive trade costs, this implies higher equilibrium variety and thus higher per capita welfare. For the native stayers in the non-OECD, the losses from lower variety due to emigration are in most cases more than offset by the fact that their emigrants experience large increases in earnings, and a fraction of those is being shared with the native stayers through remittances.

We now isolate the roles played by changes in population size, international trade, and remittances. Figure 2 presents these results using scatterplots. On the horizontal axis is the percentage change in the total population in the counterfactual relative to the baseline (column 3 of Table 1 and column 1 of Table 2), with positive values corresponding to increases in population. On the vertical axis is the percentage change in welfare in the no-migration counterfactual relative to the baseline. Solid dots depict the long-run welfare change (the first column of Table 5). As discussed previously, most countries in the OECD suffer a population loss as migrants return to their home countries, while most non-OECD countries gain population. Among the OECD countries there is a clear positive association between the population change and the percentage change in long-run welfare: the countries with the largest population losses suffer the largest welfare losses. For instance, Australia would lose 22.6% of its population, leading to a −11.63% welfare change for its native stayers. The picture is much less clear for the non-OECD countries. Most of these countries experience net population gains. However, some suffer large welfare losses while others even experience (small) welfare gains. It is particularly interesting to compare the predictions for El Salvador and Trinidad and Tobago. These two countries would experience similar population gains due to return migration, at 19% and 17.9% respectively. But while the former would suffer a welfare loss of −8.72%, the latter would experience a welfare gain of 5.70%. As we now show, the diverging effects of return migration on these two countries are explained by the role of remittances.

Figure 2 plots the results from two additional counterfactual scenarios. Hollow dots report the welfare changes that would result assuming there are no remittances. Strikingly, the relationship between population and welfare changes becomes roughly monotonically increasing, with a concave shape. In particular, we note that El Salvador and Trinidad and Tobago would now experience practically the same welfare gain (about 5%). The key is that remittances are a very large share of income in El Salvador, but not in Trinidad and Tobago. Note also that for the OECD the welfare impact remains practically unchanged. This is because the remittances originating in these countries are very small relative to the countries' GDPs, and the native stayers are not the ones sending them abroad.

Next, we examine the scenario where both remittances and international trade are assumed away. The corresponding welfare changes are depicted by hollow triangles. The relationship between population and welfare changes becomes practically linear (with a slope of 0.5), and steeper than under trade. This is because when a developing country experiences net population growth it will respond by producing a wider set of varieties. In autarky, consumers in that country clearly benefit from the increase in variety. However, in the presence of trade the resulting welfare gain is moderated by the reduction in the number of varieties that are available through imports, implying a smaller marginal welfare gain.

5.2. The Short Run

The native stayers' welfare changes in the short run are reported in the second column of Table 5. Welfare for natives in the OECD is practically unchanged in the short run (an average change of −0.46%, compared to −2.38% in the long run). In the non-OECD, all countries would experience a welfare loss (with the exception of Saudi Arabia). Furthermore, the short-run loss is uniformly larger than the long-run loss (−3.28%, compared to −2.00% in the long run). The intuition for the difference between the short- and long-run effects is as follows. The typical OECD country experiences a net reduction in its labor force. As a result, some of the firms operating in the OECD shut down. In the short run, the set of projects available in the economy is fixed. Hence, the reduction in the number of firms/varieties is attained by an increase in the productivity cutoff for operating a firm. As a result, the firms that exit are those with the lowest productivity. Losing these marginal varieties has practically no effect on the welfare of natives in the OECD. At the other end, developing countries receive a net inflow of workers. This increase in the labor force will induce a reduction in the productivity cutoff for operating a firm there, and new firms will be established. However, these are firms that did not find it worthwhile to operate before the inflow of new workers. Thus, their positive contribution to welfare-adjusted equilibrium variety is minor.

Quantitatively, in the short run, what matters crucially is *how much* less productive new entrants are relative to the firms that are already in the market. For this, the calibration to the observed firm size distribution (Zipf's Law) plays an important role. Essentially, the observed firm size distribution contains information on the relative productivity of the marginal firms compared to the inframarginal ones. The extremely skewed firm size distribution observed in the economy implies that the inframarginal firms are vastly more productive, and thus matter much more for welfare, than the marginal ones (for a detailed exploration of this result, see di Giovanni and Levchenko 2013). In comparison, the main benefit in the long run from having a larger population lies in the additional net entry of entrepreneurs—a larger n_i^s. An increase in population stimulates entry everywhere in the productivity distribution. Because the long-run entry will feature some very productive firms, it will have a much larger impact on welfare.

Three OECD countries—Sweden, Switzerland, and the United States—gain in welfare from undoing migration in the short run. It turns out that this outcome is due to the assumption that immigrants receive a per capita share of firm profits. If we instead assume that all the firm profits in the economy accrue to the natives, even in these three countries the natives are worse off without immigration.

Figure 3 reports the short-run results graphically and isolates the roles of remittances and international trade. As was the case in the long run, not taking into account remittances, the relationship between population and welfare changes becomes roughly monotonic. As illustrated by the hollow dots, with trade but no remittances, larger population *gains* in the counterfactual lead to larger welfare *losses* among developing countries. In the OECD the relationship appears practically flat. In other words, in the short run the increase in domestic varieties experienced by developing countries is not enough to compensate for the loss in imported varieties. The main reason for this is that return migrants are leaving high-productivity OECD countries to go back to their low-productivity countries of origin, which entails a large loss in worldwide efficiency units of labor. Turning now to the role of international trade, in the counterfactual exercise without either remittances or cross-border trade, the relationship between population and welfare changes again becomes roughly linear and now features a weak *positive* slope. This reflects the fact that the increased labor force in the non-OECD will deliver a net increase in varieties available for consumption, obviously with no change in imported varieties.

5.3. Distributional Effects

Our model features imperfect substitutability between skilled and unskilled workers, and thus the potential for migration to generate distributional effects to the extent that

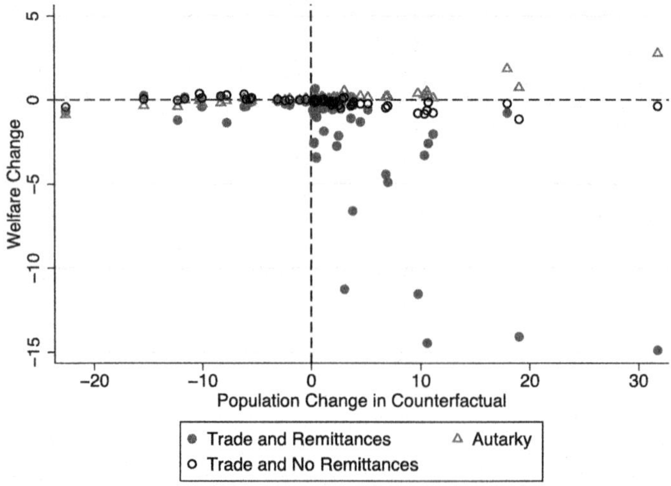

FIGURE 3. Change in average welfare in the short run: autarky, trade, and remittances. This figure reports the percentage change in welfare in the short-run counterfactual relative to the baseline (assuming $\varphi_i^\ell = \varphi_i^h = 1$ for all countries i) in three different scenarios. Solid dots depict the welfare change with both trade and remittances. Hollow dots depict the welfare change with international trade but keeping remittances constant at zero in the baseline and counterfactual equilibria. Hollow triangles depict the welfare changes under prohibitive trade costs and no remittances. The measure of welfare is the average real income of the native stayers. On the y-axis is the percent change in the population in the counterfactual relative to the baseline.

migrants differ in skill composition from natives. To isolate those distributional effects, Figure 4 plots the welfare changes of the unskilled native stayers against the welfare changes of the skilled native stayers. If a country observation is on the 45-degree line, the skilled and the unskilled experience identical welfare changes.

The top panel presents the results for the OECD. Overall, welfare changes for the skilled and the unskilled are similar: the observations tend to be relatively close to the 45-degree line (Figure 4a). Thus, in the long run the welfare gains from new varieties dominate the changes in the skill premium. A notable exception is Australia: the unskilled stayers lose 13.6% in the no-migration counterfactual, compared to 7.8% for the skilled. This reflects the fact that immigrants to Australia are more skilled on average than natives (Table 1).

However, in the short run the distributional effects come to the fore (Figure 4b). In many OECD countries, the welfare changes for the skilled and the unskilled have opposite signs, and are an order of magnitude larger in absolute value than aggregate welfare changes. For instance, in the short run the United States is 0.14% better off without migration (Table 5). Separating by skill, it turns out that the unskilled are 1.03% better off in the absence of migration, but the skilled are 0.45% *worse* off. In Australia, the numbers are even larger, and the identity of winners and losers is reversed. While

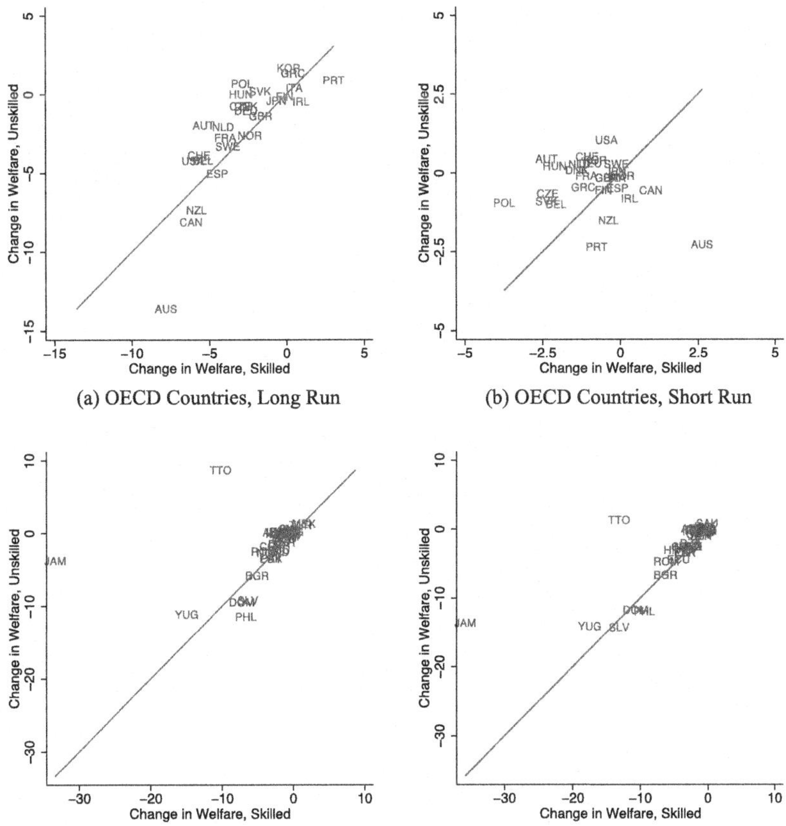

(a) OECD Countries, Long Run
(b) OECD Countries, Short Run
(c) Non-OECD Countries, Long Run
(d) Non-OECD Countries, Short Run

FIGURE 4. Distributional effects: welfare changes of skilled and unskilled natives. Units on both axes are in percentage points. These figures present scatterplots of the percent change in welfare of the unskilled native stayers against the change in welfare of the skilled native stayers, for the OECD (top half) and the non-OECD (bottom half) countries respectively, in both the long run (left side) and the short run (right side). The line through the data is the 45-degree line in each plot.

in the aggregate, Australia would be 0.68% worse off in the absence of migration, unskilled Australians would be 2.28% worse off, while skilled Australians 2.63% better off. The identity of winners and losers across countries corresponds closely to the relative skill levels of natives and immigrants. In the United States, immigrants are comparatively unskilled (Table 1), and thus in the short run migration benefits the skilled at the expense of the unskilled. The opposite is true for Australia. This is a general pattern: in the short run, the correlation between welfare changes for the skilled and the unskilled is negative at −0.22. (By contrast, in the long run the welfare changes for those two groups are strongly positively correlated at 0.81.)

For the majority of non-OECD countries, the distributional effects are negligible both in the short run and in the long run. This is intuitive: as discussed previously, for these countries the welfare effects are dominated by remittances, which are the same in the short and the long run. Only a couple of countries—Jamaica and Trinidad and Tobago—exhibit large distributional effects. In these countries, reversing emigration leads to large welfare losses for the skilled among the native stayers, with a much more subdued (or even a positive) impact on the unskilled. Table 2 reveals that emigrants from Jamaica and Trinidad and Tobago are overwhelmingly more skilled than the native stayers. These large disparities, coupled with large observed emigration, imply that returning emigrants home to these countries will significantly change the relative supply of skill there, leading to large distributional effects.

6. Extensions and Sensitivity

This section briefly discusses a number of extensions and sensitivity checks on the main results. Online Appendix B describes these exercises in detail.

6.1. Native–Immigrant Productivity Differences

Migrant productivity may differ from that of the natives of similar skill levels for a variety of reasons. On the one hand, it is well documented that migrants suffer a reduction in human capital associated with imperfect transferability of skills across countries, at least temporarily. If this is indeed the case, the findings described previously may overstate the effects of migration on the effective labor force (in efficiency units) of the host country. On the other hand, some immigrants may be permanently more productive (i.e., earn higher wages) than natives with similar schooling levels. This could be due to positive selection into migration: migrants may be above-average in terms of unobservable skills (such as talent or ability) relative to individuals that are observationally equivalent in terms of education, work experience, gender, and so on. Of course, negative selection into emigration is also possible, and the type of selection may well vary substantially by origin country.[23] Online Appendix B.1 presents two approaches to calibrating native–immigrant productivity gaps, and shows that the results are quite similar to the baseline.

6.2. Imperfect Substitution Between Natives and Immigrants

The baseline framework assumes that native and immigrant workers in the same skill category are perfect substitutes. Recently, several studies have questioned this

23. Borjas (1987) explores the conditions for one type of selection or the other to take place.

assumption (Manacorda, Manning, and Wadsworth 2012; Ottaviano and Peri 2012). Online Appendix B.2 implements a model in which natives and immigrants of the same skill level are imperfect substitutes. As expected, assuming imperfect substitutability between immigrants and natives increases the gains from immigration for the typical host country since now natives and immigrants do not compete head to head. The cross-country pattern of welfare changes is very similar to the baseline.

6.3. Additional Sensitivity and Welfare of Migrants

We examine the sensitivity of the main results along a number of additional dimensions. First, the key mechanism through which natives in the destination countries gain from migration is increased product variety. Since equilibrium variety responds endogenously to market size, and larger markets exhibit greater equilibrium variety, individuals living in larger markets enjoy greater welfare, all else equal. This phenomenon is often referred to as the "scale effect". Scale effects are common and well studied in both economic growth (e.g., Romer 1990) and international trade (e.g., Krugman 1980). Nonetheless, it is important to justify this type of mechanism in our quantitative exercise, and to benchmark it to existing empirical estimates of scale effects. Online Appendix B.3 (i) compares the magnitude of the scale effect implied by our model to existing empirical estimates, (ii) implements an alternative calibration that targets a scale effect at the bottom of the range suggested in the literature, and (iii) implements a model with explicit congestion effects to counteract the positive effect of country size on income.

Second, it may be that the share of the skilled in the population has a direct effect on TFP. For instance, Jones (2002) and Benhabib and Spiegel (2005) develop theoretical models that feature a positive link between human capital and TFP growth, while Ciccone and Peri (2006), Moretti (2004), and Iranzo and Peri (2009b), among others, provide estimates of these human capital externalities based on subnational evidence. This force may affect the welfare impact of migration because the migrants are frequently less skilled on average than the natives of their destination countries, and more skilled than the staying natives of their origin countries.

Online Appendix B.4 discusses the results of an extension that incorporates this effect. The results for the OECD remain qualitatively unchanged, whereas the conclusions for the non-OECD turn out to be sensitive to the assumption that TFP is not directly affected by the skilled share. Of course this outcome is very much dependent on the specific parameterization we adopted. Since there is considerable uncertainty regarding the nature of the link between the skilled share and TFP, these results should be interpreted with caution. The exercise suggests that this is a potentially important mechanism that should be explored further in future research.

In Online Appendix B.5, we use our baseline model to perform more realistic policy counterfactuals. Specifically, we compute the welfare effects of reducing the stock of immigrants in each country by 10%. We also evaluate the sensitivity of our baseline results to assuming a much lower elasticity of substitution between skilled and unskilled labor. Finally, Online Appendix B.6 discusses the welfare impact of migration on the migrants themselves.

7. Conclusion

The cross-border movements of people are large relative to the overall population of many countries. This paper develops a global-scale quantitative assessment of the welfare impact of migration in a large cross-section of both sending and receiving countries. Our main finding is that the long-run impact of observed levels of migration is large and positive for the remaining natives of *both* the main sending countries and the main receiving ones. Relative to the counterfactual scenario in which no migration takes place, some countries in both groups are as much as 10% better off. Interestingly, while the overall numbers are similar, the salient reason for the welfare changes is different. For the countries with the highest immigration rates (Australia, New Zealand, Canada), migration raises welfare through increased equilibrium variety. For the countries with the highest emigration rates (El Salvador, Jamaica), the staying natives are better off because of remittances. These forces are also at work for all other countries, but the relative strength of each varies substantially. Our findings also suggest that failing to account for the role of remittances would produce a welfare evaluation that would be severely biased for a number of migration-sending countries.

All in all, our analysis provides a fairly positive view of the welfare effects of international migration, both for origin and destination countries. We note, however, that our analysis does not take into account the effects that immigration may have on the provision of public goods and government-mandated redistribution. Implicitly, we are assuming that immigrants contribute to tax revenue and use public services at the same rate as the natives, and that immigrants do not alter the political equilibrium that determines the overall degree of within-country income redistribution. While this may be a reasonable assumption in some countries, it may not apply universally (Dolmas and Huffman 2004; Ortega 2010). Relatedly, our analysis ignores any impact of migration on social capital such as trust or social cohesion.[24] Incorporating the fiscal, political, and social channels into the quantitative welfare assessments of immigration remains a fruitful avenue for future research.

24. De la Rica, Glitz, and Ortega (2014) provide a comprehensive survey of the economic effects of immigration in Europe, including the fiscal consequences. Alesina and La Ferrara (2002) find that within the United States, individuals living in localities with high ethnic fractionalization and income disparities exhibit less trust. Using a large cross-section of countries, Ortega and Peri (2014) show that immigration does increase ethnic fractionalization, but any negative economic effects of increased fractionalization appear to be more than offset by other sources of gains.

References

Alesina, Alberto and Eliana La Ferrara (2002). "Who Trusts Others?" *Journal of Public Economics*, 85, 207–234.

Alvarez, Fernando and Robert E. Jr. Lucas (2007). "General Equilibrium Analysis of the Eaton–Kortum Model of International Trade." *Journal of Monetary Economics*, 54, 1726–1768.

Anderson, James and Eric van Wincoop (2004). "Trade Costs." *Journal of Economic Literature*, 42, 691–751.

Axtell, Robert L. (2001). "Zipf Distribution of U.S. Firm Sizes." *Science*, 293(5536), 1818–1820.

Barro, Robert J. and Jong-Wha Lee (2010). "A New Data Set of Educational Attainment in the World, 1950–2010." NBER Working Paper No. 15902.

Benhabib, Jess (1996). "On the Political Economy of Immigration." *European Economic Review*, 40, 1737–1743.

Benhabib, Jess and Boyan Jovanovic (2012). "Optimal Migration: A World Perspective." *International Economic Review*, 53, 321–348.

Benhabib, Jess and Mark M. Spiegel (2005). "Human Capital and Technology Diffusion." In *Handbook of Economic Growth*, Vol. 1, edited by Philippe Aghion and Steven Durlauf. Elsevier, Chap. 13, pp. 935–966.

Bergin, Paul and Giancarlo Corsetti (2008). "The Extensive Margin and Monetary Policy." *Journal of Monetary Economics*, 55, 1222–1237.

Berry, R. Albert and Ronald Soligo (1969). "Some Welfare Aspects of International Migration." *Journal of Political Economy*, 77, 778–794.

Borjas, George J (1987). "Self-Selection and the Earnings of Immigrants." *American Economic Review*, 77(4), 531–553.

Borjas, George J. (1995). "The Economic Benefits from Immigration." *Journal of Economic Perspectives*, 9(2), 3–22.

Chaney, Thomas (2008). "Distorted Gravity: The Intensive and Extensive Margins of International Trade." *American Economic Review*, 98(4), 1707–1721.

Ciccone, Antonio and Giovanni Peri (2006). "Identifying Human-Capital Externalities: Theory with Applications." *Review of Economic Studies*, 73, 381–412.

Davis, Donald R. and David E. Weinstein (2002). "Technological Superiority and the Losses From Migration." NBER Working Paper No. 8971.

De la Rica, Sara, Albrecht Glitz, and Francesc Ortega (2014). "Immigration in Europe: Trends, Policies and Empirical Evidence." Forthcoming in *Handbook on the Economics of International Migration*, edited by Barry R. Chiswick and Paul W. Miller. Elsevier. Also IZA Discussion Paper 7778.

di Giovanni, Julian and Andrei A. Levchenko (2013). "Firm Entry, Trade, and Welfare in Zipf's World." *Journal of International Economics*, 89, 283–296.

di Giovanni, Julian and Andrei A. Levchenko (2012). "Country Size, International Trade, and Aggregate Fluctuations in Granular Economies." *Journal of Political Economy*, 120, 1083–1132.

Dixit, Avinash K. and Joseph E. Stiglitz (1977). "Monopolistic Competition and Optimum Product Diversity." *American Economic Review*, 67(3), 297–308.

Docquier, Frédéric, B. Lindsay Lowell, and Abdeslam Marfouk (2009). "A Gendered Assessment of Highly Skilled Emigration." *Population and Development Review*, 35, 297–321.

Docquier, Frédéric, Joël Machado, and Khalid Sekkat (2012). "Efficiency Gains from Liberalizing Labor Mobility." Working paper, Université Catholique de Louvain and Université Libre de Bruxelles.

Docquier, Frédéric, Abdeslam Marfouk, Çağlar Özden, and Christopher Parsons (2010a). "Geographic, Gender and Skill Structure of International Migration." Working paper, Université Catholique de Louvain, World Bank, and University of Nottingham.

Docquier, Frédéric, Çağlar Özden, and Giovanni Peri (2010b). "The Wage Effects of Immigration and Emigration." NBER Working Paper No. 16646.

Dolmas, Jim and Gregory W. Huffman (2004). "On the Political Economy of Immigration and Income Redistribution." *International Economic Review*, 45, 1129–1168.

Dustmann, Christian (2003). "Return Migration, Wage Differentials, and the Optimal Migration Duration." *European Economic Review*, 47, 353–369.

Dustmann, Christian (2008). "Return Migration, Investment in Children, and Intergenerational Mobility: Comparing Sons of Foreign- and Native-Born Fathers." *Journal of Human Resources*, 43, 299–324.

Dustmann, Christian, Itzhak Fadlon, and Yoram Weiss (2011). "Return Migration, Human Capital Accumulation and the Brain Drain." *Journal of Development Economics*, 95, 58–67.

Dustmann, Christian and Albrecht Glitz (2014). "How Do Industries and Firms Respond to Changes in Local Labour Supply." *Journal of Labor Economics*, forthcoming.

Eaton, Jonathan, Samuel S. Kortum, and Francis Kramarz (2011). "An Anatomy of International Trade: Evidence from French Firms." *Econometrica*, 79, 1453–1498.

Facchini, Giovanni and Anna Maria Mayda (2009). "Does the Welfare State Affect Individual Attitudes toward Immigrants? Evidence across Countries." *Review of Economics and Statistics*, 91, 295–314.

Facchini, Giovanni, Anna Maria Mayda, and Prachi Mishra (2011). "Do Interest Groups Affect US Immigration Policy?" *Journal of International Economics*, 85, 114–128.

Facchini, Giovanni and Max Friedrich Steinhardt (2011). "What Drives U.S. Immigration Policy? Evidence from Congressional Roll Call Votes." *Journal of Public Economics*, 95, 734–743.

Fairlie, Robert W. (2012). "Immigrant Entrepreneurs and Small Business Owners, and Their Access to Financial Capital." Small Business Administration Office of Advocacy Working Paper No. 396.

Ghironi, Fabio and Marc J. Melitz (2005). "International Trade and Macroeconomic Dynamics with Heterogeneous Firms." *Quarterly Journal of Economics*, 120, 865–915.

Hamilton, Bob and John Whalley (1984). "Efficiency and Distributional Implications of Global Restrictions on Labour Mobility: Calculations and Policy Implications." *Journal of Development Economics*, 14, 61–75.

Helpman, Elhanan, Marc Melitz, and Yona Rubinstein (2008). "Estimating Trade Flows: Trading Partners and Trading Volumes." *Quarterly Journal of Economics*, 123, 441–487.

Hendricks, Lutz (2004). "A Database of Mincerian Earnings Regressions." http://www.lhendricks.org/Mincer.htm.

International Monetary Fund (2007). "Directions of Trade Statistics."

Iranzo, Susana and Giovanni Peri (2009a). "Migration and Trade: Theory with an Application to the Eastern-Western European Integration." *Journal of International Economics*, 79, 1–19.

Iranzo, Susana and Giovanni Peri (2009b). "Schooling Externalities, Technology, and Productivity: Theory and Evidence from U.S. States." *Review of Economics and Statistics*, 91, 420–431.

Jones, Charles I. (2002). "Sources of U.S. Economic Growth in a World of Ideas." *American Economic Review*, 92(1), 220–239.

Kennan, John (2013). "Open Borders." *Review of Economic Dynamics*, 16, L1–L13.

Klein, Paul and Gustavo Ventura (2007). "TFP Differences and the Aggregate Effects of Labor Mobility in the Long Run." *B. E. Journals in Macroeconomics*, 7, 1–38.

Klein, Paul and Gustavo Ventura (2009). "Productivity Differences and the Dynamic Effects of Labor Movements." *Journal of Monetary Economics*, 56, 1059–1073.

Krugman, Paul (1980). "Scale Economies, Product Differentiation, and the Pattern of Trade." *American Economic Review*,70(5), 950–959.

Lewis, Ethan (2011). "Immigration, Skill Mix, and Capital Skill Complementarity." *The Quarterly Journal of Economics*, 126, 1029–1069.

Manacorda, Marco, Alan Manning, and Jonathan Wadsworth (2012). "The Impact of Immigration on the Structure of Wages: Theory and Evidence from Britain." *Journal of the European Economic Association*, 10, 120–151.

Mayda, Anna Maria (2006). "Who Is Against Immigration? A Cross-Country Investigation of Individual Attitudes toward Immigrants." *Review of Economics and Statistics*, 88, 510–530.

Melitz, Marc J. (2003). "The Impact of Trade on Intra-Industry Reallocations and Aggregate Industry Productivity." *Econometrica*, 71, 1695–1725.
Merkle, Lucie and Klaus F. Zimmermann (1992). "Savings, Remittances, and Return Migration." *Economics Letters*, 38, 77–81.
Moretti, Enrico (2004). "Workers' Education, Spillovers, and Productivity: Evidence from Plant-Level Production Functions." *American Economic Review*, 94(3), 656–690.
Ortega, Francesc (2005). "Immigration Quotas and Skill Upgrading." *Journal of Public Economics*, 89, 1841–1863.
Ortega, Francesc (2010). "Immigration, Citizenship, and the Size of Government." *The B. E. Journal of Economic Analysis and Policy*, 10, 26.
Ortega, Francesc and Giovanni Peri (2014). "Openness and Income: The Roles of Trade and Migration." *Journal of International Economics*, 92, 231–251.
Ortega, Francesc and Javier Polavieja (2012). "Labor-Market Exposure as a Determinant of Attitudes toward Immigration." *Labour Economics*, 19, 298–311.
Ottaviano, Gianmarco I. P. and Giovanni Peri (2012). "Rethinking the Effect of Immigration on Wages." *Journal of the European Economic Association*, 10, 152–197.
Pritchett, Lant (2006). *Let Their People Come: Breaking the Gridlock on Global Labor Mobility*. Center for Global Development, Washington, DC.
Ratha, Dilip and William Shaw (2007). "South–South Migration and Remittances." World Bank Working Paper No. 102.
Rauch, James E. and Vitor Trindade (2002). "Ethnic Chinese Networks in International Trade." *Review of Economics and Statistics*, 84, 116–130.
Rauch, James E. and Vitor Trindade (2003). "Information, International Substitutability, and Globalization." *American Economic Review*, 93(3), 775–791.
Romer, Paul M. (1990). "Endogenous Technological Change." *Journal of Political Economy*, 98, S71–S102.
The World Bank (2007). "Doing Business Indicators."
Trefler, Daniel (1993). "International Factor Price Differences: Leontief was Right!" *Journal of Political Economy*, 101, 961–987.
Trefler, Daniel (1995). "The Case of the Missing Trade and Other Mysteries." *American Economic Review*, 85, 1029–1046.
Yang, Dean (2008). "International Migration, Remittances and Household Investment: Evidence from Philippine Migrants' Exchange Rate Shocks." *Economic Journal*, 118, 591–630.
Uy, Timothy, Kei-Mu, Yi, and Jing Zhang (2013). "Structural Change in an Open Economy." *Journal of Monetary Economics*, 60, 667–682.

Supporting Information

Additional Supporting Information may be found in the online version of this article at the publisher's website:

Online Appendices for "A Global View of Cross-Border Migration"

CPSIA information can be obtained at www.ICGtesting.com
Printed in the USA
BVOW06*0805160916

462284BV00003B/6/P